THIRD EDITION

MACRO/MICRO: A Brief Introduction to Sociology

Lorne Tepperman
University of Toronto

Michael Rosenberg
Dawson College

Prentice Hall Allyn and Bacon Canada
Scarborough, Ontario

Canadian Cataloguing in Publication Data
Tepperman, Lorne, 1943-
     Macro/micro : a brief introduction to sociology

3rd ed.
Includes index.
ISBN 0-13-857897-4

1. Sociology.   I. Rosenberg, M. Michael.   II. Title.

HM51.T47 1998   301   C97-930710-4

Allyn and Bacon, Inc., Needham Heights, MA
Prentice-Hall, Inc., Upper Saddle River, New Jersey
Prentice-Hall International (UK) Limited, London
Prentice-Hall of Australia, Pty. Limited, Sydney
Prentice-Hall Hispanoamericana, S.A., Mexico City
Prentice-Hall of India Private Limited, New Delhi
Prentice-Hall of Japan, Inc., Tokyo
Simon & Schuster Southeast Asia Private Limited, Singapore
Editora Prentice-Hall do Brasil, Ltda., Rio de Janeiro

ISBN 0-13-857897-4

Vice President, Editorial Director: Laura Pearson
Acquisitions Editor: Rebecca Bersagel
Developmental Editor: Lisa Berland
Editorial Assistant: Shoshana Goldberg
Copy Editor: Liba Berry
Production Editor: Marjan Farahbaksh
Production Coordinator: Sharon Houston
Photo Research: Sarah Wittman
Cover and Interior Design: Monica Kompter
Cover Image: Stock Illustration Source Inc./Charlene Potts
Page Layout: Hermia Chung

1 2 3 4 5   CC   01 00 99 98 97

Printed and bound in USA

Visit the Prentice Hall Canada web site! Send us your comments, browse our catalogues, and more. **www.phcanada.com**. Or reach us through e-mail at **phabinfo_pubcanada@prenhall.com**.

CHAPTER FOUR

Deviance and Control   92

DEFINING DEVIANCE AND SOCIAL CONTROL   93

Social order and rules   93

CHAPTER FIVE

Class and the Economic Order   123

IS INEQUALITY A FACT OF LIFE?   124

Development of the class system   125

A new outlook on society   126

THEORIES OF SOCIAL STRATIFICATION   127

CHAPTER SIX
Work and the Workplace   158

CHAPTER SEVEN
Ethnic and Race Relations   191

CHAPTER EIGHT
Gender Relations   226

CHAPTER NINE
The Family   259

CHAPTER TEN
Population and Environment 292

CHAPTER ELEVEN
Politics, Protest and Change 323

CHAPTER TWELVE
Methods of Research   357

Preface

Readers liked the first two editions of MACRO/MICRO. That meant, in revising the book for a third edition, that we faced a hard choice: should the book stay the same, with a few minor changes, or not? Staying the same would be easy for us and, we think, okay with our readers. But that is not what we ended up doing.

Why did we take the not-so-easy path? The reason is, since the second edition came out, we have changed, Canadian sociology has changed and the world has changed. Like the second edition, the third edition of MACRO/MICRO reflects these changes. Specifically, you will find some of the following changes:

- Weblinks: a new feature at the end of each chapter that gives students a list of useful Web sites relating to the chapter;

- boxed inserts that carry over from chapter to chapter:
  - "Applied Sociology,"
  - "Far and Away,"
  - "Everyday Life," and
  - "Social Profiles";

- more discussion of classical and modern theorists throughout the book;

- more discussion of religion in the chapter on culture (Chapter 2);

- more discussion of the mass media and its stereotypes, both in the chapter on culture (Chapter 2) and in the chapter on socialization (Chapter 3);

- a reorganized chapter on deviance and control (Chapter 4), with more depth and more examples; and

- a discussion of health in relation to inequality (Chapter 5).

We have been particularly eager to satisfy requests for more discussion of the major ideas and theories introduced in the work of feminist scholars. In the first edition of MACRO/MICRO, we scattered feminist scholarship throughout; in the second edition, we centred feminist scholarship in the chapter on gender relations. In this edition, we have increased the feminist material in both places.

Despite these changes, we have kept the book the same length by removing old material, to make room for new material. We have also eliminated most in-text references to the literature, to save space and increase readability. We have retained newspaper inserts, in the belief that they illustrate important sociological principles and are well-written — indeed, better written than most sociological scholarship. Our only regret is that space limitations prevented us from delving further into feminist theory and other theoretical developments in sociology, as well as innumerable areas of substantive research which merit serious attention. But after all, this is only a brief introduction to sociology, not the final word.

When we wrote the first two editions, we assumed that it is possible to explain anything sociological to anyone who wants to understand it. The book's popularity proved us right. In writing the third edition, we continued to make this assumption. The result is an even richer, more provocative conversation about sociology than before — but a book that is still reader-friendly. We think we got it right. Tell us what *you* think and, most important, enjoy!

Acknowledgements

We are grateful to a variety of students, friends and colleagues who helped us with the third edition of MACRO/MICRO.

At Prentice Hall Canada, we received encouragement from sponsoring editor Rebecca Bersagel, and concrete assistance from developmental editor Lisa Berland and production editor Marjan Farahbaksh. We also thank the copy editor, Liba Berry, who was enormously helpful.

Several years' worth of students in the introductory sociology courses at the University of Toronto and Dawson College provided lots of ideas for change and improvement. Some, however, have done much more than that. In particular, we are grateful to Toronto undergraduates Sarah Wittman (for organizing the photographic inserts and proposing editorial cuts), Megan Bockus (for helping to select the journalistic inserts) and Charles Tepperman (for creating preliminary charts and diagrams, taking care of permissions, and compiling the index). Thanks also to Toronto graduate students Nancy Nazer and Sandra Colavecchia who helped prepare the Instructors' Manual and Study Guide.

We are grateful to those — especially, *The Globe and Mail* — who gave us permission to reprint portions of their articles in the boxed inserts that appear in the book.

Finally, we want to thank everyone who read and commented on earlier drafts of this manuscript. They include Murray Pomerance, professor of sociology at Ryerson Polytechnic University in Toronto, and Jim Curtis, professor of sociology at the University of Waterloo: both provided much encouragement and many useful suggestions. Reviewers — who included Tom Callaghan, St. Clair College; Soma Hewa, Mount Royal College; Dalton Irwin, Sir Sandford Fleming College; and Vincent Salvo, Grande Prairie Regional College — provided many useful and provocative suggestions, and we thank them too. And to the readers of the second edition who have taken the trouble to give us their thoughts, thanks to you too!

We apologize for the shortcomings that remain in this book, despite so many good suggestions from so many quarters.

As before, this book is dedicated to our students — the ones at the University of Toronto and at Dawson College on whom we crash-tested our material, and students elsewhere who are reading the ideas contained between these covers. We hope they find them interesting and provocative.

SOCIOLOGY: THE STUDY OF SOCIETY

C H A P T E R   O U T L I N E

Each person is unique, but through their interactions people form social structures.

WHAT IS SOCIOLOGY?

Personal Troubles, Public Issues   Why does someone become a sociologist? There are probably as many answers as there are sociologists. But all sociologists have one thing in common: somehow, at one time or another, they got fascinated with trying to understand their own lives and the lives of people around them. They soon discovered that "common sense" wasn't enough: it gave them incomplete explanations about people's behaviour and the society they live in.

For many people, for much of what we do, our common-sense understanding of the world is just fine. But for anyone who really wants to understand how society works, it isn't good enough. We will consider the strengths and weaknesses of common-sense knowledge later in this chapter, but you may already realize that there are many questions that common sense cannot answer adequately: Why are some people rich and others poor? Why is there still war? Why haven't we put more dollars into finding a cure for AIDS? What's love? How should Canada deal with the danger of Quebec seceding?

Some of these "big" questions may interest you, others may not. But even when it comes to your personal life there will be many questions for which common sense has no answer: Why should I keep going to school? How will I know the right person to marry? Should I choose a job that pays a lot or a job I am likely to enjoy?

Sociologists spend their lives thinking about these questions, and many more. Sociologists, however, are not satisfied with common-sense answers. They want to replace their common-sense understanding with scientific explanation. To do this, they study people's lives and social relationships more thoroughly than anyone else. Why? Because sociologists want to understand how all of us are affected by the society in which we live. They are fascinated by big "public issues" such as poverty, race and the impact of technology. But they recognize that there is another side to these public issues, a personal side. Sociologists know that your "personal" problems are similar to many other people's problems. Often, these are problems society ought to deal with because individuals cannot deal with them on their own. In that sense, many of our problems are really the personal side of public issues.

Sociologists know that understanding and finding solutions to both public issues and personal problems requires clear thinking and careful research. For this reason, they have developed a variety of concepts, theories and research methods. These allow sociologists to describe the social world in ways which are unbiased, to explain how and why things happen the way they do, to critique existing social arrangements which promote inequality or have other negative effects, and to work towards effecting social change.

Our starting point is a formal definition of sociology and the connection sociologists make between personal problems and public issues.

MACROsociology/MICROsociology   Scholars have defined **sociology** in a great many ways, but most sociologists think of it as the scientific study of human society and social behaviour.

Humans are "social" beings in the sense that most of the things we do are done with other people. That's why sociologists take as their subject matter the social **groups** we create when we join together with others. They range from small groups — as few as two people — to large corporations and even whole societies. When looking at social groups, sociologists study the various ways in which group membership affects the behaviour of individuals and individual activity affects the behaviour of the group.

As you can see, sociology is an enormous area of study. However, most of what sociologists look at, and most sociological ways of looking, fall into one of two related but distinct subfields: macrosociology and microsociology.

Macrosociology is the study of social institutions (for example, the Roman Catholic Church; marriage; sport) and large social groups (for example, ethnic minorities or college students). It also includes the study of social processes and patterns that characterize whole societies (for example, social control and social change), and the system of social arrangements that makes up a society. Macrosociology, then, studies the large and somewhat abstract patterns that large groups of people form over long periods of time.

Microsociology, by contrast, examines the processes and patterns of face-to-face interaction that take place among people within groups. Generally, then, microsociology is the analysis of small groups (for example, your classroom). It studies the daily struggles for power — the interactions and negotiations we discuss later in this chapter — which, together, produce the stable and enduring patterns that macrosociologists like to study.

Macrosociology takes a broad view of society and a long view of social change, often in terms of decades, centuries or even millennia. By contrast, microsociology studies social processes that are more localized and faster moving. For example, it studies what may happen in the course of a conversation, party, classroom lecture or love affair.

The differences in perspective show up in a variety of ways. For one example, macrosociologists are likely to emphasize how slowly things change and how remarkably persistent a social pattern is as it imprints itself on one generation after another. By contrast, microsociologists are likely to emphasize how rapidly and subtly things change. They see people constantly creating and refining their relationships and in this way, creating and refining the social order. Combining macro and micro approaches can improve our understanding of the world.

Consider a common social phenomenon: racial discrimination in the workplace. From the macro perspective, racial discrimination is a large-scale social process affecting millions of people. Yet, from the micro perspective, it only occurs because (some) people make certain assumptions about skin colour in some concrete situation. Thus, individual people who assign values to physical features are at the root of the discrimination problem. Yet they do this assigning because of widespread and pervasive social values.

For this reason, microsociologists might study why and how certain physical features come to have those meanings. Or they might study how people act out those meanings by engaging in discrimination in a particular workplace. However, discrimination is not only an individual issue. It is perpetuated because discrimination benefits certain groups economically. That's why macrosociologists might study *how* face-to-face discrimination provides ongoing economic advantages for the dominant racial group.

C. Wright Mills (1959) wrote that the **sociological imagination** is the ability to see connections between large and small, fast changing and slow changing, portions of social life. It requires an awareness of the relation between individuals and the wider society. It helps us to look at our own personal experiences in a different, more objective way. It forces us to ask how our lives are shaped by the larger social context in which we live. Finally, the sociological imagination helps us to see society as the result of millions of people working out their own personal lives.

VARIETIES OF SCIENCE

It may seem strange to begin a discussion of a discipline that claims to be a science, as sociology does, by referring to the importance of imagination. Before going on, then, we had better clarify what we mean by "science" and in what sense we can consider sociology a science.

All of us are able to remember our experiences and draw lessons from them. We do not need scientific study to make ordinary, everyday decisions. In fact, common sense and remembered experience build up over a long time into something people call folk wisdom. This folk wisdom contains many "rules of thumb" — rules of behaviour that people have found useful over the course of time. Rules of thumb often become pieces of popular advice; for example, "Don't go swimming right after eating a heavy meal." We would not consider this to be a scientific statement, even if it makes sense to us and seems true. Why not? One difference between common sense and science is that common sense is *not* carefully tested with data; scientific knowledge is.

The danger in relying on common sense to understand society is clear when we examine some of the "common-sense" ideas expressed in Everyday Life (page 5). The excerpt comes from a newspaper column known for its common-sense approach to people's problems. Not only do many of the ideas expressed in the article sound familiar, they sound believable. You feel good after reading Ann Landers, as if, now, you can put your life in order and everything will be okay. That's what common-sense advice is *supposed* to do for you.

But sociological research would lead us to disagree with most of the advice offered in this excerpt, which is based on what might be called a "voluntaristic" view of life: it suggests that people are in a position to live as they would wish to, and this suggestion is deeply flawed.

According to the voluntaristic view, people's lives reflect what they *want* them to reflect. People with good ideas, attitudes and values will have good lives; people with bad ideas, attitudes and values will have bad lives. This excerpt says

The Rules for Being Human

Some sociologists do research that directly addresses the problems many people have to face in their everyday lives. Other sociologists apply this knowledge when counselling people with problems, whether educational, marital, work-related, a result of addiction, or otherwise. In doing so, however, they compete with people — such as the writer of this letter to Ann Landers — whose advice is not based on research and is probably wrong.

Dear Ann Landers:

Your advice reaches millions of readers daily.

I ran across these rules for being human and have been passing them along whenever I get the chance. –M.M., Ashland, ORE.

You will receive a body. You may like it or hate it, but it will be yours for as long as you live. How you take care of it or fail to take care of it can make an enormous difference in the quality of your life.

You will learn lessons. You are enrolled in a full-time, informal school called Life. Each day, you will be presented with opportunities to learn what you need to know. The lessons presented are often completely different from those you *think* you need.

There are no mistakes, only lessons. Growth is a process of trial, error and experimentation. You can learn as much from failure as you can from success. Maybe more.

A lesson is repeated until it is learned. A lesson will be presented to you in various forms until you have learned it. When you have learned it (as evidenced by a change in your attitude and ultimately your behavior), then you can go on to the next lesson.

Learning lessons does not end. There is no stage of life that does not contain some lessons. As long as you live there will be something more to learn.

"There" is no better than "Here." When your "there" has become a "here," you will simply discover another "there" that will again look better than your "here." Don't be fooled by believing that the unattainable is better than what you have.

Others are merely mirrors of you. You cannot love or hate something about another person unless it reflects something you love or hate about yourself. When tempted to criticize others, ask yourself why you feel so strongly.

What you make of your life is up to you. You have all the tools and resources you need. What you create with those tools and resources is up to you. Remember that through desire, goal setting and unflagging effort you can have anything you want. Persistence is the key to success.

The answers lie inside you. The solutions to all of life's problems lie within your grasp. All you need to do is ask, look, listen and trust.

You will forget all this. Unless you consistently stay focused on the goals you have set for yourself, everything you've just read won't mean a thing.

Source: Abridged from Ann Landers, "One person's guide to being human," *The Boston Globe*, Sat., June 26, 1993, p. 39

---

explicitly "What you make of your life is up to you" and "The answers [to life's questions] lie within your grasp." But can that really be demonstrated to be true? Most sociologists would disagree that such voluntaristic common sense is sound analysis, pointing to examples like the following:

- certain kinds of people (e.g., people who are poor) get sick more often and die at younger ages than other kinds of people, even though they don't want to. This also happens with people who aren't poor; and

- certain kinds of people (e.g., people who are black) are less likely to get hired for jobs than other kinds of people, though they don't want *not* to get hired.

Are we really to think that poor people *want* to die younger? or that black job-seekers *want* to be unemployed? or that these people lack the right attitudes and values, as the common-sense argument seems to say? That if only they changed their ways of thinking they would live longer or get better jobs? Or, on the other hand, might we think that the circumstances within which they live cause, or even force, them to experience conditions they would rather avoid?

This question is at the heart of sociology — indeed, all social science. It raises additional questions like: Why do some people get more choice in their lives than others? Why do more unpleasant things happen to some people than others? Where do the ideas contained in "common sense" come from? Are these ideas likely to benefit some groups (e.g., rich white men) more than others (e.g., poor black women)?

By the end of this book, you will have a beginner's answer to these questions. But for the time being understand that, because of their biases, common-sense explanations are more likely to be wrong than right. Sociology, both macro and micro, is about seeing beyond these biases. That's why sociologists take a scientific, instead of common-sense, approach to understanding everyday life.

What Is Science?

Science is the discovery, explanation and prediction of events in the world of our experience, and the analysis of relations between these events. Science requires *research* — the application of logical, systematic methods to verifiable evidence. The **scientific method** requires us to follow a systematic, organized series of steps that ensures as much objectivity as possible in researching a problem.

Objectivity is a way of interpreting events, or the relations among them, by using reason and the best evidence possible. Seen another way, objectivity is a way of looking at the world that is outside, or beyond, the impressions of a single viewer. To study something objectively means, as much as possible, avoiding personal bias, prejudice or preconception. The opposite, *subjectivity* is a tendency to interpret reality from a viewpoint shaped only by our own experiences, emotions, opinions, values and beliefs.

The scientific process forces us to construct theories, collect evidence and test predictions against careful observations, and accurately record our findings. If our predictions fail, we must change or reject our original theory.

To give a better idea of the difference between science and common sense, let's consider an issue about which most people already have an opinion: namely, the ways men and women drive automobiles. Insurance companies have long known that young men have more automobile accidents than young women do, but there are two competing, and quite different, explanations:

- in a given year, young men drive more often, and longer distances, than young women do. This means they are on the road longer and have more opportunity for getting into an accident; or

- young men drive more dangerously than young women do, no matter how long their trips may be.

It is worth knowing which answer is more correct and which cause of accidents is more important. If we know the right answer, we can take steps to reduce traffic accidents and fatalities. But we cannot know the answer without collecting data. For example, we can collect data on how many kilometres people drive, and how many accidents they have, per year. With these data, we can calculate an annual accident rate: the number of accidents per 10,000 kilometres driven. If the annual accident rate is the same for young men and young women, then there is no difference in the "dangerousness" of male and female driving.

On the other hand, if the annual accident rate is *not* the same for young men and women, then the first explanation is not valid and there may be support for the second. If so, we now have to collect data on the *ways* that men and women drive cars: how often they drink and drive, how quickly they drive, whether they obey the traffic rules and so on.

Researchers of driving behaviour have done this work and found that, in all of these respects, young men drive more recklessly than young women. A scientist then wants to ask *why* they do that. Is it genetic, something to do with the hormone levels in young men? Is it a universal feature of men growing up in Moncton or Moscow, one of the ways young men grow into adulthood, a *rite of passage* that involves risk-taking, danger and luck? Or is it a feature of our own society's view of adolescence, masculinity and the relationship between people and machinery?

These are the questions that go through a scientist's mind after someone has asked an interesting question. As you can see, science is not just a matter of technique or methods, it depends also upon the imagination, interest and insight of the scientist. Yet imagination and insight by themselves, too, are not enough because science tries to be objective, not subjective.

Scientists recognize that, in their own everyday lives, subjectivity is bound to creep in. As human beings, we all run the risk of jumping to conclusions without enough regard for evidence or reason. Being scientific in all aspects of our daily life may be impossible. What's more, it denies the part of us that is, and ought to be, intuitive and emotional. Nevertheless, if science is to be more than a collection of personal prejudices and anecdotes, the scientist must strive to be as objective as possible.

Objectivity is needed if we are to create and test theories — a major concern of sociology. A *theory* is an explanation of the causal relationship between various phenomena or events. An effective theory will not only have explanatory power; it will also enable the scientist to predict future events.

A well-reasoned theory provides *hypotheses* (or hunches) that allow us to test the theory empirically, with data. A hypothesis takes the form of a proposition or prediction about the relation between two or more events. When we make hypotheses, we predict the future. When we collect data to test our predictions, we find out if the data support our theory. If the data do not show what we predicted, our theoretical explanation is thrown into doubt: we need to revise the theory.

Let's see how this works in our previous example by looking at some possible explanations for the high rate of male auto accidents. One possibility is that the behaviour is genetic. Young men just can't avoid stomping on the accelerator pedal. Another is that it is cultural: in our culture, young men feel their manhood is in doubt unless they risk their lives while driving. They *choose* to stomp on the accelerator pedal because, as they understand their situation, they will risk losing something important to them — their macho image or self-esteem — if they don't.

Now, if the cultural explanation is valid, we should be able to prove it in any number of different ways. For example, we should be able to find cultures where people have conceptions of masculinity that do not involve fast driving. In those cultures, young men and women will have the same accident rates. We would do this research by collecting data from a variety of different societies. This is called *comparative (or cross-national) research*. Similarly, if the cultural explanation is valid, we should be able to distinguish among young men in our own culture and predict their respective driving records. According to our theory, young men who feel secure about their manhood won't feel they have to prove their bravery to anyone. As a result they will have a lower accident rate than young men who feel unsure about their manhood. We would do this research by carrying out a *survey* of young men, using questionnaires or interviews to find out their attitudes and self-images.

Finally, if the cultural theory is valid, we should be able to change people's behaviour with a new kind of driving instruction. In our driving school — maybe even in our movies and in our casual discourse — we would try to change young people's attitudes about cars, driving and masculinity. We would predict that young men learning to drive under these conditions would have a lower accident rate than young men who have learned the "rules of the road" in a macho context. (Young women would have the same accident rate, regardless of the driving school they graduated from.) An *experiment* would tell us whether the theory was valid or not.

We will discuss all of these research methods at length in Chapter 12. For the time being, we want to emphasize that sociology is concerned with testing theories, and all theories can be tested in a number of different ways.

Is Sociology a Science like Every Other Science?

Perhaps you are wondering if sociology really can be scientific. After all, the popular image we have of science is based on physics and chemistry. When we hear the word "science" we often imagine people wearing white coats in a laboratory, surrounded by expensive equipment. In fact, what we are imagining is not science, but the artifacts of a particular science at a particular time and place.

Sociology doesn't use these kinds of artifacts, but it *does* take a scientific approach to problem solving nonetheless. Like any scientific research, sociological research works by collecting, organizing and interpreting data, for the purposes of testing a hypothesis or discovering new relations among phenomena. Frequently, however, sociologists are more limited than researchers in the physical sciences in the research methods they can use. For example, it is often difficult for sociologists to carry out the kinds of experiments they would like to, such as the driving-school experiments we discussed earlier. That is because public institutions (like high schools) are often unwilling to cooperate. Their motives are humane, if not scientific: they believe you shouldn't set up a new educational program (like a driving school) if you don't know the likely outcome. If you know the program will *harm* people, you definitely shouldn't do it. If you know it will *help* people, then everyone should be permitted to take part; there should be no excluded comparison (or what experimenters call "control") group.

Fortunately, the scientific method does not always require experimentation: there are other scientific ways to carry out research. Some fields that study human behaviour — for example, psychology — use experiments almost exclusively. Other fields that study human behaviour — for example, history, economics and anthropology — use no experiments at all.

A second major problem facing sociology as a science is the problem of involvement by sociologists in some of the things they study. Physicists, chemists and astronomers study phenomena which are important but have no emotional impact on most peoples' daily lives. In contrast, sociologists often study problems which they know about first-hand and which may have an emotional impact on their own lives. For example, a sociologist studying divorce may be going through one.

As human beings, sociologists are bound to be prejudiced, emotional and irrational at times. A science of social behaviour is possible only if sociologists come as close as possible to ensure that their work is *value free*. Value-free re-

SOCIAL PROFILE 1.1

Work Harder, Get Less!

Minutes of work* required to pay for:

	1974	1994
Fleecy (litre)	5.33	6.22
Pork chops (kg)	23.42	38.93
Kraft dinner (box)	2.70	4.19
Ground beef (kg)	23.13	13.88
Nectarines (kg)	9.78	8.29
Shredded Wheat (box)	7.95	18.15
Chicken legs (kg)	11.46	13.88
Movie ticket	24.26	33.86

Hours required to pay for:

Men's dress shirt	2.70	3.17
Men's slacks	2.02	4.23
Men's off-the-rack suit	13.50	17.64
Timex watch		
(low-end)	3.13	1.76
(high-end)	10.10	5.29
Hood-mist hair dryer	6.49	4.23
Vacuum cleaner	39.95	28.21
18" electric mower	20.22	12.69
26" colour TV	19.10	49.36
Trendy child's bike	9.86	7.76
Kenmore clothes washer	65.16	38.72
Kenmore clothes dryer	42.69	26.73

Years required to buy a resale house (average price):

	1975	1995
In Canada	3.18	2.82
In Toronto	3.88	3.88
In Vancouver	3.89	6.00

*Calculations based on the average weekly salaries for 1974 ($178.09) and 1994 ($567.02).

Source: Based on Statistics Canada data appearing in *The Globe and Mail*, Sat., Dec. 16, 1995, D5

search is research that excludes all ideological or unscientific assumptions, as well as all personal judgments or biases. The problem of achieving value freedom faces all of the social sciences — namely, anthropology, psychology, political science, geography, economics and social history. That is because the things that we study often include subjects of political debate, religious teaching or personal commitment. We have to avoid setting up a research problem in a way that protects our own beliefs.

There are many cases where sociologists have formulated a research problem inadequately, or ignored it completely, because of a narrow way of seeing the world. Consider this example: Our society is dominated by men, so men define what is valuable and "important." As a result, until about twenty-five years ago, no one had done much serious research on housework. Yet housework is a job that has historically occupied more people than any other. Why had it been ignored? The answer is that, until recently, most sociologists were men and men rarely do housework.

Not surprisingly, women sociologists have led the way in doing research on this activity. This is why some sociologists argue that you need female researchers to give a female perspective on society, and to make sure important problems are not ignored. Similarly, people belonging to racial minorities, or growing up in poverty, have claimed there is a need for members of their own groups to study society from their own perspectives. There is great merit in this point of view. On the other hand, a researcher who is too closely tied to a problem risks losing the objectivity that a more "distant" observer might bring to the study (in the same way that a divorced person might study divorce less objectively than a single or married person).

If sociology has fallen far short of value-free research in the past, this does not prove that we should give up trying. Value freedom in sociology may be very difficult, but it is, and should be, the continuing goal of all sociologists. This view has implications for sociology students as well as for professional sociologists. It means that when you study sociology, you must be alert to the hidden assumptions that are shaping your argument.

Value freedom is even more important to good research than carefully collected facts and powerful statistical techniques. It is vitally important in all sociological expression, not just in research *per se*. The need for value freedom is most important when you are applying social research to public issues. Such research can play an important part in making policies to deal with child abuse, racial discrimination or school reform, for example. Good science is always possible, but the personal limitations of the researcher and the biases of those who are funding the research are always in a position to threaten value freedom.

We will see this point illustrated throughout the book; but perhaps nowhere is it clearer than in the area of gender relations. As you will learn in Chapter 8 (Gender Relations), there is still a great deal of controversy about the extent and causes of (1) domestic inequality (i.e., who does what around the home, and for what reward); (2) workplace inequality (i.e., the hiring, pay, promotion and treatment of men and women on the job); and (3) violence between intimates, both inside and outside marriage. As you can imagine, these are all complex, emotionally charged topics in which sociologists of both sexes must struggle to find out the truth despite their personal limitations and anxieties.

To repeat, sociology is a science, like physics or biology, though as a science, sociology is more like the other fields called *social sciences*.

HOW SOCIOLOGY IS DIFFERENT

In many ways, sociology is a lot like the other nonexperimental social sciences — especially anthropology, political science and economics — from which it also borrows a great deal. Yet sociology is also distinct from other scientific fields, even from the other social sciences.

Sociology is characterized as a distinctive discipline by its subject matter, its basic concepts and the way it approaches its subject matter. The biggest difference between sociology and the other social sciences is its subject matter, which is usually described as the relation between individual and society; between **social structure** and the socialized member of society.

Social Structure: The Subject Matter of Sociology

Concepts are the key to understanding any field: they are the tools of thought and argument. They make the work of study and research easier. You can come to understand road building, for example, by studying the tools road builders use: jackhammers, dump trucks, graders, tar trucks and steamrollers, among others. In the same way, you can come to understand sociology by learning the conceptual tools that sociologists use. Of these, **social structure** is the most important concept in sociology and you will soon see why.

Social structure is any enduring, predictable pattern of social relations among people in society. There is a lot of debate about how social structure works, but this much is clear: social structure is important because it *constrains* and *transforms* people's behaviour. First, it causes people with very different personalities to act the same way. That is, it shapes their action in a way that is dictated by the situation and, in that sense, it constrains them. People with very different personalities and lifestyles, for example, all behave similarly when they are sitting in a place of worship.

Second, social structure causes individual people to act in very different ways at different times. In that way it is transforming. So, for example, the black-robed judges who behave so decorously in their courtrooms may behave just like you or I — loudly, crudely and aggressively — at a hotly contested baseball game between the High Court judges and a select group of criminal lawyers.

The most fundamental transformation of all occurs in childhood, as we internalize the norms, values, attitudes and beliefs that are a part of our society. We will consider this process of socialization in detail in Chapter 3.

Note that these assumptions about social structure are precisely opposite to the assumptions that underlie genetics, biology and personality psychology. According to those fields, people don't change much from one situation to another, and they are fundamentally different from one another in unbridgeable ways. Sociologists argue the other side of the story, so sociology has a quite different approach to social behaviour, compared to those fields.

Consider the sociological approach to suicide, an example we will consider repeatedly in this book because of its association with one of sociology's founders, Emile Durkheim. Some might think that suicide, which is intensely personal, would not be socially structured — that is, subject to social influences. Yet what Durkheim showed in his classic work *Le Suicide* (1897) is that suicide *is* socially structured. For example, divorced people (especially men) without children are much more suicide-prone than married people (especially women) with children. Suicide, then, isn't an idiosyncratic act as common sense causes us to suppose.

This observation leads the sociologist to ask what is the *constraining* power of marriage and parenthood? And what is the *transformative* power of divorce? Durkheim's research shows that marriage and divorce are social experiences, among many, which shape people's most important and personal actions. Moreover, focusing on the social element of suicide gives us more ability to predict rates of suicidal behaviour than does focusing on the personal, psychological aspect.

In the abstract, these ideas about social structure may sound difficult, but in practice they are familiar and simple. Consider a more common example — the relationship between a doctor and a patient — that was the topic of a classic analysis by the sociologist Talcott Parsons (1951). When you visit a doctor for a check-up, you take along very specific expectations. You expect the physician to act in a serious, concerned and knowledgeable manner. The doctor also expects certain behaviours from you as a patient — that you show concern for

People resist scattering randomly and form small groups instead.

your health, pay attention to the diagnosis and follow the professional advice you receive.

How do we know that people really have such expectations and that these expectations are enduring and predictable? We can often see otherwise invisible expectations by taking note of the social disturbance caused by their violation. If we violate doctor-patient expectations, both doctor and patient alike will feel uncomfortable, even upset or disoriented. The interaction will stop flowing smoothly. Both doctor and patient will start wondering what to say and do next.

There are many reasons that social relationships, from the (two-person) **dyad** all the way up through a complete society, are enduring and stable. We learn to value stable relationships. Often, we lack the knowledge or courage to change relationships. Sometimes those in power develop a strong investment in the way things are and stand to lose something if they change. People with the most to gain urge us to meet other people's expectations. These reasons, and many others we shall discuss, help to maintain the social relationships of the society in which we live.

APPLIED SOCIOLOGY

The Dangers of Internet Addiction

Addictions pose a problem for sociologists, just as they do for psychiatrists, psychologists and social workers. Addictions have important social consequences — at work and at home, for example — and, often, they have social causes too. In the case of an addiction to the Internet, the particular form of social interaction itself is the object of the addiction. This makes it all the more important that sociologists apply their theoretical knowledge to understand the source and nature of this growing problem.

Counselling centres report a dramatic increase in calls — usually from a concerned spouse or other family member — relating to addictive computer behaviour. For people with little direction in their lives, cyberspace has proved engaging. At greatest risk are people with poor social skills or low self-esteem. These people, with unfulfilling social lives, are most likely to look to the Internet as a source of meaning in their lives.

However, Internet addiction is hard to control. E-mail junkies get annoyed when their children interrupt conversations with friends on the Internet. Likewise, friends and family members can never get through on the telephone — the line is always busy. The effect on (non-electronic) social relationships can be destructive.

As with any addiction, Internet addiction manifests increased tolerance and withdrawal phenomena. Addicts need to spend more and more time on the Net, like alcoholics who need to drink more every day to reach the same level of intoxication. Are you becoming a computer junkie? You may be at risk if you:

- promise to quit or cut down, then break your promise;

- mount energetic defences of your frequent computer use;

- lie about how much time you spend on the computer;

- enter E-mail relations you would shun in face-to-face contact;

- feel (alternately) euphoric and guilty about your computer experiences;

- feel depressed or anxious when you lose time on the computer;

- feel preoccupied with the computer when you are away from it;

- routinely use the computer when you are feeling uncomfortable, irritated or sad about something happening in your life;

- find you are spending too much money on computer hardware or on-line charges.

Source: Adapted from Gordon Arnaut, "Hooked on cyberspace: The danger of the Net," *The Globe and Mail*, Tues., Oct. 15, 1996, p. C1

Sociologists have found that what we learn about one social relationship —
for example, the doctor-patient relationship — can help us understand other,
quite different social relationships. Sociology is fascinated by the similarities
and differences between relationships. It is also fascinated by the structures they
form when fitted together. Sociologists can readily apply sociological concepts
across a wide range of different relationships because these relationships are
similar and interconnected. What we learn about conformity, power, persua-
sion, exclusion, belief or engagement in one relationship often applies to many
other kinds of relationship.

This willingness to generalize is one of sociology's most distinctive features.
In the end, sociology is the study of all social structures — two-position (or
dyadic) relationships like marriages, or doctors and patients; or larger sets of
relations like business enterprises or political campaigns, all the way up to total
societies and global empires.

Try your hand at this. First, read Applied Sociology above to find out about
people's responses to the Internet. Then ask yourself what it is about the Internet
that is socially structured, therefore *constraining* and *transforming*. How do people learn to deal with one another in this new social space? What is it that they
find so appealing that they get hooked on it?

Sociology's Other Main Concepts

The terms **social structure** and **social relationships**
are two basic concepts used by most sociologists. **Social structure**, you will remember, is any enduring, predictable pattern of social relations among people in
society. **Society** in this sense is the basic large-scale human group. Members of
a society interact with one another and share a common geographic territory.
To some degree, they also share a common culture and sense of collective existence and they take part in social institutions together.

A social institution is one kind of social structure, made up of a number of relationships — stable patterns of meaningful orientations to one another. Typically,
people use institutions to achieve their intended goals, as schools do for students, or hospitals do for patients. Within a social institution, people are thus part
of one or more social relationships, such as the connections between teacher
and student, doctor and patient, or parent and child.

Being a parent or a student or a doctor defines one's status in an institution.
Statuses are socially defined positions that determine how the individual should
relate to other people (such as their mutual rights and responsibilities) and with
whom the individual will interact. Roles are actual patterns of interaction with
others. Thus, being a doctor is a status, while acting like a doctor is a role performance. *Role expectations* are shared ideas about how people — any people —
should carry out the duties attached to a particular status, regardless of the personal characteristics of those people.

The concept of social relationship is the meeting point of the macro and the
micro. Each of us participates in social life in terms of the statuses and roles we
have adopted or have been assigned. Being a "student," for example, carries with
it a lot of learned behaviour patterns, expectations and motives. We all learn to
be students in elementary school. Once that role is learned, we carry around
with us expectations of what it means to be a student and how to do whatever it
is that students do. We also carry around with us expectations about teachers and
how and why teachers do whatever it is that they do.

For an individual, being a student does not mean carrying out some impersonal set of duties, obligations or expectations. We each have our own reasons for

doing things. We are all individuals, and we experience and act out our roles and statuses in our own particular ways. Yet, despite this, classroom behaviour is still largely predictable. Sociologically speaking, one class of students is pretty much like another. It is remarkable how slowly social structures change and how little they vary from one place to another, as we shall see repeatedly in this book.

At the same time, social roles and relationships don't just exist: they are enacted through interaction and negotiation. By *interaction* we mean the processes and manner in which social actors — people trying to meet each other's expectations — relate to each other, especially in face-to-face encounters. Interaction includes a wide variety of forms of communication, such as words, body language, attentiveness (or inattentiveness) and what some sociologists have called "face-work." By *negotiation* we mean all the ways people try to make sense of one another, and to one another: for example, by conferring, bargaining, making arrangements, compromising and reaching agreements. Though often hidden or masked by habit, processes of interaction and negotiation are what make roles and relationships work. They are the mechanisms underlying social structure.

Sociology's Perspectives

Sociology developed as a scientific discipline in the late 19th and early 20th centuries, as European thinkers tried to understand the dramatic changes that accompanied industrialization. For most of human history, change was slow and few people wondered much about their society. Things were as they always had been (or so it seemed), and people who wondered why were most likely to look to God for an explanation.

This attitude began to shift in the face of technological, political and religious changes within the last two centuries. People began to try to understand their society and to ask if these dramatic changes could be predicted and controlled. Chief among them, three individuals are typically credited with founding sociology as a scientific discipline: they are Karl Marx, Emile Durkheim and Max Weber.

Karl Marx (1818-1883) was not, strictly speaking, a sociologist. Nevertheless, sociology derived many of its key concepts — such as the term **class** — from his work. The questions Marx asked and the answers he provided remain important in contemporary sociological thought. In his writings, Marx (for example, *The Communist Manifesto; Capital*) developed a theory of society and of social change based on economic processes — what he called *modes of production*. For Marx, economic processes are the most fundamental ones in society and explain a great deal about how society is organized. Indeed, for Marx, most other social phenomena can be explained in terms of economic processes.

These three scholars were among sociology's most sophisticated people-watchers. In his own way, each set the stage for the work all sociologists do today. Pictured from left to right are Max Weber, Emile Durkheim, and Karl Marx.

A mode of production such as hunting will produce a different set of social relationships than will industrial production. In a hunting society, there is no private property because the animals which are hunted do not belong to anyone. They are outside the boundaries of the society and are hunted for the benefit of all. Basically, hunters are equal in this society; they even make and control their hunting tools, so they are self-sufficient.

By contrast, factory workers are not self-sufficient. A factory is a means of production that is owned by someone else, rarely by the factory workers themselves. This means the factory workers do not even own their tools; they cannot work, earn a living or feed themselves without the use of the factory's facilities. Owning the tools and controlling the worker's income puts the factory owner in a different social category or *class* from that of the worker.

Consider another difference. Because all benefit equally in a hunting society, there is little social (or group) conflict among people. But in an industrial society, owners and workers will have different interests, leading them to benefit unequally, and this will result, inevitably, in class conflict. However much an owner and a worker admire one another as individuals, owners and workers as groups are bound to conflict with each other.

Marx's work was noteworthy for a number of reasons. He made the first attempt to uncover objective, scientific laws with which to understand society. He also made the first significant attempt to use history to predict the future course of economic and social change. Marx's questions about how society works remain relevant today, even for scholars who reject his answers.

One of those who rejected some of Marx's answers and modified others was the French scholar Emile Durkheim (1858-1917). Durkheim was one of the first European academics to describe himself as a sociologist, and he devoted much of his career to establishing sociology as a distinct and respected social science.

The starting point of Durkheim's sociology was the predominance of society over the individual. Society, Durkheim insisted, creates, constrains and transforms the individual. All of our values, beliefs and attitudes — even our ways of thinking — are derived from society. As an illustration, Durkheim (1951) took the case of suicide, as noted earlier. He showed that suicide is not only an individual act, it is also a social act: suicide rates change in accordance with social factors such as place of residence, religion, marital status, age and gender.

Equally, Durkheim recognized that suicide is not only an indication of personal problems, it is also a sign of social problems. Because of the rapid pace of social change, modern society is characterized by what he called **anomie** (or normlessness). In this condition, society no longer effectively regulates people's desires and aspirations. People in an anomic condition may become profoundly depressed and are more likely to kill themselves; but the depression is social, not individual, in origin.

In Durkheim's analysis, suicidal depression — a personal problem — is shown to be the outcome of broader social forces. Durkheim's consistent ability to link such phenomena as crime, suicide and religion to broader social processes has served as a source of inspiration to later generations of sociologists. Sociologists have also admired Durkheim's (1938) attempts to develop rigorous and consistent sociological research methods, such as his use of suicide *rates* to uncover the link between suicide and social factors. Though some of Durkheim's assumptions and findings are rejected today, his image of sociology continues to inspire sociologists.

Like Durkheim, Max Weber (1864-1920) modified or rejected much of Marx's approach, but he did so for different reasons. In particular, Weber rejected the idea that any one factor or set of factors determines either society or the individual. Weber saw society as an extraordinarily complex set of social relationships. In his view, society can never be completely explained and its course never completely predicted. All we can do is try to understand the more important factors and identify the impact these factors have had on society.

For this reason Weber looked not only to economic factors to explain society but to such other factors as religion, the growth of cities, changes in the law, science and technology and different types of political organization (Weber, 1961).

To a large extent, Weber's sociology focuses on domination and power. This makes Weber typical of German thinkers at the turn of the century. However, he stands out in his remarkable historical and technical knowledge, and in his ability to link together vastly different social processes. Like Marx and Durkheim, Weber had a flair for what was not obvious: the uncommon insight and the use of sociological imagination.

For example, Weber (1974) linked the rise of capitalism to religious doctrine, especially the so-called *Protestant ethic* of hard work (see Chapter 2 for a fuller discussion). He also linked the rise of capitalism to other factors: for example, the tendency of European monarchs during the Middle Ages to ally themselves with large cities in order to gain tactical control over the independent feudal nobility. In return for their support, monarchs granted the cities many rights which freed them from feudal obligations. This allowed their "citizens" (i.e., "city-dwellers") to experiment with new forms of production (such as factories), commerce (such as banking and insurance) and government (such as elected rulers).

Weber's impact on modern sociology is immense. Many key areas of sociological research, such as stratification and bureaucratic organization, are indebted to his pioneering work (Weber, 1958a). Perhaps the most enduring legacy, however, is his lesson to sociologists to be suspicious of easy answers and to avoid looking for simple, universal explanations (Weber, 1958b).

Today, sociologists still differ in what they consider to be the most fruitful approach to the study of society. Some prefer to follow Marx, others Durkheim and still others Weber. In fact, most sociologists fall into one of several main groups which embrace different sociological "paradigms." A **paradigm** is a general way of seeing the world. It embodies broad assumptions about the nature of society and social behaviour. A paradigm suggests which questions to ask, and how to interpret the answers obtained by research. To some degree, different paradigms are associated with different founding figures of sociology.

FOUR SOCIOLOGICAL PARADIGMS

Structural Functionalism   One of these paradigms is **structural functionalism**, often just called *functionalism*. Inspired partly by Emile Durkheim, structural functionalism looks at society as a social system — a set of components or structures that are organized in an orderly way and integrated to form a whole. The term *whole* is important here and, as you can probably guess, functionalists are typically concerned with macrosociological issues.

The main assumptions of structural functionalism are as follows: each social system has certain basic needs that must be met if it is going to continue to survive; the various interdependent structures in a social system exist in order to fulfill one or more of these needs; under normal conditions, the social system has a tendency to be in "equilibrium," a state of balance, stability, harmony and consensus; because all the structures are interrelated and integrated, changes in one will provoke changes in others, so that a new equilibrium is reached.

Structural functionalists depict society as orderly and stable — an "organism" that works to meet the needs of the social system as a whole. In doing so, it also meets many of the personal, irrational or subjective needs of its members. Functionalists assume that, among all the members of society, there is widespread agreement or consensus on what values should be upheld, on what is functional and dysfunctional in society, and on the preference for stability over change.

Because the existing social system is generally seen as beneficial, change is thought more likely to disrupt society than to provide benefits. That's why functionalists emphasize order over change. Confronted with a social event or relationship, functionalists ask one basic question: How does this event or relationship help to maintain the social system?

What is most distinctive about functionalism is its tendency to identify and explain "puzzling activities" which have no obvious explanation: for example, Why do 20th-century Canadians still pay respect to Santa Claus at Christmastime? Why do young men drive in death-defying ways? and, Why are pregnant women treated in a ritualistic, almost sacred manner? To explain a puzzling activity, functionalists first describe the society or group within which this puzzling activity occurs, then show that the activity has beneficial, though often hidden, consequences for the "system." These consequences are held to be the "function" and the explanation of the activity. Thus, functionalists explain social behaviours in terms of their consequences for the group or society as a whole.

Look at the description of some puzzling activities reported in Far and Away on the next page. The newspaper report described them as "lunacy" — mere craziness. Can you find a way to explain any or all of these activities in terms of their function or meaning for the people involved? In terms of their function for society? If so, from a sociological standpoint they are not mere lunacy.

In a functionalist explanation, the consequences, or functions, of a behaviour are its causes. To uncover the functions of a given structure or behaviour, sociologists look at its *actual consequences*, not at what the behaviour is popularly supposed to do. When we do this, we often discover that any social event or relationship may have consequences other than those that were intended.

Manifest functions (Merton, 1957) are functions that are obvious and intended. For example, the manifest functions of a school system are to educate the young and teach them to be responsible citizens. By contrast, *latent functions* are unintended and often unrecognized but have significant social effects nonetheless. For example, the latent function of schooling may be: to provide free baby-sitting services, which helps working parents; to teach obedience and conformity to rules, which helps future employers when the students join the work force; and to supply employers with credentials identifying which students were adequate. It may be that schools survive in their present form *not* because of their manifest functions (which are generally *not* met) but because of their latent functions (which *are* met).

Since society is a system of interrelated structures, changes in one part of society always produce changes — often unintended — in another part. Society is always reacting and readjusting to new inputs, even when people do not intend the changes that occur. This fact is important for sociology and also for social planning. Unless we are aware of the likely consequences of a planned change — the latent as well as the manifest functions, and the dysfunctions as well as the functions — we are likely to end up with changes we did not want. One sociologist (Sieber, 1981) has coined the term "fatal remedies" to describe attempts at

Lunacy or Just Puzzling Events?

What seems inexplicable or mere craziness to some makes perfect sense to others. See if you can figure out what social functions were served by the following strange behaviours, reported recently in the newspaper.

- Camels are fitted with tail lights in the Australian tourist town of Broome. Town council member Elsta Foy says the beasts, which carry tourists for sunset rides along Broome's famous Cable Beach Road, posed an unacceptable hazard to traffic. Tour operators agree to outfit their camels' rear ends with flashing, battery-operated bicycle lights.

- Police investigate the suspicious death of a goat running for mayor in a north-eastern Brazilian town. Frederico the goat had been leading in opinion surveys in Pilar since owner Petrucio Maia launched the animal on the campaign trail as a protest candidate in the municipal elections. Mr. Maia says he thinks his goat was poisoned by a political rival.

- Italian police caution three men who strip their clothes off in a laundromat in the northern city of Bologna to wait while their clothes are being washed. The laundromat owner, who put up a sign after an earlier incident asking customers not to strip, calls the police when the three men, all in their 20s, undress. One takes off all his clothes, another keeps on just his shoes and the third his shoes and underwear.

- One thousand talking condoms meant for a Las Vegas convention are mistakenly sent to various mail-order catalogues and pharmacies in the United States. Instead of "Merry Christmas," the talking condoms say, "Thanks for your business." Marc Snyder Co., which makes the condoms, says it will provide free replacements to customers with proof of purchase.

- The brown plastic front door at the centre of a two-year legal battle is allowed to remain at a house in a northern English village. Britain's state-funded architectural watchdog body, English Heritage, argues that the polymer portal is unsuitable in a conservation area boasting wooden front doors and could set a dangerous precedent. But its arguments are rejected by Britain's High Court and the door on the modest three-storey house in the village of Wirksworth remains. The door's owner, Patricia Harman, says English Heritage has so far spent $178,000, about twice the value of her home, trying to remove her mock-Georgian door in simulated mahogany.

Source: Philip Jackman, *The Globe and Mail*, Sat., Jan. 11, 1997, p. D4

social planning that fail to think through the consequences. In the end, they do more (unintended) harm than they do (intended) good. Why? Because any society is an extremely complex, somewhat unpredictable social system.

Conflict Theory

Many sociologists who identify strongly with the works of Marx and Weber find the structural-functional emphasis on order, harmony and stability one-sided and misleading. **Conflict theory**, by contrast, is a paradigm that emphasizes conflict and change as basic features of social life. For conflict theorists, change is the only constant in society. Conflict and change are inevitable because society is composed of groups which differ in their power, status and influence. These groups are always trying to maintain or improve their respective positions.

Conflict theorists reject the functionalist emphasis on the coherent social "whole." They explain that different groups in society come into conflict because the goods that people value highly and desire — wealth, prestige and power — are scarce. For some to gain control of these valued things means that others must be denied them. Conflict develops between groups whose goals differ or even oppose each other — for example, the rich and the poor, men and women, workers and management. These categories of opposing people differ in at least one social characteristic: respectively, the amount of wealth they have, their gender, or their relationship to power at work. In each case, it is the key difference that sets the conflict in motion.

Conflicts also arise out of different conceptions of what is valuable, desirable or good. Groups often struggle with one another over the right to define good and bad, valuable and worthless. Conflicts over the legalization of marijuana or the abolition of the death penalty reflect such differing conceptions of good and bad.

For a conflict theorist, there is one basic sociological question: Who benefits from the existing social order and who suffers? Like structural functionalists, conflict theorists pay attention to the consequences of behaviours or relationships. However, the conflict theorist does not suppose that any behaviour or relationship will benefit the whole society, and does not look for such a benefit. Instead, the conflict theorist looks for particular groups that will benefit most and have the power to seize this benefit.

Thus, a typical piece of research by conflict theorists will focus on a conflict, inequality or disadvantage — for example, the reason why some people favour affirmative action (or employment equity) for women and racial minorities while others oppose it. The explanation put forward will attribute different interests to the contending groups, explaining why less educated white men are particularly opposed. It will analyze the distribution of power among groups with opposing interests and discuss the ways they pursue their interests, for or against affirmative action.

Likewise, a conflict theorist might examine the ways racial or gender stereotypes are employed, political parties court the vote of the disaffected and rhetoric is used in the mass media to degrade or dehumanize opponents on one side of the debate or the other. The questions to be answered are: By what means does one side or another prevail in a struggle of competing interests? And how does the struggle and its resolution fit into the larger structure of racial, gender and class inequality in our society?

Conflict theorists do not consider conflict to be a destructive force; instead, they believe it focuses attention on social problems and brings people together to solve these problems. Conflict is the source of the women's movement, civil rights movements and trade unionism, among others. The native rights and Quebec separatist movements also focus public attention and bring about social change. As a result, conflict serves as the vehicle of positive social change.

As we have seen, this outlook on social life focuses attention away from shared values and towards ideologies. An **ideology** is a coherent set of interrelated beliefs about the nature of the world and of people. It guides a person's interpretation of, and reaction to, external events. For example, many people in our society believe they are responsible for their own success or failure. They think, "I am free to choose the path I will take; if my choice turns out badly, I have only myself to blame." This thinking is part of what is called the "liberal ideology." (Perhaps you can see how this is related to the Ann Landers column we looked at earlier.)

Liberal ideology affects the way people behave in a wide variety of situations. On the macrosociological side, it influences which political party they will vote for and whether they will support welfare benefits for the poor or capital gains taxes for the rich. On the microsociological side, it influences how they will react if they are thrown out of work, battered by a spouse or mistreated by the government. In all cases, this ideology encourages people to "blame the victim" and support the *status quo*.

In conflict theory, the *dominant ideology* is the ideology of the dominant group, justifying its power and wealth. The rest of us do not rebel because we have come to believe in the dominant ideology. Young people are taught this ideology in schools, churches and through media; we hear it repeated throughout life. However passively, we learn to live with the *status quo*.

Marxist theorists embrace a particular version of conflict theory. They claim that the dominant ideology promotes "false consciousness," a perception of the world that is not in accord with objective reality. We see this when people blame the shortcomings of other people, and not the way society is organized, for causing widespread problems. For example, they may think, "Women who wear revealing clothes have only themselves to blame if they get raped." Views like this, which hold the victims responsible for their own misfortunes, illustrate what conflict theorists consider "false consciousness."

Often, even victims of the system blame themselves. For example, many chronically unemployed people display this false consciousness and subscribe to the dominant ideology. How else can we explain the large number of unemployed people who fail to vote for radical politicians, if they vote at all?

Conflict theorists vary in what they consider to be the central conflicts in society. Some believe that there are many possible sources of conflict. These may include differences in wealth, gender, position at work, ethnicity, race and religion. Others, especially Marxian theorists, see these conflicts as secondary to, and connected with, one central conflict in capitalist society: class conflict.

In Marxist terms, a **class** is a set of people with the same relation to the means of production. People who control the means of production — the organizations that hire workers and own the capital that finances these organizations — control the lives of everyone else. These capitalists are the ruling class, and their view about how the world works serves to justify their position. They also influence huge social institutions that perpetuate the capitalists' position at the expense of others.

Class, then, is important because it gives rise to different "life chances" — chances of gaining wealth, prestige and power, or even good health and a steady job. It does so because one class, the capitalist class, has control over everyone else.

The work of Weber also inspired sociologists who follow the conflict paradigm. Weber argued that conflict arises as much over such intangibles as values, status and a sense of personal honour as over tangibles such as money or good health. From Weber's point of view, even modern corporations with no identifiable "owner" experience conflict. The bureaucratic managers of the corporation come to think of themselves as a status group and act to further their own group interests. That is why, Weberian theorists argue, conflict can be found in *any* society, not only in capitalist societies.

Symbolic Interactionism

Symbolic interactionism is a theoretical paradigm that sees society as a product of continuous face-to-face interaction among individuals in different settings. To understand this approach, let us consider the words that make up its name: "symbol" and "interaction."

In simple terms, a **symbol** is something that meaningfully represents something else. It can be a written or spoken word, a gesture, or a sign (such as a raised fist). *Interaction* refers to the ways two or more people respond to one another. Most interaction among human beings is symbolic, in the sense that it depends on words and actions that have meanings beyond themselves. A frown, a kiss, a smile — all have meanings which are learned, shared and changed through interaction. Some acts even have hidden meanings and double meanings.

Symbolic interactionism focuses on the processes by which people interpret and respond to the actions of others. It studies the way social structures, as patterns of behaviour, arise out of these processes. When naming the approach "symbolic interactionism" in 1937, Herbert Blumer described the basic elements of the paradigm in terms of three propositions: (a) "human beings act towards

FAR AND AWAY

Short versus Tall: What is the Conflict About?

In Canada, height does play a part in people's lives. Research has found that, other things being equal, taller people gain positions of higher authority and receive higher wages than equally qualified people who are shorter. But discrimination against short people in Canada is less extreme than in China. This makes one wonder whether the differences in life chances due to height are a roundabout way of penalizing people of particular social classes, racial groups or genders who are more likely to be short.

In this nation of height-disadvantaged people, shorter citizens face blatant discrimination. Many schools and jobs require above-average height. Short people are considered an unattractive sub-species. And Chinese often discourage intermarriage for fear the union will result in short children — who will in turn endure life-long prejudice.

Being tall here is disproportionately important. Heightism is so bad that people often fib about their height, the way Westerners might lie about their age. One magazine in the western city of Xian runs an advice column especially for short people. High heels are popular not just with women but also with men. Wannabe-tall types send for mail-order "height-increasing machines" that purport to stretch limbs. And anxious parents dose their children with "height-increasing medicine."

At a recent showing of a Hong Kong hit film in Beijing, the audience tittered when a short actress, playing the role of a secretary, appeared on the screen. "Look how short she is," someone yelled.

Chinese aren't used to seeing short people in the movies, or short secretaries in real life. Acting classes at the Beijing Film Academy, for instance, enroll only those of above-average height. And many offices hire secretaries for their looks, which invariably includes above-average height.

According to a recent national survey, the average 15-year-old Chinese urban male is 5 foot 5, slightly taller than his Japanese counterpart and only an inch or two shorter than the average adult North American male, according to insurance-company statistics. The average 15-year-old urban Chinese female is 5 foot 2.

A better diet means that Chinese have been growing taller during the past few decades. The average for a 15-year-old male, for example, is three-quarters of an inch taller than five years earlier, according to the ministry of health, which sponsored the survey.

But dreams keep outpacing reality. Ask a Chinese the ideal height, and the answer invariably is 5 foot 7 for a male and 5 foot 5 for a female. And for no apparent reason, China recently issued what is called "standard weights and measurements" for Chinese people. For males the standard height is 5 foot 7; for females 5 foot 3.

Like racism or sexism, heightism seems an absurd waste of talent. Last year, 17-year-old Zhang Jinxia committed suicide by drinking insecticide after a college in Jiangsu province barred her because of her height. Ms. Zhang had scored top marks in the entrance exam, but her letter of acceptance was annulled when she showed up on registration day and officials realized she was 4 foot 7. Her death and other cases of discrimination have led to the first calls for laws protecting short people in China.

Source: Adapted from "Getting short end of stick just part of life in China," *The Globe and Mail*, Thurs., Feb. 3, 1994, pp. A1, A11

things on the basis of the meanings that things have for them"; (b) these meanings "arise out of social interaction"; and (c) social action results from a "fitting together of individual lines of action." Said another way, symbolic interaction wants to understand how it is that we know what is "going on" and how we contrive to act together and know each other.

Unlike the other paradigms discussed so far, symbolic interactionism is not associated with a single founding figure of sociology. Most sociologists agree that this paradigm arose from the work of a group centred at the University of Chicago in the 1920s, 1930s and 1940s, among them, George Herbert Mead, W. I. Thomas and Robert Park. A second generation of this Chicago group included Everett Hughes, who influenced Canadian sociology in the years he taught at McGill University in Montreal. Third and fourth generations included Erving Goffman and Howard Becker, whose work we discuss in later chapters.

Like the other paradigms discussed so far, symbolic interactionism has its own typical set of research interests and approaches. Often, symbolic interactionist research focuses on an interactional problem that results from a "bad fit" between the ways that people see themselves, others, situations or relationships. For example, symbolic interactionists are interested in the way couples come to redefine their relationship during and after a divorce. Obviously the old ways of thinking and behaving won't work anymore; the participants need to agree on some new ways.

The symbolic interactionist wants to understand how new meanings, and perhaps new relationships, arise as people interact with one another in a state of conflict or confusion. To understand this may mean analyzing conversation, for example. Ultimately, a new meaning does arise, providing a new agreed-on basis for interaction. The previous "bad fit" gives way to a new "good fit." Even though the divorced couple may not like each other, they at least have a settled way of talking to each other.

The main assumption of this approach is that people do not respond to one another directly. They respond to *interpretations* of one another. These interpretations rest on meanings that people attach to the various events, gestures, words and actions around them. The meanings are social because, through interaction, people create them, share them, learn them and often pass them down from one generation to the next.

The need to understand an actor's point of view is captured in another important concept, the *definition of the situation*. We must understand an actor's definition of the situation, because people will act meaningfully in relation to *their* definition of reality, not ours.

Take a simple illustration: self-destructive behaviour. At one time or another, we have all seen an intelligent, attractive person act in an obnoxious way; call this one Heathcliff. We may know Heathcliff wants to have friends, but his obnoxious behaviour causes other people to stay away in droves. We begin to wonder if Heathcliff is crazy to act in such a self-defeating way.

Our view may change once we get to understand Heathcliff's point of view. He feels ugly and undesirable as a friend: maybe his parents labelled him the smart but nerdy son. In any event, he avoids interactions that might end in rejection. Obnoxious behaviour poses a difficult test for anyone who wants to be Heathcliff's friend, so someone surviving this "ordeal by obnoxiousness" would surely be a friend worth having. Once we understand Heathcliff's reasons, his obnoxious, self-destructive behaviour makes perfect sense and does not seem irrational at all.

Now, you will recall that Durkheim also studied self-destructive behaviour (namely, suicide) and thought it was unnecessary to know what was in people's minds. One only needed to know the "social facts." For certain kinds of self-destructive behaviour and certain kinds of understanding, especially for purposes of predicting behaviour, this may be true. However, you can see that Durkheim's approach may not help us in many other situations. Certainly, it would not help us counsel someone who had attempted suicide or was contemplating it.

Note one other feature of the scenario we just sketched out: it is that behaviour, whether obnoxious or nice, often produces the very reaction that is expected or feared. A person who expects rejection often gets rejected; indeed, often causes rejection. A person expecting friendship, on the other hand, often gets friendship. This led sociologists (Thomas and Thomas, 1928) to conclude that "a situation that is believed to be real is [often] real in its consequences." This simple theorem applies in a wide variety of situations.

In short, social interactions produce relationships that reflect the beliefs and expectations people bring to them. But how can social order emerge from two (or sometimes many more) different beliefs, expectations and definitions of the same situation? The answer, as we indicated earlier, is through *negotiation*. According to symbolic interactionists, social arrangements require continuous negotiation, dialogue, bargaining and compromise. Negotiation takes place in the House of Commons when a law is being changed or a new law is

---

APPLIED SOCIOLOGY

The Social Meaning of a Dangerous Ritual

Sociologists are aware that behaviours often have symbolic meanings which must be addressed in solving a social problem. Take the example of needle sharing by drug addicts: this dangerous practice reminds us that drug abusers are not only looking for a drug high, they are also seeking a sense of community and a chance to show their fearlessness.

In the AIDS-haunted world of drug addiction, sharing needles to shoot up is often a communal and sexual ritual that addicts won't part with, a new study shows.

That is just one of the alarming findings of two University of Alberta researchers who have spent the past four years investigating factors leading to the spread of AIDS among intravenous drug users, believed to be North America's fastest-increasing population and the major reason the disease is spreading to heterosexuals and children.

Lois and Ann Marie Pagliaro also were told by about one-third of intravenous drug users they interviewed in Alberta that they would not use free needle-exchange programs intended to keep addicts from sharing needles and spreading AIDS and other diseases.

That sobering news is especially troubling for natives, identified as one of the groups most at risk because of the deadly spiral of poverty and intravenous drug use identified as a major problem for inner-city natives. In a survey of 47 natives in jails or treatment centres who are or were users of injected drugs — two-thirds of whom were women — 68 per cent said they shared needles during drug use. Sharing needles is considered one of the primary ways of spreading the human immunodeficiency virus, precursor of AIDS.

Addicts who took part in the study told the Pagliaros they sometimes shared needles because they could not wait even 15 minutes for a needle to be delivered. Some also disliked disinfecting with bleach, felt too intoxicated to bother with new needles or were too "lazy" to worry about it.

Others simply felt fatalistically that they were going to die anyway, Ms. Pagliaro said.

Source: Miro Cernetig, "Sharing of drug needles a valued ritual," *The Globe and Mail*, Wed., July 15, 1992, p. A7

being voted into effect. It also takes place when people are deciding what movie to see on a Friday night, and when one person holds out a teacup for a second to fill.

As you might imagine, negotiation requires a great many social skills, and we all learn these skills in interaction throughout our entire lives. We learn them the same way we learn language. With practice, most of us become good at understanding other people's definition of the situation, because we have to. Someone else's definition of the situation is the terrain in which we must pitch our own action. To communicate effectively with people, we have to see the world the way they do, however imperfectly. Communication is often easiest if we can lead people to redefine the situation: to see the interaction in *our* way.

The feminist paradigm

A fourth paradigm that is becoming more and more influential in sociology is the *feminist paradigm*. Like other sociological approaches, the feminist approach is composed of a wide variety of different points of view and diverse, sometimes conflicting, theories. Nevertheless, there are a number of common themes and concerns which can be identified in the work of feminists.

Note first that feminism is not something new. It is a paradigm that goes back at least two centuries, to the English philosopher Mary Wollstonecraft. Since the 19th century there have been numerous bursts of visible feminist activity followed by periods of near invisibility. The first wave of feminism occurred between the middle of the 19th century and the early 20th century. It culminated in women gaining the right to vote in many Western countries. Then two strands of feminism emerged: one concerned with the objective of gaining equal rights with men in the public sphere, and another with gaining recognition of women's difference from men and improving their position in the private sphere of the family. This second wave, or reemergence of feminism, occurred in the 1960s. It is this wave which created the modern women's movement and has influenced sociology through a feminist critique of the male-dominated discipline.

Up to the late 1960s feminism was concerned with understanding the oppression believed to be commonly experienced by all women. More recent feminist scholarship has emphasized the diversity of women's experience as members of different countries, classes, racial and ethnic groups. As a result, we have seen the growth of varied "feminisms" which focus on one or another type of female experience. However, one widely accepted distinction is that between radical feminism and materialist (socialist or Marxist) feminism.

Radical feminism — arguably the dominant form of feminism in the United States — is characterized by a belief that **patriarchy** is the main and universal cause of women's oppression, owing to the superior power of men over women. This view has promoted the notion that women must organize separately from men to protect their own interests and foster a distinct women's culture. *Materialist feminism* — which is equally important in Canada, and dominant outside North America — traces its roots to Marxism and, like Marxism, views gender relations in a historical, economic context. It sees social class relations as determining the conditions women experience within capitalism. This approach calls for women to organize alongside men of the same social class to solve the problems women are suffering.

What the two main types of feminism have in common is a belief that the subordination of women is *not* a result of biology but, rather, a result of socioeconomic and ideological factors. Though they differ in thinking about the ways change might be achieved, both types are committed to eliminating the continued social inequality of women.

Feminism's general goal is equality between the sexes: to promote political, social and psychological changes by calling attention to facts and issues many have neglected. As we have noted, the application of feminism in sociology calls attention to the androcentric (or male-dominated) history of sociological thinking. To remedy this, feminist sociologists emphasize the experiences of women, "because there can be no sociological generalizations about human beings as long as a large number of such beings are systematically excluded or ignored" (Sydie, 1987: 360).

In practice, feminist research is a mixture of symbolic interactionist and conflict approaches. However, feminist research is informed by the following unique set of assumptions about reality:

- all personal life has a political dimension;

- the public and private spheres of life are both gendered (i.e., unequal for men and women);

- women's social experience routinely differs from men's;

- patriarchy — or male control — structures the way most societies work; and

- because of routinely different experiences and differences in power, women's and men's perceptions of reality differ.

So, for example, men and women typically have different views about divorce since the experience of divorce is very different for men and women. For men, it typically means a brief reduction in the standard of living, if any reduction at all, and a huge reduction in parenting responsibilities. For women, it usually means a dramatic, long-term loss in income and standard of living; indeed, poverty is common among single mothers and their children. Divorce also means an increase in a woman's parental responsibilities, since mothers usually retain custody of the children. For all these reasons, divorce has a very different meaning for women than for men. For similar reasons, sex, love and marriage all have different meanings for men and women, as we will see in later chapters.

To be a woman in our society is to act out a role that is defined by others. It is also to participate in a set of social relations that define one's status vis-à-vis others. This is true for males too, but with this difference: the "feminine" role in our society places women in a subservient role to men, in which they are sometimes degraded or victimized. Along with children, women are relatively powerless and often in danger of their lives. Women and children are far more often killed by men than men are killed by women and children, for example. Thus, women's acceptance of the female role is far more costly — even more dangerous — than men's acceptance of the male role.

Feminist scholars have also opened up new lines of enquiry about "puzzling activities" that might otherwise have gone unnoticed. For example, consider the problem of witchcraft. In general, social science has long held that concerns about witchcraft, sorcery and magic revealed tensions in the society that needed to be resolved. But precisely what tensions do concerns about witchcraft reveal? From a feminist perspective, the crackdown on witches in medieval Europe and colonial America was a gendered conflict. It focused on women in particular. It may have been aimed at reducing women's independence or even at limiting the spread of information about techniques of birth

Even women who work for pay are still responsible for most of the household chores.

control. From this standpoint, it was patriarchal behaviour (of which we will say a great deal more in Chapter 8, Gender Relations.) The point is, it took feminist scholars to make this connection.

Sydie (*ibid.*) points out that feminist sociology is political because "it reveals the manner in which past sociologists have provided intellectual justifications for the persistence of gender inequalities." So, for example, male sociologists were quick to defend gender inequalities in the family by creating theories — the so-called "functional theories" we shall discuss in Chapter 8 — that made gender inequality seem not only inevitable but desirable. Feminists emphasize that our notions of what it means to be male or female and our dealings with one another as male or female are a result of the social arrangements prevalent in our society. No one is ever "naturally" male or female, because gender is neither biological nor "natural."

Feminism is also a form of political activism that attempts to change the circumstances within which men and women lead their lives. Feminism, then, has an emancipatory goal. If gender relations always reflect the larger pattern of social relations in a society, then changing gender relations requires changing those social relations as well. In this respect, feminism is one of the "new social movements" which, alongside the antiwar, youth, civil rights and antiracism movements, have in the last three decades reshaped modern politics. Like these movements in both spirit and organization, feminism has looked for grass-roots support, affirmed subjectivity and spontaneity in politics and sought to dramatize its struggle rather than submerge its efforts in the traditional party system, using traditional electoral methods.

And, like these social movements, feminism has appealed to the social identity — the personal life experience — of its supporters. More than that, by arguing that "the personal is political," feminism opened up new domains of social life — sexuality, housework, child-rearing and so on — to political debate and legislation. It also forced us to examine the very roots of our being as gendered subjects: that is, how we get to be, and think of ourselves as, men versus women or mothers versus fathers. Thus, in a century, feminism moved dramatically from demanding equal access to social positions defined and dominated by men, to demanding that we reexamine the organization of roles, identities, even knowledge about reality, in a gendered society.

How Important Are the Differences Between Paradigms?

There is no denying that there are many differences among the major paradigms of sociology. However, this book is going to blur the differences between paradigms and stress the similarities. We do this because the similarities are more numerous and important than the differences.

There is no simple relationship between the four main paradigms (functionalist, conflict, symbolic interactionist, and feminist) and the two levels of analysis (macrosociological and microsociological). True, symbolic interactionism tends to specialize in microsociological analysis and functionalism and conflict theory, in macrosociological analysis. Yet each paradigm has valuable insights to contribute at both levels of analysis. Certainly this is true of the feminist approach. And this is not surprising since, as we have argued, the two levels of analysis are merely different ways of looking at the same thing.

All four paradigms have explanations for both order and change, consensus and conflict. In one situation, the structural functionalist or feminist explanation may provide valuable insights. In another, the conflict paradigm or symbolic interactionist paradigm may be better. No conclusive evidence proves that one paradigm is always or never appropriate, or that combining paradigms is misleading and fruitless. On the contrary, many sociological researchers — especially sociologists working on applied questions with a practical significance — use all four paradigms interchangeably. They would gain nothing by ignoring other paradigms. Fortunately, the connections among paradigms are clear enough that switching among them is possible.

EVERYDAY LIFE

Four Paradigms and a Refrigerator*

Like refrigerators, paradigms are something we use all the time. And just as any given refrigerator can be used to store a wide variety of foods, so any sociological paradigm can be used to analyze any social phenomenon — even the use of refrigerators.

- **The functionalist** sees a refrigerator as part of the economic and technical structure of a kitchen, household and family. It contributes to the survival of that household and family unit by contributing to the flow of food, nurture (e.g., chicken soup), love and protection from want.

- **The conflict theorist** sees that some people have better refrigerators than others. Unequal access to refrigerators — hence more food spoilage for some (typically the poorest members of society) than for others — both symbolizes and maintains a class inequality in life chances.

- **The feminist** sees the refrigerator as a tool which subjugates and isolates women in domestic work. Though technologies like the fridge promise to make housework easier, they also raise up the performance standards. Identification of women with domestic technology maintains a gendered inequality in life chances.

- **The symbolic interactionist** sees the refrigerator as something people learn to use together — as in negotiation about rights of access. The fridge's contents convey information about family lifestyle, and its outer surface (via magnetized doodads) is a storehouse of family culture and means of communication.

* We are indebted to Murray Pomerance, Ryerson Polytechnic University, Toronto, for this analysis.

SOCIOLOGY AS A FORM OF CONSCIOUSNESS

One thing all the paradigms have in common is a tendency to evaluate and question the existing order. As the feminist and conflict paradigms make particularly clear, sociology is not only a science. There are other, probably better, ways our society could operate. We can only make the necessary changes if we understand the flaws in our current way of doing things, and sociology provides this understanding.

Some have argued that this makes sociology not only a science but an outlook, or form of consciousness. This outlook has several characteristics, among them cosmopolitanism, a sense of irony, a disregard for disciplinary boundaries, a tendency to question the basic assumptions of daily life and a desire to use our knowledge to improve the social world. Most important, doing sociology means critically paying attention to the two relationships highlighted at the beginning of the chapter: the relationship between public issues and private troubles, and the relationship between macro-events and micro-events in people's social lives.

All sociologists, whatever their perspective and whether they seek to change society or simply to understand it, refuse to take the "facts" of ordinary, daily life for granted.

Instead, sociologists continually question everyday assumptions. For a sociologist these common-sense "facts" are part of our subject matter. Understanding the assumptions of daily life, without being subjected to them, is an essential part of sociological analysis. This makes sociology inherently critical and contentious. For just as sociologists refuse to take the received wisdom of everyday life at face value, they refuse to accept the received wisdom of sociology itself at face value. Sociology's multiple perspectives and theories are a result of this critical tendency. It makes sociology less unified (and dignified) than other sciences, but it also generates the energy and excitement we enjoy in good sociology.

Closely related to this critical tendency is a sense of irony usually found in good sociology. As the dictionary will tell you, *irony* is an incongruity — a bad fit or contradiction — between what people expect and what actually happens. In the case of sociology, irony can be a bad fit between what we intend and what actually happens, between what we believe and what is really so, between what we've always assumed without looking and what we can see when we look hard, or between activities and claims.

Because sociological research is directed at what people are *really* doing, not what they claim to be doing, sociologists know that life is full of ironies. To study sociology is to look at everyday life with an eye to its contradictions. It is to explore how different we really are from the roles we play; and how, and why, the actions we take not only fail to produce the outcomes we expected, they often produce the exact opposite.

CLOSING REMARKS

To study social life, sociologists find they must take into account history, geography, economics, politics and so on. We cannot understand family life without studying economic life: the two systems continually influence each other. Likewise, we cannot understand crime and deviance without understanding the political system. Nor can we begin to make sense of cities or workplaces without understanding modern technology. Whether it be the Industrial Revolution in 18th-century England, ethnic relations in the Balkans, the ritual processes underlying a handshake, or debates over an anti-smoking by-law in Toronto, sociologists feel free to examine *any* kind of evidence that seems promising.

Sociology, by its nature, is cross-disciplinary. There are many different factors to take into account when trying to understand any aspect of social life. For this reason sociologists may find any social phenomenon relevant, regardless of the specific discipline which lays claim to it.

As to making use of what we find out, not all sociologists are as committed to promoting social change as feminists or conflict theorists. Yet most see sociology as having a practical benefit, even if this benefit is only that of allowing people to better understand the circumstances of their own lives. Knowledge can be power and a better understanding of our lives can empower all of us.

As you can see, sociologists are involved in a wide variety of research activities, many having great practical significance to people's lives. If you think about it, you will probably realize that there are many good reasons to study sociology. In general, sociology will help you gain a broad perspective on the social world. There are careers in sociology for people who become interested in continuing their studies; for example, teaching, market research, political polling and organizational analysis. As well, sociology, as a science, will help you see that things are not always what they seem to be.

By helping you better understand social order and social change, sociology will provide you with useful life skills. After studying sociology, you will be able to put your own problems in a broader context, which will help you understand the groups you are part of — your family, friends, school classes and work groups. Sociology will give you tools that allow you to collect and analyze data about the social world. Finally, sociology will help you think about the world and its problems more objectively.

It is now time to examine one of the most important and basic topics in all of sociology: culture.

Review Questions

1. How do microsociology and macrosociology differ?

2. What is a science?

3. What problems face sociology as a science?

4. What is meant by the terms "social structure" and "social relationships"?

5. What four sociological paradigms are discussed in the chapter?

6. How do the sociological perspectives of Karl Marx, Emile Durkheim and Max Weber differ?

7. What are the main assumptions of functionalism?

8. What is the basic sociological question asked by conflict theory?

9. What are the main assumptions of symbolic interactionism?

10. In what ways is feminism both an academic perspective and a form of political activism?

11. What is an ideology?

Discussion Questions

1. Have people write anonymous messages on slips of paper which, in a sentence or two, explain a personal problem they are having right now. Select one or more out of a hat and discuss. Is this personal trouble the flip side of a public issue? If so, what kind of issue?

2. Does sociology study different things than other disciplines, or does it simply study the same things in different ways? Support each side of this argument with examples.

3. Is it really possible for sociology to be value free, and should it be value free? Why, when people in

the physical sciences (for example, physicists, biologists) are becoming increasingly concerned about the ethics of their research and its consequences, should sociology be striving for value freedom?

4. Conflict theorists believe that most of us suffer from "false consciousness." What do they mean? Why do structural functionalists and symbolic interactionists not agree with this belief? What is your position on this?

5. If people really have "free will," as many people assume, does this mean they choose the lives they

lead? Are they personally responsible for being poor, for example?

6. What are some of the main differences between pure research and applied research in sociology? Which kind of research do you consider more important to society? Why? Should sociologists be prevented from doing certain kinds of pure or applied research?

7. How would Marx, Durkheim and Weber differ in their analysis of the causes of separatist sentiment in Quebec?

Suggested Readings

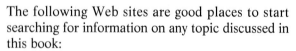

Archer, M. (1991) "Sociology for one world: Unity and diversity" *International Sociology*, 6 (2), June, 131-147. An interesting essay on the challenges and problems of creating a world sociology. In particular, Archer warns us away from the notion of "modernization," because of its hidden assumptions.

Collins, R. and M. Mayakowsky (1989) *The Discovery of Society*. New York: Random House. A brilliant short history of the development of sociology, set against the backdrop of 19th- and 20th-century social and political change.

Giddens, A. (1987) *Sociology: A Brief but Critical Introduction*. San Diego: Harcourt Brace Jovanovich. A short, interesting book on one central debate in sociology: whether contemporary social problems are due to capitalism (as Marx would say), industrialism (as Durkheim would say), or bureaucracy (as Weber would say).

Mills, C. Wright (1967) *The Sociological Imagination*. New York: Oxford University Press. This classic work in sociology is written from the conflict perspective. It emphasizes the close connection between personal troubles (private experience) and public issues (the wider social context).

Nisbet, R. A. (1966) *The Sociological Tradition*. New York: Basic Books. Wonderfully written, this long book organizes much of the history of sociology around the "unit-ideas of sociology," or its founders' key concerns: community, authority, status, the sacred and alienation.

Tepperman, L., J. Curtis, S. J. Wilson and Alan Wain (eds.) (1997) *Small World: Readings in Sociology*, second edition. Scarborough: Prentice Hall Canada. This collection of 45 readings provides interesting case studies that illustrate many of the points made in MACRO/MICRO. Despite the differences among people of different cultures, what are most impressive are the similarities in the problems people face and the solutions they use to solve these problems.

Internet Resources

The following Web sites are good places to start searching for information on any topic discussed in this book:

Universal Codex for the Social Sciences contains a plethora of links relating to every field within the social sciences.
http://www.carleton.ca/'cmkie/research.html

Annual Reviews: Sociology Online has a searchable and comprehensive collection of sociological abstracts.
http://www.annurev.org/soc/home.htm

A Sociological Tour through Cyberspace offers general and specific links to sites of sociological interest as well as essays and general theory.
http://www.trinity.edu/'mkearl/index.html

Sociological Abstracts, Inc provides a searchable listing of sociological abstracts.
http://www.accessinn.com/socabs/index/html

InterLink provides links to electronic sociological journals available on the Web.
http://accessinn.com/socabs/html/17websa.htm

Electronic Journal of Sociology offers the entire journal online, not just the abstracts.
wysiwyg://ejsmain.45/http://129.128.113.200:8010/frametoc.html

Sociological Research Online offers articles dealing with applied sociology.
wysiwyg://502/http://kennedy.soc.surrey.ac.uk/socresonline/

Upstream is a non-peer-reviewed publication dealing with many current issues from a sociological perspective.
http://www.cycad.com/chi-bin/Upstream/Issues/index.html

Sociology Resources on the Network is exactly what it claims to be, a listing of scholarly, sociological Web sites.
http://blair.library.rhodes.edu/anthhtmls/socnet.html

The Canadian Journal of Sociology Online offers a sample of the journal as well as a forum for students and faculty to discuss sociology.
http://gpu.srv.ualberta.cal/'cjscopy/cjs.html

Sociology Electronic Library offers links organized by type of resource.
http://129.97.58.10/discipline/sociology/index.html

A Sociological Resource Centre is an organized listing of general, topical and associations Web sites.
http://www.socioweb.com/ ~ markbl/socioweb/

Culture

C H A P T E R   O U T L I N E

Rudeness in Cyberspace

APPLIED SOCIOLOGY

As we saw in the last chapter, the Internet is creating new social problems — but addiction isn't the only one. As a system of un-regulated information flow, the Internet is liable to suffer "traffic problems" and out-breaks of social conflict. Sociologists, as experts in social organization and conflict resolution, will eventually have a lot to say about the solution to these problems. For the time being, the problems are going un-solved as networkers try to work out their own "netiquette" for social control.

Cyberspace can be a very impolite place, as anyone dismissed as "you moron!" after posting an opinion to a newsgroup well knows. Why do so many people post nasty comments, or "flames"? What makes people resort to anger so easily? Is cyberspace killing rational discourse? Some random thoughts:

- Cyberspace blurs notions of public and private personae. In cyberspace a surfer rubs shoulders with thousands, perhaps millions of people, while in fact he or she is sitting at a desk, at home or at the office, surrounded by familiar objects and people. Behaviour appropriate to the real world can be stripped of all this context in cyberspace.

- The Net does not transmit subtle emotions, hence the need for "emoticons" — smileys — to assure those whose prose is weak that their comments are taken in the intended manner. The vast majority of emoticons are intended to soften aggression in the language. Flamers, however, rarely use emoticons.

- Paper is real, but flimsy, a constant reminder that the ideas on it are perishable, and therefore precious, just like the trees from which the paper is made. In cyberspace, however, ideas are written with electrons, which are ephemeral, and therefore anything written with them must be ephemeral too.

- The very ephemerality of cyberspace is what starts so many flame wars — an idea can be ignored or put down by members of a newsgroup or a mailing list, leaving the writer feeling dispirited, rejected and aggrieved; flaming can attract attention. Trolling for flames — inviting nasty responses by posting provocative comments — achieves the same effect.

- "Unlike human conversation, where there is constant visual, verbal and oral feedback," says Electronic Frontier Canada president David Jones, "people posting their opinions on the Internet rush into an argument not thinking of the way it will be accepted.

- On the Net, many people present themselves in different guises, or avatars. Avatars can be heroic, some can be hilarious. An avatar can argue from a point totally alien to the actual writer's position and spew vile language. On the other hand, an avatar can also allow a repressed personality to emerge in the "public arena" of cyberspace and allow that personality to flourish where the real person would wilt in fear.

Source: Abridged from Jack Kapica, *The Globe and Mail*, Fri., Aug. 2, 1996, p. A6

CLOSING REMARKS

The sociological study of culture offers a prime example of the connection between macro and micro perspectives. On the one hand, culture is a macro phenomenon. It exists outside and "above" individual people, in their language, institutions and material artifacts. In this sense, culture is all-encompassing and slow changing, like a huge glacier. The main elements of a culture outlast individuals and even generations of individuals. On the other hand, culture is inside all of us and, as the symbolic interactionists remind us, something we all change or reproduce every day. Culturally accepted patterns change over time because dozens, then thousands, then millions of us change our way of doing things.

Likewise, the study of culture — especially the visible gap between ideal and real culture — recalls the importance we have placed on the connection between "private troubles" and "public issues." Few people manage to live up to the supposed goals and values of their society; as a result, almost everyone has something to hide, something to feel ashamed of. For many, this blameworthiness, real and imagined, may contribute as much to the maintenance of conformity as people's actual commitment to leading "worthy" lives. We will say more about this when we discuss the notion of "stigma" in Chapter 4.

At the beginning of this chapter we said that culture can best be understood as a symbolic environment within which we live. As we looked more closely at this environment, however, we discovered that it differs radically from one group to another. The culture of poor people is very different from that of rich people (we will say more of this in Chapter 5, on social classes). The world of an atheist is different from that of an adherent to Hare Krishna. The world of the Italian Canadian is, in many important ways, different from the world of the Inuit. All of us, living together in the same country, are living in different cultures. Understanding these cultures, and how and why they are different, is an important task for sociologists.

This issue of people's similarities and differences becomes ever more pressing in a rapidly changing world. We shall have more to say about social and cultural change in the midst of "globalization" in Chapter 11. In particular, we will consider the various factors — social, economic, political and technological — that change our culture and change our lives.

In the next chapter we consider the process by which people become members of their culture and society.

Review Questions

1. What is culture?

2. What are some examples of cultural universals?

3. What are the differences between ideal culture and real culture; between material and non-material culture; and between high and popular culture?

4. What are "signs" and "symbols"?

5. What values are prominent among Canadian teenagers?

6. What are the different types of norms?

7. In what ways is language a system of signs and symbols?

8. How is cultural integration promoted?

9. What is ethnocentrism?

10. How do subcultures and countercultures differ?

11. How are cultural capital and cultural literacy unevenly distributed in society?

12. Is there a distinctive Canadian culture?

Discussion Questions

1. Self-destruction in various forms — for example, setting oneself on fire, or self-imposed starvation — is a common way of dramatizing political frustration. Are all self-destructive acts symbolic? That is, are they likely to have different meanings in different cultures?

2. Are people using less sexist language in the media today? What about in private conversation? Have changes in the use of language changed people's behaviour towards women?

3. Is multiculturalism a good thing for Canada, a waste of the government's money or positively harmful to the country?

4. What conditions are likely to produce a subculture? For example, are you likely to find subcultures formed by drug addicts? antique collectors? people who love pizza?

5. How does the widespread belief that "winning is everything" support the ruling class? Is it possible

for Canadians to compete economically and politically with other nations if we reject that belief?

6. Given the ways our technology and population are changing today, what changes in cultural values do you think will occur before the year 2010? What do you think it would take to cause a major cultural change?

7. Anthropologist George Murdock identifies a number of cultural universals, which include laws, numerals and counting, personal names, religion, sexual restrictions and tool making. Identify the "issues" or concerns each of these deals with.

Suggested Readings

Berger, P. (1969) *The Sacred Canopy: Elements of a Sociological Theory of Religion*. New York: Doubleday. A beautifully written exploration of the various ways religion influences and is influenced by society, this book also examines the process of secularization.

Bibby, R. W. (1993) *Unknown Gods: The Ongoing Story of Religion in Canada*. Toronto: Stoddart. The most comprehensive sociological treatment of religion in Canada, based on national surveys which Bibby conducted from 1975 onward and a large amount of research by other scholars as well. It considers what religion means to the individual and projects the future of religion in Canada.

Brand, S. (1987) *The Media Lab: Inventing the Future at MIT*. New York: Viking Penguin. This book about major advances in information technology, storage and communication will especially appeal to "techies" who feel that cultural change is driven by technological change. One of its strong points is the sense it gives of how people work to develop new communication technologies, media and networks.

Burke, J. (1985) *The Day the Universe Changed*. Boston: Little, Brown. A fascinating and popular account of major changes in the cultural history of the world (an ambitious goal!) that

was the basis of a PBS television series a few years back. This book gives you a different slant on the issue of "globalization" and global culture by reminding you just how tightly tied together people have been for centuries, if not millennia.

Fussell, P. (1983) *Class*. New York: Ballantine Books. A witty book on culture in general, and upper-class culture in particular, this book shows — among other things — how you can judge a person's class from living-room decoration.

Lipset, S. M. (1990) *Continental Divide: The Values and Institutions of the United States and Canada*. New York: Routledge. This is Professor Lipset's latest and most comprehensive effort at describing what he considers to be deep and fundamental value differences that characterize Canada and the United States (hence, the title of his book.) You may disagree with his conclusion, but you can't escape dealing with his argument.

Willis, P. (1977) *Learning to Labor: How Working Class Kids get Working Class Jobs*. New York: Columbia University Press. This ethnography brilliantly describes the school subculture (or is it a counterculture?) of working-class children. Its purpose is to explain how and why these young people reject the school's demands and, accordingly, reject the opportunities that conformity would bring them.

Internet Resources

In addition to the general resources provided in Chapter 1, the following Web sites are good places to find more information about topics discussed in this chapter:

Canadian Culture Discussion Group is a newsgroup for general discussions about culture in Canada.
USENET: soc.culture.canada

CultureNet hosts information for a number of Canadian cultural organizations and maintains a directory of Canadian cultural resources.
http://www.ffa.ucalgary.ca

Index of Native American Resources is a comprehensive directory of cultural, educational and art-related resources that includes several Canadian links.
http://hanksville.phast.umass.edu/misc/NAresources.html

Quebec Culture Discussion Group is a newsgroup for general discussion about Quebec society.
USENET: soc.culture.quebec

Culture provides links to homepages dedicated to cultural studies.
http://www.pscw.uva.nl/sociosite/TOPICS/Culture.html

Cyberspace Links provides links to literature and journals dedicated to cyberspace and the virtual culture that it has created.
http://www.usyd.edu.au/su/social/cyber.html

Japanese-Americans, Immigration & Cross Culture explores the experience of Japanese-Americans.
http://www.saitama-j.or.jp/'nexus/nisei/nisei.html

Mennonites in Canada includes information on demographics, food, education, literature, politics and agriculture among the Mennonites.
http://www.mennonitecc.ca/mcc/menno ~ guide/index.html

Ontario Centre for Religious Tolerance provides general information about religious topics and controversial social issues.
http://www.kosone.com/people/ocrt/ocrt_hp.htm

TV Net contains links to hundreds of Web pages for television shows and resources, with some Canadian content.
http://www.tvnet.com

SOCIALIZATION

CHAPTER OUTLINE

The mass media teach children roles, beliefs and skills that may not benefit society.

Socialization Is a Lifelong Process

All of us are, to a large extent, products of our society. Society determines many of the ways we think and act, much of what we say and the values and norms we live by. But as human beings, we are also free in important ways to create ourselves. Much of who we are and what we do is a result of our own activity. As we shall see, both of these tendencies — freedom and determinism, transformation and constraint — are central features of socialization.

Socialization is often defined as the social learning process a person goes through to become a capable member of society. The process is "social" because it is through interaction with others and in response to social pressures that people acquire the culture — the language, perspective and skills, the likes and dislikes, the cluster of norms, values and beliefs — that characterizes the group to which they belong. As a result, socialization is one of the most important processes by which social structure constrains and transforms us.

Primary socialization is learning that takes place in the early years of a person's life. It is extremely important in forming an individual's personality and fixing the course of future development. Very often, primary socialization takes place within the context of a family. Here, a young child learns many of the social skills needed to participate in a wide variety of social institutions.

Because primary socialization is a fundamental social process both for individuals and for society as a whole, it interests both macrosociologists and microsociologists. Among the former, structural functionalists see primary socialization as the means by which people are integrated into society, coming to take their allotted role and learning to fulfill socially necessary functions. In their eyes, human babies are a "blank slate" waiting to be imprinted with socially meaningful information. It is through this effective social imprinting — for example, the teaching and learning of language — that society manages to continue itself.

Conflict theorists, by contrast, emphasize the ways in which socialization perpetuates domination. They see socialization, a tool of the dominant class, as teaching people their "place" in society and convincing them that this "place" is inevitable. Poor people learn to blame themselves for failing and praise the rich for succeeding. In this way, socialization contributes to the survival of dominant groups. We will have more to say about this "legitimation" of power in Chapter 11.

As microsociologists, symbolic interactionists study the processes by which people are actually socialized, particularly those that lead to the development of a social "self." Through these processes people come to think of themselves as good or bad, competent or incompetent, normal or deviant, and so on. We will discuss the interactionist view of the "self" later in this chapter.

Finally, feminist sociologists combine the interests of conflict theorists and symbolic interactionists with a particular focus on gender issues. In respect to socialization, they are interested in the learning of gender identities (or gendered selves) and gendered patterns of domination and submission. This will be discussed in Chapter 8.

Socialization does not end with childhood. It is a lifelong process because we continually undergo new experiences and change in reaction to these experiences. The socialization that occurs after childhood is called **secondary socialization**. It is much more limited than primary socialization and usually involves the learning of specific roles, norms, attitudes or beliefs. Secondary socialization has less effect on self-image or sense of competence than primary socialization, but we should not underestimate its importance. We all differ in the ways we respond to other people's efforts to socialize us. Yet all of us, at least in our early years, possess an almost endless ability to change and adjust to change.

NATURE VERSUS NURTURE

Where does this human adaptability come from? How much of it is due to our genetic makeup, unique among animals? Consider the recent research, reported in Everyday Life below, that found a genetic basis for "novelty seeking." People with this personality trait are also likely to be remarkable in other ways too; for example, they may be extroverted and impulsive. Does this mean that our human ability to invent and continually change the social environment is ultimately genetic?

No, it doesn't. Much of what we are is due to the training we receive that helps us learn and re-learn as we pass through life? But what makes each of us the kind of person we are? This centuries-old question is at the heart of what is called the "nature versus nurture" debate. People holding to the "nature" position believe that human behaviour is genetically determined. Such **biological determinists** argue that the diversity found among individuals and cultures exists because nature has selected for diversity, in the same way it has selected for our enlarged brains and upright walk.

Consider the sociological approach to bio-determinism, called *sociobiology*. Sociobiology looks for the explanation of human behaviour in animal behaviour, on the assumption that much of our behaviour traces back to our animal origins. So, for example, sociobiologists might look for the explanation of human warfare in the animal instincts of aggression or territoriality. Equally, they might look for the explanation of human mating practices in animal mating and reproductive strategies.

Rather than focus on cognitive processing — as symbolic interactionists do — sociobiologists focus on inborn, probably genetic, practices. For example, in discussing human inequality, most sociologists argue that ideologies serve to legitimate and stabilize unequal relationships. However, sociobiologists would point out that such animals as chickens also have stable hierarchies of dominance

EVERYDAY LIFE

The Genetic Basis of Novelty Seeking

By now you will have noticed that some of your classmates are shy, while others are outgoing; some are content to stick with the "traditional wisdom," while others are always seeking new ways of thinking and doing things. What accounts for these differences? How much is due to nature, how much to nurture? We can only hope to answer this question through genetic research of the kind reported below.

Genetic researchers have reported finding a partial explanation for a personality trait called "novelty seeking." Novelty seeking is one of four building blocks of normal temperament, the other three being avoidance of harm, reward dependence and persistence. All four are largely attributable to a person's genetic makeup. They are the aspects of human nature that mark one person as a pessimistic worrywart, another as an outgoing team player. In addition, people inclined to novelty seeking also tend to be outgoing, impulsive and excitable.

Novelty seekers tend to have a particular variant of a gene that lets the brain respond to dopamine, an essential chemical communications signal. This dopamine receptor accounts for about 10 per cent of the difference in novelty-seeking behaviour between one person and another, according to scientific reports.

Any person contains varying degrees of the four temperamental elements. However, once established, temperament remains fairly stable throughout life, which means the shy and anxious boy is likely to be the shy and anxious grandfather. Therapy and other adult experiences may shape and modify the genetic input. Most important is the way the temperament-mix is permitted to express itself. Random experiences and circumstances that an individual encounters in childhood, and chance exposures to reward or punishment, strengthen or weaken people's innate tendency toward avoidance of harm, novelty seeking and the like.

Parents have a major effect on their children's character by influencing their attitude toward themselves and other people, their capacity for empathy, their goals and values. Parental attitudes also help a child mature into a reasonable adult. A child may not be born a *blank slate*, but there are plenty of ways for a parent to push the child in one direction or another.

What this means is that novelty seeking, or innovative, behaviour has both genetic and social roots. The job of parents and society is to find ways to nourish and harness the creative potential of natural novelty seekers.

Source: Adapted from an article by Natalie Angier, *The Globe and Mail*, Tues., Jan. 2, 1996, pp. A1, A6

(called "pecking orders" among birds), yet they don't seem to need ideologies to achieve this. For sociobiologists, then, human "pecking orders" would exist without ideologies because it is "natural" for some to dominate others.

Most sociologists reject the sociobiological approach for a variety of reasons. A central concern is that sociobiology ignores history, ignores social, economic and political forces and, just as important, ignores the motivation, character and reasoning of human individuals. Unlike chickens, human beings have a culture which can be passed on to descendants, independant of genes, through learning. Culture, as we have seen, is the product of our actions, our past, and our hopes and plans for the future.

Advocates of the extreme "nurture" position take an approach directly opposite to sociobiology and attribute all character traits and all the diversity among people of different cultures, to learning. According to this point of view — called **social** or **cultural determinism** — infants are born without any significant genetic predispositions or instincts, and no innate personality. As children, they learn the "*dos* and *don'ts*" of their culture, which they then act out. Culture, not genes, determines their behaviour. However, in the end, the debate between nature and nurture seems impossible to resolve and most social scientists have put it aside, recognizing that both factors have an effect on socialization.

Nature and nurture interact and together have an effect that could not be guessed from either of the factors individually, as we saw in the excerpt on "novelty seeking." Members of a group are bound to share genetic characteristics because, over a long time, they live and reproduce together. This makes it likely that genes will differ from one group to another and even influence personality; but this influence is limited to forming a behavioural potential. The extent to which people fulfill this potential will depend on the social setting within which they live and learn.

Consider language as a case in point. The capacity to use language is genetic in origin. Human beings have the vocal cords necessary to produce the sounds out of which words are formed. The human brain is able to differentiate those sounds and identify their appropriate meanings. But while the ability to use language is genetic in origin, language itself is not. If language *were* genetic in origin — that is, if the sounds used and their appropriate meanings were innate — everyone on earth would use the same language in the same way. Yet there are thousands of different languages and they differ in important ways. Moreover, languages are constantly changing as new words are added, meanings get altered and old words are dropped. At the extreme is a "street language" like Ebonics, recently put forward by some as a legitimate "second language" for urban African-Americans. This illustration is particularly important because, as we saw in the last chapter, language is the means by which we communicate our experience of the world. It is also the way we learn from others and the way we teach others. Not least, it is the key to primary socialization and, in this way, to adult competence.

Perhaps nothing illustrates the importance of language and primary socialization as well as the case of feral children. These are children who have grown up lacking contact with other people. They have not undergone the typical experiences of socialization, and, in crucial ways, they never become full-fledged members of society.

Feral Children

History has recorded many tales and anecdotes about "feral" children — children raised outside society, unaffected by human relationships and values. One of the best documented cases is the "Wild Boy of Aveyron" — well documented because of a Dr. Itard who studied the Wild Boy closely and recorded what he found. (You may want to watch a film by François Truffaut, *L'enfant sauvage* [*The Wild Child*] which tells this story eloquently.)

The boy, called Victor, emerged from the woods in southern France on a winter morning in the year 1800. He had been caught digging for vegetables in a terraced garden. Though eleven or twelve years old, Victor, who was almost naked, showed no modesty and was not housebroken. He would relieve himself wherever he wanted, squatting to defecate and standing to urinate. He could not speak and made strange, meaningless cries.

Three or four months after Dr. Itard took over his training, the boy began to respond. Eventually, Victor could pay attention, understand and follow verbal instructions, play games, care for himself and even invent things with familiar objects. He soon wore clothes and used a chamber pot to relieve himself, but still felt no shame or modesty. He kept up many of his earlier habits, continuing to avoid other people and escaping company whenever he could. His old, "wild" reactions to nature — to wind, the moon and snow — never disappeared. In Dr. Itard's hands, the boy's training was, at best, a superficial success. Still, Victor showed

Families teach values and behaviour that children carry with them into adulthood.

affection to the people who protected him and did what they expected.

After spending five years with Itard, Victor lived another twenty-two years with a devoted woman named Madame Guerin in a little house near an institute for people who were deaf-mutes. In this period, no one, not even Itard, tried to train Victor further and no one followed his progress closely. By 1816, his civilization had largely eroded. Victor was once again fearful and half-wild, and still could not speak. He had few links to the rest of the community. A state pension kept Victor alive until 1843, when he died, unnoticed.

What does the story of the Wild Boy teach? An obvious lesson is the importance of primary socialization. Despite the attempts Dr. Itard made to teach him, Victor never learned to speak and never fully adjusted to civilization. There is no way of knowing now what Victor's abilities were, but we suspect that by missing the crucial years of childhood socialization he was never able to achieve his human potential. He had grown up as an animal and could not, after childhood, be fully socialized as a human.

Victor's life reminds us that we are social beings who only fulfill our human potential and achieve socially defined goals as members of society. Socialization imposes society's rules on us, it is true; but that is not all. By providing us with knowledge and skills, society also gives us the tools and resources we need to think independently, act creatively and take advantage of opportunities.

After infancy, all of us take an active part in our own socialization and are socialized by a broad range of people and circumstances. Nursery-school children display this readily. We can see them discussing, at length, aspects of adult culture which they do not understand, in an effort to slowly take personal ownership of that culture. In this sense, socialization is a collective process: people socialize one another. Families, schools and workplaces merely provide times and places where this learning can occur somewhat predictably.

ACQUIRING SOCIAL KNOWLEDGE

Learning and Behaviour   Socialization is a form of learning, so understanding how socialization works requires that we understand how people learn.

To start, learning is a natural human process in the sense that we all have the ability and the will to learn. All of us learn without anyone forcing us to do so. In fact, we learn best when we learn freely. As you know from school, things we are forced to study are not really learned at all. If they have been memorized, they are only remembered until the next test, then quickly forgotten. By contrast, we quickly learn something that is meaningful for us or useful to us. This has an implication for teaching too: to be a good teacher, you have to show the student why something to be learned is meaningful or useful!

Learning can occur in many different ways. We learn by observation, by experiment and by imitation. We learn from friends, parents, relatives and passersby.

We learn from television, radio, books, computers and billboards. As you can see, much of life's learning takes place beyond school, as well as in it.

Before the 18th or 19th century, few people had formal education and almost *all* learning occurred informally through other people. This kind of informal learning can still be seen in traditional Hawaiian culture which puts great emphasis on the informal, apprenticeship transfer of knowledge and skills. Hawaiian adults feel comfortable about teaching their children household skills, because they perform them routinely and expertly and because housework is cooperative. School learning is a different matter. Not only is it hard to teach literacy through observation, but school learning tends to benefit the individual over the group and does not fit into the helping framework that is congenial to Hawaiian culture.

Inuit learning is also informal and different from our own in important ways. Among the Inuit, various forms of play are important, especially dramas in which children act out real-life dangers and decide how to deal with them. By doing this, they learn how to solve adult problems in an independent manner. More than that, these children come to see the world as problematic and they develop skills for experimenting in different situations. The Inuit example illustrates how childhood experiences are a good preparation for the development of adult skills. Let's consider the developmental approach to socialization more fully, focusing particularly on cognitive development.

Cognitive Development

A *developmental approach* to learning examines both the inner workings of a person's mind and observable behaviour. As people go through the socialization process, they actively participate in learning. They do not merely respond to rewards and punishments, like dogs or trained seals. They respond on the basis of their interpretations of situations. Learning is more than a matter of knowing what to do, how to do it, and when; learning also involves understanding *why* we do, or avoid doing, certain things.

Observation, drama, exploration and dialogue are all ways of learning, thinking and communicating symbolically. As sociologists, we need an approach to socialization that takes this into account. That is why theories of **cognitive development** are valuable. The term *cognitive* refers to intellectual capacities such as thought, belief, memory, perception and the ability to reason. Cognitive development, then, refers to the development of these various abilities.

Consider the ways in which children learn a language. They do not simply copy what they hear others saying. Instead, they generalize, apply rules and use language in a creative way. It is unlikely a child ever heard an adult say "he runned" or "it's the goodest" or "my foots hurt." Children make such mistakes because they detect rules in our language and make up words according to those rules. In short, mistakes do not occur because children are failing to follow rules: they occur because the English language does not follow rules consistently. It's *easy* to make mistakes in English because of the great number of idiomatic uses that we learn only from many years of practice.

Idioms — cultural and linguistic practices which do not conform to obvious rules — are the hardest things to learn. A familiar example would be knowing how to pay someone a visit. On occasion, you have probably visited the home of a person you want to impress — a teacher, a boss, the parents of a girlfriend or boyfriend, for example — and you have become painfully aware of your ignorance of the relevant norms. You may have wondered how to dress for the visit. Should you bring a gift, and if so, what? Should you arrive on time, or early, and if early, how early? If offered alcoholic beverages, how many should you accept?

Most troubling of all, since you do not want to offend the hosts by leaving too soon or bore them by staying too long, how will you know when it is the right time to leave? All of us learn to speak a "silent language" as part of our cultural learning.

If you can think through questions like these and come up with answers — and you do, each day, in one situation after another — then you have achieved a high level of cognitive development. More likely than not, you have also learned, however unconsciously, the idiomatic rules that govern visiting behaviour in our society.

Moral Development

It has been difficult, in such a limited space, to describe the acquisition of social manners and language. Just think how much *more* difficult it is to describe the learning of *moral* behaviour.

Swiss psychologist Jean Piaget was a pioneer in studying the development of morality. Piaget (1932) researched the way children think about social norms by asking them to discuss a game of marbles. He studied their moral thinking by telling them stories and asking them for comments. From these simple methods, Piaget drew powerful conclusions.

Among children aged about four to eight years old, Piaget found what he called *heteronomous* morality — a respect for adult authority. A behaviour is "wrong" if the children have seen adults punish or threaten to punish it. Young children consider adult rules and moral values absolute and unchangeable. As a result, they favour punishing rule-breakers severely. Finally, they show little interest in the motivations of wrongdoers: why they did what they did.

However, this changes as children get older. Among older children, Piaget found that *autonomous* morality prevails. Older children have already begun to think about and follow their own rules of conduct. They see rules as products of group agreement that promote cooperation within the group. From this viewpoint, justice is a matter of mutual rights and obligations. Often, justice is served best by repairing the harm done, not punishing the wrongdoer. Finally, in their eyes, moral ideas are relative, not absolute. They change as the group wishes them to change.

These developments in moral thinking are a result of interactions between children, their parents and peers. As well, some social conditions promote moral development more readily than others. Children in highly politicized communities — Northern Ireland or the Middle East, for example — become politicized themselves early in life. While North American youth are spending their time on dates, after-school jobs and Nintendo games, these other children are engaged in political acts (for example, in the Middle East, boys throwing stones at Israeli soldiers). Moral development comes earlier in societies where children are encouraged to consider political issues. (Politics is an adult issue only in places where children are excluded from it!)

The kind of discipline parents use on their children also has an effect on moral development, though it is indirect. There is a lack of consensus among Canadian parents about the appropriateness of physical punishment and whether it improves children's behaviour. However, most social scientists would say that physical punishment is likely to backfire. It teaches children aggressive behaviour and injures their sense of self, instead of helping that sense of self to develop. It teaches that physical force is more important than reasoning or compassion, which is a profound (and wrongheaded) message to teach children.

Parenting well is difficult, as we can see in Applied Sociology on page 70. There are many errors parents can make — things they may do and things they

Why So Much Worrying?

Sociologists are experts in the study of social relationships. One relationship that seems to be getting more complicated is the parent-child relationship. There is no evidence that parents are doing a worse job than in the past. Quite possibly, a sense of failure in this relationship is related to many people's sense of failure in all areas of life — work, marriage and otherwise. In turn this sense of failure may be due to changes in the economy — especially the time crunches suffered by two-career families. (The excerpt below suggests other causes.) As a sociologist, how would you deal with this problem?

Here's a paradox for you: Along with giving their offspring the most privileged and loving upbringing in the history of childhood, today's parents are the most anxious and guilty parents in the history of the human race.

The sources of parental guilt and anxiety are inexhaustible. It starts in the womb. Sneaked a glass of wine? Took an Aspirin? Shame on you. If your neonate somehow emerges intact despite what you do to it, are you bonding properly? How can you tell?

Then there are the million and one pitfalls of childhood. How bad *are* Barbies? Weapons? Power Rangers? Day care? Mommy's career?

Why do so many parents feel so guilty? One reason is the general climate of social panic over the fate of our children. Many kids *are* in distress. They have chaotic home lives, or they're poor, or they're neglected, or all three. The stresses and rootlessness of modern life disproportionately hit the most vulnerable, and we hear a lot about them.

Another reason is that we are bombarded as never before with alarming information about the perils of childhood, from sex abuse to attention-deficit disorder. Few of these perils are new, but many never had names or diagnoses before.

And another reason is that child-rearing has become the biggest battleground of all in the gender/culture wars. No surprise there. It's the most important thing that human beings do.

We're also the first generation in history to have children by choice. We can decide when to have them and how many to have, or not to have any at all. Having children is no longer something that happens to you whether you like it or not. Now it's something you plan, like your career, and something in which you are supposed to have expertise. In an age that heavily favours the nurture side of the nature/nurture debate, you are judged by your kids.

And now people have two kids instead of eight. Consequently their per-child investment — in time, money, love — has soared. Combine that with our powerful belief in nurture, and you understand why people play Mozart to their fetuses.

Besides, guilt (unlike greed) is good. From an evolutionary point of view, it is highly useful because it builds better parents. In other words, who can tell where guilt leaves off and love begins? Fortunately for parents, feeling guilty doesn't mean you are.

Source: Abridged from Margaret Wente, *The Globe and Mail*, Sat., Apr. 27, 1996, p. D7

may fail to do — so parents can be forgiven for feeling overanxious at times about whether they are doing a good enough job. Regrettably, some parents, perhaps overwhelmed by the task, give up altogether, as we will see in Chapter 9, on families.

DEVELOPMENT OF THE SELF

All sociologists view socialization as a social process, but symbolic interactionists are most concerned with understanding *how* socialization actually works. How do people come to take on the norms, values, attitudes, beliefs and behaviour patterns of the people around them? How do they, in technical terms, internalize their culture? And how do they do so while maintaining their own personal identity and sense of worth? Many sociologists believe that the key to answering these questions can be found in the concept of the *self*.

Everyone has a sense of self. By *self*, we mean a person's experience and awareness of having a personal identity that is separate from that of other people. Seen another way, a *self* is an image of an organism possessed by that same organism. Sociologists believe that the process by which people develop this sense of self is the same as the process by which they internalize their culture.

A child is not born with a sense of self, any more than he or she is born speaking English or knowing how to play baseball. As Piaget showed in his research, young children are *egocentric*; they have no sense of self distinct from other people. They assume that everything happens because of them, that everyone is interested only in them and that whatever they experience is all that there is. Above all, egocentric children are unable to think about themselves objectively, or consider how others think about them.

Children only become aware of themselves as they become aware that other people (such as their parents or siblings) are distinct from them. They learn that these other people have expectations of them, and that they are required to adapt to these expectations.

This means that the self is a social product. It emerges as people interact with others, even with people they hate or admire from afar (such as movie stars or heroic ancestors). The person's experiences in life, the groups to which he or she belongs and the socio-historical setting of those groups all shape a person's sense of self. Because the self is a social product, it changes throughout life. Adolescence, in particular, is a critical period for the development of self. During adolescence people become more concerned with their appearance, for example, and this makes them feel vulnerable and shy.

People's experiences and self-conceptions change throughout life, due to secondary socialization. Though we emphasize childhood socialization in this chapter, we do not mean to underestimate the role of adult experiences in continuing to change a person's values, norms and perceptions. In this respect, the workplace — which we discuss in detail in Chapter 6 — is particularly important. It is a place where we learn and exercise our skills, defer to authority and (occasionally) exert authority, participate in a work group and work culture and, not least, earn an income.

Perhaps just as important, in the workplace we, as adults, continue to develop our conception of "self" — who and what we are. Increasingly, we become what we do for a living and become like the people we work with. Social theorists differ in their accounts of the emergence of the self, but on one thing they agree: social interaction is central to its growth.

The Looking-Glass Self

American sociologist Charles Cooley (1902) was the first to emphasize the importance of the self in the process of socialization. Cooley developed the notion of the looking-glass self, which emphasizes the role of the social environment in the development of a self-concept.

According to Cooley, people form concepts of themselves as they see how other people react to them. People live up, or down, to the expectations others (such as parents or friends) have of them. They come to see themselves as they believe these significant others do. For example, a little girl will traditionally be told to "act like a lady." After a while, she will come to see certain activities, such as playing baseball, climbing trees or boxing with other children as inappropriate or beyond her capacities, since they are beyond the capacities of the imaginary lady being held up to her as a mirror image. But of course feminist theorists question precisely this "lady" and what she presumably can and cannot do, as a key tool in promoting unfavourable gender disparity in our culture.

The **looking-glass self** is the name Cooley gives to a phenomenon we all know intuitively: the process of seeing ourselves as others see us. The way we think and feel about ourselves reflects the way we believe others think and feel about us. We behave in ways designed to gain a favourable response from the people who matter most to us. We do this because we rely on others to provide us with a positive self-image.

However, the notion of a looking-glass self is problematic. There are limits to what we will do for approval. Parents know that few of their wishes for their children will come true. As children grow up, they rebel against many of their parents' expectations. This rebellion is not limited to adolescence; for example, child-care experts refer to a two-year-old child as being in the midst of a stage they call "the terrible twos," a stage also known as *negativism*. Parents of children at other ages have their own horror stories to tell, and pet names for other stages.

In the end, Cooley's views illustrate what sociologists have called an *oversocialized* view of the individual (Wrong, 1961). It fails to account for the spontaneity, creativity and independence of real human beings. Moreover, parents, the supposed socializers, are also being socialized by their children. In short, socialization is a two-way process.

Mead on Internalization

A more complete approach to socialization can be found in the work of the American social theorist George Herbert Mead (1934). Mead's particular interest was in the process of **internalization**. How, he wondered, are the rules, norms and values which others impose on a child internalized so that the child becomes committed to them and feels guilt or shame when violating them?

The road to guilt and shame is a long one: Mead suggests a child goes through a number of phases as he or she learns to internalize social expectations. The first is called the *preliminary phase* because internalization has not really begun yet: the child does not have the capacity to engage in true social behaviour. During this phase — the first year or so of life — a child's social behaviour is largely limited to imitation. Infants imitate their parents, their siblings, even themselves, repeating gestures or sounds they made at first by chance. A game such as peekaboo illustrates the repetitive and imitative nature of an infant's social interaction.

We see a higher level of social behaviour in the *play phase*, when the child engages in solitary play. This stage is roughly equivalent to the egocentric stage described by Piaget. Both Mead and Piaget emphasize that, even if children are playing in each other's presence, play at this age is solitary because it involves no real interaction. Two three-year-old girls playing with their dolls are each in a world of their own. Each talks to her own doll, feeds her own doll, scolds her own doll. These girls are incapable of having one be the "mother" and the other the "child." Said another way, there is no "division of labour" between the children. That is why Piaget referred to conversations among children at this stage as *collective monologue*.

The next phase, the *game phase*, involves a higher level of social behaviour, for it means coordinating social roles. Games differ from play because play is largely spontaneous but games have rules that people must follow. Moreover, games always involve other people and game positions, so each participant has a role to act out in relation to other players.

A good illustration of an early game is hide-and-seek. Here children learn to take on one of two roles, hider or seeker ("it"). There are rules to follow and winning the game means coordinating one's own actions with those of others. In this sense, there is a "division of labour," which is the essence of all grown-up social life.

Mead called the process of taking others into account *taking the role of the other*. It is the prerequisite for competent social interaction. During interactions, we all take the role of the other when we orient our actions towards others so that we can be understood. Before teachers stand in front of a class, for example, they ask themselves how they can get the lesson across so that students will understand it. Then, while lecturing, they monitor the students' faces, body language and questions to see if they *do* understand what is being said. They imagine themselves to be students listening to this lecture, as now we authors can imagine ourselves to be readers perusing this text.

To return to our earlier example, when we play hide-and-seek, we cannot hide unless we can take the role of the other. We have to know what the other person is seeing and thinking when they look for us. Otherwise we do as very young children do, hiding without realizing that an arm or a leg may be visible or that we have hidden in the first place someone is likely to look.

Mead believed that taking the role of the other in this sense is an essential preliminary to coming to see yourself as others see you and to thinking about yourself in terms of your relationship to other people. Mead coined the term **generalized other** to refer to a person's general idea of society's attitudes and perspectives — of how the larger social group expects an individual to act. Having a concept of the generalized other is possible because there is a rough consensus among members of the society or subculture to which we belong. It is in relation to this sense of the generalized other that we develop conceptions of ourselves: how we are similar to, and different from, other people. When we take the role of the generalized other, it is no longer Mummy who gets upset when we spill soup; now *we* are the ones who get upset. We feel ashamed or even guilty.

But there is more to us than the socialized player of these internalized roles. Coming to see yourself objectively means realizing that who and what you are depends on the context in which you are interacting with others. Remember hide-and-seek. We do not simply and literally act out other people's expectations, because we have plans, goals and interests of our own that, to some extent, separate us. For example, a good player of hide-and-seek will also be watching where others are hiding, partly to learn appropriate, acceptable places to hide, but also because when it is the player's turn to be "it" she will know where the other players are likely to be hiding.

Mead tried to incorporate this "something more" that has goals, plans and interests by distinguishing between the **I** and the **Me**. All of us have an aspect of the self that Mead calls the *I*. The *I* is spontaneous, impulsive and self-interested. All of us also have a *Me*, a part of the self that is the result of socialization and is therefore conscious of social norms, values and expectations. The *Me* is the socialized player of social roles and, unlike the *I*, it is conformist and socially aware. But the good player of hide-and-seek is one who has integrated an *I* with a *Me*. Having interests of our own, we pay attention to how others are acting out the rules, both in order to be able to imitate them and to catch them imitating themselves.

Mead and Cooley's symbolic interactionist theories continue to dominate the study of socialization. Structural functionalists also use Mead's theory to explain how people learn to accept the values, goals and norms of the society around them. However, Mead's theory does not really mesh well with structural functionalism, because it views people as active participants in their own socialization. This point of view, which is essential to symbolic interactionism, is foreign to functionalism.

Socialization as an Active Process

We noted earlier the importance of avoiding an oversocialized image of people, for people are not puppets or robots. Socializing a person is not the same as programming a computer. Humans act in terms of personal and group interests, and they evaluate their interests themselves. Moreover, people cannot simply follow the norms or rules of society, for these are merely guidelines — general goals — and not explicit instructions. In practice, people have to develop their own strategies for achieving goals and obeying the rules.

Take being a student. As students you are aware of the many factors that affect your chances to perform well in school. There is a program of study which specifies the courses you may take. But the course you want is already full or conflicts with a part-time job that forces you to take a course or study with a teacher you really didn't want. Normatively, in theory, "school" means studying things you want and need to learn. In actual practice, it may be very different. Even such factors as family size and birth order can affect what you study and how well you perform; so do social-class background, family problems or pressures from peers. Finally, there are the many norms and rules which define how students are supposed to behave in class, in the library, even in the cafeteria. In fact, if we look, we find that these same norms are often followed only in a very loose and general way.

Consider the creative ways children struggle against the rules their parents create. Generally, creating and enforcing rules produces resentment and fosters conflict. Children often resist socialization. They fight back against parental pressure, often literally kicking and screaming, to get what they want instead of what their parents want. This conflict is difficult for parents, but it is essential for the

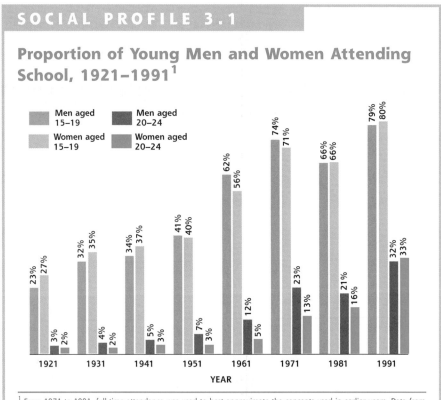

SOCIAL PROFILE 3.1

Proportion of Young Men and Women Attending School, 1921–1991[1]

Legend:
- Men aged 15–19
- Women aged 15–19
- Men aged 20–24
- Women aged 20–24

Year	Men 15–19	Women 15–19	Men 20–24	Women 20–24
1921	23%	27%	3%	2%
1931	32%	35%	4%	2%
1941	34%	37%	5%	3%
1951	41%	40%	7%	3%
1961	62%	56%	12%	5%
1971	74%	71%	23%	13%
1981	66%	66%	21%	16%
1991	79%	80%	32%	33%

YEAR

[1] From 1971 to 1991, full-time attendance was used to best approximate the concepts used in earlier years. Data from 1921 to 1961 exclude Newfoundland, and the Yukon and Northwest Territories.

Source: Reproduced by authority of the Minister of Industry, 1997, Statistics Canada, Canadian Social Trends, 11-008, Winter 1995, p. 20.

From childhood on, we are socialized into the roles of man and woman, husband and wife.

child. We noted earlier that children seem to go though a stage known as "negativism" at about the age of two. During this stage they purposely challenge the rules, become obstinate and insist on having things their own way. They seem to go around saying "no" all the time, which is why the stage is called "negativism."

This difficult stage is necessary for the child's development because this is the way a child begins to develop a sense of self and to differentiate itself from others. Negativism helps in this process by teaching the child what it can get away with and what it can't. By testing the rules repeatedly, children find out when parents really mean what they are saying and when they are willing to give in. These are important lessons, not only in learning to get along with parents, but in learning to get along with other people in later life.

Finally, remember that parents are also being socialized by this process, since knowledge of parenting is no more innate for them than knowledge of being a child is innate for a child. For their part they, too, are learning what *they* can get away with and what kind of demands they can make. In the end, parents do not get the child they expected, but they usually end up liking the child they get.

GENDER SOCIALIZATION

CBC 🅒

"Teen Magazines: Girl Talk"

Sociologists pay a great deal of attention to primary socialization. It is during this early phase of life that we learn all the fundamental roles, especially how to think and act like a competent member of society. In the first few years of life, we also learn such basic facts about ourselves as whether we are male or female and what that means about *who* or *what* we are or should be. In this sense, gender socialization stands as an example of all primary socialization.

Masculine and Feminine Ideals

As we will see in Chapter 8, gender is a social construction — a manufactured dichotomy which is learned through the socialization process. (Even the dichotomous character of gender is socially constructed; in many senses, sex-based characteristics range across a wide continuum which we are taught to ignore.)

Given the sexual categories of male and female, **gender roles** are the socially defined expectations people have of appropriate behaviour for individuals of each sex. What we mean by **gender socialization** is simply socialization into gender roles. It is the process of learning the attitudes, thoughts and behaviour patterns that a culture considers to be appropriate for members of each sex.

In everyday life we almost never make use of physiology to decide who is male or female because there are few people whose genitals or genetic structure are visible to us. We decide who is male or female on the basis of appearance, which is a matter of social convention. But appearance configurations such as use of hair length and personality differences, such as the greater aggressiveness of males, are primarily social constructions — elements of dramas we put on for one another. We know this because gender roles change over time and vary considerably from one culture to another. They are *not* permanent and inevitable.

People learn gender roles early in life. Infants are identified as male or female at birth. By the age of three, little boys and girls are playing separately, at different kinds of games. Already, they have learned to want different toys, enjoy different games and avoid relating openly with the opposite sex. A few years later, children who violate this last rule are ridiculed. In our own society, the masculine ideal has traditionally included toughness, reason, action and access to weaponry. Conversely, the feminine ideal has traditionally included softness, emotion (or intuition) and passivity.

In many societies, traditional gender roles have gone largely unchanged. In Islamic Iran, the fundamentalist (religiously orthodox) government has had an enormous effect on gender roles and socialization. Since the revolution of 1979, it has stressed a return to segregation of the sexes. School textbooks discuss women less often than they discuss men. Women, when discussed at all, are shown within the family context, not doing paid work. This is a change from the more egalitarian portrayals of women before 1979, when a secular (non-religious) government ruled Iran.

But Iran is no exception. Throughout the world, fundamentalist governments and religious authorities have struggled to maintain traditional gender roles and socialization. In transitional societies like Singapore, traditional gender roles have started to break down, though school books continue to present men and women as if they were still playing these roles. For example, they show women in the home, never in the workplace. But in North America, masculine and feminine ideals, and male and female gender roles, have changed dramatically.

The Change of Gender Roles   This change of gender roles takes a variety of forms. First, few Canadian women today model themselves on the traditional image of femininity. Likewise, few Canadian men today model themselves on the traditional image of masculinity. The male ideal mainly persists among boys in the five- to fifteen-year-old range. They are the people who watch WWF wrestling, read X-men comic books and buy Nintendo war games, GI Joe–style clothing and miniature soldier figures. Even here, changes are occurring, as miniature play figures include active Princess Leia, bazooka-toting Ripley and strong, active female fighters of other kinds.

Second, men and women are sharing more duties and activities than in the past. More women work for pay in jobs that, traditionally, only men were allowed to hold. In their work settings, women prove as able as men to be tough, rational and active. Men, at the same time, are assuming greater responsibility for child care and housework than they did in the past. At home, they are learning to behave with softness, emotionality, and, if not passivity, then at least greater tranquillity.

EVERYDAY LIFE

Beauties and Beasts: The World According to Walt Disney

Walt Disney Studios has been producing cartoons and films for more than half a century. They have been viewed by more North American children — perhaps more children worldwide — than cartoons and films coming from any other single source. Given the importance of media images for children's socialization, what effect are Disney products likely to have on children's images of women?

This was the question researcher Sarah Teres (1996) asked herself. To answer it, she closely viewed thirty Disney animated films (in English), from *Snow White* (made in 1937) to the *Hunchback of Notre Dame* (made in 1996). She focused on the main characters — their personalities, activities, physical appearance. Here are a few of the things she observed:

- A majority of the central characters are male.

- Female characters are secondary and decorative, if not altogether invisible.

- Young female characters typically combine lovable, childlike Kewpie-Doll faces (large foreheads, large eyes, tiny noses, and soft roundish noses) with sexualized bodies: large breasts, small waists, straight hips and tiny feet.

- The ultimate goal for female characters, often achieved with the help of magic, is marriage. Unmarried female characters are often the villains in these stories.

- The most attractive female characters are submissive and/or self-sacrificing. Those who behave otherwise are punished, then redeemed when they change their behaviour.

- For female characters, disobedience to authority leads to disaster. However, male characters must disobey authority to attain adulthood and their rightful power.

Teres concludes that, despite some evidence of change over time, the Disney image of females has remained pretty constant. What kinds of conclusions are children likely to draw from these films and cartoons?

Source: Adapted from Sarah Teres, "Negative gender stereotypes in Disney animation," pp. 167-176 in Murray Pomerance and John Sakeris, eds. *Pictures of a Generation on Hold: Selected Papers*, Toronto: Media Studies Working Group, Ryerson Polytechnic University

Gender roles are also changing, slowly, in schools. For example, Canadian girls and boys both wear pants — especially, jeans — to school. A generation ago, a large proportion of girls were still wearing dresses or skirts. And girls and boys wear a similar range of colours, fabrics and jewellery, unlike a generation ago. These are signs that we are not meant to make the same sorts of gender distinctions; we are to distinguish among people on other grounds. Around the world, an increasing number of roles are gender-blind, in the sense that we do not *automatically* associate a particular gender with the role. (Quick: Is a pharmacist male or female? How about a comedian? a real estate agent? a public-school teacher? a house painter? a sociologist?)

However, many mass media presentations, especially movies and television shows, continue to be heavily gendered. What effect does this have on people's roles and identities? What is the effect on gender identity of our recent revivals in film of 19th-century Jane Austen plots and characterizations?

The Effect of Media on Gender Roles

Many believe that media portrayals of men and women represent a type of sex-role socialization, with profound effects on people's sense of self. If this is true, it is worrisome, for dozens of content analyses of media portrayals of women find that images of women portrayed in the mass media are still mainly traditional and stereotypical.

Verify this for yourself by watching a soap opera or commercial advertisement on television. Researchers (see, for example, Bretl and Cantor, 1988; Rudman and

Hagiwara, 1992) report that they continue to find the following differences in the depictions of male and female characters:

Power Dimension: men are powerful, strong and dominant; women are powerless, weak and submissive.

Competence Dimension: men are competent, mature and rational; women are less competent, immature and irrational.

Activity Dimension: men are busy outside the home as producers of wealth and product sellers; women are busy in the home, as consumers of wealth and product users.

Expressiveness Dimension: men are unemotional and relatively unexpressive, but communicate verbally (if at all); women are emotional and expressive, and communicate both verbally and nonverbally (e.g., body language).

Sexual Dimension: attractive men are sexually experienced and aggressive, and a man's character is in his face; attractive women are sexually inexperienced and shy, children with mature bodies (or body parts).

What is the likely effect of such distinct — and female-unfriendly — gender images? This is a big question, so consider just a small part of it: the effect of movies showing violence against women. Research shows that such movies have the effect of empowering and disinhibiting men who view them, increasing the likelihood that they will act in a violent manner towards women. But what of the effect on *women* who view these movies? Psychologists (Reid and Finchilescu, 1995) conducted an experiment to find out whether these movies had the reciprocal effect of inhibiting and disempowering women.

The subjects, all college women, were asked to answer a series of questions indicating their sense of control (or power) over their own lives. Then, one half — Group 1 — were shown clips from commercial films containing violence of men against women. These movies tended to have a sexual content or undertone, though there was no explicit sex. The other half — Group 2 — were shown clips from commercial films containing violence of men against men. Here the sexual content was minimal. Finally, all the subjects were asked to answer a second set of questions, again indicating their sense of control or power over their lives.

Not surprisingly, the researchers found that subjects in Group 1 identified strong gender themes in the movies they watched; subjects in Group 2 did not. Second, subjects in Group 1 reported strong feelings of anxiety, tension and anger while they were watching the movies; subjects in Group 2 did not. Most important, subjects in Group 1 were much more disempowered by seeing the movies than were subjects in Group 2. That is, they were much more likely than before to say they had little control over their lives.

The conclusion? Portraying women as powerless victims makes women viewers feel that victimization is imminent and inescapable, and that they have little control over their own lives. Presumably, portraying women in other demeaning conditions — for example, as incompetent, irrational, overly emotional, consumers rather than producers of wealth, or as mere collections of shapely body parts — likewise persuades women that this is indeed who they are.

However, not everyone would agree with these conclusions. People who defend the media claim that media images of gender have less effect than is commonly believed, and that their effect is conditional or interactive. Just as men who are already hostile to women are most susceptible to the empowering influence of movies featuring violence against women, so women with low self-esteem are most susceptible to the *dis*empowering influence of these same movies.

Media defenders say people get the media they want, including the portrayal of characters they find appealing and believable. If there is too much violence against women in our movies and too much violence against women in our society, then blame our culture, not the media. The media are merely symptomatic of this cultural problem, not its cause. Many critics and students of media disagree, however, saying that the media does *not* respond to audience demand in structuring its content, and in fact markets a point of view.

So far, we have ignored the nuts and bolts of socialization — the ways in which people learn to adopt the values and roles that will be important to them. We now turn to a closer consideration of these processes by focusing on the crucially important *agents of socialization*.

AGENTS OF SOCIALIZATION

Agents of socialization are the social institutions and structured relationships within which socialization takes place. The most important of these are the family, school, peer group and mass media. In modern industrialized societies, these institutions socialize almost everyone. However, religious groups, work groups and voluntary associations also play a significant role. Often, the effects of various agents of socialization are complementary or reinforcing. Yet conflicts among them — say, between the family and the peer group — are common too. That is why we must consider these agents one at a time.

Families

Most of us are born into families and have an idea of what "family life" means. A child's first emotional ties are usually to family members. They begin to teach the child the language, norms and values of the culture in a variety of ways. And it is worth noting they do so from a distinct position of power.

Some families, for example, are stricter than others. In fact, some societies are stricter than others. In societies that value conformity highly — Indonesia and Nigeria, for example — parents are more likely to use physical punishment to discipline their children. They are also more likely to lecture their children and maintain close overall control than parents in Canadian society, which values self-reliance.

Yet, little of what a family transmits through socialization is transmitted directly. For example, in India children are taught to be passive through a speech pattern called "causing to be overheard." In this pattern one person is addressed in speech, though another person — in this case the child — is meant to overhear what is said.

As well, children are taught the rules of the community in miniature when parents repeat traditional stories, poems and word games to their children. This roundabout way of teaching rules can be gentle and soothing or quite different as in, say, the 19th-century European way of teaching children by means of frightening fairy tales, which the Grimm Brothers gathered together.

Much of family socialization is unspoken. We first learn the meaning of "woman," "wife" and "mother" by watching our own mother. Later, after an opportunity to observe other versions of "woman," "wife" and "mother" in friends' homes or on television, we begin to generalize — to learn which elements are shared among people playing these roles and which ones are not. Once generalizing begins, conscious choice becomes possible and the self can develop more rapidly and uniquely.

Of course, different kinds of socialization take place in different kinds of families, with different effects on the children. For example, living with both your parents is different from living with only one of your parents, or with a step-parent. Social class also shapes the course of family socialization. For example, some research shows that middle-class parents place a greater emphasis on children's interpersonal skills than do working-class parents.

Nothing's Wrong with Our Schools

Since you're reading this book, we assume that you have likely survived a primary and secondary education, which many say is inadequate preparation for college (and life after that). You are living proof that our educational system is a good one — or at least, not too bad. Why then has criticism of the educational system become a growth industry in North America?

For about a decade, an increasingly shrill chorus of politicians, corporate "stakeholders," journalists and "parent activists" has accused Canadian and American schools of failing in their tasks. Educators have typically responded by assuming the criticisms were true and offering lame-sounding excuses — most notably that the schools are overwhelmed by immigrant students and by students who watch too much television and aren't read to at home, or disciplined, or loved, or properly fed.

A more useful response is to examine the critics' "evidence" and discover that it is faulty. Indeed, whether judged by exam scores or real-life accomplishments, North American schools and their "human product" are magnificent, the best they've ever been and probably the best in the world.

The misuse of statistics to inflate dropout rates and libel our kids' reading ability and math skills, the push for a return to "standardized" tests, the indefensible argument that education was better 30 years ago is part of a wrong-headed effort to discredit and disinvent a school system that produces more highly skilled people and independent thinkers than business and government know how to employ.

There are two (sometimes) legitimate uses of testing: providing quick mutual feedback and blackmailing students into studying. But teacher-made tests spaced through the term function better than "external exams."

What produces a good exam-taker is the opposite of what produces a citizen of literate habits. Canadian and American studies, including a 1971 Toronto Board of Education report, have found a negative correlation between scores on standardized reading, writing and math tests and the number of times a student visits a public library, or reads a book without being forced to by a teacher.

Exam-haunted U.S. school boards have reacted to these findings by axing the once widespread rule that no student could pass English or history without showing the teacher a valid library card. Some suburban schools ask parents to forbid "unnecessary" library visits and to let their children read only for school assignments, vouched for by notes from school.

Another tactic of the education-bashers is to suggest that reading is on its way out. The truth is that library use virtually doubled in Canada as a whole from 1972 to 1992, and tripled in Quebec. (Ontario, with its notoriously "permissive" system of education, achieved a higher proportionate increase than English Canada as a whole.) Statistics Canada says the most frequent library users, not counting full-time students, are adults under 35.

Source: Abridged from William A. Hynes. The full text of this excerpt appears in the Focus section of *The Globe and Mail*, Aug. 31, 1996, pp. D1, D3

Parents' willingness to give their children some freedom also has an important effect. In North America, teenagers who see their parents as accepting and warm, and as less controlling, tend to have higher self-esteem than teenagers who do not view their parents this way. In turn, parents with higher self-esteem are more likely to give their child freedom and acceptance, and to have better communication with the child as a result.

People exposed to family violence as children are more likely than other people to end up abusing their own spouse and children. In this respect, childhood experiences can have a negative influence on adult behaviour. Similarly, children who have been punished physically are more likely to grow up to be aggressive towards other family members. A particularly explosive recipe is infrequent reasoning and frequent spanking by the parent. Treating children this way dramatically increases their potential for violence as teenagers (on this topic, see Felson and Russo, 1988; Larzelere, 1986; and Newson, Newson and Adams, 1993).

These are only a few of the factors that influence family interaction and socialization. Much more can be said and the importance of the family's influence cannot be overestimated. However, parents are never in complete control of the socialization process. As we noted earlier, children also socialize their parents, especially when the topic turns to sports, leisure, sexuality, drug use and attitudes towards minorities.

Schools

Schools are important agents of socialization too. In recent years, schools have been criticized severely for failing to deliver what children need and parents and employers expect. Everyday Life, above, discusses some aspects of this debate about the methods and outcomes of schooling. But evaluating the methods and outcomes means we must first understand what the social functions of schooling really are.

Some of these functions are obvious and well-understood by all. For example, schools provide us with information, help us understand ourselves and others, and give us skills to function effectively as citizens and workers.

Most important perhaps, schools also open the door to a new social world. Unlike families, schools are populated by strangers. Some of these strangers — the teachers — hold positions of authority. They expect obedience and punish deviation (even if not as firmly today as in the past). Unlike parents, teachers exert control without delivering affection. They expect compliance without exception and will not make special deals of the kind that children usually make with their parents. This is part of treating each student equally, as one of many. In these respects, teachers are the first truly impartial rule-enforcers a child is likely to have met. In that sense, the school is a child's first exposure to the "rule of law."

The school also offers a child a first exposure to inequality. The classroom is a structure of unequal power, over which the teacher presides. At least in theory, this power is not shared, nor is it up for negotiation, although in practice, social order within the classroom is constantly negotiated between teachers and their students. The school is also a child's first experience of economics and of status inequality. The school distributes scarce resources unequally. Some children will get more of the teacher's time and attention than others. Some children will get high marks and special honours; other children will consistently do poorly and end up in a slow learning track. Students are fully aware of this unequal allocation of rewards and punishments.

Despite the chance for negotiation between teachers and their students, children enjoy relatively little control over a school's rules and practices. This powerlessness at school provides real-life training for the adult workplace, but it also undoes some of the good that socialization accomplished in the family home. The school setting typically reduces opportunities for control and makes children feel *less* competent. This is especially troublesome for children who enter school with worse than average skills.

Conflict theorists argue that the most important part of formal education is what they call the "hidden curriculum." The *hidden curriculum* is all that is presented informally to pupils, and it includes rules that students learn to survive and, more generally, an approach to living and to learning. Learning the hidden curriculum means learning how to identify who holds power, know which behaviours are rewarded, fake interest and ability, show deference and accept humiliation, and cope with boredom and repetition.

From the conflict perspective, the hidden curriculum prevents important social change by supporting the concept of hierarchy and legitimate inequality. It encourages a passive acceptance of authority, a belief in external rewards and a

Since the 1950s, school classrooms have changed dramatically. Which kind did you experience? How does the form of a classroom communicate and structure the classroom culture?

high value placed on conformity and competition. By teaching students to accept the fragmentation of learning into disconnected subjects and topics, it prepares them for the fragmentation of work and for workplace alienation: in short, for the reduction of experience into incompleteness.

Taking the longer view, the hidden curriculum prepares young people for a class division based on "credentials" and evaluation standards devised by those at the top. In this way, it justifies high rewards for the more educated and guarantees a low self-image for the less educated. Some children adopt the hidden curriculum; other children — often, working-class children — challenge the school with truancy, disruption and other forms of counterculture rather than willingly following a middle-class conception of conformity and upward mobility. Their rebellion against authority is socialization too: a kind of preparation for working-class jobs.

Feminist theorists, for their part, consider the ways schools teach girls and boys differently, in this way preparing them to accept different and often unequal roles in adult life. Some believe that males and females have different educational needs. They note, for example, that in most schools, females are underrepresented in mathematics, science and computer courses. Some researchers argue this is due to inborn (i.e., genetic) differences, such as the possibility that females favour less abstract subjects. It seems more likely this difference reflects social influences: parents giving their sons more science-related toys, for example, or science teachers providing more encouragement for male students.

Research indicates that girls start out with as much interest in science and math as boys, but lose most of it by high school. Among girls who study science and mathematics in high school, research shows they do better in these subjects in one-sex schools, with strong teacher encouragement, and when teachers emphasize the creative problem-solving and communicating aspects of these subjects. As a result, sex differences in performance disappear among students who attend one-sex schools.

Beyond that, girls in female-only schools are likely to have higher academic achievement, to participate more in school activities, enroll in more science courses, have more female-faculty role models, consider their school more "supportive" and gain more in self-esteem. No wonder the single-sex "7 sister" American colleges — Vassar, Radcliffe, Barnard, Smith, and so on — have historically produced higher-achieving women graduates than the best co-educational American colleges.

But not all of the learning at school, hidden or otherwise, takes place within the classroom. In the schoolyard, many children have their first exposure to bullies, team games, much older and younger children and same-age children of the opposite sex. The school population provides experiences that are unlikely within the family (for example, team games). The variety of students — their peers — forces children to re-assess the rules and roles they learned in infancy.

Peers

Peers are important agents of socialization and are particularly influential from late childhood through adolescence and early adulthood. The **peer group** is a group of interacting companions who usually share similar social characteristics (age, gender, social class and religion, among others), interests, tastes and values.

Members of a peer group treat one another as individuals. This means that they are able to get to know one another in terms of interests, activities and tastes, which become the foundation for close friendships (as well as strong enmities). The friendships of youth are particularly intense because children and adolescents spend so much time together engaged in identical or similar activities. Like parents and teachers, peers are also part of a child's *reference group*, people to whom the child mentally refers when evaluating his or her own thoughts and behaviour. A reference group provides the standards against which people and behaviour are evaluated. All reference groups act as agents of socialization by giving people clear illustrations of how to behave and, occasionally, by rewarding them for behaving that way.

Consider the attempts young children make to dress like their peers, their older siblings and parents, even the people they see on television. Their sense of what or who is "cool" or "beautiful" comes from these sources, and sometimes their excessive efforts at imitation are laughable. Sometimes, as when we see a ten-year-old smoking cigarettes, the imitation is depressing. Laughable or not, by dressing and acting like "the big guys," these children are declaring a desire to *be* like the big guys: indeed, to be accepted by them, and also to be viewed by others as one of them.

Peers start to be an important reference group as soon as children start school, and they become more important through adolescence and early adulthood. The importance of peers as a reference group does not depend on school, however. For example, gangs of delinquents provide each other with emotional support and aid by providing a positive sense of self when schools or parents cannot. Why are street gangs so numerous, large and significant in certain parts of the world? It's precisely because they give their members certain kinds of experiences and opportunities for a positive self-image that no other social groups do.

By studying peer groups, we learn about the basic social processes of interpersonal attraction and repulsion, expressed in cliques, friendships and mating

FAR AND AWAY

Amusing Themselves to Death

In Canada, teenage boys seek thrills and danger in a variety of ways: some use drugs or alcohol, others minor crime, others sexual adventure. For some, the motivation is boredom, a desire to prove manhood or a need to indicate group solidarity. In Brazil, all of these motives play a part. But there a sense of hopelessness also motivates a far more dangerous pastime — train-surfing — which is described in the excerpt below.

Train-surfing is a popular sport among the teenage boys who live in *favelas* (shanty-towns) in this city's industrial northern zone. The lanky boys, some of whom are over 20, climb on top of the commuter trains and "surf" while the train is in motion. Every once in a while, a few get electrocuted and die when their bodies come into contact with a live wire or over-hanging cable. But the risk is part of the thrill, they say.

Train-surfing has become a grim metaphor for Brazilian youth in an inflationary, corruption-riddled society. In a country where the currency loses about 1 per cent of its value per day and role models elicit nothing but scorn, the future is in jeopardy. The country's youth, the majority of the population of 150 million, seem doomed.

What's it like to grow up in Brazil? If you're young in an inflationary economy, it's hard to save money and your job prospects are extremely limited. Middle-class professionals such as doctors and teachers make on average $150 (U.S.) a month — hardly enough to survive in urban centres where the cost of living is, in many ways, equivalent to that in large U.S. cities. Indeed, most middle-class kids rarely dream about working hard to build a career in Brazil. They dream of going to Miami.

Although Brazil's constitution guarantees every child's right to a free education, nearly five million children never go to school. There are excellent free universities, but because entrance requirements are so rigid only those whose parents can afford to send them to private high schools have that opportunity to attend. Kids from the teeming *favela* neighbourhoods don't really have a fighting chance to get good schooling, largely because the federal government spends a pittance on public education at the primary and secondary levels.

[I]n Brazil, where the older generations have racked up a huge foreign debt, violated democratic principles and left the country morally bankrupt, there seems little hope. For young people, it's becoming harder and harder to have faith in Brazil's democratic institutions or exercise their responsibilities of citizenship. Gilson, 19, who can be found most days "surfing" at the Central do Brasil station, recently summed up the predicament of youth in his country: "We surf because it's fun. What else do we have to do?"

Source: Abridged from Isabel Vincent, "For Brazil's young people, life is a train trip to nowhere," *The Globe and Mail*, Mon., Nov. 29, 1993, p. A14

patterns. We also see displayed the best and worst features of a society. So, for example, the fatalistic and violent activity of "train surfing," as shown in Far and Away above, tells a great deal about contemporary Brazil.

Mass Media

Socialization by mass media is a major type of secondary socialization and it influences people's behaviour through modelling and imitation. Surveys show that North American teenagers spend a lot of time listening to music and watching television. Because they consume so many media messages, teenagers are significantly influenced by song lyrics, television stories and plot lines of music videos. But *how* the mass media influence behaviour, and *whether* this influence is good or bad, are hotly debated issues.

Does television cause youthful violence? Earlier in this chapter we noted that violent movies with a sexual content have a disempowering effect on women. Do violent media also increase youthful violence? In the last decade social scientists have made major efforts to pull together the findings of hundreds of careful studies of media effects on violence. Generally, the results have been critical of the media (see, for example, Centerwall, 1992; Comstock and Strasburger, 1990; Gerbner et al., 1980; Phillips, 1980; and Rosenthal, 1986).

The networks have counterattacked with their own research, arguing that television is not to blame for bad behaviour. They claim that laboratory experiments showing television causes violence are not realistic; that correlations between media consumption and violent behaviour are not demonstrations of causation; and that the effects of television violence on children's behaviour, if genuine, are small. And, as we noted earlier, the "television effects" are conditional, with the biggest effects being reported for American boys and men.

The effects are also greater when they reinforce everyday experiences of violence, whether at home or in the neighbourhood more generally. Finally, the networks claim that whatever harmful effect television does have will decrease in the future, since television violence has decreased in the last decade. The new practice of rating TV programs for violence and other objectionable behaviours may help to further reduce TV's antisocial effects.

However, the research community is united in its belief that television violence, which they say is not decreasing, does have a harmful effect. More studies have moved outside the laboratory. More studies are also longitudinal and naturalistic, and they all show that the more television violence people view, the more violently they behave. Television violence, researchers say, also produces a generalized fear of crime and a distrust of other people.

Television stories that are most likely to trigger aggressive behaviour are those suggesting that violence is (1) safe, painless and unpunished; (2) justified, uncriticized and motivated by revenge; (3) exciting, sexy and fun; and (4) a major part of real life, involving people just like the viewer.

Other research on the effects of mass media has to do with the way advertising secretly manipulates our desires. Products are advertised in ways that appeal to people's longing for social acceptance or status. Sex is also a powerful attention-grabber; advertisers even imply that their product — whether jeans, beer or even soft drinks — will improve a consumer's sex life.

The effect of such advertising on prosperous North America is problematic enough; it has more serious effects where people are less prosperous. Teenagers in developing countries have also been socialized by the media and peers to have a materialistic outlook. Yet these teenagers are keenly aware of their relatively disempowered position as consumers in the world economic system. This awareness makes them feel inadequate because they have fewer material goods (but not less craving) than teenagers in other parts of the world and less opportunity to participate in the world economy.

Other Agents

There are many other agents of socialization in our society. They include religious institutions — such as churches, synagogues and mosques — which propagate the religious values we discussed in the last chapter.

Attendance at many religious institutions has fallen during the course of the 20th century, as part of the process of secularization mentioned earlier. And there is ample evidence that religion exerts a less powerfully emotional hold over Canadians than it does over Americans, who are much more likely to believe in heaven, hell, and a personal relationship with God (Lipset, 1990). In some parts of Canada, especially Quebec, the response to Church teachings is closer to outright rejection than it is to indifference. Despite this, we would be wrong to write off religion as an agent of socialization in Canada.

First, as Northrop Frye showed in his classic work *The Great Code*, religious thinking as manifested in the Judaic and Christian Bibles supplies us with metaphors, parables and exemplars which, imported into everyday "common sense," continue to shape our thoughts and actions. Second, religious institutions (including schools) play a particularly important role in the development of immigrant communities and ethnic identities. (We will have more to say about this in Chapter 7, which is on ethnic and race relations.)

Finally, religious ideas and affiliations continue, as they have done in Canada for nearly two centuries, to motivate regional protest movements and "Third" political parties. Today's New Democratic Party evolved out of the Co-operative Commonwealth Federation (CCF) — a party influenced by the "social gospel" values of its founders. Today's Reform Party evolved out of Social Credit — a party founded by the religious leader William Aberhart. Today's Bloc Québécois owes as much to the nationalist sentiments promoted by Quebec's Catholic Church before 1960, as it does to social critics like René Lévesque after 1960. In spreading their political views, these parties are also spreading religion-based ideas, often to followers with religion-based sympathies for these ideas.

However, as an agent of socialization, religion is far more likely to work through the agents of primary socialization we have already discussed: especially through families and primary schools. Professional schools and workplaces, by contrast, provide secondary socialization. Because modern societies have so many different social institutions, secondary socialization, particularly within professional schools and work groups, is critical. Here the socialization process centres more on specific goals and activities than it does in a peer group, family or primary school.

These agencies prepare people for a coming change of roles. As such they provide anticipatory socialization. **Anticipatory socialization** prepares people for roles they will eventually perform by helping them to understand these roles. Most adult socialization is of this character.

Both job training and professional education are types of anticipatory socialization that prepare people for the work they will do after graduating. Equally important, these programs teach the attitudes, values and beliefs associated with a future activity. A law-school education, for example, teaches students the values of the legal profession and shows them how to think about legal problems. It also teaches students how to speak, dress and deal with clients in an appropriate professional manner. On the negative side, it may induce young people who aren't quite lawyers yet to spend money or adopt an attitude toward others as if they are.

The practice of medicine requires professional socialization too. A medical education teaches students the parts of the body, types of diseases, the medical language, diagnoses and possible cures. As well, students learn the ethics of medical practice and ways to give the patient a reassuring show of competence in every situation.

Often anticipatory socialization is self-training because, as we have noted, the students have freely chosen to enter this educational stream. This makes professional education different from lower levels of education which students have *not* chosen voluntarily and where they are often socialized against their will. *Workplace socialization*, sometimes voluntary but often not, is the process of learning what is and what is not acceptable behaviour within a workplace. It includes the process of adopting the values, goals and perspectives of those with whom a person interacts at work. Workplace socialization also includes learning the specialized language (or argot) of the people at work. This gives the new worker a sense of belonging and of loyalty to the group. It also helps the worker "fit in" better and improves the individual's chances of holding on to the job.

Much of this learning is imitative and unconscious. For example, junior executives frequently pay close attention to the way senior executives dress, speak and act, and model their actions after them. A person who prepares for career advancement in this way is more likely to advance than someone who does not. A few are also lucky enough to have *mentors* who provide them with advice and support. Mentors can help by giving ambitious young workers more opportunity, contacts, advancement, recognition and work satisfaction than they would otherwise have.

SOCIALIZATION OVER THE LIFE CYCLE

What Is the Life Cycle?   As you can see, there are many socialization experiences in a lifetime. In fact, the development of the self and the learning of social behaviour are lifelong processes. In life, personal change is constant. And we have noted that current theories of socialization see development occurring in many phases or stages. The notion of developmental stages implies that people's lives follow a pattern as they age and pass through typical social roles.

These three people-in-suits learned how to dress, talk, joke and (generally) get along on the job through workplace socialization.

What sociologists call the **life cycle** is a socially recognized, predictable sequence of stages through which people pass during the course of their lives. Each stage is characterized by a set of socially defined rights, responsibilities and expected behaviour patterns. The recognized sequence in North American society includes infancy, childhood, adolescence, maturity and old age.

However, stages of the life cycle are socially, not biologically, defined. Adolescence, for example, is not a biological fact, it is a social invention. Adolescence as we know it today did not exist before the 19th century. Two hundred years ago, fifteen-year-olds spent their time in the same ways as people who were twenty-five or thirty-five: in adult work. If unmarried, they were all equally subject to domination by the head of the household. Likewise, old age is not a biological reality so much as a social and psychological one. Today, few people of fifty, sixty and even seventy years of age think of themselves as "old," or do the things "old" people used to do. People of these ages are much more physically active, travel more and enter new roles more readily than people of the same age fifty years ago. They divorce and remarry, have sex, go on exotic vacations if they can afford it, keep working if they are permitted, and so on. It is the behaviour of eighty- and ninety-year-olds today that is similar to the behaviour of sixty-year-olds a century ago.

Because the life cycle is socially defined, life cycles vary across cultures and over history. Different cultures identify different stages of life and expect them to last different lengths of time. Our own society has recently recognized a distinct stage between adolescence and mature adulthood: people are calling it the "youth stage," or "young, single and independent stage." This new stage has emerged because fewer young people are moving out of their parents' homes to marry and form new families. Some remain in their parents' home, while others move out and live on their own or with a roommate. Many delay marriage while they "find themselves," learn to be independent or simply have fun.

Even this modified picture of the life cycle is too simple. It leaves the impression that people pass through life in only one way and doing otherwise is wrong or abnormal. In fact, the life cycle is just a statistical summary of what people are doing, not a social law. People vary around the average enormously and they are varying more all the time.

Is There Anyone You Cannot Be?

We began this book by stating that social structure is what constrains and transforms everyone, even the most different kinds of people. And this chapter has shown that throughout life we change our behaviours, goals and values. In some cases we are even resocialized, which means we change fundamental parts of our personalities, not merely our attitudes or skills. **Resocialization** causes the person to adopt a new outlook on the world and a new sense of self. Such basic changes come about through the learning of radically different values, norms and role expectations from those learned earlier.

Resocialization can be voluntary or involuntary. For example, resocialization is becoming more necessary for people who want to get jobs in a tight economy. Other people, who seek psychological counselling, may also want to be resocialized — to have their personalities "remade." In both cases, resocialization is voluntary. In other cases, resocialization is involuntary, as it is for people who live in **total institutions**. A total institution, as described by sociologist Erving Goffman (1961), is an organization which is set apart physically or socially from the rest of society. Included in this category are prisons, mental hospitals, boarding schools, concentration camps, military barracks and convents. Inmates in these institutions have little, if any, contact with the outside world.

Here, they learn new modes of thought and behaviour that the people in charge deem appropriate.

People do change fundamentally when they are in fundamentally different settings, especially if they have entered them freely. But does this mean there are no limits on how much you or anyone else can change? Does it mean there are conditions under which a gentle person might willingly become a killer, for example? Or a loyal person, a traitor?

The answer to this question is often "yes." Warfare, for example, commonly teaches gentle people to systematically kill. As a total institution, the military teaches people to kill enthusiastically and efficiently. In such circumstances, most people find ways to justify their change of attitude and behaviour. They may even find reasons to betray their own family and friends: it has happened many times, in many places. However, you should remember that early socialization is, in many respects, more critical than later socialization. If we get the early parts wrong, it will be much harder — perhaps, impossible — to make them right later on (and vice

APPLIED SOCIOLOGY

Growing Up Angry

As we noted at the beginning of this chapter, people turn out the way they do as a result of their genetic predispositions and the experiences they have in life. There is little we can do about the genetic mix, at least at present, but lots we can do about people's life experiences. In particular, sociologists can play an important role in diagnosing family pathologies: the ways social and economic organization may distort family life, and the ways a distorted family life distorts a young person.

Two 11-year-olds, identified as Child A and Child B, went on trial in Britain for murder yesterday. The prosecutor said in his opening statement that they knew they were doing evil when they stoned and beat a two-year-old boy to death. The killing has touched off a major debate in the country over increasing incidents of youth violence.

Schools across the U.S. are rapidly implementing violence-prevention and conflict-resolution programs. In Canadian schools, too, the need for conflict-resolution programs is pandemic. Increasingly, our children are turning up in the classroom with an impaired ability to resolve their conflicts, frustrations and psychological turmoil through other than aggressive means.

Let's begin to look at what might be behind this. Dr. Paul Steinhauer, senior staff psychiatrist at Toronto's Hospital for Sick Children, has written a paper called, "Youth in the Eighties and Nineties — A 15-Year Trend." Dr. Steinhauer says children have two crucial biological and social drives which are often not met. The first is the need for a satisfactory and continuous attachment to a parental figure. The second is the universal need to learn to tame and diffuse our inherent aggression.

The development of a sense of right and wrong and the ability to contain and discharge aggression in a controlled manner — both of which are fuelled by a successful attachment to, and consistent structure and reinforcement from, the parents — are important in helping children learn to deal successfully with aggression, and contribute to their behaving in a socially acceptable manner.

An inadequate attachment to a parent can result from parental lack of interest, neglect or abuse. It can result from "lack of continuity of parental figures" (through separations, and especially multiple separations, including repeated changes of caregivers — e.g. nannies — which tear children away from those to whom they are attached.) Dr. Steinhauer writes: "Children experiencing an unsuccessful attachment or multiple separations frequently have their level of biologically derived aggression greatly increased by the excessive rage resulting from the frustration of their attachment needs."

So let us all read this and think about what we are doing to family life — how many of our kids we have relegated to single-parent families, how many of our kids we think of as interruptions to our work life, how much we are relying on outside caregivers whom we know little about, and how many problems we are loading onto the schools.

Source: Michael Valpy, "Youth in the 1990s: growing up angry," *The Globe and Mail*, Tues., Nov. 2, 1993, p. A2

versa). For example, it may not be possible to re-socialize the children described in Applied Sociology on page 89, though they are only eleven years old.

CLOSING REMARKS

Like the sociological study of culture, the study of socialization demonstrates an important connection between macro and micro perspectives.

On the one hand, socialization is a macro phenomenon: something imposed on people (especially infants and children) by more powerful agents of socialization. In this sense, socialization is a top-down process that moulds us in society's image. On the other hand, socialization is a process that we often willingly take part in and even initiate. As symbolic interactionists remind us, we all have the desire to learn, speak and interact with other people. From this standpoint, socialization merely gives us the tools to do what we already want to do. As long as we continue to meet new people, we continue to discover new things about ourselves and others, and learn new ways of using this knowledge.

And like the sociological study of culture, the study of socialization reminds us of the important connection between private troubles and public issues. For example, the "hidden curriculum" we study at school is a source of great frustration to many young people. We (mostly) suffer the discipline, regimentation and routine of our early schooling in silence, as though it is our own personal nightmare. But, as we have seen, there is a social logic to that nightmare. It serves a purpose beyond itself — notably, the lesson of subordination — and that is a public issue far more important than we may have thought as children.

Good sociology never loses sight of the broad social processes which affect all of us, or the intricate circumstances which are unique to each of us. That's why good sociology avoids determinism and leaves some room for "free will." As we see in the chapters that follow, social determinism causes more theoretical problems than it solves. How can we explain social change if we assume that all people are programmed to value only the existing social order? Equally, how can we explain deviance if we assume that all people are socialized to conform to society's norms and values?

Some claim that deviance results from incomplete or imperfect socialization. Others claim that deviance is conformity to the expectations of an unusual subculture. To some degree, both of these claims are valid. By now, it should be clear that what we call "deviant acts" are a normal part of social life: acts that people practise and often give up as they pass through life. We explore these issues further in the next chapter.

Review Questions

1. What is socialization?
2. Why is primary socialization considered so important by all of the sociological paradigms?
3. What is cultural determinism?
4. What do feral children teach us about the importance of primary socialization?
5. In what way is learning a natural human process.
6. What is cognitive development?
7. What is the self?
8. What did Charles Cooley mean by the "looking-glass self"?
9. Why did George Herbert Mead consider "taking the role of the other" to be so important when interacting with others?
10. What are the stages in Mead's theory of internalization?
11. In what ways is socialization an active process?
12. How does gender socialization differ for boys and girls?
13. What are the different agents of socialization?

Discussion Questions

1. Everyone pays the cost of having people in society who have been inadequately or harmfully socialized, if they end up criminals or mentally ill as adults. Should this give society the right to direct the ways parents socialize their children?

2. "If the school exposes a child to rules that apply equally to everyone and rewards for merit, is this doing the child a disservice? After all, it is preparing the child for a world that does not exist outside the school." Discuss this statement.

3. Currently, childhood is a time of play and freedom from responsibility, while adulthood is a time of little play and a lot of responsibility. How might lives be organized in future to mix play and responsibility throughout the life cycle? How would childhood gain from this? How would adulthood gain?

4. Old people seem more satisfied with life than younger people, though they may have less money and poorer health. How do they learn this approach to life, and could younger people learn it too?

5. Is there any change people cannot make through resocialization? Give examples of where this change is limited or impossible.

6. What are the arguments in favour of providing separate schools for males and females? Discuss these.

Suggested Readings

Elkin, F. and G. Handel (1989) *The Child and Society: The Process of Socialization*, fifth edition. New York: Random House. This is a classic reference work for anyone interested in knowing more about the topic of socialization.

Ellis, D. and L. Sayer (1986) *When I Grow Up: Expectations and Aspirations of Canadian Schoolchildren*. Ottawa: Labour Canada. This study of more than 700 Canadian schoolchildren examines their opinions (stereotypes) of various occupational choices and their future plans. The authors find that children seem to understand that both boys and girls can work in non-stereotyped fields, but their *own* job choices do not reflect this diversity.

Handel, G. (1988) *Childhood Socialization*. New York: Adeline de Gruyter. This is a collection of 19 articles dealing with such topics as the family, schools, peer groups and television as agents of gender and class socialization. Several of these articles look beyond the North American context.

Kostash, M. (1987) *No Kidding: Inside the World of Teenage Girls*. Toronto: McClelland and Stewart. This Canadian study is a rich analysis of the teen years, based on lengthy interviews with teenage girls who talk candidly about boys, friends, family and sex.

Shattuck, R. (1980) *The Forbidden Experiment: The Story of the Wild Boy of Aveyron*. New York: Pocket Books, Washington Square Press. Critic and poet Shattuck makes this case history into a general enquiry on the meaning of civilized life: what it gains us and what it loses.

Wrigley, J. (1994) *Other People's Children*. New York: Basic Books. This is a qualitative study of men and women who look after other people's children. It examines private child-care arrangements from the point of view of both parents and employees.

Internet Resources

The following Web sites are good places to find more information about topics discussed in this chapter:

Adult Education Resources contains links to sites for general adult education, distance education, literacy, training and human development.
http://tenb.mta.ca/sau/aed

Canadian Homeschooling Resource Page provides information on homeschooling in Canada, support groups for home-schooling and shared experiences.
http://www.flora.ottawa.ca/homeschool ~ ca

National Adult Literacy Database maintains a comprehensive, up-to-date database on adult literacy programs, services and activities.
http://www.nald.ca/index.htm

Social Identity is a Web page dealing with construction and presentation of self from a symbolic interactionist perspective.
http://online.anu.edu.au/psychology.socpsych/socindent.htm

The Presentation of Self in Electronic Life describes how people negotiate and validate their chosen identities on the Internet.
http://www.ntu.ac.uk/soc/psych/miller/goffman.htm

TeenLine includes links to music, sports and games sites, as well as information on relationships, family problems, sex, drugs and alcohol for teens.
http://www.cyberlink.bc.ca/ ~ teenline/

Deviance and Control

CHAPTER OUTLINE

Police officers are moral custodians, as are religious leaders, teachers and parents.

DEFINING DEVIANCE AND SOCIAL CONTROL

Social Order and Rules   At times, all of us have done things we should not have, things that have made us ashamed, anxious, or that gave us a secret thrill. We may even admire people — say, political rebels or environmental activists — who break the law and risk serious penalties in order to act on their principles.

How do sociologists account for this common tendency to break rules or flout laws? How, in other words, do sociologists account for deviance? By now you know enough about the field to realize that what is most likely to interest a sociologist is not the deviant behaviour itself, but how deviance and conformity are related to each other. Deviance, as we shall see, is another aspect of social order. *Society creates deviance* by expecting, insisting upon and enforcing social order.

Think about it! If you occasionally put your dirty laundry on the bookshelf, books in the fridge and pickles in the washing machine, this will seem disordered, perhaps even to you. (You may even forget where you left the pickles.) If you do this regularly, it may not seem disordered to you but will seem so to most other people, and ultimately it is society's definition that matters. For society creates the rules which define a "proper" order, and order is what creates the possibility of deviance.

Deviance, then, is not a special topic of study but a measure of how a society is organized. Every area of social life provides a chance to deviate. Deviance occurs in all the tiny activities of daily life. Whenever we lie, cheat, seduce, disgust or simply annoy one another, we are deviating from *someone's norms*. Deviant acts even occur in many subcultural groups, such as juvenile gangs. The dominant view is that these acts are deviant and, often, they are also perceived as harmful.

Most of us think of **crime** when we think of deviance, more specifically, the major crimes such as murder, armed robbery or rape. However "deviance" covers a much wider variety of actions. It includes criminal organizations such as the

Mafia and those "legitimate" organizations which engage in criminal acts by bribing officials, cheating customers or selling hazardous and defective products. Deviance ranges from murder at one extreme to pushing ahead of a line of people waiting for a bus at the other. Deviance also includes keeping a dog off-leash in prohibited areas, taking one's clothes off in the lobby of a doctor's office, bargaining at a department store, and eating poached worms in Regina.

As you might gather, the study of deviance is the study of everyone — the entire society — seen from one particular angle. This is why the sociology of deviance brings to light *all* the controversies that sociologists, and sociology students, are ever likely to meet in the discipline.

Deviance and Social Control

What all behaviours termed "deviant" have in common is that members of one group or another claim to feel their cherished values or their security are threatened by them. To sociologists, then, **deviance** is a general term referring to any behaviour that leads to a negative reaction by some part of the community. When no one feels threatened by an uncommon behaviour — for example, by the wearing of a polka-dot bow tie — people are likely to see it as simply an expression of individuality. Such behaviour may be considered eccentric, even charming, but not deviant. There is a lot of room in North American popular culture for the acceptance, sometimes admiration, of people who are eccentric (like Mother Teresa) or who rebel in fashionable ways (like k.d. lang).

Let us consider the teenager who sits at the dining-room table burping without cease. Whether or not the behaviour is deviant will depend on whether those who are listening think and call it so; and this may depend on whether they are parents, the church fund-raising committee, the older sister's fiancé's parents, other teenagers engaged in a burping contest or a pack of improvisational musicians trying out fascinating new sounds.

This means that reactions to uncommon behaviour depend largely on how the behaviour is perceived. Still, perception by itself is not enough; for an act to be deviant, perception must be turned into action. How much weight that action carries will depend on how much power people have to *enforce* their own views of acceptable behaviour. Enforcement at the microsociological level translates into agencies of social control at the macrosociological level. *Social control* refers to the institutions and procedures that make sure members of society conform to rules of expected and approved behaviour. The operation of social control is most obvious when it is *formal*, especially when laws are enforced through the police and the courts.

Formal social control gives specific people (such as police officers) the responsibility of enforcing specific rules or laws, while following specific control methods. And formal control varies widely across countries. Even policing varies, from the localized police system of the United States to the centralized system of France.

Few people have much contact with the police or other agencies which wield formal social control. Our knowledge of formal control usually comes through the media, not personal experience. But we do have first-hand knowledge of another kind of social control. We see it whenever ordinary people exercise **informal social control** through gossip, praise or blame. In small communities, informal social controls are the main way of keeping social order. Yet informal controls are not only effective in a village or small town.

Japan is a good example. Though highly industrialized and urbanized, Japanese society continues to have a low crime rate. The importance of family life, group membership and community harmony lends support to the informal control of deviant behaviour. Local debating societies, neighbourhood newspapers and conferences of special interest groups also help to enforce the rules. Informal control works in many societies because people often seek the approval of others for a feeling of self-worth. Informal controls teach us to obey the rules and gently prod us in the direction of conformity when we show signs of deviating.

Along with the threat of legal sanctions (e.g., fines or imprisonment), feelings of guilt can be an important means of social control, where crimes like tax evasion, petty theft and drunk driving are concerned. But guilt and shame are not very effective in Western society. They work best in societies like Japan, where people consider "saving face" to be very important.

The Relativity of Deviance

In North America, except for major crimes, we find little agreement about what acts should be considered deviant. In a survey conducted in 1965, American sociologist J. L. Simmons asked 180 people what they considered deviant. They replied with a total of 252 different forms of behaviour. The answers ranged from homosexuality to atheism to divorce (Thio, 1983: 3). This broad range of answers suggests there is little agreement about what is deviant and what are the norms or rules of the society.

We may interpret this evidence in several ways. First, it suggests that in North America people hold widely different, often uncertain views about a variety of acts. Over time, they may change their views profoundly. For example, standard North American views on homosexuality and premarital sex have changed in the last few decades. In 1975 only 14 per cent of surveyed Canadians said that homosexuality was "not wrong at all." By 1995, 32 per cent held that view. And though most Canadian respondents still disapprove of homosexuality, three-quarters of all surveyed Canadians support the idea that homosexuals are entitled to the same rights as other Canadians (Bibby, 1995: 72, 73). Likewise, approval of premarital sex has increased in the last twenty years. In 1975, only 39 per cent of surveyed Canadians thought it was "not wrong at all," compared with 57 per cent in 1995 (Bibby, *op. cit.*: 69). By contrast, people disapproved of extramarital sex even more in 1995 than they did in 1975.

At the same time, North American views on some deviant acts are divided. Views on homosexuality and premarital sex, for example, tend to vary with the size of community and religiosity and educational level of the respondent. Typically, the most religious and least educated residents of small towns are the least likely to approve. In Canada, Quebecers hold the most liberal attitudes towards premarital and homosexual sex, followed closely by British Columbia. The lowest approval ratings are found in Atlantic Canada (Bibby, *op. cit.*: 76).

As well, there may be a conflict between the official and unofficial norms. For example, research reported in Applied Sociology below shows a reluctance on the part of many people to pay their taxes, especially the Federal Goods and Services Tax (GST) on purchases they make. Some groups are particularly vocal in their resistance to paying and, within these groups, non-payment is almost an unofficial (subcultural) norm. Given the difficulty Ottawa has enforcing tax payment, it will need to change these unofficial norms before it can hope to see conformity to the official norms (i.e., laws) governing tax payment.

Even for crimes against persons, we find a lot of disagreement. For example, surveys in the United States asked people, "Are there any situations that you can imagine in which you would approve of a man punching an adult male stranger?" Between 1968 and 1988, the proportion of people indicating they

The Tax Anarchists

Sociologists are experts in the study of social conformity and control. Though the Canadian government offers people substantial leeway in the conduct of their personal lives, it insists that certain social obligations be fulfilled, among them, the paying of taxes. However, many people try to avoid paying their rightful taxes and many get away with it. How might you, as a sociologist, advise the government to change people's attitudes towards taxpaying? And how would you suggest the government improve enforcement of the laws relating to taxpaying?

A hard-core minority of Canadians, especially members of Generation X, are a worrying breed of virtual tax anarchists, a new survey of attitudes toward taxation indicates. Researchers say these people are young and single and resent paying taxes so much that they would readily cheat, and they believe those who play by the rules are fools. They also think tax evasion is rampant in Canada but oppose any crackdown by Revenue Canada.

The anarchists are just 14 per cent of the total adult population, but they are overrepresented among males aged 18 to 24, the survey by the Ottawa-based marketing-research firm Canadian Facts and chartered accountants KPMG Peat Marwick Thorne found.

David Hoffman, vice-president of Canadian Facts, said it is striking that a significant chunk of the population has such a negative attitude toward paying taxes. The phenomenon may be a manifestation of a wider malaise among that age group, he suggested.

"It could very well be related to the feeling that the whole system — political and economic — is not offering them the same opportunities that they had imagined, or certainly that their parents had," Mr. Hoffman said.

The survey found, for example, that 18-to-24-year-olds are twice as likely to cheat on their taxes as the average Canadian. Nearly 28 per cent said they would not report some income on their tax return, compared with 16.4 per cent for all Canadians. Similarly, 34.2 per cent said they would buy smuggled liquor or cigarettes, compared with the national average of 17 per cent.

Nearly one in two Canadians are willing to pay cash to avoid the federal goods and services tax. The rate is highest among the young at nearly 63 per cent. More than 23 per cent of 18-to-24-year-olds also agreed that people who pay all their taxes are fools, compared with 17 per cent for all Canadians.

In general, Canadians' attitudes toward taxes have become slightly more positive since the initial [1994] survey. People defined as "model citizens" make up 29 per cent of the population, up from 22 per cent in the previous survey. Model citizens pay all their taxes, think they're getting good value for what they pay and say the present system is fair.

Source: Abridged from Barrie McKenna, *The Globe and Mail*, Jan. 9, 1996, pp. A1, A2

approved of assault under *some* conditions rose from 51 per cent to 63 per cent. This suggests a growing public acceptance of assault as a way of settling disputes. In many instances, people would even approve of what the courts would consider criminal assault.

In other words, there is widespread *dis*agreement with the written law. This is due to the social and cultural relativity of deviance. As we will see, deviance is always relative to the group which defines the behaviour. Cannibalism is considered deviant in our society, but among the warlike Iroquois and Pawnee it was sacred — an accepted means of seeking revenge (Abler, 1992; Harris, 1991). *Socio-cultural relativity* means that sociologists cannot treat deviance as if it were an inherent property of an act, the way physicists can treat atomic bonding as an inherent property of matter.

Another form of relativity is *situational relativity*. Take the example of cannibalism just mentioned, then think of circumstances in which people in our society would consider cannibalism acceptable. If people were stranded without food far from civilization, would cannibalism be acceptable? Probably, it would be. A decade ago, survivors of a plane crash in the Andes were forced to eat the flesh of their colleagues. They did so reluctantly, but had little choice. Many people might say yes to cannibalism then, with the proviso that the only people to be eaten were already dead and had not been killed for use as food. In this case, it is unlikely the police would make any effort to reveal and punish cannibalism. This proves that, as the context changes, so too do the social definitions of the act as deviant or as normal (or at least, necessary). In other words, deviance is not only culturally relative, it is also "situationally relative."

Given these variations in culture and situation, it is not surprising to find rampant disagreement about deviance. Even sociologists disagree over what should be considered "deviant." But remember, it is not the sociologist's job to decide what deviance really is, much less to pass judgment on "right" and "wrong." What sociologists do is look at how deviance is understood in society and what social processes lead some people to define and treat others as deviant.

MAJOR PERSPECTIVES ON DEVIANCE

There is no one theory of deviance any more than there is one theory of society. Because there are different forms of deviance, there are different reasons for deviant behaviour and different theories about it. The study of deviance was one of the first areas of interest for sociologists, and research on deviance helped develop the four paradigms which we have been presenting in this book.

Social Disorganization

One early sociological approach to studying deviance, crime and control was the *social disorganization* approach, developed by sociologist W. I. Thomas (1928) in Chicago. Social disorganization theorists claimed that modern industrial societies are more liable to deviance than others. They argued that the industrialization, urbanization and immigration that accompanied modernization had shattered society's traditional order. This in turn spread social ills, crime and "vice," especially among the working class and the poor. Only a reestablishment of order — especially in urban settings — could reform society, and thereby cure it.

This view made a lot of sense a century ago, when people were first struggling to come to terms with city life, large-scale immigration, mass production, mass literacy and the rise of the working class. It held a particular appeal for the Chicago "school of sociology," whose members studied a city that was growing and changing rapidly and where the crime rate was high. However, this approach is still used today, for example, to explain the self-destructive behaviour of Canada's First Peoples.

CBC

**"Davis Inlet:
Moving from Misery"**

To see that this is appropriate, let's begin by considering the social order that existed before social disorganization set in. White Europeans arrived in the Americas by boat 500 years ago. However, Asians had arrived in the Americas on foot 10,000 years ago (across a land bridge over the Bering Strait). Today, their descendants Canada's native peoples, include Indians, Inuit and Metis.

No written records survive from the earliest periods of settlement. However, so far as we can tell, in North America most native peoples became hunters and trappers, food-plant gatherers or fishers. They lived in a great many small communities or bands which varied widely but which had certain features in common. These included a close tie to nature, a migratory lifestyle with no land ownership, little division of labour or inequality, no capital or wage labour, small settlements and no cities and oral cultural traditions (i.e., no written record).

Rates of Death for Selected Types of Injury, Registered Indians and Total Population, 1989–1992

	Registered Indians		Total population	
	Male	Female	Male	Female
Motor vehicle accidents	59.7	24.7	20.0	8.3
Accidental falls	9.9	7.1	6.1	6.3
Fire	12.1	6.6	1.6	0.8
Drowning	20.8	3.1	3.0	0.6
Suicide	51.5	15.1	19.2	4.9
Homicide	18.2	6.8	2.7	1.5
Poisoning	21.1	11.7	3.0	1.2

Note: Death rares per 100,000 population

Source: Report of Royal Commission on Aboriginal Peoples, Vol. 3, *Gathering Strength*. Ottawa: Supply & Services, 1996. Catalog Z1-1991/1-3E.

Despite differences in language and culture, they all lived in *gemeinschaft* communities, which we discussed in Chapter 2. Thus they were stable groups whose members had similar personal histories and intimate enduring relationships. A strong sense of community, and moral custodians who stood guard over the group's traditions, promoted the sharing of moral values.

Before the white people came, there were some wars, but native life was mainly peaceful; there were some federations, but mainly there was local rule; and there were some illnesses, but mainly people led healthy lives. *After* the white people came, there were new diseases and famines, wage labour and private land ownership, state-building and empire-building and large-scale war with advanced weapons. Not by chance, by the end of the 19th century the native population had shrunk. The natives, forced off their traditional hunting lands and onto reserves, came to depend on trade and foreign markets. Without a secure economic base, native society was shattered.

Many native children were forced to attend distant residential — especially mission — schools. In these **total institutions** run by whites, native students were totally controlled, isolated from their home community for months or years at a time. Worst of all, the native family system had been destroyed. The white educational plan deprived parents of the chance to teach their own children, and the children grew up not knowing how to parent. A generation of badly raised children followed.

Not all native children attended the distant residential schools. But in the town and city schools, native children were treated like second-class citizens. As their self-esteem plummeted, natives began to destroy themselves. Rates of suicide, accidents, alcoholism, drug abuse and violence began to rise among them. As native families and communities collapsed, native children were placed in white foster homes where they suffered new physical, emotional and sexual abuses.

Today, we can still see the results of social disorganization in native suicide rates: they are twice as high for native women as for other Canadian women, and more than twice as high for native men as for other Canadian men. Mainly young native men commit suicide: in fact, nearly two in a thousand native men ages 20-24 kill themselves — five times the rate for white men of the same age.

The problem of native self-destruction may be solved by recovering native traditions, re-instituting native social ties and ending interference by white society. There is evidence that this solution works. Natives on the Alkali Lake Reserve in British Columbia went from 100 per cent addiction to 95 per cent sobriety in fifteen years. The method that worked included addiction counselling by natives, sharing aboriginal experiences, re-learning the traditional culture and practising aboriginal rituals. Such community formation is best accomplished through self-government, which promotes native solutions to native problems, faster recovery of native traditions, less outside interference by whites, and native economic development. Hence, the native demand for self-government!

Is teenage deviance a normal product of a healthy society?

The history of Canada's First Peoples shows that social disorganization theory works to explain some deviant behaviour and to prescribe a remedy for the problem. However, the theory works better for some forms of deviance than others. It works best where we can agree that the behaviour in question is indeed harmful and dangerous. Beyond that, social disorganization theories, though suggestive, give us little ability to predict the behaviour of either individuals or groups. We cannot predict *which* individuals or *which* ethnic communities will show high rates of suicide, alcoholism or homicide.

Moreover, recent research on native peoples (Frideres, 1993; Satzewich, 1992, 1993) looks to the role of the state and state policy in perpetuating dependency as a cause of aboriginal deviance. In their eyes, the issue is not that native culture was destroyed, but that natives were prevented from creating a new culture or building a new way of life. As we will see in a later chapter, the recent Royal Commission on Aboriginal Peoples recognizes the need to limit state interference and state-created dependency.

Deviant Behaviour Theory

In at least one crucial respect, most modern sociologists think about deviance in much the same way as the average police officer. What the police see, day after day, is very ordinary rule-breaking — for example, speeding or dangerous driving. Now and then, deviance gets out of hand and results in accidents, injuries, even deaths. But this is neither "sick" nor "abnormal" behaviour. The police officer would hardly conclude that society was "getting sicker" if the accident rate went up or even if convictions for speeding increased.

What came next in the growth of sociological thinking was a vision of deviance that emphasized its "normality," not its pathology. The French sociologist Emile Durkheim led the way by breaking with the moralistic critique of modern society. He argued (1938) that, since deviance can be found in every society and every social group, it must be a normal, inevitable, even necessary aspect of society. In fact, even crime must be functional for, or beneficial to, society.

There are a number of ways, Durkheim suggested, in which deviance benefits us. For example, deviant behaviour calls attention to flaws in the social system that need mending. It may suggest new ways of getting things done, or better ways of adapting to changes in the social milieu. Minor forms of deviance serve as safety valves, allowing people to let loose in socially acceptable ways (for example, getting drunk at a weekend party). In all these respects, Durkheim believed, both deviance and social control help society to survive and change.

Deviants also provide us with vivid displays of how *not* to act. A society needs deviance to define the boundaries between good and evil, right and wrong, and what is or is not acceptable. People who are marked as deviants serve as scapegoats for social ills, as targets for repressed anger and tension. Having a common enemy helps to unite the group. The use of social control increases social cohesion and group solidarity. Said another way, the enforcement of rules ties the group more tightly together. To the degree that deviance both calls forth and justifies punishment, then, deviance is "good" for society.

Durkheim's discussion of the functions of deviance and social control gave sociologists a new way to think about deviance, one that remains an important part of the functionalist paradigm. It opposes the common-sense bias that deviant behaviour is in every sense "wrong," "bad" or "evil." Instead, it directs our notice to the social processes that produce deviance. And unlike the social disorganization approach, it helps us understand why certain forms of behaviour continue *despite* being considered both immoral and illegal.

There are, however, a number of flaws in Durkheim's approach and the most glaring have to do with the issue of "benefits." Who exactly benefits from deviance? Compare the benefits with the harms and, often, it is not so certain that deviance and social control are "functional." How can we argue that society "benefits" from rape, child molesting or murder? Punishing the deviant may strengthen the moral boundaries of society, but is this benefit worth a human life?

FAR AND AWAY

Cleansing the Leftists: Crime Control or Repression?

In Canada, the military plays little part in law enforcement and little effort is made to prevent people from organizing to express disagreement with government policies. In many other countries, Indonesia among them, the military plays a major part in actively suppressing political dissent. An effort is made to depict the dissent as a form of, or prelude to, civil war, but most impartial observers would agree that the stated goal of "cleansing of Communists" is just an excuse to eliminate political opposition.

Thirty years after a purge left as many as 500,000 suspected Communists dead, Indonesia's powerful military renewed its vow yesterday to cleanse the nation of a new generation of Communists that it held responsible for last weekend's riots in Jakarta.

As authorities detained one of the country's leading labour activists yesterday, the military issued orders to its troops, who have been stationed in the capital, to shoot at sight anyone deemed to be a troublemaker.

"History can be repeated," armed forces spokesman Lieutenant-General Syarwan Hamid told foreign journalists. "If you know the story of communism (in Indonesia), it happened in 1926, it was repeated in 1948 and it also occurred in 1965. This is a very real experience for us." He said the shoot-at-sight order was removed during the weekend riots, in which at least four people died, but was needed to keep unruly demonstrators from returning to the streets.

Military officials blamed members of the radical leftist Democratic People's Party (PRD) for sparking the riots which erupted after a violent confrontation Saturday morning between security forces and members of the mainstream, opposition Indonesian Democratic Party. The officials said they considered the PRD to be "synonymous" with the Indonesian Communist Party, which was banned in 1966 for attempting a coup a year earlier.

PRD officials, who have gone into hiding this week but still communicate on the Internet, said they were not Communists, but warned that Indonesia's rulers had missed the point of the riots. "The riots must be seen as social-political restlessness in the Indonesian community, which is accumulative," a party statement issued electronically to journalists said.

Several political analysts also scoffed at the military's efforts to create a new Communist scare. "The riots were an expression of a socioeconomic problem," and represented "hatred of the richness of the Jakarta ruling class," said Arief Buriman, a leading political writer.

Apart from the growing labour movement, the military also faces unrest in the disputed territory of East Timor and the far-eastern province of Irian Jaya, bordering Papua New Guinea, where tribal minorities have launched protests against the influx of big foreign mining companies.

Source: Abridged from John Stackhouse, *The Globe and Mail*, Thurs., Aug. 1, 1996, p. A10

Durkheim's argument fails to deal effectively with these kinds of questions. It is too easy to say that "society" benefits from any deviant act. After all, in any social act, but certainly in deviance, it is always specific people who benefit while other specific people are harmed.

Equally, the enforcement of rules is not always "for the good of society," as the report in Far and Away on page 100 suggests. In many societies, political rule is dictatorial and brooks no opposing point of view. Is the "cleansing of Communists" in Indonesia likely to increase social solidarity or is it merely an exercise of power in the interest of the ruling class? In the Indonesian case, it would seem to be the latter.

Today, many still hold by the view that "good" and "bad" are objective judgments, especially where acts like homicide or suicide are concerned. But in public statements at least, very few bemoaned the prison murder of mass killer Jeffrey Dahmer. Very few publicly deplored the suicide of Reverend Jim Jones in Guyana. The moral reading of "negative" behaviour is thus a drama itself, dependent on the meaning of the act, the scene, the supporting cast, the light in which we see it.

Today, we are far more likely than in the past to view deviant behaviour as conscious behaviour based on a choice among available options. Thus we are likely to think of robbery or embezzlement as a "line of work" rather than a symptom of personal pathology or social disorder. Whether a person becomes a robber or embezzler, or leads a law-abiding life instead, reflects the different opportunities and influences that people face throughout their lives.

Merton's Anomie Theory

A prime example of this outlook is Robert K. Merton's functionalist theory of anomie. According to Merton (1957b), the cause of deviance does not lie in the individual but in society's unequal opportunity structure. In Merton's theory, like Durkheim's, deviance is normal (not pathological), societal (not individual) in origin and supports the survival of the existing order. But in Merton's theory, unlike Durkheim's, deviance is driven by a basic conflict or paradox: a gap between culturally defined *goals* and socially approved *means* for attaining those goals.

Merton uses American society as his example. He argues that one of the primary goals of American society is success, especially in obtaining money, material goods and "the good life." Most people have been taught to value success. Yet social inequality ensures that most people will not succeed because they will not have access to the socially approved (i.e., legal) means and resources that allow them to attain success. Therefore, if they are very serious about reaching their goal (i.e., good citizens), they may have to find other means.

Merton calls this gap between goals and means *anomie*. This state of anomie allows for a variety of solutions, which Merton calls *adaptations*. They include *ritualism*, *retreatism*, *rebellion* and *innovation*. People try one or more of these solutions to bridge the gap.

Most people are conformists, recognizing that they will probably never "strike it rich," and simply live out their lives as best they can. For these people, Merton's anomic gap is not an organizing principle. Others *seem* to conform, but they are just "going through the motions"; they have given up all hope of personal success. Merton calls this adaptation *ritualism*. Such people, Merton suggests, are too well trained to give up, but they no longer have any hopes for themselves.

Other people, realizing that they will never achieve their goals, just give up. They become *retreatists* — alcoholics, drug addicts or suicides, among other things. Still others *rebel* against inequality and reject the norms and values upon which it is based. They may try to change the political order. Youths in India have, largely, taken this approach to anomie. There, crowding, poverty, hunger and noise all induce cynicism and nihilism. For young people from poor homes, education is alienating because it reveals the extent of social unfairness. Community youth organizers, often from middle-class homes, are pledged to wipe out poverty. But they are suspicious of politicians and big business; they realize they will have to bring about changes on their own.

A final adaptation to anomie is *innovation*. As Merton describes it, innovation occurs when a person has internalized the cultural goals but has not internalized a duty to the institutional norms — the legitimate "ways and means" of attaining these goals. In its simplest form, innovation is crime; the use of dishonest means to attain wealth and success. In American society, the many pressures on people to gain success often make other norms seem trivial. The "Robber Barons" who grabbed corporate power and wealth in the United States towards the end of the 19th century believed that they had to lie, cheat and steal in order to succeed. And indeed, their success bred esteem. It not only confirmed people's beliefs, it inspired others to follow the robber's road.

Merton claims that innovation — crime — is the form of adaptation most likely to be found among the lower class. While all classes share the same goals, Merton sees the lower class as most lacking in access to the approved means necessary for achieving these goals. That's why, according to Daniel Bell (1960), crime is as American as apple pie. (Now, with the breakdown of its economy, crime is also as Russian as beet *borscht*.) It is a tried-and-true method of social ascent in a society where people's hopes are high but opportunities are scant.

The Making of a Juvenile Delinquent

Since you're a college or university student reading this book, you probably are not (and never have been) a repeat-offender juvenile delinquent. However, by this point in the book, you know that, but for a different roll of the dice, you could have been. It would have taken a slightly different set of life chances from the ones you've had so far. Here are the factors that made a difference: the reasons you didn't become a repeat delinquent and someone else did.

Where did it all start? Probably in a family characterized by little affection and cohesiveness, poor parenting — for example, little supervision or discipline — and often physical abuse. In many cases, the delinquent's parents and siblings also abused alcohol or drugs and committed crimes. There is some disagreement about whether social class played a part: the evidence indicates that low income, especially long-term welfare reliance, is a modest contributing factor.

Given the family problems described above, it is no wonder the delinquent had school problems. With a low level of achievement and interest, and no concern for the job future, the delinquent racked up a below-average performance in school, complete with conduct problems.

The typical "repeat delinquent" started committing crimes of various types at a very young age. This delinquency was part of a lifestyle that included alcohol and drug abuse and an aimless use of leisure time. Rejected by non-delinquent peers and, in the end, indifferent to their opinions, the delinquent surrounded himself with antisocial, drug-using peers.

What is most characteristic of the repeat delinquent is his values. They include a rejection of the validity of law, a tendency to rationalize law-breaking, antisocial thinking and a quick temper. But these ideas and attitudes are the end product of a long development and many experiences. The problem began much earlier, in what the baby saw and heard.

Source: Adapted from *Review of the Profile, Classification and Treatment Literature with Young Offenders: A Social-Psychological Approach*, Don Andrews, Robert Hoge and Alan Leschied. *The Globe and Mail*, Sat., Apr. 1, 1995, p. A6

EVERYDAY LIFE

And far from being strange, deviant behaviour is a perfectly logical response to a striking lack of means coupled with a passionate commitment to social goals.

Merton insists that a combination of cultural and structural factors produces deviance. By itself, a rigid social structure that limits access to opportunities does *not* beget deviance. Only when such a structure is combined with cultural goals that urge people to strive for success do we get an increase in deviance.

Since his argument is functionalist, Merton does not see innovation as posing a threat to social order. Criminals may threaten other people, but they neither challenge the goals of society nor try to change them. Instead, their adaptation supports cultural goals. The criminal embodies success and proves that anyone can "make it" in American society. By their flashy display of wealth and power, criminals advertise the pleasures of success among the lower class and keep the American dream alive.

Like Durkheim, Merton fails to specify who benefits from any given adaptation to anomie. Crime supports the existing social order by supporting cultural goals, but it does so at a heavy cost. Equally serious, Merton's theory promotes the myth that crime is just a lower-class activity — a cliché that the mass media and the powerful seem content to uphold. As we shall see later, there is more to crime than lower-class "innovation." Like the other theories we have discussed so far, Merton's anomie theory has little ability to predict which individuals will select which "adaptations" — whether deviant or law-abiding.

All the theories of deviance discussed so far have obvious connections to the structural-functional paradigm. The connection is evident in their emphasis on society's need for order, balance and harmony; on the role of deviance in fulfilling a social need; and on the value of certain "puzzling activities" — even seemingly irrational acts of crime or deviance — within a given social context. And, because in structural functionalism all the structures are interrelated and integrated, changes in one will provoke changes in others. Deviance is often viewed as a step towards reaching a new equilibrium. Finally, the theories we have examined so far have been macrosociological, just as functionalism tends to be macrosociological.

Labelling Theory

Unlike the functionalist approach, the interactionist approach to deviance is microsociological. It examines the ordinary social processes that generate deviance. More important, it examines the impact social control has on the experience and self-identity of people who are considered deviant.

Recall that, in symbolic interactionism people are viewed as acting towards things on the basis of shared meanings which arise out of social interaction. Social interaction, in turn, means fitting together individual lines of action by means of communication and negotiation. Through symbolic interaction, people make sense of reality together and solve problems of a "bad fit" between the ways that individuals see themselves, others, situations or relationships. Appropriately, then, the symbolic interactionist approach to deviance focuses on the process by which labels such as "deviant" get attached to people and activities.

Not surprisingly, the most significant attempt to understand deviance which emerged out of this interactionist approach is called **labelling theory**. This approach to deviant behaviour matured in the 1950s and 1960s and embodies a major break with the older theories. Unlike the earlier theories, it assumes that "good" and "bad" are subjective, relative judgments. Everyone deviates sometimes, and for labelling theorists the question of interest is "Why are some people who break rules caught and labelled 'deviant' while others are not?" From a labelling position, further, the real problem to be solved is not what researchers call "primary deviation," of which everyone is guilty at some time or another; the problem is "secondary deviation" — repeated deviance and, even, a deviant career.

In this regard, labelling theorists are likely to look for causes of deviant behaviour in labelling practices which make some acts particularly shameful in some societies and not in others. Some sociologists, like Edwin Lemert, ask how deviance becomes a "Master Status" which comes to define, more than any other personal feature, the way a person is viewed in the community. Others, like Howard Becker, ask how labelling results in the exclusion of "outsiders." Others still, like Erving Goffman, ask how stigmatization damages an individual's identity and increases the chance a person will continue to deviate.

Labelling theorists stress the relativity of deviance. They believe that no behaviour is innately deviant; deviance is always socially defined and created. So, for example, many people in our society consider having tattoos to be deviant. Some people even believe that tattoos are a sign of a pathological need to deface or deform one's body. Typically, we find tattoos in *macho* subcultures, such as prison, the armed services or delinquent gangs. Historically they have indicated male bonding, a denial of mainstream culture and a tolerance for pain, since the process of tattooing is painful. Yet these negative views of tattoo-wearers are not produced by tattoo-wearers themselves but by outsiders who point, using what Becker calls "conventional sentimentality." To use "unconventional sentimentality" — to assume tattoo-wearers have perfectly sensible rationales for what they do — is to do sociology. As Earl Rubington and Martin Weinberg (1968: v) tell us, ". . . deviance is in the eyes of the beholder . . . [it] is defined by what people say and do about persons, situations, acts, or events." This process of defining and treating others as deviant is what sociologists refer to as "labelling."

As we have noted, one effect of applying a deviant label is stigmatization. A *stigma* is a social trait that acts as a mark of shame or social disgrace, and dis-

Graffiti has shed its deviant image; some even consider it an art form.

credits an individual or group. The stigma of being labelled a deviant reminds others of what happens to people who violate social norms.

Often, newspapers create a stigma by the ways they report on race in crime stories. Just by reporting on the race of an arrested person, the newspaper is implying that race is an important part of explaining why the person committed the criminal act. So, for example, reporting that a criminal is black is likely to strengthen stereotypes of black people as tending towards crime. Reporting that a criminal is white (a fact which is rarely reported) is unlikely to have the opposite, positive effect on perceptions of blacks. Therefore, disclosing the race of a criminal does not break down stereotypes and even bolsters them by labelling certain groups as more likely to commit crimes.

A person labelled as deviant by others may come to see themself as the labeller does. Unexpectedly, the person is then more likely to engage in deviant behaviour, because that fits in with his or her new self-image. Sociologists would say a deviant identity is being developed.

Of course, there is nothing destined about this. For example, a study of alcoholics indicates that the number of times a person had been labelled "alcoholic" by family and friends had little bearing on that individual's subsequent drinking behaviour. Frequently, alcoholism is related to other problems, of which labelling is one of the least important. That's why we are not able to cure an alcoholic by simply saying, "Now you are no longer an alcoholic!" nor turn an abstainer into an alcoholic by saying, "You have a serious drinking problem." There must be a compounding of (1) the possibility of a problem (for example, excessive drinking); (2) the person's own perception or fear that there *may* be a problem; and (3) other people's confirmation, through labelling, that there really *is* a problem.

Labelling theory has been criticized from a number of angles. As noted above, there are many instances in which labelling is *not* an important influence on people's behaviour. Some continue their deviant acts even though they have never been labelled. Others give up their deviant acts even though they *have* been labelled. As well, labelling theory can be censured generally for promoting an image of the deviant as a victim of society, or of society as uniformly brutal in its labelling. Sometimes this is a correct view, but often it is not. Most important, labelling theory doesn't work well in explaining "major" crimes like rape, homicide or armed robbery — crimes which most people agree are serious and deserve harsh penalties.

Nonetheless, labelling theory points researchers in some useful directions. It leads them to ask, "Are some people more likely to be singled out and accused of deviance than others? And if so, why?" Why, commonly, do the law, the press and public opinion tend to stigmatize and punish powerless people? That question engages sociologists who use the conflict paradigm and researchers who take the "social constructionist" approach to deviant behaviour.

Social Constructionism

Like the labelling theorists, social constructionists believe that "good" and "bad" are *not* objective judgments of human behaviour. Rather, these judgments are created by some people and imposed on others. The question is, who is making these rules and judgments, and why? This kind of question is more suited to sociologists who work in the conflict paradigm.

Recall that conflict theory emphasizes conflict and change as basic features of social life. Conflict theorists believe that conflict and change are inevitable because social groups which differ in power, status and influence are always trying to maintain or improve their respective positions. Conflict is inevitable because the goods that people value highly and desire — wealth, prestige and power — are scarce. What is of interest to the conflict theorist, then, is the strategy or mechanism by which one group comes to prevail over another. Viewed this way, the creation of "deviance" or "crime" is a way of imposing and justifying control exercised in the interest of the powerful.

Thus, the focus of this (macrosociological) approach is not on deviance so much as it is on social control and lawmaking. It seeks to explain how laws get made and enforced — why certain social groups or subcultures dislike certain acts and how they gain and wield control over other people's behaviour. Like labelling theory, social constructionism works best to explain control where people disagree about the "seriousness" of a deviant act. Typically, social constructionists study the making of social problems. This includes studying how the mass media mould public feelings, how laws are made and carried out and how people Howard Becker calls "moral entrepreneurs" promote moral causes to the point where they can change the labelling habit of society. Everyday Life, below, reviews some of these influences.

A good example of the social construction of deviant behaviour is provided in sociologist Joseph Gusfield's (1963) study of the symbolic crusade that led to Prohibition in the United States. Prohibition consisted of a ban, from 1920 to 1933, on the sale and public consumption of alcohol in the United States. Gusfield (1963) argues that the successful lobbying effort organized by the American Temperance Movement which led to Prohibition was an example of what he calls "status politics."

Status politics reveal "a struggle between groups for prestige and social position." Defending their position in the status order is as important to people as protecting or expanding their economic power; indeed, the two are often related.

The clash between drinkers and abstainers dramatized a deep conflict in American society. Between 1880 and 1920 the United States changed from a rural, small-town society to an urban, industrial power. During that time, huge numbers of immigrants poured into American cities. They shifted economic and political control of American society away from the native-born, white Protestant, small-town middle class, which had run the United States up through the 19th century. The new immigrants were foreign-born, mostly Catholic, city dwellers who, because of their numbers and differentness, many native-born Americans found menacing.

American Protestants had made a virtue of "temperance," but the new immigrants saw nothing immoral in the use of alcohol. For this reason, small-town, middle-class Americans came to identify immigrants with the drinking, making and shipping of alcohol. Symbolically, the attempt to impose temperance through Prohibition was a bid to turn the clock back to a time when the United States was a uniform society dominated by middle-class Protestants. Its goal, however unconscious, was to show the immigrants who ran the country. But Prohibition proved unenforceable and was generally unpopular. Rural small-towners had lost the battle and, in doing so, they lost their symbolic status.

This analysis fits well with the conflict approach to sociology. From the conflict point of view, both deviance and social control are the result of conflicting interests among competing groups. The conflict paradigm takes as its starting point the idea that creating and enforcing rules leads to people being defined as deviant. And since deviance only comes into being when we apply rules to behaviour, understanding how, why and by whom rules are created is the key to understanding deviance.

The Sky Is Falling (Again)

How serious is the crime problem? According to the following excerpt, it's very serious; but that isn't the main purpose of the article (or the reason we selected it). Rather, it demonstrates "moral entrepreneurship" — in this case, an attempt by Canada's most influential, establishment-oriented newspaper to raise public fears about crime. Its target is not the criminals themselves, but "criminologists, sociologists and pundits." See if you can figure out the writer's motivation.

Every year at about this time, Canada's statistical authorities announce that the probability of becoming a victim of crime — especially violent crime — has decreased. Since 1992, the national crime rate has gone down every year.

Then why are we all so worried about crime? A number of surveys show that most Canadians believe they are at greater risk from crime, especially violent crime. As the rate falls, our anxiety rises. Why?

Every summer a parade of criminologists, sociologists and pundits are rolled out to blame ordinary Canadians for their myopia, gullibility, paranoia and cantankerousness. Take your pick: either we're all dopes, or we're all duped. Several theories prevail:

- *The media.* Much attention has been given to a chart produced this week by the National Media Archive, a wing of the Vancouver-based Fraser Institute, which shows an extreme increase in the proportion of murder stories on national television networks in 1993, 1994, and 1995. But closer analysis will likely show that this was the result of one particular murder story, the Paul Bernardo case, which was of great interest to Canadians, and that crime coverage is otherwise stable. Murder will always receive greater attention than other crimes because of its grave and tragic nature, but there is no evidence that the media have misled Canadians.

- *Politicians.* Populist political leaders of a certain ilk will always try to inflame our passions with tales of terrible crimes, only to blame the reigning authorities for the "crisis" and to promise tougher-than-thou remedies. Such strategies rarely get much response in Canada, though. Federal parties with tough-on-crime platforms have never fared well, and provincial leaders, whatever their views, are almost always elected on economic or fiscal grounds.

- *Old people.* When people get older they commit considerably fewer crimes, and that's a major cause of the falling rates. But University of Toronto sociologist Rosemary Gartner went a step further, telling *The Globe and Mail* that people "start to see the world as a more threatening place" when they get older.

Perhaps the world *is* a more threatening place. [E]ven though crime rates have fallen since 1992, they had risen dramatically between 1962 and 1982. Your chance of becoming a crime victim has increased almost fourfold in that time. If you were alive during this interval, you watched crime change from a minor to a significant factor in Canadian life.

It remains significant. Non-violent crimes are a distressingly familiar part of life, and violent crimes, while rare, are more prevalent than in many Western nations.

Source: Abridged from *The Globe and Mail*, Thurs., Aug. 1, 1996, p. A14

This view has several interesting implications. The first is that societies seemingly plagued by deviance actually suffer from too many rules. Often, an outbreak of rule-making begins with what sociologists call a "moral panic." But if we lived with fewer rules and less rule enforcement — if we adopted a live-and-let-live attitude — we would have less deviance to worry about. By trying to enforce too many laws, the law-makers and police create more problems than they can solve. The argument to legalize marijuana makes this important point clearly. The so-called war on drugs cannot be won so long as poverty, inequality and racism plague millions of North Americans. And keeping marijuana illegal profits an enormous criminal drug industry which does more harm than the drug itself.

A second point conflict theorists often make is that social control extends social inequality into the realm of law. In all societies, some people have more power than others. They work to ensure that the government makes, and the police enforce, laws that guard their own interests. The powerful also make sure that crimes *they* commit are treated as less serious than crimes that the powerless commit.

As a result, we have little in the way of law enforcement against large environmental polluters. A corporation dumping toxic waste into a river that serves as the water supply for millions of people will be treated less harshly than a disturbed person who poisons a product on a grocery shelf. In the last decade especially, governments supposedly cracking down on crime have been lenient with corporate crime. Indeed, to the extent that crime is "advertised" through mass-media fictions, it tends to be associated with particularly noticeable individual characters — criminals — and corporate crime becomes relatively unthinkable because corporations are diffuse, bureaucratic and amorphous. Leniency with corporate crime reflects the pro-business attitude of North American governments throughout the 1980s, despite a "get tough" policy in relation to the sentencing and jailing of lower-class street criminals. If we included white-collar and corporate crimes (which, dollar for dollar, are far more costly to society than lower-class street crimes) in the "Official Statistics," then the popular image of the typical criminal would become older, whiter, more middle- and upper-class than it is today.

From the conflict standpoint, the study of deviance and control is the study of law-making: why governments make certain laws at certain times, and whom these laws favour. By this reasoning, social control serves one group in society — the powerful — at the expense of everyone else. Deviants are the main victims of this inequality.

Like the functionalist and interactionist approaches, the conflict approach helps us to understand a lot about deviance. However, when we look at the conflicts over deviance, it is hard to interpret many of them as involving the "powerful." Some are conflicts based on religious beliefs, as is the conflict over abortion or marijuana. Others mirror concerns about personal security, such as the demand by police that the death penalty be re-introduced for the killing of police officers.

As for criminals being victimized by the law, most people feel that the real victims are poor, young and powerless people. They are the most likely to be robbed, murdered or raped, usually by other poor, young and powerless people. In an abstract sense, crimes may be revolts against the social order and, as even the functionalists would agree, a useful byproduct of social inequality. Yet this is no proof that all laws repress the poor in order to protect the rich.

The Feminist Approach

Recall that all feminist research is guided by the notion that all personal life has a political dimension — very much like sociology's central idea of the connection between private troubles and public issues. It sees an inevitable connection between the public and private spheres of life, which are both gendered, and notes that in both spheres women's experience routinely differs from men's. Because of different experiences and differences in power, women's and men's perceptions of reality differ. Most important, for feminists, patriarchy — or male control — structures the way most societies work.

Given these starting points, we are not surprised to find that feminists emphasize the gendered nature of both deviance and control: for example, the relationship between events in the private sphere (e.g., domestic violence) and events in the public sphere (e.g., the cultural and legal tolerance of domestic violence); the gendering of law-enforcement practices (e.g., how the police treat prostitutes compared with how they treat prostitutes' customers); and the evidence of patriarchal values in the legal system (e.g., the centuries of failure to concede that husbands might be guilty of raping their wives). Here, as in other areas of sociology, the feminist approach combines macrosociological and microsociological perspectives — fitting for an approach which emphasizes that personal lives and political issues are intertwined.

Feminists have made important contributions to the study of deviance by deromanticizing the image of the criminal that distinguishes the work of both labelling theorists and social constructionists. They have done this by turning their attention to the study of victims: who gets hurt, why are some kinds of people more likely to get hurt than others and what can be done about it?

Gartner (1992), for one, looks at violence against women and children — criminal acts which are usually committed within the home or between intimates. Unlike other types of crime and deviance, here we find little doubt about the victims, the crimes or the wrongdoers: the key question is "Why did they do it?" Or asked in a sociological way, "What are the social conditions under which people are more likely to do that kind of thing?"

Gartner finds, across a wide range of societies, social patterns that predict higher and lower risks of violence. Among other things, these "risk factors" include women's education and participation in the paid work force — in short, women's freedom from and equality with men. Violence against women is likeliest in those societies in which women are in the midst of becoming legally,

SOCIAL PROFILE 4.2

The Child Killers

The killers of children up to the age of 18 (Jan. 1, 1991 to Dec. 31, 1995):

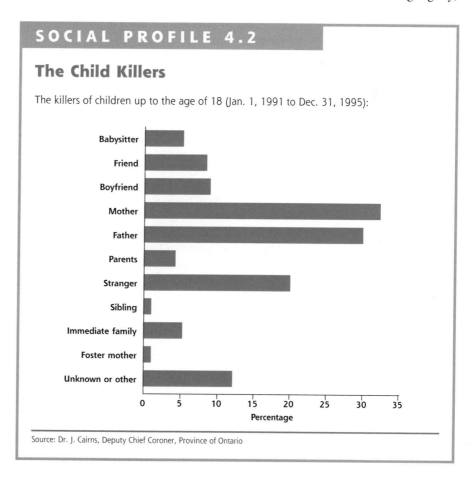

Source: Dr. J. Cairns, Deputy Chief Coroner, Province of Ontario

economically and socially free. In societies where women have achieved equality and freedom, the rate of violence is lower.

Feminists are also at the forefront of attempts to change the laws that cover crimes against women. One area in which there has been much publicized progress is in reforming the law against sexual assault. Canada now has one of the strongest laws against rape and other forms of sexual assault. Yet many questions remain about how well the new laws really work and whether they meet the needs of Canadian women.

Feminists have focused on rape and other forms of sexual assault for a number of reasons. First and foremost, rape is a terrifying, violent and embarrassing experience which many women undergo and almost all women fear. Changing the laws related to rape, providing help and other services to women who have been raped and finding ways to prevent rape are therefore important tasks facing society. Some feminists assert that rape is disturbingly typical of our society, in the sense that it symbolizes and reflects the pattern of our gender relations. While few men are rapists, most men benefit from the power over women our society permits them. The rapist's power is analogous to that power. Feminists argue that fear and dependence mark women's social relations with men at work, on dates and in the home, and that women can never be equal to men as long as fear and dependence continue.

Rape, a crime which most women would agree is of urgent and personal concern, has been a rallying issue for feminists. It has served to sensitize both women and men to the goals of the feminist movement. The media have helped by raising people's awareness of violent crimes against women. People are more aware of victimization and victims today than they were a generation ago, thanks largely to the media and to feminist researchers.

KINDS OF DEVIANT BEHAVIOUR

Deviance, as we have seen, includes a variety of behaviours that range in frequency and gravity from crimes down through what sociologists call norm violations and social diversions. We shall now look briefly at each of these categories of deviance.

Crime

Along with the state of the economy, crime has been among Canadians' top five concerns for most of the last twenty years (Bibby, 1995: 95). Usually considered the most serious form of deviance, a *crime* is any act formally prohibited by law, specifically by the Criminal Code of Canada. Defining certain acts as crimes gives the state the authority to seek, apprehend, try, convict and punish offenders, and the Criminal Code specifies a suitable range of punishments for each crime.

Within the bounds of the Criminal Code, we find many different kinds of crime. Some are crimes considered extremely harmful by most people, such as murder, armed robbery, extortion, arson, sexual assault and kidnapping. In general, there is widespread consensus in Canadian society, and in most other societies, that these forms of behaviour are improper and should be severely punished. (This has not always been the case, however; for example, forced sex within marriage has only recently been recognized as a form of sexual assault and, thus, a crime.)

In contrast, there are crimes such as the possession of marijuana over which people disagree so much that the law has, in effect, lost control. Then there are the more standard crimes. Most people consider them wrong but do not wish to debate or increase the severity of punishment. These include offences against property like breaking and entering, automobile theft and shoplifting; minor assaults and drunken driving; and "white-collar" offences like embezzlement and

Keeping Count of Drug Users

There can be no effective social policy without good social research, and no good social research without a careful assessment of the problem to be solved. Often this means a very costly and laborious head count, as in the excerpt that follows. For decades, sociologists, psychologists and epidemiologists at the Addiction Research Foundation of Ontario have tracked trends in drug use among the young. If they say drug use is up, it's up!

Drug use has increased dramatically among Canadian high-school students, with fewer teen-agers seeing any harm in trying such drugs as marijuana, the Addiction Research Foundation says.

[A] survey conducted the past spring found that 22.7 per cent of students had tried marijuana at least once in the previous 12 months, compared with 12.7 per cent in 1993. Use of other illegal drugs is up as well, in what Dr. Kendall describes as a "very disturbing" situation that is not limited to Ontario.

"A nation-wide Health Canada survey is expected to find similar results. The same trends have also been reported in some European nations as well as the United States, where student drug use peaked in the 1970s followed by a steady decline that lasted until the 1990s, when a resurgence began," Dr. Kendall said in a news release accompanying the report.

ARF researchers report a marked change in attitudes from even two years ago. "More students now entertain a more liberal view of drug use, es-

pecially for cannabis, than did their predecessors, and more believe that drugs such as cannabis are readily available," the report said.

Stephen Melemis, a Toronto doctor who specializes in addiction medicine, said in an interview that "marijuana use is fairly closely connected with smoking. There certainly has been an increase in smoking. And it's going to get even worse when the restrictions on cigarette advertising are lifted," Dr. Melemis said. "Teen-agers, of course, are the most impressionable."

In addition to the dramatic increase in marijuana use, researchers found that the use of methamphetamine (speed) has increased to 4.6 per cent of the surveyed students from 2 per cent two years earlier. Cocaine use has climbed to 2.4 per cent from 1.5 per cent; glue sniffing has risen to 2.4 per cent from 1.6 per cent.

"Alcohol remains the drug of choice for students, with 58.8 per cent reporting use, although there was no significant increase in use since 1993," the [Addiction Research] [F]oundation reports. One-third of the surveyed students had consumed beer with high alcohol content during the 12 months before the survey, and 10.4 per cent typically consumed six or more bottles on those occasions. About 38 per cent had attended a "bush" or "field" party. On average, those attending "bush" parties at remote locations away from parental scrutiny consumed 4.2 drinks per occasion.

"Overall, these findings are very disturbing, and it's clear that there must be more effective efforts put into discouraging all forms of drug use," Dr. Kendall said.

Source: Abridged from Virginia Galt, *The Globe and Mail*, Nov. 3, 1995, p. A10

Social Diversions

There is the most uncertainty surrounding a third class of deviant acts we call social diversions. A *social diversion* is a type of behaviour that few people would regard as violating norms and fewer still would consider a serious violation. The Criminal Code does not forbid these social diversions, nor do formal institutions — the courts, hospitals or health professionals — try to control them. Social diversions are mainly acts whose main purpose is recreation, stimulation and subcultural integration (Hagan, 1989).

A diversion among North American children is painting fake labial hair on their faces with milk. Lacking cows, Eskimo children don't do this, but they do play with frozen water. Rural housewives in the Midwest compete to see who can most efficiently roast a pig at a fair or bake a pie. And millions of Canadian adolescents and young adults spend hours each week staring at pictures of adolescents

Members of the Hell's Angels share a highly developed subculture, which includes group rituals and special ways of dressing.

and young adults on a screen in a dark room. All of these diversions would be thought odd, at least, in Siberia or in Zimbabwe.

There are many sexual behaviours which one would list as deviant social diversions. Some people would consider them "odd," "weird" or "sick" but a large number of people enjoy them anyway. Homosexuality is an obvious example: today it is the most visible and accepted form of alternative sexuality. Other examples would include sadomasochism, fetishism and cross-dressing. Similarly, oral and anal sex are more commonly accepted now than they were a generation ago.

When Prime Minister Pierre Elliott Trudeau came to office in the late 1960s, he declared that the Canadian government had "no business in the bedrooms of the nation." He meant that official efforts to control homosexuality, non-marital and marital sex were going to end; and they have. Today, condom use is publicly promoted to combat AIDS, birth control is open to everyone and gay rights are protected in the Human Rights Code of Ontario and, possibly, by the Canadian Charter of Rights and Freedoms. Sexual variations remain exceptions and the less common forms still raise eyebrows among many Canadians. But in some groups, even eyebrow raising is a kinky activity. Informal controls on such "odd" behaviours have also waned since the 1960s. Again, the "oddity" is all in the perspective. Homosexuals do not find homosexuality odd; wearers of nose studs are not among those who wince to see them.

Other social diversions include styles of dress, speech and behaviour that are uncommon among middle-aged, middle-class people. Take, as an example, multiple earrings and those nose studs we just mentioned. Such fashions are more common among the young than among the old. "Odd" clothes and speech often denote membership in a group holding values and norms that are uncommon and offend other people.

Deviant behaviour, as we see, takes many forms, and all of us at one time or another engage in behaviour that some people would consider deviant. Still, most of us neither commit crimes nor engage in other forms of serious deviance on a regular basis.

PARTICIPATION IN DEVIANT ACTIVITIES

Young Single Men   In the case of serious crimes, the most common offenders by far are young, single men. By a wide margin, men continue to outnumber women in crimes against the person (Hagan, 1994: 28, 29). Similarly, boys are far more likely than girls to appear in youth courts.

Why are criminals so often young, unmarried men? Many believe the reason is that young men lead less structured lives and are more used to acting aggressively than are young women. Additionally, in poor communities, a high proportion of young men are frustrated by unemployment. This combination of frustration and a macho masculine role makes them more likely to "act out" physically. It also makes them more willing to take risks with their own, and other people's, lives. And because a lack of opportunity frustrates young men who are eager to prove themselves, social inequality is among the best predictors of a country's homicide rate across nations.

Research in Britain shows a correlation between rates of violent crime, illegitimacy and dropping out of the work force by young, healthy men. All three indicators are on the rise and serve as warning signs of the growth of a chronically unemployed and (possibly) unemployable class of people. Once an underclass exists, it is hard to solve the problem with social reforms.

In addition, ethnic and racial inequality are important predictors of homicide rates in a community, even after taking poverty, general economic inequality and other factors into account. Inequality and subordination, whether economic or racial, especially increase the frequency of violence. Not only are the perpetrators of violence typically poor, young single men, so are the victims — usually students and the unemployed. These young men are most likely to be out in public places and engaged in evening activities outside the home, the conditions often connected with assault and robbery.

Delinquent Boys   Research suggests that despair, born of social and economic inequality, are at the root of much crime. To a degree this is true of juvenile delinquents too; but often delinquency reflects no more than a desire for adventure, thrills and the respect of peers. Many delinquents also use drugs and alcohol, which loosen their inhibitions against socially disapproved activities.

Delinquent activities by teenage boys and young men often display a tough, active, unemotional masculine image. They also display traits associated with the culture of poverty discussed in the next chapter: a belief in fate, danger, luck and taking risks. Generally, delinquent activities range in seriousness from vandalism, petty theft (such as shoplifting), breaking and entering, illegal alcohol and drug use, auto theft and dangerous driving, up through drug dealing, robbery and gang fighting. Some of these acts are aimed at making money but most are intended to gain or defend status, protect gang turf or prove manliness. Their symbolic value lies precisely in their danger to life and liberty and lack of practical payoff.

Research in juvenile delinquency was hampered for a long time by the belief that delinquency is only a lower-class problem. So, much of the effort given to policing and preventing delinquency has focused on lower-class youth. A prime example was the costly program the United States government mounted in the 1960s to prevent delinquency, by offering delinquents opportunities to get ahead by legitimate means: in a phrase, a job-creation program.

The program did not work. Perhaps the lower-class youths did not really want to obey socially accepted norms, even if doing so brought them a weekly paycheque. Perhaps the bait offered them — a dead-end job at low pay — was too small to lure young people into a law-abiding life. Perhaps they had learned delinquent skills and values which they were unable to give up. Or perhaps the program ended too soon for us to know whether it might have worked.

Whatever the reason, juvenile delinquency remains a problem in large cities throughout the world. An Israeli study concludes that a certain minimum number of juveniles must be in an area to provide the necessary group dynamic.

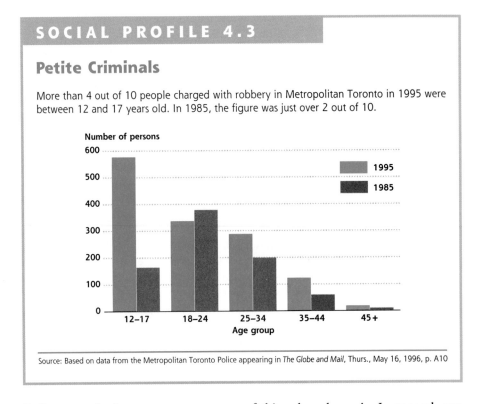

Source: Based on data from the Metropolitan Toronto Police appearing in *The Globe and Mail*, Thurs., May 16, 1996, p. A10

Delinquency is, in part, a consequence of this urban dynamic. In general, our understanding of delinquency is greater than it once was. We now have better measures of how much unreported delinquency occurs. We also have theories that help us see how similar delinquent culture is to the dominant culture.

More and more criminologists have been using self-report surveys to measure delinquent behaviour among young people of different social classes. Clearly, some respondents misreport their behaviour in this kind of survey, as in any other; some under-report their past misdeeds, to appear more virtuous than they really are; others overstate them to appear more rebellious.

Like most studies of deviance using non-official statistics, the self-report studies show a weaker relationship between social class and delinquency than studies based on official records. In that sense, official records overstate the connection between social class and rates of deviant behaviour, yet:

Evidence reviewed indicates that forms of deviance considered serious and treated as such are unequally distributed through the class structure, with the lower class experiencing more than its fair share of serious crime and delinquency, hard drug use, problems of alcohol abuse, and mental illness (Hagan, 1984: 79).

Middle- and Upper-Class Men

There are many other kinds of criminals whose actions are at least as harmful to the public good. These people commit the domestic crimes and white-collar crimes (or *suite* crimes). Compared to its way of handling street crimes, the legal system is less vigorous in dealing with domestic crimes and white-collar crimes.

White-collar crimes are committed by high-status members of the community, often in the course of their work. This category includes fraud, forgery, tax evasion, price-fixing, work-safety violations and embezzlement. Generally, the difference in types of crimes people commit is related to a difference in their opportunity to commit them. It is easier for an accountant or auditor to embezzle money than it is for a sociologist, clerk-typist or bartender. Lawyers are in a particularly good position to swindle people, and the law societies of Canadian provinces often have to decide whether to disbar lawyers who have used clients' funds for personal gain.

Such white-collar crimes, like domestic crimes, are hard to detect and almost impossible to prevent. They are also hard to punish. For one thing, the business and legal communities close ranks to prevent the criminalization of acts that should be considered serious crimes. Yet acts of corporate deviance, such as dumping toxic waste, bribery of officials and violating work-safety rules, have many victims. They deserve prosecution and punishment more than many acts we routinely consider crimes worth punishing.

In many countries the law has simply never treated corporate crime as a real problem. This can have serious results: tax evasion by corporations, for example, is a form of theft and can lead to a loss of tax revenues and uneven economic development. Yet, for a long time, tax evasion was more or less universally accepted in Italy. It is only in the last few years that progress has been made towards stopping political corruption and organized crime (the two are closely related in Italy) in that country.

Like most forms of deviance, white-collar or business-oriented crime varies along sociocultural lines. In Japan, corporations have a group mentality that discourages corporate crime for personal gain (a common practice in the United States.) But when a white-collar crime benefits the group, the Japanese are more willing to commit it, and the act is deemed more acceptable by peers. Since in Japan a white-collar crime is often considered acceptable because it is "socially responsible" to the group, it is easier to hide.

Women

As we noted earlier, women are less likely than men to commit crimes. Evidence shows some increase in female criminality and this reflects more social and economic activity outside the home than in past generations. But in general, female crime has *not* increased relative to male crime except for (1) teens and young women, where the gender gap has closed somewhat in many crime categories; (2) minor forms of property crime, such as property theft, shoplifting and welfare fraud; and (3) some forms of white-collar crime, like embezzlement. For the most part, women continue to stay away from crimes of violence and major property crimes.

The most accepted interpretation is that, with the feminization of poverty (which we will discuss in later chapters), women have turned to minor forms of property crime. This is particularly true in cities, where property crime is relatively easy to commit. Even in developing countries, as women gain opportunities to commit property crimes, their rate of criminal activity goes up. With economic modernization, there are simply more consumer items for women (and men) to steal.

The rise in women's crime also reflects a greater willingness among police to arrest and lay criminal charges against female offenders, especially teenage girls. In the past, these women would have benefitted from a popular belief that they were "the gentler sex," and therefore unlikely to commit crimes. Earlier in the 20th century, female offenders were also more likely to be thought mentally ill — hence, blameless — than criminal. Boys were defined and treated as delinquent whereas girls were, at worst, considered "wayward." The delinquency of boys was, of course, a form of virile *action*.

BIASES IN THE SELECTION PROCESS

Changes in policing have played a part in the way society deals with female law-breakers. Where there may have once been a bias against arresting and prosecuting women accused of minor property offences, for example, women are now treated more like men, with a consequent rise in arrests and convictions.

Other biases may be more persistent: for example, the alleged bias against lower-class lawbreakers. Some believe this is the reason for the often noted relationship between crime and social class. But are law enforcement officials biased when they select out some rule-breakers and not others, for systematic treatment? Or is crime primarily a lower-class adaptation to inequality, as Merton thought? And are lower-class youths the most likely to be socialized into criminal subcultures?

The perceived seriousness of a deviant act and the number of prior convictions in an offender's past record often influence the type and severity of societal response. So does the offender's social class. An important part is played by what we call *social resources*.

Middle- and upper-class people have more of these social resources — more knowledge of the law, self-confidence, money for lawyers, social connections, the capacity to produce a more respectable appearance and successful demeanour. In short, social resources are cultural capital that can be used in a legal setting. As we know from Chapter 2, our society distributes social resources (including cultural capital) unequally among the members of different social classes.

Because they are of a higher class, perpetrators of corporate crime are treated leniently by employers. In fact, people from higher classes are less likely even to lose their job over such infractions. This reveals the inequable attitude many employers show towards white-collar crime. What's more, people who commit large-scale offences are even less likely to suffer the loss of their job than those who commit small-scale crimes.

Social resources help people avoid labelling and punishment by the police and courts. For example, in assault or property-damage cases, the police and courts try to interpret behaviour and assess blame before taking any action. They are less likely to label people with more resources as "criminal" or "delinquent" and more likely to label them "alcoholic" or "mentally ill" for having committed a criminal act. For middle- and upper-class people, being labelled "sick" may be embarrassing, but it is far less harmful than being labelled "criminal."

This is one particular example of a much broader phenomenon Erving Goffman (1964) calls **impression management** — the use of such social resources to avoid stigmatization. Impression management can be defined as the control of personal information flow to manipulate how other people see and treat you. Everyone practises impression management, and people with more social resources and cultural capital are better at it.

In giving preferential treatment to people who are better impression managers, police and judges are simply inferring moral worth from visible class position. As members of our culture, police and judges are no more or less likely to do this than anyone else. Even primary-school children do it (Baldus and Tribe, 1978). There is no hard evidence that officials prefer people with more social resources because of bribery, threats or conscious discrimination.

The process we are describing is a circular one: some have called it a self-fulfilling prophecy, others a revolving door. Official rule-enforcers (including police and judges, but also social workers, psychiatrists and the whole correctional and treatment establishment) define as serious the deviant acts in which poor people engage. On the other hand, they tend to "define away" the deviant acts of rich people as signs of illness, not crime. They are more likely to consider those actions morally blameless.

No wonder, then, that criminals and delinquents are people who start out and end up without social resources. The act of labelling them criminal completes the circle and creates a secondary problem, **recidivism**, the tendency to repeat criminal behaviours and get into more trouble with the law.

LEAVING CRIME

Few juvenile delinquents become career criminals, but once police have recorded a contact with a juvenile, the probability of another recorded contact is high. It may be that police only make records for juveniles they think are likely to get into more trouble. They may certainly treat as "usual suspects" those whose names are easily found in their files. A recorded contact may lead the police to keep a closer watch on a particular juvenile. With closer observation, the police will probably detect more deviance. Yet, for all this, most delinquents stop breaking the law when they get older though, as Becker points out in discussing "falsely accused" deviants, not breaking the law is not the same as not being labelled.

A small group we might call *violent predators* do not stop. They continue to commit serious crimes: among them, robberies, assaults and drug deals. These offenders are, on average, below age twenty-five when they are first imprisoned. By their mid-twenties they have been committing violent crimes for six years or more. Evidence suggests they are less socially stable than other offenders — for example, less likely to hold a steady job or be married. Drug use is also common among violent predators. The explanation is more often sociological than not: their violence is often a response to the conditions in which they live.

Together, violent predators and juvenile delinquents dominate the public's image of the deviant. In part, this is because the legal system focuses its main attention on the *street crimes* they commit, which range from public violence down through theft and auto offences to victimless crimes. In part, it is because the media tend to focus on young people in general and, among deviants, on gangs in particular. Violent and malicious imagery is, after all, more dramatic than pictures of sedate bureaucrats boringly using telephones to embezzle millions.

Efforts to break people of their criminal tendencies, whether violent or not, have had notoriously little success. The violent predators, in particular, resist all attempts at change through treatment. Indeed, each day the prison subculture undoes any efforts at reform. Nor do professional criminals have any desire to change; in fact, they have good reason *not* to. For their part, really clever embezzlers don't get caught.

Deviant subcultures like the one described in Far and Away on the following page provide benefits for their members and keep out people who shouldn't be there. Remember, not everyone who is a member of a deviant subculture breaks rules all the time. In fact, communities which are very deviant from one perspective are very safe and rule-abiding from another.

But some lawbreakers, especially the amateurs who make up the vast majority of criminals, gradually draw away from law-breaking. The reasons are simple. Unless they are professionals, people have less time and opportunity for crime as they get older. For example, they have less time to spend with friends in public places because they're spending more time at home with their families. Also, as they get older, people have less physical energy for crime: it is too demanding and the "high" a person gets from engaging in risky acts isn't there anymore.

As they age, most people, deviants included, develop a larger *stake in conformity*, a stronger motivation to stay out of trouble. They have a family they want to support, a mortgage to pay, a job they like or income they need. Many feel less hostility towards society at age thirty-five than they did at fifteen. Certainly, they have more to lose. So people obey the rules more consistently, whether they believe in them or not. In the end, most law-breakers stop breaking the laws or, at least, appear to do so. And aging professional criminals may find rule-breaking more expensive or risky.

Giving people more opportunities and rewards helps keep them from being motivated to commit crimes in the first place and gives them a stake in conformity. Indeed, it could be argued by conflict theorists that conformists *do* get the highest rewards. Still, the fact that most of the people who get caught are poor

---

Safe among the Gangsters

Most of us are afraid of gangsters; but as we have learned from The Godfather *saga — a thinly fictionalized account of how the American Mafia works — you're safe so long as you don't cross them. Generally, they don't need us dead. Likewise, in the* favelas *of Rio de Janeiro, you're safe among the drug traffickers. In fact, you're safer among the drug traffickers than in many other parts of the city.*

I bought my first house a few months ago. It's a small, three-room dwelling perched on a mountain overlooking one of Rio de Janeiro's exclusive neighbourhoods. The house is located at the highest point of Rocinha, a *favela* [shantytown] of 250,000 inhabitants that has one of the worst records in Brazil for drug trafficking and violent crimes related to drugs. It also has the reputation of being one of the most secure and safe places for a person to live, if they keep their nose out of other people's business.

For instance, there is virtually no crime against property or individuals in the *favela*. While there are shootings nearly every night in the shantytowns — most of Rio's 4,000 murders last year occurred in the *favelas* — the victims are almost always members of the tiny minority involved in the drug trade. Mr. Batista and other residents say they sleep with their doors unlocked at night and have no fear of assault, something unheard of in Rio.

Protecting them are the self-same drug traffickers involved in nightly altercations with police. For gangs, who have made Rio an important corridor for the export of cocaine from Colombia's Cali cartel to Europe and North America, pour thousands of dollars every year into improvement projects to win the support of the *favelas*. They throw community-wide Christmas parties, provide the poorest people with food and bus passes, and finance day-care centres. They even "help" local youth by allowing them to work as "airplanes," which is Brazilian slang for drug couriers.

The other side of gang generosity is the iron-fisted control they wield over their *favela* domains, which one Rio newspaper recently described as "republics of white powder." Residents are prohibited on pain of death from telling police about drug activities and many are forced to store arms and drugs, and even hide gang members during police raids.

In using their power, the traffickers operate a "justice system" far swifter and harsher than the government's. Informal tribunals dispense penalties of biblical proportion to residents who commit crimes against neighbours or disrupt the drug trade. Rape and robbery are often punished by expulsion or death. Stoning, burning (with a flaming tire "*neclace*"), decapitation or being tossed from a cliff are not uncommon penalties.

Favela citizens fear the traffickers but many are more afraid of Rio's corrupt military and civil police forces, who regularly harass them during searches for arms and gang members. "When *favela* residents are forced to choose between a bad situation by siding with the traffickers or a worse situation by siding with the police, most of them prefer the bad situation," says Francisco Alves Filho, a journalist with Brazil's *Isto* E newsmagazine.

Source: Abridged from Isabel Vincent, *The Globe and Mail*, Sat., Dec. 18, 1993, p. A16

only means that poor criminals are less able to avoid detection for the crimes they commit.

CLOSING REMARKS

Deviance is one of those topics that are popular with students. As with all human differences, there is something exotic about deviance. Few of us view ourselves as deviant, so we tend to find the underside of the social order fascinating.

The sociological study of deviance offers another good example of the connection between macro and micro perspectives. On the one hand, deviance is a macro-phenomenon. It is something that exists outside and "above" individual people — a result of what Durkheim called "social facts" like poverty, social integration (versus isolation) and social regulation (versus anomie). In this sense, deviance is an indication of social inequality, social change and new social strains. It has, seemingly, little to do with particular people and their unique motives and opportunities.

On the other hand, the potential for deviance is inside all of us. We all deviate and conform. As the symbolic interactionists remind us, conformity to the social order is something we negotiate every day. There is no rule, no belief, no taboo so sacred that it is not violated hundreds of times every day; and in every instance, we have to get inside the mind of the deviant actor through that process Weber called *verstehen*, to understand what the particular act of deviance "means." For without such understanding, we can scarcely hope to make effective theories that explain or predict deviant behaviour. *Verstehen* implies taking the rule-breaker's point of view, to see the behaviour as that individual does.

Seen from another angle, some deviance is "innovative behaviour" and that gives us a new slant on the issue of social change. The unequal structuring of opportunities and influences in our society almost makes such innovation inevitable. Often, behavioural innovations will seem threatening at first and people may respond with attempts to control and stigmatize the new behaviours. Some innovations will be truly harmful and call attention to the social pathologies of the age; others will seem (and be) less harmful as time passes. What this tells us is that, often, we cannot judge the meaning or value of an innovation until long after it has appeared.

As shown in this chapter, understanding deviance and control requires understanding how inequality is organized in our society. However, the organization of inequality in our society is an issue whose significance goes far beyond the issues of crime and deviance, as we shall see in the next chapter.

Review Questions

1. What is deviance?
2. What are "formal" and "informal" social control?
3. What is meant by a "social pathology" perspective on deviance?
4. Why did Durkheim believe deviance could benefit society?
5. What are the flaws in Durkheim's approach?
6. What does Merton mean by anomie?
7. What are the adaptations to anomie Merton discusses?
8. What is the labelling approach to deviance?
9. How does the conflict perspective on deviance differ from the other perspectives?
10. What issues are of greatest concern to feminist criminologists?
11. What are "crimes," "norm violations" and "social diversions"?
12. Who is most likely to commit serious crimes?

Discussion Questions

1. *Grokking* is a form of deviant behaviour that was unknown twenty years ago, was barely mentioned ten years ago, yet today is as widespread as the common cold. We have limited funds to study this change. To understand most about the rise of this new behaviour to prominence, should we spend our money studying Grokkers or the Grok-police?

2. Some believe sociology took a great stride forward when it rejected the social — and personal — disorganization explanations of deviance in favour of labelling theories. Others believe it was a step backward. What do you think?

3. How might different theorists we have discussed go about explaining the observed differences in crime rates between Canada and the United States? What evidence would we need to test which one was right?

4. Many kinds of crime and deviance are apparently more common in the lower classes than in the upper classes. Given what we know about the reasons for this, for which kinds of crime and deviance would class differences be *least*?

5. The debate over how to reduce crime and delinquency keeps polarizing people. One group says punish the criminal, the other group says treat the criminal. Where do you stand on this issue? Now, organize the most persuasive argument you can for the *opposite* position.

6. Why don't we put organized crime out of business by decriminalizing all the goods and services they offer?

Suggested Readings

Becker, H. S. (1963) *Outsiders*. New York: Free Press. In this widely read classic, Becker spells out the labelling theory of deviance, then applies the theory to a variety of outsiders including jazz musicians and marijuana smokers.

Erikson, K. T. (1966) *Wayward Puritans*. New York: Wiley. By panicking about witchcraft, the early Puritans in Massachusetts "created" deviants where none really existed. As Erikson shows, this strengthened their solidarity and sense of normality.

Goffman, E. (1961) *Asylums*. Garden City, New York: Doubleday. Through the eyes of participant-observers and inmates, we learn about life in "total institutions" which dramatize the boundary between insiders and outsiders.

Hagan, J. (1991) *The Disreputable Pleasures: Crime and Deviance in Canada*, third edition. Toronto: McGraw-Hill Ryerson. This brief yet comprehensive textbook by one of Canada's leading researchers in crime and deviance is rich in description and theoretical insights. Particularly interesting are the cross-national comparisons.

Levinson, D. (1989) *Family violence in cross-cultural perspective*. Frontiers of Anthropology, Volume 1. Newbury Park: Sage Publications, pp. 9-38. This essay uses the Human Relations Area Files to find out typical characteristics of societies in which family violence is common, and to address why domestic violence is justified in different ways in different societies.

Stebbins, R. A. (1993) *Deviance: Tolerable Differences*. Toronto: McGraw-Hill Ryerson. An amusing book that discusses some of the forms of deviance which are tolerated by most people. These "tolerable differences" include deviant sexual practices, gambling and recreational drug use.

Internet Resources

The following Web sites are good places to find more information about topics discussed in this chapter:

Cop Net and Police Resource List keeps track of police and security resources, with many links to the home pages of Canadian police departments.
http://police.sas.ab.

National Crime Prevention Council profiles initiatives that take a proactive approach to the problems of crime, disorder and insecurity, as well as the underlying causes of crime.
http://www.web.net/ ~ ncpc/welcome.htm

Royal Canadian Mounted Police Museum provides a verbal and pictorial history of Canada's national police force and its organization.
http://spider.regina.ism.ca/RCMPRCMPhome.htm

CSIS–Canadian Security Intelligence Service reports on Canada's spying and anti-spying mandate, organization and history.
http://www.csis ~ scrs.gc.ca

Department of Justice of Canada Home Page provides news releases, an overview of the justice system and recent bills and statutes, with links to other legal resources on the Internet.
http://canada.justice.gc.ca

Law and Justice Links offers lists of links by subject.
http://www.acjnet.org/resource/sub.html

At the Wayne County Boot Camp inmates are rehabilitated in a minimum security prison using a disciplined, military-style program.
http://www.state.tn.us/correction/wcbc.html

Deviance and Control offers a bullet review of theory relating to deviance as well as links to other related Web sites.
http://www.umsl.edu/ ~ rkeel/010/deviance.html

Sex Workers Alliance of Vancouver provides a clearinghouse for information about law on sexual health, commerce and culture as these topics relate to sex work.
http://www.walnet.org/swav

CLASS AND THE ECONOMIC ORDER

Food banks, like the one pictured here, are becoming a sad fact of Canadian life. So are astronomical salaries and bonuses for corporate elites.

IS INEQUALITY A FACT OF LIFE?

These days, we see more people sleeping outdoors, despite the cold winter temperatures in most of Canada. On the streets, we are more often approached by people asking us for a dollar. We hear more about mothers on welfare being evicted for failing to pay the rent, food banks being unable to meet the demand of the hungry, and public institutions — including colleges and universities, the Canadian Broadcasting Corporation (CBC), the United Way and dozens of others — cutting back their services. We meet more unemployed men and women — many of them highly educated and in their thirties, forties and fifties — still trying to figure out how to make a living in a rapidly changing, relatively unforgiving economy.

At colleges and universities, more and more students work long hours for pay so they can afford to continue their education. In class, they are often sleepy or irritable because of the workload they are carrying. When asked what they plan to do after graduation, many admit to uncertainty and anxiety. They just don't know what will happen to them once they finish school, so many stay on longer and longer.

How should we react to the homeless, the beggars and others who come to us asking for help? How to react to the downsized workers and would-be clients of food banks, inexpensive day-care centres and women's shelters? To the students who drowse in our classrooms or, in private, suffer from depression? None of us wants to lead these lives and none knows how to be sure of avoiding them. Moreover, none of us wants to feel guilty about the privileges and pleasures we are able to enjoy. So we all have to "make sense" of the suffering that surrounds us and, if possible, reduce and prevent it. This chapter attempts to make sense of the problem, and as we shall see, opinions differ about its causes and solution. As we shall also see, the problem comes down to socially structured inequality and unequal life chances.

Sociologists use the term **life chances** to describe the effects of inequality, and few terms do as well in capturing the link between large macrosociological processes and private lives. What we mean by the term are the chances a person has of sharing in the economic (or material) and cultural (or symbolic) goods of a society. People who belong to different class or status levels of society have different access to these material and symbolic goods. This chapter is about the reasons why this is so and the effects of unequal life chances.

Social inequality includes all the differences in life chances that arise out of social characteristics and relationships. It includes unequal access to social rewards like wealth, prestige and influence. The factors influencing inequality are social because they are a result of the way a society is organized and the kinds of social connections which affect people's experiences.

Development of the Class System

Canadians are not in the habit of thinking much about inequality. We live in one of the wealthiest and freest countries in the world. One result of this is that Canadians are more likely than people in other nations to attach either praise or blame to the individual, instead of to society, for success or failure in life. Still, not all Canadians have equal life chances. Learning to recognize inequality as a built-in feature of social life, not a result of fate, hard work or good character, is an important part of learning sociology.

Most social inequality arises out of the normal working of the **economic order** — the social system that produces, distributes and consumes material resources. People learn about the economic order first-hand whenever they shop for groceries, buy or sell a house, lose a job or get moved to another city, pay taxes or fill the car's tank with gas. The link between inequality and the economic order becomes more evident if we think about how inequality changes as the economic order changes. Consider, for example, the impact on inequality of the Industrial Revolution

The term **Industrial Revolution** refers to a set of economic and social changes that started in England in the last quarter of the 18th century and later spread to other parts of the world. Before then, people produced most goods at home, on farms, or in small shops with simple tools they owned. The use of new sources of energy, such as water, steam, and later, electrical energy, allowed large-scale production to evolve. This proved more efficient than the old handicraft method. Plenty of inanimate energy made it possible to develop machines for mass production. This increased the size, complexity and cost of productive technology.

Mass production, as the name implies, is the production of goods in large numbers. It centres manufacturing in a large self-contained area such as a factory. The work involved in producing an item is broken into small, specialized steps, each carried out by different people or machines in sequence. The use of machinery to do routine tasks is especially important.

The growth of mass production changed social life. First England, and then other Western European societies, were altered from rural, agricultural communities into urban, industrial states. These changes not only moved people around, they transformed the ways in which people experienced society and their place in it.

Before the Industrial Revolution, societies had changed slowly and few people thought about *why* society was organized as it was. Their lives were the same as those of their parents and neighbours. Most people assumed that their form of social life was "natural," or that God had so ordained it. That no such assumption could be made about the "hellish" working conditions of early industrialism escaped the notice of those distanced from them.

Gradually, conditions improved and the pace of social and economic change increased strikingly. Soon it was obvious to everyone that these changes were a result of human acts, not the work of God or nature. There developed a new outlook on society: that society is created by human beings and society changes because of what we choose to do or fail to do.

A New Outlook on Society

The spread of this new outlook altered the way people understood themselves and their ties to one another. It even fostered the development of sociology and the other social sciences.

The new outlook influenced all of the different groups in society. For most workers, the factory was their first exposure to power-driven machinery and highly specialized work. That exposure created a group awareness of common problems that centred around work and relations with the employer. Workers realized they could solve the problems only by changing these relations. The stage was set for class conflict and, later, for the growth of labour unions.

In this way, the new outlook on society also fostered what Karl Marx called *class consciousness* among the bourgeoisie, or capitalist class. Class consciousness refers to an awareness of class interests and a willingness to act to attain those interests.

Before the Industrial Revolution, a master craftsman and his workers were tied together by mutual obligations. Workers were usually apprentices or journeymen entitled to a customary level of pay, often including room and board. Most important, they were entitled to learn the skills of the craftsman.

But with industrialization and the introduction of machinery, cheap, untrained workers replaced craftsmen and their apprentices. The breakdown of customary relations between employers and employees ended all notions of obligation. Employers exploited their workers and paid them the lowest wage possible. And employers acquired attitudes to justify this exploitation. These included a belief in unlimited opportunity and inevitable progress. According to this ideology, no one should put limits on either profits or output, and any exploitation leading to vast profits is reasonable.

Social theories of the age in turn justified these attitudes. The destruction of religious dogma and traditional belief meant that people could develop their own explanations of the world more freely. Most social theorists came from the same social background as the factory owners, so it is not surprising that their views of how society "works" suited (and justified) the attitudes of that class.

In 1776, the English philosopher Adam Smith published *The Wealth of Nations*, the key work in what scholars call classical economics. In it, Smith argues in favour of *laissez-faire* economies — markets in which people could buy and sell anything at an unregulated price. The term *laissez-faire capitalism* refers to an economy that is free from hindrance (especially by the state). Smith believed that such free markets would allow materials and products to fetch a just price. As a result of this, more people would receive more benefits from the economic order.

Classical economists also promoted a new view of social life. According to this view, everyone was driven by a desire to maximize their own well-being in the marketplace. Ideally, people would cooperate and *everyone* would benefit. Economic exchanges were to be stripped of aspects that were not "rational," such as customary obligations, ethnic loyalties or religious beliefs. Social life was to be based only on what Karl Marx later called the "cash nexus."

The idea that people can create the lives they want by choosing wisely in a competitive system is part of an outlook called *liberal democracy*, or the *liberal ideology*. It grows out of this philosophy of laissez-faire capitalism.

Liberal democracy rests on free choice and free competition in a market where people trade labour, goods and ideas (Macpherson, 1962). But given social inequality — unequal starting points — freedom conflicts with fairness. That is because, in a liberal democracy people are expected to protect their own interests. This ignores the fact that some people are less able than others to protect these interests. It also denies that any shared interests — for example, environmental safety and world peace — may be more important than individual interests.

By destroying the old economic and political order, liberal thinking gave people new chances, freedoms and rights. But it also produced an economic system distinguished by insecure jobs, terrible working conditions and poor pay. It was in this climate of conflict that Karl Marx evolved his analysis of capitalism, the first of the modern theories of stratification.

THEORIES OF SOCIAL STRATIFICATION

Class Theory   The theory of class conflict was first developed by Marx as part of his theory of society and social change. This theory of class is often described as a form of economic determinism. Marx saw the stratification system as set by the means of production to be found in a society. The means of production are the tools, objects, techniques or skills that are used in the production process.

Marx (1936) and Marx and Engels (1955) described our kind of society as "capitalist" because of the important role capital plays in production. **Capital** includes money and other forms of wealth which are invested in a business to increase yield and profits. In Canada, the means of production are technology, labour and capital. People's position in the class system of social inequality depends on their link to the means of production.

In Marx's theory, a small group of people, the bourgeoisie, own the capital and control the labour of everyone else. As owners, they are able to create and destroy jobs, hire and fire people, and extract "surplus value," or profits, from other people's work. This profit becomes capital when it is re-invested. A second group, the petty (or petite) bourgeoisie, includes small-business owners who have a few employees and work alongside them. Like the bourgeoisie, they own the means of production. Unlike the bourgeoisie, they extract few profits from other people's labour.

Most people belong to a third group, the proletariat, and work for the bourgeoisie. They own none of the capital and sell their own labour power to bourgeois employers for a wage.

People in the same social class share the same relationship to the means of production. Thus, they have similar wealth, authority and power, and thus, have similar lifestyles and life chances. All members of the proletariat, or working class, are exposed to the power of the bourgeoisie. They all — construction workers, sales staff, secretaries and professors alike — sell their labour for wages. All could be thrown out of work, find themselves without an income and have to rely on savings, welfare or charity to survive.

As a result, class affects the ways people think of the future. Middle-class people are more devoted to values like self-growth, achievement and activism than people in the working class. For their part, poor, powerless people tend to think less about the future than people with more wealth and power, defending themselves psychologically against the knowledge that they lack the ability to do much about their problems. Instead of organizing themselves as a social class to demand changes in society, they often retreat into silent self-blame (see, for example, Sennett and Cobb, 1973).

Problems arise when we try to apply class analysis, as Marx originally stated it, to North America today. First, many people in the proletariat do not think of themselves as "workers," and identify instead with the "middle class" or even the bourgeoisie. They model their attitudes, goals and lifestyles on middle-class, not working-class, ideals.

The class consciousness of blue-collar workers depends on many factors outside work itself. For example, union membership plays a part in forming a person's identity as a member of the working class, but many working-class people do not belong to unions. Besides, the effect of union membership is limited. For example, marrying a woman with a middle-class background increases the chance that a working man will develop a middle-class identity and support non-socialist political parties.

In North America, people fail to identify with their real social class. The concept of class has little meaning for people's sense of identity. That is why few workers vote for working-class political parties. In fact, so weak are people's class identities that a survey of worldwide voting data has led Clark, Lipset and Rempel (1993) to conclude that social class is no longer useful for predicting political behaviour.

A second problem with Marx's theory is that, in modern capitalism, ownership and control are largely distinct. Millions of small stockholders own a great many large businesses. These businesses make huge profits and pay few taxes, returning large dividends to their stockholders (see Everyday Life, below). But senior management and elected directors control these businesses. This separation of ownership from control is not something Marx had foreseen. It makes understanding the structure of inequality more difficult, since it is less visible.

Third, the differences between wage-earning people may be more "real" and more important than Marx had imagined. Not all wage-earning people share the same market position: they may receive very different material rewards and life chances, in terms of pay, security and chance of promotion. And not all share the same work tasks and production technology, or amount of supervision on the job. The working class is therefore divided.

Finally, in a society with fairly high rates of social mobility, class lines are blurred, making people even less likely to identify with their social class (Clark and Lipset, 1991). For all these reasons, we may benefit from another approach to studying social inequality, and that approach is provided by Max Weber.

Weber's Approach

In cataloguing classes in modern society, Weber (1958a) added to Marx's list. He included the propertied class (Marx's bourgeoisie); the traditional petty bourgeois class of small business people, shopkeepers and farmers; and the working class (Marx's proletariat). As well, he identified a wage-earning intellectual, administrative and managerial class. Within each of these four classes we find the similarity (and awareness of similar interests) that Marx expected to find.

Both Marx and Weber believed that changing historical conditions would produce new forms of domination. For Marx, the crucial changes were those in the means of production. New means of production create new classes which come into conflict with the old ones. History, to Marx, was the record of class conflict and revolutions in which new classes overthrow old ruling classes.

For Weber, many more factors could change the forms of domination; these include changes in cultural and religious values. More important, Weber was the first to stress the independent role of authority. Though class has a huge impact, electoral politics and government bureaucracies also give the state a central role in people's lives.

EVERYDAY LIFE

The Taxman Doesn't Come Here Much

Around March and April a lot of people's thoughts turn to paying taxes — that annual tussle with the government over who owes what, and why. Out comes the calculator, shoeboxes of old receipts are spread across the dining-room table — with T4 slips off to one side — and the arithmetic begins in earnest. How much nicer it is to be rich: not only are there accounting firms to do the job, but in the end there's also less to pay.

A report by the Ontario Coalition for Social Justice and the Ontario Federation of Labour found that 450 major corporations paid less tax in 1993, 1994 or 1995 than the average worker. The share of federal government revenue received from corporate tax has fallen steadily to 8 per cent in 1994 from 23 per cent in 1954. At the same time, taxes on individuals rose to 58 per cent from 35 per cent. Today, hundreds of Canadian corporations pay lower income taxes than the average worker, and many paid no tax at all in spite of earning millions of dollars in profit.

Among the companies paying less than a 15 per cent tax rate in 1994 are Air Canada, which paid 3.2 per cent tax on $157 million; Canadian National Railways, which paid 4.7 per cent on $256 million; Telus Corp., which paid 2.9 per cent on $218 million; and Thomson Corp., owner of *The Globe and Mail*, which paid 12.9 per cent on $527 million (U.S.). Many large companies were also able to defer tax payments without any interest charge: in fact, a total of more than $40 billion (Canadian) in deferred taxes outstanding in 1994. Companies benefiting in this way include Alcan Aluminum Ltd., with $914 million (U.S.) outstanding; BCE Inc., with $2 billion (Canadian); Canadian Pacific, Ltd., with $1.8 billion; Shell Canada Ltd., with $867 million; and Thomson Corp., with $313 million (U.S.).

This generosity towards corporate debtors is in stark contrast to the treatment of ordinary citizens who are told endlessly about the need for fiscal responsibility. Massive cutbacks in health, education and social welfare are justified on the grounds that there's not enough money to pay all the bills. But wouldn't there be enough money if some of the corporate tax loopholes were closed. Alternatively, we could spread the wealth by allowing ordinary workers to write off many of their operating costs, development costs and depreciation, just like the big companies. After all, everyone operates, develops and depreciates.

Source: Adapted from an article by Greg Ip, *The Globe and Mail*, Wed., Feb. 7, 1996, p. B5

And unlike Marx, Weber believed that social (or "status") groups are able to control markets too. Like social classes, ethnic, racial, religious, professional and national groups all have the power to do this. Said another way, all societies use gender, ethnicity and race, as well as class, to distribute wealth, power and prestige (or social honour). But unlike other groups (for example, ethnic groups) classes rarely organize politically in industrial societies. We have already noted the lack of political action among working-class people. As a result, there is no destined change from a shared economic position to shared political interests, as Marx expected.

As for status, Weber claimed that most of the important forms of stratification in the past, such as caste systems and slavery, were based on cultural and religious values, not class. He was not entirely right: the Indian caste system is remarkably intricate, and any full treatment of it needs to include class as well. Though the Indian government has officially disbanded the caste system, traditional practices like "untouchability" continue to shape social relations in Indian villages (Sharma, 1986). But caste and class are at work at the same time, with the result that Indian society is even more hierarchical than Canadian society.

In fact, as Weber pointed out, all systems of inequality are complex. They are based not only on class, or values, or politics: they are based on all of the

Boundaries between the bourgeoisie (or capitalist class) and proletariat (or working class) were easier to define in the 19th century, when Marx was writing.

above and many more factors. That means that any useful theory of stratification has to examine all of these dimensions.

Combining Marx and Weber

Many of the newer theories of stratification are referred to as neo-Marxist or neo-Weberian because they modify the older theories by combining key elements drawn from Marx and Weber.

In large part, we need to do this because the world has changed radically since Marx and Weber's time. To understand the kinds of inequality we face today, we need to take into account the kinds of social and economic organization that people face, at work and at home. A first step in this process is to bring together the insights of Marx and Weber.

Erik Olin Wright (1985), among others, has changed the Marxian scheme of class analysis to include Weber's views, especially the stress Weber places on domination. In Wright's scheme, there are capitalists and petty bourgeoisie. However, there are also four types of wage-earners. Some exert workplace control over other wage-earners and others do not. At the same time, some wage-earners are controlled in the workplace and others are not. The wage-earners who are controlled but control no one else — call them workers — are closest to Marx's proletariat. Similar in many respects are the wage-earners called supervisors, who are controlled at work but also control other workers.

Two other wage-earning groups differ from the supervisors and workers in their social origins, educational attainment, pay level and workplace autonomy. One is the group of managers and technocrats that controls other workers but enjoys a lot of freedom from control on the job. Another is the group of workers — academics, salaried professionals and technical personnel — who enjoy a lot of freedom on the job and have no control over other workers. Call them semi-autonomous employees.

This last type of worker, including mainly salaried professionals, has grown in the 20th century and poses a special problem for Marxist analysis. Consider, as an example, Supreme Court judges. They enjoy high salaries, high job security and a great deal of prestige. They also have a lot of power over the way Canadian society works: their decisions govern all law-making and law enforcement. Once appointed, they are free to act as they wish; but they don't own any capital or exercise any direct control over other workers.

Objectively, salaried professionals like the Supreme Court judges are workers. As workers they lack complete control over the labour process: what they produce, how they produce it and who gains a profit from that work. But subjectively, they are not workers: they think of themselves as independent and, in some respects, they are.

For this reason, two class-related attributes — income and the chance for self-directed work — may be thought to determine people's class identity and their attitudes towards business and labour. Typically, people who earn high salaries and have a lot of freedom at work (whether self-employed or not) tend to be more friendly to business than they are to labour. Though they lack power, they increasingly come to think like "bosses" and reject resistance to power and class conflict.

Few employed Canadians — probably fewer than 3 per cent — can be considered members of the capitalist class. The petite bourgeoisie make up about 12 per cent of all employed Canadians. Managers and technocrats comprise another 7 per cent, supervisors 11 per cent, semi-autonomous employees 8 per cent, respectively. Finally, workers form the vast majority — over 50 per cent — of the employed population (Ornstein, 1988: 194).

Despite their small numbers, capitalists average the highest rate of pay, twice that of all wage-earners and nearly three times that of workers. Even controlling for education, age and gender, the average capitalist earns nearly twice as much as the average wage-earner and more than twice as much as the average worker. (These numbers, derived from a survey by Ornstein [1988], probably underestimate the differences in income and more so, the differences in wealth.)

Neo-Marxism argues that every type of society has a distinctive form of exploitation. This is why it is important to study groups of similarly exploited people, with similar amounts of control over their lives: we will continue to call them social "classes." However, it is no longer possible to do a class analysis of a society without exploring how economic position combines with gender, ethnicity, religion and other social factors (Clement, 1991).

Neo-Weberian theory sees what is often called the North American middle class arising from a capitalist investment in worker discipline (i.e., supervision and "management"). Comparative research shows that, where domination is concerned, the Swedes and Finns differ from North Americans. The former give their workers more autonomy, spend less money controlling and punishing their workers and are less afraid of new technologies in the workplace.

The Functionalist Approach   Sociologists Kingsley Davis and Wilbert Moore (1945) are credited with developing an explanation of inequality which sociologists call the functional theory of social stratification. In contrast to the theories of Marx and Weber, it says that social stratification is inevitable and, even, desirable in society.

The argument goes like this: There are certain positions that are more important to society than others. Performing well in these positions requires special skills, but few people are likely to invest enough time and money to acquire these skills. Only through a system of special rewards and privileges is society able to motivate some few people to get the skills needed to fill the most important positions. These special rewards include wealth, prestige and power.

Now let's take an example that shows off the theory in its best light. Consider brain surgery. If you are going to have surgery done on your brain, you want it done by someone who is very skilful. You want to know that this person has a steady hand, a good knowledge of the human body, and an up-to-date familiarity with surgical techniques. You would not be surprised to learn that such training had required ten or more years of post-secondary education. Indeed, you

SOCIAL PROFILE 5.1

How Canadians Spend Their Money

		Household annual income			
	All households	Under $10,000	$10,000–$14,999	$15,000–$19,999	$20,000–$24,999
			$		
Average income before tax	46,076	6,358	12,392	17,535	22,456
Average expenditure per household	45,548	13,116	14,427	20,082	24,965
Total current consumption	32,416	12,186	13,347	18,009	21,311
Food	5,686	2,379	2,810	3,635	4,111
Shelter	8,102	4,281	4,640	5,583	6,056
Principal accommodation	7,624	4,236	4,513	5,427	5,909
Rented living quarters	2,279	2,547	2,814	2,916	3,017
Owned living quarters	3,912	985	856	1,467	1,702
Water, fuel and electricity	1,433	704	843	1,045	1,190
Other accommodation	478	45	128	155	147
Household operation	1,974	767	931	1,175	1,394
Household furnishings and equipment	1,372	297	439	688	736
Household furnishings	699	119	211	313	351
Household equipment	593	159	199	335	345
Services related to furnishings and equipment	80	19	29	40	40
Clothing	2,222	530	642	915	1,179
Transportation	5,640	1,611	1,528	2,445	3,339
Private transportation	5,198	1,374	1,302	2,126	3,005
Public transportation	442	237	225	320	334
Health care	867	347	359	514	718
Personal care	844	268	372	497	600
Recreation	2,300	496	511	856	1,075
Reading materials and other printed matter	248	117	96	134	160
Education	430	156	96	140	245
Tobacco products and alcoholic beverages	1,410	570	626	901	1,033
Miscellaneous	1,322	368	298	525	666
Personal taxes	9,378	404	393	991	1,988
Pensions, life and unemployment insurance	2,289	57	129	299	627
Gifts and contributions	1,464	469	558	783	1,039

Household Spending, 1992

Source: *Canada Year Book 1997* © Minister of Industry, 1996, p. 181

would be desperately insecure if you heard your surgeon had spent only two weeks in university after completing high school.

So if someone told you that brain surgeons earn a lot of money, this would not seem unfair. Obviously, they possess a rare, important and exacting skill which cost a great deal of time and money to develop. Without the prospect of large rewards, few people would be willing to become brain surgeons.

			Household annual income				
$25,000– $29,999	$30,000– $34,999	$35,000– $39,999	$40,000– $49,999	$50,000– $59,999	$60,000– $69,999	$70,000– $89,999	$90,000 and over
			$				
27,450	32,304	37,348	44,748	54,548	64,605	78,748	119,563
29,870	34,583	38,563	45,721	54,350	61,689	73,558	106,005
24,382	27,154	29,183	34,204	38,498	41,559	48,220	63,046
4,618	4,906	5,321	6,102	6,585	6,862	8,207	9,864
6,710	6,668	7,347	8,410	8,912	10,027	10,613	14,641
6,465	6,431	7,021	8,006	8,301	9,457	9,814	13,015
2,920	2,795	2,632	2,472	1,797	1,594	1,511	884
2,321	2,325	2,994	4,047	4,871	6,145	6,422	9,907
1,225	1,311	1,395	1,487	1,632	1,718	1,881	2,224
245	237	326	404	611	570	799	1,626
1,474	1,619	1,804	2,018	2,236	2,535	2,882	3,850
938	1,103	1,223	1,387	1,672	1,788	2,169	3,107
435	549	617	661	875	861	1,176	1,719
443	501	546	646	719	822	860	1,183
59	53	60	80	78	105	132	206
1,463	1,723	1,755	2,266	2,595	3,065	3,708	5,281
3,959	4,710	5,266	6,269	7,255	7,409	8,831	11,319
3,616	4,398	4,870	5,851	6,843	6,900	8,213	10,308
343	312	397	408	412	509	618	1,011
727	852	868	930	1,072	1,029	1,166	1,421
678	757	755	872	1,014	1,047	1,253	1,552
1,271	1,628	1,877	2,352	2,902	3,437	4,026	5,461
196	194	212	249	283	333	357	526
169	318	274	390	565	671	740	1,110
1,174	1,446	1,367	1,597	1,686	1,665	2,056	2,114
1,007	1,230	1,113	1,361	1,719	1,692	2,212	2,800
3,291	4,596	6,109	7,904	11,202	14,568	18,715	33,409
1,017	1,387	1,822	2,318	3,090	3,882	4,662	6,047
1,180	1,445	1,449	1,294	1,560	1,680	1,960	3,503

Equally, without the prospect of large rewards, few people would be willing to accept the costs and risks of becoming entrepreneurs and innovators. So functionalist theory also assumes that inequality is likely to produce new ideas and inventions, by producing the people who produce them.

However, the evidence does not fully support these assumptions. First, few cases are as clearcut as that of the brain surgeon. We can all agree that brain surgery is important, but is it possible to rank *all* occupations according to their importance to society? Beyond that, are even the contributions made by brain surgeons all that important to society, even if they are to the subjects of the surgery? Using the term "rewards" implies, perhaps wrongly, that people "deserve" what they receive.

Even if we could agree that brain surgeons are more important to society than truck drivers, and thus should be better paid, we would have trouble applying the same logic to explaining the salaries earned in organized crime, professional sports and popular entertainment. (There, perhaps, "plunder" and "booty" are precisely the words we are looking for.) Or the low salaries, by comparison, earned by teachers, librarians or ambulance drivers rushing their patient to the brain surgeon.

Even if we could get past that hurdle, we would have trouble using the functional theory to account for non-occupational inequalities: why, for example, men dominate women, whites dominate non-whites, and rich nations dominate poor nations. As to innovation, it may be true that the chance of large rewards motivates some people to try new things and take new risks. However, a high degree of inequality also makes it impossible for most people to risk innovating. So it is more likely that a high degree of inequality puts a damper on innovation.

Inequality is too complex and, usually, too unfair for the functional theory to handle. Generally, most sociologists today explain stratification using some form of the conflict approach.

Feminist Approaches

According to feminist theorists, to understand inequality it is necessary to consider gendered patterns of domination both at home and in the workplace. One must try to understand how the suppression of women at home contributes to the suppression of women at work. Like the neo-Marxists and neo-Weberians, feminist sociologists have tended to stress the interaction between class, gender and racial inequalities.

One simply cannot study class and status inequalities without recognizing the importance of gender differences. For example, in studying Canadian workers Ornstein (1988) found large differences in background, pay and working conditions between manual and nonmanual workers: namely, manual workers:

- are more likely to be men than women;

- have less education (on average) than non-manual workers;

- report a much less settled work history than nonmanual workers; and

- are more closely supervised than nonmanual workers.

In short, manual workers have less autonomy and job stability than nonmanual workers. On the other hand, the typically "pink-collar" (female, nonmanual) workers earn about 20 per cent less than their "blue-collar" (male, manual worker) colleagues. This shows that a person's place in the stratification system is not just a result of the relations of production. Women doing the same jobs as men are sometimes paid less than men, even substantially less.

Also, women doing the same work as men usually have less chance for promotion than men.

Beyond that, women typically have a different work history than men. For example, they are more likely than men to choose part-time work, and they are more likely to interrupt their work lives for familial or educational reasons. This reflects women's heavier family duties, which some sociologists have called working women's "double day." It also reflects the way "women's work" evolved, as part of North America's administrative revolution in the early part of the 20th century

The *administrative revolution*, between 1911 and 1931, included a huge increase in the clerical sector of the work force, a dramatic shift in the sex ratio (towards female clerks) and the rationalization of office work by scientifically oriented office managers. At the forefront of this growth of white-collar work was an increase in the total number of clerks, who today comprise more than 15 per cent of the labour force. With feminization, clerical jobs became fragmented and routinized. The popularity of the dictation machine and the typing pool signified the rationalization of office work. It also had the effect of reducing the skill level, prestige and pay of secretarial work.

The spread of large central offices reflects the parallel spread of industrialization and capitalism. The main purpose of modern management was to regulate labour and reduce class conflict; here it was accomplished in an office, not a factory, and the main objects of control were women. Clerical work could be mass-produced, rationalized, controlled and poorly paid.

As our society has moved away from a manufacturing economy towards a service economy, women have entered poor-paying, insecure and low-status jobs in large numbers. For example, women, along with teenagers and recent immigrants, are particularly numerous in the fast-food industry (Reiter, 1986). As in the highly controlled offices we just described, their work is specialized but lacks challenge or creativity.

Interactionist Approaches

Symbolic interactionists have done little work on class and other forms of inequality. A microsociological outlook is unfit for developing a full-fledged theory of inequality. However, interactionists and other microsociologists have made important contributions to our understanding of the symbolic and interactional aspects of domination, status and class differences. For example, Stone (1970) studied the ways people use appearance, such as clothing, to establish and display their social status.

One interactionist, David Karp (1986), studied aspects of the social psychology of upward mobility. He discusses some of the experiences and views of upwardly mobile people — individuals from lower-class families who have become professionals. Among the intriguing results of his study is evidence that the upwardly mobile feel like "strangers in a strange land." Because they did not grow up in families of professionals, they are not as likely to share the same values and lifestyles as people from such a background, and they are not always comfortable with their success. Indeed, there is some evidence that the upwardly mobile do not feel they deserve their occupational success. Some even avoid going still further up the occupational ladder for this reason.

Interactionists have also shown an interest in micropolitics, which is concerned with interpersonal struggles for advantage or control in face-to-face groups. This concern is illustrated in Goffman's (1961) study of a mental hospital, which examined a "total institution." In this institution, an "underlife" develops as a way of "working the system." The study gives a good example of the way dominated people can avoid submitting to authority with limited strategic resources. Beyond that, interactionists have been particularly sensitive to the use and meaning of "status symbols." But it is important to note that all stratification and inequality is actually embedded in concrete social situations where an interactionist analysis can nicely reveal imbalances in the social resources available to participants for mobilizing action.

A symbolic interactionist looking at inequality in a classroom, for example, can show how certain capacities for verbal expression are predictive of success; and how these capacities are unequally distributed or evaluated. By knowing exactly how, and with what materials, people work in a situation we can understand why some people are ill-equipped to succeed.

LIFE AS AN UNEQUAL CONTEST

Let's use all of these approaches to clarify the processes which cause and maintain inequality. To do so, begin by considering a set of sporting contests. Who do you think is likely to win in each of these contests between Jones and Smith?

- Jones and Smith are racing to see who is fastest in the 100-metre dash. Jones starts at the 50-metre line and Smith starts at zero. Who will likely win the race?

- Jones and Smith are racing to see who is fastest in the 10-kilometre marathon. Jones has new, well-fitting shoes and Smith has shoes that pinch his feet. Who will likely win the race?

- Jones and Smith are lifting weights to see who is strongest. Jones is permitted the assistance of three strong friends in lifting the barbell. Smith must lift the barbell himself. Who will likely lift the heaviest barbell?

If you guessed that Jones is going to win every time, you're right, and the reasons are clear. The same reasons make it likely that some people will (almost) always win and others will (almost) always lose in society's contests for wealth, power and social standing. And here's what you have to remember: the wins and losses are due to social structure. If you are born a "Jones," you will win, but if you are born a "Smith," you will lose. Accidents of birth will determine your life chances. Social structure will constrain and transform your life, here as everywhere else.

And as in sporting contests, so too in social contests for better life chances; poorer starts produce poorer finishes because unequal social origins — origins in environments with unequal resources — mean unequal prospects in the contest for better life chances. Even when the opportunities are equalized so the contest is "fair" as, for example, when bigotry is banned, unequal social origins mean unequal outcomes.

Here's some evidence that life chances are unequal, from a study (Corak and Heisz, 1996) of the incomes of fathers and their sons. It links the tax records of fathers in 1978-1982 (when the sons were teenagers) and their sons in 1993 (when they were in their late twenties). Specifically, the study looks at 440,000 father-son pairs, examines the father's income group when the son is a teenager, then asks what income group the son is in roughly fifteen years later. Fathers are compared with fathers in 1978 and sons with sons in 1993, using constant dollars.

The data show that teenage sons of fathers who were in the top income decile (i.e., 10 per cent) in 1978-1982 grow up twice as likely to be in the top income decile (when they are earning an income of their own) as they are to be in the bottom income decile. As adults, they are more likely to be in the top income decile than in any other decile, and more likely than anyone else to be in the top income decile. In fact, sons of wealthy fathers are four times as likely to be in the top decile than sons of poor fathers.

Sons of poor fathers grow up three times as likely to be in the lowest income decile themselves as to be in the top income decile. In effect, they inherit poverty in the same sense that rich boys inherit wealth. Thus, sons at the top and bottom of the income hierarchy inherit their father's income level. Very few go from "rags to riches," or from riches to rags, contrary to our most popular mythologies. Income inheritance among the very wealthy and the very poor is a common event, even more common in the United States and the United Kingdom than in Canada.

In the middle of the income pyramid, on the other hand, there is a lot of change in incomes, both upward and downward. Middle-income boys are as likely to do better or worse than their fathers as they are to stay in the same income decile.

This study by researchers at Statistics Canada tells us a great deal. However, it doesn't answer some vital questions that we will have to consider below: for example, How *do* sons benefit from their fathers' incomes to attain high incomes of their own? Would a study of daughters show the same results as this study of sons? How do other family assets (e.g., mother's income, father's cultural capital, family property) affect a son's inheritance? Does getting a higher education change the odds of inheriting the father's income? And does the endowment of power, authority and prestige work the same way, and work to the same degree, as income inheritance?

Unequal Origins = Unequal Destinations

There are many different types of social inequality, but there are also many links among them. Indeed, social inequalities overlap and reinforce one another so that some people enjoy a great many advantages and others, a great many handicaps. How would we go about equalizing the advantages? Our answer depends, first, on what we mean by equality.

Many people favour **equality of condition** — equal portions of wealth, prestige and power for all members of society. Other people favour **equality of opportunity** — equal access to those things valued by society. Equal opportunity means that all positions in society are equally open to all people, regardless of age, race, gender, religion or class of origin. In principle, recruitment is done according to merit or on the basis of personal talent. Inequalities of opportunity are differences in the chance that people (or their children) will get to enjoy an improved social condition: more wealth, authority and prestige; better health; more happiness.

However, in no society do we find complete equality of either kind. To say that inequality is apparently universal is not to say that it is natural or inevitable; and the extent and forms of inequality vary widely across societies. Nonetheless, equality has so far proved elusive in human societies. As a result, we find inequalities of wealth, authority and prestige. These translate directly into differences in food, shelter, physical security, health and education. Indirectly, they also translate into differences in mental health and happiness.

So it's better to be rich than poor, and some people are very rich indeed. In the entertainment industry (see Everyday Life on page 138), the richest stars earn a hundred times more in a year than you may earn in your entire lifetime. The figures for leading bankers and industrialists, though less public and sometimes less dramatic, are equally striking.

EVERYDAY LIFE

Thank Goodness for Inequality

Do you remember the functional theory of stratification we discussed a few pages back? It argued that inequality is necessary for society, since it ensures that the most able people are motivated to develop and use their talents to the utmost. Well, when Forbes Magazine *came out with its list of the 40 highest-paid entertainers (estimated gross income for 1995-1996), we saw this as a great opportunity to put functional theory to the test.*

- **Item: Highest-paid entertrainer is Oprah Winfrey ($171 million)**

  Now let's say that a really good brain surgeon makes $500,000 per year. Oprah seems to have the value of 342 brain surgeons. Problem is, we're not sure what she does for this amount of money. Write to us if you find out.

- **Item: The Beatles ($130 million) versus the Rolling Stones ($77 million) and the Eagles ($75 million)**

  The Beatles *were* a great group but they don't perform anymore — not surprising since John Lennon has been dead for more than a decade. So what makes the Beatles worth nearly twice as much as the Stones and the Eagles, who at least are still performing?

- **Item: Michael Crichton ($59 million), Stephen King ($56 million), John Grisham ($43 million) and Tom Clancy ($31 million)**

  Call us snobs, but where are the novelists — Margaret Atwood, Saul Bellow, Robertson Davies, Michael Ondaatje and so on — who win prizes for their writing? Aren't they providing more social value than Crichton and the others listed? If not, why the prizes?

- **Item: Men versus women**

  There are only four women (Oprah Winfrey, Roseanne, Mariah Carey and Sandra Bullock) on the list of the top forty earners, compared with thirty-six men. Are men really nine times more socially valuable, or more entertaining, than women?

- **Item: White versus non-white**

  Only four out of the forty, or 10 per cent — Oprah Winfrey, Michael Jackson, Bill Cosby and Denzel Washington — are non-white. This underrepresents African Americans and other visible minorities in the North American population. Is that because Caucasians are more socially valuable or more entertaining?

So you see, there are some problems with the functional theory of stratification.

Source: Based on data provided in *The Globe and Mail*, Mon., Sept. 19, 1996, p. C3

The entertainment, sports and crime industries are unusual in one respect: they are routes of significant upward mobility for a tiny number of lucky people, born without much money. For most other people, it takes money to make money. As we have already seen, better conditions and better opportunities for improving those conditions go together. People cannot have much chance to win the contest for what they want if they start out with little wealth, power and respect. This means a society cannot equalize the odds without greatly reducing the range of unequal starting points. Only if people were all born with the same social position, social connections and amount of money, would they all have an equal opportunity to improve their condition.

Social Status

There is no denying that income and material well-being are important aspects of inequality, but they are not everything. Status is a distinct aspect of the system of inequality and it is also very important to people.

Status is a measure of social worth or honour, and that makes it peculiar in several ways. First, status is relative: one person's worth or honour is always set by comparison with another person's. This makes status harder to measure than material wealth. As well, our desire for status has no limit. Wealthy people spend vast sums of money to gain higher status (for example, through charitable work or fund-raising for the arts). Second, status is symbolic. This means that status involves the unequal distribution of **symbolic** resources. Some of these resources, like cultural capital, allow people to acquire even more status. People often display their social status through what Thorstein Veblen called the conspicuous consumption of symbolic (and material) resources.

Our society has a multidimensional **stratification system** — a system of inequality that integrates income and status with other forms of differentiation, such as gender, race, ethnicity. That means people can, at the same time, occupy positions giving them different levels of social status. Often, one result is **status inconsistency**. For example, a person who is highly educated yet works in a low-paying job, belongs to a racial minority or has a criminal record, can expect to undergo status inconsistency. So can a self-educated stevedore who authors a best-selling book of social criticism.

However, major inconsistencies are rare and people tend to rank similarly on income, job prestige, authority at work and educational attainment. People who rank similarly on clusters of different dimensions are said to belong to the same social **stratum**. Within each stratum, people share similar life chances and outlooks on life. Across strata, we find striking differences in life chances and outlook.

Sociologists use the term **socio-economic status (or SES)** to refer to a social ranking which combines various types of scarce resource: particularly prestige and wealth. It takes into account a number of factors that govern a person's social status: income, type of occupation, level of education attained and place of residence, among others.

In North America, wealth, power, intelligence, athletic competence and physical attractiveness are all highly valued and all sources of prestige. **Prestige** is social honour. As such, it is a way of measuring social status and how much respect will be shown a person who has it. In our society, a person's job is that individual's main source of income, authority and prestige. Being the president of a large corporation is prestigious and provides a person with great authority. However, winning an Olympic gold medal is also prestigious, though not authoritative. So, both the president of a corporation and an Olympic athlete enjoy high status, though different amounts of authority.

Research has found that a good way to estimate one's SES is by measuring the person's **occupational prestige**. The most prestigious jobs are usually those which pay best and are filled by highly educated people. That's why we can predict how much prestige a person will receive from a job by knowing what the job usually pays and how much education it usually requires.

With few exceptions, occupational prestige rankings are very similar from one industrial society to another. The gaps in prestige between medical doctor, door-to-door salesperson, machinist and unskilled construction worker are similar whether we are considering Canada, Finland, Switzerland or the United States. What's more, with few exceptions, prestige rankings are similar in 1997 to what they were in 1977 and 1957.

Social Mobility

As we have seen, in the middle of the income hierarchy — among "middle-class" people — there is a great deal of upward and downward social mobility.

It is easier to move up the career ladder in some fields of work than in others.

Social mobility is the movement of people to and from different levels of the social hierarchy. Usually this mobility is measured in terms of occupational or socio-economic status.

Many sociologists study **vertical social mobility**, the change from one occupational status to another that is higher or lower in rank: from lawyer to bartender, or short-order cook to architect. Some movement is upward, to a higher stratum than the person (or person's parents) held before, and some is downward. Typically, sociologists will measure the relative amounts of upward and downward mobility.

When studying inequality, sociologists routinely find out what fraction of upward mobility is structural and what fraction is exchange mobility. Most upward mobility is **structural mobility** — a result of growth in the number of "good" jobs available in the economy. Only a small amount of upward mobility is **exchange mobility** — a result of some people vacating their social positions so that others can enter them.

Finally, social mobility may be intergenerational or intragenerational. **Intergenerational social mobility** is the change in a family's social (occupational or economic) condition over the course of generations. Usually, it is measured as the difference between a parent's SES and grown-up child's SES at the same age. By contrast, **intragenerational social mobility**, also called "career mobility," is the change in SES over the course of a person's lifetime. Concretely, we could measure John Smith, Jr.'s *intra*generational mobility by comparing his status at, say, age forty-five with his status at age twenty-five. We could measure his *inter*generational mobility by comparing John Jr.'s status at age forty-five with John Sr.'s status at age forty-five, when John Jr. was about fifteen — still a dependent member of the family.

As in the study of income mobility by Corak and Heisz, the most commonly studied patterns are of vertical intergenerational mobility among men. Doing such studies, researchers find similar patterns in all industrial societies. The amounts of mobility are remarkably similar. What determines the overall amount of social mobility is economic growth. During an economic recession almost no one gets ahead, regardless of education, hard work or good values. Since most upward mobility is structural mobility, when there is no economic growth no one gets ahead except through the deaths and retirements of people who are higher up.

Given the slowdown in economic growth and social mobility in the last quarter of the 20th century, it should come as no surprise that the system of inequality has changed too. And given the variety of viewpoints and paradigms in sociology, it is not surprising that sociologists disagree about the nature of these changes. One example is the debate about whether the middle class is disappearing. Given our current economic troubles, it is no wonder people fear the "death of the middle class" and a coming generation of children who are downwardly mobile, compared to their parents.

IS THE MIDDLE CLASS DISAPPEARING?

Debate over whether the middle class is disappearing is timely and important. Our difficulty in answering this question stems, in large part, from a lack of agreement about what counts as "the middle class." There are at least four competing definitions of "middle class": we shall call them the statistical, relational, cultural and institutional definitions.

People who use a *statistical* definition answer the question about the disappearance of the middle class by examining income distribution. By "middle class," these statistically minded analysts mean people whose incomes are near to the average: for example, people who earn between 50 per cent and 150 per cent of the average annual income. The question is, what percentage of people are in this "middle range" and is it declining? If many people are being driven downward into poverty, and a few are floating upward into wealth, the statistical middle-income group may indeed be disappearing.

Other analysts use a *relational* definition. They follow Karl Marx's notion of social classes, focusing on power and control, and search for signs of the disappearance of the middle class by examining the working conditions of the traditionally white-collar workers. In particular, they look for evidence of the "proletarianization" of clerical, service and professional workers, about which we will say more shortly.

The Class System Lives On

FAR AND AWAY

In Canada, attitudes towards social welfare are mixed. On the one hand, one finds greater acceptance of government intervention to solve social problems than in the United States. On the other hand, one finds more support for individual responsibility and a free market approach than in many European countries. Britain is caught between traditional beliefs in government assistance and more recent, conservative demands that public spending be cut, whatever the human cost.

The roots of reliance on government or figures of authority in Britain go back centuries. But for the bulk of the British public, they go back to the Second World War, when the Ministry of Information issued propaganda about a unified society shorn of its crippling class system.

National solidarity suited the war government's aims. Many of today's elderly people were in their formative years then, and they believed it. Such public largesse was the price the upper classes grudgingly paid for the support of the middle and lower classes during the war. But in the face of growing social spending and government debt, that feeling of obligation has evaporated.

While spending on the National Health Service continues to rise, hospitals are being closed and beds are disappearing because costs are increasing in other areas of the service. The government has cut back on pensions paid to the elderly, who currently receive about half of all social-security payments. And their numbers are swelling; the average life span in Britain is increasing by two years every decade.

Unlike many European countries, Britain does not legally oblige people to look after parents or siblings who cannot provide for themselves. And everyone has an enforceable entitlement to state benefits — what Canadians call welfare. "There's an assumption in Britain that at 65, suddenly people should be the responsibility of the [government] care services," says Wally Harbert, who works for the charity organization Help The Aged. "Since 1948 there's been no requirement for family to look after an older relative."

By comparison, Germans assume that the family is responsible. If one of the family is living on social assistance, the government can pressure family members for contributions. Canada is like Britain in having no statutory obligation for citizens to look after aging parents or siblings.

While critics in Britain say the current system is not sustainable, even the slightest cut by the government is greeted with hysteria by the working and lower-middle classes, who feel they have been betrayed. The public anger is fuelled by stories of growing social inequality in Britain, where massive wage increases have been given to the bosses of privatized gas, water and electrical utilities and a separate health-care system is emerging for those who can afford it.

In short, the class system that was supposed to have died in the war is still very much alive.

Source: Abridged from Madelaine Drohan, *The Globe and Mail*, Sat., March 25, 1995, p. D4

A third group of analysts use a *cultural* definition. To define the middle class, they build on Max Weber's research on the Protestant ethic and its contribution to capitalism's growth, focusing on distinctive class values. To determine whether the middle class is disappearing, they look for signs that the traditional Protestant ethic virtues are losing their hold — virtues including asceticism instead of hedonism; thrift; a tendency to plan for the future; and so on.

Others still use an *institutional* definition. They are concerned with the people who create and use institutions to maintain distinct class identities. Thus, they look for signs that middle-class people are becoming more or less separated, geographically and socially, from capitalists and working-class people than they once were.

The different definitions of "middle class" lead us to answer this question in slightly different ways.

Yes, It Is Disappearing

Some who say that the middle class is disappearing note a widening gap between the rich and poor in North America and, to a lesser extent, in Europe. The percentage of the population that earns between 50 per cent and 150 per cent of median income is decreasing. That is, a smaller percentage of people are "middle-income earners."

With downward pressure on their jobs and incomes, increasing numbers of middle-class Canadians are calling for assistance from public welfare agencies that were originally established to serve poor people. This decline in real wages and salaries, which brought about the shrinkage in the number of middle-class families, has only been partly offset by the contribution of working wives to family incomes.

Personal incomes have become more unequal in North America since the 1970s. Working-class incomes have stagnated while managerial-sector income — especially compensation for corporate executives — have risen. Data from the (American) Panel Study of Income Dynamics confirm that, between 1977 and 1987, the middle classes shrank in size, the income distribution became more skewed towards lower incomes and mobility out of the middle class was more likely to be downward than upward, so that the class system became more divergent, or unequal and polarized.

One common measure of income equality is the Gini Index, which ranges between zero (indicating total equality) and 1.0 (indicating total inequality). The United States has the highest Gini Index of all industrial countries, followed by Australia, New Zealand and Switzerland. (Japan, Sweden, Belgium and Holland, by contrast, have the least income inequality.) Canada is nearer the middle.

Evidence shows that the Gini Index for earned incomes in the United States has risen continuously since 1980 from about .38 to .42. This indicates that the middle class is, indeed, shrinking. Since the 1950s, there has been a shift in the kinds of occupations that are considered to be "middle class" and "working class," respectively. While the boundary was once easily drawn between manual and non-manual labor — the former being working-class and the latter middle-class — the distinction between the two classes has come to be based on additional features of work. These include income (both the amount and whether it is paid in wages or as salary), job security, opportunity for upward mobility and degree of autonomy given to do the job.

Jobs that are secure and well-paid, that provide a chance for upward mobility and allow people some freedom on the job are considered "middle-class" occupations. Jobs that score low on these criteria, even if they do not involve manual labour, have fallen into the "working-class" category. Examples include clerks, secretaries and day-care teachers.

Since the start of the 1980s, downward mobility has become a common experience for middle-class Canadians. Many have lost their jobs and have had trouble finding new ones. Along with this, many have lost their faith in the ideology that hard work is rewarded.

Some even claim that many professional jobs — for example, lawyers, pharmacists, architects, engineers and even doctors — have been "proletarianized." In general, the jobs have become less autonomous, secure or well-paid. Aspects of proletarianization for clerical labour include the actual removal of supervisory functions from a position, the loss of autonomy and "career prospects" and a decreased opportunity to play a part in decision-making.

Thus, by definition, some people who were once considered to be "middle-class" are now no longer so considered. There has been no trend in the opposite direction; that is, no occupations that used to be considered working-class have now been granted middle-class status. So it is safe to conclude, at least in terms of income and job ranking, that the middle class is smaller now than it was before.

One defining feature of the old middle class was that it differed culturally — in beliefs, values, attitudes and lifestyle — both from the rich and the poor. Not only were these middle-class values distinctive, they were also the dominant values in politics and the mass media. Middle-class culture was characterized by the belief that family life should hold a high priority. Other features included the so-called Protestant work ethic, respect for the law and for government and a strong belief in individualism as a philosophy of life. (There was also at least lip service paid to tolerance and respect for differences among people.)

The past two decades have witnessed a decline in general support for some, if not all, of these values. Widespread economic insecurity has made people less tolerant of others, particularly if these "others" are thought to pose a threat to their economic well-being. Family life is now an ideological battleground in which some forms — for example, poor lone-parent families — are singled out for criticism and close observation.

The visible decline in income equality discussed earlier is a result of corporate "downsizing," more unemployment and underemployment and downward social mobility for many middle-class people.

At the same time, there has been a gradual reduction in union memberships among blue-collar workers. This is due mainly to the migration of industrial jobs to low-wage, traditionally non-unionized areas of the United States and threats to move jobs offshore in case of difficulties with the

SOCIAL PROFILE 5.2

International Income Inequality* in Selected Countries, 1947–1992

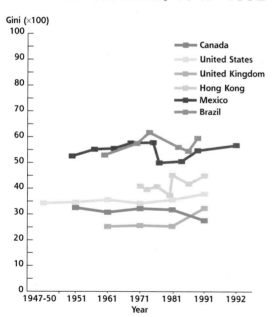

Gini (×100)

Legend:
- Canada
- United States
- United Kingdom
- Hong Kong
- Mexico
- Brazil

*As measured by the Gini Index of inequality. In this graph, 0 indicates perfect income equality (everyone gets the same amount of income) and 100 indicates perfect income inequality (one person gets all the country's income).

Source: Adapted from data provided in the Deininger-Squire data set, at Web site http://www.worldbank.org...dmg/grthweb/ddeisqu.htm. See the "high quality" sample, Klaus Deininger and Lyn Squire, "Measuring income inequality: A new database," The World Bank, Policy Research Department, June 1996.

local work force. White-collar jobs have also become more numerous. Customarily, these jobs have not been unionized and unionizing them has become more difficult than ever, given the economic recession.

Stagnant or falling wages, weaker middle-class prospects for upward mobility and weaker working-class unions have blurred the lines separating the two classes. It has also become harder for middle-class people to keep up other distinctions, like different neighbourhoods, clubs or schools for their children. Increasingly, the line between working-class and middle-class people has disappeared or at least been smudged.

From all four outlooks, then, we can argue that the middle class is disappearing. However, and as usual, there are arguments on the other side.

No, It Is Not Disappearing

Statistically speaking, the middle class is far from disappearing. Though the fraction has fallen, most Canadian households still earn between 50 per cent and 150 per cent of the average income. A bimodal income distribution is nowhere in sight and may never develop. Though there has been a small decline in wages since the early 1970s, the average worker is no worse off in terms of total pay per hours of work, nor has there been a large change in the distribution of earnings for the labour force as a whole.

People who say that the middle class is not disappearing point out that industrialized countries all over the world have entered the Information Age. This change has meant a huge job loss in the manufacturing sector. At the same time, there has been a big increase in the number of jobs that require technical knowledge. However, research also suggests more "bad" (i.e., service-sector) jobs are being created than "good" (i.e., technical-expert) jobs. There has also been a shift in the occupational structure, so that more people provide services, particularly professional and helping services. An increasingly large fraction of the work force is employed in white- rather than blue- or pink-collar work. This means that the middle class is swelling, not shrinking.

Indeed, Daniel Bell claims in his classic book *The Coming of Post-Industrial Society*, we have only begun to change the economy from one that is based on capital and labour to one based on expert knowledge and information technology. (Of course, expert knowledge and information technology would be seen by conflict theorists *as* capital.) Class categories which were developed to describe the old industrial order may no longer capture the new economic reality. In any event, by this account, the fortunes of highly educated "middle-class" people will improve, not worsen, with the shift Bell describes.

Some sociologists suggest, therefore, that the withering away of the middle class may not be a pressing problem. The distribution of income has not changed a great deal. Rather, the composition of the middle class has changed, with fewer opportunities for low-educated, low-skilled workers and greater stratification of the work force along educational lines. The condition of the core middle class continues to differ very clearly from that of the working class. A marginal middle class combines both working-class and middle-class features.

By some accounts, middle-class culture is not in decline: it is merely changing, due to socio-structural and economic changes. Millions of middle-class Canadians are still hardworking, ambitious, thrifty and tolerant. And individualism, though tempered by a greater awareness of society's role in shaping opportunities, is still alive and well. Nor has the work ethic been lost. Most middle-class people still believe that one must work hard to get ahead. Indeed, many sociologists voice a concern that individualism is excessive in North America. So long as individualism remains central to people's dreams, it is hard to claim that middle-class culture is truly dead.

We also find much evidence of middle-class culture as a lifestyle distinct from working-class culture. So, for example, travel is increasingly important to the new middle classes. Green or environmental politics are of great interest. So are natural fabrics: advertising campaigns to shift consumers away from polyesters were one process of gentrification marked by gentle class warfare and snobbery.

Historically, middle-class life has been characterized by distinctive approaches to work, consumption, residential location, voluntary associations and family organization. These have been aimed at distinguishing middle-class life and thought from that of the peasantry and working class. Central to middle-class culture is the emphasis its members put on achieving control in their own lives.

Even today, well-educated middle class (or professional) parents are more likely than working-class parents to expose their pre-schoolers to lessons and conversations, and to encourage early goals related to independence, self-control and environmental control. In fact, many sociologists have pointed out that the amount of education a young person gets is better predicted by his/her parents' own educational attainment and attitudes towards education than by the parents' income level. By contrast, nonprofessional parents place a higher value on good manners, obedience and getting along with other people.

These value differences are strong enough that they cut across ethnic identities, allowing us to see a vast structural similarity among persons in the middle class. Thus, class identities compete with ethnic and racial identities.

As the "new economy" (the globalization of jobs, more information-dependent technology, privatization of services, job insecurity, decline of unions, and so on) takes its toll on personal lives and class institutions, one thing continues to amaze us: the tenacity of optimism and faith in the future. Historically, the expansion of the middle class was closely linked to a growing economy and increasing equality of opportunity. The reversal of these conditions, evident from the 1970s, may undermine the well-being of the middle class and its notable tolerance and civility. For middle-class people, a sense of powerlessness produces opposition to economic redistribution. For working-class people, it produces support. As a result, powerlessness produces political polarization between social classes and support for different political parties.

Middle-class people have tried, despite adversity, to maintain a distance from the poor and from the working class. Note that it is precisely with the downward pressure on middle-class incomes and the blurring of actual differences between classes that we have seen a middle-class backlash against welfare recipients and other vulnerable, relatively powerless people.

Writing about middle-class opposition to labour legislation in 19th-century Europe, Abram Swaan called this phenomenon "downward jealousy." Those whose status is in the greatest danger — people who are downwardly mobile or already in the lower middle class — are ready to use any means to draw distinctive class lines. Though not benefitting financially by treating the people below them more harshly, these (marginal) superiors gain status by pushing others downward.

The welfare backlash shows that middle-class people are still acting as though they are different from working-class people (and from the poor). New institutional boundaries between the classes are also being established in the political arena, just as they still are in schools, clubs and neighbourhoods.

Summing Up the Debate

As we have seen, the answer to the question "Is the middle class disappearing?" is "no," regardless of how we define "middle class."

People who say that the middle class is disappearing point out that a smaller percentage of the population are "middle income earners," that fewer people fit the traditional middle-class label and that middle-class culture and values are not as prominent as they once were. Those who claim that the middle class is not disappearing note that while working-class jobs are being lost due to the automation and computerization of production and service delivery, the same forces are creating new middle-class jobs. They add that middle-class culture is not in decline: it has merely changed in character.

Our analysis suggests that (so far) the middle class is far from disappearing statistically, culturally, relationally or institutionally. Despite major economic changes, social institutions and major groupings (such as social classes) change very slowly indeed.

POVERTY

CBC 🔲
**"Davis Inlet:
Moving from Misery"**

Defining and Measuring Poverty

We now turn our attention to the poor. Everywhere, the recession has meant an increase in the numbers of working poor, unemployed poor, homeless people and beggars.

In studying the topic, sociologists distinguish between relative and absolute poverty. We speak of **absolute poverty** when people do not have enough of the basic necessities — food and shelter — for their physical survival. So, for example, in Meherchandi (Bangladesh), poor households spend 97 per cent of their income on food and shelter. Only 3 per cent is left to be spent on health, medicine, recreation and charity. These poor people are surviving, but barely. They are living in absolute poverty.

In contrast, researchers define **relative poverty** by reference to the general living standards of the society. Since not all societies or groups within a society are equally wealthy, what people consider "poor" varies too. In industrial societies, we consider people to be "poor" if they have much less than the average income. To measure this, statisticians have established a Low Income Cut-off (LICO) Point.

The LICO Point is the income level below which a person (or family) is judged to be living in poverty. Judgments of what constitutes "poverty" vary over time and from one region (or social group) to another. They also vary with family size and the size of the community in which a family lives. Larger families who live in larger communities require more income to live at the same level as smaller families in smaller communities. The guiding principle is that a low-income person or family spends more than 58 per cent of its income on food, shelter and clothing.

Some believe that the line ought to be set much higher, with the result that a great many more people are shown to be "in poverty." Such a finding would suggest government has mismanaged the economy. On the other side, government supporters argue in favour of lowering the poverty line, to suggest that there are fewer poor than we had believed. In the end, what we mean by "poverty" and how we choose to measure it is a result of our ideology and political agenda.

But, for now, we have no better measure of poverty than the LICO Point. At least this method allows us to compare groups within Canadian society and see which are doing worst.

Who Are the Poor?

In 1996, 5.2 million Canadians lived below the LICO poverty line. Health and Welfare Canada reports that among families, the incidence of low income is highest in families with three or more children, families headed by mothers

SOCIAL PROFILE 5.3

How Poor is Poor?

Based on a family of four living in a large city in 1995.

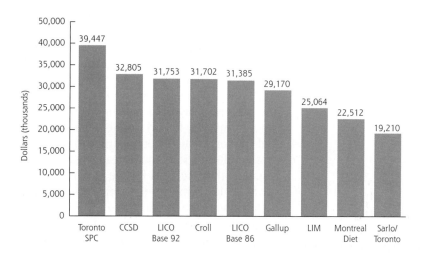

Toronto SPC, the description of the first bar of the above graph, refers to the budget guides of the Metropolitan Toronto Social Planning Council updated to the year 1995. *CCSD* refers to the Canadian Council on Social Development's income guidelines, which are based on one-half of average family income and do not vary from one area of the country to another. The LICO Base 92 and 86 bars are the Statistics Canada low-income cut-offs. The calculation for the bar labelled *Croll* uses the methodology first proposed in 1971 by a special Senate commit-tee on poverty headed by Senator David Croll. The *Gallup* bar is an update of responses to a public opinion poll that asked: "What is the minimum weekly amount of income required for a family of four, consisting of two adults and two children?" *LIM* means the low income mea-sures of Statistics Canada, an alternative measure based on one-half of median family income with no geographic variations. *Montreal Diet* refers to the income needed for a minimum ad-equate standard of living for a two-earner couple with a 15-year-old son and a 10-year-old daughter in Montreal as calculated by the Montreal Diet Dispensary. The group also has basic needs guidelines strictly intended for short-term assistance that are somewhat lower. *Sarlo Toronto* is the poverty line for Toronto calculated for 1994 by Christopher A. Sarlo and updated to 1995 by the National Council of Welfare. Professor Sarlo also has "social comfort lines" that are twice as high as his poverty lines.

Source: *Poverty Profile 1995*, A Report by the National Council of Welfare, Spring 1997

(usually, single parents) and among elderly widows. For example, nearly two-thirds of all families headed by single mothers had low incomes and this per-centage has increased since 1981. Indeed, families headed by lone female parents make up about one-third of all low-income families.

This growing problem is what people have called the "feminization of poverty." The incidence of low incomes among families headed by lone male parents is also growing. Yet it remains about half as high as for families headed by female lone parents. What's more, families headed by a lone parent are far more likely to have a female than a male family head. After divorce or separation, women usu-ally get custody of the children. So the female-headed family is likely to remain poor unless the state takes strong measures to change things.

Worst of all, in 1996 just under 1.5 million of the poor were children under the age of eighteen. Over one Canadian child in five lives in a low-income family — a fraction that has increased from just over one child in seven in 1981. Children living in single-parent families are at the highest risk of living in poverty, and many proposals have been made to remedy the situation. For example, there is a need to increase support from absent fathers, improve job training for single mothers and increase supports other than welfare (such as high-quality, low-cost day care).

Children are clearly not to blame for their poverty. So child poverty shows the general error in thinking that poor people have only themselves to blame. The poverty of children does not result from bad values or bad behaviour but from forces beyond their control. About 40 per cent of poor children live with a mother who is divorced, separated or single, for example. They suffer from their parents' inability to find work or stable partners and from the insufficiency of social supports which would permit their parents to work. It is a growing lack of steady full-time jobs and a steady decrease in transfer payments (like family assistance) that accounts for the growth in poverty.

Since 1981, the greatest increase in numbers of poor children has been among children with two parents (aged 25-44) at home. Their poverty problem is not due to marital breakdown. Like the female lone parents, these parents cannot find work or, if they work, they are not paid above the low-income level. A study by the Canadian Council on Social Development, released in 1997, reports that in 1994, 450,000 families were below the poverty line even though *one* adult in the family had worked the entire year. Another 100,000 families were poor even though *two* adults in the family had worked all year. The reason: many jobs pay wages which are too low to allow full-time workers to support their families adequately. Other families whose adult members were unemployed or unable to work were even worse off.

In many countries the homeless are another group making up a large fraction of the poor. Observers have suggested that homelessness is mainly the result of an inadequate housing supply which caused housing costs to skyrocket. By definition, if more good cheap housing were available, fewer people would end up homeless. Yet this misses the main issue, which is the gap between the cost of housing and the amount of income certain kinds of people can spend on housing.

In less economically developed nations, a scarcity of food complicates the homelessness problem. For example, in the poorer countries of Latin America live an estimated 25 million street children. Their lives are marked by violence, drug abuse and prostitution. In a few of these countries, measures are being taken to provide housing which draws on the resources of homeless people themselves.

Wealthier nations like Canada and Britain have developed complex social welfare systems, but many homeless people have trouble getting help from them. The United States does even worse, with mainly stopgap measures, such as emergency shelters, which are not intended to solve the problem. Comprehensive and, perhaps, long-term services will be needed to address the needs of the growing numbers of homeless poor.

Public Attitudes to Poverty

Public attitudes to inequality are mixed and confused, and so are public attitudes to poverty. People occasionally see themselves as victims of forces beyond their control. They are then willing to believe that poverty resulting from unemployment, old age or ill health deserves assistance. At other times people see themselves voluntaristically, as masters of their own fate. They then hold the poor responsible for their own poverty and feel that these people do not deserve public assistance.

The amount of assistance a province makes available to poor people varies with the perceived causes of poverty. The elderly and persons who are physically challenged receive the most help, since people tend to consider them the blameless "deserving poor." They often consider single mothers and chronically unemployed people the "undeserving poor." To some extent, their thinking operates on the sexist assumption that women are naturally responsible for children. As a result, these two groups receive less generous and secure assistance. Social assistance payments to this latter group fail to meet actual living expenses, especially for people who live in large cities like Toronto and Vancouver, where rents are high.

People in countries with undeveloped social security systems have even greater problems. In India, for example, there are estimated to be over one million beggars in the major cities. Large-scale migration from the countryside to the city and a lack of social security for people who cannot find work once they reach the city contribute to the prevalence of urban poverty.

In Canada, there are fewer beggars and the problems of poverty, unemployment and worker training are more manageable. Yet many believe that, if social assistance payments exceeded the minimum wage level, unemployed people would be reluctant to get off welfare and take a job, though hundreds of thousands cannot find a job. Throughout the 1990s, the unemployment rate has hovered around 10 per cent. In some regions and for some groups the rate has been much higher. Certain groups, such as female lone parents of small children, cannot afford to pay the day-care costs that would allow them to take a job. Others, such as persons who are physically challenged, cannot find a job that fits their abilities.

Poverty and Health

There is a reluctance among middle-class Canadians to pay taxes that — redistributed in the form of welfare or family assistance — will benefit the poor. And increasingly, there is a reluctance to pay for good-quality universal health care. These two issues are related in several ways. First, both universal health care and welfare are costly social institutions. Second, low-income people have both the greatest need for welfare and the worst health.

Research in Canada and elsewhere shows that the poor health of poor people is due to a number of factors that include higher levels of stress and anxiety, worse working conditions, worse food and housing, higher rates of accidents at work and exposure to physical violence in their community. When health care is privatized, as it is in the United States, the poor get less of it. Even when health care is public, poor communities typically have fewer services available than wealthier communities. There is some evidence that professionals take the health-care needs of the poor less seriously than the needs of middle-class and wealthy patients. Finally, the poor are less able to take time off work to visit a doctor or recover from illness.

As a result, poverty is generally correlated with higher risks of poor health. The sociological problem lies in explaining precisely why poor people have worse health. One explanation is that ill health among the poor is due to unemployment. Research by Brenner (1984) suggests that unemployment causes a wide range of social and personal pathologies. For example, Brenner estimates that a 10 per cent increase in the unemployment rate — for example, from 10 per cent to 11 per cent — directly increases the rates of homicide by 2 per cent, of arrests

Health Problems of the Homeless

APPLIED SOCIOLOGY

Applied research, at its simplest, means describing social problems in ways that point to a need for social change through legislation, improved services or grass-roots social organization. Testimony at the Toronto Coalition Against Homelessness inquiry provided this list of common physical and mental illnesses of homeless people. What course of action does it suggest to you?

A. *Common physical problems:*
   Head injuries from falls and assaults
   Headaches
   Second-degree sunburn from May to September
   Hypothermia and frostbite from November to March
Extensive dental problems
Pneumonia
Tuberculosis (an estimated 40 per cent)
Liver disease
General and local blood poisoning
Kidney and heart disease
Diabetes and cancer (significantly higher than in the general population)
Pre-natal complications
Foot infections (e.g., skin ulcers, circulation problems)
Malnutrition
Lice

B. *Common psycho-social problems:*
Sexual assault
Clinical depression (an estimated 50 per cent)
Anomie (i.e., lacking accepted standards of social behaviour)
Schizophrenia
Extreme sleep deprivation
Suicide (10 per cent have attempted it, 25 per cent considered it)
Drug and alcohol abuse (an estimated 33 per cent)

Source: Adapted from a report in *The Globe and Mail*, June 1, 1996, p. D2

and psychiatric admission (each) by 4 per cent, and of incarcerations of young men by 6 per cent. It also increases the suicide rate of young men by nearly 1 per cent, the overall mortality rate by more than 1 per cent and deaths due to cardiovascular disorders (strokes, heart attacks) by nearly 2 per cent.

This suggests that unemployment causes both poverty and ill health. Poverty only appears to cause ill health and it is really unemployment that is to blame. These figures tell us that, if a society does not invest money in jobs for the poor it will have to invest money in more jails and more health care. However, the effect of unemployment is not the whole story.

Unemployment aside, inequality itself may cause ill health — a conclusion suggested by British research on the experiences of 10,000 employed civil servants. In Britain, as elsewhere, life expectancy varies directly with socio-economic status: the higher your status in the social order, the longer you can expect to live. And British data going back as far as 1911 show that there has been *no change* in this correlation, despite improvements in public health, medical care, drugs and treatments and repeated efforts to equalize people's life chances.

To study the persistent correlation between status and health, British researchers carried out a longitudinal study of 10,000 British civil servants, to measure ten-year rates of survival for men aged 40-60 at the start of the study. At the end of the decade, they found that the chance of surviving was highly correlated with rank in the civil service. Indeed, mortality rates in the ten-year period were 3.5 times higher among men in the (low) clerical and manual grades than among men in (high) senior administration positions.

This study shows that differences in survival rates are not always due to unemployment (since everyone in the study was employed, at least until retirement), nor to absolute poverty (since none was absolutely poor). Nor were the differences due to variations in smoking or lifestyle (e.g., cholesterol or blood pressure levels), since the differences in survival rates persisted even when smoking and lifestyle were controlled.

The study concludes that there is indeed a health gradient by socio-economic position. There is something about inequality that makes people sick (if they are low-ranking) or well (if they are high-ranking). However, there is no obvious connection between rank and risks of death from one particular cause. The researchers believe that diseases are merely "pathways" to death, not causes of death *per se*. The real cause of death may, instead, be inequality. Future research will find out why; perhaps it will show that inequality affects the immune system which, in turn, makes people more or less susceptible to a wide range of death-causing diseases.

Thus, inequality is a matter of life and death. The question is, what can you do about it?

SOLVING THE INEQUALITY PROBLEM

As we have seen, rich people are likely to inherit wealth, poor people are likely to inherit poverty and middle-class people can go either way. If you are not rich and are worried about your own prospects, what can you do to minimize the disadvantages associated with inequality?

In short, there are two options. One is to seek personal solutions by which you can improve your own position in an unequal structure of life chances. The other is to seek collective solutions; that is, to improve the position of the group to which you belong, or strive to decrease inequality for everyone. We shall consider each of these options in turn.

Personal Solutions

Among the more popular solutions are getting a higher education. Status attainment research has shown that a father's socio-economic status (or SES) — more than any other single factor — influences the amount of education a person gets. In turn, a person's education — more than any other single factor — influences adult SES. Most important, if we control for the amount of education a person gets, a person's class of origin (father's SES) has no effect on a person's class of destination (that individual's own SES in adulthood). Said another way, two people with the same amount of education can be expected to attain the same socio-economic status, regardless of the class into which they were born.

For people at the top and bottom of the stratification system, class and SES coincide, and people's statuses—income, occupation, education, place and residence— are fairly consistent.

What this tells us is that at the top and bottom of society's stratification system, incomes and educations are inherited. There, educational inequality legitimates income inequality. Poor people get little education, largely because they are poor. Because they get little education, they earn little income and they are blamed for getting too little education, an instance of what social researcher William Ryan calls "blaming the victim." Rich people get much more education and inherit much more income. Their high incomes are justified by high levels of education.

In the middle ranks of society, higher education reduces the disadvantages of birth. Many middle-income Canadians get a great deal of education, and equalized education tends to equalize incomes. Thus, within the middle 80 per cent of Canadian society — people who are neither desperately poor nor fabulously rich — the most mobile are those people who are well-educated. Despite unequal opportunities, most people fight to "get ahead." They consider upward social mobility to be a realistic goal and devote much of their time and energy to improving their position in the social hierarchy. It is this ideal that has kept enrolments at colleges and universities increasing while the actual number of traditionally school-aged persons in the population pool has declined.

Repeated studies of social mobility in Canada have confirmed the results obtained elsewhere. They show that formal education is the single most important factor in overcoming the disadvantages of birth into a lower class position. Even in a country as culturally different from Canada as Chile, education is the most important means of upward social mobility. As in Canada, in Chile a large part of the population (just under half) is upwardly mobile, thanks to education and a growth in jobs due to industrialization. The better education a person obtains, the more likely that person is to get ahead (given the existence of new jobs which industrialization has made available).

The "status attainment" studies show that people with equal amounts of formal education tend to get jobs of roughly equal prestige, whatever their class of origin. This is because the best-paying, most prestigious and secure jobs require education. Higher education provides skills and credentials for obtaining a good job, and also cultural capital which is useful in advancing a career.

Given the importance of higher education, the most upwardly mobile Canadian is likely to be a professionally educated male born into a middle-class family. The least upwardly mobile person is likely to have a high-school education or less. That person will live in a small town or city where educational and job opportunities are limited. (We shall discuss women's mobility, and the mobility of ethnic and racial minorities, in later chapters.) Note, however, that there is still evidence of gender and race discrimination. This means that the investment in education pays off best for white males.

Even so, the investment in higher education doesn't work as well to solve a person's inequality problem in a stagnant economy, or when higher education is common. The reason is that most social mobility is structural, not exchange mobility. Positions of wealth and power are rarely vacated by the rich. For most people, mobility is produced by economic growth, but economic growth is flagging.

Moreover, the mobility value of education depends on scarcity. Educational "credentials" are mainly useful because they provide employers with the ability to distinguish among candidates for a job. But when the economy is stagnant and higher education is common, higher (rarer) degrees are needed to impress a job recruiter, schools and universities inflate grades in order to pacify students and their parents, employers come to doubt the information value of credentials and every degree declines in value.

EVERYDAY LIFE

Get Your Very Own Welfare Mom

Often we can see (and expose) the nastier bits of a social policy if, using sociological imagination, we think them through to their real-life logical conclusion. That's what University of Toronto psychologist Jonathan Freedman has done to Ontario Premier Mike Harris's "common sense revolution" in this letter from an imaginary friend.

A lot of us in town are really looking forward to the Ontario tax cuts. [But] I have been a little concerned about how [people on welfare] may react to the tax cuts right after their own incomes have been cut. I am also concerned about the notion of workfare. My friends and I are worried that the government will have to spend a lot of money and hire lots of people just to find jobs for all those on welfare, and we just hate more government bureaucracy.

I think I've found a solution to both these problems. We should institute a kind of buddy system that matches welfare cuts with tax cuts.

Here's how it would work. I figure my tax is going to be cut about $300 a month and a single mother on welfare has had payments cut by almost the same amount. Once the tax cuts start, instead of the welfare mother's cheques being reduced, she would get the same amount as usual, but every month she'd send the $300 directly to me. That should make her feel much more a part of the system; no faceless bureaucrat is taking the money from her, she is sending it out herself to a real person. It should also make her feel closer to me and people like me.

When this scheme really clicks, I expect "the buddies" to exchange cards or notes. So my welfare mother might send me a note saying how she and her three-year-old daughter are doing, with maybe a picture of her daughter enjoying her plain noodle dinner. And I sure would send her back a card thanking her for the cheque, along with a picture of the family around the pool sitting on our new lawn furniture. I don't really expect the buddies to send notes or pictures every month, but I hope she'll send them pretty often.

But that's only the beginning. The true beauty of the scheme is how it deals with workfare. [U]nder the buddy system, the welfare mothers simply go over to their buddies' place to do their work. My buddy could mow my lawn, mend my socks, do some house-cleaning and laundry, take out the garbage, pick up my shirts and provide other kinds of personal services. There would be no end of work, and I'd be real happy to pay her something under minimum wage.

It would be perfect. I'd save a lot of money because I wouldn't have to pay the outrageous wages that regular cleaners and gardeners charge, and I could get some services that are hard to find right now. She would have all the work she can handle and the government wouldn't have to worry one bit about finding her work. The only problem might be if she didn't want to do the work or didn't do it well, but I think we could deal with that. After all, she has to do it or she loses her welfare.

It's a good deal all round; I sure hope the Harris government goes for it.

Source: Abridged from Jonathan Freedman, in the *The Globe and Mail*, Thurs., Dec. 7, 1995, p. A25

Given these facts, what should you do to improve your position? Well, you can accept your fate and try to find happiness within the existing structure of inequality. As Everyday Life above suggests, the middle class and wealthy among us can all "adopt" unemployed people, producing personalized versions of workfare for the poor.

Or, you can get as much education as possible, fight against mark inflation and the devaluation of degrees, and find other ways to distinguish yourself (for example, develop social or cultural skills). And you can support government efforts to increase economic growth — but no one seems to know quite how to accomplish this. Alternately, you can turn your attention from personal solutions to inequality and pursue collective solutions instead.

Collective Solutions

Collective solutions to the problem of inequality aim to improve your group's position in the stratification system and/or reduce overall inequality in society.

Strategies for doing this include: (1) mobilization — for example, union formation, native community development and women's movement formation; (2) demanding new laws — for example, better income redistribution programs, anti-discrimination and affirmative action laws; and (3) social disruption — for example, strikes and even rebellions.

These strategies work. It is clear that income inequality and poverty decrease when there is more income redistribution and more unionization of workers. (We know this by comparing societies with higher and lower levels of income redistribution and unionization.) It is also clear that members of ethnic minorities do better economically if they mobilize as groups and do not assimilate culturally. Finally, the available evidence shows that women and racial minorities have done much better economically and socially since they started to mobilize as groups in the 1960s.

For these collective strategies to work, it is necessary for people to understand that their own best interests are tied to the interests of others. They must also come to see that they are not to blame for their poverty or low status in society. Finally, they must come to realize that conflict over scarce economic resources is both normal and necessary.

Since personal solutions don't work well to solve the inequality problem, why don't people use collective solutions more often? Marx identified the reasons for this more than a century ago when he counselled the English working class on ways to improve their situation. First, collective protest is opposed by powerful people who stand to lose their wealth and power if the stratification system is reorganized. We can look to public ideology and the media to see the controlling class's defence system against class action.

Second, protest is often opposed by powerless people who fear they will lose what little they have. (This accounts for much of the opposition by white working-class men to efforts to improve the status of women and visible minorities).

Third, there is often inaction by powerless people who stand to gain from protest. Part of this is due to a lack of resources and skills needed for organizing. Beyond that, some of the powerless are victims of *false consciousness* — a failure to perceive the true nature of their interests — largely because they have adopted the dominant ideology's view that "losers" deserve to lose and "winners" deserve to win. Related to this, many powerless people suffer from low self-esteem and a sense that they cannot control or even influence the way their society works. Finally and ultimately, many lack an awareness of their shared interest — what Marx called a **class consciousness**. This means that they lack a group identity, and without this identity they cannot form a cohesive group.

What if these problems were overcome and there was more collective organization against inequality? Sociological research suggests the result would be an increase in conflict; therefore, a new basis for social order would be needed. There might also be an extreme backlash by the powerful and the fearful powerless, raising the risk of oppressive political changes, even fascism. The best possible result would be a reduction in social inequality and a different organization of inequality. However, there is no evidence to suggest that all inequality or all conflict could ever be eliminated, once and for all.

In the end, collective solutions are a more effective way of dealing with inequality than are personal solutions. However, they are hard, slow and imperfect ways of dealing with the problem. They are never final and never accepted by everyone. And, in the context of a global economy, it will be increasingly necessary to carry out collective actions on an international scale. This too is something Marx foresaw more than a century ago.

So long as we understand the difficulties involved and do not give up the effort after failing to achieve a classless society, collective solutions will bring about change in the system of inequality.

CLOSING REMARKS

The sociological study of class and status offers another good example of the connection between macro and micro outlooks. On the one hand, a class and status (or stratification) system is a macro-phenomenon. Especially for the poor and powerless, it is a world they never made or agreed to, something outside and "above" their control. In this sense, stratification, like culture, is all-encompassing and slow-changing, like a huge glacier. By means of laws, dominant ideologies and property rights, stratification systems outlast individuals and even generations of individuals. They press down on the poor and powerless, depriving them of a sense of worth and dignity.

On the other hand, social stratification, like every other element of culture, is a human product. We are all changing or reproducing stratification every day. Practices of social inequality change over time because dozens, then thousands, then millions of us change our ways of doing things. In the most dramatic cases, change occurs by means of a revolution — the overthrow of one stratification system and its replacement with another. In less dramatic cases, change occurs through social mobility, protest and legislative reform.

We began this chapter by noting that although inequality is a fact of life for all of us, few Canadians are in the habit of thinking much about it. Most just assume that some people are better off financially because they work harder, plan better and stay out of trouble. Poor people, they assume, do the opposite and that's why they're poor. The idea that there is a "stratification system" — a set of impersonal forces beyond our immediate control that shape our life chances — is foreign to most Canadians.

But, however unfamiliar, this idea is basic to understanding Canadian society and the way our own lives fit into the society. Most sociologists would see our place in the stratification system as the most crucial component in our life chances. And as we have seen, the stratification system is much influenced by the economic order, which we discuss in greater detail in the next chapter.

Review Questions

1. What is meant by social inequality?
2. In what ways is social inequality social in origin?
3. Define "domination" and "submission."
4. What are some of the symbols of domination we are likely to see in everyday life?
5. How do functionalists explain social inequality?
6. What is the role of class in Marx's theory of stratification?
7. What factors did Weber consider important in understanding inequality?
8. How have Marx's and Weber's theories been combined by more recent sociologists?
9. What issues have feminists raised about the relationship between gender and inequality?
10. What issues have interactionists addressed in looking at inequality?

11. How do equality of condition and equality of opportunity differ?

12. What is social mobility and what factors lead to upward social mobility?

13. What is the difference between absolute poverty and relative poverty?

14. Who tends to be poor in Canadian society?

Discussion Questions

1. Research shows that people who are physically attractive enjoy better opportunities than people who are less physically attractive. Why is that? Is this a "social inequality," as we have defined the term?

2. Who has control over *your* access to the necessities of life — your food, shelter and clothing? Who has control over that person's access? Are you in the same relation to the means of production as the person who controls your access to necessities?

3. How might one argue that the failure to eliminate inequality in the former Soviet Union does *not* prove Marx's theory wrong? Make the strongest case you can for that view. Then consider what evidence would be needed to prove Marx's theory wrong.

4. Are the connections between Canada's ruling class and foreign ruling classes likely to become stronger or weaker in the next fifty years? What influences are likely to strengthen or weaken these connections?

5. Is there anything you can do to reduce the risk you will fall into poverty? If so, will you blame yourself if you fall into poverty nonetheless? Which poor people do you *not* blame for their poverty?

Suggested Readings

Curtis, J., E. Grabb and N. Guppy, eds. (1993) *Social Inequality in Canada: Patterns, Problems and Policies*, second edition. Scarborough: Prentice Hall Canada. Contains a series of articles that show how patterns of social inequality are rooted in ideological supports (including the law) and that changes in an egalitarian direction have usually required political struggles between have-nots and haves.

Lewis, O. (1961) *The Children of Sanchez: Autobiography of a Mexican Family*. New York: Vintage. A poignant story of a poor Mexican family, told in the family members' own words. This book illustrates the experience of a culture of poverty.

Marchak, P. M. (1988) *Ideological Perspectives on Canada*, third edition. Toronto: McGraw-Hill Ryerson. Provides discussions of various ideologies in Canada, and their interpretations of relations to elites, class protests and nationalism.

Palmer, B. D. (1993) *Working Class Experience: Rethinking the History of Canadian Labour, 1800-1991*. Toronto: McClelland and Stewart. A historical survey of the way class relations developed in Canada over nearly two centuries. It emphasizes working-class culture and class struggle as the best way into understanding the history of relations between labour and capital.

Rossi, P. H. (1989) *Down and Out in America: The Origins of Homelessness*. Chicago: University of Chicago Press. A penetrating analysis of why, in North America, homelessness and extreme economic hardship increased markedly in the last decade. The author puts forward policy suggestions based on the analysis.

Tepperman, L. and J. Curtis, eds. (1994) *Haves and Have-Nots: International Readings on Social Inequality*. Englewood Cliffs, NJ: Prentice Hall. A selection of edited readings from around the world that focuses on class, ethnic, racial and gender-based inequalities. Of particular interest are the different ways people resist and protest against their conditions.

Internet Resources

The following Web sites are good places to find more information about topics discussed in this chapter:

Community Action on Poverty (CAP) is maintained by an anti-poverty coalition in Winnipeg, Manitoba. It provides statistics on poverty, poor-bashing and the efforts being made to fight poverty.
http://www.freenet.mb.ca/capov

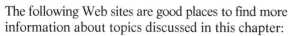

Winnipeg Harvest provides information about the history and programs of this community-based food bank, facts about poverty and links to other anti-poverty organizations.
http://www.Xpressnet.com/harvest/

The Web Spinner's Index to Canadian Equality-Seeking Groups on the Web offers links to various equity groups.
http://fox.nstn.ca/ ~ nstn1439/eq-main.html

The Canadian Council on Social Development contains statistics and information on historical poverty lines, poverty rates, income, welfare and more.
http://www.ccsd.ca/facts.html#

Karl Marx, etc. provides access to a variety of sites having to do with Marx, Marxism and the movements Marx's theories provoked.
http://www.socioweb.com/ ~ markbl/allstuds.html

Myths on Homelessness provides information about homelessness and the homeless in Canada, with links to other related Web sites.
http://totem.sd7.bc.ca/Homelessness/Myths.html

Global Stratification and Conflict provides data and related links on the topics of global inequality and conflict.
http://www.sscf.icsb.edu/soc/honors,strat/GlobalConflict.html

WORK AND THE WORKPLACE

CHAPTER OUTLINE

As our economy has changed over the last two hundred years, so has our social life.

THE ECONOMIC ORDER

We all know something about work, whether from first-hand experience or the accounts of others. Young people work at going to school, then most move on to work at a job or career. Some people work in the home, keeping house or caring for children; normally, they get no pay for doing this. Others work at home and earn an income by selling a good or service outside the home. Most of us work in large organizations — in factories or offices — to earn a living. Working together in large numbers, we create goods and services, earn a wage for ourselves and produce a profit for the company.

The daily work routine is so common that people who break the pattern seem abnormal. No wonder so many unemployed and retired people feel like outsiders to the "real" business of society. For the same reason, many people have trouble relaxing at night, on the weekend or holidays. For some, stress and sleep disorders have become a constant problem. For many full-time homemakers, the problem is boredom and a sense of worthlessness; many look to alcohol or anti-depressants for solace. In short, as work has become more and more central to our society, it has also become a main source of stress in our lives.

Of course, some conflict theorists would argue that members of one particular class do not, and do not need to, work. The bourgeoisie, owning the means of production and hence the labour power (and desire) of the proletariat, do not work, experience no ill effects themselves from not working, and indeed compel others to work. Other theorists, working from Max Weber, like Hannah Arendt, suggest that the ethic and spirit of making and doing are basic to the human condition.

In the previous chapter we noted the importance of the economic order and its impact on the life chances of Canadians. But most of us think of the economic order in terms of a job. It is in the realm of work that we can easily see the choices and chances the economic order provides. For most, work life, like family life, is a social context where macrosociological processes meet microsociological experiences.

It is at work that we experience control or freedom from control, social integration or isolation. We form unions or associations to look after our interests; in this way we develop a sense of ourselves as workers, managers or employers. In the end, our job identity is a key part of our social selves.

The Four Major Paradigms

Because work is so central to our daily lives, all of the major sociological paradigms have a great deal to say about it. Yet, as usual, they focus on different issues and study them in different ways.

The functionalists, for example, follow Durkheim's lead and focus on specialization, industrialization and the division of labour. They ask such questions as, Are all industrial societies alike, and if so *how* are they alike? Do all societies become the same when they industrialize? If so, why? And, what are the human costs of too-rapid change? of over-specialization? of unregulated industrial conflict? For that matter, what is the right balance between too many and too few economic rules? How do new technologies change the way work (and social life more generally) are organized? Finally, is it possible to increase the efficiency of work without over-regulating the economy?

For their part, conflict theorists focus on inequality and power. Work efficiency, for example, is seen as an interest of managers, not workers; or of managers in a radically different way from workers. Below we discuss the view of the workplace as a "contested terrain" where managers struggle to find better ways of controlling workers and workers struggle to find better ways of resisting control.

Symbolic interactionists focus on interpersonal processes in and around the job site. These processes include workplace socialization, professionalization, the content of workplace subcultures and the ways people negotiate order at work. Given the conflict of interests between workers and managers, how, they ask, does the work actually get done? As well, how do men and women get along at work? or whites and visible minorities? part-time and full-time workers? and so on.

Finally, feminist sociologists advance our understanding of job "ghettos" such as the "pink-collar" world of female office workers. As well, they turn our thoughts to the (gender-based) differences between primary and secondary labour markets. They raise questions about job equity and different jobs of "comparable worth." And they study the reasons women with children are likely to take part-time work rather than full-time work, or choose jobs rather than careers.

Types of Work and Workplaces

Whether they gather in offices, stores, workshops, supermarkets or factories, everyone discussed in this chapter has one thing in common: they do work.

By "work," we don't just mean "paid jobs." School work is as much work as the part-time job many students take to cover their expenses. And don't forget housework — the most common work in our society. But not all kinds of work are treated the same. So, for example, most people ignore housework when they speak of work: they focus mainly on membership in the labour force. The *labour force* includes all the people over the age of fifteen who work for pay, and people who do not now work for pay but who want to and are looking for paid work.

Payment does not prove the social value of work done, only the ability of the worker to turn effort into money. And even *within* the paid labour force, workers vary in this ability. The same effort spent in one part of the economy or labour market will bring far more money than it will in another. Similarly, the same educational degrees will earn twice as much in one part of the economy as they will in another. Consider, for example, twenty hours of a young person's time spent either (a) working for $6 an hour at Wal-Mart, or (b) writing an essay the professor gives a D-.

People compete for their jobs in a *labour market*. There is not one big labour market in which every person who is willing to work competes for the same jobs. On the contrary, there are *many* labour markets and segments within each of these.

According to the so-called "dual labour market" model, national labour markets contain two (or more) subdivisions: a primary and secondary labour market. These subdivide by geography: by region, province and size of community.

The **primary labour market** consists of jobs which offer good wages, chances to get ahead and job security: jobs like lawyer, plumber, teacher. The **secondary (or marginal) labour market** consists of jobs that pay low wages, offer little chance to get ahead and promise little job security: jobs like taxi driver, secretary, bank teller.

People with different social traits, backgrounds and skills can be found in different markets. For example, there are far more women and visible minorities in the secondary labour market, and far more white men in the primary labour market than could have occurred by chance.

The big difference between primary and secondary markets tends to blur important differences among jobs in the *same* market. For example, though both are in the primary labour market, few teachers feel they have the sort of benefits and opportunities that doctors do. And, though both are in the secondary labour market, few bank tellers would consider their work to be the same as that of taxi drivers. Still, the difference between primary and secondary markets gives us a crude indicator of the differences in life chances that they afford.

Another major aspect of any job is the sort of organization in which a person works. As we have seen, managers organize work in different ways, depending on the work being done and current theories about the best way to manage (or control) workers. As a result, schools are different from automobile factories in the ways they organize work. And school work is organized differently today from the way it was organized fifty years ago.

Organizations also contain different labour market segments. Some jobs are well-paying and secure, while others are not. As we see from the data in Applied Sociology, below, different educations lead to different kinds of jobs, with very different incomes. The chance to move across segments within the organization is rare, if possible at all. The promotion from secretary to manager in a business is just as rare as a promotion from private to lieutenant in the military, or nurse to doctor in a hospital.

What we have to say about work in this chapter is not about all kinds of work in all kinds of societies. In fact, it is about some kinds of paid work in one particular kind of society: namely, a corporate capitalist industrial society. So, much of what we will have to say about work will be in the context of discussing what we mean by "corporate capitalism" and "industrial society."

Corporate Capitalism

Corporate capitalism is an economic system in which the key players are corporate groups and their directors. In terms of people's beliefs, it is a form of economic organization that enshrines the profit motive and the ideal of free competition motivated by personal gain. Corporate capitalism not only permits greed, it encourages it. A capitalist culture sees the acquisition of wealth as a central goal

What Is a University Degree Worth?

The following illustrates a very simple calculation that reveals what many of us already know and all of us suspect: namely, that education makes a huge difference in the current economy.

Recently, the consulting firm KPMG surveyed more than 300 employers in Canada to find out what they typically paid new employees — graduates of the class of 1996 — with different levels of educational attainment and no relevant experience.

The pay schedule is as follows: $40,000 for the possessor of a Master of Business Administration degree; $38,400 for a master of arts or sciences; $36,900 for the possessor of a bachelor's degree in engineering; $31,600 for the possessor of a bachelor's degree in any other field; $29,400 for the graduate of a community college or technical institute program; and $23,100 for

a high-school graduate. Presumably, new hires without a high-school diploma will earn less than that.

Doing a bit of arithmetic tells us that investing an extra five years in education after high school to get an MBA degree almost doubles your starting salary. Though now shown in these statistics, such an investment will more than double your lifetime earnings: the average MA holder's income will rise faster, for a longer time, to a higher peak than will the average high-school graduate's income.

In case you think this is a fluke, the KPMG survey also found that starting salaries for the highly educated, and differences in income from the less educated, were expected to increase from their 1995 levels. MBAs showed the biggest increase, with expected starting salaries jumping 11 per cent to $40,000 from $36,500. Graduates with any other master's degree jumped 5 per cent. But graduates of a community college or high school aren't so lucky: their average wage was not expected to change.

Source: Adapted from *The Globe and Mail*, Tues., March 5, 1996, and from KPMG *1996/7 Pay Adjustment Report*

---

of life. Newspapers, magazines, television and the other media glorify people who have achieved this goal.

Some people in our society make huge fortunes by helping the economy grow; for example, by inventing new technologies that produce goods more cheaply, or by finding new markets overseas. However, most fortunes are made at other people's expense; for example, through currency or stock-market gambling, which adds nothing whatever to the output of the economy.

Another important feature of corporate capitalism is the spread of monopolies and oligopolies. When one company controls a hundred per cent of the market, it holds a **monopoly**. And when a company holds a monopoly, the consumer has no choice but to buy its product at the asking price, or do without. Those who control monopolies wield a vast amount of control over people who need their goods or services. So, the state tries to limit monopolies in the interests of consumers.

In an *oligopoly*, which is far more common, a few large firms control an entire industry. We find oligopolies in banking, insurance, the oil industry and (until recently) the auto industry. Oligopolies are common in all industries where competitors have each invested a large amount of money.

In principle, there could be lively competition among these firms. In practice, there isn't. Ask yourself when a North American automobile company or cable company willingly offered consumers something new or better at a lower price? On the contrary, there is often *price-fixing* — an illegal activity that the state rarely prosecutes. Canada has laws aimed at limiting monopolies and oligopolies. Yet monopolies and oligopolies remain; for example, in the mass media where a few companies control a majority of newspapers, television and radio stations, and therefore, the intelligence and representation of life made available to an enormous audience.

As you can see, there are serious problems with liberal ideology — in particular, the belief that people can protect their own interests with no one else needed to act on their behalf. Even during the heyday of 19th-century capitalism, governments regularly protected the interests of business and inherited wealth, not those of workers and consumers (Polanyi, 1944). Eventually, governments came to realize that other interests also needed protecting. Widespread poverty threatened the social order; it was a problem which called for more complete "poor laws" and, eventually, current welfare laws.

Poor laws provided for public relief and support of the poor. Up through the first decades of the 20th century, they were the only public income assistance available to poor people. But because poor laws typically required a proof of poverty (what we would call a "means test"), they degraded people receiving the assistance, and required them to live and work in harsh conditions.

During the worldwide Depression of the 1930s, states learned to intervene more usefully. British economist John Maynard Keynes argued that capitalism could not survive without more and better state involvement in the economy. Government needed to "prime the pumps" and stabilize earning, spending and saving.

Today, all industrial economies operate through an extremely complex mechanism of laws and assistance to both business and private citizens. Almost no sphere of life goes unregulated.

Some would say that the type of businesses and societies that exist today are too different from those to which the 19th-century term "capitalism" referred to still be called capitalist. In his writings Marx describes the form of capitalism common during the mid 19th century. Then, an individual entrepreneur typically ran his business himself and made all of the decisions affecting it. But in the past century, the economic order has evolved into corporate capitalism. Under corporate capitalism, individuals have influence only as officers in the corporate bodies to which they belong, especially as directors of the business. As we shall see, there are also large differences among capitalist societies and large similarities among industrial societies which may or may not be "capitalist" in the traditional sense. For this reason, many sociologists believe that our society is now better described as an industrial society.

INDUSTRIAL SOCIETY

The term **industrial society** refers not only to a society in which industrial (or mass) production prevails, but to a whole packet of associated features we consider basic to contemporary life. In the shift to an industrial society:

- subsistence farming disappears;

- the number of people in farming declines;

- people produce for exchange with others, not for their own consumption;

- workers begin to produce goods in large factories;

- large machines increasingly assist production;

- jobs and workers become highly specialized;

- the number of wage-labourers increases;

- more people come to live in large cities;

- more people learn how to read and write;

- scientific research changes industrial production; and

- people become more concerned with efficiency.

In these respects, societies as different as Canada and China, Russia and Argentina, are all industrial societies. Whatever the political system or economic ideology, industrialization leads a society to develop the above features. Sociologists have spent a lot of time identifying these features of industrial society. The factors which lead societies to industrialize are so many and complex that we can only discuss three main ones here:

Human Capital

One key feature of industrial society is a concern with improving human capital. Human capital theorists show that people's general well-being improves through better health, education, welfare and public security associated with industrialization. After all, they argue, people are key to creating wealth in an industrial order. Money invested in human well-being (that is, in human capital) is money invested in future economic growth.

Problems related to developing human capital are described in Far and Away, below, where the problems of patriarchy and poor cultural capital are compounded by a caste system.

Investment in human capital is expensive and slow in bringing expected payoffs. As well, such investment changes many parts of the economy and society in unexpected ways. One such change is the effect on class structure and the class struggle. Generally, an investment in human capital unsettles the population and mobilizes protest.

Class Structure

We have already noted one way that the rise of an industrial society changes class relations: the "cash" relations replace customary feudal ties of mutual oblig-

For Canada, geographically vast as it is, railroad construction was a central part of industrialization and the creation of a market economy.

FAR AND AWAY

The Girls of Tamil Nadu

In Canada, most girls of 14 spend most of the day in school. There, they study, socialize, fool around and generally take their time developing mentally and physically. But in many parts of the world, children of this age and even younger are not so lucky. Child labour — especially by girls (whose schooling is considered a low priority) — is common; it is also dangerous and harsh. While this pattern may make sense to impoverished parents, in the long run it hurts their daughters and the future prospects of their society.

Six mornings a week, Panjankani walks down the road from her family's one-room house, her two sisters beside her, three brothers behind. It might seem like a normal start to a school day, until the boys veer down one path to Mamsapuram's school and the girls follow another trail to a nearby matchstick factory.

For the next 12 hours, Panjankani and her younger sisters sit on dank, concrete floors in a room heaving with toxic fumes, shuffling matches into a mound of matchboxes before them. They work so quickly that often the matches ignite. "I don't know how many times I've been burned," Panjankani, 14, says, opening palms scarred by four years of match-factory work. "When it happens, I cry, but my mothers scolds me and says, 'You must keep working.'" All this, for just 15 rupees (65 cents) a day. On these drought-stricken plains of Tamil Nadu in Southern India, close to 100,000 children — three-quarters of them girls — go to work every morning in match factories, fireworks plants, rock quarries, tobacco mills, repair shops and tea houses. Together, they make up the single biggest concentration of child labour in the world.

In an age when child labour has disappeared from much of the world, it continues to be rampant in South Asia. The Operations Research Group, a respected Indian organization, has pegged the number of full-time child workers at 44 million in India, with perhaps 10 million more toiling in neighbouring Pakistan, Bangladesh, Nepal and Sri Lanka — a total almost equal to the population of Britain.

But this isn't just child labour. It is predominantly girl labour: Extensive research shows that two of three child workers in the subcontinent are female. A government survey of Tamil Nadu's main districts published this year found 70 per cent of boys attend school while 80 per cent of girls work full-time. "The problem of child labour is also a manifestation of the problem of the girl child," the report concluded.

Most important of all [to eradicate child labour] is education, compulsory if need be. "The theory that it is the poorest of the poor who cannot afford to send their children to school and that until poverty is eliminated, there is nothing educationists can do, is unfounded," concludes a recent Unicef study of Tamil Nadu.

[However] the roots of child labour appear to spread far deeper and wider through the soil of Indian society. By many counts, three-quarters of the children at work in the Sivakasi matchstick bet are from landless backward castes. "If the adults got higher wages, then they would not bring their children to work," says R. Vidyasagar, a child-labour researcher at the Madras Institute of Development Studies.

Source: Abridged from John Stackhouse, "The girls of Tamil Nadu," *The Globe and Mail*, Sat. Nov. 20, 1993, pp. D1, D3

ation. New social classes, especially the bourgeoisie and proletariat, emerge as a result.

But the class structure changes in other ways, too. For example, industrialization pushes and pulls the rural peasantry into cities and factories. Change of the peasantry to a wage-earning proletariat can be gradual. More and more peasants are forced off the land and into wage labour as land holdings become larger and privatized, producing cash crops rather than subsistence crops. Many of these peasants work part-time on the land and part-time in factories.

However, some believe this changeover from peasant to part-time worker may not be entirely desirable. The interests of a permanent working class are different from those of part-timers who return to the farm as soon as job opportunities worsen in the cities. Back-and-forth movement weakens the proletariat.

Another condition affecting class structure is the evenness of economic growth. Under conditions of *un*even growth, industrialism produces a multilayered working class, in which the layers have different problems and conflicting interests. This too fragments the working class, making it less able to oppose policies which work to its disadvantage.

Convergence

The contrasts between Canada and India, Brazil or Nigeria point up differences between industrial societies (as a group) and nonindustrial or developing societies. Generally, industrial societies have: (1) a secular culture focused on efficiency, consumerism and a high standard of living; (2) a highly developed state which provides health, education and welfare benefits to its citizens; and (3) a class structure dominated (numerically) by the urban, middle class.

As a result, there are important similarities between industrial societies like Canada and Japan which, a century ago, had almost nothing in common. The growing similarity of industrial societies around the world has produced what sociologists call the *convergence thesis*. Supporters of this thesis argue that as societies industrialize, their social patterns converge or become more similar, despite differences that existed before.

The convergence thesis is an important part of the theory of industrial society. It rests on the idea that industrialization gives rise to changes — like mass literacy, a nuclear family and respect for the rule of law — that are linked to economic life. The linkages are easy to understand. For example, as people become literate, they become better informed, more politically active and more eager to demand political liberties. The result is participatory democracy.

Another common feature of this convergence is the growth of a political rights-seeking middle class which manages large businesses. One emerged in Korea in the 1980s and another in Thailand in the 1990s. Similar changes seem to occur in *every* industrial society, though not always in the same sequence.

What is remarkable about convergence is the certainty of the process. The convergence thesis plays down capitalism as a crucial feature of economic life and puts industrial society in its place. It argues that what is important in world history is industrialism, not capitalism. With exceptions, non-Western experience has provided much support for the convergence thesis. Developing societies differ mainly in whether they merge selected "modern" ideas with their existing culture, as Japan has done, or rearrange their cultures around these ideas, as Singapore has done. However they do it, industrialization everywhere has certain key features. But it is not clear whether industrial societies converge because they must satisfy the same societal needs (e.g., for literacy) or because social practices spread from richer to poorer societies. There is evidence to support both views.

Cultural Factors

In Chapter 2, on culture, we discussed Max Weber's theory of the Protestant ethic and its role in the rise of capitalism. Much research has been done to test and extend Weber's insight that culture influences economic growth, taking into account local differences in cultural tradition.

Consider the difficulty in applying Western ideas of scientific management, productivity and discipline in a Chinese silk factory, for example. Because of China's traditional culture, industrialization will not follow the European model exactly, nor does it need to. But one cannot ignore the importance of cultural factors in helping or hindering economic growth. Or, take the importance a cul-

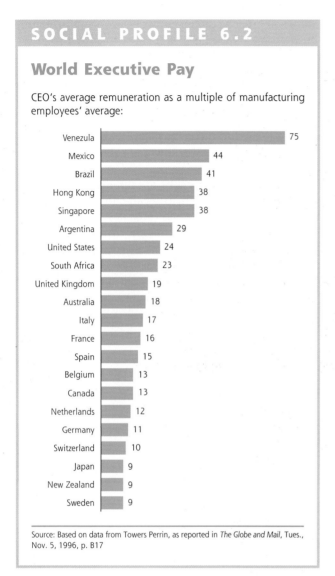

Source: Based on data from Towers Perrin, as reported in *The Globe and Mail*, Tues., Nov. 5, 1996, p. B17

authority (the boss, the master plumbers and the apprentice plumbers) and a span of control of three (that is, each superior controls three subordinates). Joe controls twelve workers, and the chain of command is clear: Joe commands the master plumbers, who command the apprentice plumbers.

The path of information flow is also clear. Joe receives reports from only three employees: his master plumbers. This limits confusion and gives Joe time to find new customers and think about "company policy." In turn, each master plumber receives reports from only three employees: his or her apprentice plumbers. This limits confusion and gives the masters time to deal with customers and supervise the apprentices' work. (The apprentices do most of the work, and don't have time for anything else.)

Even in such a small organization with thirteen members, there are seventy-eight possible dyadic (or pair-wise) communication paths. But with a clear chain of command and reporting, only a few paths are used formally. And, the maximum communication distance from the bottom of the hierarchy (an apprentice plumber) to the top (Joe) is two links — the number of levels in the organization, minus one.

Now let's apply the same logic to a larger organization with a similar "tree-shaped" communication structure. Imagine the Wooten Motor Car Company, with a span of control of six (not three) workers and nine (not three) organizational levels from top to bottom.

Do the calculations and you will learn that the CEO of this company, Elsie Wooten, has, roughly, two million employees. With *only* nine levels of organization and *only* six subordinates reporting to each superior, Ms. Wooten commands a work force the size of, say, Philadelphia. Yet Ms. Wooten receives reports from only six subordinates, leaving her free to pursue new business and lunch with important people.

The maximum distance from Ms. Wooten to her lowest-level worker — the front-line of the operation — is only eight links. This means that if a problem arises on the factory floor, there will be no more than eight telephone calls before Ms. Wooten hears about it. Some might say that's seven phone calls too many. On the other hand, only eight calls is not bad. In the Wooten Motor Car Company, the number of *possible* dyadic communications is 2×10^{12} or two thousand billion — a number that is unfamiliarly, unimaginably large.

The point is that a "tall" (many-level) bureaucracy, with a clear chain of command and information flow, effectively controls vast numbers of workers and conveys vast amounts of information upward and downward. For its size, no other kind of organization has yet shown it can do better.

WORK SATISFACTION AND ALIENATION

Sociologists who follow Marx's approach see current work problems as mainly a result of capitalism. These problems would disappear, or at least improve greatly, they say, if socialist economic organization replaced capitalism. Those who follow Durkheim's approach see problems as primarily the result of over-specialized labour, large organizations and rapid change. And those who follow Weber's approach see problems to be the result of rationalization and too-rigid bureaucratization.

These different outlooks are related to different theories about work satisfaction and alienation: why many people hate working and some people love it.

Work Satisfaction: Its Causes and Effects

Many jobs are mindless and boring, yet evidence shows that most North Americans *say* they like their jobs. Four in five workers are satisfied to some degree, and one in three describe themselves as "completely satisfied." Three in four people even say they enjoy their work.

Yet we have good reason to doubt these findings. Most married people *say* they are satisfied with their marriage, yet roughly four in ten will divorce at least once during their lives. When asked their opinions in surveys, people put a pleasant face on unpleasant situations. Moreover, there is widespread evidence of dissatisfaction with work. This evidence includes high rates of absenteeism, indifference to what happens at work, the attitude that life begins when work ends, industrial sab-

EVERYDAY LIFE

Hard Times Cause Stress and Depression

Canadians are suffering disturbingly high levels of stress and depression because of employment and financial pressures associated with the decline in the economy. Almost half of the 1,500 respondents surveyed on the topic said they feel "really stressed" anywhere from a few times a week to all the time, while one-third said they're "really depressed" at least once a month. And why do they feel this way? Fifty-eight per cent cited problems related to work and money.

The survey shows that people who make up the backbone of the economy — those between 25 and 54 — are experiencing the highest levels of stress, while young people are most prone to outright depression. About 40 per cent of respondents between 18 and 24 reported feeling "really depressed" once a month or more.

The survey also found marked differences based on income. While 48 per cent of people earning less than $30,000 a year reported frequent depression, a mere 18 per cent of those earning more than $100,000 feel the same. On the other hand, stress was a problem for 66 per cent in the high-income

bracket, compared with 45 per cent of the low-income group. Men and women reported almost identical levels of both depression and stress, the results show.

Dr. Gosselin, one of the researchers, said, "Left unchecked, stress and mild depression can escalate into more serious or chronic conditions. Our immunological system goes down the drain." Illnesses such as heart disease, high blood pressure and cancer have been strongly linked to stress. "We estimate that about 50 per cent of depression goes untreated," he said. "The cost to society for lost productivity and ill health is staggering."

Depression afflicts about 675,000 workers in Canada. The Canadian Mental Health Association says a person with depression will exhibit any number of the following changes: irritability or hostility, withdrawal from or extreme dependence on others, hopelessness or despair, slowness of speech, chronic fatigue, or alcohol or drug abuse. In the workplace, look for the following signs of depression: difficulty making decisions, decreased productivity, inability to concentrate, less dependable, unusual increase in errors, accident prone, lateness, increased sick days, lack of enthusiasm for work.

Source: Adapted from *The Globe and Mail*, Thurs., May 9, 1996, p. B14; and from Joan Breckenridge, "Canada suffering bad case of blues," *The Globe and Mail*, Thurs., Oct. 1, 1992, pp. A1, A10

otage and attempts by workers to increase their control over the production process through strikes and working to rule.

What causes people to be satisfied or dissatisfied with their job? Most research into causes of job satisfaction has focused on objective job characteristics. Generally, job satisfaction results when work "is varied, allows autonomy, is not physically fatiguing . . . is mentally challenging . . . allows the individual to experience success, and . . . is personally interesting" (Locke, 1976: 1342).

The social acceptability of a job also makes a difference. Consider the problem that arose among caretakers at an urban university when they were forced to change from the night shift to the day shift. This change put them in contact with the building's higher-status daytime occupants, creating problems in status management. You see, "clean work" done at one time of day (e.g., at night, in isolation) becomes "dirty work" when done at another time. When they looked at themselves through the eyes of professors and students (their new reference group), the caretakers became less satisfied with their job.

So, objective job characteristics are not the only things that matter. Even satisfaction with rewards depends on "the fairness or equity with which [rewards] are administered and the degree to which they are congruent with the individual's personal aspirations" (Locke, *op cit.*). Along similar lines, the more central a task is to the organization's normative and technical structure, the more highly workers will rate its intrinsic value. Said another way, people like to do something important.

Occasionally, people can learn to accept work conditions they don't like and adapt to the frustrations of their job. People are *often* able to commit to, and identify with, new job demands. So, for example, the factory worker promoted to supervisor gradually learns (and tries to adopt) the viewpoint of management. The young academic leaves behind the viewpoint of student for that of teacher. In these and other cases, people learn to change their goals, standards and behaviour.

However, human adaptability has its limits. The high rates of turnover and absenteeism even among well-paid automobile workers make that point. Feelings of work dissatisfaction run deep and their causes are complicated.

The Problem of Alienation

Marx thought dissatisfaction reflected a problem of unequal social relations in a capitalist society. At the core of his theory is the concept of **alienation**. As Marx describes it, alienation has both objective and subjective sides, because work has a great importance in our lives. Marx viewed work as the most important means we have to express and develop ourselves. It is an activity in which people can express their uniquely human qualities. Both objective and subjective consequences follow from this.

The objective side of alienation has several aspects:

- an estrangement of workers from the product of their labour — the inability of the worker to buy what one makes;

- a lack of control by workers over the labour process itself — the inability to make things in a comfortable, sensible way;

- separation of workers from their own humanity — the sense of being treated only as an employee, not as a person; and

- the distancing of workers from each other — the sense of being alone in one's employee status.

These aspects of alienation are "objective" in the sense that they are inevitable consequences of social organization (and, in Marxist theory, inevitable consequences of capitalism). They are real, not imaginary, troubles, rooted in real relations of power and production. As you can see, they include subjective aspects, but they are centred on the objective problem of workers being distanced from their own labour sufficiently that the wage paid is far too little to make up for what is lost.

"Subjective" alienation varies from one person to another. In that respect, alienation looks more like a personal trouble than a public issue. In Canada today, some workers experience alienation in the form of stress, while others experience depression. Stress, often indicated by a feeling that one is late or short of time, suggests an absence of control over the work process. Depression — seen by many as anger turned inward or converted into hopelessness — also suggests a lack of control over the work process, and a feeling of being trapped. Both stress and depression are common among Canadian workers.

Cures for Alienation

We get nowhere treating the symptoms of alienation if we leave the causes unchanged. The only way of curing the illness is by abolishing the causes of powerlessness, meaninglessness and estrangement. This means giving people power, meaning and social contact. At the very least it means giving people a chance, at work and elsewhere, to express their creative selves and make the workplace truly human. Researchers have come up with various ideas for doing this.

One idea involves the re-skilling of workers. Many industries show evidence of Braverman's "de-skilling" due to technological innovation, as we noted earlier. However, research also shows that in some countries, de-skilling tendencies have been short-lived and rare. In Germany, for example, employers have pushed for re-skilling that is based on trust and responsible autonomy in the workplace. National programs of vocational education are shaping and redesigning Germany's work culture. There and elsewhere, the Quality of Working Life approach to industrial organization has pushed for job enrichment, enlargement and rotation. In this way, not only do workers attain more useful and usable skills, they also feel more involved in their work and in the workplace.

Throughout the developed world, businesses have become places of learning as well as of production, providing an urgently needed supply of new skills. New skills are a precondition for economic success, but in order to ensure that workers learn new skills, management and unions must cooperate. The production of the will toward re-skilling among workers will need union approval. But management will have to pay for it as a new component of workers' activity. In the end, it is an interplay of managerial goals and established shop-floor subcultures that decides the balance of new skill levels. All de-skilling or re-skilling depends on the struggle for control in that "contested terrain," the workplace.

WORK AND THE NEW TECHNOLOGY

Computerization and Knowledge Work

No one can doubt that we live in a period of constant and sweeping changes in the nature of work. Some of these changes are a result of the tools we use, some are a result of the purposes for which we use them. More and more often, people are doing work that requires the acquisition and use of knowledge. Thus it is that people's relative abilities to learn — to acquire and use information and modes of thought — is itself a form of social capital affecting job success.

Knowledge is central to the professions. Professionals gain their status and autonomy through a knowledge of and control over techniques and information. The physician, for example, has the knowledge to diagnose and deal with illness. More generally, we find that collecting, interpreting and controlling information are crucial features of the way we organize work in our society.

Think about the high-tech industries: they include software producers (who make video games for Nintendo or data analysis packages for IBM), database producers (who create mailing lists for advertisers, check your credit for banks, or keep up-to-date information on stock-market listings) and hardware producers (who create computerized weaponry for the armed forces). All of these jobs manipulate and apply information.

In the fast-changing, high-technology industries, "There is less formality and fewer layers of bureaucracy; financial risks are more often shared with employees" (von Glinow, 1988). That is because of the uncertainty in these industries. Causes of uncertainty include a dependence on outside capital, young and inexperienced managers, foreign marketing and competition, a short product life and the frequent introduction of innovations. To survive this uncertainty, high-technology industries spend a large part of their earnings on research and development. They value knowledge even when the immediate practical benefits are not readily apparent.

In industrial society, knowledge constantly alters what we do and how we do it. As a result, we find ourselves undergoing dramatic changes in the work we do over our lifetimes. Some of us will find that our jobs disappear as new tools or skills take over. Secretaries, for example, found in the early 1980s that word processors were replacing typewriters. To keep their jobs, they had to learn how to use the new machines. Yet, by the late 1980s, computers had almost completely replaced word processors, requiring yet more training and the gaining of new skills. Today, a secretary's desk will contain drawers filled with software guides, a booklet on how to fix the photocopier and a manual on how to use the fax machine.

Computers also decrease the need for secretaries because they can store "boilerplate" — phrases which appear repeatedly in a variety of documents. Now, for example, a lawyer can use a computer to generate a will or a contract — which consists largely of boilerplate — and simply add whatever specific information is needed. Other computer systems can obey spoken commands. Once these systems are perfected, they will further reduce the need for secretaries.

For similar reasons, computers have rendered the work of many supervisors and middle managers redundant. Computers can easily monitor the work of employees. If necessary, they could provide a single manager with easy-to-understand statistics on even hundreds of workers.

Technology in the Workplace

Having said that, the effects of technological change largely depend on the social context within which a change takes place. As a result, it is impossible to make general rules about the effects of technological change.

SOCIAL PROFILE 6.3

Canada's Labour Force Participation Declines in the 1990s

Percentage of participation in the labour force

Source: *Canada Year Book* 1997 © Minister of Industry, 1996, p. 188

The effect of technological change at a high-technology firm is different for managers and computer professionals, than for computer operators and secretaries. Generally, people higher up in the organization experience more positive effects, and fewer negative effects, than people lower down. Computer operators, specialty professionals and secretaries report being the most controlled by the work process; they are right to expect the fewest chances of advancement.

Everywhere, social factors influence the pace and outcome of technological change. Technology is not class-neutral. In the end, new technologies embody the dreams and plans of the industrially powerful. However, these industrialists have to manipulate actual work practices within particular industrial settings. Technologies are never the deciding factors in the way in which work is organized; they are only tools that can be used in different ways and for different purposes, depending on who is controlling them.

So, whether a technology will improve or worsen work depends on the organizational milieu in which people use the technology and the economic climate surrounding the organization. The social and economic effects of computer-based technology, for example, are *not* determined by the technology itself. All the actors involved have a say, according to their relative power. Culture also plays a part, forcing organizations to adapt technologies to local uses, instead of directly copying other organizations.

Stock markets around the world, for example, have quickly adopted similar computerized techniques of collecting, storing and analyzing financial data. The result is that capital circulates at increasing speed, while labour remains trapped within national borders. What this shows is not the awesome importance of technology so much as the awesome importance of *power* wielded by capital. Conflict theory would show that computing and other technologies are themselves capital or at the service of a dominating class to control and exploit the labour of workers. And this, of course, brings us back to Marx.

The Future of Work

No crystal ball is needed to foresee the continued southward migration of Canadian jobs. This is especially true of manufacturing jobs, although service jobs — record keeping, computer programming and telephone services, for example — can also migrate. Already, thousands of jobs have migrated due to economic globalization and the lowering of trade barriers.

As workers, we all want well-paying jobs. As consumers, we all want cheap products. Asked to choose between a car made by well-paid workers in Canada and an equally good, cheaper car made by poorly paid workers in, say, Korea, most people choose the latter. As the Korean firm sells Canadians more of its cars, it hires more Korean workers. As the Canadian firm sells fewer cars, it lays off Canadian workers. The result is a booming economy in Korea and a slump in industrial Canada.

The governments of high-wage countries like the United States have tried various strategies to reverse this trend: among others, threatening countries (like Japan) which enjoy a huge export surplus, insisting on favoured access to foreign markets or slapping tariffs on the exports of trading partners like Canada. In the long run, none of these strategies works. Wealthy investors don't want them to work. They want the freedom to invest their capital wherever it can earn the biggest profit. Trade barriers and trade wars interrupt the flow of capital and profit-making by wealthy investors.

For these reasons, lower-paid foreign workers will continue to take manufacturing jobs away from Canadians. The only way to reverse that trend is for

Canadians to lower their standard of living and settle for the same wages paid in Korea, Mexico and Poland, for example. But such a process would require the wholesale redefinition of a value system that teaches us that it's great to get rich.

Machines have been taking people's jobs since the Industrial Revolution began, more than two centuries ago. That's the whole point of machines: to do a job more quickly, cheaply and uniformly than people can. And on balance, the mechanization of work has helped humanity. Today, we live better materially than even the richest people lived three centuries ago. Generally, our work is also safer, cleaner, quicker and (often) more interesting than it was in the past. Machines have done away with a lot of drudgery.

The displacement of people by machines has not pleased everyone, however. In England, the Luddites began attacking machines almost as soon as machines made an appearance, for Luddites saw what was in store. They were ridiculed for their short-sightedness. It was clear to consumers, if not to Luddites, that mechanization was a good thing. Many people also felt that machines could go only so far. They would take away the horrible jobs and leave the interesting ones for people to do. Worklife would improve as a result.

Many people still think so today. However, increasingly, computers are taking even white-collar jobs. With the refinement of "expert systems," machines will also take professional jobs, like diagnosing illness, giving legal advice or drafting plans for an office building. Children can already get some of their education at home, studying from a compact-disc library or interacting with a mechanized "teacher" over the Internet. This sounds exciting if you are a consumer, but menacing if you are a job-holder or job-seeker.

In this way, entire professions are reduced to semi-professions and para-professions, or eliminated altogether. Already we see a surplus of engineers, architects, teachers, nurses, pharmacists, lawyers, managers, even doctors. Where these professionals are still employed, many are underemployed — working below their level of skill and training. "Proletarianization" has greatly reduced the status, salary, autonomy and security of what used to be "good" jobs. And our social value system, embodied in our media, begins to back away from the public admonition to get rich, replacing it with advertisement for brute power, pleasure, escape. If getting rich can be shown publically to be *not* for everyone, there will be less anomie, less strain, even if more resentment and opposition, from workers whose income is drained away.

Machines and global competition will not take all the jobs. Some — like haircutting — still need to be done here, where the customer is. Other jobs, at present, are too complex to be mechanized. For example, programming a computer to provide toddlers with day care would be absurdly expensive; hiring live caregivers is much cheaper.

The competition for jobs that remain will intensify, for there will be more people seeking fewer jobs. The "information economy" will also provide new kinds of jobs, eventually even the job of programming a machine that cuts hair (to replace barbers) or plays with infants (to replace caregivers). However, most displaced workers will lack the education and skills needed to do these new jobs. An unemployed barber knows a lot about cutting hair, for example, but doesn't know how to program a machine to do it.

To judge from recent events, the shortage of skilled people will coincide with a large number of unemployed, underskilled people; a migration of skilled people to North America or skilled jobs overseas; and the creation of machines to do human work. In the end, it may be a machine, not an ex-barber or human pro-

SOCIAL PROFILE 6.4

Fewer of Us Are Part of the Work Force

Labour force participation rates show young people are the main cause of the decline.

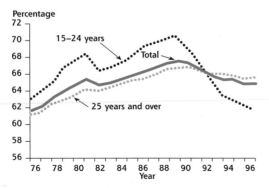

More of Us Are Working Part-Time

Part-time work as a per cent of all jobs.

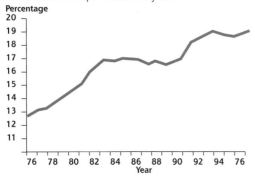

More Part-Timers Are Unhappy

Those wanting but unable to find full-time jobs, as a per cent of all part-timers.

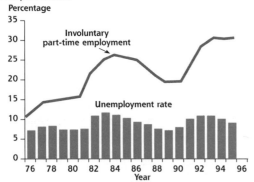

Source: (Top and middle) Adapted from Statistics Canada, "Historical Labour Force Statistics," Catalogue No. 71-201, 1996, pp. 1–7; (bottom) adapted from Statistics Canada, "Perspectives on Labour and Income," Catalogue No. 75-001, Autumn 1994, p. 28

grammer, that figures out how to program a machine to cut hair. Or how to compose a sociology book to discuss all of this.

In a future with few jobs to do, more people will rely on welfare or a guaranteed annual wage. And given the popular view of welfare, discussed in the last chapter, more of us are likely to be poor. The "underclass" will grow, further increasing the gap between the unemployed poor and the employed well-to-do.

Under these conditions, would the economy collapse through overproduction? If there were lots of products to buy but no one to buy them, the economic system would crash. In the event of an economic disaster, we would see the behaviour associated with demoralization: more addiction, violence and crime, among other things. We would also see more behaviour associated with rapidly rising unemployment: escapes into fantasy, political extremism, religious fanaticism, hatred of foreigners and racism. All this happened in the 1920s and 1930s: we know how the story turns out. Right-wing political movements like Nazism flourish.

A bleak picture, yes. But not everyone imagines the future in this way. There are at least two reasons why people will still have jobs in the future. First, people will want to avert the disaster associated with a large-scale loss of work. Second, work has always changed, so it will continue to change.

Without a reorganization of work, capitalism will collapse. No one — especially capitalists — wants this to happen. Governments will collapse too. No one — especially politicians — wants this to happen. And without reorganization, society will collapse. No one — not even the consumers of cheap goods and services — wants this to happen. No one wants an upsurge of fanaticism and racism, crime and poverty. When it is clear that these are on the way, people will take ameliorative steps. The reason for thinking so is that education and work organization have always changed to meet new needs and dangers.

Just over a century ago, most Canadians farmed. With the rise of manufacturing, farmers' children became blue-collar workers. With the rise of clerical and managerial work, blue-collar children became white-collar workers. And with the rise of employment in the public sector — in

Mechanization and specialization were both central to the development of industrial society. But is it any wonder that many workers felt endangered— at the mercy of their machines?

government, teaching, social services, policing and the like — white-collar children entered public service.

Each shift was wrenching, at the time. But in retrospect, each seems perfectly natural, almost inevitable. We cannot easily see ahead to the next major shift. But we can assume that, as in the past, the children of today's workers will flow into new kinds of work as new opportunities open up.

Expected Changes in Work

Over the past century people have reduced the fraction of their lives they spend at paid work. Today, people get more education, enter paid work later and retire from work earlier than their great-grandparents did. The average workday is only seven or eight hours, the work week only five days.

It takes little effort to imagine the coming of a four-, five- or six-hour workday, a three- or four-day work week and a work life that is only thirty, instead of forty or fifty, years long, as it was in the past. Or, it may turn out, as many are discovering today, that we have to work longer and harder when we are working at all.

One way to solve the shortage of jobs is to share them. Sharing fits in well with people's competing obligations: with needs for more schooling, job training and childcare, among others. People with the most family obligations have led the way in job-sharing and (accordingly) income-sharing. Parents of young children have been the most likely to take part-time work for part-pay, sometimes willingly and sometimes not so willingly. (Critics say this is just another way of exploiting a powerless group.)

What began as exceptions — part-time work and work-sharing — are gradually becoming more common. The same can be said of increasing numbers of people who piece together a living from a combination of part-time jobs.

Public-sector work expanded rapidly in the 20th century, in response to the Great Depression and Second World War. People needed jobs and the state supplied them, at least to certain varieties of people. For example, better public services — roads, sewers, teachers, social workers, police and so on — were needed and large numbers of workers were hired to provide them.

The concept of public service will expand in the foreseeable future. In the past, many community services were provided informally or voluntarily. Homemakers were particularly active in this way. They provided attention, care and assistance to the neediest and most vulnerable community members: the old, the young, the infirm, the newcomers. However, as large numbers of women have entered paid work, less community work has been done voluntarily. Critics fear the loss of community spirit and communal association.

To fix that, the state will have to pay people for community work which, in the past, they did voluntarily. Unlikely as it may seem, the state will do so because the work is important and it is not being done. So, for example, people will be paid to tutor school dropouts, take meals to shut-ins, help organize community activities and welcome immigrants who don't speak English.

The state will pay an annual income for this "nonprofit" work, expanding the nonprofit sector. Doing so will prepare us to replace welfare (or workfare) with a guaranteed annual income for everyone.

Recession Creates a Lost Generation

EVERYDAY LIFE

The first and continuing victims of the revolution in work have been those with the weakest foothold in the economy — people who hold secondary labour-market jobs or entry-level jobs in the primary-labour market. Typically, that means less educated people, immigrants, minorities and the subject of this excerpt: young people. Some fear that the recession which has marred their transition from school to work may have done permanent damage.

The recession has had such a disastrous effect on the job prospects of young Canadians that it may actually have created a lost generation. Unprecedented numbers of young Canadians have been wrestled out of the work force. Proportionately, more of them lost their jobs than adults [and] it will take years longer for them to gain back jobs than it will for adults.

[I]n 1989, before the recession hit, 62.3 per cent of Canadians aged 15 to 24 were employed. By November of 1992, the number had fallen to 50 per cent. Adult employment, meanwhile, had overtaken the levels it had reached before the recession.

Young Canadians also began losing jobs fully eight months before the beginning of the recession, the Statistics Canada study says. And by November of 1993, 16 per cent of Canadians aged 15 to 24 had never held a job, a sharp increase from the 10 per cent who had not worked in November 1989.

And while more young Canadians are turning to school to fill their days (Statistics Canada says 56 per cent of young people were in school full time in November of 1993, compared with 49 per cent in November of 1989), this avenue, too, is being barricaded with steep increases in tuition fees and much tougher entrance guidelines.

Not only that, this additional education does not guarantee a good job if the jobs are nowhere to be found, said Lars Osberg, an economist at Dalhousie University. "Going back to schoool only delays the problem. It doesn't actually solve it."

Dr. [Gordon] Betcherman [director of a labour research group at Queen's University in Kingston] said that this generation of Canadians may not find its niche in the job market until the end of the century, when the oldest batch of baby boomers begins to retire.

The boomers "are sort of jamming up the system," he said. He said he believes that the government should step forcefully into the issue by devising policies to help young, skilled Canadians into what he called the "good-jobs" sector.

Source: Abridged from Mitchell, Alanna, "Recession creates lost generation," *The Globe and Mail*, Thurs., March 3, 1994, pp. A1, A2

If work life changes in these ways, *then* there will be important consequences. First, the relationship between work and leisure will change. Fewer hours will be spent in paid work, so people will take their leisure more seriously, spending more time visiting friends and relatives, joining voluntary associations and just relaxing in public places. Second, communal, cooperative activities will count for more, and individual, competitive activities for less.

Finally, the relation between industry and schooling will change. For example, educators will make a clearer distinction between schooling for jobs and schooling for education.

Consider the following possible scenario: In 2050, most adults will still have jobs. However, their work lives will be much more varied than they are today. We have seen this "individualization" process in the lives of women who entered the work force in rapidly growing numbers in the last three decades. What we notice about the lives of North American women is the variety, fluidity and idiosyncrasy of their job patterns. Compared with their mothers and husbands, women do a wider variety of jobs today. Over their work lives, they often move in and out of jobs. As we have noted, temporary, short-term and part-time employment is increasing, especially for women. Finally, it is becoming ever harder to predict who does what kind of job. Education, marital status, parental status and age are no longer good predictors of a woman's job status they once were.

Following this pattern to its logical conclusion, in 2050 each person will uniquely mix education, domestic work and paid work over a lifetime. No two patterns will be the same. Few people will have a single lifelong career. People will need to be educated, re-educated and re-trained, again and again, as the market changes its demands for job skills. This pattern of individualized work lives, already evident among millions of North American women, will come to characterize the work lives of more and more North American men.

With so much variety, fluidity and idiosyncrasy, it will be hard for us to identify people's social class. As a result, class identification and cohesion will be even weaker than they are today. One consequence is that labour unions, which depend on stable class identification, will also be weaker than they are today. And social class affiliations may weaken. Critics may view such job individualization as yet another control strategy to divide and conquer the working class.

As men's and women's lives individualize, gender lines will blur further. The life chances of women and men will be more similar than they have been in the past. As a result, male domination will diminish and gender identities will weaken.

Educational institutions, particularly colleges and universities, will contain an even more varied and fluid mix of people. No longer primarily places for young people, they will increasingly bring together people widely experienced in the "real world" and people lacking such experience. Under these conditions, students will challenge their teachers more.

This imagined "Canada in 2050" is an exciting place, and we may get there sooner than expected. But if we get there, it will not be without conflict and stress. The major changes we have described are on their way, yet no one is really ready. Delayed public responses to what appear to be personal problems — unemployment, poverty and demoralization, among others — will hurt people. An awareness of possible changes and the need to prepare makes the process easier. One thing is certain: change is coming and we have to get ready for it.

CLOSING REMARKS

What will happen to the close link in our society between work and identity when people routinely have to change their jobs or careers, possibly several times, during their working lives? Will we see even more people engaged in free-floating "consultancies," working for a variety of employers, with no permanent loyalty to any company or, even, to any line of work, just as we already see people working in tall bureaucracies with no particular loyalty to clan chiefs or feudal lords?

Japanese research reveals that occupational self-direction has the most powerful effect on work-related attitudes. Self-direction — in effect, being one's own boss — decreases alienation and improves attitudes towards one's own work. So, in the long run, it may be a good thing if workers are less locked into particular organizations. (In Chapter 11, we will further consider the economic and social changes which are transforming the world.) However, the point is that the rapid and dramatic pace of change initiated by the Industrial Revolution has not abated; it is continuing still.

These changes in work — from pre-industrial to industrial, then from industrial to post-industrial society — illustrate once again the importance of linking private troubles with public issues. Every individual in society has been affected deeply by these changes, yet not a one can hope to deal with the problem on his or her own. The private troubles associated with work — alienation, anomie, danger and depression, among others, can only be dealt with collectively, after people have seen it is in their common interest to do so. For, as in other areas of sociology, change at the macro-level of society more often than not brings important changes at the micro-level. And that, once again, is why we have to have both macro-sociology *and* micro-sociology.

Ensuring a collective response to new problems, the Industrial Revolution brought people a new perspective on society: in particular, a willingness to doubt traditional authority and try to control their own work lives. But even as workers became more organized and powerful, so did employers. Unions were developed under traditional bourgeois capitalism. But at the same time as workers were perfecting their unions, bourgeois capitalism was being replaced by globalized corporate capitalism.

Throughout the industrial world, we have seen the same kinds of social changes, and this fact has several implications. First, it means that we can predict the ways newly developing nations will change as they industrialize. Second, we can predict an increasing similarity among industrialized nations of the world. Third, we can expect cultural influences to pass from older industrial nations, like the United States, to newer ones, like Japan.

Specialization and a detailed division of labour continue to characterize industrial society. So do anomie and alienation. As new efforts are made to solve the problem of the anomie Durkheim described, bureaucracies and professions continue to change form.

This chapter has examined a variety of innovations in the workplace. Some were inventions like the computer or computer-assisted technology. Others were social innovations like bureaucracy, professional associations or trade unions. We have seen that all innovations arise at a particular time and place, for sound social, economic and political reasons. Many are responses to other innovations — part of a continuing contest to control the "terrain" of the workplace.

For many workers, the most important innovations at work seem to be technological; for example, the adoption of computerized aids to production and decision-making (or expert systems). However, as we have said repeatedly, the structure of power determines how technology will be used. No matter how much the technology changes, little will change in the workplace until power is used differently.

The previous chapter discussed class inequality growing out of economic relations, as a backdrop to understanding the world of work. In the next chapter, we discuss inequality growing out of ethnic and race relations.

Review Questions

1. What is the "economic order"?
2. How have the four major paradigms approached the issue of work?
3. What was the "Industrial Revolution"?
4. What was the new perspective on society that developed during the Industrial Revolution?
5. What is liberal democracy?
6. What is corporate capitalism?
7. What are the characteristics of an industrial society?
8. What is meant by the convergence thesis?
9. What are the characteristics of Japanese industrial organization?
10. How does specialization produce anomie?
11. What are "mechanical" and "organic" solidarity?
12. What are the characteristics of a bureaucracy?
13. How do simple control and professionalization differ from bureaucratic control?
14. What are the "primary" and "secondary" labour markets?
15. What impact are the new technologies having on work?
16. What effect does alienation have upon work satisfaction?

Discussion Questions

1. Weber argues that the elimination of tradition, intuition and superstition from decision-making played an important part in the rise of modern economic and political life. On balance, did social life improve?

2. Durkheim recognized that anomie is a problem of modern societies that will not go away easily. New ways of attaching people to one another, and to new rules, are needed. Is the problem of anomie getting better or worse in Canada?

3. Would people be alienated from their work in a non-capitalist society? Suppose you were studying a non-capitalist society—past, present or future. What evidence would you look for to determine whether alienation was stronger or weaker than it is in Canada today?

4. Does the laissez-faire (or liberal) ideology increase or decrease people's sense of alienation from their work? From society as a whole?

5. Why would workers with the same amount of education who work equally hard make less money in the secondary labour market (for example, as waiters or taxi drivers) than in the primary labour market (as plumbers or lawyers)? And why would a well-educated, hard-working person be working in the secondary labour market?

6. Is it still appropriate for men and women to make different kinds of educational and occupational (or career) plans in our society?

Suggested Readings

Bell, D. (1973) *The Coming of Post-industrial Society*. New York: Basic Books. This key work on the future of economic organization pulls together a great deal of earlier writing, and is full of interesting ideas. The major debate about work started by this book has never ended.

Edwards, R. (1979) *Contested Terrain: The Transformation of the Workplace in the Twentieth Century*. New York: Basic Books. This exciting book about the evolution of worker-employer relations in North America explains how our own ambitions keep us doing what the boss wants us to do.

Hamper, B. (1992) *Rivethead: Tales From the Assembly Line*. New York: Warner Books. This lively, gritty and often funny book is written by a man who spent several years working on a General Motors assembly line. He offers an insider's perspective on why this kind of work can be, at different times, boring, challenging, ridiculous and tragic.

Howard, R.(1985) *Brave New Workplace*. New York: Viking. In many countries, there has been a growing trend toward more employee participation in workplace decision-making. This volume critically analyzes that development. The author concludes that most cases of this approach are really managers manipulating their employees. Workers *believe* they have control and autonomy, but the most important result is more managerial control over workers.

Krahn, H. J. and Graham S. Lowe (1988) *Work, Industry and Canadian Society*. Toronto: Nelson. An excellent introduction to work and industry in Canada, which includes up-to-date discussions of labour markets, women's work and industrial conflict.

Sennett, R. and J. Cobb (1973) *The Hidden Injuries of Class*. New York: Vintage. The psychological costs of having a low-status, menial job in a class-conscious society are examined in this book. The authors interviewed blue-collar workers to find out their feelings about their own work and work in general.

Internet Resources

The following Web sites are good places to find more information about topics discussed in this chapter:

Human Resources Development Canada (HRDC) contains labour statistics, fact sheets and papers on social security reform, and general information about the organization's library.
http://hrdc ~ dhrc.gc.ca

Ontario Workers' Compensation Board contains facts and figures about employees and employers, and their responsibilities in the event of injury.
http://www.wcb.on.ca/

Canadian Council on Rehabilitation and Work provides information about employment opportunities for people with low vision or blindness, psychiatric disabilities, learning disabilities and other disabilities.
http://www.ccrw/org/ccrw/

Canadian Auto Workers (CAW) provides information on Canada's largest private-sector union, representing more than 200,000 workers in 12 different economic sectors.
http://www.web.apc.org/caw/

Public Service Alliance of Canada contains information about one of Canada's most important public-sector unions and offers links to other related Internet sites.
http://www.psac.com

The McDonaldization of Society contains essays and links relating to rationalization.
http://www.wam.umd.edu/ ~ allan/mcdonald

International Development Research Centre Home Page describes research that meets the priorities of developing countries and the basic needs of the world's poor.
http://idrc.ca

Social Indicators of Development, as its name suggests, provides social and economic data on 170 economies, plus links to related data.
http://www.ciesin.org?IC/wbank/sid-home.html

ETHNIC AND RACE RELATIONS

CHAPTER OUTLINE

Growing up in different ethnic groups often means having different life experiences.

A WORLDWIDE CONFLICT

If you have been paying attention to the news lately, you will know that ethnic and race relations are a major source of conflict both in Canada and worldwide. In Quebec, the 1995 referendum defeat of the sovereignty option was blamed by the former premier, Jacques Parizeau, on "money and the ethnic vote." Since the Oka crisis of 1990, there have been several tense encounters between police forces and native groups seeking to redress long-standing grievances. In Toronto, the influx of visible minorities has generated anxiety and animosity among some members of the white population. Indeed, Canada today is a country with a fair share of ethnic conflict, most of which, thankfully, has not been violent.

Other countries have not been so lucky. In recent years, lesser ethnic conflicts have broken out in nations which, just a few years ago, seemed to have subdued "tribal" divisions within their borders. Despite years of "Russification," ethnic conflict played a large part in the collapse of the Soviet Union in 1991. Ethnic conflicts also smoulder in other parts of Eastern Europe such as Romania (where conflicts involve the Hungarian minority) and the former Yugoslavia (where conflicts involve the Serbs, Croats and Muslims).

Other places experiencing ethnic conflict include Rwanda and Sri Lanka. The conflict in Rwanda has killed thousands and driven countless others to seek refuge outside the country. The conflict in Sri Lanka shows the danger and explosiveness of ethnic feeling. It began as a rivalry between elites, then grew. The elites provoked strong feeling on both sides by appealing to ethnic loyalty and escalated the conflict into a civil war.

Like the former USSR, many of these countries once had socialist rulers who rejected ethnic origin as a proper basis for people's loyalties and feelings. With the current global stress on democracy and self-rule, many ethnic groups are fighting to define themselves as free nation-states. And with the release of nationalist feelings, old conflicts rise to the surface. No longer held in check by force or communist ideology, these conflicts have flared up all over Central and Eastern Europe.

As for racial conflict, South Africa will take a long time to heal from the racial tyranny and violence of *apartheid* — the policy of racial segregation and discrimination against non-European groups in South Africa. Although apartheid is no longer legal in South Africa, many Afrikaners still support the historic racist policies, despite disclosures of murder and mayhem carried out against non-whites by the white governments in the 1970s and 1980s.

These global conflicts remind us how hard it is to organize a peaceful, democratic state, composed of many linguistic, cultural and religious groups. They also demonstrate the need, in many countries, to develop political arrangements which honour ethnic differences.

This chapter will explore ethnic and race relations and consider some of the reasons for the conflicts which so often erupt. We will begin with a definition of the terms "ethnicity" and "race" — terms that are too often a source of confusion and conflict.

The Concepts of Ethnicity and Race

From a sociological point of view, both ethnicity and race are socially constructed. They are ideas we have about ourselves and others which affect how we perceive and interact with one another. They are similar in that both terms imply some kind of common biological origin that ties people together: people who share a common **ethnicity** or **race** are usually considered to be related by "blood" or to have had some common ancestor. The terms differ in that ethnic identity is likely to form among people with a common culture, language, religion or national origin. Members feel they are culturally and socially united, and that is how others see them.

By contrast, members of a race are identified on the basis of presumed physical traits, especially appearance. A race could include members from many ethnic and social backgrounds and is defined in terms of shared appearance rather than shared history or culture.

Neither race nor ethnicity are objective concepts. Interethnic and interracial contacts have been taking place for thousands of years. As a result, no supposed racial group is genetically pure and racial divisions do not reflect genetic realities. They reflect the assumptions, biases or stereotypes with which people categorize one another.

Consider a child of a mixed-race couple, such as a child who has one white and one black parent. Is this child black or white? In the United States such a child would almost certainly be considered black. Yet the child is as much white as black. In much of Latin America the child would be considered white or as the member of a category that falls between black and white. The truth is, the child is black or white or some mixture of the two not because of innate biological traits, but because of how the people in a society identify and categorize that individual. Being black or white is a social construction.

The same is true of ethnicity. A recent premier of Quebec, proud of his Quebecois family's long and illustrious history, was Daniel Johnson. Among his many francophone ancestors there was a "Johnson" and another long line of English ancestors. Yet Daniel Johnson is firmly and unhesitatingly a francophone Quebecois. In other words, both race and ethnicity are social constructs, not biological facts. The point is made forcefully by research reported in Applied Sociology below.

But even though they are not biologically meaningful, group markers such as appearance carry social meanings and people respond to these markers. If people see themselves, and others see them, as members of a unique biological

APPLIED SOCIOLOGY

Race Is Just Skin-Deep

Racial differences have played an enormous part in world history. Many of the world's conflicts have pitted one racial group against another and, in some instances, the conflicts have been justified by the propagation of elaborate theories about racial superiority or inferiority. Sociologists have long argued that racial differences are socially constructed and, finally, geneticists have supplied evidence that supports this view.

Many people think that races are distinct groups — biological categories created by differences in genes that people inherit from their parents. However, genetic researchers don't think so. Drawing on evidence accumulated since the 1970s, eminent geneticists and anthropologists have finally concluded that race is a social, cultural and political concept based largely on superficial appearances.

The idea that races are *not* the product of human genes may seem to contradict common sense. People don't seem to want to believe this, largely because it contradicts the evidence of their eyes. Some groups do look different from other groups. And scientists concede that people do look different, but this may be primarily due to the environments in which their ancestors lived. Besides, differences in appearance may have little to do with other, more consequential differences in thinking or behaviour.

Most important, scientists agree that race matters a great deal as a social concept. That a person's skin colour and hair texture can be sources of love or hate, respect or disrespect, pride or shame, is a sociological fact. People take note of such visible differences and attach meanings and values to them.

In turn, misconceptions about race — about its deep or innate character — have fuelled forms of racism that have caused much social, psychological and physical harm. Even recently, government policies concerned with fairness in employment have treated racial minorities differently than majority whites. But efforts to redress centuries of racial discrimination have created a backlash in certain parts of Canada and the United States. Resentment over "employment equity" (or "affirmative action" in the United States) has become highly politicized, as certain segments of the population — especially working-class and lower-middle-class white men — feel they have been hurt by these policies.

In large part, the problem has arisen because what should have been treated as a class issue — namely, poverty and unemployment — was treated as a racial issue.

But even though race, in the social sense, is a reality, in the scientific sense, it is not. The characteristics that we can see with our eyes that help us to distinguish people from different countries — Africans from Asians or North Americans, for example — are, in reality, skin-deep. Beneath the surface, at a genetic level, there's really not much difference at all.

Source: Adapted from an article by Robert Boyd, *Toronto Star*, Sun., Oct. 13, 1996, p. A14

category, then in practice they form a race. Race is real in the sense that its effects are real. As we will see, people often choose their friends and spouses, places of work and lodging, even hire workers and elect representatives, on the basis of the "race" they perceive.

How to Study Race and Ethnic Relations

Like everything else in this book, ethnic and race relations can be explored from both a macro and micro perspective. The choice of perspective usually reflects the particular issue that interests the researcher and the paradigm being used.

Ethnic and racial relations are social relationships. Sometimes these are individual relationships, but usually they are relationships among groups. Minority people who suffer from political and economic bias often react by organizing themselves as groups. In doing so, they hope to gain political power, change the laws or gain an economic edge. Those who already enjoy political or economic power are also organized in order to retain what they have.

Macrosociologists, especially conflict theorists, build theoretical "models" to explain why ethnic groups mobilize and conflicts occur. They specify the circumstances — such as competition, discrimination and perception of threat — under which an ethnic conflict is likely to break out. These models provide a good place to start studying both modern and historical cases of ethnic conflict.

Surprisingly, functionalists tend not to take a macrosociological approach when it comes to ethnicity. Because of their stress on common values, functionalists expect most ethnic differences to disappear — a common "modern" industrial lifestyle would eliminate differences. Those that remain, functionalists assert, are largely "symbolic" (Parsons, 1975). That is, they are a part of one's identity but have few practical consequences. A second-generation Italian Canadian may feel pride when an Italian wins an Olympic event, but in most respects an Italian Canadian is very much like any other Canadian.

Macrosociological research on ethnicity is underdeveloped because traditionally, like the functionalists, most sociologists have expected ethnic differences to disappear. It was assumed that modern society is either a class society or an industrial society in which ethnic distinctions are becoming less and less important. To a large extent, ethnicity was simply ignored. Indeed, it was the virulent ethnic conflict that suddenly appeared after the breakup of the USSR in 1991 which reawakened interest in ethnicity among macrosociologists.

Microsociological research on ethnic and race relations has been more common. Such research centres on the personal experience of minority status, asking questions like: What impact does a negative ethnic stereotype have on a person's sense of self? How, for example, does a young Sikh boy respond when classmates mock his ceremonial turban and dagger? How does a native (or Chinese or black) person feel about the lack of role models on television or in politics? How does the ongoing ordeal of death and violence affect the ethnic loyalties of Northern Irish, Palestinian or Bosnian children?

Symbolic interactionists in particular stress the links between ethnicity and identity. They are especially interested in how ethnic identities are socially created and maintained. Some, such as Shibutani and Kwan (1963) have sought to develop an integrated theory of ethnic relations and an understanding of why ethnic relations so often lead to conflict and violence. Calling their approach a theory of "ethnic stratification," Shibutani and Kwan show that ethnic conflict is not inevitable, but the result of cultural differences and prejudices. Interestingly, they too argue that ethnic differences would disappear in time as communication among people of diverse backgrounds became more common. Unfortunately, as the example of Bosnia shows, people who have been neighbours for many years, who speak the same language and have communicated on a regular basis can still maintain and even amplify deadly hatreds and animosities.

Feminist scholars, such as Daiva Stasiulis (1990), have made important contributions to understanding the dynamics of ethnic and race relations by stressing the links between ethnicity, class and gender. Stasiulis argues that white middle-class feminists must overcome their own ethnocentrism and take into account the experiences of immigrant and visible-minority women who face different problems and need different solutions than do the majority.

Canadian sociologists enjoy a rich tradition of research on ethnicity, especially in stressing the links between ethnicity, race and inequality. Most make use of a conflict perspective, and most of this chapter presents ideas and research that take this approach.

ETHNIC PLURALISM IN CANADA

Canada has always been a *pluralist* society made up of sundry groups. Some ethnic groups have been eager to keep their special cultural features, preserve their identity and remain conscious of who they are and where they came from. Others have been more willing to merge with the rest of society. For the most part, Canadian minorities have kept their culture alive while living among members of other ethnic groups. This **pluralism** grows out of a founding fact of Canadian history: the union of two distinct cultures, French and English.

Increasingly, Canadians have found it useful to distinguish between traditional (or liberal) pluralism and **multiculturalism**. Traditional pluralism protects the rights of minority people through provincial human rights codes and other legislation. By contrast, multiculturalism treats each of us as a member of an ethnic or racial group — a proxy for the groups we belong to. In this case, it is the group, not the individual, that is protected by law.

The difference between these two approaches is important. By its nature, traditional pluralism focuses on civil liberties. But where traditional pluralism protects individual job-seekers against bias, multiculturalism supports blanket preferences, such as employment equity, to promote the hiring of disadvantaged groups. Likewise, traditional pluralism would forbid the issuing of certain pre-trial information in criminal cases if it threatened the right of the accused to a fair trial. By contrast, multiculturalism flatly opposes the gathering or issuing of statistics on the ethnic or racial origins of criminals.

In the following discussion we distinguish among four major types of ethnic group, each with its own place in Canadian society. These four types are the native peoples, the Charter Groups, European ethnics, and visible minorities.

The Native Peoples

CBC ◉

"Davis Inlet: Moving from Misery"

Canada's native peoples come from a variety of geographic locales and cultural backgrounds. There are many variations among the groups that comprise this population. Perhaps because they have different languages and cultures, they have historically thought of themselves as belonging to different ethnic groups or "nations." A nation can be seen as a sociocultural entity comprising people who identify with one another linguistically, culturally and ethnically, and that does not necessarily have a country or government of its own.

The variations are partly a result of living in different physical settings: forests versus plains versus coastal regions, for example. As well, **band** and **reserve** sizes differ greatly from one group to another, and from one region to another. The average reserve (or settlement) in Ontario is about ten times the size of a reserve in British Columbia. Both distance and differences of language bolster the cultural differences between groups. In the past, political and economic conflicts, even wars, have increased the differences between groups even more.

Today we can divide Canada's native peoples into three main groups: Indians, Eskimos and Metis. Each of these groups includes several subgroups.

The first main group are *registered* or *status* Indians, who belong to bands. They fall under the rule of the Indian Act. Indians who lack band membership can still sign up with the Department of Indian Affairs and Northern Development. About 70 per cent of Canada's roughly 620,000 status Indians live on nearly 2,300 reserves. Most of the other 30 per cent have moved to cities, in hopes of realizing better economic chances.

A subgroup of native people, *non-status* Indians, lost their Indian status through marriage to non-Indians or as the children of such marriages. There were fewer than 100,000 such Indians in the Canadian Census of 1991 and many do not live on reserves. Bill C-31, passed in 1985 by the federal government, allows some non-status Indians to regain their status.

A second main group, the Eskimo people, include the Inuvialuit of the western Arctic and the Inuit of the eastern Arctic and Labrador. Most of these approximately 57,000 people still live in small native communities. Unlike the Indian peoples, they have not moved to big cities in large numbers. The Inuit — the most distinct of Canada's native peoples — have a cultural system unlike that of most Canadians. Even their system of writing differs from the predominant Canadian system; it uses symbols unlike those used in English to denote what are in some instances unfamiliar (to us) sounds. Like other aspects of their culture, this difference makes it hard for people to converse across the native – non-native divide.

A third main group, the Metis, are the offspring of native–French couples who never obtained registered Indian status. The 1991 Census counted fewer than 100,000 Metis. Most live in small rural communities or among the non-native people of larger communities. Though few live in ethnically separate communities, the Metis maintain an identity that is distinct from that of Indians and Eskimos.

All three types of native people undergo problems we usually associate with Third World conditions. For example, they receive little schooling and few get a post-secondary education. They are more likely than white Canadians to live in poverty and their urban unemployment rates are higher than average. On reserves, many of their homes fail to meet national health-and-safety standards. Overcrowding is common, so infectious diseases spread through the population. Native peoples are much more likely than white Canadians to die of infectious (especially respiratory and gastrointestinal) diseases, or from accidents, poisoning and violence. They are less likely than other Canadians to die of chronic diseases, cancer or stroke. And native peoples also have the highest rates of alcoholism, suicide and crime in Canada. Given these conditions, rates of mortality among native peoples are substantially higher than the national average and life expectancy at birth is much lower.

At the same time, the native population is growing very quickly through high birth rates. This means that it is the youngest of Canada's population groups, and some of the troubles it faces — such as violence and suicide — are due in part to the large fraction of young people.

Federal and provincial governments try — somewhat half-heartedly, many believe — to deal with these problems. For example, the federal government provides native peoples a range of services at almost no cost. But, for the most part, these efforts fail. In return for the "handouts" they get, native peoples pay a high social cost: primarily, disrespect from white society and little control over their own lives. As well, they confront barriers that others do not. For example, because they don't own property on the reserves, they don't pay property taxes. But they also cannot secure mortgages and business loans as easily as Canadians who *do* own property.

Many natives feel that Canadian governments have little commitment to solving their problems, and little idea of how to go about doing so. This is one of the reasons that many native people seek self-government. The blockades Mohawk Warriors built at Oka, Quebec, in the summer of 1990, dramatized this effort. Many native peoples feel they must take charge of their own lives if they are to improve their life chances. Despite the ostensible benevolence of governments, native peoples cannot forget a long record of conquest, trickery and betrayal.

The active role played by native peoples in constitutional discussions shows that they will not remain the victims of paternalism and neglect.

The six-volume Report of the Royal Commission on Aboriginal Peoples, published in December 1996, calls for sweeping changes to the treatment of native peoples in Canada. Among other things, the report recommends an acknowledgement of past mistakes by the government of Canada, an inquiry into the effects on native children of residential schooling and into the harm done to native peoples by relocations, the overhaul of land-treaty and land-claim settlements, arrangements to stimulate aboriginal economic development and, most important, measures to establish aboriginal self-determination, including the creation of an aboriginal parliament called the House of First Peoples.

From a sociological standpoint, the issue of what to do about the First Nations is intriguing: though from the outside they may look like a single, unified entity — a distinct society — viewed from the inside, the native peoples comprise scores of distinct social and cultural groups. Finding a common viewpoint among them is almost as difficult as finding common ground with the mainstream non-native society. And, from a political standpoint, the issue of what to do is equally difficult. If one acknowledges native rights to self-determination, one can scarcely deny the same to Quebec francophones. Conversely, if one denies this right, on what grounds can we argue that any society, however distinct, needs political independence from any other such as, for example, Canadian political independence from the United States? We will continue to struggle with these questions well into the 21st century.

The Charter Groups: English and French Canadians

The term **Charter Groups** signals the important status British and French groups enjoy in Canadian society. It is a status that makes them politically, economically and socially dominant over everyone else. The source of this status is historical: *Charter Groups* are the groups that first conquer and colonize a land. They set up the institutions and rules which serve as a framework for the new society, often neglecting the claims of those who were conquered and colonized. Conquered groups like the native peoples, and people who immigrate after the period of conquest, are expected to go along with these plans as though they were inherently compatible with everyone's needs.

Both British and French Charter Groups shaped Canada's institutions during the country's first century of nationhood. However, their sway over Canadian society has declined as their numbers have dropped. Since 1871, the fraction claiming British (that is, English, Scottish, Welsh or Irish) ancestry has dropped steadily, from about 60 per cent to less than 40 per cent today. The fraction claiming French ancestry has remained almost constant at 30 per cent. This means that about one-third of Canada's present population has ethnic origins that are *neither* French nor British.

Though they are now a smaller fraction of the population, Charter Group members retain control for several reasons. For one thing, they are still the largest of Canada's ethnic groups. As well, some of Canada's other ethnic groups have spread themselves unevenly (and sometimes thinly) around the nation. By contrast, most French Canadians live in Quebec, where they constitute over 80 per cent of the population. In Quebec, the numerical majority gives French Canadians control over the Parti Québécois–led provincial government and allows them to take steps to clinch their political, economic and cultural control.

Reacting to the Royal Commission's Report

Sociologists are likely to view the reports of Royal Commissions as demonstrating the value of applied social science, and in this respect the Royal Commission's Report on Aboriginal Peoples is no exception. Never before has so much good evidence been collected and analyzed to reveal the problems facing people who belong to the First Nations. However, one might then ask, what good is applied research that lacks a communication plan and an agenda for implementing the report's recommendations?

With last week's long-awaited release of the report from the Royal Commission on Aboriginal Peoples, communication issues have been brought into even sharper focus. Unless a great deal of sustained "noise" is created around the report's analyses and 400 recommendations, its 3,500 pages will gather the same dust as decades of broken treaties and dozens of unresolved land claims.

The report outlines for Euro-Canadian society what Indians have known for generations: that repeated government attempts to eliminate them as distinct peoples have failed miserably. Canadian and colonial law-makers have created an Indian underclass plagued by poverty and despair, and mired in a cycle of dependency on the very government that tried to make them disappear.

But if this is stale news to Indians, their partners in the Canadian confederation need a steadier dose of headlines to awaken them to the reality of what passes for life in Indian country. How else can one hope to overcome the abject ignorance indicated in a recent survey showing that fully 40 per cent of Canadians think Native people enjoy a standard of living as good as or *better* than theirs?

Many of the Aboriginal stories that must be told are not dismal accounts of despair and suffering. How strong must be the courage of people who, in the face of government-sanctioned genocide, still stand proud and point to many successes: the banning of alcohol from many reserves, the insertion of traditional teachings and customs into everyday activities, and the increasing prevalence of Aboriginal language instruction.

More Canadians need to hear about success stories such as the healing circle of Hollow Water, a Manitoba reserve achieving virtually unblemished results in dealing with sexual-abuse offenders. By treating episodes as problems for the entire community to solve instead of passing them off to an impersonal court system, the program has so far saved taxpayers an estimated $6-million in legal costs. The financial implications should interest Canadian citizens and their elected representatives, who persist in treating Indians as little more than economic millstones around their necks.

How persistently members of the national press corps now pursue the stories in the commission's final report remains to be seen.

Source: Abridged from Maurice Switzer, *The Globe and Mail*, Thurs., Nov. 28, 1996, p. A23

Quebec's motto of *Je me souviens* ("I remember") reveals both French Canada's history and its social agenda. What Canadians of French descent remember is that, in their view, almost all of Canada was once theirs. Today, many French Canadians feel threatened by the possibility of a decrease in their numbers through language loss. And, before it is too late, they want to ensure that they win the political and cultural rights to which they feel entitled. This accounts for the lasting strength of sovereigntist movements in Quebec, and a near vote in favour of independence in the 1996 referendum.

Like the native peoples, French Canadians see themselves not as an ethnic group so much as a "national" group with its own viable economy. Many feel Quebec is "their country." A large minority does *not* want to stay a part of Canada. But if they are to stay, Quebecers believe that it must be as equal partners in a state uniting two "nations," one of them French Canadian. (The *state* is a set of public organizations that makes and enforces decisions. It includes the elected government, civil service, courts, police and military.)

Like the United States, Israel, Australia and Argentina, Canada has always been a nation of immigrants, with enormous numbers entering (and often leaving) every decade. It is impossible to exaggerate the impact of so much population movement on our national identity.

Other countries have pluralistic arrangements that are like Canada's. Many of these, like Belgium and Sri Lanka, suffer from ethnic conflict. Others, like Guyana, Malaysia and Fiji experience less conflict; their history suggests that ethnic groups co-exist most peacefully when group members disperse and there are no territorial bases for a split.

For 200 years, British and French Canadians have tried hard to avoid conflict by leading separate lives. Canadian novelist Hugh McLennan portrayed this separation in his aptly named novel *Two Solitudes*. In Quebec, the contact between British and French Canadians was, for a long time, limited to politics and work. Even after non-British immigrants began to arrive in Canada (after Confederation), this pattern of quiet isolation endured. Today, French- and non-French Quebecois seem to get along well interpersonally but remain divided on the issue of political control.

European Ethnics

The settlement of Canada has always mirrored the country's changing need for labour power. At times when the country needed a greater number of farmers or workers, the Canadian government made more spirited efforts to attract immigrants. But in the country's early years, there was a preference for people much like the English and French: first for northern (Protestant) Europeans and then for eastern and southern (Catholic) Europeans. Immigration has always been used by a dominant class to satisfy its need for an exploitable labour resource.

After Confederation in 1867, the national government braced itself against threats of an American invasion. It did so by building a railroad from coast to coast and bringing settlers to the sparsely peopled Prairies. In the first decade of the 20th century, about one and a half million immigrants came to Canada. The people Canada gained through immigration more than made up for the number it lost in the prior four decades, when more people left Canada for the United States than entered it from all sources. Large numbers of immigrants arrived in Canada from Austria-Hungary, Germany, Poland, Russia (including the Ukraine) and Scandinavia. A majority came to Ontario and the Prairies, most of them to farms or small towns. But even by 1911, over one-third had chosen to live in cities of more than 25,000 people. The lure of city life would grow throughout the 20th century.

Immigration to Canada slowed between 1914 and 1945 because of two world wars, the Depression of the 1930s and a decline in the demand for labour. But after the Second World War, immigration entered a new phase. As before, large numbers came from Britain, Northern and Eastern Europe. As well, throughout the 1950s, 1960s and 1970s, vastly increased numbers came from Southern Europe: first Italy, then other Mediterranean countries (Greece, Portugal and Spain). Most of these immigrants settled in the quickly growing cities of central Canada. And from the 1970s onward, Canada has taken in a great many immigrants who are unlike the Charter Groups in important ways.

Visible Minorities

Anxiety about culturally and racially different immigrants has long been a main feature of Canadian life. Nowhere is this clearer than in the head tax imposed on Chinese aliens in 1885, a tax that increased to a forbidding five hundred dollars in 1903. An even more explicitly limiting Chinese Immigration Act was passed in 1923. Until 1947, this act continued to bar all but a few new Chinese immigrants.

Today, people of Chinese ancestry have been living in Canada for more than a century. Some came from China to work on the construction of Canadian railways and then settled in the West. Because of this, in the first half of the 20th century nearly every small town on the Prairies had a Chinese laundry and a Chinese restaurant (Li, 1982). But it was not until after the Second World War that the repressive immigration act was repealed and the Chinese were made welcome in the country.

The rejection of the Chinese signified a general dislike of visible minorities, whether from Asia, Africa, the Pacific islands or the Caribbean. But from the 1970s onward, non-white immigrants began to pour into Canada. Many Chinese came from Hong Kong. As well, for the first time many Asians came from other parts of the British Commonwealth, especially India and Pakistan. Soon, the numbers of immigrants from Latin America, the Caribbean and Southeast Asia also grew dramatically.

Many of these people were fleeing poverty or political unrest. Yet, entry into Canada has never been open to all. After a brief period when "family class" immigrants were welcome, Canada's policies once again stress economic value, using a "point system" to grade applicants for immigration. As it has through most of its history, Canada puts the needs of business and industry first, and immigrants have to bring skills that suit current economic needs. Some immigrants also bring large amounts of capital, and this wins them a high standing with immigration officials. Only since the 1980s have refugees, who are exempt from the point system, begun to enter Canada in large numbers.

Today, business needs the skills, hard work and capital of city-dwelling visible minorities. It is this need that has changed Canada's well-known preference for white Northern Europeans. It seems likely that, in the future, labour needs will continue to shape Canada's immigration policies. Thus, immigration continues to change Canada's ethnic and racial makeup and the country's economic needs continue to change immigration policies.

Immigration Issues

Given high rates of unemployment, many people are contesting the wisdom of current policies, and some are demanding far lower rates of immigration. There has been too little reliable research on the effects of immigration. What happens to immigrants after they come to Canada? Who gains from high rates and who loses? How have immigrants helped the country's economy? the culture? the social life? Uncertainty about the answers to these questions is causing conflict in our race and ethnic relations and a lack of clear policy.

However, research suggests that immigrants generally help the economy grow. Because of selective immigration policies, many immigrants are highly skilled or highly educated; they provide a cheap source of talented people which this country has not had to pay a cent to train. Many are also ambitious; just think how much courage and energy it takes to travel to another country and culture, and start life all over again. Since many (even most) are young and skilled, immigrants tend to enter the work force and remain in it. They do not increase the general unemployment rate; indeed, they often take jobs that native-born people are unwilling to do. On balance, the evidence shows that immigrants pay more in taxes than they draw in public services and benefits.

Beyond that, immigrants confer a demographic benefit on the country. In Canada and the rest of the Western world, fertility rates are near or below replacement. That means there is no danger of too many people. In fact, even with 5-10 per cent unemployment there may be a danger of too few people. Among other things, a shrinking population means a shrinking work force and, therefore, a shrinking economic base. Immigration provides more people to consume, as well as make, the economy's goods and services.

More important still, a population with fertility near or below replacement is an aging population. Low fertility, not increased longevity, is mainly what increases the average (or median) age of the population because statistically, there are relatively fewer youngsters to bring the median age down. Currently, the median Canadian is nearly forty years old (half the population is older, half younger.) While fertility remains low or even shrinks, the median age rises even more. This means a large and growing fraction of old and retired people, and a shortage of young people.

A society can have too many young people, as we saw in an earlier chapter, but it can also have too few. Population aging can be a bad thing. First, older people are less productive economically than younger people. A large proportion are retired, though some not by choice. Many require costly services, especially health care, in the last years of their lives. Most draw old-age pensions. We need young workers to pay for these pensions and other services. The fewer the young people, the more each one has to pay to cover the costs of our old people.

Moreover, there is evidence that older people are more rigid in their ways, and less innovative than younger people. This is bound to affect the economic, social and cultural life of the country. Increasingly, as we noted earlier, the country (and world) needs flexibility and adaptiveness: new ideas, new technologies, new ways of relating to other "kinds" of people and so on. Young people can adapt in these ways more easily than older people.

High rates of immigration supply the needed young people in two ways. First, a high proportion of immigrants are young — often in their teens or twenties. Second, immigrants from less developed societies tend to have higher rates of fertility than native-born Americans (or other Western peoples). This means that immigrants will supply more babies per capita, and this too will keep the country's median age from rising at a rapid rate (though it is likely to rise nonetheless).

THE HORIZONTAL DIMENSION OF PLURALISM

How do members of different ethnic groups get along with one another in a pluralist society like Canada? How are the various ethnic groups absorbed into Canadian mainstream culture? And what makes some ethnic communities more cohesive than others? These are questions that arise when we consider the "horizontal dimension" of ethnic pluralism.

By *horizontal dimension*, we mean the ways in which ethnic communities come together or stay apart from one another. Imagine a "map" with Canada's ethnic groups located on it, then ask: Which groups are "closest" to which others and which are most distant? Second, how tightly linked are people within each of those ethnic groups? Finally, how can we explain the closeness or distance *between* groups, and the strength of linkages we find *within* groups?

Broadly, all horizontal ethnic relations in a society take the form of either **assimilation** or **segregation**. When ethnic groups assimilate, their members adopt the dominant social patterns. Doing so often results in a growing likeness between the lives of the minority and those of the majority ethnic group. In time, the minority loses itself within the dominant group. Thus, the economic and cultural features of the two groups become similar.

Acculturation, one form of assimilation, means adopting a new culture — usually the dominant culture. People do this by learning new behaviour, language, customs, values, norms and roles. This is only possible if minorities are willing to interact with members of the dominant culture, and vice versa. Usually, acculturation is required for assimilation to be complete.

Today, the mass media play a central role in this process. Television and radio weaken ethnic and cultural identities by exposing widely disparate peoples to the same kinds of influences. At the same time, more ethnic groups are urging their members to retain a strong ethnic identity. The result is puzzling: as groups assert their cultural uniqueness in more militant ways, they become more alike than ever before. One current issue in the area of race and ethnic relations is how to fulfill people's needs for cultural uniqueness while admitting that, around the world, people's cultures *are* becoming more similar.

Amalgamation is the means by which different racial or ethnic groups blend in a new cultural mix, with all groups giving equally of themselves. For example, the United States is the product of such an amalgamation. It sees itself as a *melting pot*, where people from many ethnic backgrounds learn to think of themselves as individuals (not members of ethnic groups) and Americans. At least this is the way the process is supposed to work; in practice, ethnic identities are as strong in the United States as they are in Canada.

The reverse process is **segregation**. Segregation separates two or more groups of people who live within the same territory. It may take the form of social separation, as when one group avoids mingling with another. Or there may be forced physical separation. Then, the groups live in distinct geographic areas, whether in ghettos or in separate but equal neighbourhoods. *Apartheid* in South Africa was an extreme and horrible form of forced segregation where the different races lived unequally and apart.

What we mainly see in Canada is *self-segregation* — separation chosen and practised freely by the members of a given ethnic group. Neither the larger society nor the dominant Charter Group imposes it. Groups that separate themselves from the mainstream of society — such as the Hutterites, a rural religious group in western Canada, or the Amish in Ontario — exemplify the process of self-segregation. Many other ethnic groups in Canada practise a less extreme form of self-segregation. They join into mainstream Canadian life but also keep alive

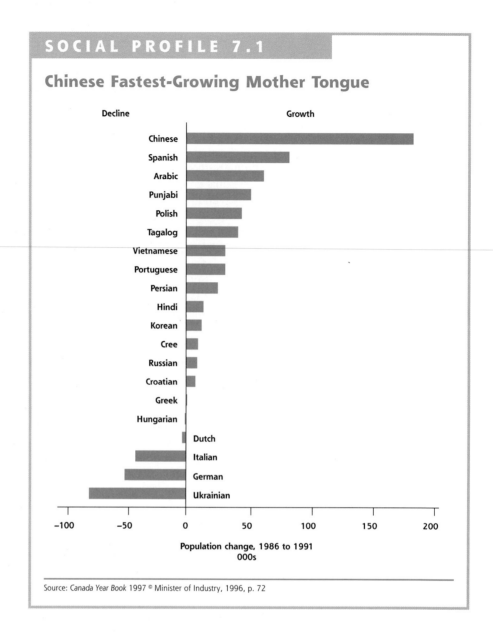

SOCIAL PROFILE 7.1

Chinese Fastest-Growing Mother Tongue

Source: *Canada Year Book* 1997 © Minister of Industry, 1996, p. 72

their own institutions and culture. One ethnic group that is very close to invisible in Canada is Americans living away from home. Every year on the Fourth of July, they can be seen identifying themselves with traditions, a cultural heritage, an ethnicity that under normal conditions disappears easily into the fabric of Canadian life.

As we said earlier, the model for this process of self-segregation has been French Canada. Despite efforts at encouraging bilingualism, Quebec and the rest of Canada are becoming more distinct linguistically and culturally. But as the French-English split has become more extreme, other cultural and language groups have found a way to combine economic assimilation with social and cultural segregation.

This practice of self-segregation has not harmed Canada's ethnic minorities. In fact, it may have helped them. So we must ask how minority groups achieve successful self-segregation and how this practice helps them survive as mini-societies.

Language and Culture

Why do some ethnic communities survive longer and "better" than others? In a study of ethnic communities in Canada, sociologist Jeffrey Reitz (1980) surveyed ten groups in five Canadian cities. He wanted to find out which factors cause some groups to remain cohesive and others to vanish through the assimilation of their members into mainstream society.

Reitz measured many aspects of people's attachment to their ethnic group. To know how well an ethnic group is keeping up its community and culture, he found, one must look at patterns of interaction and patterns of language use. These two patterns are closely linked; moreover, they are both important ways that people stay involved in their ethnic group.

Living in an ethnic neighbourhood, though also important, is a somewhat weaker way of staying involved if you do not speak the ethnic language. That's because people can stay involved even if they move away from the ethnic community, *if* they keep up their ethnic language use. However, living near other members increases the chance of using the language and staying involved with other group members.

Knowing and using the language, then, is a key to ethnic cultural survival. So it makes sense that language would play a central part in maintaining the ethnic community. First, the use of a minority language excludes linguistic "outsiders." In that way, it forms an invisible border around the group. This influences social interaction: who is friends with whom, how often people interact outside their group, and even who marries whom. Second, in Canada, the chance to speak one's native language decreases the pressure on immigrants to learn and use English or French and, thereby, to acculturate. Third, as discussed in Chapter 2 (Culture), language is a way of viewing the world. Use of the ethnic language maintains ethnic traditions of thinking and acting, and traditional values. It also signifies a connection with, and loyalty to, those cultural values and ways of thinking. Ancestral language thus helps to define the "self" as a member of an ethnic minority. A sign of the role that language plays in cultural survival is the importance francophones in Quebec attach to the use of French.

Not only does language use increase people's ethnic loyalty, ethnic loyalty also increases people's language use, according to a study of Welsh-speaking bilinguals in Wales. People who feel strongly about their ethnic identity make a point of speaking their ethnic tongue, as much for symbolic as for practical reasons.

In the United States, rap music provides another interesting example of cultural survival through language. Though rap grows out of African traditions and most rappers are black, audiences are often white. This has led to debates over rap as cultural or ethnic property: who "owns" rap, who has a right to "use" it, should it be dominated by blacks, and so on. As a language, rap is able to cross over ethnic lines, but even as it does so it keeps many of its customary African aspects. The question is whether the adoption of rap music by whites lessens its cultural value for blacks.

The Role of Religion

Ethnic language use is only one part of a community's effort to keep alive a distinct identity and tradition. Ethnic religion often plays the same role.

Like language use, attendance at an ethnic place of worship is a good predictor of attachment to the ethnic community. A person who attends the ethnic church (or synagogue or mosque) regularly is likely to live in an ethnic neighbourhood, hobnob with other members of the group and use the ethnic language. Like language, religion encodes a system of cultural assumptions about life, the world and the spiritual. Moreover, attending one church means not attending another: like language use, attendance at a place of worship draws an invisible border around the group.

Involvement in an ethnic religion also shapes people's values and goals, thus limiting their cultural assimilation. And by limiting their assimilation, ethnic religion promotes the survival of the ethnic group.

This influence is greatest where ethnic religion is in control of the group's ethnic education, as it is in parochial schools. For example, before the Quiet Revolution of the 1960s, Quebec's Catholic school system played a major role in maintaining a traditional humanistic outlook on life. One result of this was to steer Quebec francophones away from scientific or business careers by limiting their chance to do otherwise.

Ethnic church attendance also limits mixing with other groups and, in that way, slows down assimilation. For example, Filipino, Indonesian and Malaysian Christians in Canada have their own churches, although church authorities are doubtful about the value of this practice. However, these separate churches discourage the mixing of ethnic groups and, in this way, help to maintain segregation. Separate ethnic parishes also maintain inequalities between groups, a topic we discuss shortly. So contrary to the professed beliefs, being Christian does not notably encourage social equality, at least not in Canada.

In the former Soviet Union, the government tried to limit ethnic cohesion so as to reinforce loyalty to the state. For this reason, it also tried to limit religious identification and practice. But over the past few decades, religion has crept back into Russian life, promoting a return of ethnic nationalism. It was this ethnic and religious nationalism that fed anti-Russian demands for self-rule and the overthrow of communism.

Residential Segregation

We noted earlier that Canada's ethnic groups are spread unequally throughout the country. For example, many Ukrainian Canadians but few Chinese Canadians live in rural Manitoba. On the other hand, many Chinese Canadians but few Ukrainian Canadians live in downtown Toronto.

This reflects different histories of immigration — what jobs immigrants could find, and where they could find those jobs when they arrived in Canada. It also reflects *chain migration*, the process by which people come to areas where similar, often related, people are already living. Segregation also reflects long-lived preferences. For example, certain groups favour urban over rural life, or seem to, as their cultural capital fits them for urban living here and incapacitates them for survival in our self-enclosed

People deeply involved in their national or ethnic group usually keep up their cultural traditions.

rural towns. In Canada, this is particularly true of visible minorities (excluding native peoples), Jews, Italians and Greeks. The urban preference feeds on itself: visible minorities like to live in neighbourhoods made up of people like themselves, so they continue living in cities.

Ethnic segregation is as highly developed in Canadian cities as it is in American urban centres. Indeed, we can see the phenomenon all over the world. So the segregation of ethnic and racial groups is not uniquely Canadian. Nor is it recent; sociologists have studied it for generations. But, in Canada, the extent of ethnic residential segregation — that is, who you live near to and, as a result, who you interact with, befriend and marry (among other things) — is very great in major cities.

Further, ethnic segregation has a huge impact on people's lives and identities. Consider the results of a study of Toronto's ethnic groups by Raymond Breton (1964) and his colleagues. Usually, the study found, segregation decreases with each passing generation. Also, groups segregate themselves less as their social status improves and level of schooling increases. But the Toronto Jews are an exception in both respects: over generations, they have continued to segregate themselves, despite rises in social status.

Residential segregation is important to an ethnic group because it limits who you get to know. After all, you have to meet someone before you can become a friend or acquaintance. If you are mainly meeting people of your own ethnic group, these are the people who are likely to become your friends. For similar reasons, segregated people are more likely to marry within their own group. As a result, Toronto Jews are very endogamous (or, in-marrying). This penchant to marry within the group has persisted across generations and research shows it is one of the most important differences between the Jewish, Ukrainian, Italian and German communities in Toronto.

People who segregate themselves are also more likely to keep up their ethnic language use. Accordingly, Ukrainian Canadians, Italian Canadians and Jewish Canadians are more likely to keep up their ancestral language than members of other groups in Canada the same length of time. They not only know and use the language, they also urge their children to learn it. German Canadians, by contrast, are much less likely to keep up their ancestral language because they do not traditionally practise self-segregation.

Economic factors play a part in maintaining ethnic segregation, too. When the Jews first settled in Toronto (1910-1930s), they suffered from anti-Semitism. Bigotry against the Jews then was as severe as the bigotry facing non-white immigrants today. The Jews dealt with this in several ways. First, they entered professions or created businesses which would let them be their own bosses. Even today, many Jews are self-employed. Second, they drummed up business within their own ethnic group, so they wouldn't have to rely on members of other groups for economic survival. As a result, even today, Toronto Jews are much more likely than other businesspeople to report that their customers belong to their own ethnic group.

To judge from these data, an ethnic identity thrives when people surround themselves with others of the same ethnic group, marry them, befriend them, sell to them and buy from them. Under these conditions, it is easy to keep up the traditional ethnic language and customs. And this process feeds on itself. Strong ethnic identities increase the likelihood of continued segregation, especially in groups featuring a high degree of what sociologist Raymond Breton calls **institutional completeness**.

Institutional Completeness

Institutional completeness is a measure of the degree to which an ethnic group provides its members with the services they require through their own institutions. These organizations include places of worship, schools, banks and media that are separate from those of the larger society. In a group with strong institutional (or community) completeness, members do not need to depend on the services of ethnic "outsiders."

Full community completeness is rare, however. Whether an ethnic group can develop a complete range of institutions depends on many factors. These include the size of the ethnic group, its assets, and the ties of friendship, family and work among group members. Ethnic harmony and loyalty are also critical. Not least, community completeness depends on the range of jobs that are available in the ethnic community.

In turn, a community's degree of completeness influences the number of members who carry out most of their activities within the ethnic group. Ethnic organizations — schools, day-care centres, camps, places of worship, business groups, social clubs, mutual-aid societies and credit unions — all give people a chance to meet other group members. They also promote group goals and make people more aware of their ethnicity.

The kinds of problems immigrants face on arrival in Canada influence the degree of completeness a group develops. Many visible-minority immigrants, and their native-born children, may feel discriminated against, as the data in Social Profile 7-2 indicate. Immigrants may be unable to speak English or French. They may be new to city life or lack marketable skills and job contacts. On the positive side, they may have brought from their homeland social contacts they can use to cultivate business and friendship ties here. So new immigrants create a community that plays to their strengths and hides their weaknesses, useful in the face of a dominant culture that is stronger still.

This is bound to be important for groups that face serious prejudice and discrimination. Settling in a "complete" community can protect immigrants from a hostile social milieu outside it. Jews and Chinese in Canada, both victims of prejudice in the past, have used this self-protective tactic for generations. And for generations, Jews and other self-segregating minorities have been exploited by dominant groups against whose power that self-segregation has acted to protect them.

However, self-segregation is not restricted to Jews and Chinese, nor to Canada. The same phe-

---

SOCIAL PROFILE 7.2

Attitudes to Visible Minorities

A. "Visible minorities often bring discrimination upon themselves by their own personal habits and attitudes."

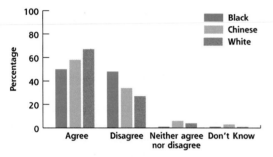

B. "It's got to the point where visible minorities often get better treatment than other Canadians."

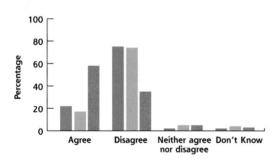

C. "If companies have few visible minority workers, they should be made to hire more visible minority workers when they hire new staff."

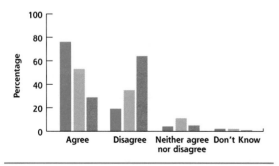

Source: Based on statistics appearing in York University, Institute for Social Research *Newsletter*, Winter 1996, Vol 11 #1, p. 2. Study of Torontonians' attitudes conducted on behalf of the Commission on Systemic Racism in the Ontario Criminal Justice System.

nomenon is practised by East Indian people in South Africa, for example. Over time, the East Indian community in that country has prospered and many members have become successful businesspeople. Like Canadian Jews and Chinese, they have used family businesses and a strong ethnic community to amass their capital.

Such ethnic groups keep to themselves in separate communities even after the discrimination has diminished or disappeared. The community continues to defend its members against discrimination and pressures to assimilate. It also maintains group cohesion by creating institutions, gaining control of resources and providing a variety of cultural and social services. Thus the community is self-maintaining: institutions within it create a demand for the services they provide. For example, ethnic schools foster the belief that they provide a better or richer education for their students. They also keep children in contact with others of their own group.

The mere survival of an ethnic community does not prove that discrimination is occurring. Neither does the absence of an ethnic community prove it is *not* occurring. Some groups which suffer from bigotry have little chance to protect themselves in this way, despite good reasons to do so. For example, Canadian blacks lack the community completeness that would help them prosper. Coming from many birthplaces and cultural backgrounds, blacks have so far been unable to unite to develop common institutions.

Canada's pattern of ethnic pluralism and self-segregation has led sociologists to describe Canada as a "mosaic." But because of the link between ethnicity and life chances, sociologists have also made a close study of the inequality among ethnic groups. This leads to additional questions about ethnic and race relations that stress the conflict perspective.

THE VERTICAL DIMENSION OF PLURALISM

In a pluralist society like Canada, how do the members of some ethnic groups get to control the members of other groups? And why do some ethnic groups enjoy a higher social status, higher average income and greater chance to set the cultural and political agenda than other groups? These are some of the questions we ask when we consider the "vertical dimension" of ethnic pluralism.

By *vertical dimension*, we mean the ways in which ethnic communities are ranked from top to bottom in relation to wealth, power and prestige. This is referred to as the system of *ethnic stratification*, a social ranking of people based on ethnicity. In a society that is ethnically stratified, each ethnic group occupies a well-defined position. And at the top of the ranking system are people with the power to define which qualities are most socially desirable. These qualities are usually their own. Other groups are judged on their similarity to the top group and in that particular sense, to be ethnic is synonymous with relative powerlessness.

Ethnic stratification only occurs in a society whose members attach cultural meanings to physical and ancestral traits — to skin colour, birthplace or preferred foods and clothing, for example. There is nothing about the features themselves that naturally signals "good" or "bad," "smart" or "dumb," "hard-working" or "lazy." Ethnic stratification exists because people attach meanings to these features and base their behaviour on these meanings.

In Canadian sociology, the study of ethnic stratification took centre stage when sociologist John Porter published his classic work *The Vertical Mosaic* in 1965. His view of Canadian society stressed the historic link between class inequality and ethnicity.

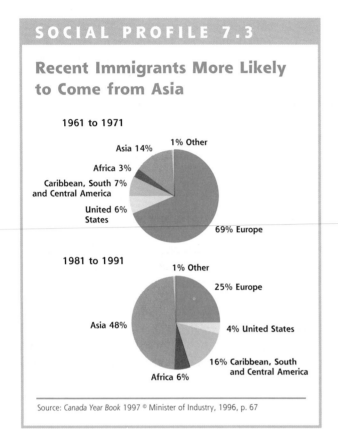

SOCIAL PROFILE 7.3

Recent Immigrants More Likely to Come from Asia

1961 to 1971

Asia 14%
1% Other
Africa 3%
Caribbean, South 7%
and Central America
United 6%
States
69% Europe

1981 to 1991

1% Other
25% Europe
Asia 48%
4% United States
16% Caribbean, South and Central America
Africa 6%

Source: *Canada Year Book* 1997 © Minister of Industry, 1996, p. 67

The finding that ethnicity and race, along with social class, are part of Canada's stratification system led Porter to describe Canada as a **vertical mosaic**. Since then, that metaphor has become a part of our national identity. A *mosaic* is a pattern made of small, distinct pieces. Sociologically, a mosaic is a society in which members of different ethnic groups keep up their distinct identities and cultures.

Porter called Canada a "vertical" mosaic because he found that people's ethnic backgrounds determine their place in the system of inequality. According to Porter, ethnic groups have unequal access to all sectors of the economy and to entry into the economic and political elite. Porter showed that Canadian society is stratified along ethnic lines, with the English and French Charter Groups at the top of the social ladder. Other ethnic groups are ranked according to how closely they resemble Anglo-Saxons, who form the dominant group.

Because of this, Porter argued, you can predict a person's socio-economic status — that is, education, income and job prestige — just by knowing that individual's ethnic origin. People's life chances are largely set by their ethnic origins.

This link between ethnicity and social status arose from Canada's pattern of immigration, discussed earlier. Certain groups had come to do certain kinds of work: the Ukrainians to farm the Prairies, the Italians to build Canada's cities, and so on. Over time, they and their descendants had stayed at the same economic level, even in the same industry. The reason, Porter believed, was ethnic bias and lack of educational opportunity.

Though Porter focused on Canada, the same processes have operated in many other countries. Take Germany, a country which has admitted many Southern European immigrants over the past few decades. Studies show that Germans rank these immigrants, putting those from Southern Europe (e.g., Sardinia, Greece or Turkey) at the bottom of the social ladder. German companies prefer to hire native German workers, thus keeping immigrants from blending into the German economy. As in Canada, immigrants are admitted mainly because native-born workers lack the skills or willingness to do the available work.

The United States, unlike Canada, has never willingly been a vertical mosaic. It has always tried to be a *melting pot* which assimilated its citizens. People were taught to consider themselves Americans first and ethnic minorities second, if at all. The U.S. has always fought to create a new national identity, not a mixture of old identities.

Given this goal, there have been criticisms of the American trend towards multicultural education. Critics of the new multiculturalism believe that public education should unify Americans of all cultural backgrounds, not protect and shelter distinct identities.

For their part, Canadians have always been less certain of their national identity than Americans. By default, ethnic and regional identities have always been much more important in Canada than in the United States. Yet Porter believed that a modern society should break down ethnic identities by increasing the chances for post-secondary education and helping minorities to get this education. This is why he strongly supported the growth of Canada's university and college systems in the 1960s.

Then, most sociologists thought that as educational inequalities lessened, economic inequalities would lessen too. As economic inequalities lessened, ethnic affiliation would weaken as well. However, data from many countries cast doubt on this theory.

For example, in Malaysia, educational reformers tried to weaken the link between ethnicity and social status. As in Canada, they hoped that expanding the educational system would increase educational equality and in turn, lead to more equal incomes. Instead, an enlarged educational system *widened* the income gap between native Malays and other groups. This sharpened ethnic tensions.

We now know that economic inequalities often *increase* with the spread of higher education. The reason is that educational credentials go mainly to middle-class people. They serve to justify, not reduce, inequities that already exist in the society. As well, a higher education is no guarantee that people will give up their ethnic identity. Many upwardly mobile people keep a strong ethnic identity *despite* their higher education and prosperity. As mentioned earlier, the Toronto Jews are one group that does this. So it is hard to argue that attachment to an ethnic identity disappears with upward mobility. And there is no proof that expanding higher education solves the problems of social inequality.

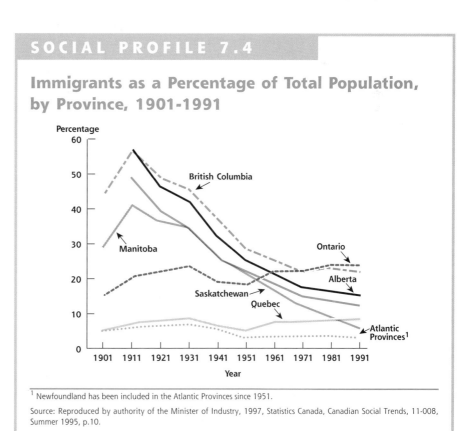

SOCIAL PROFILE 7.4

Immigrants as a Percentage of Total Population, by Province, 1901-1991

[1] Newfoundland has been included in the Atlantic Provinces since 1951.

Source: Reproduced by authority of the Minister of Industry, 1997, Statistics Canada, Canadian Social Trends, 11-008, Summer 1995, p.10.

Like Canada, most multi-ethnic societies are a vertical mosaic, at least for a time. For example, Israel is a multi-ethnic society made up largely of immigrants. *Within* the Jewish population of that country, the "Charter Group" — Jews who were living in the area before 1948, the time of statehood — are more privileged than other Jews. The Jewish groups arriving in Israel more recently — from Asia, Northern Africa and Eastern Europe — are worse off. Not only are they poorer and less educated, but their investments in higher education do not pay off as well as equal investments by the Charter Group.

Some multi-ethnic societies like Nigeria manage to achieve a better balance between the ruling group and other groups. The groups interact cautiously to avoid conflict and help ensure economic success. People from the secondary ethnic groups rarely challenge the dominant Hausa group, even when that means swallowing their own ethnic pride. However, this balance of power is also sustained by a repressive military government and we should not underestimate the importance of force in maintaining the peace.

At the other end of the continuum is Rwanda, where minority Tutsis have tried in vain to control the majority Hutus. The two groups have repeatedly slaughtered each other in a civil war that has nearly destroyed the country and spilled over into neighbouring Burundi and Zaire. The example of Rwanda shows what happens when an ethnic rivalry is ignited and the state is unable to contain it politically or militarily.

Social Distance

Status differences between ethnic groups are also likely to show themselves in **social distance**. This is a restraint placed on interactions between people who belong to groups ranked as superior and inferior in status. All socially "distant" relationships are unequal relationships. As such, they are governed by norms which specify the way superiors and inferiors should relate to one another. Even when such relations do become close, the norms still oblige people to keep their "proper place."

In race and ethnic relations, fear, suspicion and hostility often accompany social distance. E. S. Bogardus (1959) created the most commonly used measure of social distance. It asks people to say to which steps on the following scale of intimacy they would admit members of various ethnic and racial groups:

1. to close kinship by marriage

2. to my club as personal chums

3. to my street as neighbours

4. to employment in my occupation

5. to citizenship in my country

6. as visitors only to my country

7. would exclude from my country

Social distance measures *both* the horizontal and vertical dimensions of ethnic relations. On the horizontal side, social distance between two groups is influenced by the internal cohesion of each group. Some evidence suggests that groups which are highly cohesive tend to maintain a larger (average) distance from others than groups which are less cohesive.

Social distance is also influenced by the degree of familiarity between the ethnic groups. Thus, it reflects past experiences of intimacy: we prefer to be close to people we have been close to before. Conversely, we avoid people we have had little contact with in the past. For example, Australians show the most social distance to ethnic groups that immigrated most recently; notably, the Vietnamese. They show the least social distance to ethnic groups that immigrated longest ago: that is, Europeans. Asians, Indians and Middle Eastern peoples score between these extremes on the distance measure. So people we scarcely know are (usually) not people we want to imagine being close to.

Because of this link between social distance and familiarity, many believe that social distance can be reduced by learning more about other ethnic groups. It is hard to hold fanciful ideas when you have good information about the ways people really behave. In support of this view, a study of black Ethiopian immigrants to Israel showed that the more contact a person had with the newcomers, the less social distance that person wanted from them. Therefore, ignorance *is* a factor in distance ratings.

Research shows that familiarity reduces fear and hostility between groups, especially when interactions between "different kinds" of people are (1) gradual, relaxed and repeated; (2) cooperative, not competitive; (3) guided by norms of friendliness; (4) between people of equal status; and (5) supported by legitimate authorities (e.g., government officials, teachers, clergy). Such interactions are particularly beneficial when they contradict the stereotyped notions groups hold about one another.

The worst inter-group problems are likely to arise in fundamentally competitive situations: for example, work settings. Problems are more easily avoided

Like other Canadian groups that have been oppressed, native peoples have sometimes taken their grievances to the streets.

among young people in social or educational settings. This puts a special onus on teachers and others in contact with young people to create the best possible conditions for inter-group understanding and cooperation.

On the vertical side, social distance is influenced by the value, prestige or attractiveness a culture attaches to one or another ethnic group. Measures of social distance confirm other measures of social ranking. We prefer being close to others who possess the qualities we idealize (if not possess). As discussed in Chapter 3 (Socialization), values are learned; and at least from a conflict perspective, they service the ideology of the dominant class.

Research on vertical distance has found that people of different income, regional, educational, occupational, and even ethnic group show similar patterns of preference in rating other groups. In an American study, the most admissible groups — those granted the least distance on average — are most like the dominant white, Anglo-Saxon group: namely, the (white) English and (white) Canadians. Most people would accept them as citizens, neighbours, even family members. At the other extreme, white respondents put Hindus, Turks and blacks at the greatest distance, on average.

In a similar Canadian study, respondents put "Canadians" (meaning WASPs), British and Americans at the least social distance. Northern Europeans and French Canadians followed closely, then Eastern Europeans. At the bottom of the ranking were visible minorities: in descending order, Chinese, Japanese, West Indians, Eskimos, East Indians, native Indians and Metis. On average, respondents wanted twice as much social distance from the visible minorities as they did from "Canadians."

To some degree, the results vary depending on who is doing the rating. People typically rate members of their own group higher on the list, according them less social distance, than people outside the group do. However, minority group members usually conform to majority views, proving that acculturation imposes similar values and perceptions on all of us, whatever our ethnic or racial background.

Social distance is also affected by social class. For example, Egyptian research showed that upper-class students want less social distance from (high-status) Westerners than they do from (lower-status) Arabs. By contrast, lower-class Egyptian students want less social distance from fellow Arabs and more from Westerners. This shows the two groups of students had different goals: the lower-class students wanted to protect themselves against (possibly hostile) Westerners and to offset assimilation; the upper-class students were prepared to cross ethnic lines in order to form alliances with people of the same social status. A brief glance at the economic positions of the two groups might show how their preferences are in line with their greatest likelihood of material advantage.

In the United States, a growth in respect for cultural and social diversity over the last sixty-five years has produced a roughly 50 per cent reduction in the average social distance that people say they want to maintain. Everyone is getting closer to everyone else and even the distance between whites and blacks is much less than it once was. In "horizontal" terms this seems to mean that ethnic groups are opening up to outside influences and tolerance is increasing. More people accept "different" kinds of people as neighbours, workmates, friends and spouses than ever before. In short, ethnic diversity isn't obviously and "naturally" a problem, but we can make it one.

In "vertical" terms, the reduction in social distance means that there is less inequality based on ethnicity than in the past. Since Porter released his findings on the vertical mosaic in 1965, sociologists have researched every corner of this question. They have done so with better data and more powerful techniques of analysis than Porter had available. As a result, they have concluded that (1) Ethnicity is not a particularly good predictor of either socio-economic status or of mobility; (2) Ethnic inequality seems to be decreasing over time; (3) The members of many ethnic groups do experience considerable "net" upward mobility; and (4) The effect of ethnicity on "status attainment" becomes weaker as immigrants become more "acculturated" (Brym and Fox, 1989: 107).

Brym and Fox concede that "these generalizations do not hold as strongly for members of some groups — especially some racial minorities — as they do overall." Canada remains a vertical mosaic along racial, if not ethnic, lines, then. Considering how much Canadian society has changed since 1965, we cannot now know if Porter was simply wrong in his analysis of Canadian society or if his analysis was right for the period of time in which it was produced and times have changed.

Ethnic Politics

Many different factors, including religion, language, residential segregation and in-marriage, help people to form a border around the group and fight to increase their relative standing. When such factors overlap with political divisions, ethnic groups are likely to compete for control over state institutions and entitlements. Sociologists call this ethnic competition for control "ethnic politics."

In Canada, the reality of Quebec as a mainly French province has spurred the practice of ethnic politics throughout the country. Groups are very jealous of their rights. Beyond that, ethnic groups with strong community completeness, like the Hutterites we spoke of earlier, are almost self-sufficient. Often, members of such groups interact with members of other groups only through their communal leaders. Even groups that are less self-sufficient often assign to leaders the burden of *political* contact with other ethnic groups. But this can lead to problems.

Just imagine a society in which there were, say, three of everything: three primary-school systems, three college and university systems, three public broadcasting systems, three banking systems, three public-service unions, three charitable organizations like the United Way, three Scouts organizations, and so on. If you have been able to imagine this, you are coming close to imagining Holland, with its three parallel structures (for Catholics, Protestants and nonbelievers). In fact, Holland is more complex than that. So is Canada.

In Canada, not only do we find parallel systems based on religion, we also find parallel systems based on ethnicity: for example, different sets of institutions for Irish, Portuguese, Italian and Chinese Catholics. Cross-cutting this are provincial and federal rules which increase the separation of, and competition between, these subsystems.

The degree of parallelism also influences what kinds of matters become public issues in ethnic communities and what bargaining takes place. These problems often arise because groups think they are in a *zero-sum* game, with one ethnic group ultimately gaining power only at the expense of another. The greater the parallelism, the more likely it is that ethnic communities will want access to the same resources and rewards, and the greater the threat one community poses to another. As well, the greater the parallelism, the more conflicts will likely arise over authority and the more effort each group will have to make to capture control of the larger political system.

The question sociologists ask is, What connects all these parallel structures together into a single country? The answer is ethnic leadership, which plays a central role in Canada's social life. The political process requires that group leaders reach accords with other leaders. In a society like Canada, made up of many parallel social structures, politics is based on competing ethnic groups and colluding leaders — what sociologists call "accommodating elites."

In the end, ethnicity has more sway over Canadian politics than class does. People are far more likely to vote for a candidate of their own ethnic group than for a candidate of their own occupational or income class. As a result, ethnic leaders can more dependably get community members to vote as a bloc than union leaders can. This gives ethnic leaders great power.

In the struggle for organizational power, people use the networks they have at their command. Community leaders gain the most power from ethnic parallelism, but they are not the only ones. Members gain too from belonging to a highly organized and powerful ethnic group.

These comments on ethnic politics apply most to French Canadians in Quebec but, increasingly, they also apply to other well-organized ethnic groups like Italian Canadians, Ukrainian Canadians, Jewish Canadians and Chinese Canadians. As their numbers, capital and community completeness grow, these ethnic groups become more potent forces in Canadian politics. The political party most skilled at getting the support of ethnic elites has the best chance of winning elections in Canada today.

In many countries besides Canada, politicians have to seek votes across ethnic lines, and often interethnic relations benefit from this need. The process demands political compromises and avoids making any one ethnic group feel left out. So, for example, Malaysia (like Canada) has a possibly explosive ethnic situation. Yet because of the need to form political alliances across ethnic groups, there is little actual conflict.

At the other extreme is Sri Lanka, where no such compromise occurs and ethnic conflict is ongoing. This could be a valuable lesson for the developing Pacific Island nations mentioned earlier. Some, like Fiji, have the added problem of trying to harmonize the ideas of Western democracy with the traditional customs and group rights of native peoples.

It is easy to see the social, cultural and political benefits that group members can gain through self-segregation. However, the flip side of inclusion is exclusion. What one person considers a mere preference for "people like myself" seems like discrimination or prejudice to someone else.

Prejudice

Although many people confuse the two terms, social scientists treat prejudice and discrimination as different. **Prejudice** is a negative, hostile social attitude towards members of another group. All members of the group — because of their group membership — are assumed to have unsuitable qualities. **Discrimination** refers to actions carried out against another person or group because of that individual's group membership. In particular, it means denying opportunities that people would grant to equally qualified members of their own group.

An important element in prejudice is the use of **stereotypes** — fixed mental images that prejudiced people believe embody members of a given group. When we make use of stereotypes, we categorize people on the basis of only some characteristics which we exaggerate in importance.

For example, one study compared the ways American sportscasters report the achievements of white football players and black football players. It found that white television announcers reproach black NFL players more and praise them less than they do white players with similar abilities, playing the same positions.

The announcers also describe black players more often as targets of aggression and white players as initiators. Finally, they portray the white players as more intelligent than the black players. By inference, the successes of the black players are due to instinct or luck, for which they deserve no credit.

Note the striking features of these findings, for they are found in all cases of racial prejudice. Typically, prejudiced views are negative views based on *hidden assumptions* about the way race is related to intelligence, morality or other valued qualities. Sometimes these slanted views are even worded like praise, as in "Jewish accountants *really* know how to juggle the books" or "Black boxers can *really* take a lot of punishment" or "French Canadian women can *really* cook."

Most stereotypes *are* both prejudiced and prejudicial. They justify our prejudices against racial and ethnic minorities, giving them shape and order. In doing so they justify prejudice. There is no clearer evidence of the harmfulness of prejudice than the effect of Nazism's anti-Semitic policies on Germany itself. In the 1930s and 1940s, German society made huge sacrifices to carry out its racist policies. Leaving aside the moral issue, this was money, time and effort that could have been spent improving the lives of average Germans.

Instead, racist prejudice destroyed the German universities, fine arts, professional, scientific and engineering capabilities, and even Germany's business community and civil service. This was all part of the obsessive effort to keep non-Aryans out of public life. Germany and the Germans had to pay a heavy price for their prejudice, and from that episode most Germans have learned the folly of racism. Unfortunately, a violent minority continues to threaten and harm visible minorities, such as Turkish "guest-workers" and Asian refugees.

Discrimination

Prejudice is the outcome of many different factors and it may be inevitable. What's more, prejudice may even be tolerable if it does not grow into discrimination. As human beings, we all like some people and dislike others. We feel drawn to some people and repelled by others, often for no good reason. This happens even among our neighbours, school friends and relatives.

Many stereotypes are built into our popular culture and we rarely think about them. So, for example, there has historically been a stereotyping of blondes in our society. On the one hand there is the idea that blondes have more fun (and *are* more fun!). Alongside this, there is the image of the female "dumb blonde" popularized by Marilyn Monroe. She is either unintelligent or keeps her intelligence from showing, in the interest of having good relations with men. (And from a male-dominant perspective, this reticence or actual lack of intelligence may be perceived as fun.) In some societies where natural blondes are particularly rare, these ideas may be taken to extremes that are both racist and sexist. Even in our own society, these ideas complicate life for all women, blonde and otherwise.

A problem only arises when we transform our prejudiced views and feelings into action as, for example, when a teacher gives a student he or she does not like an unwarranted lower grade. That is discrimination. Discrimination takes a variety of forms: job segregation, unequal pay for equal work, or denial of promotion, among others. It is hard to measure the effects of discrimination, as they are often subtle. However, we can usually show that the members of some ethnic and racial groups enjoy advantages over the members of others. When people with the same ability receive different rewards for doing the same work, we can claim that, logically, discrimination exists.

It took field experiments by Henry and Ginzberg (1985) to show the *true* extent of job discrimination. In one set of experiments, they sent two job applicants

Dyeing To Be Blond

In Canada, with many people of Northern European ancestry, there are many natural blondes. And (partly) because blondes are common, we pay little attention when people use hair dyes to "help" their blondness along or switch to blond from red-, brown- or black-coloured hair. But in Brazil, with few people of Northern European ancestry, natural blondness is a rarity and switching to blond conveys a clear, not so subtle message. The message it conveys is about stereotyping in Brazil and, perhaps, in Canada, as well.

"Below the equator blondes gain a fascinating quality that they would never have in Europe or North America. They become a symbol of purity and paradise," says Fausto Fawcett, a Rio writer and professional bohemian who hosts a late-night television show called *Basic Instinct*.

Mr. Fawcett's program is popular in Brazil because it features several scantily clad blond women dancing and posing while the host recites his poetry about — what else? — blondes.

Despite the popularity of *Basic Instinct* and Xuxa [an entertainer], many in Brazil say the fixation with blond women is sexist and even racist. Black activist Cristina Rodrigues goes so far as to say that the country's fascination with light-skinned blondes is a major symptom of racism. "People want to be blond and white in Brazil because it is a symbol of power and wealth," says Ms. Rodrigues, a member of the black cultural and social activist group Olodum.

"In Brazil, nobody wants to be black because the mass media equates black with poor and stupid," says Ms. Rodrigues, adding that among the black population there are 53 different words for black. Depending on the shade of their skin, many black or mixed-race Brazilians will classify themselves as "chocolate" or "bon-bon" or "coffee with milk" rather than call themselves black, she says. During the last census in 1991, the federal government launched a nation-wide campaign to encourage black Brazilians to take pride in their roots and count themselves black in the census.

"In a *mestizo* society, the darker people are always stigmatized. The higher you get in Brazilian society, the whiter it is. Ever since the last Brazilian emperor married a blond Austrian woman, the aristocracy has always been very white and very blond," Brazilian anthropologist Roberto Damatta says.

For one of Rio's top hair stylists, Eduardo Meckelburg, the Brazilian fascination with blondes is good for business. At his tony salon in Ipanema, Mr. Meckelburg, known as Dudu to his clients, says that more than 40 per cent of his customers are blond. Of that number only 5 per cent are authentic blondes; the others come in to colour their hair on a regular basis, he says.

Source: Isabel Vincent, "Success-seeking women are dyeing to be blonde," *The Globe and Mail*, Mon. Feb. 7, 1994, pp. A1, A2

matched with respect to age, sex, education, experience, style of dress and personality to apply for the same advertised job. The applicants differed in only one respect: race. One was white and the other black. In all, teams of applicants sought a total of 201 jobs in this way.

Some applicants were young male or female students applying for semi-skilled or unskilled jobs — server, gas-station attendant, store clerk — that people might expect them to seek. Other applicants were middle-aged professional actors. Armed with fake résumés, they applied for positions in retail management, sales jobs in prestigious stores and waiting and hosting jobs in fancy restaurants.

In a second set of experiments, researchers called 237 telephone numbers published in the classified-job section of the newspaper and presented themselves as applicants. The jobs they were seeking ranged widely from unskilled up to highly skilled, well-paying jobs. Henry and Ginzberg report that callers phoned each number four times, using different voices. One voice had no discernible accent (it sounded like a white-majority Canadian), the second had a

Slavic or Italian accent, the third had a Jamaican accent and the fourth had a Pakistani accent.

Men who did the calling (no women took part in this study) presented themselves as having the same characteristics: the same age, education, years of job experience, and so on. As before, the applicants were suited in age and (imaginary) experience for the jobs they were seeking.

With data collected in this way, the researchers created an Index of Discrimination that combined the results of in-person and telephone testing. They found that, in twenty calls, black applicants would be offered thirteen interviews yielding one job. By contrast, in twenty calls, white applicants would be offered seventeen interviews yielding three jobs. Henry and Ginzberg conclude that *The overall Index of Discrimination is therefore three to one. Whites have three job prospects to every one that blacks have*" (*ibid*: 308).

This study and others like it prove that racial discrimination is not the result of a few bigoted employers. There is a general bias against hiring non-whites. That is why many immigrants, especially the visible minorities, become "middlemen." Important "middleman minorities" around the world include the Chinese in Southeast Asia, the Jews, Greeks and Armenians in Europe, the East Indians and Arabs in East Africa, and the Koreans in North America. All of these groups display a high degree of ethnic cohesion, and their members tend to achieve more than usual economic success in societies where they have been, at least at first, unwelcome.

Research on "middleman minorities" indicates the following historical pattern is typical. A culturally or racially distinct group immigrates and suffers discrimination. Members of the group come to see themselves as "strangers" in the country and, to protect themselves, settle in the larger towns and cities. There, they become self-employed as merchants or professionals. As a result they come into competition with local capitalists of the dominant ethnic group. Their economic success depends upon thrift, a high degree of education and organization, and the use of family and community ties in business. By these means the group achieves a middle-class standard of living.

Socially, members of the group keep apart from other ethnic groups. They maintain their traditional values and institutions and form strong ethnic communities. Some also form alliances with members of the ruling group. Their successes often draw the hostility and envy of the poor members of other groups. And this hostility strengthens a feeling of rejection which, in turn, strengthens the minority group's resolve to maintain its self-reliance and succeed economically.

Late-arriving ethnic groups — like later-born children — must be creative to find a niche for themselves in the society, so innovation plays an important part in their relations with other groups. Since these middleman minorities have less stake in the existing social order, they are more open to social and political change. And because they have a stronger need to protect themselves from bigotry, they are more open to new ideas which help secure their position in business, the professions and other walks of life. Often, they are also overrepresented in progressive political causes for the same reasons: a weak commitment to traditional ways and a strong sense of connection with "underdogs."

Given the value of such self-protective behaviour, both for the minority group and (through innovation) for society as a whole, why don't *all* minority groups become middleman minorities? The answer is that some — for example, Northern and Eastern European immigrant groups — lack racial distinctiveness and are less subject to discrimination. Others — for example, black Canadians or native

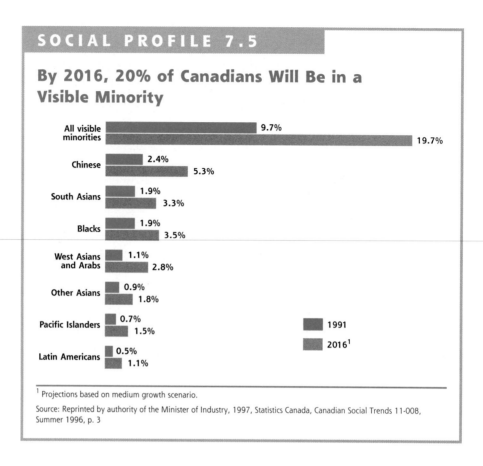

SOCIAL PROFILE 7.5

By 2016, 20% of Canadians Will Be in a Visible Minority

	1991	2016[1]
All visible minorities	9.7%	19.7%
Chinese	2.4%	5.3%
South Asians	1.9%	3.3%
Blacks	1.9%	3.5%
West Asians and Arabs	1.1%	2.8%
Other Asians	0.9%	1.8%
Pacific Islanders	0.7%	1.5%
Latin Americans	0.5%	1.1%

[1] Projections based on medium growth scenario.

Source: Reprinted by authority of the Minister of Industry, 1997, Statistics Canada, Canadian Social Trends 11-008, Summer 1996, p. 3

peoples — are racially distinct and socially vulnerable. However, they lack traditions of trade and cooperation that are usually based on cultural unity. As well, they may lack enough members or group assets to found a self-reliant community.

No less serious than blatant and intentional discrimination is what people have called **systemic**, *community*, or *constructive* **discrimination**. This is unintended discrimination that is so deeply embedded in a society's institutions and customs that it is hard to see. It shows itself in practices whose "naturalness" and fairness we take for granted, and whose hidden assumptions we very often forget to question.

One example is the height requirement for police officers and firefighters. Because northern racial and ethnic groups are often taller, this rule unintentionally discriminates against southern groups. Taking a height requirement for granted is part of the problem. Once people realize that such a rule is unnecessary — that shorter people can do just as good a job as taller people — the basis for racial discrimination disappears.

Similar problems have arisen with respect to work scheduling. Christians will want to have Sunday off, but orthodox Jews will want Saturday off, and Moslems Friday. A rigid rule that Sunday is the only acceptable Sabbath excludes all non-Christian applicants for the job. But often there is no reason for the rule. Once the rule goes, unintended religious discrimination goes too.

Discrimination is harmful in many ways — not least that it encourages reverse discrimination. Until all institutions are kept from practising discrimination

Nazism destroyed Germany and much of the rest of the world in this century. Neo-nazism is now, once again, threatening the peace and security of minority peoples.

against minorities, minority groups will discriminate in their own favour. As in the past, their best strategy is to rely on community completeness and the formation of subeconomies. But as we have noted, some racial minorities like the blacks still have trouble doing this. They continue to lack the wealth, connections, education and community completeness of Canadians of Jewish, Chinese, Italian, Greek and Ukrainian background.

Like social distance, the problem of discrimination is starting to change for the better. With provincial human rights codes and the federal Charter of Rights and Freedoms in place, the 1990s has seen one victory over discrimination after another. Not only ethnic and racial minorities, but women, the elderly, the physically challenged and homosexuals have all called for protection against direct and systemic discrimination. Almost without exception, the courts have decided in their favour.

Racism

As we saw in Chapter 2, *ethnocentrism* is a tendency to view the world from the perspective of one's own culture: in effect, to use one's own culture as a measuring stick. **Racism** is ethnocentrism carried to an extreme — a belief that one's own biological group or race is superior to all the others.

Over the course of history, there have been many motives for racism. Often, racism has served to justify inequality, whether economic, political or symbolic. But the case of Nazi Germany showed that racism can be a manifestation of nothing more than irrational, sadistic, violent emotions. There, the claims to be furthering political and economic domination served as *excuses*, not causes of the racism.

However, conflict theorists argue that unequal racial and ethnic relations are mainly a consequence of economic inequality. People with the most wealth, prestige and power — the dominant group — maintain their position through exploitation. To do this in large numbers, some ethnic or racial groups exploit other groups. The exploiters use racism to justify this inequality so they can feel good about themselves. Thus, racism develops out of a group's need to justify the exploitation of another group. Members of the dominant group blame the misfortunes of the subordinate group on an inferior genetic constitution (laziness, stupidity, aggressiveness, and so on), bad cultural values, or both.

People with the most intensely racist feelings are not always the ones to gain most from a system of inequality. Often, they are people who feel they have the most to *lose* should the targets of their racism gain equal status. Swaan (1989) calls this "downward jealousy." Economic competition from minorities poses the greatest threat to low-status members of the dominant cultural group — "white trash" in the southern United States or Afrikaner farmers in the Transvaal, for example.

Consider the experience of Japanese Canadians on Canada's West Coast. In 1941, most Japanese Canadians were taken from coastal British Columbia to isolated interior camps and settlements. Officials gave the excuse that Japanese Canadians, of whom three-quarters had been born in Canada, posed a national security threat during Canada's war with Japan.

Yet there had been ample evidence of hostility towards Japanese Canadians before the war. Most of the hostility came from people lower down the social scale. Social distance and stereotyping were evident on the West Coast even before the First World War. Among the victims were Japanese, Chinese and East Indian Canadians. The success of Japanese Canadians in fishing, farming and lumbering threatened the ordinary Canadians they competed with.

Anti-Japanese feelings culminated in the Vancouver Race Riots of 1907. Economic recessions usually produce feelings of insecurity among local workers who fear that immigrant or native-born minorities take jobs away from them. Concerns that the Japanese would take away their jobs led the white Anglo-Saxon majority to press for an agreement with Japan that would limit further immigration to Canada. It is against this historic backdrop of competition and dislike that we must understand anti-Japanese actions during the Second World War.

As we have said, racism develops out of a need to justify the exploitation of another group. Unfortunately, it does not disappear after the conditions that produced it disappear. When people have learned to think that social inequality reflects real differences in people's moral values or moral worth, they have trouble thinking differently about a group whose oppression they used to consider natural. Moreover, they have to deal with guilt about their own past acts of discrimination against other supposedly inferior groups.

In a roundabout way, ethnic and racial conflict — even serious conflict that includes riots — can have a positive effect on society. That's because such conflicts finally focus public attention on group relations. In turn, this forces politicians to take action. In the long term, there are likely to be improvements, as happened with race relations in Great Britain. As well, racism and exclusion from participation in the dominant society plays an important role in the formation and maintenance of minority identity and cohesion.

Canadians pride themselves on having avoided large-scale race riots of the kind that occurred in the United States, Britain and other countries. This success, along with the country's formal commitment to multiculturalism, has led many to assume there is no "race problem" in Canada. But sociologist Jeffrey Reitz (1988) draws a different conclusion. He argues that, in fact, there *is* a race problem in Canada that is no different, and no less, than that which exists in Britain. This is shown by comparing the results of Henry and Ginsberg (1985), who studied job discrimination in Canada, with the results of identical research in

Britain. They indicate that there is no less discrimination against black people in Canada than there is in Britain.

This conclusion would be contested by the results of an analysis by the Applied Research Branch of Statistics Canada which determined that the earnings gap between Canadian-born visible-minority and other men is very small. In fact, the Canadian-born visible minorities earn only 3.5 per cent less, and discrimination accounts for only about one-third of that. According to research done by Arnold de Silva and Craig Dougherty (1996), among immigrants, where the visible minority earns very much less than average, "the earnings gap is largely a reflection of quality differences in education, language proficiency and experience."

However, researchers for the Commission on Systemic Racism in the Ontario Criminal Justice System drew a conclusion more similar to Reitz's, citing a great deal of worrisome evidence about discrimination against black men by police, prosecutors and judges (see Applied Sociology, below). So, overt racial conflict may be lacking in Canada, but discrimination is not!

Factors which limit racial conflict today may disappear in the future, leaving Canada to play out Britain's racial conflicts of several decades earlier. As Reitz points out, young, single, native-born minorities are more likely to rebel against bigotry than their older, married, immigrant parents. As the fraction of native-born minorities grows, so does the risk of open conflict. We may even be facing the creation of a black underclass of the kind found in the United States.

APPLIED SOCIOLOGY

Systemic Discrimination in the Canadian Justice System

Sociologists know that social institutions rarely work the way they are "supposed to." Finding out how they actually work, and why they work that way, is a major concern of applied sociology. So, for example, the Canadian justice system is supposed to apply the laws of the land in a fair, unprejudiced manner. However, sociologists conducting research on behalf of the Commission on Systemic Racism in the Ontario Criminal Justice System found this is not the case. They found that, other things being equal . . .

- Black males are much more likely than other males to be harassed by the police:

  Black males report being stopped by police much more often than whites or Chinese males. These reported stops, particularly multiple stops, support complaints made to the commission and previous inquiries that the police single out black men. They appear to see black men as warranting more scrutiny than other people.

- Blacks charged with crimes are much less likely than whites to be granted bail:

  For example, blacks are twenty-seven times more likely to be imprisoned before their trials on charges of drug trafficking and importing charges and about twenty times as likely as whites to be imprisoned for drug-possession charges.

- Crown prosecutors put an undue emphasis on the accused black person's immigration status and ties to the black community:

  As a result, a great many blacks imprisoned before their trials have their bail set so high it is equivalent to an outright denial of bail.

- Many blacks in the community believe that racial discrimination is rampant:

  A belief that the justice system discriminates against blacks is widespread in the black community. That it is not a small, vocal minority which holds this view suggests that many have experienced this discrimination or heard about others who experienced it.

Source: Adapted from an article appearing in *The Globe and Mail*, Tues., Jan. 16, 1996, pp. A1, A7

If Reitz is right, at the very least we should stop being complacent. We also need to take steps to fight discrimination in the workplace and elsewhere; this may avert the disaster Reitz is projecting. And even if he is wrong, the country has lost nothing by opposing racism: it has simply made good on the promise of multiculturalism.

CLOSING REMARKS

Like other topics we have discussed so far, the study of ethnic and race relations offers a good example of the connection between macro and micro perspectives. On the one hand, ethnic (and racial) groups are macro phenomena: large categories of people that exist outside and "above" individuals in their language, institutions and material artifacts. National identities and customs are slow to change; indeed, many civilizations have lasted for thousands of years. Generation after generation is steeped in the traditional wisdom and taught what it means to be a Quebecer, a Jew, a Buddhist or a black person in a white-dominated country.

On the other hand, notions of ethnicity and race are mental constructs. Every day, we play out these rigid and outmoded ways of thinking and behaving. At any time, we can change or even reject the ideas we have learned about race and ethnicity. As a result, accepted ways of thinking, speaking and behaving do change over time. People marry out of their group, change religions, ignore the traditional ways. Slowly the traditions bend and change because dozens, then thousands, then millions of us rethink our way of doing things.

As we have seen in this chapter, Canada is a society built on differences. The British and French of North America built the country to preserve their cultures against American influence. From the beginning, ethnicity, language and religion were central to the creation of Canada and to the ways Canadians thought about themselves. It is not surprising, then, that ethnicity became tied into the politics and stratification of the country. The result was a vertical mosaic.

However, the vertical mosaic appears weaker today than it once was avowed to be, thanks largely to the immigration of minorities who became highly mobilized and highly educated after arriving in Canada. These groups have been important innovators in Canadian social life, since their group survival has depended on carving out a niche for themselves.

In the next chapter, we look at the third in our trio of major inequalities: gender inequality, and the relations between men and women.

Review Questions

1. What is ethnicity?
2. What is race?
3. In what sense is Canada an ethnically "pluralistic" society?
4. Why do Canada's native peoples today demand some degree of self-government?
5. What is a "visible minority"?
6. What is assimilation?
7. What different forms can assimilation take?
8. What is the connection between residential segregation and ethnic identity?
9. What is institutional completeness?
10. Why did John Porter describe Canada as a "vertical mosaic"?
11. Is Canada still a vertical mosaic?
12. What factors contribute to ethnic group cohesion?
13. What is the difference between "prejudice" and "discrimination"?
14. What is meant by "social distance"?
15. What is racism?

Discussion Questions

1. How are Canada's native peoples like, and how are they unlike, colonized Third World peoples?

2. Given Canada's history of immigration, what kinds of people — and how many — are likely to immigrate in the year 2025?

3. How might you test whether language loss within an ethnic minority leads to a decline in ethnic group cohesion?

4. Racism is only one possible response to economic difficulty. Other historical examples have been crime, political protest, escape into drugs and al-

cohol, and strengthened religious belief. What determines whether racism will be the response chosen at a particular time and place?

5. Worldwide, has there been more ethnic and racial conflict in the second half of the 20th century than in the first half? If so, how do you account for this upsurge?

6. Is the amount of intermarriage between two groups a good measure of the prejudice one group feels for another? If not, why not? Would more intermarriage cause prejudice to decline?

Suggested Readings

Breton, Raymond (1991) *The Governance of Ethnic Communities*. New York: Greenwood Press. This important book by one of the most influential and respected researchers on ethnicity in Canada examines the way in which the nation's ethnic communities are organized to govern themselves.

Driedger, Leo (1989) *The Ethnic Factor*. Toronto: McGraw-Hill Ryerson. A clear, concise, integrated text on ethnicity in Canada. Perhaps Driedger's greatest merit lies in having mastered, and being able to synthesize, the many diverse theoretical perspectives on ethnicity.

Frideres, James S. (ed.) (1993) *Native Peoples in Canada: Contemporary Conflicts*. Scarborough: Prentice Hall Canada Inc. Now in its fourth edition, Frideres's book not only is packed with a wealth of facts and figures, but also provides an insightful and comprehensive discussion of the difficult issues presently troubling relations between native peoples and the various levels of government.

Li, Peter S. (1988) *The Chinese in Canada*. Don Mills: Oxford University Press. One of the few books that examine an ethnic group in the context of its interactions with others. In particular, Li looks at the role played by racism in shaping the Chinese Canadian community

Porter, John (1965) *The Vertical Mosaic*. Toronto: University of Toronto Press. In the most widely celebrated work in Canadian sociology, John Porter shows the connections between social class and ethnic status. He explains why ethnic groups have had trouble improving their standing in society.

Satzewich, Vic (1992) *Deconstructing A Nation: Immigration, Multiculturalism and Racism in '90s Canada*. Halifax: Fernwood Publishing. This collection of papers by some of the foremost researchers on ethnicity in Canada is a particularly good source of information on current issues in the study of ethnicity.

Internet Resources

The following Web sites are good places to find more information about topics discussed in this chapter:

Aboriginal Links puts you in touch with over 200 links to Web sites operated by and for the Aboriginal people of Canada and the United States.
http://www.bloorstreet.com/300block/aborcan.htm

Black Web spotlights the heritage, achievements and business interests of the black community in the Greater Toronto Area, including a section devoted to black heroes.
http://www.black ~ web.com

Canadian Human Rights Commission provides information about this organization that has been fighting racial (and other) prejudice since 1978. You can reference the CHRC library online.
http://www.chrc.ca

Asian Canadian Newsgroup is intended to discuss issues affecting Asian-Canadian culture.
USENET: can.community.asian

Fighting Racism—The Communist View provides a communist perspective on racism and its solutions.
http://www.hartford-hwp.com/cp-usa/archives/96-02-17-3.html

Aboriginal Studies WWW Virtual Library contains links to information facilities on Australian Aborigines as well as ones pertaining to indigenous peoples.
http://coombs.anu.edu.au/WWWVL-Aboriginal.html

Migration and Ethnic Relations is a collection of links to major Web resources on migration and ethnic relations and features a keyword search.
http://www.ruu.nl/ercomer/wwwvl/index.html

Multiculturalism offers an essay explaining the origins of Canada's policy on multiculturalism and its effect on the rest of society.
http://infoservice.gc.ca:82/canadiana/faitc/fa26.html

GENDER RELATIONS

CHAPTER OUTLINE

Cultural artifacts express people's values. Paintings done in the late 19th century force us to wonder why fine artists then often portrayed women as sickly, sleeping or dead. Why did they, and their audience, equate sickliness with femininity and virtue?

GENDER DIFFERENTIATION

Like class and ethnicity, gender distinctions create a system of social differences which have important effects on people's lives. At their most trifling, gender differences are pleasant and enjoyable. As the French say, *Vive la difference!*, meaning "How wonderful it is that men and women are different in such delightful ways!" But many differences are neither delightful *nor* trifling.

You may not have thought of gender differences as part of a system of inequality. After all, to most of us being male or female seems to be natural, an inevitable result of human biology. But, just like class or ethnic differences, gender differences disadvantage some and advantage others. Indeed, in Canadian society, class and ethnic disadvantages are often entwined with gendered disadvantages. For example, other things being equal, women are more likely to be poor than men. Yet there is nothing "natural" or inevitable about being poor. We need to take gender into account in understanding inequality. Failing to do so prevents us from gaining a complete and precise picture of inequality in Canada.

You will find discussion of gender throughout this book. This chapter presents an overview of the topic: it is concerned with many of the forms that gender inequality and gender conflict take in society, and the ways they affect our social relations in general. But first we need to define the key terms **sex** and **gender**.

Gender as a Social Construction

CBC ⊛
"Educating Girls"

Sex is a biological concept. People are male or female from the moment of conception, with biological differences between the sexes that are anatomic, genetic and hormonal. These differences have few, if any, inevitable effects on modern social life. Men and women have different reproductive functions, but there is no scientific proof that there are biologically based psychological differences (such as a "maternal instinct") between human males and females. And as women spend less and less of their lives bearing children, the reproductive difference becomes less socially relevant to a definition of people's roles.

In contrast to biological sex, **gender** refers to culturally learned notions of masculinity and femininity. **Gender roles** are learned patterns of behaviour that a society expects of men or women, and they are a widespread aspect of social life. By **masculinity**, then, we mean that package of qualities that people in our society expect to find in a typical man. By **femininity**, we mean that package of qualities that people in our society expect to find in a typical woman.

So, for example, in our culture, as parents, few men have become as nurturant as women, with the result that fathers behave differently with their children than mothers do. As we learn from Everyday Life, below, there is some indication that younger men are learning to *seem* like more devoted fathers. However, as we also learn, most men continue to behave in traditionally gen-

EVERYDAY LIFE

The Sensitive New Age Guy Mystique

A lot of research shows that good parenting is important but that a lot of men don't seem to know, or care, much about the fathering role they have taken on. On the other hand, we do see evidence, especially among younger fathers, of greater sensitivity to their children and more willingness to put in time being a "good father." Is this change rare or widespread, real or just an illusion?

A recent theory has it that things have changed. It is a new world, people say, and the old ways are no more. The relations between men and women are more equal, and the responsibilities shared. The watchwords are sharing and caring.

Young fathers are one visible barometer of this shift, and certainly you can see the evidence of change all around. Fathers are assuming a level of responsibility and competence in child care and household duties that few of their fathers ever contemplated. It is one of the images of the generation — young fathers with infant children and paraphernalia in a variety and complexity that is wondrous to behold.

Indeed, the world really has changed, or part of the world. But in contemplating this brave and good new order, it's maybe useful to acknowledge that when people talk about a Sensitive New Age Guy, otherwise known as a SNAG, they usually snicker. And even when they talk of the New Man or the New Age, they add an inflection that puts quotation marks around the words.

Jack Wayne has been teaching sociology at the University of Toronto for almost 30 years. The university is a perfect laboratory, which he describes as an intersection of rampant hormones and knowledge. His unhappy judgment is that what looks like change may be just veneer.

"The students are learning how to behave in different ways, which may be a start — just learning to appear more liberal, having a less sexist or a non-sexist attitude. But when the discussion gets going in class, some of these more conventional attitudes pop up."

Perhaps most fascinating of all, he concludes that the image of change has its own particular rewards: "I think to get the girls these days, you need to be a New Man, at least around campus. The people who do really well are single fathers or guys with dogs. You know, people who appear to be nurturing." In other words, you get the babes by being careful not to call them babes.

A parallel skepticism comes from another sociologist, Gillian Ranson at the University of Calgary. She points to the current North American culture of fatherhood and suggests that there is a difference between the culture and the conduct. There certainly is a new definition of fatherhood — "an androgynous, shared-parenting kind of guy; you know, the Sensitive New Age Guy" — that you find in everything from comic strips and television sit-coms to films. And Ms. Ranson says there is a general understanding that this prototype is what should be happening. But it isn't, really. "What we think about what fathers might be doing and what fathers are actually doing is different. There is a gap."

The reality checks are everywhere. A man well known to his friends for his sharing and caring asks with a furtive leer whether you've seen the real babe three tables over. It's not quite 'Check the jugs on that one over there,' but this is the same old animal speaking.

Source: Abridged from John Gray, *The Globe and Mail*, Sat., June 15, 1996, p. D1

dered ways, still spending less time with their children and spending their child-care time differently, as well.

Since gender is learned, gender roles vary from one culture to another. For example, it was men who dominated domestic service in colonial Zambia. This challenges Western views that housework is always low in status and always implies the subordination of women. It shows that housework is not everywhere, nor at all times, defined as a woman's activity, nor is housework always considered innately demeaning. There are historic and cultural reasons why women are at times excluded from domestic service, as they were in colonial Zambia. At other times and places, domestic service comes to be seen as "women's work" — again, for historical and cultural reasons.

In short, beliefs about masculinity and femininity are not linked to sex in the same way in all societies. Like race, gender is a social construction which varies across societies. And like race, gender is largely an imposed social construction, which confers more benefits on some people (in this case, men) than it does on others (namely, women.)

Sociology and the Study of Gender

Three sociological perspectives — functionalism, conflict theory and interactionism — have not been very effective at explaining gender or gender relations. Indeed, considering the central role gender plays in society, it may surprise you to learn that few sociologists paid attention to gender issues until the last ten to twenty years. In part, this was because most sociologists shared the traditional assumptions and stereotypes about gender that characterized Western society. A second reason is that most sociologists, until recently, were males. As such, they paid less attention to issues related to gender and were less sensitive to the problems women faced.

It is not that male sociologists completely ignored gender, only that their views usually took for granted traditional assumptions about it. These traditional assumptions about the "naturalness" of gender differences showed up in the theories and explanations produced by male sociologists, whatever their sociological perspective. Male sociologists lacked the interest needed to address gender issues effectively.

Functionalists, for example, took for granted not only that gender differences were natural, but also that they benefited society as a whole. They argued that the different roles assigned to men and women fulfilled both personal needs for emotional support and social needs for reproduction and child-rearing. From a functionalist perspective, therefore, gender roles support and contribute to the integration of society.

Such an idealized view of gender relations, however, ignores some harsh realities. Men's and women's roles are not only different, they are also unequal. Moreover, today, the middle-class ideal of the wife who stays home to look after the family is not a reality for millions of women who work away from home in addition to doing all the household tasks expected of them. As for the women who do stay home, many of them find that a life of cooking, cleaning and looking after a family does not allow them to feel either fulfilled or valued in a society which does not consider housework to be "real" work.

Marxists have tended to consider gender differences in society as less significant than class differences. They believe that a male and female worker have more interests in common than a male worker has with a male employer, or a female worker with a female employer. Indeed, most Marxists see gender differences as largely a consequence of class and property relations. Friedrich Engels (1962), for example, linked gender stratification to the development of private property. According to his theory, male domination reaches its peak under capitalism by forcing women into the role of homemakers at work for no pay. In this view, traditional gender roles, which reflect a conflict of interest between men and women, will change as women gain more economic power.

Other evidence suggests, however, that men and women may experience the same class positions in different ways. What's more, there is no proof that class awareness and solidarity lead to more cooperation between male and female members of the same class. Historically, even the progressive Canadian labour union movement has ignored women's concerns and focused on the well-being of men.

The other major influence on conflict theory, the work of Max Weber, also shows little concern with gender issues (aside from a largely ignored essay on intimacy). This is particularly surprising because Weber's wife, Marianne Weber, also a sociologist, was very interested in gender issues. Perhaps it shows the degree to which male sociologists of the past were unable to free themselves from the fundamental biases about gender that characterized men in their society.

Male interactionists, too, have had difficulty "taking the role" of the female other. W. I. Thomas, one of the most influential of the early interactionists, wrote a book entitled *The Unadjusted Girl* to examine the effects of rapid social change and the breakdown of traditional norms on young women. Thomas saw these as having negative effects upon women in particular. Clearly, he saw males and females as naturally different from one another with a separate explanation needed for why women may become deviant. Girls become "unadjusted" when they no longer have standards to guide them. Boys simply become delinquent.

There were some women sociologists in the 19th and early 20th centuries, such as Harriet Martineau, who emphasized the significance of gender relations in society. But they were few in number and marginal to the mainstream of sociological work. This is not surprising. How could women recognize themselves, their experiences or their concerns in the male-centered theories which dominated sociology?

The rapid increase in the number of female sociologists in the 1970s, therefore, was accompanied by a widespread rejection of traditional, male-centered sociology. Instead, female sociologists developed a new view of society — feminist sociology — which is grounded in women's experience of inequality in everyday life. This led to a greater awareness of the role of gender in society on the part of all sociologists, male and female.

As far back as the 1950s, some male sociologists, such as C. Wright Mills, had already commented on the inequality which is built into our system of gender relations. Feminist sociologists have gone beyond this to uncover the ways in which gendered inequality has been maintained and reproduced. It is one thing to say that women are disadvantaged, quite another to show how women's concerns, interests and experiences have been systematically excluded from public recognition or academic debate. In addition, Mills, like other male sociologists, made little contribution to the task of overcoming gender inequality. Again, it is feminist sociologists who have taken the steps necessary to promote equality, in their own lives and that of other women, and in their suggestions for how society must change.

A key contribution of the feminist approach has been to show how gender roles are socially constructed and maintained. Two crucial components stand out in this respect; one is the ideology of gender, the other is the reality of patriarchy. We will consider each of these in the next two sections.

THE IDEOLOGY OF GENDER

The *ideology of gender* is an element of the socialization process that serves to explain and justify how and why males and females are different, treating the sexes as two distinct and separate kinds of persons. Men, for example, are assumed to be more aggressive and competitive than women, yet at the same time more rational and objective than women. It is men who invent, explore and explain. Women are considered more passive and supportive than men, yet at the same time more emotional and dependent. It is women who consume, nurture and create.

The maintenance of such a sharp dichotomy between men and women is facilitated if we conceive of separate locations for the two groups. Women's "place" is in the home, for example, while men have a place in public affairs. Men and women have separate activities and schedules. They wear different kinds of clothing (i.e., uniforms), with women's clothing often discouraging vigorous physical activity. Historically, men and women were also treated in different ways, as in the idealized phenomenon of "gallantry," whereby men's caring attentiveness has emphasized the weakness and dependence of women.

The ideology of gender describes and explains the weaknesses of women and complementary strengths of men. Not only are men taught the ideology to justify their privileged and authoritative role; women are taught the ideology too, to justify their subordination. For example, the structure of rock videos and rock performance can legitimate the female fan's powerlessness by displaying females as mindless (therefore powerless) collections of body parts. Acceptance of the ideology becomes a central part of membership in the culture. Violation of the norms is taken as a demonstration that the violator is immoral, unmanageable or sick. Most people expect women in our culture to be submissive. For a woman to behave otherwise is for her to risk being labelled unfeminine or a "bitch." Conversely, people expect men to be dominant. For them to act in a submissive manner is to risk being called a "sissy" or a "wimp."

The ideology of gender is not just a system of beliefs, it has very real consequences in the lives of men and women. The result is that gender differences become part of the very structure of society. For example, women's clothing is regarded as dainty, vulnerable to destruction and vital to presentation of self; men's clothing is regarded as rugged and casual, in general. Accordingly, professional cleaners are in a position to argue that a woman's blouse is twice as difficult to clean as (and should therefore cost twice the price of) a man's shirt. Even those men and women who reject traditional notions of gender find themselves forced to accommodate to a society which is patriarchal.

Patriarchy

A degree of **patriarchy** exists in every society. By "patriarchy," we mean male dominance over women that has been justified in the society's system of values. The phenomenon is itself tied to the ideology of gender.

Most known societies are patriarchal to some extent — a fact that has never been satisfactorily explained. Perhaps the universality of patriarchy is due to the universality

Men are socialized to express themselves physically rather than verbally.

of social differentiation by sex, due in turn to the physical vulnerability and dependence of women under conditions of frequent pregnancy and childbirth. If so, it follows that with the worldwide reduction in childbearing (described in Chapter 10) we should see a worldwide reduction in patriarchy; in fact, this change is evident. An increase in women's educational and job opportunities makes it possible for lower fertility to translate into less male domination.

Like class inequality, the degree and form of inequality between the sexes already varies a great deal from one society to another. So too does the excuse or justification for gender inequality. In many societies, the excuse is sacred (based on religious texts and teachings). Major religions of the world — Catholicism, Judaism and Islam among them — give different and less powerful roles to women compared to men.

In our own culture, common ways of expressing gender inequality are also the least tangible. One way of expressing domination is to assume decision-making powers in a relationship. In a marriage, one spouse may control the way money is spent. In a dating couple, one person may decide how to spend an evening or whether there will be sexual intercourse. In conversation, one person will cut off or break in on the speech of another.

People learn their gender-based habits of behaviour through *gender socialization*. The socialization process links gender to personal identity — in the form of *gender identity* — and to distinctive activities — in the form of gender roles. The major agents of socialization we discussed in Chapter 3 — family, peer groups, schools and the mass media — all serve to reinforce cultural definitions of masculinity and femininity.

Consider the very obvious difference between men's and women's interest in football. Men are more likely to play football and watch football games than women, but the difference doesn't end there. Men also use football playing and watching as an occasion for male-bonding. Televised football games model a certain style of male talk and behaviour. In the end, football is an exemplary instance of masculine behaviour in our society.

Gender-based communicative difference extends into all areas of life. For example, male and female doctors typically exhibit different attitudes towards their patients, which shows up in the way they communicate. Female doctors may seem more interested in their relationship with the patient, whereas male doctors may appear to be more interested in getting and giving information.

Learned gender differences in communication also show up in our intimate relations. For example, women are taught to behave in a demure, innocent and uninterested fashion when sex is the topic of discussion with men. (They are more forthcoming in discussions with other women.) In short, learned patterns of communication create and maintain gender distinctions and reinforce social arrangements between the sexes. Often they complicate our understanding of what is going on between the sexes.

However, such differences in communication between the sexes are socially created. They are frequently maintained by the different positions men and women hold in the occupational structure. Since "bosses" are more often men than women, women have to adopt "men's" ways of doing things if they are to succeed. For example, people resolve conflicts differently at home and at work, using more competitive styles at work and more accommodating styles at home. But at work, at most managerial levels, men and women tend to do it the "male way" because that is the way in which women have been able to achieve promotion in male-dominated workplaces. In female-dominated workplaces, women use a somewhat more consensual, less hierarchical style of management. In her many studies of gender and talk, feminist social scientist and conversation specialist Deborah Tannen suggests that conversation itself is hierarchical with men and consensual with women.

As we have said, several agents of socialization ensure that the sexes learn proper gender characteristics. The most important of these agents are the family, schools and mass media; each reinforces existing patterns. Gender socialization begins as soon as an infant's sex is identified and continues through pre-school and primary school. Young children learn gender identities when they experiment with hair and clothing styles, role-playing games and body decoration, and also by observing others at nursery school or day care. Their imitative efforts all reflect enormous pressures to conform to assigned gender identities.

Parents routinely assign more household tasks to daughters than to sons. The tasks people assign to their sons are more usually "handyman" tasks, not cleaning, childcare or meal preparation. Not surprisingly, children form traditional, gender-based attitudes towards housework before the end of high school. In this way, they perpetuate age-old stereotypes without being aware of doing so. Men, older people and poor people are particularly likely to hold and teach traditional, gendered attitudes. As a result, fathers raising teenage daughters demand more help from their children than fathers who are raising teenage sons.

Even parents who believe they treat their children equally often treat boys and girls differently. And even the children of parents who reject traditional gender roles are affected by the stereotypes around them. For example, where gender identity, role and sexual orientation are concerned, the adult daughters of lesbian mothers do not differ from those of heterosexual mothers. Children in these "nontraditional" families learn essentially the same gender attitudes as their peers.

Media images of gender roles still influence children, who end up holding stereotyped ideas of male and female behaviour. So, for example, when asked to write stories on any topic, students aged nine to sixteen show strong evidence of media-influenced sex-role stereotyping. They depict men in a variety of occupations, using violent means to resolve conflict. They portray women in more traditional female roles, where they are less active, and where they use less violence to resolve conflict.

Sexism and Social Structure

We typically think of patriarchy as something that belongs to social structures of the past. But even today some governments act in ways that prolong patriarchy. Iran and Pakistan, for example, both have patriarchal religious and family systems supported by the state. These countries provide examples of instances where partial modernization has worsened women's position. Members of traditional groups, fearing that development may cost them their cultural identity, call for the restoration of women to their "proper place." In many cultures, there remain fully sanctioned social processes of denigrating, often physically abusing, women.

Gender-role differences continue to exist in North America, and they are expressed both in learned personality traits and in the division of labour. The socio-economic conditions that supported patriarchy have largely disappeared from industrial societies. However, male dominance continues to be defended by **sexism**, just as racial dominance is defended by racism. "Sexism," like other ideologies, is a belief system that upholds the status quo, and it carries important costs and consequences. For example, traditional gender roles prevent part of the population from playing an effective part in the economy. They also have undesirable social and psychological effects on both men and women.

Many women, as well as men, believe sexual inequalities are rooted in biology. In this respect, some women contribute to their own subordination. Like men, women are socialized to accept sexist ideologies. Gender socialization has the effect of controlling access to rewards and opportunities by discouraging women from competing for the rewards everyone desires. As a result, many women don't think of themselves as able to compete.

This may explain the small proportion of Canadian women who enter engineering, a traditionally male field of work. In fact, women are nearly six times more likely to attain an engineering degree in Belgium, for example, than they are in Canada. Nevertheless, it would be incorrect to say that all women have accepted the traditional ideology of gender found in our society. The traditional belief that a woman should stay home to look after her children has never been shared by everyone.

Since they are cultural in origin, traditional ideas about the relative value of males and females can change. An example is parents' preferences for male children, which is still strong in many parts of the world such as India, China and the rest of Southeast Asia. In India, parents display their bias by bringing daughters for their first immunization at a significantly later age than sons. Indian girls also have poorer nutrition than boys, indicating that parents do not feed them as well. And female infanticide is still practised in cultures where male children are regarded as more desirable than female children.

In China, every year there are about 500,000 fewer recorded births of girls than we would expect to find, given the Chinese birth rate. A possible reason for this is the country's one-child policy, which has the unintended consequence of encouraging parents, particularly in rural areas, to abort, murder or conceal baby girls so they can legally proceed to bear sons. Sons are preferred because they are considered better able to take care of their parents in their old age. The combination of government policy and traditional notions about gender poses a danger to the safety of girls and women in China.

This situation notwithstanding, there *is* evidence of growing equality for women in China. Today, for example, many Chinese women aspire to higher education, and they are more active in their communities than were their mothers and grandmothers. Chinese society, however, still shows a strong preference for sons. Rural areas will have to develop socially and economically before traditional Confucian ideas disappear and women receive the same treatment as men.

Canadian parents, too, at one time preferred to have male children. Today, however, most Canadian parents care little whether their children are boys or girls. In fact, they prefer a mixture of boys and girls, a sign that males and females are equally valued.

Indeed, in our society, traditional notions of masculinity and femininity seem to be breaking down. In addition, consciously designed social or state policies have altered gender roles in many other industrial and developing societies. As a result, women today are, in many respects, acting in ways people would have considered "unfeminine" a mere generation or two ago.

Other women continue to act in "feminine" ways which have fallen into disrepute. In Everyday Life, on page 235, we see evidence of the controversy that has come to surround topless waitresses, lap-dancers and other women who use their sexuality to lure big-tipping customers. The clients at Hooters and similar establishments are men, and the main detractors, women, just as might have

EVERYDAY LIFE

Hooter Girls

When was the last time you saw a scantily clad man on a magazine cover? Got a good look at a naked guy on a TV screen? Or had your restaurant food order taken by a young man wearing short-shorts with a big bulge in the front? Probably, it was quite a while ago, if ever. The fact is, women's bodies are displayed for commercial purposes much more casually, obviously, and often than men's bodies. In fact, that's the whole point of "Hooters" — a place that urges you to ogle "their" women while you eat.

Since opening last month, they've been packing them in at Hooters, a large and controversial U.S. restaurant chain that features buxom waitresses in tank tops and has been the subject of discrimination charges in the United States for not hiring men as waiters. The reason for the large crowds in Edmonton, says restaurant manager Hank Hampton, is the large volume of foot traffic from Canada's largest mall.

Inside, the place is heavy with double-entendre and innuendo. On one wall, hangs a pogo stick, upon which it is rumoured a waitress will occasionally vault across the restaurant. A newspaper clipping of the daily Sunshine Girl hangs in the bathroom, and the menu is dotted with adolescent humour.

The name of the place is a matter for personal interpretation, executives say. The restaurant mascot is an owl with two oversized eyes represented by the two Os in the word Hooters. The logo also appears on the T-shirts worn by the waitresses.

The women who make up the restaurant's staff claim not to be bothered by the fact that their customers may be in the place for more than just a simple burger and a beer. "A lot of people ask, 'Does it feel degrading?'" said an 18-year-old waitress in her first stint at waiting tables. "Well, you know, go to a beach some time. People are wearing a lot less there."

If the waitresses aren't bothered, a lot of others are.

City newspapers have been sprinkled with letters from Edmontonians who say they will boycott the mall because of the restaurant. Women's groups says Hooters' success stands on the restaurant's willingness to portray its employees as sexual objects. The waitresses are, of course, the place's big drawing card, so accusations of sexism are generally shunted aside. Described by one employee as "the Dallas Cowboy cheerleaders and the surfer girls of waitressing," the women are involved in promotions across the city, many of them sports-related. Hooters workers appear in calendars and trading cards, as well as the chain's own magazine.

"Women have the right to use their God-given sex appeal to support themselves and their families," said company vice-president Mike McNeil from the company's Atlanta headquarters. If Cindy Crawford and Naomi Campbell can flash some skin and make a buck, why not the Hooter Girls?

Eating a meal at the place is something like contemplating a peek at the Playboy magazine floating around the local barbershop. Gawk if you dare, but be assured that someone walking by is uttering the words, "Repent, sinner" while you do. "This is great sitting here having people stare daggers at you," said a friend while shoppers trudged past the restaurant's patio.

Are company officials worried that patronage may eventually dry up, given the uncomfortable feeling some may have eating at their establishments? Not likely, if the firm's expansion plans are any indicator.

Source: Abridged from Brian Laghi, *The Globe and Mail*, Fri., Aug. 2, 1996, p. A2

been the case a century ago. But today, criticisms of such practices and places have less to do with their immorality or the dangers they pose to family life, as they would have a century ago, and more to do with the belief that such practices are degrading to women, discriminatory and associated with outmoded thinking about gender relations.

GENDER INEQUALITY

The dramatic increase in women's labour-force participation has signalled a major change in gender roles. Yet women still tend to do "women's work." These are jobs that pay less, have lower prestige and require longer hours of work than jobs in which most workers are men. This is part of what sociologists call a **gendered division of labour**.

A gendered division of labour, and more generally, inequality, in the relations between men and women, are not necessarily caused by attitudes held by the particular people involved. Instead, a gendered division of labour is structural. It is part of a system of **gender stratification**. That means it is built into the expectations and obligations attached to different roles found in particular institutions.

Consider the work relationship between nurses and doctors. Traditionally, doctors have been male and nurses have been female. Historically, men have tended to demand and receive more authority than women. By tradition, the nurse has been the "handmaid" of the doctor. The doctor is viewed as the professional who possesses the most training, expert knowledge, authority and prestige. The nurse's role is to carry out the doctor's wishes with an attitude of obedience, competence, selflessness, loyalty and total dedication to caring for patients. In short, the nurse serves as an "instrument" or "tool" of the doctor — not as the doctor's co-worker.

Kerr and MacPhail (1991: 21) point out that "Sex stereotyped views of nursing emphasize subservience, lack of assertiveness and domination of nurses who are primarily female, by physicians, who are primarily male." From a feminist perspective, nurses form a minority group who are kept powerless by doctors and hospital administrators. The domination of (usually female) nurses by (usually male) doctors and administrators is only one form of a general domination of women in our society.

As we would expect, the occupational domination of women has economic consequences. For example, a registered nurse makes only about a third as much money as a doctor and half as much as a hospital administrator. Most people do not consider the work of nurses to be as valuable as that of physicians and hospital administrators. Perhaps because most nurses are women, and women are expected to be nurturing, nurses are also expected to settle for low pay and high emotional satisfaction for a job well done. Also, because most of them are women, nurses are often assumed to be working to supplement their husbands' incomes, not working to earn an income in their own right. Because these false ideas about women's work and women's worth persist, women's concerns, financial and otherwise, are viewed by some people as less serious than those of men.

As we see, the patterns of gender inequality in the relationship between doctors and nurses are structural. They have nothing to do with the virtues or weaknesses of particular doctors or particular nurses. Rather, they are built into how particular types of organizations "work," how different tasks are valued and how roles are assigned. An individual doctor may be male or female, sympathetic to the concerns of women or indifferent to them. Nevertheless, hospitals and the practice of medicine are arranged in such a way that nurses remain subordinate to doctors. (However, some changes do seem to be taking place in the relations between doctors and nurses, an issue that is addressed later in the chapter.)

Since gender inequality is structured into many sectors of society, the experience of inequality is common among women in two important areas of everyday life: the family and the workplace. Moreover, family and work are linked for many women. Whether they work for pay outside the home or whether they don't, the home is a work setting for most women. Additionally, work and the family are often intertwined. A women's family obligations may affect her ability to work for pay, while work obligations may affect her family relations. We will look at both settings, the workplace and the family, in turn.

The Family and Domestic Inequality

The organization of family life has changed dramatically in the second half of the 20th century. Family changes and changes in the organization of paid work have had more impact on women than on men. Women have entered the labour force in large numbers. However, many men have not made the parallel shift to assuming an equal responsibility for domestic work. One result is that wives typically have less free time than their husbands and often feel overburdened.

Within the household, we usually find a gendered division of labour. Some jobs are done exclusively by women, other jobs exclusively by men, and some jobs are shared or rotated between them. However, studies of domestic labour find that husbands get more say in financial matters, and take less responsibility for the children and household than their wives. Also, spouses who earn more have more say at home than spouses who earn less, and wives are usually the spouses who earn less.

For the last few decades, most women in the paid labour force have suffered from responsibility-overload. Terms like the "double day" or the "second shift" remind us that, despite a job outside the home, women continue to do or organize the largest share of housework and childcare. Canadian wives who are employed full-time still do most of the housework. The situation is even worse in traditional societies. There, wives can avoid conflict with their husbands over paid work only if they are willing to accept full responsibility for the housework.

Such conditions of domestic inequality prevail in many parts of the world, even in many parts of Canada. However, things are starting to change. For example, in two-earner couples, more and more spouses are spending equal amounts of their time on productive work, though this work is gender-specialized. The rule seems to be: Whoever does less paid work does more housework. In the time left over, gendered expectations determine *who* performs *which* household tasks.

In the early 1990s, Canadian working women were doing only twelve minutes more housework than their husbands. Inequality in domestic work is becoming a thing of the past for many women, to judge from these data. However, Canadian women continue to have the main responsibility for most domestic tasks, even though their husbands help out. Part of the increase in men's housework "is due to the fact that divorced and never-married men are a growing share of all men, and these men are responsible for all their own housework. Husbands and fathers are also spending more time on overall housework. But these increases are primarily in the areas of child care and shopping . . . Household cleaning has yet to become trendy among married men" (Crispell, 1992: 40).

Trendy or not, men are starting to do a little more around the house. For example, time budget data since the 1970s reveal a change in men's housework and childcare activities in Canada. In fact, fathers in dual-earner Canadian families appear to be moving from a traditional fatherhood role in which their main responsibility was economic, to one in which they contribute to homemaking and caregiving as well as providing economic support.

Not all husbands or other family members are willing to do their share of domestic work. Some men see housework as women's work and refuse to help out. Wives can try to force their spouses and children to cooperate more, but that works only up to a point. They can also risk their mental and physical health by working harder. Or they can opt for part-time instead of full-time paid work, especially while their children are young. Many rely increasingly on paid domestic and childcare services (day care, fast food, house cleaners and so on). And many others set their aspirations and expectations low and think of work they are doing for pay as a job not a career.

The Domestic Division of Labour

Though the balance is shifting, women still perform the bulk of household chores in Canada. On average, women spent 1,482 hours doing unpaid work in 1992, compared with 831 hours for men.

*Never-married child living with one or both parents.

Source: *Statistics Canada, from "Household's Unpaid Work: Measurement and Valuation," Catalogue No. 13-603, No. 3, 1993, p. 48*

It is difficult to have a serious career *and* a serious marriage if you are a woman, since you are expected to carry a full load in both activities. Women who carry heavy domestic responsibility find it hard to compete effectively with men at work. Moreover, employers expect women to be carrying this domestic responsibility and, therefore, see women as less valuable (since less available) employees. This means that continued gender inequality at home will almost ensure continued gender inequality in the workplace.

Gender Inequality in the Workplace

At one time, people expected women to have the primary responsibility of caring for young children and looking after a home. These responsibilities made working women more likely than men to quit paid work and stay home to raise their children. Today, few women quit work when they have children, though many interrupt it for a maternity leave. Two out of three mothers of pre-schoolers and 70 per cent of mothers of school-age children are employed. Nevertheless, many women find that the old expectations have not disappeared and that their status and needs in the workplace are not treated as seriously as those of men.

Worldwide, it is hard to determine precise rates of labour-force participation by women. That is because much of women's work is done in the informal economy (the exchange of goods and services that are not paid for in cash) and so it is not included in official estimates of economic activity. In 1990, the highest rates of paid economic activity by women were in the former USSR (60 per cent), Eastern Asia (59 per cent) and North America (50 per cent). Lowest participation rates were found in Latin America and the Caribbean (32 per cent), Southern and Western Asia (24 per cent and 21 per cent respectively) and Northern Africa (16 per cent) (United Nations, 1991: 84). Like the domestic division of labour, occupational segregation is universal. In Western societies, women typically work in clerical, service and sales jobs. In Africa and Asia,

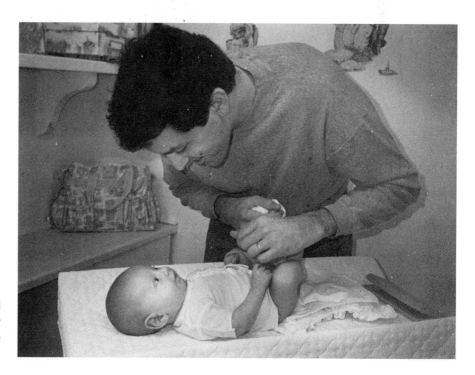

Men are slowly and sometimes grudgingly taking a larger part in the care of children.

women typically work in agriculture. It is no accident that these "women's" jobs all have low status and are poorly paid.

Does a **double standard** exist in North America when it comes to hiring, promoting and paying women? Is there a **glass ceiling** that keeps women from moving up the ladder as far as similarly qualified men? Do bosses treat women differently from men? Are women *discriminated* against, victims of a "double standard" in the workplace? These are hard questions to answer.

The average wage of women, across all occupations, is about 68 per cent of what men receive. True, the wage differences are most marked among men and women over the age of fifty. For younger men and women with equal years of education and work experience in the same occupation, there is little, if any, wage difference. What difference remains can be largely ascribed to marital status. Married women suffer a wage disability (in relation to married men) that single women do not.

Still, a difference in male and female wages continues to exist for a number of reasons. First, more women than men in paid employment are in part-time, not full-time, jobs. Second, most women work in sectors of the economy that contain mainly insecure, poorly paying jobs requiring skills that are undervalued or easy to acquire. Third, as we have seen, women have more of the responsibility for housework and childcare than men.

To see the effect of marriage and housework on women's wages, we need only look at the data on men's and women's incomes in Canada's ten best-paying jobs. They include jobs like judge, physician, lawyer, dentist, senior manager and university professor. The data show that women working full-time at these jobs in 1990 earned about 60 to 70 per cent of what men earned working full-time in the same jobs, during the same year. Even among dentists, who are mainly self-employed (and don't discriminate against themselves!), there is a roughly 30 per cent income gap between men and women.

Let's consider some possible explanations. Some women who work "full-time" do in fact work fewer hours per week, or fewer weeks per year, than men who work "full-time." This is because they take more time off work to attend to family business (e.g., taking sick children to the doctor).

As well, women in a particular occupation may have less experience and seniority than men in the same occupation. Since income is often a function of age, experience and seniority, women will earn lower incomes than men, on average, until they acquire more seniority.

Women may hold jobs in worse-paying organizations or geographic locales than men. So, for example, a doctor or dentist in a small town is likely to earn less than a doctor or dentist in Montreal, Toronto or Vancouver. Likewise, a manager in a small company is likely to earn less than a manager in a large company, and women may be more likely than men to get work in small towns or small companies. If so, they will have lower incomes than men, on average.

Women are also at a disadvantage in the work world because few have received the kind of education that would win them well-paid, highly skilled jobs. Historically, women were excluded from higher education; now women form a slight majority of all college students and receive half of the master's degrees awarded. Most doctorates and professional degrees still go to men. However, as women continue to improve their educational credentials, they will continue to improve their position in the work force.

A sizeable percentage (in the United States, over 40 per cent) of the difference between male and female starting salaries is due to differences in the college major of the employee. In other words, men and women specialize in different fields; men tend to specialize in the better-paying fields. For example, there is evidence that mathematical fields (e.g., physics, engineering, computing) are still dominated by men. Though this pattern is changing, the process is slow because gender-differentiated aspirations are formed in high school, if not before. We are left wondering how much wage inequality is due to acceptable factors like occupational choice and how much is due to discrimination — a double standard in the work world.

All the factors described above are plausible explanations of income inequality between men and women. All would result in women having lower incomes than men even *without* there being prejudice or discrimination against women employees. Some social commentators like Andrew Coyne, in Applied Sociology below, have taken this finding to imply that pay equity is unnecessary. Some believe the labour market, via laws of supply and demand, assigns a proper value to people's services, and governments should not interfere in the workings of the market. Others, however, see hidden biases in the way that market works.

One study, based on American data which appears to take a variety of factors into account, claims that between 40 per cent and 60 per cent of the gender wage gap in professional occupations is due to discrimination. Likewise, data from a study done by the Bank of Montreal (1992) suggest that between 5 and 20 per cent of the wage gap cannot be explained by anything but discrimination.

In the West, the consequences of gender inequality are most dramatic for women caught between domestic and wage-earning responsibilities. For example, the single mothers of young children often cannot earn enough both to maintain a decent standard of living and cover their childcare costs. Welfare payments are below the poverty line and people are penalized for earning over a minimum amount. Not surprisingly, single mothers face a higher risk of poverty than any other group and make up a high percentage of Canada's poor.

Elderly women are another group of women at particular risk for poverty. Since few of them had paying careers when they were younger, few have incomes from job-based pensions when they get older.

Because of their experiences of inequality, all women can be considered members of a "minority group." This is not to suggest that they are a small segment of the population — in fact, they are a numerical majority — but, instead, to note their distinctive identity and socially disadvantaged position. And like other victimized "minority groups," women suffer from oppression because of ideologies which justify gender inequality.

Ways of Viewing the "Glass Ceiling"

As we mentioned earlier, one of the problems facing women in the work force is what has been called the **glass ceiling** — an invisible but real limitation on women's advancement in large bureaucratic organizations.

The problem originates in a set of assumptions, common in our culture, about the nature of women (versus men), bureaucracy and rationality. Following Weber's "ideal type" version of bureaucracy, our culture supports the views that in a modern society: (1) "rationality" is good, and (2) bureaucracy is rational; (3) therefore, bureaucracy is good; (4) and since men are assumed to be more rational than women, (5) therefore, men are better suited to work in a bureaucracy, so (6) women are less suited for top positions in a bureaucracy. In this way, the "glass ceiling" can be defended as a necessary consequence of a modern society's values and "natural" gender differences.

Wage Gap Disparity

APPLIED SOCIOLOGY

Sociologists have devoted a great deal of attention to the study of comparative wage data, to determine whether the inequality between men's and women's wages was narrowing. But as this excerpt shows, even when the gap does narrow, there may be reason to suspect systemic discrimination against women. A sociologist would want to explain why marriage has more negative consequences for women's wages than it does for men's. Is the reason women's "double day," especially when children are present?

The remarkable political success of pay equity as an idea is directly related to the widespread belief that there is a difference in wages between men and women that can be explained only by their sex. This in turn is based on a single, seemingly telling, calculation. In 1993, Statistics Canada reports, women working full-time earned 72 per cent of what their male counterparts earned: $28,392, compared to the men's $39,433.

And that 72 per cent is simply an aggregate: it takes no account of genuine differences in the personal characteristics and work patterns of men and women. For starters, even women working full time put in 12 per cent fewer hours, on average, than men: 38.7 hours a week compared to 43.8. Likewise, because so many women have entered the labour market so recently, the necessary mathematical consequence is that men will have, on average, more work experience. Even the Ontario Pay Equity

Commission estimated that only a quarter to a third of the wage gap was due to systemic discrimination — which is to say, the residual left over after a few such easily identified variables are factored in.

There is no significant gap, for example, between single men and single women: Single women working full time earned 96 per cent of what single men earned in 1993 (in 1992, it was 99 per cent). The situation is much the same for new entrants to the labour force: Women under the age of 24 working full time earn 91 per cent as much as men of the same age. And while female university graduates overall earn only 75 per cent as much as male graduates, among more recent graduates, a Statscan study has found, the wage gap has closed. Indeed, single female university graduates working full time actually earn more than their single male counterparts: $40,024 to $39,342. The significant predictors of wages, then, are not sex, but such mundane factors as age, education and work experience.

The most striking "wage gap," indeed, is not between men and women, but between married men and everyone else. Single men earn much the same as single women, but both earn much less than married men. There would seem to be two ways to explain this. Either there is a vast unseen system of discrimination against single people, or else people in different circumstances — mortgage-burdened married men, for example, versus footloose bachelors — make different choices in life. Their jobs, and thus their pay, may simply reflect those choices.

Source: Abridged from Andrew Coyne, *The Globe and Mail*, Wed., June 14, 1995, p. A12

Efforts to deal with the problem have revealed a variety of viewpoints about gender and social change. In short, different ways of thinking about the "depth" of the problem have led to different ways of thinking about the necessary "depth" of the solution. Consider first the liberal critique of the glass ceiling, which is based on attacking principle (6); namely, women are less suited for top positions in a bureaucracy.

Liberalism, which emphasizes the rights of individuals, would argue that discrimination against women in hiring and promotion is bad, first, because it is unjust. It unfairly deprives people of equal opportunities on the grounds that they belong to one sex rather than another. Second, liberalism would argue that a glass ceiling wastes human capital; talented women are deprived of the opportunity to develop and display their abilities. This short-changes the society and economy, and cheats talented women themselves. Finally, discrimination, like other forms of unfairness, is likely to cause resentment, low morale and even work-place sabotage. In the end, this hinders the productivity of any organization.

For all these reasons, the glass ceiling on women's work should be eliminated. Liberals would propose doing this through employment equity (or affirmative action) laws which force organizations to hire and promote women just as they do men. Often, however, such laws are not enough and it is also necessary to reform the organizational culture. Ideally, in the future, male supervisors will hire and promote women not because they have been forced to, but because they see the advantages in doing so.

The liberal approach has succeeded in reducing the effects of the glass ceiling to some degree, but success has been far from complete. A second approach has been provided by the liberal-feminist critique of the glass ceiling. This approach attacks principles (4) and (5), namely, men are more rational than women and men are better suited to working in bureaucracies.

Liberal-feminists argue that men are no better suited than women. First, men are no more rational than women, if what we mean by "rational" is the ability to reach decisions through the use of reason. Men differ from women chiefly in their communication styles: men tend to be colder, more openly aggressive and competitive. They appear more rational (to some observers) because they hide their feelings more than women typically do. If bureaucracies really require the male style of self-presentation, women can learn it — in fact, a great many female managers have already done so. But research on different approaches to management suggests that organizations may benefit in equal measure from the co-operative and sociable style women often bring to management positions.

For these reasons, the glass ceiling can and should be eliminated. Doing this would require male bosses to re-evaluate the skills and interactional styles women bring to an organization. If necessary, women could be taught male skills and interactional styles. Additionally, they could be included in (male-dominated) old-boy networks, and provided with "mentors" who could advise and help them in developing their career. Like the liberal approach, the liberal-feminist approach has succeeded in reducing the effects of the glass ceiling to some degree; but again, success has been far from complete.

A third approach to the problem has been provided by the (radical) feminist-interpretive critique of the glass ceiling. This approach attacks principles (1), (2) and (3); namely, the ideas that rationality is good, bureaucracy is rational, and therefore bureaucracy is good (Ferguson, 1984).

One part of this approach is to argue that bureaucracies are a much-overrated form of organization. After all, they are hierarchical, restrictive and dehumanizing — not the kind of place most people would choose to work. Research has shown repeatedly that bureaucracies often don't produce the desired results; for example, they are not as efficient or effective as people like to believe. Often they even produce unwanted results (such as goal displacement, which we discussed in Chapter 6.) Weber's "ideal type" version of bureaucracy is far from describing what actually happens in real bureaucracies, where merit often counts for less than politicking, trickery and backbiting.

If real bureaucracies don't work like the "ideal type" and don't achieve the desired results, why do people continue to hold positive views of this form of organization? The answer, some argue, is that people have been brainwashed by powerful bureaucratic organizations, among them government, the educational system and large private corporations. They have been taught to believe that bureaucratic organization is good and that we ought to comply with its demands, whether as students, workers, citizens or otherwise. Thus, bureaucracies are instruments for controlling their workers and, also, their supposed clients or customers.

Along similar lines, the interpretive feminists argue that "rationality" itself is much overrated. Here, they are referring to what Weber called "formal rationality" — thought or action intended to facilitate chosen means and procedures, whatever the outcome. So, for example, our criminal justice system is "formally rational" in the sense that it follows a set of well-established procedures. It is performing rationally even if it wrongly convicts an innocent person or acquits a guilty person, just so long as it follows the established procedures. Or, take a primary-school system: it is performing rationally if it teaches children in ways that experts believe *ought to* help students read and write. No matter what the outcome — even a 50 per cent illiteracy rate among graduates — the process is formally rational if it follows the established procedures.

Can you see the built-in stupidity of formal rationality? First and most obviously, it separates means from ends, sometimes completely losing track of what an organization was set up to accomplish. By emphasizing *how* a thing is done rather than *what* is accomplished, formal rationality also leads people to believe that value freedom is possible. Formal rationality hides our goals (or values), then promotes the belief that if they are hidden, they don't influence the way we behave. It also, secretly, ranks different ways of knowing, preferring so-called reason over emotion or intuition. In doing so, formal rationality not only promotes a bias against women, it also encourages us to fragment our personalities, to emphasize our "rational" side above all else.

To survive in a formally rational society, we all learn to be diligent role-players and expect others to do the same. But deep down, we know that there is more to social relationships — indeed, more to life — than playing roles in the presence of other people who are also playing roles. To live this way is to live as slaves to conformity, alienated from ourselves and others. To see modern society as committed to formal rationality, as Weber does, not only gives a wrong picture of people and social life, it also makes sociological theory an accomplice in oppression.

For these and other reasons, the glass ceiling on women's work should be eliminated. But it should be clear by now that, in the eyes of interpretive feminists, the solution will not be simple or superficial. What is needed is nothing less than a deep change in formal organizations, in modern society and its inhuman culture. Included in this profound change is a need to rethink our sociological knowledge and methods, perhaps using family life, not bureaucracy, as a metaphor for healthy social life.

As sociologists, we need to avoid seeing people as mere role-players (or worse, as bundles of variables playing out universal rules of cause-and-effect.) As we discover in Chapter 12, on research methods, there is a feminist approach to research which embodies these concerns. Clearly, these concerns take us a long way from the issue of a glass ceiling as originally conceived by liberal sociologists. But they also give you some idea of the way that feminist theorizing has contributed to the overhaul of traditional sociology.

Prejudice and Discrimination

As we have seen, men and women draw unequal rewards, whether we measure these as income, prestige, authority, power or otherwise. In some societies, these differences in treatment are literally matters of life and death, as illustrated by the case of Rani, described in Far and Away, below. In others societies, like our own, the differences in treatment are often symbolic or, if material, questions of degree. Yet that is no reason for complacency: prejudice and discrimination are as serious a problem in gender relations as they are in race and ethnic relations.

Often, the extent of prejudice and discrimination is hard to measure. Remember from Chapter 7 that researchers (Henry and Ginsberg, 1990) needed to run experimental field trials to gain compelling proof that there was racial discrimination against blacks. Mere inequality was not proof enough.

One kind of evidence of prejudice and discrimination is a so-called "double standard" of the kind we mentioned earlier. The basic idea behind a **double standard** is that two groups are judged against different standards of conduct — a patently unfair thing to do. Imagine, for example, that you are writing an examination in this course and the teacher tells you that men and women will be graded in different ways. Women's exam papers will be graded only for content: that is, how many right answers they give. Men's exam papers will also be graded for quality of handwriting, imaginativeness and neatness. Under these conditions, women will end up with higher average grades than men: after all, they were graded according to an easier standard. The men would, rightly, feel they had been discriminated against. That's the sort of thing that happens to women in many areas of life, most especially where sex is concerned.

Let's compare China and North America on this. Chinese people are more opposed to premarital sex than North Americans are. The Chinese place a higher value on female virginity than Canadians and Americans do. In China, many more survey respondents, both male and female, say virginity is a girl's most valuable possession. This suggests a double standard for men and women in China. Women are expected to be virgins at marriage though men are not.

North America is different in this respect; here, attitudes have changed radically in the last thirty years. Until the late 1940s or early 1950s there *was* a double standard: non-marital sex was permitted for men and prohibited for women. From about 1950 to 1970, there was a period of "permissiveness with affection," during which premarital intercourse was acceptable so long as it occurred in a love relationship that was expected to lead to marriage. But since about 1970, there has been a general acceptance — certainly among young people — that sexual intercourse is a natural and expected part of a relationship for both men and women, whether or not that relationship is expected to lead to marriage. (Physical or emotional exploitation of the sexual partner is still considered unacceptable.)

So, in North America today, people put little value on female virginity at marriage. And even in China there is a conflict between what we would call ideal culture and real culture. Female virginity at marriage is part of China's ideal culture. In reality, a large fraction of Chinese men and women do have sex before marriage. So it would appear that the Chinese are endorsing an ideal norm like the one North Americans held before 1950, but are following an actual norm like the one that North Americans held between 1950 and 1970.

With changes in the status of women, this kind of double standard in China will diminish. Yet there is often what sociologists call *culture lag* — a tendency for cultural ideas to change more slowly than real behaviour. So, despite the increased equality of women in modern China, there is still a strong attachment to a pre-modern, non-egalitarian idea.

Interconnections with Race and Ethnicity
We noted earlier that gender differences are not only interconnected with class differences, but with racial and

Female Infanticide in India

It's hard to believe but it's true: in Canada, parents rarely kill their children, and when they do, the community is outraged. Punishment of infanticide is swift and harsh. But in many other parts of the world, infanticide is widespread and rarely punished. The reasons vary but, fundamentally, they have to do with poverty and (often) patriarchy. Children — especially girl children — are a drain on poor people's resources.

It has been more than a year since Rani killed her six-month-old daughter by pouring poisonous oleander berries ground in oil down her throat. "There is no money in our family," says Rani, 37, her knot of hair shining in the moonlight. "I just could not keep her." The baby was Rani's second daughter.

She wouldn't consider adoption. Who knows, the new parents might beat the child, or sell her into prostitution. The baby girl, Rani says resolutely, was *kuzhipappa* — "the child that was meant for the burial pit."

Despite repeated government attempts to stop female infanticide, it continues to thrive in pockets of rural India. There are no large factories in Usilampatti, and therefore female children are of less use than they are in the plains, the heartland of the child-labour belt.

In a survey of 1,250 families last year by the Community Services Guild in Tamil Nadu's Salem district, one-third admitted killing at least one female baby. In one village after another, people talk openly about the methods employed: oleander berries, tobacco paste, boiling liquids, pesticides, suffocation.

In the Community Services Guild study, two-thirds of the families, most of whom owned property, said they considered girls an asset. But the costs of a girl child, built up by centuries of tradition, can be prohibitive even for the wealthy.

In the Gounder tribe, parents are required to throw elaborate celebrations at virtually every turn in a girl's life: when they name the girl, when she reaches puberty, when she is married, when she sets up a home, when her first child is born, and, if the parents are still alive, when she reaches menopause. And if their daughter has a daughter, they must give the paternal grandparents up to 10,000 rupees ($450).

What disturbs researchers is that infanticide may be increasing, as some tribes open up to other cultures, resulting in the adoption of customs such as dowry and divorce, which turn parents against daughters.

To halt the practice, the state government last year began arresting couples, including a Salem forestry official, although prosecution is difficult in a land where infant mortality already is high. The state has also set up a 2,000-rupee trust for new-born girls that matures to 10,000 rupees by the time they reach marrying age.

Another group, the Women's Emancipation and Development (WED) Trust, offers women loans for sewing machines, dairy cows and basket-making, and has trained 58 women in tailoring. The loan money comes from women's savings co-operatives that WED organized in the villages. So far, 415 women have saved about 40,000 rupees ($1,800).

One of the savings co-operatives this year attracted a new member: Rani. She has managed to put away 200 rupees and hopes to buy a cow. More important, say WED officials, is that Rani this year gave birth to twins, both girls, and she says she will let them live.

Source: Abridged from "Killing unwanted baby girls continues in pockets of India," *The Globe and Mail*, Sat., Nov. 20, 1993, p. D3

ethnic differences, as well. Immigrant women are another group that is disadvantaged in Canadian society. Stasiulis (1990: 287) points to the symbolic images which underlie the treatment of immigrant women in Canadian society:

Images of sturdy, asexual, and subservient Black domestics and of exotic, sexually dextrous, and compliant Asian women are pervasive in Western popular culture and mass-media advertising . . . Such racially and culturally specific notions of femininity play an important role in elevating women of different "races" and ethnicities to specific occupa-

tions, in barring them from entry into others, and in conditioning managerial strategies of control.

Immigrant women are often relegated to the lowest-paying, lowest-status and most tedious occupations — as domestics or in manufacturing. They are far more susceptible to exploitation in these circumstances because immigrants are often unfamiliar with Canada's laws or the agencies designed to protect their rights. Moreover, they often lack any kind of social network to look after them should they lose their jobs. As a result, immigrant women fear unemployment more than discrimination in the workplace. The powerless and poor immigrant woman is likely to work unofficially — for cash — thus putting rights and protections at risk. This makes it difficult to unionize immigrant women in many industries.

At home, too, immigrant women face major disadvantages. Married women often have to work long hours at low pay, then are still expected by their husbands to perform the household tasks which, traditionally, they would have been expected to do in their country of origin. They are still expected to do all the cleaning, cooking and childcare activities. Immigrant men often find that they, too, are working long hours for low pay at jobs much lower in status than their skills or education would lead them to expect. As a result, they are often frustrated and sometimes become aggressive and violent towards their wives and children.

VIOLENCE AND VICTIMIZATION

In discussing this topic, we must note at the outset that within the sociological community a great deal of controversy surrounds the issue of violence. There are two main approaches which are, as you will soon appreciate, bitterly opposed. The first, sometimes called the *sociological* approach, argues that intimate relations between men and women are often conflictual and even violent. Though the forms of interpersonal violence may differ, women are as likely to use violence against men as men are against women. Thus, taking the sociological approach, the question of interest is: What conditions, situations or characteristics of the participants are most likely to set off violent episodes? In answering this question, researchers look at variables such as age, education, income, unemployment, stress level in the household, childhood socialization experiences and so on.

The second, *feminist* approach argues that violence against women by men is different in kind from violence by women against men. To lump the two together under the rubric of "domestic violence" is to equate the two and, in so doing, to make violence against women seem not only similar but also less blameworthy. And to attempt to account for episodes of violence against women in terms of sociological variables like age, education or stress is flawed in at least two respects. First, it gives the appearance of "explaining away" or condoning a social behaviour which is dangerous and morally wrong. Second and more important, it tends to underestimate what feminists consider crucial in explaining violence against women: namely, a patriarchal culture and social structure.

Feminists argue that it is only within a system of patriarchal inequality that factors such as age, education, stress and so on will express themselves in the form of violence against women. Men, whatever their social characteristics or stress level, are far less likely to beat up other men — especially bigger men or men in authority — than they are to beat up their wives and girlfriends. In short, our culture gives men licence to express their frustrations in an anti-female manner: that is what patriarchy is finally about. (In a similar fashion, Nazi culture once gave frustrated people a licence to beat up Jews, and to racists in the American South a licence to beat up blacks.) If we do not deal with the problem of patriarchy, we can never hope to control violence against women. And in using violence against men, women for their part are simply using the limited means of self-defence available to them in a patriarchal system. Again, the problem of "domestic violence" is due to patriarchy.

In writing this section, we have tried to incorporate both viewpoints since we see merit on both sides of the argument.

In our society, violence against women runs a gamut from verbal and psychological harassment to physical assault, sexual assault and homicide. Research on criminal victimization in Canada (Sacco and Johnson, 1990: 21) shows that "rates of personal victimization are highest among males, the young, urban dwellers, those who are single or unemployed . . . Risk of personal victimization is also greater among Canadians who frequently engage in evening activities outside the home and among heavier consumers of alcohol." Most recorded victimization is male victimization in public; but this is not the *female* experience of crime or victimization.

This issue of "experience" is important. It puts into focus the concerns and fears with which women in our society must deal and that men, for the most part, can ignore. Women fear to go out to a park at night, for example, or even to take a stroll in their own neighbourhood. Women at universities in Montreal and Toronto have arranged for escorts to accompany them to the subway station after late classes, or wait with them at a bus stop. They are always aware of the potential danger of attack, which most men do not feel they need to take into account.

Without ever taking a sociology course, young women soon learn the truth of what we noted in Chapter 4 on deviance; that is, the most dangerous, crime-prone (including violence-prone) people in Canadian society are young, single men. Yet the danger to women is *least* likely to come from strangers outside the home. More often, it comes from intimates: spouses, dates, male acquaintances

By changing the name "fireman" to "fire fighter" we make it easier for girls to imagine entering this traditionally male-only job.

and workmates. In particular, family life has the potential for both physical and mental abuse since stronger family members have the power to take out their frustrations on weaker ones.

Domestic Violence

We have no reliable figures on *all* the violence that takes place, but domestic violence and rape appear to be much more common than the official statistics reveal. Likewise, sexual harassment directly affects a large but undetermined number of Canadian women. Expert estimates range from at least one woman in ten to one in four having been beaten by her partner. Repeated severe violence is believed to occur in one out of every fourteen marriages. People who work in shelters for battered women believe that roughly nine times out of ten it is men who abuse their partners or their children.

For a variety of reasons, the data on domestic violence are somewhat uncertain. For example, research done by York University's Institute for Social Research (1992) shows that women's reporting of sexual abuse on a survey is significantly affected by (1) whether another person is present at the time of the interview, and (2) whether the respondent likes or does not like the interviewer. This evidence of an "interviewer effect" on the reporting of abuse reminds us that *all* data are gathered in a social environment. All data are "social facts" in more than one sense. Therefore, they are always open to debate and re-analysis.

Generally, research on abuse shows that violence often occurs at the same time as alcohol abuse, a spillover of work stress, and a loss of control over anger. But these psychological effects are not more important than social structural ones. For example, the state's attitude towards violence against women significantly affects domestic conditions women have to face every day. Often, police are reluctant to intervene when the neighbours call to complain of a noisy family dispute, or even if the wife herself complains. Many people, police included, still believe that family members should be allowed to work out their problems for themselves. Police and social workers, they believe, should stay out of the picture until there are overwhelming grounds for outside involvement.

As a result, within affluent groups violence may be hidden. The affluent rarely use shelters and legal clinics, even though they may suffer from just as much domestic violence as other women.

According to both the (American) National Survey of Families and Households and the (Canadian) General Social Survey, in much of the reported violence between married partners *both* partners are perpetrators. In other words, women as well as men commit violent acts in married couples. However, data indicate that the probabilities of injury for male and female respondents differ significantly. Since men are usually stronger than women, wives are more often injured than husbands, even when both partners are acting violently.

Recent concern about violence by men against women has stirred to action even such relatively conservative organizations as the World Bank, which commissioned a report on the topic. As we see from Far and Away on the next page, physical and sexual violence against women are all too common throughout the world. Some violence against women has a political purpose, as in the mass raping of Bosnian Muslim women by Bosnian Serb soldiers. More usually, the violence has no purpose whatever and is carried out on a woman with whom the man involved has been intimate and loving, often for years.

One survey of self-reported domestic violence in Canada shows that (1) younger people are more violent to their spouses than older people; (2) unemployed people are more violent than employed people; but (3) lower-income and less educated people are no more violent than higher-income, highly educated people. There is also a relationship between a belief in patriarchy and wife battering. Husbands who believe men ought to rule women are more likely than other husbands to beat their wives. In turn, a belief in patriarchy appears to depend on educational and occupational level. Specifically, the belief appeals to lower-status, less educated men.

The most revealing and significant finding in this study is that high rates of domestic violence are associated with high levels of domestic stress. Concretely, the more stressful events a person reports experiencing in the previous year, the more violence will have taken place within the household.

FAR AND AWAY

Violence Against Women: A Global Crisis

According to the writer of this article, "25 per cent of Canadian women surveyed reported being physically assaulted by a current or former male partner since age 16." The statistics are even more disturbing for other countries, making clear that the abuse of women is an international problem not limited to one culture, religion or form of political or economic organization. However, there are reasons to think the problem will diminish.

Away from the rhetoric of the [United Nations] Fourth World Conference on Women, which opened yesterday in Beijing, women almost everywhere have struggled against what many say is the greatest silent crisis of the 20th century: domestic violence. From the United States, where an average of 240 women a day are raped, to Papua New Guinea, where two-thirds of women report physical abuse at home, violence against women has continued apparently unabated into the 1990s.

Since the previous international women's conference in 1985, the same disturbing pattern has been documented on every continent.

- One-half of suicide attempts by black American women are preceded by abuse.

- 20 per cent of women surveyed in Colombia said they had been abused physically; 10 per cent said they had been raped by their husbands.

- Of 2,000 cases recorded in 1987 at an all-women's police station in the Brazilian city of Sao Paulo, more than 70 per cent involved domestic violence.

- 42 per cent of women surveyed in Kenya said they were beaten regularly. In 1991, when schoolboys raided a girls dormitory, raping 71 girls and killing 19, the school's principal was quoted as saying, "The boys never meant any harm to the girls. They just wanted to rape."

- Nearly 60 per cent of women surveyed in Japan reported sexual abuse.

Domestic violence is so widespread that it is called the silent crisis of the 20th century. Some governments have made efforts to punish offenders and to set up services for victims. Others have enacted legislation that effectively reduces women's protection. Women's organizations, including some of those attending the United Nations Fourth World Conference on Women, are raising the profile of domestic violence and seeking to force governments to respond to the problem. [The question is] will governments attending the UN conference in Beijing be able to agree on and follow through with action to reduce domestic assault?

"But violence is not inevitable," the World Bank says. "Cross-cultural research shows that, although violence against women is an integral part of virtually all cultures, there are societies in which gender-based abuse does not exist." The World Bank study found that domestic violence tends to decrease as women gain economic and social power outside the home. Community intervention and sanctuary for women victims can also be important, the study said.

Source: Abridged from John Stackhouse, *The Globe and Mail*, Tues., Sept. 5, 1995, p. A12

It is easy to imagine how these events might cause intense frustration and, in this way, violence. And not surprisingly, since we have been living through a period of economic recession, rates of spousal assault appear to be rising dramatically. Still, if stress and frustrations give rise to violence, they do not excuse it. The real problem underlying violence is not stress or frustration but the fact that some men find it acceptable to channel their frustrations into violence towards family members. A marriage licence is not a licence to batter. As long as our society tolerates and even condones family violence, it will continue.

Date Rape and Sexual Inequality

Another current concern is "date rape." A survey was conducted on forty-four college and university campuses across Canada by sociologists Walter DeKeseredy and Katharine Kelly (1992). It found four women in five claiming they had been subjected to abuse by a dating partner. Overall, nearly as many men admitted having acted abusively towards their dates.

The validity of the findings were attacked because the study listed a very wide range of behaviours under the heading of "abuse." These behaviours included insults, swearing, accusations of flirting with others or acting spitefully, as well as violent and grotesque acts such as using or threatening to use a gun or knife, beating, kicking or biting the dating partner. So it is best to separate out the violent from the less violent abuses before we attempt to analyze the results.

When we do this, certain patterns fall into place. Where *violent* abuses are concerned, women are more than twice as likely as men to acknowledge their occurrence. Where less violent abuses are concerned, men and women acknowledge them equally often.

For example, 65 per cent of women report being insulted or sworn at by a date, and 63.6 per cent of men report having done that to a date. On the other hand, 11.1 per cent of women report being slapped by a date, yet only 4.5 per cent of men report slapping a date. Likewise, 8.1 per cent of women report being kicked, bitten or hit with a fist, yet only 2.4 per cent of men report having done any of those things. This consistent discrepancy leads to one of three possible conclusions: either (1) violent and abusive men date a lot more women than gentle, non-abusive men; (2) women tell a lot of lies about their dates; or (3) many men are ashamed to admit the things they have done to their dates.

The data also show that violent abuses on dates are not only physical, they are also sexual. As before, male respondents are only about one-half or one-third as likely to report doing these things as women are to report having them done.

Bear in mind that most instances of forced sexual activity occur between people who know each other. The result is, too often, that women blame themselves for the experience. Because they know the assailant, they react passively to the sexual assault. Because they react passively, they blame themselves for not reacting more forcefully. A few even continue the dating relationship.

Sexual harassment is another form of sexual assault, and is especially prevalent in schools and workplaces. As evidence in the Social Profile below indicates, in the halls of their schools Ontario's female high-school students regularly experience harassment which ranges from unwanted staring and rude or embarrassing remarks, to unwanted touching. The result is a frequent, if not constant, sense of discomfort — even dread — about being at school.

Part of the problem is that perceptions of sexual harassment vary by gender. High-schools boys may have little idea just how much they are upsetting the girls. College-aged men are much less likely to label behaviour "harassment" than their female peers. But after exposure to the work force, men's awareness

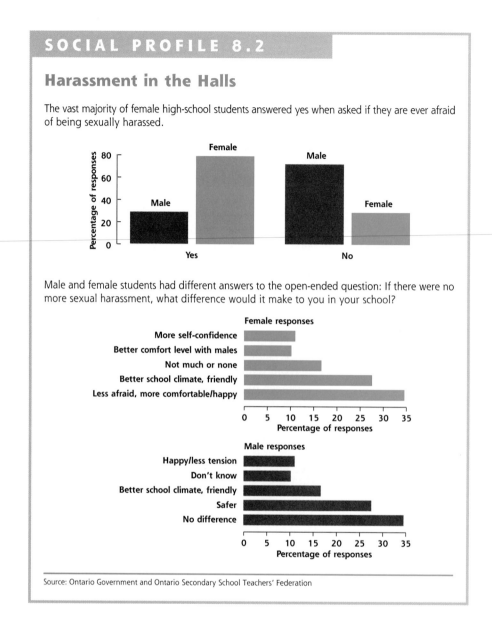

SOCIAL PROFILE 8.2

Harassment in the Halls

The vast majority of female high-school students answered yes when asked if they are ever afraid of being sexually harassed.

Male and female students had different answers to the open-ended question: If there were no more sexual harassment, what difference would it make to you in your school?

Source: Ontario Government and Ontario Secondary School Teachers' Federation

grows and they, too, come to see certain behaviour as harassment. Overall, women label more behaviours as harassing than men do, but this discrepancy decreases with experience in the work force, as women become accustomed to "the norm."

CHANGE AND RESISTANCE TO CHANGE

The main force changing gender relations today is feminism. Challenging the cultural division of humanity into masculine and feminine worlds, feminists seek to eliminate the social disadvantages women have historically faced.

But does the acceptance of feminist ideology and attitudes reduce gender inequality in ordinary, everyday social relationships? The evidence says it does — somewhat. For example, newlyweds in New Zealand who said that they accepted feminist ideas expected to allocate household tasks on a more equal basis than those who said they did not accept feminism. However, backsliding occurs.

Behaviour often changes in a more traditional, less egalitarian direction after marriage, with the result that a great many women with children (but half as many men with children) still feel highly "time-crunched." In the end, a combination of egalitarian sex-role attitudes and wives working outside the home does bring about some change in the household division of labour, including a change in the father's involvement in childcare.

Yet the goal of equality remains elusive and the persistent economic instability which has created a climate of anti-feminist sentiment, is another obstacle to achieving that equality. People's patriarchal attitudes about men and women resist rapid change, despite legislative attempts to limit systemic discrimination. After all, our assumptions about what it means to be male or female are among the most fundamental to our sense of self and our perception of others. Changing such a crucial part of our own identity and our way of dealing with one another does not come easily.

Until recently, women's job histories were very different from those of men. A generation ago most women spent little of their lives in the paid work force. Many worked for pay only before having children or after all their children were in school full-time. Even then, they fitted their work lives around their family responsibilities and avoided careers requiring too much time away from home. As a result, the majority had jobs, not careers. As well, women suffered discrimination in the labour force. This made it harder for women to get good jobs or promotions when they competed with men, or even equal pay for equal work.

Under these circumstances, most married women held the social rank their husband, the "breadwinner," had been able to attain. As a result, women would gain their greatest social mobility by marrying and supporting their husbands' efforts. Some women married up while others married down. Not so long ago, British data analyzed by Heath (1981: 114) showed that "a woman's class fate is more loosely linked to her social origins than is a man's," and conversely, more tightly linked to her spouse's fortunes.

Until recently, women's fates in the job market have also been more "loosely linked to social origins" than men's fates. In enormous numbers, women have filled a small variety of low-to-medium-prestige jobs. These jobs have been chiefly in sales, clerical work, service and light manufacturing, while some have been in professional work (like nursing and schoolteaching). To women from working-class backgrounds, these jobs have often meant upward mobility. To women from middle- or upper-middle-class backgrounds, these jobs have meant downward mobility.

In the United States, most women's occupations are confined to the lower 66 per cent of the prestige scale. This reflects the traditionally male-dominated job market. These patterns have begun to change as women attain higher levels of education, have fewer children, spend more years in the labour force and experience less discrimination. Increasingly, women's patterns of social

SOCIAL PROFILE 8.3

A Woman's Work

Percentage of respondents who say they are highly time-crunched (full-time workers):

Source: Based on Statistics Canada data, as reported in *The Globe and Mail*, Jan. 8, 1997, p. A6

mobility grow more similar to those of men. Yet the patterns are far from identical or equal.

The problem is similar, though of varying magnitude, in most industrial societies. For example, since the fall of communism in Poland, women have been facing job discrimination that is leading to high rates of unemployment. This anti-woman initiative is supported by Roman Catholic politicians and nationalists, who are promoting a "traditional Polish family." As well, with women out of the work force, the official unemployment rates are lower.

Such sentiments as these find a sympathetic response from *some* Canadians, but *most* Canadians would consider them backward, sexist and unacceptable. As a result, discrimination against women in Canadian workplaces is hidden and hard to measure.

We spoke earlier about traditional relations between male doctors and female nurses. Even these relations are starting to change, illustrating the general process of change that is taking place in gender relations. We are finding a more collaborative relationship between nurses and doctors, men and women. In this newer relationship, the doctor and nurse are professional co-workers who form a team and cooperate in the design and application of a treatment plan. The physician is still responsible for diagnosing the illness but the nurse plays a more important part in planning and providing the treatment. There is less tendency in this kind of relationship to see nursing care as trivial. Here, the doctor and nurse work hand-in-hand, not as "master" and "maid." Another factor contributing to the change in relations between doctors and nurses is that, more and more, males are choosing nursing as a career.

This is not the final stage in the process of change in nursing. A third kind of relationship is evolving in some places. Especially in the United States, the nursing role is developing into that of "independent practitioner" or "nurse therapist." In this situation, the nurse takes on "sole" responsibility for patient *care*. A doctor continues to be responsible for diagnosis and prognosis. The independent nurse practitioner plans, carries out and evaluates all parts of the treatment plan.

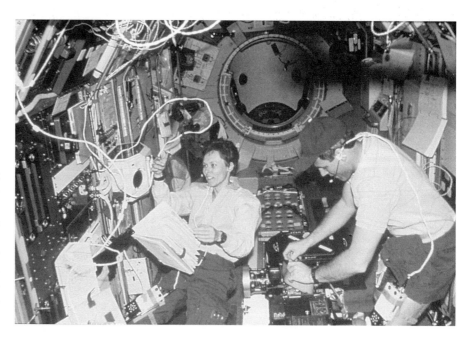

As professional rocket scientists, women in the paid work force will win higher wages and more respect than in the past. But can they rely on their husbands to get the children to the dentist or put dinner on the table by 6:30?

This nursing approach has many advantages over the other two. It gives the nurse more autonomy, more money and higher status as a caregiver, but nurses are not the only beneficiaries. The change also leads to more specialization of nursing activities: for example, to specialization in obstetrics, emergency, chronic care and so on. In community clinics, many nurses work as specialists in family practice nursing. (On the other hand, many nurses resist this change. They feel they are becoming second-class doctors instead of first-class nurses.)

In short, the doctor-nurse relationship appears to be changing from one based on a paternalistic model, through a model based on collaboration, to a model in which the nurse works as an independent practitioner. Still, the dominant model continues to be paternalistic, and most nurses remain subordinate to doctors.

What is particularly insidious about the gendered division of labour is not only that women are restricted to work which is subordinate to and lower in status than that of men, but that jobs often lose their status and authority as more women enter them. For example, nursing, teaching and secretarial work were largely male occupations in the 19th century. The movement of women into these occupations coincided with a dramatic decline in status and authority in each of these positions.

One wonders whether the same thing will happen if and when women succeed in persuading the Catholic Church to begin ordaining female priests, after two thousand years of refusing to do so. The international debate on this topic is discussed in Applied Sociology on the next page.

Or take a less unusual example: doctors. Once the symbol of the autonomous, high-status professional, doctors are more and more often being transformed into employees of the state. This change has structural causes and affects the status of all physicians, not just women. But it does indicate that women are always playing "catch-up." They often succeed in moving into a previously restricted occupation or role only to find that many of the benefits to be gained from the occupation have moved on, as well.

Traditional gender roles have both positive and negative consequences. The negative consequences for women of traditional gender roles have fuelled efforts by the feminist movement and others to press for change. As a result, North American women have indeed gained. However, unless these hard-won legal rights are enforced, women and men will still not have equal access to social rewards and gender stratification will continue.

Men and women may never have identical lives, but it is critical that, one day, they enjoy equally fulfilling, equally free lives. Discrimination has advantages for men, and for employers, who pass along the consequences — such as female poverty — to the taxpaying public. It is not so advantageous for women, nor is it just. On the other hand, it is hard to devise a way of measuring "comparable worth" so that we can give each kind of work the rewards it deserves.

In reality we all — men and women alike — lose from the persistence of gender inequality. Justice and fairness aside, we are not using the talents of our population effectively, not taking advantage of the knowledge, enterprise and skills possessed by both men and women. The movement of large numbers of women into the labour force means that many issues, such as inadequate day-care facilities for children, now affect both husbands and wives. The failure of our society to provide supports for the new problems husbands and wives are facing contributes to high divorce rates and increased gender conflict.

Female Priests

Sociologists know a great deal about the workings of formal organizations; we got a small glimpse of this in discussions of bureaucracy in Chapter 6 (Work and the Workplace). But how do you go about changing the 2,000-year-old practices of what is, arguably, the world's oldest, largest and most conservative formal organization: the Roman Catholic Church? That is precisely what women, both within and outside the organization, are trying to do.

An attempt by the Pope to end all discussion about ordaining female priests has spurred women in Canada, the United States and Europe to join forces to fight for full equality. The women want a priesthood that unreservedly welcomes women. In 1994, the Pope declared in a letter that the church had no authority to ordain women as priests and that "this judgment is to be definitely held by all the church's faithful." Because he didn't use the word 'infallible' church members were left leeway to challenge the declaration.

To rectify that situation, the Vatican Congregation for the Doctrine of the Faith said last November that this teaching has been taught "infallibly" by the Pope. That means it is not simply a rule but a deposit of faith that must be unquestioningly accepted. For many Catholic women, that will never be possible, says Frances O'Connor, a nun and guest scholar at Notre Dame University's Kellogg Institute for International Studies. "In society, women have had more freedom over the last 30 years whereas in the church, we get a pittance or what I call 'crumbs from the table,'" Sister O'Connor said during a telephone interview from Indiana.

Catholic women can now be lectors, theologians and scripture scholars, they can sit on parish councils and hold retreats.

"While the church has given us some good-sized crumbs, we don't have the whole loaf yet," she said. "And that's very painful for those women who really feel called to the priesthood."

What frustrates women even more is that the church does allow women to preach and minister to Catholics in exceptional circumstances. For example, Catholic women function as chaplains at universities and hospitals and perform all priestly functions except for administering the sacraments, like the Eucharist, in churches affected by a growing shortage of priests.

"But, for the most part, this is entirely at the behest of the occasional empathetic priest," said Mary Malone, a feminist theologian at St. Jerome's College at the University of Waterloo. "It can change in the wink of an eye if the priest gets changed."

Dr. Malone, a prominent and highly respected academic, shocked the Catholic community last year when she decided that she could no longer call herself a Christian. She had worked relentlessly for years to get the church to deal with issues like inclusive language and its patriarchal character.

One day, she said, she realized that she had lost all hope that the church would change in her lifetime. "If you're in church every day and you are being addressed as a man and a brother and a son, it really doesn't make a lot of sense," said Dr. Malone, who has only recently gone public with her decision. "I cannot worship a male God . . . I felt I had to leave Christianity when I no longer saw any hope that my inclusive vision would ever become a reality in practice."

Source: Abridged from Joan Breckenridge, *The Globe and Mail*, Sat., May 4, 1996, p. A11

CLOSING REMARKS

What is most important to remember in closing is that gender relations offer us the best example yet of C. Wright Mills's view that public issues are really the other side of personal troubles. As a public issue, gender inequality is in a confused state indeed!

On the one hand, people experience the recent shifts in gender relations as personal troubles. As Luxton (1983) found on returning to Flin Flon (a mining town in northern Manitoba), traditional work patterns are eroding and new ones are emerging. More women are working for pay, and as they begin to do so, their views are changing on how domestic labour should be divided by spouses.

This leads wives into personal struggles with their husbands. Seeing change in terms of personal conflicts, rather than as a public issue or sociological trend, increases the tension between men and women.

On the other hand, we can all see major changes in women's lives during the 20th century. Consider, for example, the influx of women into wage labour, which merged the market and domestic economies in a new way. Now, market and domestic economies — paid and unpaid labour (formerly, men's work and women's work) — must be viewed as two poles in a larger framework of production. And the growing importance of unpaid, home or informal work has an enormous impact on the formal economy. We buy more goods instead of services, for example.

We all need to catch up with, and reflect upon, the wide-ranging changes that have already taken place in every area of our private lives. Most important, we need to know how to apply our macrosociological understanding of the "battle of the sexes" to our personal lives. Nowhere is this need to rethink personal relations in the light of large structural trends more momentous than in the realm of family life. Turn to the next chapter for a discussion of this topic.

Review Questions

1. Define sex and gender.

2. How do these two concepts differ?

3. What is meant by patriarchy?

4. What are the consequences of gender socialization?

5. Why did most sociologists in the past not pay much attention to gender issues?

6. Which sociological paradigm has paid the most attention to gender issues?

7. In what ways does gender inequality disadvantage most women?

8. In what ways is gender inequality present in family relations?

9. Are changes in the family structure altering the patterns of domestic gender inequality?

10. In what ways is gender inequality present in the workplace?

11. Is increased participation by women in the labour force altering the patterns of workplace gender inequality?

12. What is the "double standard"?

13. How are prejudice and discrimination against women interconnected with racial and ethnic discrimination?

14. What effects does the fear of violence have upon women's experiences?

15. What does the incidence of date rape tell us about sexual inequality?

16. How are traditional gender roles changing?

17. Has feminism had an effect on traditional gender roles?

Discussion Questions

1. Why do you suppose North Americans are shifting away from preferring sons to preferring one son and one daughter?

2. What evidence would prove that capitalism is responsible for the growth of inequality between men and women? What does the *actual* evidence indicate?

3. What social changes led to the elimination of a sexual "double standard" in North America? Do you think the change was a good one? Why or why not?

4. To what degree is discrimination responsible for the earnings gap between men and women?

5. Name several other male/female pairings in the workplace that illustrate, as well as doctors and nurses, the structure of gender inequality in our society.

6. Do you agree that "the battle of the sexes" is both more violent and more important than class or racial conflict in our society today?

Suggested Readings

Armstrong, P. and H. Armstrong (1993) *The Double Ghetto*, third edition. Toronto: McClelland and Stewart. Married women inhabit a "double ghetto," which means that, unlike their husbands, they work a double day. Their freedom to work for pay, pursue a career and be economically independent does *not* mean freedom from domestic work. Instead it means a double burden.

Brownmiller, S. (1986) *Femininity*. London: Paladin Books. A witty survey of what we mean by the term "femininity" in our culture, and how (historically) the term came to take on that meaning. Includes sections on body, skin, hair, clothes, voice, movement, emotion and ambition.

DeKeseredy, W.S. and R. Hinch (1991) *Woman Abuse: Sociological Perspectives*. Toronto: Thompson Educational Publishing. An excellent review of the literature on wife abuse, dating abuse, rape and sexual assault by two Canadian sociologists, one of whom (DeKeseredy) is a co-researcher on the dating-violence study cited earlier in this chapter.

Hochschild, A. (1989) *The Second Shift*. New York: Avon Books. The author thoroughly and eloquently explains the important relationship between domestic equality and marital satisfac-

tion. She concludes that the happiest two-job marriages are between men and women who do not load housework onto the woman, nor devalue that work: they share the burden.

Kanter, R.M. (1977) *Men and Women of the Corporation*. New York: Basic Books. The first of Kanter's books to explore the reciprocal benefits between organizational openness (e.g., gender equality) and collective well-being. In short, everyone's happier and more productive, and the organization also does better, when women are numerous and included at all levels.

Luxton, Meg (1980) *More Than A Labour of Love: Three Generations of Women's Work in the Home*. Toronto: Women's Press. Based on participant observation and interviews in Flin Flon, Manitoba, this book provides ethnographic insights into gender relations at home and work.

Mackie, Marlene (1987) *Constructing Women and Men*. Toronto: Holt, Rinehart and Winston. This book pulls together a wide range of research on relations between women and men from a symbolic interactionist perspective. Following in the footsteps of the author's earlier work, it focuses on socialization over the life course.

Internet Resources

The following Web sites are good places to find more information about topics discussed in this chapter:

Canadian Women's Internet Association gives Canadian women a central meeting place, with Internet help and Canadian resources for women, links to sites on feminism, women's studies, motherhood, health and fitness.
http://www.women.ca

Women in Canada provides a history of women in Canada, published by the Department of Foreign Affairs and International Trade.
http://www.dfait ~ maeci.gc.ca/english/html/canada/19women.htm

Whirlpool Foundation's "Women—The New Providers" examines the changing role of women within our society.
http://www.whirlpool.com/corp/foundation/women1c.htm

Gender and Society provides links to pages dealing with women's issues, feminist concerns, the backlash against feminism and violence against women.
http://www.trinity.edu/ ~ mkearl/gender.html

MensNet contains a list of links to pages dealing with any and all aspects of gender issues.
http://www.magi.com/ ~ mensnet/netsite.htm

Feminism and Women's Studies publishes women's studies and feminist works, focusing on issues of sex, gender, sexual identity and sexuality in cultural practices.
http://english-www.hss.cmu.edu/feminism/

THE FAMILY

C H A P T E R   O U T L I N E

"Family" conveys a set of meanings to all of us: ideally, it means intimacy, familiarity, support and dependency— even love. Unfortunately, not all families achieve this ideal.

THE FAMILY AS A MAJOR INSTITUTION

North Americans value family life more highly than any other part of their lives and there are good reasons why this is so. Many of the things people like to do most — sex, hugging and kissing, talking or playing with children, sleeping, or just wasting time — are most likely to take place at home. On the other hand, many of the things people like to do least — going to the dentist, shopping for groceries, commuting to work or sitting through lectures at school — are least likely to take place at home. So, from a personal standpoint, the family home is a place you want to be.

From a sociological standpoint, the family is the most basic (and some would say, most important) social institution. It is in the family that most people come to be socialized, learn who they are, what others expect of them and what they can expect of others. It is also in the family that most people learn to get along with others, to love and sometimes to hate, to express their innermost feelings and also to lie, to resent being subject to other people's authority and to use others to get what they want.

Family life embodies the relationship between our macro and micro social worlds. After all, our most intimate moments are lived within the "family" or "household" setting; not surprisingly, some people have called the family a "haven in a heartless world." This is true whether we have in mind the traditional heterosexual family or the non-heterosexual (same-sex) family — a rapidly emerging form of family life.

Yet what happens in the family is affected by what happens outside it. Family inequality mirrors inequality in the larger society. People who are more powerful *outside* the family tend to hold more power *inside* the family. People who suffer the most disgrace *outside* the family may try to disgrace and shame others *inside* the family. You may have seen the cartoon where the boss bawls out the dad, dad comes home and bawls out the mom, mom bawls out the big kids, big kids bawl out the little kids and little kids bawl out the pets. We take out our workplace frustrations on the people who are closest to us, whether they deserve it or not.

At the same time, our public lives *outside* the home are also affected by what is happening *inside* the home. Family conflict and other domestic stresses influence how we perform at school and on the job. Because of this, more employers are taking family duties into account these days, by providing on-the-job child-care, more flexible work hours, help in career planning and even programs to help employees who are having domestic problems. Employers are no longer able to ignore their employees' personal troubles if they want a high level of productivity from them.

For the first few years of our lives, the family is a microcosm of the larger society in which we will one day participate. By learning to be family members, we learn how to be members of society. Then, after we leave the shelter (or tyranny) of our family, most of us marry and begin our own adult families. The new roles we take on — as spouse and parent — become crucial parts of our identity. New, intense relationships with others afford us satisfaction and self-esteem but also limit what we can do or hope to do.

As we learn from Everyday Life below, people's family lives are changing in dramatic ways. This chapter is about many of these changes, about what is causing families to change, and the ways families cope with the conflict and uncertainty that results. These changes would not be as newsworthy, hopeful (in some cases) or shocking (in others) if not for the important place families hold in our society.

Defining the Family

Before we examine the diverse forms a family can take, we need a definition of the **family** that gives us a common starting point for analysis. We can say that a "family" consists of a group of people who are related to one another through marriage, descent or legal adoption. Family members have institutionalized roles that define what they can expect from one another and what duties they owe each other. The nature of these rights and duties is determined by cultural values; in turn, these values are influenced by economic realities and in many cases backed up by the laws of the state.

Adult family members have a legal duty to take care of their dependent children. This means tending to their basic survival needs, like food and shelter. Ideally, it includes providing love, comfort and a sense of security. Good families also teach their children the language, customs, beliefs, norms, skills and values they will need to fit into their society. To a degree, most families do these things. Yet real families fall short of the ideal in many ways, and this can cause problems. Like the society that it mirrors, a family can display selfishness and cruelty, inequality and violence.

Because "the family" is a basic social institution, membership is not limited to a particular time or place. If you move to Winnipeg and the rest of your family stays in Vancouver, you still consider yourself to be a family member. You may also consider your grandparents, uncles, aunts and cousins, none of whom may live with you, to be members.

Gathering statistical data on the family, however, requires having a clearly defined unit that can be measured and compared. Because the family can take on so many forms and can change so dramatically over time, this unit cannot be based on either the "legal" or the "ideal" model of the family. For these reasons, Statistics Canada (the source of much of our information) uses the concept of a *family household* as the basis for its analyses.

A **family household** is a group that includes an adult who shares a dwelling and keeps a household with at least one other relative, whether a spouse, child, parent or other kin (for example, cousin). The members of a family household may be related by blood ties, marriage or adoption.

This differs from the sociological definition given above, because for the sociologist, family members need not live together in order to be a family. Unlike

EVERYDAY LIFE

The End of "Leave It to Beaver"

Sometimes what we see every day, up close, is the thing we are least likely to notice. We don't see it changing because we are taking part in the change. We don't see its size and extent because our lives occupy only a small portion of the entire social structure. So it is with family life. Family life has changed dramatically and we have all been a part of it. Did you notice?

The typical Canadian family has changed its look so dramatically that married couples with children account for just 44.5 per cent of all families, while the proportion of common-law families has doubled to 12 per cent.

"It may be the end of the *Leave it to Beaver* family," said Robert Glossop, director of programs at the Vanier Institute for the Family in Ottawa. The data "tell me that people are still living in families, but they don't look like the kind of families I grew up in [in] the 1950s; it tells me that people are still making commitments to one another," he said.

Donna Lero, a family-studies professor at the University of Guelph in Ontario, said that "I think there are some causes for concern" about the changing family structure. "For many people the message is coming across that having children is a liability — economic in some cases, and a social liability if [programs like] maternity leave are not available. How friendly is Canadian society towards raising children?"

While living common law is not a new phenomenon, its substantial increase in the past 15 years in Canada "is striking," Statscan says. From 1981 to 1995, the number of common-law couples almost tripled to 997,000 from 355,000, and as a proportion of all Canadian families, rose to almost 12 per cent from 5.6 per cent.

Quebec leads all areas of the country in preference for living together. Last year, 21 per cent of all its families were common-law (versus just under 9 per cent for the other provinces) and the trend has been consistently rising in Quebec since 1981.

The prevalence of common-law couples reflects changing attitudes toward marriage, Statscan says. "It appears that common-law union is not only a prelude to marriage but also an alternative to marriage and remarriage."

More Canadians are also raising children alone. During the 1950s and 1960s, a spouse's death was the major cause of being a single parent. But by 1981, more than half of lone parents were separated or divorced, and the proportion reached slightly more than 55 per cent last year. Not only are single-parent families increasing as a proportion of all families in Canada, but their numbers leaped to more than one million from 712,000 in the past 15 years. And the number of single parents who have never married is also on the rise: Last year, almost one in four single parents fell into this group, compared to just under 10 per cent in 1981.

Last year, there were an estimated 430,000 stepfamilies — "a growing phenomenon" which will continue its upswing, the agency noted, and which now accounts for more than 10 per cent of all couples in Canada — married or otherwise — raising children.

Dr. Glossop said he does not think the statistics suggest that there's a vacuum of family values. "Canadians say in surveys that family is important to them," he said. "It tells you that . . . [i]t's not the marriage certificate we value as much as the way in which we try to care for one another."

Source: Abridged from Dorothy Lipovenko, *The Globe and Mail*, Thurs., June 20, 1996, pp. A1, A8

Statistics Canada, which needs a single benchmark, sociologists and anthropologists are interested in examining the many different forms a family can take. By looking at the differences, we hope to recognize basic features that stay the same. Also, by uncovering the social, economic and cultural factors that gave rise to these differences, we can better predict how the family will change in the future and understand why.

To accomplish this, sociologists focus on two basic activities — marriage and parenthood — which are found in one form or another in all family systems. We will discuss each of these attributes in detail. First, a few words are needed about the differences in sociological approaches to studying families.

Perspectives on the Family

Because the family is such a basic institution, it has been a central focus for research by sociologists working within all the major sociological perspectives. One result is that the family is yet another topic about which there is vast debate and contention. Yet the family is such a diverse social institution that each of the four perspectives can tell us different and valuable things.

As you might expect, the functionalist perspective emphasizes the various functions performed by the family as a social unit. Functionalists note that the family's role as a key social institution grows out of our long period of dependence on others for survival. The human infant's physical dependence requires that others feed, care for and teach it. In order to function well as adults, human infants rely more than infants of any other species on social contacts and teaching. This combination of biological and social factors makes the family a uniquely important social institution for the survival of the individual and society.

Marriage, too, emerges from a combination of biological and social factors. In all societies, women have the main responsibility for childcare, at least during infancy. That women bear, suckle and generally care for infants means that they are, at least temporarily, limited in their ability to protect and economically support themselves. The dependence of infants on women and of women on men may have given rise to the universal practice of marriage. However, the form marriage takes and the relationships and attachments that develop among family members are socially, not biologically, determined.

Functionalists identify a number of specific functions carried out by the typical family. These are the "socialization of children, sexual regulation, reproduction, economic cooperation, affection, intimacy, emotional support and status placement" (Mandell, 1987: 151). By carrying out these functions, the family ensures survival of the society and of the individual. It provides a setting within which the personality of the individual is moulded, and promotes people's integration into the culture and society. Given its central role, the family, in one form or another, is found in every society. Marriage, for example, is a cultural universal and, like every cultural universal, its form varies from one culture to another.

Although functionalists emphasize the widespread functions of the family, they recognize that the family has changed radically in the last few centuries. A leading functionalist, Talcott Parsons argued that the family's major functions in the past were economic (Parsons and Bales, 1955). A peasant family, for instance, served as an economic and productive unit. Everyone worked together to produce what the family needed to survive. This means that it was also within the family that most children learned the work they would do as adults, such as the tasks of a farmer, housewife, warrior, merchant and so on. In this way, the family was responsible for both economic production and "job training."

However, these two major functions, Parsons said, have both been removed from the contemporary family. Few people today work for pay at home and most occupational socialization has been turned over to schools and the workplace. Even primary socialization has largely shifted to day-care centres, peer groups and television. This change means that the family has lost its functions at the macrosociological level. Its new functions are largely microsociological. The family remains important for integrating people into society, and remains the setting in which people lead their private lives and maintain intimate relationships.

Whatever the merit of this argument, both conflict and interactionist critics of the functionalist approach argue that the family described by the functionalists is an ideal model, not a real family.

Instead of focusing on the functions of the family, conflict theorists have focused on the social relationships out of which the family is composed. Marxists, for example, suggest that the family remains an economic unit in our society even if it is no longer a unit of production. Relationships between men and women within the family reflect the economic conditions and forces that govern society.

They argue that once industrial capitalism took away the family's ability to function as a self-contained productive unit, family members became dependent upon the wage earned by the husband and often by the wife. The *nuclear* family, by eliminating the economic supports of the *extended* family, increased everyone's dependence: the worker's dependence on the capitalist, the wife's dependence on her husband, and children's dependence on their parents.

Thus, for conflict theorists, the relations among family members are just as likely to be conflictual and dysfunctional as they are to be loving and harmonious. Also, the relationship between family life and the economic order is bound to be conflictual. Like it or not, family life must change as economic life changes, whatever the cost to spouses, parents, children and their relations with one another.

Interactionists, for their part, have usually focused on the family as the context within which intimacy and primary socialization occurs. For this reason, they have focused their research largely on the microsociological processes of interaction among family members which lead to the emergence of identity and the "self" (see Chapter 3).

Equally important, interactionists study the family as a specific social setting within which intimates work out their lives, sometimes in harmony and sometimes

Despite the worldwide reduction in childbearing, child-rearing and socialization remain a central focus of family life.

not. For example, interactionists have used qualitative interviews to discover the difficulties women encounter in trying to balance the demands of domestic and wage labour. An example would be the process by which parents work out, with one another and with their employers, who will stay home when their child gets sick. Blain (1992) shows us that the answer to this question is never simple, and it is always structured by gender, class and workplace ideology.

As we saw in Chapter 8, feminist contributions to the study of family life are fundamental and wide-ranging. Feminists emphasize the family's role as a microcosm of the broader patterns of male domination in society. In this respect, the family becomes a political unit within which this domination is acted out on a daily basis. The family teaches and justifies the subjection of women through the roles and values assigned on the basis of gender and passed on to the next generation.

Clearly, the family is not just a major social institution: it is also an unequal and gendered social institution. Conflict within families is not simply a product of capitalist class relations outside the household's gate. As with any gendered institution, conflict is built right into the structure of family relations and family processes.

We cannot understand why a worldwide fertility decline began around 1870 and has continued ever since unless we know something about the changes in men's and women's power within families and the relative advantages of low fertility for men and women. This, too, has been a topic of interest to sociologists working in the feminist paradigm. (In Chapter 10 we will discuss international changes in childbearing, another key aspect of family life.)

MATING AND MARRIAGE

Two social relationships are central to the family. The first is *marriage*, the relationship between spouses (usually, a husband and wife.) The second is *kinship*, the relationship between parent and child. Variations in family life, then, include variations in the relationships between (1) spouses and (2) parents and children.

Types of Marriage

Broadly defined, **marriage** is a socially approved sexual and economic union between two or more people that is expected to last for a long time. People often enter this union with public formalities or a ceremony, such as a wedding.

In Canada, traditional forms of marriage and the family are going through a period of dramatic change. Many people find this change disturbing. Because the family is such a basic institution and marriage is such an intimate relationship, change can seem very threatening to some people. Yet there is no particular form of marriage or family relations that is universal or necessary. In order to understand what the change in our own society means, and what it may predict for the future, it is helpful to take a larger view of the institution of marriage and the many ways other societies provide "marriage-like" arrangements between people.

After all, societies vary in their patterns of marriage, family and kinship. For example, they vary in the range of choice given to would-be marriage partners; their reasons for marrying; the rules about premarital and extramarital intimacies; and, whether the same rules apply to both men and women. Even the desired age at marriage and the desired age difference between spouses varies from one society to another.

In some societies, people wed more than one mate at a time. **Polygamy** is the generic name for this arrangement. Within this general category, **polyandry** is the marriage of one woman to more than one man, and **polygyny** the marriage of one man to more than one woman. Polygamy was common in most pre-industrial societies and is still permitted in a few. In Nigeria, for example, half of all marriages were polygynous as recently as 1975. But polygyny is banned in all industrial societies.

Polyandry, on the other hand, has always been a rare form of marriage. It occurs in societies like Nepal, where living conditions are harsh and few men are able to support a wife and children on their own. A woman is therefore "shared" by a group of men — usually, brothers — and she is a wife to all of them. Female infanticide is practised, with the excuse that the number of women "needed" in such a society is much less than the number of men. Anthropologist Marvin Harris suggests that societies with low population pressure (the relation between population density and arable land) favour polygyny; societies with high population pressure favour polyandry.

Monogamy — marriage between only one woman and one man — is the marriage form that is most familiar in Canada. However, variations on monogamy, too, are becoming more common. One variation which is increasing in incidence is cohabitation in a marriage-like fashion between two people of the same sex. Sociological research shows that these stable same-sex relationships are very similar to stable opposite-sex relationships. Both are typified by stability and instability, peace and conflict, and varying degrees of inequality.

Another form is what sociologists have called **serial** (or **sequential**) **monogamy**. Serial monogamy is the marriage of a person over the life course to a series (or sequence) of spouses, though only one at a time. In a society with high rates of divorce and remarriage such as ours, a growing number of people practise serial monogamy.

In pre-industrial societies, marriage was rarely considered to be the concern of the marriage partners alone. Instead, people saw marriage as the joining together of two kin groups. Each group considered carefully whether the proposed match was good for all its members. This was largely because, upon marriage, family property would pass from one group to the other.

A second variation found in marriage is the expected place of residence. Anthropologists have found three basic patterns of residence: **patrilocal** (living with the husband's family), **matrilocal** (living with the wife's family) or **neolocal** (living with neither family and, often, at a distance from the spouses' parental families). Place of residence was an important issue in pre-industrial societies because the family was a unit of production. In industrial societies, where the family is not a unit of production, neolocal residence is most common.

As mentioned above, in pre-industrial societies marriage was a relationship between kin groups, not merely spouses. Usually, the kin groups arranged the marriage and the partners involved had little, if any, choice in the matter. Relationships work differently in our society, where *individuals* get married and their motivations for marriage are considered to be personal.

Romantic Love

Whether we are examining heterosexual or same-sex couples, a central feature of marriage in Canada is commitment to the ideals of romantic love. Another way of looking at this is that in our society the arrangements — geographic and economic — of marriage are framed through the ideological rhetoric of romance. Though practical concerns always play some part — more in some relationships than in others — most people who get married do so because they believe they love their partner. And often, people feel they have discovered the best, even, perfect, mate, through some destined process. Yet, for all the belief in the inevitability of love, we feel we also have to assist the process. How else to explain the enormous amount of time and money single people spend on personal display, searching for the right mate and dating candidates for the position of Mr. or Ms. Right?

The ideal of romantic love plays a small role, if any, in selecting a marriage partner in many parts of the world. Instead, marriage is usually seen as a mainly practical arrangement in which love is beside the point or a matter of luck. What is relevant is whether the likely husband will be a good provider, whether the likely wife will be a good homemaker and whether the union will supply the family and kin group with sons.

In our culture, people expect, and are expected, to marry for love. Another way of stating this is that Canadian families are ideally founded on *expressive* exchange, not *instrumental* exchange. The term *exchange* refers to a process of ongoing interaction between spouses. The exchange perspective sees marriage as a give-and-take process in which each spouse both gives and gets. The stability and well-being of a relationship is thought to depend on how well a balance is struck and sustained in this exchange between spouses.

Expressive exchanges in marriage are exchanges of emotional services between spouses. They include hugs and kisses, sexual pleasure, friendship, a shoulder to lean on, empathy and understanding. They affirm the affection and love each spouse has for the other. By contrast, *instrumental exchanges* are non-emotional. They maintain a household in practical ways, and include such services as sharing the housework, paying the bills and looking after the children.

As you would expect, every real marriage is a mixture of expressive and instrumental exchanges. As well, every culture values both types of exchange. But cultures differ in the importance they attach to each. In our society, instrumental exchanges have always been important, particularly in families raising children. Our culture considers expressive exchanges to be more important in marriage than instrumental ones, although instrumental exchanges may loom larger in tough economic times, and among people who have been married before.

In our society, people are urged to marry someone they love, not just people who would help out in practical ways. Yet no matter how much two people may love each other, married life always involves practical matters and economic concerns. Love may be central to married life, but in the last three decades, most families have needed two incomes to support a middle-class lifestyle that one income would have supported in the past. Economic and cultural influences have led many people to delay marriage, forgo intimacy or cohabit instead of marry. In Quebec, with the lowest rate of traditional marriages in Canada, the formation of married families is further hindered by laws which make marriage a less appealing option than cohabitation (see Everyday Life below).

So, in fact, the modern family still has both instrumental and expressive functions, but in our ideal culture the family is mainly expressive, directed to fulfilling emotional, psychological and personality needs. In large part, it is this idealization of the marriage and family, and the conflict between ideal and real family lives, that leads to high rates of frustration, divorce and sometimes violence.

Mate Selection

The term "mate selection" may seem like an odd one. Do we really "select" whom we shall love or marry? The answer seems to be . . . yes. Every society, including ours, has rules or laws about whom we can marry or with whom we can have sexual relations. We cannot legally decide, for example, to marry a sibling nor to have sex with a child.

Common Law Marriage Comes of Age

A recently released Statistics Canada document, "Report on the Demographic Situation in Canada, 1996," by demographers Jean Dumas and Alain Belanger, reveals that cohabitation, or common law marriage, may have come of age in Canada. No longer a rare occurrence, it has become — under some circumstances and in some parts of the country — the norm for intimate relations.

In the 1950s, cohabitation — sometimes contemptuously called "shacking up" — was relatively rare and unrespectable. The culture said it was something men did with women they would never marry, and "good girls" did well to keep that in mind. This view began to change with the sexual revolution of the 1960s and 1970s, when young people entered into sexual relations with more people earlier in life, protected against pregnancy by "the pill" and against middle-class norms by the hippie or youth culture. New living arrangements outside marriage began to flourish, and cohabitation rates began to rise.

Throughout the 1970s and 1980s, sociologists and demographers debated the meaning of this increase in cohabitation. Few thought it signalled a rejection of marriage; the dominant view was that, for most participants, cohabitation represented an extended date or "trial marriage." This view was supported by research in the early 1980s that found about half of cohabiting couples ended up marrying, usually in less than three years. Few cohabiting relationships persisted beyond three years and

even fewer had produced children. The 1984 Family History Survey also found that cohabitation was much more common in Quebec than in any other province; and that the popularity of cohabitation was growing rapidly, as evidenced by differences in the intimate experiences of young versus middle-aged Canadians.

The new findings on this topic, just released, show that Quebec continues to lead in its attachment to cohabitation. In Quebec, 25 per cent of all couples (compared with 14 per cent in all of Canada) are living common law; among people under 30, 64 per cent of Quebec couples are living common law (compared with 42 per cent in all of Canada). Between 1990 and 1994, 80 per cent of Quebecers chose a common law union when they first moved in with someone (compared with 50 per cent in the rest of Canada).

By now, more than six million Canadians have lived common law in the past two decades, and for many cohabitation continues to be a transitional relationship. After three years, about one-quarter of common-law relationships examined in 1995 had ended as marriages; another quarter had broken up; and half were still going strong. Thus the common law relationship continues to be a halfway point for many couples on the way to marrying. But among common law relationships lasting beyond three years, one-third had produced children. For more than in the past, cohabitation *is* the end point of an intimate relationship. Note, finally, that much of northern and western Europe is even further along in this process than Canada; this is no passing phase.

Source: Adapted from Alanna Mitchell, "Common-law gains cachet," *The Globe and Mail*, Wed., March 26, 1997, p. A10

Many societies have much more specific rules about who can marry whom. Some societies practice **endogamy**, which is the requirement common in small, traditional societies that people marry within their own social group (such as their own class, caste or ethnic group). Other societies practice **exogamy**, which means marrying *outside* one's social group. Exogamous societies are occasionally small and based on extended kinship, like the !Kung bushmen of the Kalahari Desert.

Marriage rules always aim at ensuring a kin group's advantage. Why endogamy? Wherever land or other immovable property might be lost through marriage, the pressure towards endogamy is strong, even today. Endogamy also increases when a group is suffering discrimination by outsiders and has to strengthen its social bonds by stressing group boundaries in marriage. By contrast, exogamy gives the members of a small society more chance to survive by increasing the size of the group they can call on in the event of a famine, war or other trouble. It is a good survival strategy where group resources are few and the group does not feel threatened by (all) outside groups; also, where there are few, if any, family properties to be lost (or gained) through marriage.

Our own society has no rules of endogamy or exogamy, but it sometimes seems endogamous, since most people tend to fall in love with and marry people who are like themselves in important ways. Sociologists call this tendency for like to marry like **homogamy**. Similarities in age, education, religion, physical attractiveness and appearance, class and social status, and geographic closeness are all important influences in homogamous mating.

There are good reasons why people tend to be homogamous. First, they are more likely to meet others who are (at least socially) like themselves than to meet people unlike themselves. This is a result of the social circles within which people move and interact with others. Second, we usually like people who think the way we do and act the way we expect them to; we feel comfortable in their presence. If we like ourselves, we will probably like people who are similar to us. Third, instrumental and expressive exchanges are easier to balance when like is marrying like. That's because people are bringing similar, hence more equal, qualities and resources to the marriage.

The research literature suggests that homogamous marriages are more satisfying marriages. For example, couples of the same religious faith have more successful marriages than other couples, as measured by lower divorce rates and higher rates of stated satisfaction. Educational homogamy is also important; in fact, its influence has been increasing over time, while the influence of social class and other ascriptive (inborn or hard to change) similarities, such as religion, has been decreasing.

Experts who provide premarital counselling note a variety of unrealistic beliefs which are common among people when they choose mates. They include the beliefs that:

- choosing a good mate is easy;

- people will find the perfect partner;

- there is one and only one good partner for each person;

- people will become perfect mates to their perfect partners;

- love is enough to smooth over the rough patches in a relationship;

- when all else fails, the mates will try harder and succeed; and

- opposites complement each other.

Why do people hold such beliefs when more useful, alternative beliefs might serve them better in the long run? The answer is that mate selection, for many, is the capture of "erotic property" and people's ability to reason is often clouded by passion.

Erotic Property

Let's take the notion of "marriage as exchange" to the limit. If we strip away the romantic ideals, marriage is like the purchase of a "consumer durable" — a house or recreational vehicle. Many feel that, by marrying, they take ownership of "erotic property," and that means sole sexual rights to someone's body.

Sociologist Randall Collins makes two main points about this system of erotic property: (1) marriage is a system of property relations, and (2) every marriage system is unequally structured — men have more property rights over women than women have over men.

As Collins (1982: 123) notes:

A couple who live together and have sexual intercourse exclusively with each other are for all intents and purposes married. If this goes on for several years, in many places they are considered legally married, as a "common law" marriage. On the other hand, a couple who are legally married but never have sexual intercourse is said not to have "consummated" the marriage. This is grounds for legal annulment, since the implicit terms of the marriage contract are not put into effect. In our society, then, marriage seems to be a contract for exclusive rights to sexual access between two people. Socially speaking, they are exchanging their bodies as sexual property to each other.

Collins believes that sexual property "is the key to the family structure; it is the hinge on which everything else turns." This can be shown, Collins argues, by our ideas about infidelity. "Traditionally, before the legal reforms of recent decades, the only way one could get divorced was by proving adultery" (*ibid.*). Adultery is considered such a serious offence because it violates the right to sole sexual access.

These ideas continue to exert a strong hold on people's thinking. A recent survey of sexual attitudes and behaviour reveals that in Quebec, apparently the most liberated province in Canada, 96.4 per cent believe faithfulness between a couple is essential, even more important than a stable relationship or active sex life; however, 22.4 per cent of men and 11.1 per cent of women admit they have cheated on their partner.

Arranged Marriages versus Love Marriages

A society that puts erotic property under kin-group control creates the practice of "arranged marriage." In most societies for most of history, marriages have not been based on love but on the needs, beliefs or desires of a couple's relatives. Thus, "arranged marriages" are most common in societies where we find extended families.

There, rights to the land are passed from one generation to the next (usually, from father to son). Since marriage is an arrangement between families — not just between individual mates — it makes sense to arrange marriages in a way that protects family assets. Parents also want to minimize conflict between the families that will be joined together by their children's marriage. For these reasons, the choice of marriage partners is far too important to be left to the whims of youth. Spouses are chosen because the union is economically advantageous, or because of friendship or kinship obligations. Now and then people marry other people they have never met.

In the West today, few marriages are "arranged" in the traditional sense. Yet an article in the University of Toronto's student newspaper *The Varsity* (Jan. 25, 1993: 7), reported the following:

Most second generation Canadian-Pakistanis grew up expecting and accepting the concept of an arranged marriage — an arranged marriage was inevitable and the social norm. And yet the definition of an arranged marriage today differs from the definition of one 20 years ago . . . In Toronto today, most individuals actively participate in selecting their

EVERYDAY LIFE

Family Live Converges

Just as the theory of industrial society (or modernization theory) we discussed in Chapter 6 (Work and the Workplace) would have suggested, family life is changing all over the world. The trends in family life listed below are for Canada, but they apply just as well — with varying time frames — worldwide. Some started changing earlier or changed faster, while others started later or changed slower. But the world's families are all going in the same direction!

In a nutshell, here are the changes that are affecting our families *and* creating a need for drastic changes in social policies related to family life:

In the last 100 years:

- people's lives have been getting longer and healthier

- birth rates have been falling in industrialized countries

- family households have been getting smaller and smaller

- nuclear families have been replacing extended families

In the last 30 years:

- more people have started living together outside marriage

- more mothers have entered the labour force

- rates of divorce and separation have exploded

- the number of births outside marriage has risen

- the number of lone-parent families has doubled

---

partners. The couple meets first with their families. If they are interested in each other, they can speak to each other on the phone and go out with or without a chaperon, depending on the values of the families . . . It's not an individual decision but a collective [one], involving six family members at least.

Modern marriage has its own complexities and raises a whole host of new problems in the relations between a husband and wife. We will return to this issue after looking at another crucial relationship, the one between parent and child.

PARENTS AND CHILDREN

Historically, the relationship between parent and child was the kernel of a broader set of relationships called *kinship relations*. We are related to many more people than our immediate family. The total network of people related by common ancestry or adoption is called a *kin group*.

In many societies, people trace their descent through one line only — either their father's or mother's line. In a *matrilineal* society, a person traces descent (or kinship) through the mother's line only. The father, his parents, brothers and sisters, and their children are not included in that person's kin group. In a *patrilineal* society, this pattern is exactly reversed. All descent is traced through the father, his brothers and his father.

Our society is neither matrilineal nor patrilineal — it is *bilateral*. This means that relatives of both of our parents are thought of as kin. We have maternal and paternal aunts, uncles, grandparents, cousins and so on. Bilateral descent fits well with an equalitarian authority structure where father and mother have a roughly equal say in family matters.

In many societies, what we consider the family is embedded in a much broader web of kinship relations, and a household will include numerous kin. In others,

The traditional view of marriage — sacred, lifelong and male-dominated — has given way in many cultures to a view that marriage is a residential or lifestyle choice, provisional and egalitarian.

such as the Canadian counterpart, a household usually consists of parents and their unmarried children. These two main forms of family household are referred to as the **extended family** and the **nuclear family**.

The nuclear family is the most common type of family household in Western society. It consists of one or two generations living together; typically, one or two parents and their children. The nuclear family is a conjugal family, in which priority is given to marital ties over blood ties. The basic relationship is between spouses, not between one or more spouses and their parents, siblings or more distant kin.

An extended family is one in which two or more generations of relatives live together. It may include grandparents and/or grandchildren, and uncles, aunts and cousins. The extended family is a *consanguine family*, since preference is given to blood ties over marital ties. Consanguine families stress the importance of relationships between parents and their children, among siblings, and with other "blood-related" members of the kin group.

Each of these forms has its pros and cons. The extended family usually serves as one big productive unit, with all able-bodied members contributing to the family's common good. The members of this unit cooperate in such productive activities as agriculture, craft work, hunting and gathering, building shelters, and other activities related to subsistence.

One benefit of such a family structure is that members of an extended family are able to rely on one another when they need emotional support. For example, children can go to aunts and uncles, cousins and grandparents when have a problem they feel they cannot talk about with their parents. Spouses can rely on their parents and siblings for comfort and support. This puts less strain on the marital relationship. And, in an extended family, grandparents can be sure they will be taken care of in their old age.

However, the nuclear family has some advantages over the extended family. For example, the nuclear family is not forced to remain in any particular location. Because it is small it can move easily to take advantage of job opportunities in another part of the country, or in another country entirely. It follows, then, that the rise of a middle class and industrial society helped shape the development of the nuclear family as a private institution. Britain and the North American colonies were among the first areas to display this form of organization.

Yet, the nuclear family also has its drawbacks. It offers its members too few people to rely on in times of financial trouble or emotional stress. Family members are liable to expect too much from each other because they have no one else to turn to. This reliance puts a lot of strain on relationships between spouses, or between parents and children.

This change in family composition has important consequences for the many immigrants to North America who have often left members of their extended family behind. For example, Korean families in North America are moving towards nuclear-family structures; as a result, many family traditions, such as filial duty, may soon disappear. Moreover, this change also weakens connections with extended kin in Korea, as well as with Korean culture.

More generally, we must recognize the wide variation in family and household types in Canadian society, due largely to the large number of immigrants and varied ethnic traditions. Though neolocal nuclear-family households are the most common form, other forms of family life are also common.

Childcare and Child-Raising

Styles of childbearing and child-rearing also vary from one group to another. Within Canada, some regional, ethnic and religious groups are more inclined to raise children than others, and they go about the task in somewhat different ways. Yet, research shows that there are better and worse ways of raising children, regardless of social background or type of family.

From the standpoint of raising children, what is a "good" family? Decades of sociological research on this topic has come to fairly consistent opinions. One of these is that family *structure* does not matter as much as family *process*.

For children, a "good family" is one that provides enough love and attachment, the right kind and amount of supervision, a sense of stability, social support for both the parents and children, and enough income that there is not day-to-day hardship or anxiety about making ends meet. Equally important, a "good family" is one that prevents and controls conflict, whether between the parents and children, or between the parents themselves. The implication of research on this topic is that to raise healthy, adjusted children, we need to ensure that parents know how to manage domestic conflict, that they have enough income, receive social support if they need it and learn how to cope with stress. And though one might not think so, some parents may need to learn how to provide their children with love, steady supervision and a sense of stability.

The point to remember here is that good family processes are possible in any kind of family, whether same-sex or heterosexual, cohabiting or married, first marriage or remarriage, two-parent or single-parent, and so on. However, family structure affects family processes: that is, some families find it easier or harder to work effectively — to interact, communicate, negotiate or limit conflicts. This is why, compared to children from intact families, children of divorce — especially children raised by single parents — are more likely to be emotionally distressed, low school achievers or engaged in delinquent behaviour.

A recently released study by Statistics Canada, titled *Growing Up in Canada* (Nov. 1996), the first report of an ongoing National Longitudinal Survey of Children and Youth, documents some of these differences. Using survey data drawn from a representative sample of children, their parents, teachers and school principals, the study shows that, compared to children ages six to eleven in two-parent families, children of the same age from single-mother families have higher rates of hyperactivity, conduct disorder, emotional disorder, behaviour problems, school problems (including repeating a grade) and what the researchers call "social impairment." The greater risk of each of these problems — and of multiple problems — in single-mother families persists even when researchers control for income by separating out low-income families from other families. Thus, income *per se* is not the whole explanation of the difference in children's experience, though it is an important part of the picture.

These signs of child distress may reflect any of a number of problems that disrupt family processes, such as marital dissolution, pre-dissolution conflict, single parenthood, poverty or remarriage. It is not easy to separate out these effects of family structure on family process and, in turn, on child well-being. However, there is little support for the notion that family structure *per se* is the problem; that divorce or lone parenthood is a bad thing for children. Faulty processes are what cause problems in children, and some family structures (such as the single-parent family, or blended or reconstituted family) put a strain on family processes.

For example, in a blended family, there is often a difference between what the child has come to expect from his or her biological parents and what is now expected by the step-parent or stepsiblings. This change in "family culture" may be a source of abiding confusion or conflict. In a single-parent family there is often less income and more anxiety about money. There is no other parent to share the work or provide social support, and it is harder to cope with stress and maintain supervision.

Put simply, parents in a single-parent family may have a harder time giving their children as much attention, love, supervision or support as they may need. Money aside, their time and emotional energy are just stretched too thin. This poses a problem not only for the families themselves, but for sociologists whose job it is to figure out what kinds of parenting strategies are likely to work best under these circumstances.

New "types" of family are becoming ever more common due to rising rates of divorce, unwed pregnancy and remarriage. Unless social programs are aimed at fostering healthy family processes, problems — mental, legal and social — will be with us for the next seventy-five years or so, as badly raised children live out troubled lives. More research is needed to determine the best ways to support good family processes. But one thing is certain: child poverty is a continuing problem that must be addressed by public spending.

Not only does the spousal relationship affect parenting, but parenting also affects the spousal relationship. Most people marry with the idea of having children. What they rarely know or admit is that, for all its pleasures, parenthood imposes a great many burdens. Family instability and conflict often arises out of the trials of parenthood.

The onset of parenthood is a trying time. Raising small children strains the marriage: quarrels become more common, both husband and wife feel they get less companionship from their mate than they once did, marital satisfaction declines and the enjoyment of parenthood is slight. "Two out of five of these mothers of small children go so far as to admit they sometimes wish they could be free of the responsibilities of being a parent, a much larger proportion than is found among mothers of older children" (Campbell, 1980: 188).

At all ages and marital durations, women without children are more satisfied with marriage than are women *with* children. Employed wives reach a lower level of satisfaction with marriage than housewives. Conversely, the husbands of housewives reach a lower level of marital satisfaction than husbands of women who work for pay. In all cases, the lowest point occurs when the children are adolescents. Husbands of housewives are more affected by parenthood than their stay-at-home spouses because their financial burden increases as their children enter adolescence. This greater need for money in middle age, just when a husband's income has started to level off, is often called the "life cycle squeeze."

The sociological evidence leaves no doubt that parenthood strains the relationship between husbands and wives. This in itself is a good explanation of why many couples are cutting down on childbearing, but it is not the only one. Parenthood has been on the decline for more than a century chiefly because it has become gradually harder to live a comfortable, middle-class urban life with many children. In fact, the financial problems which affect parents and strain the husband-wife relationship can strain parent-child relations, as well. Economic hardship can lead parents to provide inconsistent and punitive discipline which, in turn, causes the child emotional distress and other social, emotional and cognitive harm.

Given the choice between having more children and having more disposable income, most Canadians over the last hundred years have chosen the latter. With the recurring economic recessions of the 1970s, early 1980s and 1990s, the motivation to further limit childbearing grew stronger and, with the development of new contraceptive technology (the Pill, better condoms, spermicides) around the mid 1960s, the wish for a smaller family was easier to fulfill.

At the same time as contraception was making it easier for women to have only as many children as they wanted, when they wanted them, women were also getting more formal education and entering the work force in larger numbers. This meant that people who wanted to have children would have to find ways of caring for their infants until they were ready for school, and often other family members were not available to provide this care. Many mothers (but few fathers) stayed home with their children until they were ready for school; others put their children into day-care centres. Sociological research has found no proof that preschool children left in a good-quality day-care centre develop any worse than children who stay home with their mother, grandmother or a baby-sitter. However, as we see from Applied Sociology on the next page, the myth persists that in some imagined past, there were no working mothers or day-care centres.

Prolonged Dependency

For most of you reading this book, parenthood and its problems are still in the future. In your household, you are probably the son or daughter, not the mother or father. Parents and children, like husbands and wives, have different views of the family that reflect structural features of our society, not individual personality differences. These differences of view are often referred to as the **generation gap**.

The most important structural feature that has promoted the generation gap is the lengthening of the time that people are economically and emotionally dependent upon their families. In pre-industrial societies, adulthood came soon after the end of childhood, usually around the late teens. At this time, a person would get married and be considered a full adult member of society. Age categories such as "adolescence" and "youth," which we have come to take for granted, did not exist.

Several factors have led to the lengthening of the period of dependency and childhood. As we saw in Chapter 3 (Socialization), one factor that contributes to this phenomenon is modern education. In pre-industrial societies most people spent their lives doing what their mother or father had done. From early childhood on, children learned to perform the work expected of them as adults by performing tasks at home. By the end of childhood, they were ready for adult duties.

Today, we learn most of what adults need to know — especially future job skills — outside the home. And because we have so much more to learn in an industrial society, we have to attend school for many years. This means that many people are still students in their early thirties: still dependent financially on their families, often still living at home. This period of dependency has been still further extended, and filled with uncertainty, by recurring recessions.

This financial dependency prolongs the unequal relationship between parents and children past the point where young people willingly accept their parents' authority. It is difficult to attend college or university, where you are expected to act responsibly, think for yourself and succeed or fail by your own efforts, and then come home to be treated as a child again.

Myths about Childcare

It is in the nature of nostalgia to imagine there was once a "golden age" when life was simpler, families were more loving and children received better care from their parents. Unfortunately, research has been unable to unearth any evidence to support this nostalgia. But bear this in mind: uncovering and reporting inconvenient facts about family life is an important role that applied research can play in our public debates.

Research by social historians suggests that ad-hoc, private and family-based arrangements rarely worked for those in most need — mothers who worked because their earnings were crucial to family survival. It is necessary to demolish a few myths:

Myth: *Mothers who work outside the home are a new phenomenon, found only in Canada since the Second World War.*

Not so. While most families in the past solved their need for extra income by sending sons and daughters out to find employment, some mothers of young children have been obliged to find paid labour since at least the early 1800s. High death rates in Canada meant many women were widowed and, like today's divorced parents, had to find some way of supporting their offspring. Men lost their jobs, walked out on their wives, disappeared and drank up their wages in the past as in the present.

Myth: *Mothers who needed to work turned to their own parents, other relatives or neighbours to look after their offspring.*

Some did, and sometimes these arrangements worked well. Many families, however, did not have living grandparents. In poor families, relatives were often equally poor and could not help. Babysitting was most often done by other children in the family. Babies and toddlers were left with sisters as young as 6 while their mothers worked for meagre wages. As early as 1872, Toronto's truant officer complained that children were being kept at home for what he saw as frivolous reasons, including babysitting. Children continued to be the main caregivers for other children in working-class families until well into the 20th century. Often this meant sacrificing their schooling.

Myth: *Day-care centres are a recent phenomenon.*

We have had day cares in Canada for well over 100 years. The earliest were started in the 1850s and 60s by nuns concerned that the children of poor working mothers should receive adequate care during the day. Toronto's first day-cares were set up in the 1890s. Demand was always greater than the number of spaces. Most staff had little or no training; furniture, equipment and attention were minimal; and even the low fees charged made them too expensive for many families in most need. Mothers continued to rely on children, relatives and informal agreements; but compulsory schooling laws and higher ages for school-leaving made it increasingly difficult for parents to use their children as babysitters.

Since then, Canadians have sought to create a system that would not offer one kind of care to the children of the rich and another to the poor. In Ontario, parents have been able to choose between subsidized care in private homes and in group settings, with prescribed standards and regulation in each.

If Ontario moves to give parents vouchers that do not cover the cost of good-quality day care and that need not be paid to inspected care-givers, it risks overturning the important advances made in the province. There is no sense in returning to a variant of the old system. History suggests it didn't work.

Source: Abridged from Bettina Bradbury and Molly Ladd-Taylor, *The Globe and Mail*, Thurs., Nov. 23, 1995, p. A21

In pre-industrial societies, becoming an adult usually meant marrying and taking on the burden of raising your own children. Today, few couples get married until they are in their twenties. This prolongs the period of *emotional* dependence on parents. Young adults find that their parents' opinion of them continues to be an important part of their sense of self, just at the time when structural factors, such as financial dependence, lack of autonomy, joblessness and a prolonged skill-training period are lowering that opinion. They are still locked into an intense emotional relationship with their parents at an age at which, in another society, they would be independent, capable adults with a spouse and children of their own.

The result of this lengthened period of dependence is that adulthood is put off. The age categories of adolescence and youth have emerged as a result. They do not reflect a biological fact about age; they are social categories generated by specific structural features of society. This does not mean that they are not "real," however. In our society, they are as real as ethnicity, race or gender; that is, they have real social consequences.

Economic Aspects of Family Change

Traditional families continue to survive but their numbers are growing slowly, while non-traditional families — especially two-income marriages, common law marriages and lone-parent households — are increasing rapidly and show no sign of ceasing to grow. These forms of non-traditional family all have consequences for adults' experience of parenthood and, even more, for children's experience of childhood.

The rise of the two-earner family has caused many changes in the marketplace. Since both spouses work, they have less time to spend on such tasks as cleaning, cooking and taking care of the children. They look to outside services and hired help to do these tasks. Luckily, two incomes provide these couples with the extra money they need to buy leisure. Their new demands account for a growth in the sales of frozen foods, restaurant foods, household care and child-care services. Two-earner couples have also furthered the growth of the appliance industry (which makes items like microwave ovens and dishwashers) and the leisure-goods industry (which makes VCRs and sports equipment, among other things).

Childless couples have even more *discretionary income* — money to spend on things other than basic needs like food and shelter — than families with children do; and this makes childless couples important consumers. Two factors explain their large discretionary income: high earning power and low expenses. Most childless couples earn two incomes and also earn about 20 per cent more than couples with children. In part, this reflects the group's higher-than-average education: the more education a woman gets, the more likely she will avoid or delay bearing children.

Without child-care expenses to pay, childless couples have a lot more money to spend on themselves. Economist Gary Becker (1981) compares childbearing to the purchase of *consumer durables* — long-lasting, often expensive items like automobiles or dishwashers. This comparison has a lot to recommend it; but actually the lifetime expense of raising children, in energy and emotion, as well as money, outdistances most consumer durables on the market. (The only durable that demands nearly as much time and money as child-rearing is a house.)

This new family imagery — children as consumer durables, mates as erotic property — resists

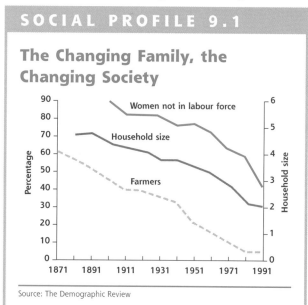

SOCIAL PROFILE 9.1

The Changing Family, the Changing Society

Source: The Demographic Review

fuzzy, emotional thinking almost to the point of cynicism. But does it help us grasp current trends in marriage and parenthood?

There is no proof that people today place a lower value on love, sex, intimacy, marriage or living with others than they did a generation ago. If anything, the greater insecurity of our economic and work lives has made such close relationships more valuable (and valued) than ever before. Yet, in the midst of this strong desire for family-like relations, families are forming, changing and breaking up at a rapid pace.

Important changes in the Canadian family since the 1960s include an increase in the number of families with both husband and wife working for pay, a decline in childbearing and family size, and — another result of the decline in childbearing — the aging of the Canadian population. Divorce and remarriage rates are high, as are rates of domestic violence. But the most striking feature of Canadian families is their variety.

Is There a Distinct "Canadian" Family?

Focusing on the variations outlined above, we can see that the typical Canadian family is nuclear, its residence is neolocal, marriage is monogamous, descent is bilateral and, increasingly, the authority structure is equalitarian. The selection of marriage partners is homogamous and usually endogamous, although not as limited as in pre-industrial societies. These features are as common in heterosexual as in same-sex families.

Researchers today are intrigued not by what is typical about the family, but by the increasing diversity of families. We have already noted important regional, ethnic and religious variations in people's marriage and childbearing practices. There are also some social class variations — not surprising since both marriage and childbearing have important economic aspects which pose more problems for some groups than for others.

Within these social groupings, individuals and couples work out their own strategies for marriage and childbearing. Where both members of a couple plan

Mating patterns, as well as family forms, are changing rapidly throughout the Western world.

to study, travel and then establish a career, the partners may put off marrying until their late twenties and not have a first child until their mid-thirties. This strategy is less necessary where neither partner, or only one partner, will have a prolonged education and/or career development.

Cohabitation

Reflecting this need for new strategies, rates of first marriage have fallen to an all-time low in Canada. The falling national rate has been led by large declines in Quebec, which has one of the lowest marriage rates in the world. The trend of younger people opting for common law unions over marriage partly explains this decline. Most people are merely delaying, not rejecting, marriage, so the average age at first marriage is increasing. Both increased common law cohabitation and delayed marriage reflect at least a temporary flight from marriage, and predict lower percentages of people ever marrying. Probably the family will survive as an institution, but not in the form we have grown up idealizing.

Cohabitation is an arrangement in which an unmarried couple lives together to determine if the partners are suitable, to cut down on living expenses or as an alternative to marriage. The major difference between marriage and cohabitation is that the former is an explicit legal commitment and the latter is not.

Even so, the law regards cohabitation that continues for more than three years as a legally binding relationship in certain respects, thus a common law partnership. Long-term cohabitants owe each other support obligations (though not the sharing of community property) in the event of a breakup. So even here, the difference between marriage and cohabitation has blurred.

Often, common law partnerships are a prelude to marriage, with about one-quarter of the people ever in a common law union ending up marrying their common-law partner. This suggests that common law unions often serve as trial marriages. However, cohabiting before marriage does not make the marriage more likely to succeed; in fact, there is evidence to the contrary. Prior cohabitation is found to be positively related to marital disagreement and an increased chance of divorce. We do not know *why* this is so. Perhaps people who cohabit are poor marriage risks before they marry. We have no proof that cohabitation itself causes a decline in the quality of a later marriage; but neither is there proof that cohabitation improves mate selection or trains people for marriage.

As we see from Applied Sociology below, out-of-wedlock births are increasingly common in Canada, and especially in Quebec. Many people assumed that a majority of such births would produce deserted women and lone-parent families, but as is often the case in sociology, the reality is quite different. In a vast majority of out-of-wedlock births, the parents are living together unmarried. The author cautions us not to imagine that the feelings or promises are any less genuine just because they are not formalized in law.

Divorce

A second significant change in North American family life is the increase of divorce. **Divorce** is the legal, formal dissolution of a legal marriage, freeing the spouses to remarry. By the mid-1980s, fewer than one-third of the persons who first married during the mid-1970s were still in their first marriages and were "very happy" with these marriages.

Divorce is widely accepted today as a valid and fitting way out of an unhappy marital situation. Many people feel that the children of such unions are better off with single parents than in a family filled with conflict and, occasionally, violence. Data collected as part of the National Survey of Families and Households in the United States (1992-93) show that recently separated women perceive a

APPLIED SOCIOLOGY

Out-of-Wedlock Births in Canada

One of the myths about family life that sociologists have addressed is the belief that children born to unwed parents are unwanted or uncared for, or that their parents, because unmarried, are living apart, or consorting with one another in casual irresponsibility. A convenient myth it may be for people who disapprove of sex (or childbearing) outside marriage, but research shows it is a myth nonetheless!

In 1993, nearly half (46%) of all births in Quebec occurred to unmarried mothers. Only a few years back, Statistics Canada would have classified these births as "illegitimate." They are now more appropriately referred to as "out-of-wedlock." Behind this more contemporary designation, most people will still picture the figure of a young single mother, left alone to bring her pregnancy to term by an equally young single father who by the time of birth will have vanished, leaving the declaration of fatherhood on the birth certificate to be filled most inaccurately as "unknown." This is simply not the case anymore.

[The] proportions of out-of-wedlock births in Quebec have seen a tremendous increase during the 1980s, growing from around 10% in the mid-'70s to nearly five times as many 15 years later. Quebec is not alone among industrialized societies to experience such a phenomenon. Although the increase in the rest of Canada remains far less spectacular (23% of all births in 1993), the level experienced in Quebec can also be observed in countries like Denmark (46%), and to a lesser degree in France (30%) and England (31%). However, births to unknown fathers have remained fairly stable, still accounting for only 5% of yearly births in Quebec. The real growth shows in children born to unmarried parents who have chosen cohabitation rather than marriage as a setting to start a family. Fifty-seven percent of all first births in Quebec in 1993 were "out-of-wedlock."

A sign that such families have acquired a certain stability comes from the fact that out-of-wedlock births are not only first-born babies but, increasingly, second and higher rank children. In Quebec in 1993, 41% of second rank births, 33% of third and 29% of fourth rank and higher were births to unmarried mothers.

And such trends also can be confirmed by considering the age of these mothers. That 92% of births to mothers under the age of 20 are classified as out-of-wedlock may come as no surprise. But we are observing something different when 41%, 37% and 37% respectively of births to mothers aged 25-29, 30-34 and 35-39 can also be classified as occurring outside of marriage.

However, these children are still being born within a family. Their parents did not tie the legal knot but, nevertheless, they seem to have committed to some form of union, at least long enough for children to be born. Studies done from surveys show that Mom and Dad are still as present as ever at the birth of their kids.

Source: Nicole Marcil-Gratton, *Transition*, Dec. 1995, pp. 10, 11

net improvement in their parenting and social lives, though less improvement in their finances and job opportunities. More than twice as many women say their overall happiness is much better since the separation than only somewhat better (or worse than that).

But divorce has its drawbacks too. The increased incidence of child poverty since 1960 has been traced to, among other factors, an increase in divorce and single-parent families. In fact, researchers judge that child poverty rates in the United States would have been one-third lower if divorce rates had stayed at their 1960 level. In particular, the high rate of single-parent black families largely accounts for the different economic experiences of black and white children.

Researchers project that newly married couples run a roughly 40 per cent risk of future divorce. Their projections assume that rates of divorce will continue to rise, or at least stay high among young and middle-aged people. Other studies also show that the factors which cause marital instability, such as health problems, lack of social integration or low income, have the strongest effect on young married couples. To make matters worse, the age at which people marry also affects marital satisfaction. As such, people who marry young are more likely to divorce. If they do not divorce, they will spend a longer time than other people feeling unhappy in their marriage.

Risks of divorce are also high among people who live in the city, have friends and relatives who did not look favourably on the marriage or (according to some research) were previously married. Low socio-economic status also increases the likelihood of divorce. Finally, divorce is more likely where the wife is economically independent than where she is not.

What causes marital breakdown, whether it ends in divorce or not? We cannot answer that question for any particular couple, but we can identify some factors which affect marriage in general in our society. Some researchers believe the major cause is too much pressure on the nuclear family. In the event of a crisis, we have few people to rely on for comfort and support. Others suggest couples have unfulfilled hopes of a love that will last forever owing, perhaps, to media fictions or influences from parents. People feel their marriage has failed when it loses its romantic lustre. Finally, researchers note that the growing economic independence of women means that more women can leave unhappy marriages today than in the past.

A related question, which has received little sociological attention to date, is: What causes marital success? We know little about the conditions of marriages which persist and in which the couple retain their commitment to each other and to their relationship. However, couples who regard each other as good friends are usually happier than average; these couples also work harder than others to maintain a good marriage. Spouses who are independent are more likely to enjoy stable marriages with each other. Perhaps they are better able to manage freedom and intimacy than other people and so require traditional sex roles less. This promotes equality in the marriage, which is more in line with modern society and also more satisfying to spouses. Finally, people who share things in common with their partner — for example, a similar degree of religiosity — tend to be more satisfied with married life. Apparently, it is the *process* of sharing with a spouse, not precisely *what* is shared, that accounts for a higher-than-average degree of marital satisfaction.

Single-Parent Families

As more marriages end in separation or divorce, single-parent families increase in numbers. A **single-parent family** is a family in which only one parent lives with the dependent child or children; however, childcare and child support may be provided by both parents.

The great majority of single-parent families are headed by women. This has caused a debate, as yet largely unresolved, over whether the absence of a male parent has harmful effects on child development. Children from a single-parent family often do feel a sense of loss about their absent parent. However, the main problems facing such a family seem to be economic: research conducted in Nova Scotia suggests that, in Canada, the main issues are related to a shortage of money. Single-parent families constitute a high proportion of all family, and especially all childhood, experiences of poverty. They are a stark reminder of what sociologists call the **feminization of poverty**: as we noted in Chapter 5, on class and status inequality, the "poor" in Canada are predominantly women and children. These women include single mothers living on welfare, who cannot work because they cannot afford day care for their children; and elderly women who spent their lives as homemakers and could not contribute to a pension plan that would support them decently in their old age.

Just as the nuclear family once embodied a separation of the tasks of production from reproduction, "the lone-parent family represents the separation of marital and child rearing processes. As the adult adapts to movement between the lone, nuclear and **reconstituted families**, children provide the continuity as they grow through all the developmental stages" (Moore, 1989: 348). As stated earlier, whether one parent or two are present, good family processes raise healthy children. Indeed, the most reliably constant relationship is between parent and child, as long as those family processes have been consistent.

PROBLEMS OF THE MODERN FAMILY

Leaving aside financial problems, many of the problems facing the modern family are a result of faulty gender relations between the spouses. As we discussed these in the last chapter, we will touch on them only briefly in this chapter.

Spousal Inequalities

Across societies, we see wide variations in the extent to which rights and responsibilities are shared equally within families. Families differ in whether they are **equalitarian** (or egalitarian), **patriarchal**, or **matriarchal**.

In the **patriarchal family** the husband/father is the formal head of the household. He has the final say in all important matters because of his gender role, not because he has shown more wisdom, or has more skill or more experience. In this type of family, maleness alone confers authority. In societies where such families are found — for example, throughout the Islamic world and in many parts of Latin America — women have a limited or nonexistent role in public life, and usually their limited status is endorsed by fundamentalist religious beliefs. Even in the United States, religious fundamentalism proves to be the best predictor of preference for a patriarchal family.

Patriarchal authority relations characterized family life in many pre-industrial societies, and patriarchal features remain in our own. The extreme alternative to a patriarchal family, a **matriarchal family** in which the woman/mother is formal head of the household, is rare in human societies. We have some examples of such families in our own society, especially where a marriage breakdown has left the mother head of a single-parent family. Sociologists report that, at least since the Second World War, this pattern has characterized the African American family in the United States, in a subculture where males have been especially transient. The result has been a large fraction of children living in mother-dominated, single-parent families.

Compared to families in other societies, most families in our society are closer in form to equalitarian than to patriarchal or matriarchal families. In an **equalitarian family**, the wife and husband make important decisions jointly. Their opinions are equally important and mutually respected. Neither has authority over the other in the eyes of the law, and both have an equal say in all family matters.

This does not mean that all families today are equalitarian. It is hard in a great many households to know if a family is equalitarian or not. Also, although spousal equality has become the ideal, it may not yet have become the practice. Especially in families of middle-aged or less educated people, there is still a lot of inequality between husbands and wives *in practice*. The result is a gender-based difference in women's and men's experience of marriage. Sociologist Jesse Bernard

(1973) calls this a difference between *his marriage* and *her marriage*. According to Bernard, marriages often contain two very different views of the relationship: the wife's and the husband's. The two perspectives are different enough, and equally distant from the objective reality, to comprise two different marriages.

These differences in marital experience have, if anything, been increased by women's large-scale entry into paid work. Now married women inhabit what sociologists Hugh and Pat Armstrong (1993) call a "double ghetto." We find this happening all over the world, wherever women work for pay. As we saw in Chapter 8, women's freedom to work for pay, pursue a career and be economically independent does not mean freedom from domestic work. On the contrary, women continue to be mainly responsible for the household chores, even after they have put in a full day's work outside the home. "Being responsible" doesn't mean that they do all the work; in many cases, husbands share it. But it does mean that, no matter what, women are obliged to make sure the work gets done.

Sooner or later, Canada will have to implement social policies of the kind described in Far and Away, below, policies practised in other industrial societies, to make it possible for parents to care for their children, and increasingly, their aging parents, while earning a living. In short, there is a need for better

Learning about Family Policy from Other Societies

In Canada, nostalgia for the old-style family has clouded our vision and kept us from recognizing the full diversity of new families and their new needs. By contrast, many European countries are far ahead in recognizing that the society has an interest in helping families to succeed, especially in the job of parenting children effectively. They have led the way in the creation of new family policies.

Programs taken for granted in other countries are unimaginable here. They include maternity leave at close to full pay for all working mothers, plentiful day care, weeks of state-legislated time off work to care for sick children, even an hour or two off work each day for breast-feeding mothers.

Yet even as families require more support, billions of dollars have been stripped from social programs aimed at families over the past several years.

"I don't think the government can continue to abdicate and erode," says sociologist Susan McDaniel of the University of Alberta in Edmonton. "I think at some point there has to be an outbreak of reasonableness."

Critics say advances in Canadian family policy have been crippled by nostalgia for the family as it was in the 1940s, 1950s and 1960s, when Canada's social-program network was built.

Then, most husbands worked while wives stayed at home to take care of the children. Policy-making on family matters was simpler because no one had to take into account a myriad of models.

Universal education and health-care programs continue to provide important security for families, says Robert Glossop, co-ordinator of programs and research at the Vanier Institute. But other policies work on the old assumption that families ought to have one breadwinner.

These include a tax system that treats wives as deductions and pension-plan rules that cut a wife's income in half after her husband dies, while leaving him with full benefits if she dies.

Still other potential programs have failed to materialize, despite women's relentless march into the work force. One is the sort of organized, standardized child-care system that families in many European countries rely on.

Canada's maternity benefits scheme — engineered to replace some of a new mother's lost wages as she cares for a baby — gives significantly less support than those of countries such as France, Germany and Italy.

Source: Abridged from Alanna Mitchell, "Others enjoy benefits unheard of in Canada," *The Globe and Mail*, Jan. 24, 1994, pp. A1, A4

FAR AND AWAY

maternity and parental benefits, more public day care for children and more flexibility in people's working lives.

Husbands and wives identify with work outside the home in more or less the same way, but they relate it to family life in different ways. Wives feel that they should give precedence to their identity within the family, rather than to their work. Husbands, on the other hand, feel no need to make any choice between the two, and strive for a balance of work and family roles. This difference is illustrated by the fact that wives are less willing than husbands to accept a promotion if it means relocating.

Generally, feminists view the family as a source of female subordination, but black feminists take issue with this: "They argue that . . . in racist societies, the family is commonly experienced by Black women as the *least* oppressive institution" (Stasiulis, 1990: 284). In general, however, people experience many more kinds of marriage than just the *his marriage* and *her marriage* described by Bernard. This variety of types of marital experience has yet to be adequately researched.

Family Violence

Because the family has long been considered the most private institution in our society, until recently few people realized how pervasive violence is as a part of family life. In the past, it was taken for granted that parents had a right to use physical force to discipline their children. Violence between spouses was less acceptable, at least in public, but many men believed that they had as much right to hit their wives as to discipline their children.

Feminists argue that wife battering and child abuse are two aspects of the same phenomenon: they both stem from patriarchy. What's more, reported incidents of physical abuse against children who receive hospital attention reveal that wife battering is also the most common context for child abuse.

Verbal aggression is another type of family violence and it commonly results from a defect in communication skills; that is, people are not able to express their grievances in helpful ways. The worst type of verbal abuse is characterized by attacks on the character of the other person. Evidence shows that character attacks correlate with physical violence more highly than any other kind of verbal aggression.

Although men are taking on more domestic duties, in most homes women are still responsible for seeing that all the jobs are done.

A third form of family violence we are beginning to learn about is elder abuse — mistreatment directed towards the elderly by their children and grandchildren. In Japan, elder abuse often takes place between wives and their mothers-in-law; in this context, verbal abuse is much more common than physical violence or neglect. At the root of such conflicts are personality differences, disagreement over disciplining grandchildren and strategic difficulties arising from sharing the same kitchen.

In many cultures family violence is not seen as acceptable at all. For example, in Fiji, physical violence occurs occasionally. But it is traditionally unacceptable, particularly within families, since women and children are seen as weak and deserving of protection. As well, such behaviour violates the expectation that family members will cooperate and help one another. To a degree, violence in Fiji is also controlled by fears of ancestral punishment. Such cultural brakes on family violence do not exist in North America. Far from being a safe haven in a difficult world, the family has been, for many people, a source of pain, shame and anger. The psychological consequences of living with the terror of family violence are only beginning to be explored. Social isolation and marginality, and repeated crises, work to promote this family pattern.

The abusiveness in family life is illustrated by the law's failure to recognize marital rape as a crime until 1983. That marital rape was not considered assault tells us that it was taken for granted that wives should be sexually available at their husband's will and that the use of violence by men was considered acceptable when directed against their wives. Conversely, the change in law that made it a crime suggests declining support for the idea of the wife as "erotic property."

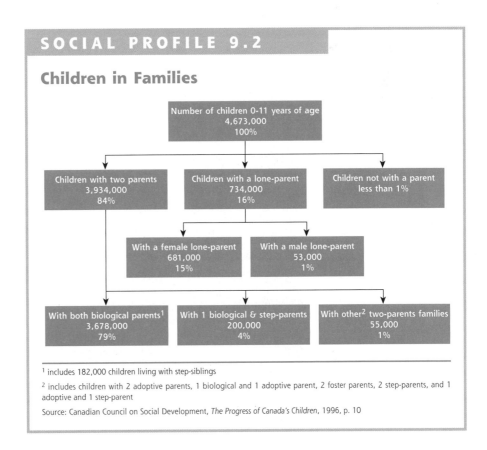

SOCIAL PROFILE 9.2

Children in Families

Number of children 0-11 years of age
4,673,000
100%

Children with two parents
3,934,000
84%

Children with a lone-parent
734,000
16%

Children not with a parent
less than 1%

With a female lone-parent
681,000
15%

With a male lone-parent
53,000
1%

With both biological parents[1]
3,678,000
79%

With 1 biological & step-parents
200,000
4%

With other[2] two-parents families
55,000
1%

[1] includes 182,000 children living with step-siblings

[2] includes children with 2 adoptive parents, 1 biological and 1 adoptive parent, 2 foster parents, 2 step-parents, and 1 adoptive and 1 step-parent

Source: Canadian Council on Social Development, *The Progress of Canada's Children*, 1996, p. 10

Although the laws and people's attitudes have changed, much family violence goes unreported. The Canadian Urban Victimization Survey conducted in 1982 showed that only 44 per cent of cases of wife abuse were reported to the police. Half the wives who did not seek help from the police indicated that they feared revenge by the offender, and about a third indicated that they "wanted to protect the offender" (Johnson, 1988: 19). Altogether, 59 per cent considered the abuse to be "a personal matter and of no concern to the police." An even smaller proportion of cases of child or elder abuse are reported to authorities.

Because of the failure to report family violence, we do not have good statistics on the prevalence of such violence. However, homicide statistics, which are usually quite complete, tell the same tale as surveys of sexual and child abuse. People are at a greater risk of physical injury from a spouse or family member than from a stranger. Forty per cent of solved homicides between 1985 and 1987 were cases of domestic homicide, and in the vast majority of these cases men killed their wives or common-law partners.

More recent studies find no correlation between violence and income or education. In other words, violence is found in the richest homes as often as it is in the poorest ones. However, as we noted in Chapter 8, men who have experienced many "stressful" life events, such as unemployment or having to work excessive amounts of overtime, are particularly likely to abuse their spouses. This does not mean that stress caused the violence. Expressing violence in this way shows that abusers see their wives as acceptable outlets for a husband's frustration.

WERE FAMILIES BETTER IN THE PAST?

There has been a lot of talk in the last few decades about the supposed "decline of the family." This discussion is related to concerns about what some have called the "sexual revolution" and the "second demographic transition." Both changes, related but distinct, reflect a division of sexual activity from marriage and procreation, and the development of contraceptive technology that makes this division possible. (The growing acceptance of same-sex marriage is also largely based on the recognition that most sexuality is *not* aimed at procreation.)

A third concern is due to problems of parenting, educational quality and the future of our children. Since the 1960s, rising divorce rates and rates of women's participation in the paid work force, combined with a traditional absence of fathers from active parenthood, have raised the fear that children are not getting the parenting they need. The weak influence of schools (and religiosity) on young people, and the strong media influence on them, prompts concern about delinquency and vocational incompetence.

But are families really getting worse? Let's try to answer this by imagining family life in the past, say, in a small town in Canada a century ago. In those days, what were people's prospects for a happy family life?

Well, there was little choice of a mate, for people had little contact with the world outside their community. On reaching their late teens and early twenties, they would have known only a few dozen potential mates. Often, they met at their place of worship. Some were "unacceptable" on class or racial grounds. Others were already engaged, in fact or in the eyes of the community. To end up with a mate they found attractive and compatible was, for most, a matter of very good luck.

Once married, a woman was financially dependent on her husband. (Women who did not marry were just as dependent on their father or brothers.) Culturally, legally and financially, men ruled their wives and children. This meant that women and children had even less protection against abuse or neglect than they have today. And with shorter life expectancies than today, many men died leaving their wives widows and single parents. Indeed, lone parenthood was as common in those days (due to death) as it is today (due to divorce). Widows and orphans were often left without financial protection and forced to rely for help on charity or kin.

Family life was governed by the uncertainties of childbearing. Poor birth control technology meant many unexpected or even unwanted children. Pregnancies and deliveries risked a woman's life. Child-raising was a strain that lasted through most of a woman's adult years. Naturally, each child had many brothers and sisters. This limited children's privacy, chances for education, access to parental attention and other benefits that children take for granted today. And the life chances were even worse for daughters than for sons.

What about the health of families today? Well, just consider the "facts of life" and you'll get a partial answer. Over the last hundred years or so, people's lives have lengthened. People are less likely to die in infancy and more likely than ever to live into their seventies, eighties and nineties. Today, death is less salient than before; that is, we spend less time observing or anticipating death. So, we can focus our thoughts and efforts on the future, and the future has grown longer for everyone. One result is we spend more time planning for the future.

Thanks to improved contraception, more people today plan their families: how many children they want to have, and when they want to have them. And because fewer children die, fewer births are needed to reach the "desired" family size. A higher proportion of children born are actually wanted. So, parents today have a stronger emotional attachment to their (fewer, longer-living, wanted) children than in the past. With reduced fertility and generally improved living conditions, wives come to outlive their husbands by wider margins than in the past. This means a longer period of widowhood.

From a child's point of view, parents are less likely to die in early or middle age than a century ago. This means there are more parents (even grandparents) living into old age. Consequences include the creation of retirement communities for both single and married elderly people, emotional dependence on adult children that lasts many decades and, for people without children, financial dependence on the state. Moreover, lone female parents aren't discouraged from keeping their children, so there are fewer orphans today. Most children today have living parents, even if those parents do not live with one another or with the child.

Most dramatic of all, since spouses are unlikely to die in early or middle age, unsatisfied husbands and wives face a new dilemma. In the past, many unhappy marriages ended when one or the other spouse died. Today, they end this way less often. Indeed, married people often face many years spent in an "empty nest," alone with their spouse. It's either that, or divorce. High current divorce rates reflect this new demographic reality, as much as they reflect women's greater economic freedom and fewer young children.

Today, marriage is not centrally concerned with childbearing and child-raising any more than it is centrally concerned with economic production (as it was in farm families of 1851). Modern marriage is about companionship, affection and emotional support between spouses.

Modern Families Are Based on Choice

In every modern family, life is a series of choices: whether to marry, when to marry, whether to have children, when to have children, whether to divorce, when to divorce, whether to remarry, when to remarry and so on. To have this degree of flexibility and choice, people need to have the means to make real choices. For example, we cannot expect people to accept the duties of parenthood, and perform these duties well, unless they have a secure financial base. As a society with an interest in the well-being of the next generation, this means keeping children out of poverty, for poverty, not lone parenthood *per se*, is the biggest problem facing children today (see Applied Sociology, below).

The modern family — hugely variable and based on personal choice — is not in decline. People still form families, though their ideas about family life vary widely. As noted, people form families for less instrumental reasons today than in the past. They form different kinds of families than in the past. Yet they still use the traditional language of family life, speaking of husbands, wives, parents, children, brothers and sisters — even when the reality is far more com-

APPLIED SOCIOLOGY

Unwed Mothers Vindicated

One of the important jobs of applied sociology is to provide accurate factual information about the way the world works, for without accurate information new and appropriate social programs are unlikely. For this and other reasons, it was important for sociological research to dispel the myth that unmarried mothers are inadequate mothers; conversely, it was important to show that money, not marital status, is key to good parenting.

The first definitive study of unmarried mothers, its results just published, shows that a mother's schooling, not her marital status, determines how well her children turn out. Poverty, it found, is the big culprit when it comes to the health and welfare of children. The study shatters a number of myths—most of them imported from the United States—about unmarried mothers and their children.

The study showed that both married and unmarried mothers with high-school diplomas, and therefore the prospect of earning higher wages, were less likely to bring their children up in poverty than women without diplomas. And conversely, mothers without a diploma were more likely to bring their children up in poverty, whether married or not.

The study also found that unmarried mothers do not have scads of children. Those who never married during the 10 years the study was con-

ducted had an average of 1.55 children, compared to the 2.40 children of mothers who were married throughout the period.

The children of unmarried mothers do not live in violence and neglect. Over the 10 years of the study, none of the unmarried mothers was reported to authorities for abusing or neglecting her child. In fact, extensive intelligence and behavioural tests showed that the children of both married and unmarried mothers fell into the normal range. They were generally well cared for.

And while the study showed that many of the mothers—both unmarried and married—drew on social assistance during the decade, it also showed that the unmarried mothers did not get on welfare and stay there. Just 3 per cent of all the mothers had been on welfare for more than nine years. In general, the study found that many of the unmarried mothers never caught up with the married mothers when it came to education and income.

[As a result] poverty rates among the unmarried mothers were dramatically higher than among married mothers. Fifty-three per cent of unmarried mothers lived in poverty compared to 18 per cent of the married mothers.

It was this poverty — whether it stemmed from unmarried or married mothers — that caused problems for the children, the report concluded. The poor children, who were 10 at the time, scored lower on tests of vocabulary, verbal comprehension, IQ determinants, reading and math.

Source: Abridged from Alanna Mitchell, "Unwed mothers vindicated in study," *The Globe and Mail*, Mon., March 14, 1994, pp. A1, A2

plex. The 1950s family — the traditionalist's ideal — was a short-lived historical accident. Briefly, it interrupted the century-long rush towards greater choice, especially fewer children and more divorce. North American families today are no worse than families at any other time or place; they are simply different and appropriate to this moment in history. In that sense, families are not in decline.

As we have seen, families today vary immensely. As never before, people are rethinking what we mean by "family life" and what we can expect from "family" as a social institution. In talking about families, we must be careful to consider how earlier expectations of family fit together with times past. As well, we must draw contrasts between what we expect from families and what families can actually give us.

Family life is becoming more, not less, important. For this reason, people want families to succeed as much as possible. Success depends on a family's ability to provide its members with security, identity, companionship and other important resources. A successful family life produces social, economic and psychological well-being, even increased longevity and good health. Healthy families are productive families and they benefit society at large as well as the individual family members. Much is known about how healthy and successful families are nourished and what works to make them successful.

Research on same-sex families reveals that the same processes are important as in heterosexual families. They too show divisions of domestic labour, even inequalities between the spouses; characteristic stresses and conflicts; and similar strategies of child-rearing. Children reared in well-functioning same-sex families turn out as well, and as varied, as children reared in well-functioning heterosexual families.

However, old ideas and old solutions to family problems — indeed, old-fashioned family forms — do not always work as desired. In many areas, we need to find new solutions to family problems. The deeper we look into the "family decline" question, the more we realize that for people in modern societies, family is both part of the problem and part of the solution.

CLOSING REMARKS

The sociological study of family life offers a good illustration of the connection between macro and micro perspectives. On the one hand, family life is a macro phenomenon. Some aspects of family life — for example, the norm of marital fidelity — are slow to change and the main elements of a culture outlast all of us. The "family" as a cultural ideal exists outside and "above" individual people, in the ways that people of a particular society think about love, marriage, parenthood, the domestic division of labour and so on.

On the other hand, family life is constantly being constructed and every family bears the unique stamp of its members. No two families portray love, marriage, parenthood or domestic work in precisely the same way. If anything, the study of families makes clear that social life is a process of continued uncertainty, variety and negotiation. We get the families we struggle for, although some family members have more power in the struggle than others do.

Yet the data we have examined show that families *have* changed dramatically since the 1960s. Accepted ways of thinking, speaking and behaving have changed because dozens, then thousands, then millions of family members have changed their way of doing things. We should not conclude that we are in the midst of a breakdown of "the family," in which a mate is no more than erotic property, or a child no more than a consumer durable. Most people continue to struggle and sacrifice for their family *as though* the family means a great deal more.

The next chapter picks up on some of the themes introduced in this chapter. It discusses changes in rates of birth, death and migration, and how these changes affect our social lives.

Review Questions

1. Why is the family such an important social institution?
2. How do sociologists define the family?
3. What role does the functionalist perspective assign to the family?
4. What aspects of the family are the focus of the conflict perspective?
5. Why do feminists consider the family to be a "political" institution?
6. What are "polygamy," "polygyny," "polyandry" and "monogamy"?
7. What is the ideal of romantic love?
8. What are "endogamy," "exogamy," "homogamy" and "heterogamy"?
9. Why has marriage been described as a system of "erotic property"?
10. What are the advantages and disadvantages of an "extended" family and of a "nuclear" family?
11. What are some of the problems parenthood poses for husbands and wives?
12. What problems does prolonged dependency pose for family members?
13. What are current trends in family life?
14. What do we know about the causes and consequences of family violence?

Discussion Questions

1. No one knows precisely why pre-industrial societies had patriarchal families. What explanation would you offer? What evidence might historians gather to test the validity of your theory?
2. Does a division of labour between spouses have to lead to spousal inequality? Discuss how spousal inequalities might be avoided or reduced in modern marriages.
3. Has the mechanization of housework improved family relations? If so, how? What other kinds of mechanization might solve problems that remain today?
4. Under what conditions might the "flight from marriage and parenthood" stop or even reverse itself? What government policies, if any, might contribute to such a change?
5. What are the ways a two-income family might re-organize its use of time to reduce the tension and conflict parents (especially wives and mothers) commonly feel due to lack of time?

Suggested Readings

Baker, M. (1990) *Families: Changing Trends in Canada*. Toronto: McGraw-Hill Ryerson. This multi-authored text focuses on changing families in Canada. Topics covered include: the origins of the family, mate selection, economic conditions and family structures, alternatives to traditional marriage, marital dissolution, family law and patterns of family violence.

Bernard, J. (1973) *The Future of Marriage*. New York: Bantam Books. This provocative book shows how the traditional marriage — in reality, an uneasy mix of *his* marriage and *her* marriage" — is giving way to new thinking and new practices.

Jones, C.L., L. Tepperman and S.J. Wilson (1995) *The Futures of the Family*. Englewood Cliffs, NJ: Prentice Hall. This short book takes a historical and cross-national approach to the research on families through the ages. Its purpose is to discuss the problems of today's families and provide scenarios describing change in family life in the next century.

Mandell, N. and A. Duffy, eds. (1993) *Reconstructing the Canadian Family: Feminist Perspectives*. Toronto: Butterworths. An important collection of the work of feminist scholars, this book puts the modern family against a backdrop of women's "hidden history." The focus is on gender inequality in family life.

Ramu, G.N. (ed.) (1993) *Marriage and the Family in Canada Today*, second edition. Scarborough: Prentice Hall Canada. This collection of pieces by a variety of authors provides an overview of Canadian families as seen from a variety of sociological perspectives.

Wilson, Susannah J. *Women, Families, and Work*, fourth edition. Toronto: McGraw-Hill Ryerson, 1996. This brief, clearly written book provides a comprehensive examination of Canadian women's changing experiences, at home and work, over the past century.

Internet Resources

The following Web sites are good places to find more information about topics discussed in this chapter:

Canadian Stepfamily Association provides information about stepfamilies in Canada as well as E-mail support groups, speakers, seminars, workshops and a newsletter.
http://www.eagle.ca/ ~ jcollar/index.html

Fathers Are Capable Too (FACT) contains news about events affecting divorce cases, stories about fathers denied access to their children and a library of information helpful to divorced fathers.
http://www.ionsys.con/ ~ fact/homepage.htm

Radical Mother Page contains information on parenting, running a home-based business and alternative therapies for breast cancer. It also advocates home birth, home learning and breastfeeding.
http://www.islandnet.com/ ~ bedford/bonnie.html

Fatherhood and Fatherlessness contains links relating to the role of the father within a family.
http://www.vix.com/men/nofather/nodad.html

LesBiGay Parenting Homepage offers advice and support for families that do not conform to society's norm.
http://www.albany.net/ ~ gelco/

YPN: Home & Family: Parenting offers links and discussions relating to families and parenting.
http://www.ypn.com/topics/430.html

Kearl's Guide to the Sociology of the Family provides discussions on cross-cultural variations in family life, institutions affecting family life and family changes over the life cycle, as well as links to related sites
http://www.trinity.edu/ ~ mkearl/family.html

Society and Culture: Families–Parenting is an omnibus site with links to other sites (books, usenet groups, magazines, organizations and newsletters) discussing mothering, fathering, childcare, single parenting and many other "parenting" topics.
http://www.yahoo.com/Society_and_Culture/Families/Parenting

POPULATION AND ENVIRONMENT

CHAPTER OUTLINE

Crowds and crowding, which are features of modern urban life, are a growing problem in the world today.

POPULATION AND HUMAN SURVIVAL

In Chapter 6 we looked at social upheavals that accompanied the Industrial Revolution and led people to adopt a new outlook on society. After the Industrial Revolution, the social world was no longer seen as a product of natural "forces" or supernatural "design," but as a human product. The results of this change in thinking were dramatic. People realized that if *we* had made society the way it is, we could also remake it. We could reshape society to fit our needs. New theories about what form society could or should take led to the development of sociology.

Today, we are in the midst of another revolution just as profound. Many of the problems historically connected to industrial development and capitalism — for example, worker health and safety — have been improved, if not solved. New organizations — labour unions, social democratic political parties, feminist groups, and a welfare state — have made important contributions to people's well-being.

However, there are new concerns about the future, many of which focus on the environment and ecology. We hear that the depletion of the ozone layer and the "greenhouse effect" are making it hazardous just to be out in the sun. The destruction of the Amazon rainforest and the emission of industrial pollutants threaten air quality. Oil spills and the dumping of industrial wastes threaten life in the world's rivers, lakes and oceans. These new social problems face us *all*, regardless of class or political system. The former Soviet Union had its Chernobyl nuclear "mishap" in 1986 just as the United States had its "accident" at Three Mile Island in 1979 (although the former cost a great many lives, while the latter did not). Developing countries suffer as much from such mishaps, and usually more, than the developed world.

Not all problems are solved when we change forms of social organization. We live in a natural environment we can no longer afford to take for granted or to dominate. In Russia, for example, despite dramatic changes in social organization, economic and health conditions have worsened significantly in the last few

Environmental Damage Wreaks Human Damage in Russia

In Canada, most people enjoy lives of seventy, eighty or more years in reasonably good health. Infant mortality is low and birth defects are relatively few — all indications of a healthy, prosperous society with a good health-care system. But in the last ten years, health conditions in the former Soviet Union have been worsening dramatically, with increasing birth defects and a plummeting life expectancy. In addition to poor economic conditions and inadequate health care, the environment itself is conspiring to make people sick.

Valentin Palma's neurosurgery ward is a world of brain tumours, deformities, cleft palates, oversized skulls and strange spinal growths. There are 30 children waiting for operations or recovering from surgery. Most are suffering from the mysterious birth defects that have increased dramatically in number in Russian cities in recent years.

In one crib, a 20-month-old girl with a grossly enlarged head is crying desperately. She has already had an operation to remove a spinal hernia and another to drain water from her head. Soon she will need a third operation on her urinary system. "This is a typical case," Dr. Palma says, showing no emotion.

The infant girl is from Rostovon-Don, an industrial city in southwestern Russia. Asked why she is so sick, Dr. Palma mentioned the heavy concentration of military factories in the region.

Industrial pollution, the toxic legacy of the Soviet Union's obsession with massive chemical and metallurgical factories, is believed to be one of the biggest reasons for the rising level of sickness and disease among Russian children.

About 10 per cent of all Russian children are born with deformities or other birth defects, and this is increasing by an estimated 2 percentage points annually. One-fifth of the birth defects are caused by pollution; according to Alexei Yablokov, the head of a Russian environmental commission.

There are other factors too. Radiation poisoning from the Chernobyl nuclear accident is still a major cause of birth defects. Uncontrolled use of fertilizers is contaminating the vegetables in the markets. Poverty and economic turmoil are making it difficult for pregnant women to get proper food and medicine. Alcohol abuse has reached epidemic levels. And the state-run health-care system is crumbling.

Even if a baby is born without a deformity, the chances of avoiding sickness are slim. Of the one million babies born in Russia in 1993, only 9 per cent were completely healthy. The doctors, like most medical researchers, are convinced that Russia's widespread industrial pollution is one of the most important reasons for the increase. At a Moscow hospital for maternal and child health, the number of birth defects has increased fourfold since 1988. Industrial pollution is believed to be one of the major causes.

Source: Abridged from Geoffrey York, *The Globe and Mail*, Mon., July 24, 1995, pp. A1, A7

---

years. Problems such as those described in Far and Away, above, are due to industrial pollution, among other things, and they are likely to get worse before they get better.

In the short term, the depletion of Canada's and the world's natural resources, such as the overfishing of the Atlantic banks, means a loss of jobs and the end of traditional ways of life. In the longer run, it may mean global disaster, hence, the rise of "green" political parties in a number of countries.

As Chapter 3 on socialization showed, we all change, and learn to change, throughout our lives. The prospect of having to change our ways of living is not threatening to most people. But *how* and *what* should we change, if we are to solve the problems facing us? And can we make the changes soon enough for them to have the desired effect?

Let's begin our discussion of the environment and ecology by looking at population issues. To a large extent the ecological problem is "us," people. Most problems, ecological and otherwise, are aggravated by the sheer number of people in the world. It is harder to solve problems of poverty and inequality, intolerance and war, environmental damage and a falling quality of life, when the population is growing rapidly. For ecological and other reasons, we must come to terms with the world's population problem — understand it, then solve it. The social science that provides materials for the study of population is **demography**.

Sociology and demography are two separate disciplines, but they are intimately linked. Demography is the scientific study of the size, structure, distribution and growth of the world's population. "Social demography," the topic of this chapter, is concerned with the effects of population on the organization of societies, and vice versa. Demographers play a central role in collecting and analyzing population data such as Census data. And sociologists rely on demographers for this information to help us understand population problems.

Demography and sociology are also linked because they complement each other. Population analysis is typically macro in scope, because it looks at large numbers of people over long periods of time. Yet the actual patterns it uncovers are often a result of millions of people making personal decisions, such as when to marry and how many children to have. It is sociology that has the theoretical and methodological tools to examine how and why people make these decisions.

In this chapter we will focus on one central issue: population growth.

Population Growth and Change

One of the traditional concerns of demography is measuring and predicting population growth. Changes in the size and structure of a population have continuing and important effects on our personal lives. For example, information on the size and age structure of society influences the demand for, and availability of, housing, education, health care and employment. No wonder, then, people were concerned when some researchers concluded that the Earth's *optimum* population size is one or two billion, but its *expected* population size in a hundred years is between twelve and fifteen billion. Still, this conclusion, like any other, is up for debate. It supposes we know what the optimum (or ideal) population is today, or a century from now. It also implies that we can accurately predict how the world's population will change over the next century.

The "population problem" takes a different shape in different parts of the globe. In 1990, the Canadian government decided to raise the ceiling on the number of immigrants allowed into the country. That decision was based on a projection of current demographic trends which suggest that unless Canada increases the immigration rate, the country's population by the year 2025 would be *smaller* than it is today. In Africa, by contrast, the population is projected to grow to over 1.3 billion people without any substantial immigration. Nigeria, for example, is expected to grow into the fourth most populous country in the world by 2025. Since Nigeria is very poor in comparison with Canada, this growth has the potential to cause serious problems.

Population growth and change take place within a political, economic and social context, with cultural beliefs and practices also affecting the size and structure of a population. Such beliefs include views on preferred family size, the use of birth control and female infanticide, among other things. Equally, the size and structure of a population affects cultural practices. For example, as the proportion of the population made up of people who are over age sixty-five increases, tolerance for older people grows. There is a greater acceptance of aging as a natural, even desirable, part of life. With the aging of the large baby boom generation (we discuss this phenomenon later in the chapter), we may even see some aspects of old age glorified.

COMPONENTS OF POPULATION GROWTH IN CANADA

Changes in the size and structure of a given population are caused by variations in the birth rate, the death rate and the net migration rate. The **growth rate** is the rate at which population size increases each year. (In the case of negative population growth, it is the rate at which population size declines.) The growth rate is calculated by subtracting the number of deaths and out-migrations (people leaving) from the number of births and in-migrations (people arriving), and expressing the result as a proportion of the mid-year population. Since about 1980, the growth rate has levelled off at a level just below zero. To understand why, we must understand changes in the three factors that influence population growth: fertility, mortality and migration.

Fertility

Since the end of the 19th century, *fertility* — the production of births — has been in a more or less steady decline. Two exceptions to this trend were the Depression of the 1930s (when many fewer children were born than demographers expected) and the 1950s (when many more children were born than expected). Otherwise, fertility has continued to plummet at a regular pace.

In the past, high fertility played a critical part in Canada's population growth. Contrary to what many believe, up until recently, immigration has *not* played the decisive role in 20th-century Canada. In fact, Beaujot (1988: 54) reports, "The net migration of 4.0 million persons from 1901 to 1981 comprised 21.2% of [Canada's] population growth over this period." The other nearly 80 per cent occurred through natural increase. Immigration had so little impact because, often, there were as many or more people leaving the country as there were entering it, and because rates of fertility were so very high.

The rapid increase of Quebec's French population illustrates the power of local reproduction. Between 1608 and 1760, a mere 10,000 French colonists came to New France. By doubling every twenty-five years until the first years of this century, they produced all of the millions of francophones in North America. Last century, this extraordinarily high level of population growth was referred to by francophone nationalists as "the revenge of the cradle." It partly made up for the failure to attract new immigrants from France. More important, it helped prevent the assimilation of most francophones into an overwhelming anglophone majority.

But today, Quebec's fertility is the lowest in Canada and Canadian fertility rates are among the lowest in the world. Continuing low fertility gives variations in mortality and migration more importance than ever in Canada's population picture. This explains why francophone Quebecers are so anxious to control how many and what kinds of people can immigrate to Quebec.

What demographers call the **fertility rate** is the number of children an average woman bears during her lifetime. Typically, different "kinds" of women bear different numbers of children — for example, religious women tend to bear more children than non-religious women because they tend to abjure birth control. Women also vary in the ages at which they bear their offspring. For example, less educated women tend to bear children at earlier ages and continue for a longer time. However, in calculating a national fertility rate we ignore these variations.

Age-specific fertility rates are annual fertility rates that we find among women in specific age groups: ages fifteen to nineteen, twenty to twenty-four, twenty-five to twenty-nine, and so on. A *total fertility rate* is calculated from these age-specific rates. By summing them, we can estimate the average number of live births to a woman who lives through the childbearing years of fifteen to forty-nine.

The study of age-specific fertility rates shows that today, women spend much less of their adult lives producing children than they did in the past. And few women today continue to bear children at the biologically possible maximum (about one child every two years). Because more women have jobs and career ambitions that take them into educational institutions and the workplace, they have less time to bear many children.

As well, contraceptives and cultural attitudes make it possible for women to delay childbearing until they have completed their education and established themselves in a career. They also make it socially acceptable for women to have fewer children overall. Even women who have a first child in their teens — often the result of an unwanted pregnancy — are unlikely to continue bearing children at a biologically maximum rate. Like women who begin their childbearing later, they want a family that is closer to two or three children than to ten or fifteen.

Childbearing norms — people's desired family size — are lower today than in the past; so are childbearing realities. Modern contraception allows women in the developed world to have the number of children they actually want, when they want to have them. They can also space their childbearing, so that births occur almost exactly when they will be most convenient. However, the use of contraceptives is relatively rare in developing countries. Often, high fertility is due not so much to a lack of knowledge about contraception as to a failure to use contraceptives. In a study done in Zimbabwe, only 14 per cent of unmarried women and 18 per cent of unmarried men used contraceptives at the time of first intercourse. Only 36 per cent of women and 29 per cent of men are currently using them. This results in a large number of unwanted premarital pregnancies in Zimbabwe and other parts of Africa. Failure to use contraception thereby affects school attendance, educational attainment and the chance to work. It also increases the risk of AIDS. In Canada, these risks of unprotected sex are much lower but they are also increasing, especially among teenagers.

High rates of fertility mean large families and rapidly growing populations.

Since the Second World War, the biggest population change in Canada was caused by the **baby boom**. This was a sudden and considerable rise in the birth rate in the 1950s and early 1960s. The baby boom was a response to the end of restraints on marriage and childbearing caused by the Depression and then the war, as well as to the rapid increase in economic prosperity after the war. The birth rate reached its peak and began to decline again around the end of the 1950s.

The baby boom of the 1950s had a large impact on Canadian society by changing the relative advantage of one generation compared with the others. At a group level, a large cohort enjoys more social advantage. A **cohort** is a group of people who share similar life experiences at the same point in time; for example, all the people who were born in the same year form a *birth cohort*. The baby boomers, a large cohort, have controlled the culture at each stage of their development — as hippies in the 1960s and yuppies in the 1980s, for example. Given the aging of the baby boom generation, it is no wonder we have heard so much about "the family" in the last ten years and are starting to hear so much about retirement and menopause today. This is because we tend to hear most about the experiences and concerns of one particularly large cohort, the baby boomers.

However, the individual members of a large cohort often suffer less social advantage. Other things being equal, it is scarcity which brings people high rewards, and the baby boomers will never be scarce. In this sense, whether you were born in a small or large birth cohort has a huge impact on your life chances in a competitive society (Easterlin, 1980). Partly because they have found it harder to get jobs than members of previous generations, members of the baby boom generation have had smaller families, and members of Generation X (who followed them) have done the same. Since the 1970s, Canadian women have postponed marriage and childbearing and have had fewer children than their mothers and grandmothers did. More of them are spending more of their lives working for pay, for obvious reasons: most couples need two incomes to maintain the standard of living they expect in Canadian cities today.

These economic difficulties will not stop when baby boomers reach age sixty-five; baby boomers will also have had more difficulty earning and saving for old age. Younger age groups are too small to be able to support the baby boomers through contributions to pension and social security funds. New solutions for supporting the aged will be needed early in the 21st century; and this is the case around the world. Even in high-fertility African countries, the numbers of people over age sixty-five are increasing. The number of elderly in Sub-Saharan Africa, for example, is expected to increase by 93 per cent between 2000 and 2020. Because these countries are poor, finding new ways to help the aged will be even harder than in Canada.

In short, that unusual burst of high fertility — the baby boom generation — has reshaped Canada's society and culture. Unfortunately, members of the baby boom generation will end up paying most of the social and economic costs of their parents' high fertility. On the other hand, analysis provided in Applied Sociology, below, suggests that retirement for the boomers will be different and, in some respects, better than it was for their parents.

Normally, the younger siblings and children of the baby boomers — variously called the "baby bust" generation and Generation X — would benefit from their small cohort size. They are, demographically, in short supply, and that ought to make them more valuable in the job market. However, this expected advantage has, so far, failed to materialize, due to a worldwide recession which

Heading into Old Age

Good sociological theories help us look into the future, predict problems before they occur and take actions to minimize the extent of those problems. Take the coming problems of a rapidly aging population. By comparing today's forty-five-year-olds with sixty-five-year-olds (twenty years ago) when they were forty-five, we can see where there are likely to be problems, and why. For example, the "old-to-be" have the advantage of more education but the disadvantage of more divorce and less chance of a spouse to help pay the bills.

For one thing, tomorrow's seniors are more likely to head into old age without a spouse. In 1973, the "traditional" family was alive and well among households headed by people in their 40s. Fully 70 per cent of households had a husband and a wife, well ahead of the 18 per cent with people living alone and 10 per cent led by single parents. By 1993, the husband-wife combination accounted for only 56 per cent of homes, while those living alone had climbed to 28 and single parents to 14.

The financial implications of that shift are obvious. Two-earners bring in more income — and can save more. Elderly people who live alone are significantly poorer than those with a spouse. So financial insecurity could be a problem for more seniors.

Among women, today's fortysomethings face brighter prospects than their predecessors. The big increase in women's paid employment means that "women who reach 65 20 years from now will have greater financial resources than the current generation of elderly women." They will have earned more; they will have made bigger contributions both to the CPP and to their own pension plans at work, and they will have saved more through registered retirement savings plans. As a result, they will have larger retirement incomes.

They may need it. Older people often count on their children and grandchildren for various kinds of support, and today's new seniors have plenty of kids. In 1973, half of the husband-wife families had three or more, compared with only one in five of their 1993 counterparts. So, the researchers say, "tomorrow's seniors may be more likely to rely on friends and community groups for social and emotional support."

Education is another big difference. In 1993, 26 per cent of the men and 17 per cent of the women had a university degree, compared with 10 and 5 per cent in 1973. Not surprisingly, a smaller proportion hold blue-collar jobs and a larger proportion hold managerial and professional jobs. Well-educated managers and professionals also have a habit of going back to work — sometimes more than once — after their initial retirement. They're also likely to help out in the community, a tendency that increases with education and income. In 1987, 22 per cent of Canada's seniors did some kind of volunteer work; get ready for more.

So, compared with their predecessors, tomorrow's seniors will be healthier (provided that today's lifestyles persist), wealthier and, if not wiser, more likely to share their life's wisdom with the community around them.

Source: Abridged from Bruce Little, *The Globe and Mail*, Sept. 30, 1996, p. A6

has kept unemployment rates high and wages low, and sent young people back to school for more and different kinds of education. Here is a clear case of economic difficulty that is *not* due to what people have called "overpopulation."

Mortality

Like birth, death has a profound effect on population growth. To measure the risks of death in a population, demographers measure a mortality rate for people of each age; paradoxically, this collection of death risks is called a "life table." From this they can calculate life expectancies at each age. The most commonly used indicator is life expectancy at birth. In Canada, a woman's life expectancy at birth is about eighty years. That is, the moment she is born, a woman can expect to live eighty years. A man's life expectancy at birth is roughly seven years less.

Canadian mortality began to fall in the early 19th century and continued falling through the early 20th century. It declined more slowly in the north, on native reserves, and in isolated parts of the Maritimes. In other parts of the country, mortality rates levelled off around mid-century.

Though mortality rates have been steadily declining, women continue to enjoy a lower mortality rate than men at every age. This is the case in all industrial countries, including Canada, and there are various reasons for it. Males have much higher mortality rates as infants and this, along with other evidence, suggests that women are biologically hardier than men. Tobacco and alcohol use, more frequent among men, also has an effect on mortality rates. As well, men typically die in larger numbers as casualties of war, from automobile accidents and from stress-related illnesses. Indeed, demonstrating male dominance can be a dangerous business.

As we saw in Chapter 5, socio-economic status remains an important factor in mortality risks. In most countries, people with high socio-economic status have the lowest mortality rates. Lower-status people are more exposed to occupational hazards. They have a generally lower standard of living, which includes less and poorer food and worse sanitation.

The poor also have less access to medical care. That's why there are large class differences in the mortality rates for diseases that are medically treatable. Gender inequality has a similar effect. Where women have much lower status than men, they are much more likely than men to die young. For example, the deaths of women during childbirth and pregnancy are generally preventable, yet annually, an estimated 500,000 die worldwide from these causes. The vast majority of these deaths take place in poor, developing countries, where women are less valued than men.

Because mortality is related to the level of economic well-being in a country, there is a long-term relationship between unemployment rates and mortality rates. In particular, the incidence of heart disease and heart attacks increases during periods of high unemployment. It remains to be seen whether public health measures can reduce these effects, or whether job creation can do so more efficiently.

Ethnicity and race are other factors that affect mortality risks. For example, Canadian native peoples have a lower life expectancy and higher rates of disability than other Canadians: the reasons include poverty and poor health care. Though mortality differences may not be as great as in the past, the differences between ethnic groups that persist are caused by lower than average income, nutrition and education among some groups. They also reflect regional variations in environmental quality and standards of living.

Mortality rates in North America's inner cities can also be much higher than the national average. For example, a study of mortality in central Harlem, New York, where 96 per cent of the population is African American, showed that men's rates of survival beyond age forty are lower than one finds in rural Bangladesh, a desperately poor, undeveloped country. In Harlem, mortality rates are double those of the general American population, even after adjustments for age difference. One reason for this huge disparity is that African American slum dwellers have limited health care available to them.

What these data show is that mortality rates are a reflection of social inequalities. People live longer, healthier lives in rich regions of rich countries. In these regions, the richest, best-educated people live longest. Race, ethnicity and religion are important factors insofar as they are associated with class position.

They also shape people's lifestyles, the health-related information they get and the care they are encouraged to take. And one of the social benefits unequally distributed in any stratified society will be access to life-saving medical technology in desperate situations.

Social class aside, a great deal of evidence shows that there are health benefits in getting married and staying married. Unmarried people have a higher risk of mortality than unmarried people. In short, marriage contributes to people's well-being, perhaps because spouses look after one another. Evidence also shows that men gain larger increases in life expectancy by marrying than women do, which may be another way of saying that, after marriage, women take care of men better than men take care of women. As the Dutch sociologist Ruut Veenhoven pointed out, if your goal is to increase your mental and physical well-being, there are two things you could do that are equally effective: win a million dollars *or* get married — especially if you're male.

The success of modern medicine in treating infectious diseases and identifying the biological bases of illness has led many to believe that we shall continue to make progress against death without significant social and cultural changes. However, there is no easy road to universal good health and longer lives. In the future, people's risks of death will decrease if and only if people have access to health-bringing care, that is, if societies reduce poverty and inequality, broadcast health information and promote some sort of marriage as an institution. On the other hand, any gains from these influences will be lost through unhealthy activities. For example, smoking continues to be a significant, avoidable determinant of high mortality rates.

Through most of this century, demographers have largely ignored mortality patterns, leaving the work to actuaries who, on behalf of insurance companies, calculate the risks of death at different ages. They may have had several good reasons for ignoring death as a factor in population change. For example, demographers may have felt that humanity has made all the major gains in the fight against mortality. Fewer and fewer people are dying each year from infectious diseases, the traditional killer in high-mortality populations. People's life expectancies have increased throughout the 20th century; but now we appear to have hit a plateau.

As stated earlier, Canadians cannot expect to live more than about eighty years; this fact has changed little for a generation or more. Some researchers believe that all living creatures produce a fixed number of heartbeats per lifetime; the life expectancy of a species is determined by the average number of heartbeats per unit of time. Smaller species, with faster heartbeats, live a shorter time; the opposite is true for larger species (like humans). If this theory is valid, there is indeed an upper limit to our lifespan; but we are far from knowing whether we have reached it yet. That is because we tend to destroy ourselves needlessly.

As familiar infectious diseases have been beaten back by medicine, nutrition and sanitation, more people in developed countries have died from causes that are avoidable and often self-inflicted. Consider the main causes of death among Canadians in the prime years of their lives, ages ten to fifty. They include suicide homicide and accidents, especially automobile accidents.

In less-developed countries, there are still a huge number of deaths from disease and malnutrition which need not occur. For example, two-thirds of the world's childhood deaths could be avoided by improving health care, education and nutrition. This view is supported by evidence from China and Sri Lanka, both of which have rapidly reduced infant mortality levels. What's more, the same strategies could be used in North American cities. Some research suggests that homicide is more prevalent in underdeveloped societies than it is in developed societies, especially within the family. Gradually, violence decreases as education increases, poverty is reduced and the state becomes more developed. The United States may be an exception to this rule, owing to the inadequate control of handguns in that country. But in general, going to school helps you live longer.

Decreases in the mortality rate are heartening. Still, much progress is yet to be made in many parts of the world. And, for the most part, the leading causes of death are still uniquely human. To prevent them means understanding the uniquely human capacity for self-destruction and the destruction of others. So far, we know little about how to reduce these causes of death. For example, we probably know less about homicide and suicide than we know about the ways to prevent death from cancer. Yet many consider cancer to be the most mysterious cause of death today!

The AIDS epidemic tells a slightly different tale. For some, the epidemic "demonstrates" that drug addicts and sexual "perverts" get "punished" for their sins. This definition of the problem, unsound though it is, continues to have a certain popularity among those who do not do sociological analysis. Yet the conception that AIDS is a geographically limited, homosexual disease was outdated at least ten years ago. And, since at least Louis Pasteur, science has given up any commitment to the primitive notion that infections are punishments. Indeed, condom use won't increase so long as sins, not sexual intercourse, are seen as the agents of contamination. Condoms don't work to correct our sins.

Demographers and policy-makers now expect dramatic increases in the prevalence of AIDS. Sub-Saharan Africa is expected to record the most AIDS-related deaths, as safe sexual practices such as condom use have not increased much since the epidemic began in the eighties. Yet, the huge and growing number of AIDS deaths has the potential to cause widespread social breakdown by creating as many as 1.2 million orphans in Africa. Even if these children find shelter in extended family networks, they are still at a higher risk of death than they would be otherwise, because of the economic and health stresses they put on their caretakers, who are often elderly people.

History shows us the futility of believing in progress towards perfect health. There will always be new health-killers to conquer. Some of them (like suicide and war) are due to avoidable social problems, while others (like AIDS and cancer) are an interaction of new viruses or contaminants and lifestyles which facilitate their transfer, such as intravenous drug use.

We have failed to decrease mortality significantly or increase life expectancy in the latter half of the 20th century. This may indicate too great a focus on high-tech medical cures which rely on expensive technology and treat a relatively small, relatively wealthy population. We have failed to address the uniquely social killers partly because

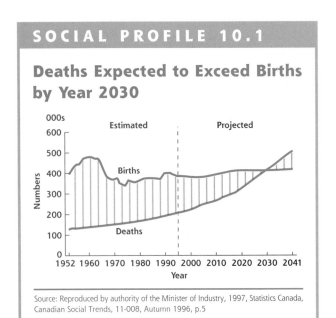

SOCIAL PROFILE 10.1

Deaths Expected to Exceed Births by Year 2030

Source: Reproduced by authority of the Minister of Industry, 1997, Statistics Canada, Canadian Social Trends, 11-008, Autumn 1996, p.5

they have not been claimed as medical problems by the rich, and therefore by the health professions. These problems call for preventive measures. However, modern medicine mainly focuses on remedying, not preventing, causes of death. Prevention means restructuring the society, not merely helping the person or persons most immediately at risk.

The health establishment will learn this lesson as it tries to deal with other causes of death which lie closer to its traditional concerns. For example, increasing evidence shows that cancers are caused by genetic mutations triggered by dangerous substances all around us as, for example, the illnesses caused by industrial pollution in Russia in Far and Away, above. Humans place many of those dangerous substances there, through auto emissions, factory smokestacks, toxic-waste dumping or badly tested manufacturing. And we can be responsible for preventing it in future.

New health strategies require a dedication to reducing the conflict between humans, in order to wage war more effectively against disease than against one another. They also require a commitment to decreasing poverty and improving health internationally, because these factors affect how long, and how well, people can live. These insights are central to the conflict approach to population studies.

Migration

The third major component in population growth is **migration**. In and of itself, migration does not increase the world's population, it merely redistributes it. Yet such redistribution can have a profound impact. In the United States, for example, migration has played a significant role in national development. Understanding the processes promoting or inhibiting migration is important for understanding the American national character. When we consider Canada, immigration (movement into an area), emigration (movement out of an area) and internal migration have also played an important part in our history. Indeed, migration will be playing an ever greater role, now that the country's fertility is so low.

The *migration rate* is the number of people who enter or leave the population in a given year (per thousand inhabitants at mid-year). The *net migration rate* is the number of immigrants, minus the number of emigrants, per year per thousand inhabitants.

Internal migration refers to people moving from one region of a country to another. Patterns of internal migration are useful indexes of changing circumstances in various regions. *International migration* refers to the number of people moving from one country to another, and these statistics also serve as useful indexes of changing circumstances in various countries. All migration is affected by push and pull factors. **Pull factors** in migration are all those factors that encourage people to move to a particular area; they make that particular location more desirable. Pull factors include better job opportunities, more tolerance for ethnic or religious minorities and greater freedom. Generally, they promise people a better life. **Push factors** are all those factors that encourage people to leave an area. They include famine, a lack of job opportunities, discrimination and fear of oppression. Migration out of an area may reflect changes in the job opportunities available around the country, a rising cost of living, a lack of affordable housing or feared discrimination against a given ethnic group.

While immigration has always been an important concern in Canada, recently it has become an explosive political issue. Many immigrants inside the country want the chance to bring their relatives to Canada. Many people outside the country want a chance to get in. But a weak economy makes many native-born Canadians resist the push for an increase in immigrant numbers. Some even want the immigration rate cut back.

As we saw in Chapter 7, postwar immigrants have been drawn to Canada primarily from Southern Europe and the non-Western countries — Asia, Africa, the Caribbean, South America. These types of immigrants are inclined to settle in large metropolitan centres. In this respect, they are following the general trend: more and more Canadians today are living in or near large cities.

Canada's population is mobile, with people often relocating as their plans and opportunities change. Every separation and divorce brings someone a change of location — at least a change of households, or even a change of cities or regions. Likewise, most marriages — matrilocal, patrilocal or neolocal — bring at least one of the spouses a change of location. Beyond these factors, changes in location often result from increases in family size (through birth), decreases in family size (through death or children leaving home) and changes in family income and new job opportunities.

With so many economic and demographic events taking place, we would expect to see a large amount of movement, and data from the 1990 General Social Survey (an annual survey coordinated by Statistics Canada) bear out this expectation. Nearly two Canadian adults in three move in a ten-year period, one adult in two in a five-year period and nearly one adult in five moves in any given year. Some of this is short distance (within-city) movement, while some of it is longer distance — movement *between* cities. Large cities and their surrounding suburbs continue to gain most from this inter-city movement.

Historically, the Canadian population has been moving westward since the early 19th century. The trend, though uneven, is well established, and in this westward movement Canada's population is not so different from that of the United States. The American population, too, has moved westward for the past two centuries. In a sense, the westward movement in Canada is almost inevitable:

Migration is the result of many pulls and probes, and war remains one of the main push factors.

few Canadians want to live farther north, and since the population is already concentrated on the southern border, further migration southward becomes international.

According to a recently released study of interprovincial migration by Statistics Canada, over the past thirty years Canada's westernmost provinces — Alberta and British Columbia — have gained 176,000 and 679,000 in-migrants, respectively, from other provinces. Conversely, Canada's easternmost provinces — especially Newfoundland, Nova Scotia and New Brunswick — all suffered fairly steady net losses of residents over the same period. However, there is more to this than a simple east-versus-west competition. For example, two adjacent Canadian provinces had quite different experiences: between 1966 and 1996, Quebec lost more than 500,000 residents, while Ontario gained more than 200,000. And in the West, while Alberta was gaining from interprovincial migration, its neighbour Saskatchewan was losing. What this tells us is that we have to make sociological sense of this westward "slide" and the exceptions to that rule.

Today, migrants are still being strongly attracted to Ontario, Alberta and British Columbia, especially to the cities. In- and out-migration are nearly balanced in Quebec, and the Atlantic provinces are losing more migrants than they take in. Though the overall trend continues to be westward, countervailing economic, social and cultural forces moderate that movement. For example, the direction of movement between Ontario and British Columbia varies with shifts in the economic growth of these two provinces.

The process of internal migration cannot be understood by focusing on the personal characteristics of those moving. Some communities attract or lose more people than others, depending on the opportunities they offer. What demographers sometimes call population "churning" is a joint result of two social processes. One is movement that results from changes in the quality of **human capital** — people's greater ability, via higher education, capital, or rare skills, to settle wherever they want to. The second process is the changing attractiveness of different locations within Canada. As Canadians become increasingly concerned with obtaining a high-quality lifestyle, more and more are drawn to communities with a pleasant environment and a wide variety of social, cultural, economic and recreational opportunities.

Changing gender relations, discussed in Chapter 8, have played an important part in changing the pattern of migration in North American society. For one thing, women have been acquiring more education. As a result, they have been getting better jobs and more opportunity for career mobility. In fact, a wife often has as much opportunity as her husband does. This has meant that, when moving, couples need to consider the demands of both partners' careers. For another thing, women's growing equality in the workplace and in the home has meant that wives' wishes concerning where and how the family is going to live are gaining more influence. While previously, relocation was based on the husband's job opportunities, now both spouses cast a vote on the issue and it is no longer certain that a husband's job and career will prevail over all other considerations.

The importance of geographic pushes and pulls is shown in a study that analyzed migration out of Canadian native reserves. It reports that involvement in mainstream employment and education "stimulates out-migration" (Gerber, 1984: 158). On the other hand, "distance from major urban centres and institutional completeness inhibit migration." Greater distance makes the move off-reserve more costly, by making it harder to stay in touch with the reserve community.

The same can be said of ethnic and racial communities in large Canadian cities. People with more education and job skills are more likely to leave these communities for other neighbourhoods and work settings. But the greater the *social distance* between an ethnic group and the outside world, the less likely people are to make that trip. If their own community is institutionally complete, they are much more likely to stay within it.

Now that we have discussed the main components of population change, it is time to consider the main theories of population growth: Malthusian theory and the theory of the demographic transition. Since both apply to the world at large, we will turn our attention from Canada to all of humanity.

THE MALTHUSIAN DILEMMA

The newspaper article excerpted in Far and Away, below, warns of a severe food shortage that can be expected to hit the Third World soon, taking many lives. Frightening as this prospect may be, neither it nor the newspaper report of the impending event is new. Such "news" has been broadcast throughout this century; indeed, it started with Malthus two centuries ago.

The idea that food shortages constitute a serious problem for humanity was first put forward in 1798, by one of the founders of demography, Thomas Malthus (1766-1834). He was the first to take seriously the possibility that the earth would eventually become "overpopulated."

Malthus argued that, while the earth's available food increases additively, population increases *exponentially* (or geometrically). A population increasing exponentially at a constant rate is adding more people every year than the year before. Consider a population of 1,000 women and 1,000 men. Each woman marries and has four children. If all survive, in the next generation there will be roughly 2,000 women and 2,000 men. If all of *these* women have four children each, in the next generation there will be roughly 4,000 women and 4,000 men, and in the generation after that, 8,000 women and 8,000 men. Thus, with a constant pattern of four births per woman, the population doubles every generation (roughly thirty years). In four generations, or about 120 years, it grows from 2,000 people to 16,000 people. In 300 years it exceeds a million people! This is the power of exponential growth.

Malthus argued that, on the other hand, increases in the food supply are only additive or *arithmetic*. The growth in food supplies is limited by the amount of land available, the soil quality and the level of technology a society has attained. Malthus believed that there is a real risk of population exceeding increases in the food supply. This possibility that food supplies will not be enough to feed the earth's growing population poses an ongoing threat to the survival of the human species.

Checks (or limits) are needed to ensure that population growth is kept in line with the food supply. Welfare schemes to help the poor are futile, said Malthus. If we feed the hungry, they will simply increase their numbers until they are hungry again. The only sure solutions are positive checks and preventive checks. **Positive checks** prevent overpopulation by increasing the death rate. They include war, famine, pestilence and disease. **Preventive checks** prevent overpopulation by limiting the number of live births. They include abortion, infanticide, sexual abstinence, delayed marriage and the use of contraceptives. Malthus urged people to use preventive checks so that they would not have to suffer the horrible consequences of positive checks.

As you can see, Malthus painted a grim picture of the world's future. But was he right? "Overpopulation" is a word that is often used but is hard to mea-

Global Food Crisis Looms

In Canada, though many people are poor and some make use of food banks, we rarely fear a shortage of food. There is a sense that the problems we face in feeding ourselves are due to social inequality, not insufficient production. Globally, however, there is a problem of insufficient production that is due to social inequality — the stratification of rich and poor nations — and an unforgiving environment.

The world is headed for an unprecedented food shortage which neither science nor current farming practices will be able to meet, a summit of leading agriculture scientists has concluded.

With two billion more mouths to feed in the Third World by the year 2025, the developing countries will need at least 75 per cent more food than currently consumed, the scientists were told. But as incomes rise and cities explode in size, especially in China and India, the demand could be far greater.

"A global wake-up call is needed," Ismail Serageldin, vice-president of the World Bank and chairman of the Consultative Group on International Agriculture Research, told the gathering. "There is a misperception the world is awash in food."

The scientists, including many who spearheaded agriculture's Green Revolution in the 1960s and 1970s, when scientific innovations led by a rapid increase in food production, said the world should not count on a repeat performance.

With a drought in the United States, and Russia's agriculture system in tatters, global grain stocks are at their lowest level in 35 years. The world must also cope with an unprecedented increase in population, with projected growth averaging 90 million people annually. "We have to produce more but we have to produce it differently," the scientists said in a statement to be released today, on World Population Day.

The group, representing 14 science academies from around the world, recommended a new approach to agriculture to address the poverty, water shortages and ecological damage that remain despite four decades of growing food supplies.

About 740 million people worldwide lack enough food to complete a full day's work. The scientists agree that access to food, rather than food production, is now the world's greatest barrier to resolving hunger. Not only do low-income households lack enough food, people in many better off families — mainly women and children — face an individual food crisis.

However, the scientists warned that food production would return as a major global crisis, especially as rapidly growing cities and industries threaten to drain agriculture of increasingly scarce water resources. Food production globally is growing at its slowest rate in four decades, and is on the decline in 90 countries, including 44 in Africa. At the same time, food aid from the West has been cut by half in three years, from 15.2 million tonnes in 1993 to 7.6 million tonnes in 1996.

Although future projections vary widely, all major estimates point to a growing food gap in the Third World. Conservatively, the UN Food and Agriculture Organization says, developing countries will need to import 160 million tonnes of grain annually by 2010 — about 76 per cent more than the 91 million tonnes imported in 1990.

Source: Abridged from John Stackhouse, *The Globe and Mail*, Thurs., July 11, 1996, pp. A1, A12

sure. An area is often thought to be overpopulated when inhabitants do not have the means available to support themselves — when there are more mouths to feed than there is food. Yet the number of people is not all that determines whether an area is overpopulated. What is critical is the *relationship* between a population and the environment in which it is located. Some environments can support more people than others. The type of technology available to exploit this environment, and the system of food distribution, are also important.

It is hard to put meaningful absolute numbers on the world's **carrying capacity** — that is, the number of people who can be supported by the available resources at a given level of technology. However, it is easy to see when a territory is far beyond its carrying capacity. Then, scarcity starts to show itself in dramatic ways — famines and epidemics, for example — and the conflict over resources increases.

Malthus did not realize that technological advances in agriculture would make it possible to vastly increase the food supply, to the point where most of the people in industrialized countries are able to live on the food produced by 3-4 per cent of the population. Today, even in less-developed countries, most people have food to eat, though many do not have enough food and others do not eat the right kinds of food for good health.

However, historical records and computer simulations used to study the effects of famine on human history suggest that, contrary to what Malthus argued, famines have *not* historically been significant "positive checks" on population size. Nor can we assume plagues or epidemics are positive checks that result from overpopulation. In fact, they may sometimes indicate economic development (even if uneven development) is taking place.

For example, one of the reasons plague took such a large toll (12 million deaths) in India in the first quarter of the 20th century was because of "imbalanced modernization," not overpopulation. On the one hand, there were many conditions which allowed the plague to spread throughout India. They included a large railway, a grain trade and considerable human mobility within the country. On the other hand, the country had few of the conditions which could have hindered the spread of disease, such as good nutrition, housing and sanitation. Because of people's opposition to mandatory health inspection, fumigation, quarantine and hospitalization for those infected, health measures were left voluntary. As a result, the illness spread quickly and over an extensive area. The problem was faulty organization, not overpopulation.

Some economists believe the reason for world poverty and the positive checks we have been discussing is that developing countries do not have enough resources (for example, arable land or minerals) or do not know how to use them efficiently. Yet this cannot be true. Industrialized countries rely heavily on developing countries for many resources such as timber and zinc, iron and copper, oil and natural gas, that they cannot get in their own countries. They also rely on these countries for foods they cannot grow, such as sugar, coffee, tea and bananas.

The less-developed countries *do* have valuable resources. However, control over these resources is often in the hands of the developed world. What's more, it is in the interest of the developed nations to keep the price of resources low. The small amount paid for resources leaves developing countries with little money to invest in their own industrial development, but plenty of margin for profit when the foods are sold by someone else. This means they cannot develop manufacturing or break free from dependence on the industrial nations for capital or manufactured goods.

In poorer nations, then, the problem is not too many people; it is a shortage of capital and the consequent difficulty of starting to industrialize. The problems of poverty, dependency, plague and famine are compounded by a large, rapidly growing population. Faced with world population concerns, many have come to advocate **zero population growth** (ZPG) as a temporary solution, until a longer-term solution is found. Zero population growth occurs when the factors leading to population growth, especially births, are exactly balanced by the factors leading to population decline, especially deaths. Under conditions of ZPG, births and deaths are equal. Then the size of the population remains constant over time.

The goal of zero population growth is realistic if the demographic changes we have seen in the industrial world continue to spread elsewhere. These changes are part of a process of **demographic transition** which began in Europe about two centuries ago and profoundly altered population growth patterns there.

DEMOGRAPHIC TRANSITION THEORY

The term **demographic transition** refers to the change a society undergoes, from *high* birth and death rates to *low* birth and death rates, usually during industrialization. This type of change began in Europe around the time of the Industrial Revolution and has continued to the present day. Currently, much of the Third World is in the middle of this transition process.

In its most general form, the transition is brought about by a package of changes called "modernization," which include, among other things, industrialization, urbanization and increases in literacy. According to the theory, modernization first causes a drop in mortality, then, after a time, a drop in fertility. To explain why, we need to back up a bit and consider the dynamics of population change.

Dynamics of Population Change

There are only a few factors that affect the size of a population. In a "closed" system with no migration in or out — like the world as a whole — only births and deaths make a population change in size.

A population's fertility rate (or Total Fertility Rate, as it is properly called) is the average number of children a woman bears in a given society. For a society like ours to replace itself — to stay the same size from one generation to the next — the fertility rate will be about 2.1 children, or 1.05 daughters, per woman. For the population to survive, each woman who gives birth must reproduce for herself and her mate, and also for the women in her generation who never reproduce because they die before they reach reproductive age, choose not to have children or are unable to do so. Some women must have more than two children to compensate for those who have fewer.

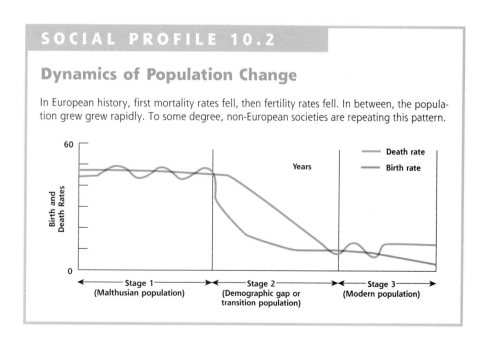

SOCIAL PROFILE 10.2

Dynamics of Population Change

In European history, first mortality rates fell, then fertility rates fell. In between, the population grew grew rapidly. To some degree, non-European societies are repeating this pattern.

Pre-industrial Population Growth

In pre-industrial societies, birth and death rates were nearly identical. Before modern medicine and sanitation, death rates were high, as you would expect, and so were birth rates. As a result, the rate of **natural increase** — the difference between births and deaths, expressed as a ratio of the total population — was nearly zero. That is, there was little change in the population size from year to year. The population was young and constantly "turning over" through births and deaths; but it was not growing larger.

Given the high death rate, women would bear as many children as possible. At that time, children were an economic asset, as they continue to be today in nonindustrial countries. In rural areas, they start to work at an early age as farmhands, doing chores in the home, or earning extra wages on other farms or in nearby factories. In parts of the world where old-age security, pension plans and welfare assistance do not exist, children are the only source of support when parents get old and cannot take care of themselves.

In a pre-industrial society, the more children a couple has, the more chance they will be looked after in their old age. Sons are especially important since, unlike daughters, they often continue to live with their parental families after marrying. In rural South Asia, for example, they provide a kind of income insurance for their parents' old age, and the failure to rear a son is often seen as a material loss. Among old people without a surviving son, one finds higher mortality risks and a higher chance of property loss in old age. The consequences are even more severe for mothers than they are for fathers, since women are more likely to survive their spouses into old age. Thus, women have even more reason for wanting many children than do men. In societies with arranged marriages, children allow a family to form economic and social ties to other families for mutual assistance. So it is also desirable to have many children because the more children one has, the more ties one will have to other families.

The pattern of high birth and death rates described above started to change in Europe in the 18th century when nutrition, sanitation and medical treatment began to improve and the death rate fell dramatically. For a time, women kept on bearing children at the traditional rate. But with many more children surviving to reproductive age, the population grew rapidly.

Eventually, women began bearing fewer children — only as many as they thought they could support. They no longer had to bear ten children in the hope that four would survive. Almost all their children survived! As well, parents began to *want* fewer children as the burden of social security shifted from the family to the state. Urbanization, extended education and social and geographic mobility all lowered the economic value of children. At the same time, the cost of raising children went up. More recently still, the changing roles of women — especially the growing availability of paid work — also made women less willing to bear many children.

Thailand provides an example of the demographic transition and its effects. In older rural areas, fertility is still at the traditional high levels. In newly settled towns, fertility has declined. The declines are associated with land-saving and labour-saving changes: for example, industrialization and high wage rates. These have made bearing children less necessary than in the past and less materially rewarding.

For these and similar reasons, the birth rate began to fall. In the West, it continued falling until, finally, it was below the death rate. As a result, the population growth rate is negative in most developed societies today. Said another way, many Western populations are shrinking, with important social consequences.

One such consequence is population aging and the effect of aging on social structure. There is an enormous difference between the relatively stable social organization of societies like Canada and Japan, which have completed the demographic transition, and the fluid organization of societies like Ethiopia and Nigeria, which have scarcely begun it. Equally important is the effect of the demographic transition on the social organization of the world. Here the issue is relative power: in the next thirty years, the poor, high-fertility, high-mortality societies will become a larger and larger segment of the world's population — a change that may well have explosive political consequences.

Limitations of Demographic Transition Theory

Demographic transition theory has great practical as well as theoretical importance. It describes what seems to be a universal process. The theory also makes an important contribution to our understanding of economic development and the way population is tied to development. Today, this theory is the dominant way of thinking about population and it is behind every forecast of world populations.

The theory reminds us that a low-mortality/low-fertility population type is critical if people wish to maintain a high standard of living. Yet research over the past twenty years has cast doubt on the theory's validity. Some data show that the theory does not apply to European history as well as people once believed. It does even worse with non-European, Third World countries. That is because the theory fails to consider many problems that are common in Third World societies.

The Industrial Revolution caused mortality and fertility to decline, but it also created major environmental problems.

One such problem is the permanent damage a long-term population explosion can do to a nation's economy or ecosystem. An example is Brazil's destruction of the Amazon rainforest — the result of migration, rapid population growth and the Brazilian state's hunger for a growth in national revenues (through the export of meat and lumber). Such damage makes transition to the final stage impossible (or may even return Brazil to high rates of mortality and fertility).

A second problem is the inability of Third World countries to provide the socio-economic conditions that make fertility reduction attractive. These conditions include social security, education, urbanization, social mobility and careers for women. So their citizens may still have many children even if doing so provides only a slight or temporary economic advantage.

A different way of interpreting the same facts is provided by several societies — among them, Costa Rica, Sri Lanka and Kerala State (India) — that have enjoyed notable success in lowering the birth rate. There, low mortality and fertility rates are the result of a long process that began with fairer income distribution, better nutrition, more education (especially for women), more autonomy for women, higher rates of political awareness and participation for all, and universal access to health services. In particular, income or land redistribution and political involvement gave people more sense of involvement in their own lives; hence, more to gain from changing their fertility decisions. This is particularly true of women who, with more education and autonomy, are no longer so reliant on children for social status and income security.

Beyond that, traditional cultural factors encourage the persistence of large families. First, although mortality has fallen in many Third World societies, people still put a high value on children. People will not adopt Western family-planning techniques unless these values change. This is one of the reasons why foreign-aid givers and financial institutions like the World Bank have felt it necessary to step into the "family-planning" debate, occasionally with the great success that is reported in Far and Away on next page.

In many countries there are people with a vested political interest in large families. For example, in Nigeria, members of the dominant ethnic group — the Hausa — prefer large families. Perhaps this is because maintaining a large population helps them remain politically dominant by producing the poverty and destitution that leads to political weakness. Moreover, less-developed countries often need to choose among competing social investments — to spend money on social security versus education versus health care versus exportable manufactured goods, for example. The theory says little about which factors are most important in the transition process and which should be given top priority.

Often, the result of so many conflicting demands is political tension. For example, many Arab countries have a problem with high fertility because it reduces per capita income. It also creates a young population and, typically, a young population is a politically explosive population. This combination of poverty, youth unemployment and the suppression of women is likely to cause political problems in the future for many Third World countries.

In China, high fertility poses a different version of the same problem. China needs reforms of almost every kind — agricultural, industrial, educational, economic and so on. Money could be usefully invested in thousands of different activities and choosing among the possibilities, though inevitable, is very difficult. Worse still, every year thirty million new Chinese babies are born — equalling the total population of Canada. To planners, these new citizens represent new demands on the public purse. This is why China has turned to the "one child" policy. However, this policy poses problems of its own. In rural areas it leaves parents with little security in their old age, for it is difficult for one child to support two aged parents. And if the one child is a daughter, she will owe her first allegiance to her husband's parents. It will be interesting to see if, with the death of Deng Xaoping in February 1997, China maintains an allegiance to this policy or switches to other tactics for population control.

By contrast, Hungary, with the world's highest fraction (25 per cent) of single-child families, has a long history of low fertility for reasons that are poorly understood. It is not, apparently, a result of modernization. Rural regions of Hungary have long had a one-child system, perhaps to keep up the tradition of peasant self-sufficiency. In the 20th century, this system came under attack, as many Hungarians feared population decline and national extinction. Yet low fertility has continued.

In the end, demographic transition theory describes the macrodynamics of many contemporary populations, yet it is unable to explain the details of demographic history in any given country. As such, it contributes little to forecasts or social planning.

Family-Planning Success Stories in Bangladesh

FAR AND AWAY

In Canada, fertility decline came gradually and almost effortlessly. Throughout the first half of the 20th century, birth rates continued to drop smoothly. Today, Canadians, with the particular help of young immigrants, are just managing to replace the population from one generation to the next. But the process has not gone as quickly or smoothly in other, less developed societies. There, until recently, there was little sign of a willingness to adopt modern means of limiting family size.

Behind the swaying palms, the villages of the Matlab region of Bangladesh have produced a remarkable demographic turnaround. In scores of remote fishing and rice-growing villages, 20 years of concerted family planning have cut birth rates by half. In the 1970s, an average woman in Matlab bore six children. Today, she has three. Once an unassuming backwater, Matlab stands as a milestone in human development and the foundation stone for Bangladesh's national family-planning program, which has become one of the most successful in Asia.

The roots of Bangladesh's demographic transition lie in Matlab's effort to treat contraception as a marketing challenge that requires good products, a trained sales force and follow-up service. Unlike the governments of many countries that believe the poor want large families, the Matlab program assumed couples everywhere wanted birth control, especially when it came as part of a bigger health package.

The link is a village health worker, a local woman with no more than a high-school education who not only sells the idea of contraception, but provides doorstep health service: vaccinating children, checking the weight of infants, dispensing basic medicines and monitoring the health of young mothers.

In Matlab's tiny, thatched-hut hamlets, where most people earn less than a dollar a day, the female health workers have made contraception a household word and reduced the child mortality rate to a level 30 per cent below the national average.

"It is a total package," said Aparajita Chakroborty, a village health worker in Matlab since 1985. "There is trust. Because I have helped people's children, I have their confidence." Bangladesh employs 23,000 women like Ms. Chakroborty, who, for a salary of about $100 a month, ensure that 200 couples around her village have access to modern birth control as well as maternal and child health care.

Amid Matlab's rice paddies, there is no obvious economic reason for young couples to practice birth control with such enthusiasm. The majority of the adult population, about 55 per cent, are landless labourers who might benefit from more hands in the fields, markets and brickyards. Yet local aspirations have changed in the last 20 years, not least because the local school system is vastly improved. When asked why she stopped having children after three, Monowara Manufa, a field labourer, said, "We can provide a better living and more education for our children this way. And my health is better," she said.

Nationally, Bangladesh's family-planning program has increased contraception use nearly tenfold without any change in the national poverty rate — a setback for the theory that economic development is the best contraceptive. In an exhaustive study of Bangladesh's success in family planning, John Cleland, a British demographer, noted in 1993 that "the poor, the landless and the illiterate have reduced their fertility at the same time and in similar proportion as the less poor, the landed and the literate."

Source: Abridged from John Stackhouse, *The Globe and Mail*, Mon., July 22, 1996, p. A8

WAS MALTHUS RIGHT?

Those who argue today that there is still a "population problem," that the world is becoming "overpopulated," or that the world is a population time bomb make some of the same arguments Malthus did nearly two hundred years ago. Was Malthus right back then and is he right today?

Yes, He Was

Today, in central Africa, women average six children or more. However, even the more modest four children per mother is common in Southeast Asia, the Islamic world, parts of Africa and Latin America. In short, millions of mothers are still producing children at this rate, often because male domination of one kind or another dictates that they should. As we have seen, with four children per mother, a population doubles every thirty years or so. Even allowing for slower growth, experts predict that in thirty years the current world population of just under six billion people will be three billion larger. Will the world be able to feed 50 per cent more people in thirty years?

Here, expert estimates vary. However, statistics collected by the research organization Worldwatch indicate that the world's grain production is falling. The store of available food is only enough to last for a short time, in the event of widespread crop failures. Other ecologists conclude that the number of people on Earth will have to drop to at least one-third the current level by 2100 in order to survive in relative prosperity. Though an optimum population is between one and two billion people, the current population is near six billion, and predictions using current growth rates put it at between 12 billion and 15 billion people in 2100.

At the current growth rate of 1.1 per cent a year, the population of the United States in 2100 could be 1.2 billion people, the current population of China. Today, each American consumes about twenty-three times more goods and services than the average person in the Third World and fifty-three times more than someone in China. A future America, with as many people as China today, might have to settle for something close to a Chinese standard of living.

One of the problems hinted at above is a growing shortage of nonrenewable resources that include land, fresh water, petroleum fuel and minerals needed for manufacturing. It is not always clear which problems are caused by overpopulation. However, some observers link growing shortages of nonrenewable resources in the developed world — even shortages of water — to the problem of overpopulation.

In recent decades, humans have dramatically transformed the environment. The entire global ecology is affected, especially the equilibrium of the biosphere and the interdependence between living systems. This raises doubts about the survival chances of humanity. The ultimate source of concern for environmental change is its potential effect on the "livability" of the globe and its ability to support the variety and complexity of ongoing human activities.

Too-rapid population growth threatens human self-regulating systems as well as natural ecosystems. Even if rapid population growth does not cause all these problems, it makes them harder to solve. In rapidly growing societies, childbearing women are also less likely to be economically active. Along with old people, children and the infirm, they require much public spending on health and welfare. So, in a rapidly growing society, health, education and welfare spending consume a large part of the national budget. And this is an expense that has to be paid by relatively few economically active adults.

Several consequences flow from this. First, high-fertility societies are often unable to afford good health, education and welfare programs. Money spent on these programs takes money away from programs to develop manufacturing or export industries. This limits the country's ability to develop economically: at best, it slows the process dramatically.

In 19th-century England the population problem Malthus had predicted seemed to solve itself. Mortality began to fall and, soon, as a result, so did childbearing because it was no longer necessary to bear a huge brood to be sure some would be reasonably likely to survive. Food production increased and people's standard of living began to improve. All of these changes were due, in one way or another, to the development of new technology. Will technology come to our rescue again in the twentieth century?

Not necessarily, for several reasons. There are limits to what we can expect technology to do. Given present levels of technology, all the world's people cannot possibly enjoy the level of affluence North Americans enjoy today. There is just not enough wealth to go around. Beyond that, technology is costly and uncertain. As well as population size and consumption (or lifestyle) patterns, technology determines the amount of pollution generated, so it plays a part in destroying the ecosystem. It depletes natural resources, contributing to environmental problems and (even) perpetuating social inequality. (Since people's access to modern technology is unequal, more rapid development of technology more rapidly increases inequality.) Evidence suggests that technology will continue to improve, yet technology also has harmful side effects. If our consumer culture is not checked, gains from technology will be offset.

Malthus noted that in a population that failed to take preventive measures, positive checks would come into play. Plagues, famines, epidemics, wars and other causes of death would increase. Eventually, a rise in the death rate would bring the population down to a manageable level. But Malthus did not realize that technological advances in agriculture would make it possible to vastly increase the food supply. Today, even in less-developed countries, most people have *some* food to eat. However, famines and epidemics continue to rage throughout the world, especially in the countries where the population is growing most rapidly.

The twentieth century is remarkable for two major shifts in human experience. One is an explosion of population growth that is still continuing. The other is an explosion of "mega-murders" — deaths by war, civil war and internal terror — that, by one estimate, have consumed 188 million lives. (Some scholars have estimated that more people have died from genocide than from all wars combined in the twentieth century!) Malthus would not be surprised by these facts. Probably, rapid population growth increases conflict, brings pressure for rapid solutions and reduces our ability to solve problems peacefully.

No, He Wasn't Those who take the opposing view — and many readers will sigh with relief to learn that there are such thinkers — believe Malthus wasn't right, after all, and challenge the "Malthusians" on many points of evidence. Few sociologists support all of Malthus's gloomy views. They realize that claims of overpopulation are sometimes used to mask issues of powerlessness and social inequality.

For example, the famines that have plagued Ethiopia and Somalia in recent years are not a result of overpopulation. Famines are often a result of improper land use, civil wars and other social and political factors, such as low prices set on foods by the state. So we cannot take famines, in themselves, as proof of overpopulation. Beyond that, many developed societies pay their farmers not to grow crops, even if this means a shortage somewhere else in the world. So we cannot take low rates of food production to indicate the maximum amount of food that can be produced in the world today. It is likely that rapid population growth slows down economic development. However, at issue is *how much* it slows development, compared with other factors. Note, for example, that economic growth has been extremely slow in the United States — indeed, much of the Western world — for the last decade or so. That cannot be blamed on rapid population growth.

There are many possible reasons for slow economic growth: they include global competition, a shortage of capital, competing economic or social goals, poor corporate planning, poor economic planning, poor political leadership, exploitation by foreign investors, internal strife, even a low level of commitment to economic growth. We cannot assume that rapid population growth is the most important influence in each, or any case.

Likewise, we cannot assume that rapid population growth is the most important influence on social conflict or environmental stress. It is true that social conflict, rapid population growth and environmental stress are often found together. But showing a correlation is not the same as establishing causation. All three may be caused by yet another factor, and at least two possible "candidates" suggest themselves: national poverty and global inequality.

National poverty and a low position in the global hierarchy of nations are correlated with each other. As well, both promote social conflict, rapid population growth and environmental stress. Take poverty: compared to rich people, poor people are more likely to invest heavily in children (their only insurance against impoverished old age). They are also more likely to overuse their land, to get the maximum short-term productivity. And they are more likely to engage in violent conflict with members of other groups or tribes, against whom they compete for scarce land, jobs or housing.

SOCIAL PROFILE 10.3

World Population Size from 1950 to 2050

Beyond 2030, fertility, mortality and migration is kept constant.

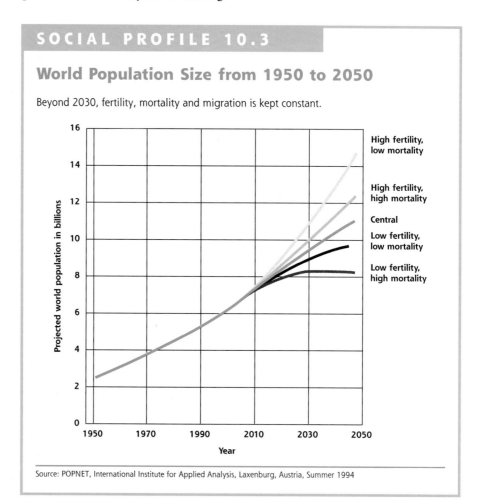

Source: POPNET, International Institute for Applied Analysis, Laxenburg, Austria, Summer 1994

To repeat, rapid population growth is part of each scenario, but it does not necessarily cause the other problems. Poverty and inequality often cause problems that are similar to those caused by overpopulation and may contribute to overpopulation too. And with the arrival of new ideas and new technology, economic development will explode once again. When that happens, we can expect rapidly growing populations to enter the "demographic transition" towards lower death and birth rates. History shows that people have much to gain by doing so, and too much to lose by failing to do so. With low death rates, they will have little need for many children, especially once old-age security and middle-class lifestyles become available.

Summing Up

In his book *How Many People Can the Earth Support?*, population expert Joel Cohen recognizes that our "population time bomb" question cannot be answered as posed. The earth can support many more people than currently live on it, but it supports them with more or less ease under different conditions. Cohen notes a number of conditions which determine when more or fewer people are feasible:

- **Equality of well-being** With more equal global resources, Earth can support many more people than it does today.

- **Technological development** With more time to prepare technologically for their arrival, Earth can support many more people.

- **Political institutions** With governments that are more honest, effective and peaceful, Earth can support many more people. (But more people might limit our liberty and political participation.)

- **Economic institutions** With safer, better-organized work, and healthier, better-educated workers, Earth can support many more people.

- **Demographic arrangements** With a higher death rate and shorter life span, Earth can support many more people. (Also, with better childcare arrangements, to allow more women to work.)

- **Level of well-being** If we can tolerate a lower level of material well-being, Earth can support many more people than today.

- **Environmental conditions** If we can tolerate more physical and biological degradation of the environment, Earth can support many more people.

- **What range of variation?** If we can tolerate more fluctuation in death rates and material conditions, Earth can support many more people.

- **What risk of catastrophe?** If we can tolerate more uncertainty about the occurrence and outcome of disasters — famines, epidemics, wars and so on — Earth can support many more people.

Two things are to be noted about this list of questions and answers. First, we cannot bank on the occurrence of changes — for example, more equality, better government or new technology — that will make Earth able to support many more people. Second, most of us would be unwilling to give up many "goods" — like material prosperity, long life, political liberty and a low-risk future — merely to have more people on Earth.

Putting these two observations together, Cohen is telling us the world *is* a "population time bomb" if we cannot do without things we like and value. If we cannot or will not change our desires — and there may be no good reason why we should — then there *are* limits to how many people the Earth can support. To put it another way, having many more people means giving up many (all?) of the gains the human race has made, economically, socially and politically, since the Enlightenment. It also means a continuing destruction of the natural environment.

The Population/Environment Connection

What we have seen in Western societies in the last ten years of the 20th century is a dramatic and justifiable growth in concern about the environment. More and more people feel strongly about the need for improvements in water purity and air quality. They want higher waste-disposal standards, including improved monitoring of landfills, recycling, packaging and toxic-chemical disposal. People want assurance that consumer products are environmentally safe. Increasingly, they support the conservation of energy, the reduction of acid rain and safer use of pesticides.

Environmental concern is as economically significant as it is socially significant. Protecting the environment requires changes in consumer behaviour, and this increases the price of consumer products. It also requires more state regulation and higher production costs, which, in turn, creates a higher risk of job losses, since a company that cannot afford to make the changes a state demands may relocate to a country with lower environmental standards.

Yet these costs, risks and changes are inevitable. In recent decades, humans have dramatically transformed the environment. The entire global ecology is affected, especially the equilibrium of the biosphere and the interdependence between living systems. This raises issues affecting the survival of humanity. The ultimate source of concern for environmental change is its potential effect on the "livability" of the globe and its ability to support the variety and complexity of ongoing human activities. Urban-industrial civilization threatens human self-regulating systems as well as natural ecosystems. For instance, some respiratory and cardiovascular health problems are related to environmental pollution. The future of humanity depends on a better understanding of natural ecosystems and their relation to human populations.

Throughout the world, international bodies (like UNESCO), governments at every level and even local movements are responding. They are developing plans for research, education, legislation and regulation of the environment. The failure to take such preventive and preparatory steps will likely lead to the positive checks Malthus associated with overpopulation — massive death and dislocation. Yet these checks are not a result of overpopulation *per se*. They are social, not demographic, in nature. That's why human societies will have to change dramatically: the Earth is unable to support our current standards of human life. But for a worldwide issue such as global warming, new types of policy-making challenges are in store. To deal with global problems like the greenhouse effect, governments will have to build international consensus, and sacrifices will be needed.

In the end, technology and development, poverty and population growth are all tied together in a knot. Poverty leads the poor to overuse, and in that way, degrade the land. Results include erosion, pollution, deforestation, the wrongful use of common lands — in short, a "destructive cycle" which worsens the long-term prospects of the rural poor and their children.

The poor also suffer in Third World cities. Environmental problems such as unsafe water, overcrowding, air pollution and hazardous work conditions all affect the poor more than anyone else. Yet aid agencies and governments pay little attention to urban infrastructure. To get the Third World's cooperation in addressing global problems, the Western world must help it address the environmental problems that affect its poorest citizens.

The population and environment problem also arises because of uneven development. By bringing capital, industry and population growth to bear on a particular geographic location, the chances are great that industrial wastes will overwhelm the natural recycling processes. Pollution is the inevitable result. The pollution could have been avoided if the process of development had been spread out more evenly over time and space.

FAR AND AWAY

Aquaculture in Bangladesh

Big problems often lead to the hasty adoption of big solutions, and more often than not, even bigger problems. So, for example, a rapid rise in the price of foreign oil may lead to the adoption of nuclear power generators, perhaps more quickly or on a larger scale than is organizationally sensible. As a result, haste makes waste or — as sociologist Charles Perrow said about nuclear power stations — "normal accidents." Described below is a normal accident that happened in Bangladesh. It involved prawns.

From the desolate yard of his farm hut, Abdul Aziz can see where Asia's Blue Revolution rolled across the once-fertile plains of southwestern Bangladesh, and where the revolution crashed to a halt.

A subsistence farmer who relies on one-fifth of a hectare of land, Mr. Aziz followed the advice of his government and some of the world's biggest foreign-aid donors when they suggested he convert his meagre rice field to a prawn farm. He was told the small crustacean known as "pink gold" would end his days in poverty.

Five years later, the Blue Revolution — the massive investment in aquaculture that was designed to help Asia's rice farmers develop new sources of income — is finished in Shyamnagar, and Mr. Aziz has lost almost everything. His animals, his vegetable garden, his bamboo tress and banana grove are all gone, ravaged like the barren landscape that now surrounds Shyamnagar. "Before the prawn farms, this was beautiful paddy field," Mr. Aziz said. "People destroyed it for money."

Mr. Aziz's story increasingly is the story of coastal Asia, from southern India to the Mekong Delta, where massive investments in prawn farming and other forms of aquaculture have meant instant riches for some but ecological destruction and social uprooting for others.

Promoted by governments, the World Bank and many large aid agencies, the Blue Revolution created huge export earnings for Asia, which accounts for 80 per cent of the world's $9-billion prawn trade. But in little more than a decade, prawn farms have destroyed an estimated 800,000 hectares of mangrove forests and created improbably saline deserts in some of the world's wettest countries.

Subsistence prawn farming has existed in Asia for at least 700 years, but only the past decade has it become an intensive industry, producing extraordinary profits and extraordinary soil damage. For Asia's large prawn cultivators, ecological damage is only a cue to move on to new territory. The industry has abandoned large parts of Taiwan, China, the Philippines and Thailand, while new farms emerge in Cambodia, Burma, Bangladesh and southern India.

Today's farms rely on constructed ponds that trap saline water in fields once used for rice paddies. Some of those farms continue to alternate prawn and rice crops, but many harvest prawns year-round in highly intensive operations. The carnivorous and highly profitable tiger prawns must be fed fish meal with large doses of chemical fertilizer and lime, and protected with antibiotics from the many organisms to which they are susceptible.

"Those investing in it are possessed by a gold-rush mentality, plundering precious resources to make big money for a short period before moving on," the British charity Christian Aid said in a recent report on the industry's spectacular expansion. "After the prawn rush, they leave untold misery and ruin in their wake."

Source: Abridged from John Stackhouse, *The Globe and Mail*, July 13, 1996, pp. A1, A10

Even the disasters at Bhopal (India), Three Mile Island and Chernobyl are a result of uneven or unconsidered development. A factory or power plant begins operating under conditions of rapid growth and prosperity but, eventually, changes occur. Speeded-up operation, sudden changes in policy, cutbacks in staff and other uncertainties occur because of political or economic change. The resulting confusion can trigger a crisis which kills people and poisons the earth, air and water for generations to come. This is the reason organizational sociologist Charles Perrow calls such mishaps "normal accidents."

A related concept is what sociologist Sam Sieber calls "fatal remedies" — solutions which cause worse problems than the problems they solved. An example, reported in Far and Away, above, is the environmental destruction which resulted from an effort to farm prawns for profitable export. The original problem to be solved was local poverty. After a brief period of extraordinary profit-making by a few, the new problem is local poverty *plus* social conflict, a poisoned water supply and soil that is unsuitable for farming.

In short, environmental problems result from an interaction of technological, social and economic factors. By itself, population plays only a small part. Nonetheless, population planning can play a part in solving these problems or making them worse. Controlling population growth helps us protect our future better than a mere reliance on new technology and new resources which are far less certain.

CLOSING REMARKS

The sociological study of population offers another clear illustration of the connection between macro and micro perspectives. On the one hand, population is a macro phenomenon which exists outside and "above" individual people. After all, the size, location, rate of growth, life expectancy and age composition of the population are all beyond the control of any individual. They are the "givens" of life in a society. In this sense, population is all-encompassing and changes slowly, over decades and generations. The main elements of a population are characteristic of a society. They change much more slowly than the people who make up the society: for example, a population "ages" more slowly than a person does.

On the other hand, *we* together are the population. Without us, there is no population. If we all kill ourselves or emigrate, there's no population left. If we have too few children to replace ourselves, the population gets older, then gradually disappears. We are the people who decide how many children to have, where to live, when (and whether) to marry, whether to live in a healthy, life-extending or unhealthy, life-shortening manner. A population changes over time because millions of individuals change their way of doing things.

This chapter is ending on a sombre note, and that may be appropriate. Yet, many observers are far more optimistic about population and environmental issues than we have indicated. They point out that, on balance, things are getting better around the world. Fertility is falling and life expectancy is rising. People, on average, have more food to eat and they are more literate; and at least some environmental problems, like the lack of control over the world production of chlorofluorocarbons, are improving dramatically. What do you think? Is the glass half-empty or half-full?

We began this chapter by referring to grim prospects facing the world. Perhaps industrial society has reached the limits of its development. Many social scientists refer to the coming of an information-based post-industrial society. The development of inanimate sources of energy led to the Industrial Revolution. Today, the development of automation, computers and robots is causing an information revolution. As a result, we need fewer people than in the past.

Are we moving in a direction that promises to change society for the better? If not, how do we go about getting started? The topic of social change, to which we now turn, addresses these issues.

Review Questions

1. What is demography?
2. What is the "Malthusian dilemma"?
3. What is overpopulation?
4. What are positive and preventative checks?
5. What is demographic transition theory?
6. What is meant by a population's fertility rate?
7. What is meant by a population's mortality rate?
8. How did population growth change after industrialization?
9. Why is there doubt about the validity of demographic transition theory?
10. How is fertility measured?
11. What role has migration played in Canadian society?
12. Why has migration become a political issue in Canada?
13. What impact does population change have upon the environment?

Discussion Questions

1. If the world's population is doubling every forty years and the population today is about five billion people, what will be the population of the world in two hundred years? Will that be too many people? Why or why not?
2. What are some of the reasons that some countries pass through the entire demographic transition process quickly and others take a much longer time?
3. Will future resource discoveries have as great an impact on the Canadian population as past ones have? Why or why not?
4. Mortality rates are an indication of social (class) inequalities, and we are all in favour of people living, not dying. Why, then, is little action taken to eliminate these social inequalities in risks of death?
5. How will the changing age composition of Canada's population change the industry that you are training to enter?

Suggested Readings

Beaujot, Roderic (1991) *Population Change in Canada: The Challenges of Policy Adaptation*. Toronto: McClelland and Stewart. A thorough and sophisticated analysis of population processes in Canada, this book considers what kinds of population policies Canada needs in order to deal with its present and future population problems.

Coale, Ansley and Susan Watkins (eds.) (1986) *The Decline of Fertility in Europe*. Princeton: Princeton University Press. Edited by two eminent demographers, this book brings together the findings of Princeton University's European Fertility Study. Readers will get a sense of that project's vast richness and the possibilities for interesting research in historical demography.

Easterlin, Richard (1980) *Birth and Fortune: The Impact of Numbers on Personal Welfare*. New York: Basic Books. Professor Easterlin's book stirred up much controversy when it first appeared, because it attributed many life satisfactions (and dissatisfactions) to a single "accident of birth": that is, whether one was born in a small or large birth cohort. Some believe he has overstated the case for demographic factors. Read his book and decide for yourself.

Foot, David K. and Daniel Stoffman (1996) *Boom, Bust & Echo*. Toronto: Macfarlane Walter & Ross. The authors of this compelling book contend that demographics can explain about two-thirds of everything. This book is an illuminating examination of how demographics has shaped and will continue to affect Canadian life.

Laslett, P. (1979) *The World We Have Lost*. London: Methuen. This classic work weaves dry statistics and historical documents into a fascinating picture of Europe (especially England) before the coming of industrialization. It asks whether we have lost more than we have gained from the change.

McNeill, W.H. (1976) *Plagues and Peoples.* Garden City, New York: Anchor Books. Written by a prize-winning author, this book shows how human history has been shaped by shifting "disease balances" and "disease pools." It will make you wonder whether people make their own history.

World Commission on Environment and Development (1987) *Our Common Future.* New York: Oxford University Press. This report (often called the Brundtland Report after its chairman) is based on work sponsored by the United Nations World Commission on Environment and Development. Fascinating facts and interesting analysis provide a major basis for the current worldwide move towards sustainable development.

Internet Resources

The following Web sites are good places to find more information about topics discussed in this chapter:

David Suzuki Foundation discusses major issues and practical projects relating to solving the root problems behind threatening environmental problems.
http://www.vkool.com/suzuki/index.html

Green Party of Canada and Ontario contains a history of the ecologically oriented party, discusses current policies and conferences, and publishes a newsletter.
http://onlinedirect.com/green/home.html

Environment Canada Home Page provides reports on a variety of environmental issues including water quality, endangered species, pollution, ozone depletion and toxic substances.
http://www.doe.ca

The Global Trajectory deals with the effect of the world's growing population on the environment.
http://atm.geo.nsf.gov/unidata/staff/blynds/globtraj/gtpt1.html

The Population Council's "Population and Development Review Abstracts" provides abstracts from the journal and of related books.
http://www.popcouncil.org/pdr/pdrabs.htm

CERN/ANU Demography and Population Studies contains more than 150 links to demographic information resources around the world.
http://coombs.anu.edu.au/ResFacilities/DemographyPage.html

Zero Population Growth Inc. contains information on this worldwide organization whose purpose is to limit population growth. It also provides links to sites concerned with rapid growth and wasteful consumption of resources.
http://www.igc.apc.org/zpg/index.html

CHAPTER 11

POLITICS, PROTEST AND CHANGE

CHAPTER OUTLINE

UNDERSTANDING SOCIAL CHANGE

Evolutionary theories

Revolutionary theories

Through the crystal ball darkly

POLITICS

The role of the state

The authoritarian state

The state and civil society

ELITES

Elite accommodation

"Our president, today, tomorrow and forever"

Class versus elite analysis

Can you get into the elite?

IDEOLOGIES

Ideology and control

Ideology and protest

SOCIAL MOVEMENTS

Relative deprivation

Resource mobilization

New violence and protest ahead?

Charisma in social movements

OTHER SOURCES OF SOCIAL CHANGE

New ideas and inventions

New technology

All information is not created equal

GLOBALIZATION

Battlefields of the new millennium

The end of history?

The macro/micro connection

Yardsticks of progress

CLOSING REMARKS

Change can sometimes take a heavy human toll, as it did in Cambodia under rule by the Khmer Rouge.

UNDERSTANDING SOCIAL CHANGE

People have an amazing ability to adjust to change. So it may be hard to convince you just how quickly the world is changing in important ways, because you have already started to take yesterday's changes for granted. But here's something to think about:

For most of human history, life was very quiet. People didn't hear many sounds and most of what they did hear were natural sounds: animals, wind and running water, for example. They didn't see large crowds or large buildings. Nor did people travel long distances very often. That's why they didn't get to know people very different from themselves. There was no reason to spend time thinking about things that didn't affect them directly. Most people just assumed life would go on forever much as it had in the past.

Our own world isn't like that. We live in a noisy age in which change is built into the very organization of society. Elections every four years or so, new car models every year, newspapers every day, television news continuously: we devour change and news about change. Whole industries — fashion, luxury goods and the mass media, for example — depend on that taste for change. Often they don't satisfy our desires; they set them afire and keep them burning.

As we shall see, social change may begin at either a macro or micro level; but eventually, its effects show up at both levels. Take the growth of high-tech industries. Automated manufacturing is gradually replacing human beings with machines and computers, changing the lives of thousands of workers and their families. For another example, consider people's decisions to delay childbearing, to have no children or only one child. These are micro-level choices that people are making one couple at a time, and their impact builds slowly. Yet taken together, these choices are changing the whole world.

Contrary to popular belief, social change is rarely the result of great men and women having great ideas. Social change is happening all the time, a result of the actions of ordinary people. This is illustrated dramatically by sociological research on people's reactions to disaster — earthquakes, hurricanes, floods, famines and the like. A review of disaster behaviour — whether the disaster is an earthquake in Mexico City or a flood in Manitoba — shows us that media reports typically mislead us. In fact, looting, price-gouging, panic flight and other deviant behaviours are rare; so is psychological dependency and disaster shock. Martial law is rarely if ever necessary. On the contrary, people often show their best side: ordinary people help to find and rescue disaster victims, and relatives and friends provide them with shelter (Quarantelli, 1996).

Both in times of quiet routine and sudden disaster, we are all busy creating, fixing and changing society. The difference between micro-change and macro-change does not lie in the number of people affected or the importance of the change. It lies in the change's point of origin. But whether a change begins at the macro or micro level, understanding it usually demands a macro level of explanation.

Evolutionary Theories

There are two types of macro-theories about change: theories of *evolution* and theories of *revolution*. Evolutionary theories see societies as systems that continually adapt to changes in the social, economic or technical environment. Changes are gradual and take place over a long time. Thus, an evolutionary theorist might refer to the Judeo-Christian tradition, or the influence of Greek culture on today's language, arts and thought.

Behind evolutionary theories of social change, from Durkheim and Spencer onward, is the idea that societies always and steadily become more complex. The world comes closer to being what communications guru Marshall McLuhan called a "global village," as distances shrink through faster travel and communication. In the end, we are all tied together in a single, complex social order.

Central to this argument is the assertion that in any social system two main evolutionary processes are at work: **differentiation** and **integration**. Differentiation is the process that splits up tasks previously performed by one person or group, so that different people or groups perform them.

The division of labour we discussed in Chapter 6 (Work and the Workplace) is one form of differentiation. Another good example is the way a modern family operates. In the past, families not only consumed goods, they also produced them and educated children. But today, the family is primarily a consuming unit. Almost everyone who works for pay works outside the family home. Schools and other institutions are mainly responsible for educating family members. That leaves the family with much less to do than in the past. One result is that the family redefines itself. Increasingly, as we saw in Chapter 9 (Family), marriage is based on love not economic exchange. Increasingly, parenthood is a lifestyle choice rather than a way to produce necessary labour power to help support the family. What the family has to do is more expressive and symbolic than instrumental or practical, as in the past.

Integration, a complementary process of social evolution, combines specialized parts or elements of a society to form a unified whole. Integration helps people to cooperate effectively as a group, and to avoid or reduce conflicts. So, for example, within the "new" family, people search for ways of integrating their very different activities. Spouses need to find time for each other and parents need to find time for their children. All family members need to integrate their domestic and paid work, their personal goals and family goals. As we noted in our discussion of anomie in Chapter 6, the more specialized people's lives become, the more difficult it is to integrate their activities. Yet people do it all the time. Differentiation and integration is not a recent development. Societies have always had to differentiate and integrate their activities. That is what we mean by the process of social evolution, which has gone on as long as societies have existed.

Or, think of the differentiation and integration visible on a modern film set. Some people who once wrote, performed, sang and designed now restrict themselves, formally, through union membership, to acting, screenwriting, cinematography, makeup, or set design. Yet all of these people performing differentiated tasks must work together to realize a shot, a scene, a complete film. What was in ancient times an art form of declaration is now a complex organization (an integration) of clearly divided (differentiated) tasks.

People who study change from an evolutionary perspective often take a functionalist approach. They focus on **social statics**, the processes that keep societies stable. Social institutions that do this include the family, churches, mass media and the educational system — all of which develop and spread the culture of a society. They also include institutions that slow change and resolve conflicts.

They argue that in tightly integrated societies, a change in one part will cause changes in the other parts. A social system continually adjusts to the flow of new, often conflicting demands — political, economic, cultural and so on — from its many subsystems. It does this by continually, but slowly, differentiating and integrating.

Not all evolutionary theories are functionalist, however. Emergent norm theory, for example, looks at the processes which bring people to a shared understanding of their situation. Emergent norms differ from one situation to another. By attaching meanings to these situations, people create appropriate norms to which they can commit themselves.

An example of this is the evolution of "netiquette." Communication through e-mail, or on the Internet, is different from face-to-face communication in a great many ways, not least because it is impossible to "read" a person's facial expression or body language and make appropriate adjustments. For this reason, people have had to learn new ways of expressing and censoring themselves — and controlling the behaviour of others. In short, to make the Internet a viable social system, they have had to invent and enforce a new social etiquette. This etiquette continues to evolve without clear planning or centralized control: it emerges spontaneously, making possible a new kind of social life.

How could it be otherwise? As we learn from Everyday Life, below, few of us — even science fiction writers who speculate endlessly about the future — are able to foresee the changes that will occur in our lives and our societies. More often than not, we find ourselves forced to adjust to changes that are already upon us and, for the most part, we adjust creatively by inventing new rules, roles and forms of organization. It is this fact of social life which led Max Weber to argue that we should never look for simple explanations or deterministic theories of social organization.

Unlike most of the theories we will be discussing, emergent norm theory is a symbolic interactionist theory of social change. It is also useful in explaining the development and persistence of **social movements**, of which we will say more later. Like other evolutionary theories, emergent norm theory views social change as the gradual result of thousands, even millions, of actions, interactions and interpretations.

Revolutionary Theories   By contrast, the other main orientation holds that social change is revolutionary in character. According to this view, the change from one social order to the next is typically abrupt and occasionally violent. The new order is differ-

EVERYDAY LIFE

Through the Crystal Ball Darkly

Truth, if you just look at it the right (i.e., sociological) way, is stranger than fiction. Everyday life is always throwing us curve balls, sliders and spitters. That's what makes predicting the future so very difficult, as the following excerpt shows. It makes us realize that some of the futures that social thinkers are so glibly predicting these days — for example, the end of history (or unquestioned triumph of the market economy), the end of work as we know it and the enhancement of human freedom by the information highway — are probably far off the mark.

What I'd like to talk about are some of the futures we sf writers could never have imagined that have come true.

The recent fuss about evidences of life on ancient Mars brings up the most obvious and appalling: In 80-some years of commercial sf, not one writer ever predicted, even as a joke, that humanity would achieve the means to conquer space — and then throw it away. None of us guessed there might be raised up a generation so dull and dreamless they would not realize (or listen when they were told) that incalculable wealth, inexhaustible energy and unlimited adventure are hanging in the sky right over their heads, a mere 250 miles away, at the upper limit of the ionosphere where one escapes Earth's gravity and it doesn't take an extra dime to reach *any* destination.

The next most obvious example: I don't think one sf writer predicted the quiet collapse of the Soviet Union. Even the most liberal of us accepted without question the seeming truism that a slave state could never collapse until the last proletarian was expended. Apparently with all our vaunted exploration of the behaviour of alien cultures, we failed to do enough homework on one of the most prominent ones available for study on *this* planet.

Many sf writers have hopefully predicted the eventual conquest of all diseases. But none of us could have dreamed that one day mankind's oldest and deadliest scourge, the taker of more human lives than any other single cause — smallpox — would be eradicated from the planet, utterly and forever and the event would arouse no notice at all. Did they have a party on *your* block when the last smallpox vaccines were destroyed a while back? Was there a parade in *your* town, honouring the heroes and heroines who avenged millions of our tortured, disfigured and slain ancestors? Are you familiar with their current efforts to do the same for polio, chicken pox, diphtheria and other diseases?

Several sf writers foresaw the VCR. Not one of us ever guessed that by the time it arrived, a sizable fraction of the populace would feel incompetent to operate one. We still have trouble grasping that there are people with shoes on who find it a challenge to set a watch, twice, and specify a channel number. Even harder to understanding why some of them seem proud of it.

I haven't checked, but I'm sure that at least some sf writers predicted the disposable lighter — and that none ever envisioned a feature mandated by law that would make the lighters virtually useless for senior citizens, musicians and invalids, while perfectly accessible to toddlers. Nor could any of the thousands of us who foresaw computers, or even the dozens who foresaw personal computers, have guessed that in the end an operating system that Spoke Human would be supplanted by one that required you to learn to Speak Computer.

Source: Abridged from Spider Robinson, *The Globe and Mail*, Sept. 2, 1996, p. A11

ent in kind from the old one and breaks with the past profoundly. Because of their interest in qualitative change, revolutionary theorists look for turning points in history — "revolutions" — whether these are political, cultural, technological or otherwise.

Revolutionary theorists, for example, would emphasize the ways in which our society *differs* from feudal England or slave-holding Athens. They would point out basic social changes caused by the printing press, industrialism, the French Revolution, nuclear energy, the population explosion, genetic engineering and changes in the ozone layer. The notion of a "Judeo-Christian civilization" would be meaningless to such a theorist.

The emphasis here is on *social dynamics*, all the factors that promote change and can be seen as turning points in world history. The best-known example of a revolutionary theory is Marxism. Marx's theory argued that as a result of changes in the means of production, Western society has undergone a number of revolutionary changes during which almost all social, economic and political relationships among people have been completely transformed.

According to German sociologist Georg Simmel, the invention of money marked a turning point in history. Simmel claims that the spread of money had an important social and cultural effect by creating links between more people than ever before. The social connections it created were new and impersonal. Money lets us do business with a lot of people we don't know and care nothing about. What's more, money lets us spend our wealth where and when we want to. Unlike perishable food and live animals, money can be accumulated and stored forever, freely exchanged when convenient and passed down from one generation to the next. In these ways, money breaks down primary social ties and encourages individualism. Ultimately, having money even becomes an end in itself, signifying freedom and success.

Revolutionary theorists look for major changes in people's ways of thinking and behaving. The sources of change can be anything. Unlike 19th-century theorists, few sociologists today try to make a single, general law they can apply to all social change. The thinking about "evolution" and "revolution" which prevailed in the past was based on Western ideas of progress and the natural law that structured relations between God and humanity, humanity and nature, one class and another, and men and women. Such general ideas are no longer very useful. Though many use the ideas of "post-industrialism" and "globalization" to cover a large variety of economic, cultural and political changes, few believe that these changes necessarily signify "progress" (in the sense of providing better lives for more people).

Most theorists recognize that the effects of change depend on the social context within which change takes place. The Western idea of progress — that people can remake society by applying reason and political will — is no longer the prevailing ideology. That is why most sociologists today have more modest goals: they examine changes within a particular society or social institution.

One important focus is on the role politics play in social change. For one thing, all social change has political consequences. And often, social change begins with a political act. So, in much of this chapter we will focus on the role played by political actors, such as the state and protest movements, in bringing about social change.

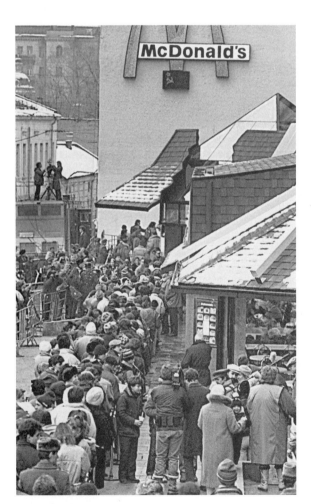

McDonald's has conquered Moscow, something that Napoleon and Hitler weren't able to do.

POLITICS Even more than political scientists, sociologists are interested in the social and cultural context of politics which leads to changes in the laws, political institutions and voting patterns of a society. This means that sociologists study a larger number of variables than political scientists usually do. Sociologists are also interested in what some call "micro-politics" — the politics of everyday life. Politics is not limited to the state. It is an activity in which people and groups struggle for control over resources, such as wealth, status and power. Schools, businesses and even families are governed by politics and, within these institutions, people vie for control. One of sociology's goals is to reveal the hidden politics of everyday life and develop political theories that apply to all social institutions.

For example, we may study the growth of feminist goals and ideas within mainstream social institutions such as the military or the Catholic Church. Or, we may observe the processes by which neighbourhoods organize to oppose group homes for the mentally ill. In this way, we discover which groups are more likely to mobilize and which are most likely to achieve their goals.

An important debate within political sociology is over the question of how power is exercised by dominant or ruling groups. Those who follow sociologist Antonio Gramsci — himself an intellectual descendant of Marx — acknowledge the importance of the state and its coercive apparatus, but place equal importance on mechanisms of social and cultural control. In their eyes, both civil society (discussed below) and ideology serve to manufacture and reinforce consent of the governed. They keep in place social obligations which personalize the need to conform — turning public issues into personal problems — and legitimate ideas that say people must keep doing what they are doing. (These are exemplified by structures like the "hidden curriculum" discussed in Chapter 3 and notions like "traditional family values" popularized in the mass media.)

But for French sociologist Michel Foucault, the structuring of power is even more subtle and consists of the elaboration of techniques and practices which shape the patterns of people's thinking. "Regimes of truth" order our knowledge, our systems of categorization, our belief and our practices. For example, the commonplace notion that "Everyone is different" is not only an erroneous assumption about human beings, at least, in sociologists' eyes; it also supports the status quo by discouraging comparison, communication and cooperation. In effect, it keeps public issues hidden in the form of personal problems. One consequence is an obscuring of the difference — indeed, the gap — between rulers and ruled. Another is the multiplication of strategies and practices of resistance. Finally, and because of these, the third consequence is increased difficulty in finding common ground among people who practise resistance.

We will return to these issues near the end of the chapter. But note that, to the extent it is possible to identify a centre of control and domination in our society, the best place to start looking is the state.

The Role of the State

To repeat, within any social unit — family, school, local community, state, or otherwise — any conflict over resources is a political conflict. But among social units, the state has a special part to play, for it always monitors and attempts to control the ways groups compete.

The *state* is that set of public organizations that makes and enforces decisions that are binding upon every member of a society (Weber, 1946). It includes the elected government, civil service, courts, police and military. The right to use violence puts muscle behind these state decisions, and only a member of the police or military has the legitimate "right" to use violence without fear of punishment. In many societies, politics converts the struggle for state power into a competition for electoral votes. Both the need to gain electoral popularity, and constitutional rules, limit the state's use of raw force. In this way, "civil society" is able to exercise some degree of control over the state.

The term *civil society* is used to refer to all of society except the state. This includes such important institutions as labour unions, churches, business organizations, charities and interest groups; also people's private (personal, family and work) lives. Sociologists have long studied the relationship between the state and civil society. In fact, the distinction between state and civil society dates back to Thomas Hobbes, an English philosopher who lived three centuries ago. It marks the attempt by liberal thinkers to "define a private sphere independent of the state, thus freeing civil society from political interference" (Held, 1989: 13). In that sense, civil society refers to relationships among people that are indepondant of state interference.

The Authoritarian State

At one extreme of political life, we find the authoritarian state, which attempts to fully dominate civil society and represses political dissent. Such states are usually made all-powerful by politically active military and police forces. Often, a military dictator rules the authoritarian state.

An authoritarian state allows to civil society no independence. It penetrates everyday life fully and, compared to the form of government we have in Canada, it is extremely repressive. Such a state intervenes in the economy and social life, for example, often by uniting some social groups and excluding others. In Argentina between 1976 and 1980, the state even controlled the dress and hairstyle of ordinary citizens. Far more chilling is the way government violently represses opposing political views. In Latin America, governments have dealt with political opponents by kidnapping, torturing, imprisoning and even murdering them. Amnesty International reports that such practices are to be found in many other countries as well. In some cases, like China, Myanmar (Burma), Indonesia and Iraq, the goal is suppression of popular dissent. In other cases, like Rwanda or Sri Lanka, the goal is victory in a long-lasting civil war.

Weak political parties and party systems make it easier for dictators to achieve authoritarian power. So does help from the large financial and agriculture-exporting elites. In his classic study of political systems, Barrington Moore (1966) argues that authoritarian fascist governments appear where the middle class is smaller and weaker than the landed aristocracy. As a result, social change typically takes place "from the top down." This describes the Latin American experience well, just as it describes early 20th-century Italy, Germany and Japan.

However, one significant change in recent years has been the success of democratic movements in challenging authoritarian regimes throughout the world. Naturally, political sociologists have tried to explain how and why this occurs.

Usually, the road to democracy requires a reduction of support for the authoritarian leader. This support decays at the point when even devoted supporters can see that the government isn't working well. For example, an economic crisis in Brazil increased patriotic, anti-government sentiments. In the end, even the military turned against the government. And in South Korea, support for the dictatorship eroded because opinions within the ruling group itself came into conflict. As well, educated, middle-class Koreans became less willing to follow traditional Confucian ideas about authority and hierarchy.

As you might imagine, the change from an authoritarian to a democratic system is a long, hard process. Usually, it demands changes in both attitudes and political bodies. In Russia, the change from authoritarianism to democracy has required economic and legal reforms. It has also required reforms to deal with the collapse of old myths and promote the acceptance of new ones. In the end, democracy needs its citizens to trust the state and believe that the state will devote itself to their welfare. However, the failure of economic reforms to bring about an improved standard of living has forced pro-democracy leaders to scale back on their promises and once again exercise powers that are not in the Constitution.

The State and Civil Society

The value of civil society is clearest wherever states try to limit it; for example, by controlling people's private lives. In this sense, the communist states in Eastern Europe controlled civil society for more than forty years. This created problems that persist today, when people need a strong civil society to help establish democracy and a market economy. Yet social relations are marked by suspicion and distrust that are slow to disappear.

Under communism, people in Poland, for example, learned to be highly dependent on the state. The result was widespread social apathy. Today, both political and social involvement are lacking in Poland. The needed civil society is developing very slowly.

The distinction between state and civil society can be useful, especially in authoritarian countries. But it tends to confuse our understanding of North American society. For example, it encourages us to view the state as always repressive and bureaucratic. It also leads us to think of relations between civil society and the state as conflict-ridden. It implies that there is an inevitable barrier between the state and the rest of society. Finally, it suggests that the state is a unified body with clear interests, goals and policies.

Many would disagree with these views of the relationship between the state and the rest of society, at least as they apply to Canada. In Canada, some see the state as an impartial referee which mediates among society's varied interest groups. Others see it responding only to the interests of the dominant capitalist class. Still others, in Canada and elsewhere, see the state as largely autonomous; though it serves the interests of dominant groups or class factions, it does not automatically obey their wishes.

The state, as Canadians experience it, is not a unified body with a clear, integrated policy. It is a set of separate agencies and agents with whom citizens interact in different ways, at different times, and for different reasons. And in Canada, the state is visibly "fragmented." Constitutional crises that have plagued the country in recent years prove that the federal government must perpetually struggle to control the wilful provincial governments. Nothing shows the fragmentation of the Canadian state more clearly than the growth of regional politics in the 1990s. The rise of the Reform Party of Canada and the Bloc Québécois to prominence in the national Parliament illustrates this fragmentation.

The fragmentation of the state can also be seen in the failure of the federal government to exercise control over the Canadian military after the killing of civilians in Somalia. An inquiry was set up because the federal government was unable to get to the bottom of the matter by the usual chain of command. Unfortunately, the inquiry too was stymied by the refusal of the military to cooperate or the refusal of senior officers to take responsibility for their subordinates' actions. While the minister of defence is supposed to be in charge of the military, it is such a large, complex and segmented organization with its own internal politics and loyalties, state control over it breaks down when operational details come to be considered.

In Canada, it is no easy matter to distinguish the state from "civil society." To assume a clear boundary exists between the two is to underestimate how much the state invades the rest of society. In truth, the state regulates *most* aspects of Canadian life. And because the state is "embedded in our socioeconomic systems," we cannot treat it as distinct from those systems (Held, 1989: 2). The state is a set of institutions or agencies that structures the relationships among all sectors of society. For these reasons, many recent theorists have stopped distinguishing between the state and civil society. In their eyes, the state is *not* distinct from society; it is embedded in our social relations. In fact, "politics" pervades all social life, and vice versa.

The educational system, for example, is part of both the state and civil society. After all, a school must follow ministerial rules, and it must also consider the relationships among teachers, students and parents. No one can understand education practices in a particular province without referring to the civil *and* state activities which make up the educational sector. Many groups — politicians, bureaucrats, trustees, administrators, teachers, students, parents, lobby groups, professors of education, journalists, taxpayers and "concerned citizens," among others — all engage in school politics.

ELITES

Despite the popular rhetoric about democracy, most states, Canada's included, reflect the activities and views of political elites. An **elite** is a relatively small group of people with power or influence over many others. Typically, the elite hold positions of authority in society's dominant organizations.

Elite Accommodation

In Canada, elites from different sectors of society struggle to promote the goals of their own groups. Each has some power in this struggle but, usually, none has enough power to prevail over all the others. Consequently, elites must cooperate to achieve their goals. Appropriately, this process is called "elite accommodation."

In the long run, *elite accommodation* furthers the interests of all the groups the elites represent. So whatever their source of power, elites are committed to keeping things as they are. They want to avoid upsetting a social order that works to their advantage. As well, they often share a common set of values. In part, that is because members of elites often interact with one another. Many are acquaintances, friends or members of the same social class, with similar school backgrounds.

On the other hand, though they are tied together socially, politically and culturally, elites often fight to further their own group or organizations' interests. There is an inevitable conflict between governing and nongoverning elites, for example. This is what makes democracy such a precarious form of government. And it is through such clashes of interest between elites that much social change comes about.

In Canada, John Porter's *The Vertical Mosaic* (1965) has given the most sustained attention to this idea of accommodating elites. The book concludes that continuity and change in Canadian society are the product of acts, or failures to act, by Canadian elites. According to Porter, Canada is controlled by five cooperating elite groups comprising people in the top positions of five broad areas of Canadian society: the major economic corporations, political organizations, government bureaucracies, labour organizations and ideological (that is, religious, educational and media) organizations.

Of the five elite subgroups, two are more powerful than the rest. In first place, the economic (or "corporate") elite has been most successful of all in ensuring that its interests are served. Canada's corporate elite, the top executives of major Canadian corporations, is Canada's dominant elite. In second place is the bureaucratic elite, made up of high-ranking civil servants — the so-called "mandarins" of government. Federal bureaucrats are the most powerful civil servants, followed closely by high-ranking personnel of the largest provincial bureaucracies.

The corporate and bureaucratic elites are powerful because of the enormous economic resources each commands and because they employ large segments of the Canadian working population. Both sectors also provide elites with better-paying and more stable careers than politicians and labour leaders typically enjoy. This enables the corporate and bureaucratic sectors to recruit many talented people for membership.

FAR AND AWAY

"Our President, Today, Tomorrow and Forever"

In Canada, people sometimes complain that our political leaders are unremarkable — even unnoticeable. There is relatively little confidence expressed in politicians and we expect little from them. And, most of our politicians make a career of running for and holding political office. How different this is from many parts of the world, where few are experienced in politics yet people expect their leaders to display remarkable, even exemplary traits. One common figure in the less-developed world is the military "strongman" who seizes power and holds on to it with a combination of charisma, trickery and violence.

In the Central African backwater of Equatorial Guinea, in the country's first so-called multiparty elections, the long-time ruler Brigadeer-General Teodoro Obiang Nguema Mbasogo seems to prefer to see his followers rigging voting lists and beating up opponents. In the country's first multiparty election in 28 years, held in February, Mr. Nguema retained his job with 99 per cent of the votes and an apt campaign slogan: "Our president, today, tomorrow and forever."

The return of the African strongman may not be surprising in countries where democracy is about as deeply rooted as satellite television. "Democracy in Africa is fairly shallow and fragile anyway, but the greater threat is the horrendous economic conditions," says Richard Sandbrook, a political-science professor at the University of Toronto. "It would be miraculous if democracy survives in many of these countries."

After 20 years of economic decline, governments across the continent have slashed subsidies, closed factories and axed thousands of coveted public-sector jobs. Add to that low literacy levels, tribal divisions and displaced societies, and you have "the worst possible conditions to develop democracy in," says Professor Sandbrook.

There are exceptions, to be sure. In two coup-prone states, Sierra Leone and the Comoros, voters lined up at polls in recent weeks to elect civilian governments to replace their military leaders. Even Nigeria says it will hold proper elections within three years, although most of the world remains incredulous.

But there can be little doubt that authoritarianism is again stalking the continent. Over the past two years, four West African governments have fallen to military coups, Niger being the most recent in January. Many more countries have managed to sidestep a multiparty system entirely. According to a study at Georgetown University in Washington, D.C., 35 out of 48 countries in sub-Saharan Africa have held multiparty elections in the past five years, but 17 of them "did not bring about significant change in the direction of democracy." In another four — Angola, Burundi, Gambia and Nigeria — election results were later cancelled. Another seven elections were "seriously flawed."

In many of these cases, a return to autocracy has been an easy sell to populations that have grown disenchanted with enduring poverty, chronic corruption and seemingly ineffective governments.

Source: Abridged from John Stackhouse, *The Globe and Mail*, Sat., April 6, 1996, p. D3

However, in other societies, other institutions provide the elites who become most socially and politically prominent. An example is the role of the military in Africa, discussed in Far and Away, above. There and in other countries with less developed economic and bureaucratic elites, the military "strongman" is a fixture of political life. But more often than not, these military dictators draw their strength from the assistance, cooperation or tacit approval of bureaucratic and economic elites in other, more developed societies. And more often than not, the reason foreign elites turn a blind eye to the violence and lawlessness of military dictators is that it suits their interests as a dominant political or economic class. So, understanding elites here or elsewhere requires that we understand the interests of the world's most powerful people.

Class versus Elite Analysis

Some sociologists disagree with Porter's analysis. They argue that Canada's dominant economic elite duplicates the capitalist class structure. Thus we need to analyze classes, not elites, to understand how power is used in Canadian society.

By this reasoning, what appear to be other elites really consists of agents of the economic elite. Thus, elite accommodation is actually cooperation among capitalists and their agents, and class interests overrule state, family, community and other interests. In the end, the economy dominates all other social institutions, and the capitalist class dominates the economy.

Class theorists further argue that: (1) the state and its offshoots (such as the courts and legislatures) serve the interests of the capitalist class; (2) schools, media and organized religion serve to "legitimate" or justify unequal economic power and give the interests of capitalism moral authority; and (3) decision-making in our society is closed and hierarchical (anti-democratic), though it is designed to appear open and democratic.

Indeed, class theorists argue that Canada's corporate elite does not necessarily take into account only Canada's economic interests. The corporate elite of a country may be tightly tied into the corporate elite of other countries, especially that of the United States. It is necessary, therefore, to distinguish between **comprador** elites and **indigenous** elites within the Canadian corporate elite. Comprador elites work for foreign-owned companies in Canada. By contrast, indigenous elites control firms that are Canadian-owned.

Porter, for his part, stopped short of concluding that there is a dominant capitalist class. He rejected this possibility because he found the Marxist theory of the state, in which "the economic . . . system is the master" (1965: 206), too simplistic. Porter remained impressed by the "counteracting power" of the other elites (1965: 522-23)

Whichever view we adopt, there is little doubt that elites play an important, if largely invisible, role in Canadian life. Elites are able to dominate, in part because they are more unified and less confused about their interests than other groups in Canadian society.

Can You Get into the Elite?

Societies vary in the extent to which their elites (political, intellectual, economic and so on) form a cohesive ruling group. Where such a group exists, the ruling elite makes decisions affecting everyone else. In most societies, the children of people who are elite members have the best chance to enter the elite themselves.

Certain general findings about elites hold for Canada as well as for India, Britain and other Western countries. However, there are also unique features that make it necessary for us to examine the Canadian elites more closely. Canada is different from many Western countries in the following ways:

- there has never been a landed aristocracy in Canada;

- a significant portion of the Canadian economy is controlled by foreign-owned (especially American-owned) multinational corporations;

- the state has always played a particularly vigorous part in Canada's social and economic development;

- Canada has always had a high rate of immigration; and

- the Canadian population and economy have grown rapidly and unevenly since the Second World War.

The fact that there has never been a landed aristocracy in Canada has probably made it much easier for people to move into elite positions. In Canada, as in the United States, great wealth and power — even recently acquired — are

SOCIAL PROFILE 11.1

Public and Elite Views on the Role of Government (Questions Asked in February 1994)

Some of the traditional roles of government are under pressure and some people are expecting different things from government in the future. I am going to read you a list of possible future roles for government. For each one, I would like you to rate how appropriate you think that role will be on a scale from 0 to 100 where 0 is not at all appropriate, the midpoint 50 means somewhat appropriate and 100 means extremely appropriate.

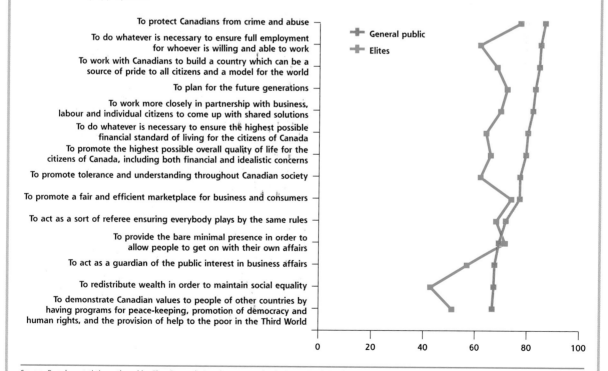

Source: Based on statistics gathered by Ekos Research Associates, appearing in Peters, *Exploring Canada Values*, CPRN Study No. F/01

enough to gain a person entry into most social circles. But converting money into social acceptance has always been harder and slower in Europe, where family lineage has counted for more.

Clement (1975) found more upward mobility into comprador elite positions in Canada than into indigenous elite positions. Most likely, this indicates that (Canadian-owned) financial institutions recruit more conservatively than (American-owned) industrial organizations.

The important role of the state in Canada's economy has meant that government (especially civil-service) elites are as important as corporate elites. So mobility into corporate-elite positions has to resemble mobility into government-elite positions. Indeed, Porter found many similarities in the backgrounds of corporate- and civil-service elite groups, including an over-representation of upper-class people in both (by comparison with their presence in the population at large.)

The Canadian elite has been changing, and so has the opportunity for upward mobility into the elite. Although Clement argues that this opportunity has shrunk since Porter's research twenty years earlier, little evidence supports that view. On the contrary, evidence suggests that new players have entered the elite in the last thirty years and this number may continue to grow.

Still, unless you are the child of a member of this elite, your chances of entering it are very small. The fact that a few people do enter the elite from below does not prove that Canada is a meritocracy — a system in which leaders are selected on the basis of talent and achievement. The key to gaining elite status is still financial capital, cultural capital, good luck and having the right parents.

IDEOLOGIES

Despite the important role that elites play in society, most Canadians do not see their society as dominated by elites. In large part that is because most Canadians accept an ideology of Canada as an equalitarian society. **Ideologies** are beliefs that "explain" how society is, or should be, organized. In North America, we are used to ideological debates on political and economic topics. People use ideologies to interpret and react to events in the real world. Ideologies are important for social change because they motivate and control people.

In a sense, "myths" and "trust" play important roles in social and political life. Before people can change their political order, they must imagine a new order worth working for. They must have faith in that vision and in the leaders they expect to carry out that vision. This means that, in changing a society, people create and accept ideologies.

In this way, ideologies influence the distribution of power. Sometimes, they prevent social protest and social change; at other times, they make change easier. Ideological debates arise in widely varying areas of life: for example, Should Canada admit more refugees? Should marijuana use be decriminalized? Is a foetus a person, entitled to legal rights like other people?

Such debates are hard to resolve. That is because most people are sure they are right and equally sure that people on the other side are wrong. Usually, both sides fail to see that their opinion is just a belief, not the absolute truth. In fact, ideologies can never be proven or falsified by scientific means. And when people adopt these ideas, they usually don't know they are learning or believing in anything at all. They think they are discovering the "truth."

Ideology and Control

There are two main types of ideology. On the one hand, *reformist* and *radical ideologies* rally the forces of change. We will say more about these in a little while. On the other hand, *dominant ideologies* support the "status quo" or existing power structure. We call them "dominant" to point out their role in controlling people. Whether an ideology is dominant is something we can learn only through empirical research. We consider it "dominant" if the most powerful or socially dominant groups in society sponsor it and if it also supports the interests of these groups.

The popular belief in "winners" and "losers" — in people getting what they deserve and deserving what they get, and in social action being a game with a scoreboard — is an ideology that is "dominant" in this sense. In turn, the dominant ideology is an important part of popular culture and entertainment. In American culture, for example, a high value is placed on heroism and war. This makes it easy for American politicians to mobilize public sentiment behind activities like the Gulf War, and before that, the long-standing Cold War.

In the former Soviet Union, the dominant communist ideology infused every aspect of social and political life. By North American standards, Soviet sociology was very biased in that it denied legitimacy to a variety of opinions. Three sets of ideas dominated what sociologists could and could not say in public. They were Marxist-Leninist theory's vision of an ideal socialist society, the Soviet ideology which emphasized the goal of political order, and a development ideology which emphasized the goal of industrial productivity.

Everywhere, dominant ideologies influence political life by shaping *public opinion*. However, there is no single "public" in industrial societies. A wide range of social types — the result of a complex division of labour, large-scale immigration and relatively easy social mobility — creates a variety of "publics." Each has its own opinions, values and interests.

Any particular "public" is an unstructured set of people. Like the members of a "cohort" we discussed in Chapter 10, the members of a "public" do not interact with one another and are rarely aware of belonging to the same group. All we really mean by a "public" is a set of people who hold certain interests in, views on or concerns about a particular issue.

In principle, public opinion should be central to any democracy since what we mean by a "democracy" is "government by the people." A Latin proverb says *vox populi, vox dei*, meaning "the voice of the people is the voice of God." In a democratic society, this proverb should be the guiding principle, and to some degree it is, since polls measure people's sentiments and politicians follow the polls. And polls measure public opinion quite accurately. However, they also manipulate or shape public opinion. As well, they impute certainty or "facticity" to opinions that often are in flux, creating something out of nothing.

The *bandwagon effect* is one example of the way opinion polls influence public opinion. People like being part of a group that has succeeded: they want to "get on the bandwagon." The bandwagon effect shows up in post-election polls, when a much larger number of voters claim to have voted for the winning candidate than did so. After the fact, people adopt opinions that are popular *because* they are popular. They may even support a politician who seems likely to win (i.e., according to the pre-election polls) just because they want to back a winner.

Political and other public-opinion polls contribute to this illusion-making, but journalists play a far larger role when they report propaganda under the guise of news. **Propaganda** is any idea or doctrine that is spread for the purpose of influencing people's opinions and actions. It includes all attempts to influence other people's thoughts and opinions. In this sense, Sunday-school lessons, advertising and election campaigns are all propaganda. In fact, propaganda is any information that represents itself as pure, unquestionable truth.

Not surprisingly, people are becoming more skeptical about the information they receive and the people who control government. Survey data show that Canadians distrust politicians more than almost anyone else (including advertising executives, who have never been famous for their honesty.) The best way to protect against a blind acceptance of propaganda is education, an openness to new information and a tolerance for ambiguity. It is particularly important to be willing to consider different views of a single issue.

Ideology and Protest

Ideologies can dominate us, but they can also empower us by helping people to form protest groups. In this way, they increase the chance that people

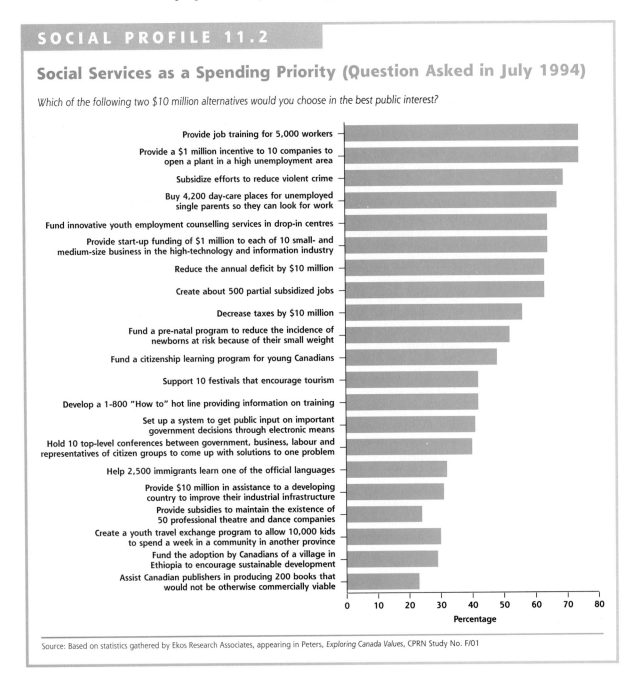

SOCIAL PROFILE 11.2

Social Services as a Spending Priority (Question Asked in July 1994)

Which of the following two $10 million alternatives would you choose in the best public interest?

Source: Based on statistics gathered by Ekos Research Associates, appearing in Peters, *Exploring Canada Values*, CPRN Study No. F/01

will protest against, and improve, their life chances. Ideologies that advocate change are either radical or reformist. Those who support *reformist ideologies* call for changes without challenging the basic ground rules. In Canada, the provision of medicare, welfare and unemployment insurance are reforms that were based on this kind of ideology. These programs were intended as "safety nets" to help people who got into trouble.

Unemployment insurance, however, does not prevent unemployment. It does not create jobs. It makes unemployment less harmful without changing the factors that create unemployment.

Radical ideologies, on the other hand, call for a complete reshaping of society. This is what the Co-operative Commonwealth Federation (CCF) — parent of today's reformist New Democratic Party — did at its founding in 1933, when it adopted the Regina Manifesto. This manifesto declared, "No CCF government will rest content until it has eradicated capitalism and put into operation the full programme of socialized planning which will lead to the establishment in Canada of the co-operative commonwealth."

The reform and radical ideologies we find in any society are what sociologists call *counter ideologies*. They are "counter" in the sense that they challenge the bases of the dominant ideologies. They also expose the interests that dominant ideologies serve and offer people a different vision of society.

Often, counter ideologies develop out of people's responses to experiences of unequal treatment. Counter ideologies call the status quo to account and deny legitimacy to customary ways of treating people. So, for example, feminism is a counter ideology that undermines sexism and traditional ways of treating people. Feminism as a *counterculture*, to which it is closely tied, promotes ideas and behaviours which are less immediately political. (For example, feminist academic and artistic works interpret women's experience.)

Groups which promote counter ideologies get their message out to people in many ways, particularly through public meetings and the media. Intellectuals and other highly educated people (called the "intelligentsia") often play an important part in promoting counter ideologies. The Polish intelligentsia, for example, played a major part in the Solidarity movement during the early 1980s. And in both Poland and Hungary, the intelligentsia has helped to create a civil society since the collapse of communism.

SOCIAL MOVEMENTS

Often, social change results from the success of social protest movements (or "social movements"). The term **social movement** refers to any form of collective act that promotes or resists change in a society. Such movements usually engage in both political acts and media campaigns to get their views across and ensure that they achieve their goals. English-rights political groups in Quebec and western-rights political groups in Alberta are two social movements that have engaged in political action.

Some social movements are more visible than others. For example, the struggle of environmentalists against clear-cut logging in Clayoquot (British Columbia) made maximum use of the mass media to gain a lot of visibility. On the other hand, social movements supporting minority rights have, in the past, lobbied behind the scenes to get laws enacted that punished discrimination based on gender or race. For them, public visibility would not have contributed to ultimate legislative success.

We do not consider such actions by people who already have power or influence to be part of a social movement. We reserve the term "social movement" for people who are seeking power or change, and who mobilize in large numbers. These are *not* defining features of the Canadian business elite.

Social movements are the result of a conscious reaction to social changes, or a conscious effort to bring about social changes. They may support any one of many social issues: abortion on demand, an end to storing toxic waste in a community, a nuclear-weapon-free Canada, an end to seal hunting, opposition to free trade and so on. Whatever its specific concern, every social movement is guided by a particular ideology and generates propaganda that explains its cause to the public.

Generally, social movements arise out of a feeling that society is not working properly and needs changing. In China, an alliance between students and workers in 1989 led to the Tiananmen Square protests and subsequent massacre. Some say this protest resulted from a lack of Western-style democracy, but it may have resulted from the entry of Western and Asian capital into China. The entry of capital raised living standards but also led to massive corruption, new (and less secure) employment practices and a wider gap between the richest and the poorest.

Relative Deprivation

One important theory — *relative deprivation theory* — argues that movements arise when large numbers of people feel deprived in comparison with other people. They feel there is a gap between the social rewards they are getting and those they are entitled to get. Or they feel cheated when they compare their own lives with those of others. Such people have a strong desire to join a social movement whose goal is to change the distribution of social rewards.

Relative deprivation is largely subjective and even temporary, compared to *absolute* deprivation — a serious, visible and lengthy lack of social rewards. Yet social scientists agree that *relative deprivation* is more likely to cause social movements to form than absolute deprivation. Indeed, social movements gain the strongest support when there is a "revolution of rising expectations" (Runciman, 1966).

People typically protest under improving conditions, not grinding, desperate poverty. For one thing, improvement makes it easier for people to protest, because they are now not so fully preoccupied with the struggle to survive. When people's lives improve, their expectations for change often grow faster than the rate at which change takes place. What this tells us is that, with much of the world yet to industrialize and achieve a reasonable standard of living, we can expect much more protest in the coming years. As we learn from Far and Away, below, there are many battles yet to be fought between the powerful and the dispossessed, and this means that, despite the end of conflicts between capitalism and communism, we are not yet entering a millennium of peace and tranquillity.

Feelings of frustration and discontent are caused by a sense of deprivation. They are *necessary* for a social movement to emerge; a movement will not form without them. Still, they are not enough by themselves to get a movement going. Many discontented people never join, let alone form, social movements. Another condition — the possibility of **resource mobilization** — must be met before a movement forms.

Resource Mobilization

Resource mobilization theory addresses the methods people use to put forward their views. This theory does not look at *why* people want to promote or resist social change, but at *how* they launch social movements. It sees social movements in terms of the ability of discontented people to organize.

FAR AND AWAY

New Violence and Protest Ahead?

In Canada, we have long been accustomed to the idea — and often the reality — of "peace, order and good government" promised in the British North America Act — so much so that it is difficult to imagine conditions which are radically and dreadfully different. But elsewhere in the world, history has been less kind, so expert observers warn of growing war and disorder in the future. In a shrinking, interdependent world, Canada may not escape unscathed.

Social scientists are predicting new levels of violence, crime, and civil protest around the world, for three reasons:

- growing inequalities of wealth, both among and within countries;

- ecological changes that intensify the competition for declining resources; and

- the emergence of a new dispossessed class in all countries.

Taken as a package, these explosive trends signal a "revolution of unfulfilled expectations" and a growing "revolt of the dispossessed." Increasingly, the world's poor are taking up arms to challenge the odds against them. And why not? One per cent of the world controls 60 per cent of its resources, while 80 per cent of the global population scrambles for a mere 15 per cent of its resources.

Most people are slow to recognize the deep divisions within their own societies, and slower still to notice even deeper divisions between societies. But thinking ahead, we all may have to prepare for a coming crisis in our political and economic institutions. Here's a safe bet: the world's wealthy will act to ensure their own security and well-being. Social dissent and public disorder on the massive scale predicted may easily produce a backlash, leading to authoritarian government within societies and a search for outside scapegoats — hence, wars — between societies.

No less explosive is the foreseeable fight over physical resources. Dire social and political problems are already evident in the world's cities, where the cost of fuel, shelter, food and water is escalating and environmental conditions are worsening. And in a rapidly urbanized world, concerns about pollution, sanitation and water supplies are bound to mobilize more and more people. An estimated 600 million people are already homeless or live in life-threatening conditions, and this number is expected to triple within thirty years unless humanity's problem-solving skills improve dramatically.

Half the world's rural poor — more than a billion people — now live without enough land to provide food for themselves. Like other peasants in history, they are starting to rise in protest when they can't take it anymore: witness the uprising of the Zapatistas in southern Mexico and Hezbollah in Syria. Since the early 1990s there have also been food riots in Haiti, Central America and the Philippines. In the end, these political acts are a reaction against global development that relentlessly pursues profits and ignores people.

Source: Adapted from an article by John Vidal, *The Guardian* (London); reprinted in *The Globe and Mail*, June 15, 1996, p. D4

Without discontent, there would be no social movements. Yet discontentment is a constant of human life: it is always lurking in the background, waiting to express itself. Without the movement of resources, discontent can never express itself as a social force. It remains hidden or comes out in nonpolitical, personal pathologies: random violence, mental illness, heavy drinking and so on. No wonder data from the United States, the Netherlands and Germany show that group mobilization and the availability of resources are better predictors of political activism than personal values and dissatisfaction.

Important elements in "getting organized" include using resources such as effective leadership, public support, money, legal aid, ties with influential officials and public personalities and access to the mass media. Occasionally, organizing also means acquiring, and learning to use, weapons. Without access to key resources, discontented people cannot change society or resist the powerful, and they rarely attempt it. Thus, the successes and failures of social movements indicate a change in access to key resources, and not necessarily a change in levels of contentment. Likewise, an absence of protest movements does not prove that people are contented. More often, it proves that the state can suppress protest when it wishes and that discontented people lack the resources they need to form a movement.

Generally, the strength of earlier political protests will influence how a state acts in the face of new protests. We also know that leadership is an important resource in social movements. Elites play an important leadership role, and so do intellectuals, as we noted earlier. As a result, political conflicts vary according to whether the elites are united or not. When elites are not united, movements are less likely to succeed. Also, the class background of the leadership has an important effect. Often, it will determine whether a social movement has reformist, radical or revolutionary goals.

Occasionally, as in 1993 Somalia, leadership and resources are all it takes to gain control of a society. Somalia is so poor and disorganized that the groups which are *least* disorganized and poor become powerful. Moreover, in Somalia, kin groups and clans lend legitimacy to a leader's claims to control. But a far more important part was played by outside powers (such as the United States) that wanted a stable leadership they could work with.

Unlike deprivation theory, mobilization theory draws our attention towards objective or material factors in movement formation. This focus on practical issues is the greatest strength of the theory.

Earlier in the chapter we noted that, due to the obscuring of domination by "regimes of truth," Foucault doubted the possibility of integrating multiple forms of resistance into overall strategies. In his view, there was no clear enemy against whom to rally and no basis for a common protest.

However, Carroll and Ratner (1996) have recently studied the survey responses of members of various social movements and come to another conclusion. They find that activists in labour, poverty, gay/lesbian, feminist, environmentalist, peace, and aboriginal groups share many common beliefs. In particular, the "political-economic injustice master frame appears to serve as a common interpretive framework for most activists across the entire spectrum of movements" (*op cit.*: 418). This set of beliefs views power as systemic, structural and materially grounded (for instance, in wealth). Oppression, in this framework, is seen as a matter of material deprivation, exploitation and alienation within a system driven by its own logic and the self-interest of those who occupy positions of power.

The authors also find variations among the members of these groups: especially a greater sympathy for "identity politics" in some of the new social movements (e.g., gay/lesbian and feminist) which shows itself in a greater concern with exclusion and empowerment than is found in the traditional labour movement.

But far more striking than such differences is evidence that members of these various movements frame similar "social visions" or images of the desirable society. For example, nearly half of all the activists interviewed support "a caring society where people are tolerant and treat each other with respect (i.e., values such as love, compassion, respect, trust, honesty, integrity, fairness and sharing are prominent)" (*op cit.*: 422-3). Moreover, large proportions in each movement show "classical left" sensibilities which emphasize the need to right political and economic wrongs and provide for material welfare and equality.

Shared ideals, then, still provide a basis for integrating social activists. Another source of integration is dynamic leadership.

Charisma in Social Movements

As we have seen, social movements usually form around a set of common interests or grievances. In some cases, however, the goals of a social movement may become secondary to its leadership. In such cases the followers will develop a commitment to their leader which may become more important to them than their particular grievances.

Weber identified such a movement as one centred on a "charismatic," inspiring leader. The history of such a social movement is, largely, the history of its leader and the successes or failures of that leader. That is not to say that each movement is just the unique product of a unique person. Nevertheless, the leader of a movement is charismatic when he or she inspires loyalty and enthusiasm among followers, despite the cost or danger this affiliation poses to them. So, for example, Mahatma Gandhi and Martin Luther King, Jr., were **charismatic leaders** who were able to create movements based on non-violence, despite the fact that violence was directed at their followers and at themselves. Other recent charismatic leaders include Jim Jones, who led his followers to mass suicide in Guyana in 1976, and David Koresh, leader of the Branch Davidians, who, along with his devotees, perished in Waco, Texas, in 1993.

CBC
"Toronto Blessing"

When this charismatic leadership is combined with social isolation (or "encapsulation") and a clearly stated belief system — especially a belief in the coming apocalypse — it may even induce a group to commit mass suicide. This happened in 1997, when thirty-nine members of the Heaven's Gate cult killed themselves in San Diego County, California. A similar mix of leadership, faith and anxiety contributed to smaller-scale cult suicides by Order of the Solar Temple groups in Quebec in 1997, and Switzerland and Quebec in 1994.

Charismatic leaders hold unshakeable beliefs about the rightness of their cause and they exert a powerful hold on their followers. Followers believe their leader's qualities of personality are supernatural, superhuman or inaccessible to common people (Weber, 1964). Such powers, which often include the claim of a gift of prophecy, make it easier for leaders to control the masses, particularly in new or developing societies.

Leaders may appeal to their followers' better instincts, or offer them higher self-esteem. In the end, some leaders abuse their followers and commit grave misdeeds in the name of a higher calling. When leaders consider themselves godlike, the charismatic movements they lead often turn into tyrannies. Happily, this was not the case in the movements led by Gandhi or Martin Luther King, Jr.

However, charismatic social movements are also self-limiting. Attachment to the leader is intensely emotional, so these social movements are unpredictable and operate at a fever pitch. They can be loving one minute and violent the next. Paradoxically, the movement becomes more stable and predictable after the leader dies or retires.

Then, the movement enters a process of **routinization**. A bureaucratic structure emerges, patterns of authority develop and day-to-day duties replace spontaneous acts. The group relies less on inspiration and more on tradition. Routinization creates institutions — for example, churches and trained clergy — that draw on people's deepest faith in the movement. Directed towards clear goals and well-organized, these institutions are strong enough to stand up against the tests of faith people suffer in everyday life. Through routinization, the movement achieves a measure of permanence. Movements that routinize charisma provide their members with friendship and help, maintaining their involvement with the group. Failure to routinize almost ensures that the movement will die out.

OTHER SOURCES OF SOCIAL CHANGE

Political and social movements are only two sources of social change in the world today. We discussed the significance of another source, population pressure, in Chapter 10. Other important sources of social change include new ideas, new technology and the globalization of world markets. We will briefly discuss each of these in turn.

New Ideas and Inventions

New ideas can be a powerful force for social change. Consider the importance of the following ideas in world history: *Liberty*, *Equality*, *Justice*, *Nation*, *God*, *Truth*. At one time or another, people have shed blood, even died, to defend these ideas. People are still doing so in many parts of the world.

Marx viewed ideas as the result and reflection of social forces, not their cause. That is, he thought ideas grew out of people's life conditions; but that ideas also affected people's life conditions. Otherwise, he would not have spent his own life writing down ideas about class relations and capitalism. He must have known that *without* these ideas and the class awareness they would provoke, the chances of revolution and communism were slight.

But ideas alone are not enough to produce social change. Throughout history, many ideas — both beliefs and discoveries — have been lost or forgotten. For ideas to spread and take root they must gain the support of people in power. Ideas spread fastest when they arise among, or gain acceptance from, the powerful; this happened with the rise of Christianity, for example. Equally, the powerful

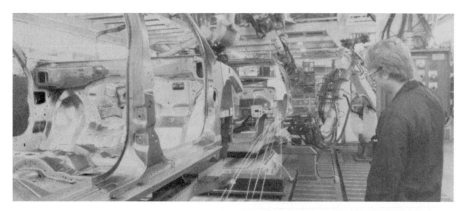

This robotic factory can sit on the outskirts of your city and replace thousands of manual workers.

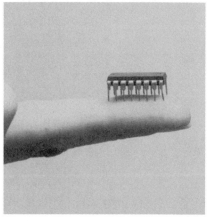

Inside the computer, this small transistor replaced the much larger vacuum tube and was soon replaced by the even smaller, more efficient microchip.

ignore or suppress ideas that oppose ruling ideologies. People who support ideas that oppose the dominant ideology must be willing to fight for them.

Technology and economics also have an effect on the spread of ideas. Generally, ideas that people cannot use are lost or ignored. Like popular movements, new ideas depend on resources for their survival. To survive and spread, new ideas must have a social movement or institution that adopts them. In that sense, they are then the few ideas (of many) whose "time has come."

Innovations are new material objects or ways of doing things that become part of a culture. There are two forms of innovation: discovery and invention.

A *discovery* involves finding out about and making known the existence of something that was always there, whose existence was unknown before. Like ideas, discoveries have social origins. Usually they are the result of patient research, which often requires a societal commitment to finding out and using new knowledge. In turn, a commitment to scientific research has particular cultural roots. In the Western world, this commitment has flowered only in the last 300 years, alongside Protestantism and capitalism. The growth of science has required funding and also a cultural commitment to ideas like "truth," "progress," "efficiency" and "productivity."

Invention also has a cultural and social basis. It is the creation or design of something that did not exist before — for example, the bow and arrow, automobile, television or Nintendo game.

Many innovations, whether ideas, inventions or discoveries, spread from one place to another through a process called *diffusion*. They spread from group to group within a society and from one society to another. Usually the diffusion of an invention or idea starts slowly, picks up steam, then levels off when a large part of society has been exposed to it.

Diffusion also increases as the means for diffusing ideas improve. Here, the media have been very important. Improvements in communication technology since Gutenberg invented the printing press have increased the cultural and scientific diffusion of ideas.

Sociologists have studied a variety of diffusion processes. One study examined Noah Webster's invention of American spelling practices in 1806 (e.g., "center" for "centre," "labor" for "labour"). Webster purposely diffused these American spellings by using them in his dictionaries and in primary-school readers of the day. His goal was to draw a cultural boundary between the United States and Great Britain; as you can see, he succeeded.

New Technology

Today, much social change results from new technology. Genetic engineering and informatics — the combination of computing and communication technologies — are two of the newest major influences on our society. However, in discussing new technology, we must be careful to avoid the dangers of technological determinism.

Technological determinism holds that social and cultural change are usually the result of changes in technology. Like other single-minded theories, this theory assumes that one particular factor — in this case, technology — always has the same effects. Technological determinists propose that technology has the same social effects, whatever the culture, society or socio-historical setting in which it is being used. A prime example of this view is Marshall McLuhan's famous slogan, "The medium is the message." By this, McLuhan meant that television influences us all by the way it conveys information, not because of the information it conveys. He believed that changes in communication technology would change the world's culture.

And, in fact, it has. Still, it is easy to overstate this view — to believe that technology does, or can do, more than is really possible. Without denying technology's importance, we cannot agree that social and cultural life are *determined* by technology. Like ideas, new technologies are neither sufficient nor necessary for social change to occur. Societies are too complex for that.

The evidence shows that people use the same technology differently in different organizations, societies or cultures. The precise effect of a new technology depends on the context into which it is introduced. The motives and attitudes of people who control the technology, and the prevailing culture — the beliefs, cultural practices and existing technology — all make a difference.

We can see this in the ways different people and different societies make use of already available technologies ranging from the telephone and automobile to

APPLIED SOCIOLOGY

All Information Is Not Created Equal

One of the growing specialties in applied sociology is the study of new technologies and their use. For it is plain that technologies do not invent or use themselves: they have a social context, and it is that context which determines their adoption and pattern of use. Even the heavily touted Internet is a two-edged sword: like any technology, it can be used to free people or to oppress them. How the technology finally gets used is of concern to applied sociologists, and to all concerned citizens.

I recently returned from a three-year adventure: I lived in the future.

How was this possible? I was a member of the Ontario Telepresence Project, a research group that created an audio/video communication environment designed to respect our belief that communication is an inherently social process. How good was it? When the project ended this January I experienced what I can only describe as "video withdrawal."

In contrast I recently returned from the American southwest where simply using the telephone was an exercise in frustration. I lost several dollars without making a single connection. Undoubtedly American technology was not the culprit. Deregulation policies that have led to fragmentation of services were the more likely suspect. I wondered: was this a glimpse of Canada's future as we head down the same path?

Communication and collaboration were the primary interests of the early users of the Internet and it evolved into a relatively democratic set of communities. But like other alternative communities that have emerged in larger cities — Toronto's Yorkville in the 1960s is one example — the Internet settlements attracted attention, "tourists" arrived and the market potential was identified.

By 1959 Daniel Bell, the Harvard sociologist, had already identified information as a commodity in post-industrial society and the Internet *is* information. Not surprisingly the Internet became a market and the Information Highway was the new metaphor.

Speed, competitiveness and the transfer of "goods" all contribute to the metaphor. It plays to our fears of being left out (no on-ramp) or, worse, wiped out (road-kill) and we forget how the construction of superhighways destroyed communities in the past. So if you're surfing the Net, get ready to pay more for your surfboard.

What is good about the Internet should be a public good, otherwise we are creating a new category of the disadvantaged. Where are the discussions about universal access or privacy for the individual amid the scramble for market share? And what about the implications for employment?

Second, if you have spent any time on the Net you will know not only how much information there is but how hard it is to find a specific item. And what might you be missing by not looking in more traditional places? All information is not created equal and it is what we actually *do* with information that transforms it. Thinking, reasoning and evaluating are where the emphasis should lie.

Source: Gale Moore, *University of Toronto Magazine*, Autumn 1995, p. 48

the computer and Internet. As we learn from Applied Sociology, above, the Internet, for example, can be used for good or ill depending on the kind of information it carries and the way that information is organized and used. In turn, the organization and use of Internet information is a social product; like all social products, it is shaped by culture, political power, class interest and the value placed on efficiency.

Even today we see a vast number of different uses made of computing technology. Computer use varies from one society to another and from one organization to another within the same society. People determine computer use, not vice versa. But some of the most influential of these people are the ones who design computers and computer software, like Microsoft's Bill Gates. Computers and other new technologies have the most impact where they are dealing with problems that are readily "technifiable." These are problems that have a few very characteristic features:

- the problems are specific and practical — for example, how to get money out of your bank account on a weekend or at 3:00 a.m.;

- ordinary people are hoping for new technology in that area — for example, cheaper, more reliable cars that do not pollute the air;

- the technology is powerful, meaning that it requires little instruction and can do a great deal for the user — for example, a microwave oven, computerized chess game or reference library on CD-ROM.

Often, making a technological change is too complicated and costly to be worthwhile. Things remain the same, even though better solutions are possible.

Nevertheless, we are in the midst of a microelectronics revolution which is transforming many aspects of society. With proper use, computers can become instruments of human betterment. With improper use, they can become instruments of domination. In the 20th century we have seen that this is true of *all* technology.

GLOBALIZATION

Many believe we have now entered a new stage of history. Throughout the world we find uneven development and conflict. **World System theory** explains the uneven pace of development in the world by looking at the unequal relations among different countries. It insists that we must study the world as a unit, not study arbitrarily selected chunks it.

If we look at the history of selected societies (for example, Germany or India) over a long period, we see that their boundaries change frequently. National boundaries offer no solid basis for the analysis of social change. In recent times, the only "society" with a clear boundary is the world system itself.

Since the world's states are integrated into a world system, changes in one will provoke changes in the others. This integration of states into a world economic system began in the 15th century, with capitalism's expansion in Western Europe. This process of integration is far from over.

Though states are all connected, they do not relate to one another as equals. Politically and economically, some dominate others. Dominant states are referred to as the *core* and subordinate states as the *periphery*. Industrial core states take much of the raw materials and cheap labour they need from peripheral states. It is because they are economically and politically dominant that core states have the power to extract an economic surplus from the periphery. This helps them develop and prosper at an ever faster rate. Meanwhile, the periphery, ever more depleted of materials, labour and capital, becomes increasingly dependent on the core region for manufactured goods. The gap between core and periphery widens.

Investors from the core states control the economies of peripheral states. As a result, profits made in the periphery drain out of the local economy and flow back to the core. Moreover, foreigners decide what kinds of businesses to operate and what resources to exploit in the periphery. They make these decisions with their own interests in mind and it is in their interest to keep the periphery dependent on the core. Dependence ensures that they will have a continued source of cheap raw materials and labour, and a market for their manufactured goods.

Core states engage in *imperialism* — the exercise of political and economic control by one state over the territory of another, often by military means. Its purpose is to exploit the indigenous population and extract economic and political advantages.

Early European imperialism occurred through colonization, the settlement and administration of foreign lands. However, domination of a foreign land does not always require colonization. In fact, *economic* domination is far safer, less costly and usually more stable. By gaining control of a nation's economy — whether through ownership of lands or industries, the purchase of stocks and bonds or monopolistic control of key resources (e.g., a long-term contract to buy all its oil, or cars, or wheat, or water at a certain price) — it is possible to control the political and social life of the country very effectively. This is precisely how, first Britain then the United States, have controlled Canada. Colonization has not been needed for the last 150 years.

As colonialism has declined, a more subtle form of imperialism, neocolonialism, has become common. Under neocolonialism, core states exercise economic control over countries that are formally politically independent.

The end of old-style colonialism and imperialism probably means the end of old-style world wars, which were largely driven by colonial interests. In turn, this means that wars of the future are likely to be smaller and more localized. And, if the argument in Applied Sociology, below, is valid, this probably means that the combatants will be terrorists and fanatics, not national armies using nuclear weapons. While the number of wars fought may increase, the number of victims may not; and without the use of nuclear weapons, there is less chance humanity will be evaporated by a nuclear firefight.

However, the number of wars and the number of victims will continue to reflect the extent of global inequality and, particularly, the effects of underdevelopment in many parts of the world.

Underdevelopment is the effect on the periphery of unequal exchanges with the core. An underdeveloped society is one that has lost its capacity to take care of its own needs. Signs of underdevelopment include:

- a dependence on the export of raw materials;
- the import of manufactured goods;
- little domestic control over the economy;
- a small industrial base;
- little economic diversity;
- settlement of most of the population in rural areas;
- high rates of unemployment;

Battlefields of the New Millennium

APPLIED SOCIOLOGY

The hallmark of a mature science is its ability to predict future events which are foreseeable because they are connected to the present by a theory about change. And when social scientists turn their efforts to predicting the future of warfare, the predicted changes are provocative, imaginable and mildly terrifying. But when the readers of this book are very old and look backward, these predictions may turn out to have been far too cautious. Applied sociologists need to spend more time refining sociological theory by finding out how past predictions went wrong.

Future wars will almost certainly not involve nuclear weapons, said a panel of experts convened at the World Economic Forum to discuss the battlefields of the 21st century. Like the 20 or more wars that rage on in the world today, they probably will not even involve states on both sides. Instead, they will be waged by terrorists, guerrilla groups, fanatics and nationalist zealots whose weaponry will range from Second World War technology to the latest software for computer sabotage.

These wars will combine widely available weaponry with what one expert calls "the lurking class," the obsessions of whose members place them beyond the reach of logic and reason. And so the wars will be bloodier, less predictable and will kill more civilians than conventional battles between regular armies.

"It doesn't mean the end of war, just a shift to a different kind of war," Israeli military historian Martin van Creveld said. The Cold War — when the United States and the Soviet Union each had a well-stocked nuclear arsenal — was a period of both high risk and high stability. The world has since become low risk, but also low stability. Now

Islamic terrorists in Paris and religious fanatics in Tokyo can turn subways into abattoirs, while car bombers in Oklahoma City and New York do the same thing to office buildings. In Afghanistan, Sierra Leone, Chechnya, Sri Lanka and other places around the world, similar attacks are taking place. Nuclear weapons have stayed out of the mix so far.

Most of the weapons being used in current conflicts are low-technology and easily available. Wolfgang Reinicke, a research associate at the Brookings Institution, said governments are encouraging dual-use technology because goods that have both a civilian and military application are cheaper and easier to buy. But that means a heavy truck that could be bought and used for commercial purposes could equally be converted to carry ground launched missiles, as was the case during the gulf war.

The same can be said for computer technology, which can have military or civilian applications, depending on who is at the keyboard. "This has made a strategy of technology-denial impossible," said Mr. Reinicke, referring to the Cold War tactic of forbidding the export of certain technologies to the Soviet Union and its satellites. It would be impossible anyway, because many of the groups seeking to amass the technology are not know to governments.

Many of the battlefields of the 21st century will be left over from the 20th century, Mr. Jenkins said. By his count, there are 27 wars at the moment. Sixteen are in their second decade and eight in their third. Ending them through diplomatic channels will become increasingly difficult if there are religious or ethnic hatreds involved, Mr. Jenkins said. "If you believe your opponents are pagans or disbelievers and will burn in hell anyway, there's not a lot of room for diplomacy."

Source: Abridged from Madelaine Drohan, *The Globe and Mail*, Thurs., Feb. 8, 1996, p. A14

- a lack of social programs such as health care;
- a high illiteracy rate; and
- a low standard of living.

Underdeveloped societies vary in the number and combination of typical characteristics they display. However, they are similar in that their condition is always a result of international differences in wealth and power, which permit other states to exploit them. The underdevelopment of the periphery is *not* due to a lack of resources, to illiteracy or to a traditional or backward mentality. It results from domination by the core.

Even semi-peripheral countries like Canada show some of the same signs of dependence. However, these countries are different in one main respect. Social movements are more important in semi-peripheral societies and, sometimes, they challenge existing social, political and economic relations. That is because people in semi-peripheral regions have the motivation and the opportunity to make major changes. These societies are fertile grounds for protest. For example, the 1993 federal election in Canada did more to challenge the status quo than the 1992 federal election in the United States, a core society. Protest movements, like those that gave rise to the Reform Party and Bloc Québécois, are much more common in Canadian politics than they are in American politics.

Sometimes elites in core societies try to avoid domestic problems by making wars abroad, focusing people's attention on foreign policy, or exporting problems like unsafe working conditions to the Third World. In the long run, however, the domestic problems explode: witness the problems of urban crime, violence, unemployment and drug use in America's inner cities.

Alongside economic and political imperialism is cultural imperialism — the mental colonization of developing societies with Western ideas. This process is subtle. Over time, exposure to Western media gradually alters cultural values, causes conflicts and changes perceptions of local and world events. Powerful, mainly American, media organizations are responsible for the worldwide distribution of a total cultural package that includes television, film, sports and consumer items.

Even the worldwide flow of "news" is shaped by the imperial connection. Galtung (1971; also Galtung and Vincent, 1992) points to four main characteristics of news flow within a colonial system, where a core nation dominates peripheral nations. First, news about the core is more common than news about the periphery (e.g., people in countries that are politically or economically domi-

Control of information flow is one way developed core countries can control less-developed peripheral countries.

nated by the United States hear more about the United States than they do about Canada). Second, news about the colonial core is more common than news about *other* colonial cores (e.g., in Canada, there is more news about the United States than about Japan). Third, news about the core is dominant even in broadcasts that originate in the periphery (e.g., Canadians hear more about the United States than they hear about other parts of Canada). And fourth, there is little, if any, flow of information between peripheral countries, unless it is provided by the centre (e.g., there is little direct news flow between Canada and Mexico). Even within a country we can use this theory; news about events in the core cities of Toronto, Montreal, Vancouver and Ottawa is far more likely to be aired than news about Madawasca, Saint-Stephen or Upper Musquodobit.

World System theory has its weaknesses. They include a failure to explain or predict the varied pathways of change in Third World countries. For example, the theory cannot explain why East Asia is getting richer and richer while Africa is getting poorer and poorer. Critics claim that World System theory fails to consider influences on social change that are internal to the state. For example, it says little about the role of social classes within the respective core and peripheral nations.

As a result, it cannot explain why Canada, a former colony and major exporter of raw materials, is not underdeveloped today to the same degree as Argentina, another former colony. In 1900, Canada and Argentina had equal levels of economic development (i.e., Gross National Product) and today Argentina is far less economically developed than Canada. World System theory cannot interpret this fact. Still, the theory reminds us that all significant social change produces conflict. No change, even change that evolves out of an earlier stage of development, can escape conflict. And no theory of exploitation makes much sense if it fails to take the global dimension into account.

The End of History?   It is difficult to predict the future in a time of such momentous change. Perhaps for this reason, some have proclaimed "the end of history." And there can be little doubt that we have entered a new phase of history with the fall of communism. So-called "industrial" civilization seems to have won the day. But, according to Lash and Urry (1987), "modern" or "organized" capitalism has given way to "late capitalism," an unpredictable form with a few main properties.

First, late capitalism is *decentralized*. Increasingly, industrial, commercial and banking enterprises are multinational and oriented to a world market. Manufacturing is decentralized, with work sites spread around the world. Proletarian jobs are exported from the old industrial world to the Third World. Decentralization also means a decline in the size and importance of industrial cities. Work itself decentralizes, with average plant sizes becoming smaller. One consequence is a decline in the importance of national unions as collective bargaining declines at the national level and increases at the company and plant levels.

Second, traditional beliefs in science, modernity and nationalism come increasingly under attack. This skepticism about reason and progress often goes under the name of "post-modernity." In the past, most left-wing movements were based on a world-view of historical or scientific materialism, and a belief in progress and human betterment, that is collapsing all around us. Today the Left is changing its focus from economic to ethical or human rights concerns, from a belief in revolution to a belief in democracy, from involvement in the state to involvement in social movements and from "vanguard" to grass-roots movements.

Throughout Europe, the past thirty years have seen a flowering of social movements. They include counterculture, antiwar, student, feminist, environmental, antinuclear and peace movements among others. At the same time, socialist movements have lost their former power to win people's support.

Finally, many herald the growth of ecological consciousness. Increasingly, the future of human history depends on the ecological future of the planet. We are reminded time and again of the social and environmental costs of economic growth. We cannot continue to ignore the ecologically destructive effects of business. Nor can people go much further without resolving the built-in conflict between (disposable) consumer culture and traditional values, arts and ways of life.

In the end, humanity will need to evolve into a race of "sustainable people." These are people who can keep the planet alive because they possess the ability to renounce present gains in favour of people who are yet unborn. "Sustainable people" also have adequate and relevant knowledge about the problems nearby, feel a moral and aesthetic commitment to humanity and the earth and believe that humanity must take control over its own future. To survive, humanity will also have to turn its back on the mass-produced brutality that has characterized social and political conflict in the 20th century.

The Macro/Micro Connection

We have just noted some of the many concerns people have about the future. They include macro-level concerns about global conflict, technological displacement, imperialism and environmental destruction. Indeed, much of this chapter has been about macro-level conflicts and changes, but we should not lose sight of the corresponding micro-processes. For example, consider the social role of optimism and courage (versus pessimism and fear). Both are causes *and* consequences of social change.

Optimism varies from one country to another for reasons that we do not yet fully understand. By international standards, Canadians are fairly optimistic: they want and expect to be happy, and they expect their lives to go smoothly. On the other hand, this expectation can be a form of smugness if it neglects utterly the deterioration produced for some people as others gain smoother and smoother lives.

Some people are even more optimistic than Canadians. Gallup polls conducted in thirty countries during the 1980s (Michalos, 1988) asked people: "So far as you are concerned, do you think that [next year] will be better or worse than [the year just ending]?" By this measure, the world's greatest optimists turn out to live in Argentina, Greece, Korea and the United States, where more than 50 per cent of the respondents expect that next year will be better. Along with Chileans and South African whites, Canadians rank just above the world's average on optimism, with 35 to 39 per cent saying that next year will be better. On the other hand, the polls showed that Canadians are twice as likely to express optimism as Germans, Austrians and Belgians.

Optimism is substantially influenced by changes in economy and society. For this reason, with the weakening of Canada's economy, Canadian optimism has slipped in the last few years. Between 1984 and 1993, annual Decima/Maclean's opinion polls saw the percentage of Canadians saying they were optimistic about their economic future drop from 79 per cent to 71 per cent (Maclean's, Jan. 3, 1994: 24).

In the same poll (Maclean's, Jan. 4, 1993: 42), just over 25 per cent of Canadian adults said that they were pessimistic or very pessimistic about their personal economic situation. More than 50 per cent believed that the generation of Canadians being born now will be worse off than their parents, and less than one respondent in five believed that the new generation will be better off (*op cit.*: 44). This change shows how macrosociological events — for example, the continuing recession and fear of unemployment — produce microsociological results.

Pessimistic people are also more fearful that immigration will take away their jobs. As a result, there is a widespread desire to limit immigration, and this de-

APPLIED SOCIOLOGY

Yardsticks of Progress

A hallmark of a mature science is general agreement on how to measure its key concepts — in sociology, concepts like inequality, development and well-being, for example. Sociologists have made slow progress in applying their insights to the solution of major social problems because of such differences in opinion. As well, controversies about the difference between average GDP (Gross Domestic Product — a measure of income commonly used by economists) and average quality of life or well-being are due to different opinions about what a "good society" looks like.

Saskatchewan politicians, public administrators and academics met in Regina last week to look for ways to measure community well-being that are better than merely counting the flow of marketplace dollars.

The GDP measures what people consume, regardless of scarcity, environmental despoilment or the byproducts of social stress. In the United States, where everyone, even the poor, seems to be enjoying increased incomes, the federal Environmental Protection Agency reports that gasoline consumption has climbed 14 per cent in a year because Americans want to buy gas-guzzlers — minivans, pickup trucks and so-called sport utility vehicles — rather than fuel-efficient vehicles.

The GDP measures dollars changing hands in the marketplace. It measures price, not value. It measures income, not quality of life. It has become the pre-eminent yardstick of perpetual progress.

Doug Norris, director of the housing, family and social-statistics division of Statistics Canada, says the search for the one big number that would more accurately measure a community's well-being than the GDP was a booming business in the 1960s and early 70s, but dribbled out of people's minds after the oil-price crisis of 1976. There is now a frenetic revived interest in it, coinciding with the disappearance of full-time jobs, the widening gulf between rich and poor, social stress and the depletion and despoilment of the natural habitat.

Statistics Canada in recent years has increased the number of social surveys it conducts, and is developing social indicators. The problem, as might be expected, said Mr. Norris, is that social and environmental things can be difficult to measure accurately, especially if the goal is to find one big number like the GDP.

[By contrast,] the United Nations Human Development Index awards such thinly sliced scores that it is hard to derive meaning from them. Canada, for example, gets an HDI of 0.951; the U.S., 0.940; Japan and the Netherlands, 0.938; Norway, 0.937; and so on.

The state of Oregon uses a composite score from about 250 benchmark indicators, such as: percentage of people commuting 30 minutes or less, percentage of streams not meeting environmental standards, numbers of homeless, numbers of pedestrians and cyclist fatalities, attendance at arts events, literacy rate and percentage of people above the poverty line.

The Genuine Progress Indictor (GPI), designed by the San Francisco public-policy institute Redefining Progress, adjusts personal consumption for income distribution. It adds the value of household work, parenting, volunteer work. It subtracts the cost (which the GDP doesn't) of crime, family stress and breakdown, pollution and commuting time. I looked at Mr. Norris's graph of a rising GDP line and a falling GPI line. The GPI looked sort of the way I feel about the country. Mr. Norris said a lot of people tell him that.

Source: Abridged from Michael Valpy, *The Globe and Mail*, Thurs., Oct. 3, 1996, p. A21

sire helped the election of Reform Party candidates in Canada in the 1993 federal election. At the same time, fears about unemployment strain ethnic and racial relations. In general then, a worsening of the economy (a macro-event) reduces optimism and confidence (a micro-event in millions of homes and offices). This, in turn, worsens the economy still more — people hesitate to spend money — and may also have political, legal and social effects on immigration and group relations (all macro-events).

As we reach the end of the millennium, we have to wonder whether the world is going to improve or worsen in our lifetimes. Most observers have given up on the ideal of "progress" that so motivated educated people and reformers at the end of the 19th century. And as we learn from Applied Sociology, above, there is even a lot of disagreement about what goals we ought to set for humanity and how we ought to measure whether we are achieving them. Sociology can contribute to the debate by reflecting on the reasons some goals get set instead of others, and some goals are attained instead of others. Equally, sociology can help measure humanity's movement in one or another direction, as we shall see in the next chapter.

CLOSING REMARKS

The sociological study of politics, protest and change offers yet another prime illustration of the connection between macro and micro perspectives.

As a macro phenomenon, politics exists outside and "above" individual people, in their laws, political institutions and traditional voting practices, and in the ideologies that substantiate the status quo. The political structure of a society can be depicted as very slow to change: political parties last for generations; rules of order, constitutions and administrative procedures can last for centuries. The main elements of a polity outlast individuals and even generations of individuals.

On the other hand, politics is the pursuit of individual or collective goals. We all participate in one or another kind of politics, and many of us are active in electoral politics, as campaigners, contributors and informed voters. As such we can sometimes effect rapid and significant changes. Who would have bet on the immense electoral success of the Reform Party of Canada and the Bloc Québécois in the federal elections of 1993? Or of the Ontario New Democratic Party (NDP) in 1991, followed by the election of an extremely right-wing Conservative government in 1995?

Politics is something we all change or reproduce every day. Often we cannot even see the immense changes we are about to create, because they are occurring so quietly, so subtly, so gradually, in millions of homes, then thousands of polling booths.

How do we know about these subtle, gradual and (often) *private* changes that culminate in momentous *public* changes? We know about them through social research, the topic of the next chapter. Finally, then, it is time to discuss the ways sociologists make and test their theories.

Review Questions

1. What is meant by an evolutionary theory of change?

2. What role do the concepts of "differentiation" and "integration" play in evolutionary theories.

3. What is meant by a revolutionary theory of change?

4. What is the "state"?

5. What are the characteristics of the authoritarian state?

6. What is the difference between the state and "civil society"?

7. What role do ideologies play in social change?

8. How do radical and reformist ideologies differ?

9. What is meant by a "social movement"?

10. What is relative deprivation theory?

11. What is resource mobilization theory?

12. What role does "charisma" play in social movements?

13. How does new technology result in social change?

14. What are the signs of underdevelopment?

15. What is cultural imperialism?

Discussion Questions

1. Why do you suppose Canada has never had authoritarian political rule and many countries have never had anything *but* authoritarian rule?

2. Where progressive thought is concerned, is public opinion usually ahead of, or behind, the views of political leaders? An example of where it is behind leaders' opinions is on the issue of the reinstatement of capital punishment. Most of the public want it, the leaders do not. Can you think of an example where public opinion is ahead of leaders' opinion?

3. Why are charismatic leaders more likely to emerge in some periods of history than in others?

4. Ideas are a powerful force for social change, but they must come from somewhere. Why are certain kinds of ideas — for example, gender equality — more likely to arise and find acceptance in some times and places and not others?

5. Computers can do great good or great harm. What factors will decide which use people make of them in your lifetime?

6. Why does the idea that we are at "the end of history" appeal to many people? Do you suppose people are always imagining that they are at a turning point in history? If so, why?

Suggested Readings

Abercrombie, Nicholas, Stephen Hill and Bryan S. Turner (1980) *The Dominant Ideology Thesis*. London: George Allen & Unwin. This detailed critique describes dominant ideologies in different historical periods and discusses the factors that influence the spread of ideology.

Carroll, William K. (ed.) (1992) *Organizing Dissent: Contemporary Social Movements in Theory and Practice*. Toronto: Garamond. This book views the dominant trends in studies of Canadian social movements from a variety of perspectives and approaches. A good introduction to the state of research on social movements in Canadian sociology.

Chirot, D. (1979) *Social Change in the Twentieth Century*. New York: Harcourt Brace Jovanovich. A brilliant and ambitious attempt to understand all social change since 1913 in the context of the "world system." Read how Canada managed, in only eighty years, to move from the periphery to the semi-periphery of world events.

Laxer, G. (1982). *Open for Business*. Toronto: Oxford University Press. In this outstanding book, the author uses a comparative approach to examine the role of the state in shaping historical patterns of foreign ownership in the Canadian economy.

Moore, Barrington, Jr. (1966) *Social Origins of Dictatorship and Democracy: Lord and Peasant in the Making of the Modern World*. Boston: Beacon. This fascinating account of elite and class alliances during the modernization of England, France, the United States, China, Japan and India fashions a general theory of dictatorship and democracy.

Skocpol, T. (1979) *States and Social Revolutions*. Cambridge: Cambridge University Press. A masterful comparison of the revolutions that occurred in France, Russia and China. Written as a rebuttal to Moore's work (see above), it also attempts to explain why revolutions occur when and where they do, and the reasons they turn out differently.

Wolf, E. (1982) *Europe and the People Without History*. Berkeley: University of California Press. A sweeping worldwide perspective on the ways that expanding European capitalism and colonialism affected pre-capitalist societies, including their structures of class and stratification.

Internet Resources

The following Web sites are good places to find more information about topics discussed in this chapter:

Canadian Political Discussion Group is a newsgroup for general discussion about Canadian politics.
USENET: can.politics

North American Institute provides news, reports and publications about the emerging relationship between Canada, the US and Mexico, focusing on the environment, trade, and socio-cultural identities.
http://www.santafe.edu/ ~ naminet/index.html

National Citizens Coalition argues for "more freedom through less government" and favours free markets, more individual freedom and responsibility, and a strong military.
http://www.FreeNet.Calgary.ab.ca/populati/communi/ncc/ncitizen.html

The Unity Links provides updated news, from both the federalist and separatist camps, on issues of separation, distinct society and renewed federalism.
http://is.dal.ca/ ~ ttyner/index.htm

The Sacramento Bee's Report: "Logged On or Left Out?" discusses the implications of the paucity of women within the computer world.
http://www.sacbee.com/news/projects/women/

Development Theory contains abstracts of many articles pertaining to economic underdevelopment.
http://www.stile.lut.ac.uk/`gyedb/STILE/t0000425.html

Culture, Power and Social Action on the Internet discusses the implications of the Internet on existing societal institutions.
http://robotweb.ri.cmu.edu/ ~ ppan/Essays/Maddox_essay.html

The United Nations' Homepage offers many resources, including an online database.
http://www.un.org/databases/

METHODS OF RESEARCH

CHAPTER OUTLINE

Focus groups help researchers to sample ideas and opinions, and to plan more systematic research.

BASIC IDEAS OF SOCIAL RESEARCH

Scientific Research Is Rigorous and Objective   We began this book by noting that everyone is a sociologist of a kind. All of us try to understand the social world in which we live, the behaviour of other people and the events taking place around us. For this reason, some of what we have discussed may have seemed familiar to you.

Almost certainly, you will have discovered for yourself much of what we have said about family life, culture, conformity, work, inequality and so on. Often, you will have made your "discoveries" when experiencing personal troubles. You may have even found out for yourself that personal troubles are the other side of public issues — just as we have been saying throughout the book.

Personal experiences help to persuade us of the truth of many sociological findings; but they are no substitute for research. We cannot create sociology simply by living. That is because much of what goes on around us is neither obvious nor easily explained. What's more, personal experiences and emotions hide as much from us as they reveal, because we are so wrapped up in certain ways of seeing things and evaluating them.

So, understanding social life requires more than experience in living; it requires careful research. Fortunately, everyone is used to doing some research in their own lives. For example, think about how we find the lowest price on a new car: we do research. Research is nothing more than carefully and systematically gathering information. Because of this, a lot of the ideas in this chapter will be familiar to you from your own experience. But be warned, many of them will not.

Types of Research

Most sociological work consists of trying to answer questions. Gathering the information to answer these questions is social research. Because questions come in many varieties, there are different kinds of research. Let us take poverty as an example. We may read in newspapers or see reported on television that poverty is a serious problem in our society. We may suspect that this is true, but we are not sure whether it really is true, or what the magnitude of the problem may be.

In that case we engage in *exploratory research* to find out whether poverty is an issue that warrants doing further research, or what kind of information is already available on poverty, or what kind of further research needs to be done on the subject.

If the information we obtain suggests that poverty is an issue that needs to be investigated further, we will ask many more questions: What is considered poverty in our society? How many people are poor? Who are these people? Where are they living? And so on. In this case we engage in *descriptive research* to find out what exactly is going on. Descriptive research provides us with the answers to specific questions about some people, activities, events or conditions in which we are interested.

But we may also want to find out *why* some people are poorer than others. In this case we engage in *explanatory research* to find the *cause* of an effect.

Explanation and Prediction

Formally defined, an **explanation** is something that gives reasons for or interprets something else. Take the issue of poverty: Why are some people poorer than others? In the process of looking for an explanation, we make informed guesses or suggest probable explanations, called hypotheses, which we then test with data. You will recall from Chapter 1 that a **hypothesis** is a proposition or tentative statement about the relationship between a specific cause X and its effect Y that we can test through research.

Previous sociological research has suggested that some people are poorer than others because they have not received enough formal education to get a well-paying job. It may be that they failed to learn crucial facts and skills, or perhaps they have learned these but lack the necessary piece of paper, or "credential," because they have not demonstrated the learning.

If our hypothesis is correct, the more education a person gets, the more income that individual should earn. We can now examine the data to verify the hypothesis — that is, test it with facts. If the data show that people with more education always earn more income than people with less education, then we have come partway towards an explanation.

However, explanation does not end when we show a connection between two activities, events or conditions, X and Y. We must also understand the reasons for that connection: *why* more education leads to higher earnings. Without understanding the process, we have only gained an ability to predict Y from X. **Prediction** is the act of forecasting an outcome. In predicting, we infer the outcome of an event or series of events from scientific — especially statistical — analyses of known events.

For example, you ask me to guess whether Frank earns more money than Alexander. I ask how much education each has completed. You tell me Frank completed Grade 12 and Alexander only completed Grade 9. Remembering my hypothesis that higher education usually means higher earnings, I predict that Frank earns more. If the hypothesis (or hunch) is valid, other things being equal, my prediction will be right. But I still haven't explained the relationship.

To give another example, we can pretty certainly predict that if a freshly baked pizza is put in front of four overworked undergraduates (desperately trying to understand this chapter), it will soon vanish. And it can turn out that this prediction is right 87.6 times out of 100. But who knows *why*?

For sociologists, the real world is more complicated. In social research, we almost never find an X that always causes Y, or a Y that always results from X. Most of the processes sociologists study are multi-causal and conditional. By *multi-causal*, we mean that many Xs combine in complicated ways to produce a single Y. By *conditional*, we mean that a particular X will cause Y under some conditions but not others.

The relationship between education and earning power is a case in point. Education is not the only factor to influence earnings. Many others — gender, race, region, even physical appearance — also affect how much money a person earns.

As well, education has more influence on earnings in some kinds of work than others. Consider two people making hamburgers at a fast-food outlet. One has a Grade 9 education, the other a Grade 12 education. They are doing the same job and earning exactly the same amount of money, so education has no effect on earnings in this case. Higher education has the greatest effect when it allows a person to enter a restricted line of work — such as a skilled trade, a profession or a managerial position — that pays higher-than-average wages. The "returns to education," or the amount of income an additional year's education will bring, vary from one sector of the economy to another.

For these reasons, it is not easy to predict something as simple as how much money a person will earn. It is even harder to *explain* an observed result. To explain something well means understanding the entire process that ties X and Y together, particularly knowing *why* X leads to Y.

Social scientists go about answering the question "why" differently from other people. Take the topic of suicide. Most of you are probably familiar with Shakespeare's play *Hamlet*. In that play, one character — Ophelia — kills herself, and another character — Hamlet — thinks about killing himself. In fact, Hamlet's famous soliloquy ("To be or not to be, that is the question") is about what supposedly goes on inside the mind of a person who is thinking of killing himself. This soliloquy contains Shakespeare's "theory" about why people do, or do not, kill themselves.

On the other hand, the sociologist Emile Durkheim, a much less skilful writer than Shakespeare, makes every effort to state *his* theory about suicide in a way that is clear and testable, though less poetic. Then, he tests his theory with data. And unlike Shakespeare, Durkheim pays no attention to what is in people's minds when they kill themselves: he doesn't think he can get good data on that matter. He also doubts that people always know the reason for their own thoughts and actions. This is partly because, as we see from Everyday Life, below, people are often confused about their own motives. It is often impossible to predict their behaviour from their thoughts — or at least, from the thoughts they express.

So Durkheim's book *Suicide* is about the conditions under which people generally do, or do not, kill themselves — and not about what they might have been thinking. Durkheim theorizes that two factors — social isolation and a breakdown of social norms — increase the chance of a person killing him- or herself. Using data, he sets out to explain variations in recorded suicide rates in a variety of countries.

To test his theory, Durkheim has to construct *operational definitions* for his concepts. An operational definition links the meaning of a concept to procedures for measuring it. Specifically, Durkheim must measure "suicide," "social isolation" and "social regulation" in each of these countries. Among other things, he uses marital status to measure social isolation. Married people are considered "socially connected," while single, divorced or widowed people are considered "socially isolated." Thus, Durkheim hypothesizes that people who are single, widowed or divorced are more likely to kill themselves than married people, especially married people with children.

EVERYDAY LIFE

"To Be or Not To Be ...?"

The Emergency Crisis Service of Toronto's Hospital for Sick Children encourages [disturbed young people] to express their emotions. One 17-year-old patient set down [the pluses and minuses of living] in careful point form:

Reasons to live

- To become a high-school graduate
- To be able to become a writer
- To have kids
- To experience new things
- To get back together with family
- My older brother might say "hi" to me
- Christmas is coming

Reasons to die

- School and getting things handed in
- Work, feeling inferior there
- Scared of the future
- Why not?

Three months later she wrote:

Reasons to live

- Might become someone famous
- Because I might discover the cure to some disease
- Life may be fun
- For the hell of it
- I might make some friends or really close friends who care
- Who knows what I'd be missing
- Graduating from high school

Reasons to die

- School and getting the work done
- Work and feeling really inferior to the other workers and I hate working there
- Friends, not sure if I will ever really make any in school
- Feeling lonely and scared about my future
- Nuclear war
- The ozone layer
- I am really ugly looking so I'll never get a husband and end up being alone
- Because I don't think there's really too much out there so why wait around to discover it
- No more [being] tired all the time, trying to get things done
- I won't have to feel confused any more, like up one minute and down the next
- It'll take the burden off everybody else
- I'll never have to worry again
- I'll never get hurt by anyone again

A few months later, just after her 18th birthday, she killed herself.

Source: Abridged from *The Globe and Mail*, Sat., Nov. 16, 1996, p. D3

He then examines data to verify his hypothesis, or test it with facts. If the data show that people with a spouse and children run a lower-than-average risk of suicide, Durkheim can conclude that the hypothesis is valid and the theory which produced that hypothesis is also valid. He will have come part of the way towards explaining suicide.

Variables

Researchers speak about Xs and Ys in a particular way, so it is worthwhile defining our terms before going further. Xs and Ys are variables. A *variable* is any trait, quality or social characteristic that can vary in size or amount over time, across individual cases, or among different groups. The Y variable we are trying to explain and predict is the dependent variable. A *dependent variable*, such as income in the first example above (education and earnings), is influenced, changed or caused by the effect of other variables. An X variable, or *independent variable*, causes a change or variation in the dependent variable. Thus, independent variable is the causal or explanatory variable. As already noted, a dependent variable can be influenced by many independent variables. As well, any independent variable can influence many dependent variables. So when we come to research a particular relationship — the relationship between education and earnings, for example — we are isolating one particular relationship in a vast network of possible Xs and Ys.

QUALITATIVE AND QUANTITATIVE DATA

Data on amount of education and earnings are examples of **quantitative data**. They are based on precise measurements in recognizable units. We can say exactly, in dollars and cents, how much a person earns. We can say exactly, in years, grades or degrees and diplomas, how much education a person has completed. Moreover, everyone knows what dollars and grades are, so we can easily share and discuss our findings. With such quantitative data, it is easy to *replicate* a study another researcher has done, that is, do it the same way in order to see if we get the same results. We know exactly what the earlier researcher was measuring, and how.

What's more, such precise and clear-cut measures allow us to evaluate the results with powerful statistical methods. They permit us to judge whether our finding could have occurred by chance alone. Quantitative measures also let us compare the relative importance of different Xs which have an effect on Y. Finally, they let researchers create mathematical models for their theory. In short, quantitative measures allow sociology to do research that is like research in economics and the physical sciences.

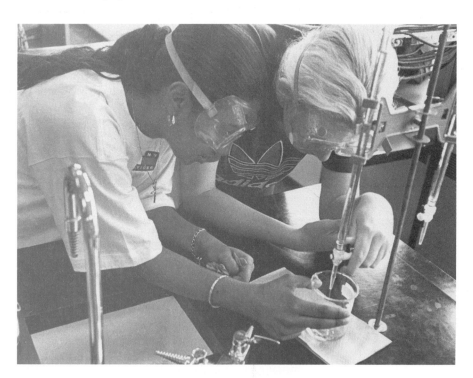

Sociology is science, but it does not require laboratory experiments.

It is not simply that quantitative sociology uses numerical measures of social variables. Beyond that, quantitative sociology is associated with a particular way of thinking about social life. Typical quantitative studies are narrowly focused on one part of the social structure. The researcher assumes that reality is stable and knowable, that reality doesn't flip around randomly: that precise hypotheses, when tested in a rigorous way, will yield reliable and replicable findings. Finally, the researcher assumes that such work will produce conclusions that can be generalized over time and from one social situation to another.

Much of quantitative research is obtrusive and controlling: the researcher sets the agenda through the questions being asked and the way these questions are put. Concepts, when measured empirically, become variables in the model, and hypotheses are derived for empirical testing. Then the researcher tests the hypotheses about these relations by collecting quantifiable data and examining relations between the variables. Statistical tests are used to decide whether or not the hypotheses are valid.

The result is a set of findings that is clear and (relatively) unarguable. Consider, for example, the theory that people today place little importance on their extended family largely because they have less extended family — fewer uncles, aunts, nephews, nieces and cousins — than a century ago. This is due to a continuing reduction in fertility over the last hundred years. There cannot be lots of uncles, aunts and so on without lots of brothers and sisters a generation earlier. So low fertility always means fewer kin. In turn, fewer kin means more importance for the nuclear family. It may also mean more demands being placed on spouses and children for economic or emotional support. Perhaps it means a growth in the importance of friendship over kinship. It may also mean a growth in the value placed on those few non-nuclear kin who *are* available.

Note that these speculations or hypotheses are all logically related, testable with data and possibly even correct. The best way of testing this theory is by collecting survey data on kinship relations in the past and comparing them with survey data on kinship relations in the present. Once the data are in, we will be able to draw firm conclusions; there will be little room for doubt.

However, much of what sociologists study cannot be as easily quantified. Consider something like "team spirit" — you know whether it is present or absent from a group you are observing but, often, you are hard-pressed to say precisely how you know it. Unlike quantitative data, **qualitative data** do not easily lend themselves to precise measurement. But they have other strengths. To do good qualitative research, what we need is a clear, detailed description of people's behaviour, including information from people about their own experiences. This usually involves observing people, talking to them and trying to understand them. Think of qualitative research as a kind of pre-industrial handicraft: not quite as precise as quantitative research, but much more painstaking and unique to the particular researcher.

Qualitative data are useful for exploring relationships and developing new theories. We get a subtler, more complex picture of people and their relationships when we do *not* try to compress their actions or feelings into a simple measurement. All research needs this sensitivity of understanding; some research cannot be done without it.

In particular, microsociologists often use qualitative data: verbal rather than numerical descriptions. However, qualitative researchers also tend to look at research in a different way from macrosociologists. They want their research to

What Seems Risky to You?

Percentage of Canadians in a 1992 survey who said they considered these a high risk to the public:

Source: *The Globe and Mail*, Thurs., April 13, 1995, p. A14

be as naturalistic and unobtrusive as possible so as to avoid disturbing and changing the subtle nuances of the social life they are studying.

Qualitative researchers, unlike quantitative researchers, usually assume a dynamic, rapidly changing reality; they are more interested in social processes than in social structures. Casting their net widely across a wide range of behaviours and sentiments, they explore and discover all the relationships among members of a group. There is no certainty that the cases they study in such depth will yield generalizable results. What is far more important is that the results obtained by this method will be valid, real, "rich" or deep. A good example is sociologist Howard Becker's study of medical students (1961), or his study of jazz musicians (1963).

Such research often rejects the underlying premises of the quantitative approach: namely, that people can be usefully viewed as collections of variables; that there is a clean separation between the researcher and the object of study; that findings can be precise and unarguable. From this standpoint, the role of social science is to evoke and provoke deeper understanding, not find immutable social laws!

In this light, consider research by Anne Kasper (1994) conducted on women with breast cancer. She asks: How do women cope with the social and emotional conflicts caused by the onset of breast cancer, its effects and treatment? To answer this question, Kasper uses largely unstructured interviews with twenty-nine women who are facing breast cancer for the first time.

From Kasper's qualitative and feminist point of view, the woman studied is in control of the interview, since she is the "expert" on the topic of study. The woman with cancer is the best interpreter of her own story. In this context, the researcher must be informed about technical issues and language (e.g., symptoms of illness, types of treatment used) but avoid all preconceived notions. The researcher must earn the respondent's trust and help the respondent connect her views into a single "story line." It is the researcher's job to make sense of what is remembered and forgotten, said and left unsaid.

The researcher tapes dozens of hours of interviews with each respondent, then transcribes the interviews and looks for "themes" in each woman's "story." Then she looks for common themes among the stories she has heard from her respondents. Finally, she attempts to make sense of these themes — for example, feelings of powerlessness, physical violation or loss of sexuality — in terms of dominant social expectations about health, youth and femininity.

Other examples of qualitative research are Keniston's study of alienated youth (1965) and Garfinkel's landbreaking study of "Agnes," a transsexual (1967). Perhaps the most astonishing work is done through participant observation. For example, we could cite Goffman's studies of mental hospitals — he passed himself off as an inmate to do this research (Goffman, 1961). Good research, whether qualitative or quantitative, is persuasive and enlightening. But it is hard to do. It requires careful planning; an ability to define a workable problem and to find a feasible approach that suits the problem; and systematic follow-through.

DESIGNING A STUDY

Types of Research Design

Planning and carrying out research requires the preparation of a research design. A **research design** is an orderly plan for collecting, analyzing and interpreting data. The design chosen will depend on the nature of the problem that is being studied. It will also depend on the time, money and skill that are available.

We can do research on any question in a number of different ways: there is no one "right" way to do research. However, a good research design will match an interesting question with the skills and resources we actually have available.

Sometimes, we lack the resources to study what we want to study in an effective way. Consider the following example. Research has suggested that migrants are more dynamic and ambitious than the people they leave behind. This hypothesis makes sense: after all, emigration does carry risks, and taking risks requires courage, energy and ambition. So we have a theory that explains the hypothesis; now we need data to test whether the hypothesis is valid. How should we measure whether immigrants really are more ambitious and dynamic than average; and whom should we measure? We shall consider questions of measurement a little later. For now, let us consider the second question: *whom* to measure.

The researcher realizes that in the time available it will be impossible to study all immigrants. She decides to study immigrants from Portugal who live in Montreal. She makes her decision on the grounds of convenience: it happens that she speaks Portuguese and lives in Montreal. That's fine for her, but do *we* have any reason to suppose that Portuguese immigrants in Montreal represent all immigrants living everywhere? Unless she can give us a satisfactory answer to that question, or define the question more narrowly, the researcher should not go any further with this project.

Suppose the researcher does go on. She has a test that measures, on a scale from 1 to 10, how dynamic and ambitious a person is. She tests fifty Portuguese immigrants in Montreal and finds they score an average 6.5 out of 10. Is this score high or low? Does it prove her hypothesis right or not? To answer this, she must compare their score with another group's. But which group is appropriate: (a) Canadian-born people of non-Portuguese ancestry; (b) Canadian-born people of Portuguese ancestry; (c) Portuguese immigrants who avoided going to Montreal; or (d) people born and continuing to live in Portugal?

The answer is (d). The researcher needs to compare these Portuguese non-immigrants — the people who stayed behind — with Portuguese immigrants, to see whether they differ in their dynamism and ambition. If the immigrants score significantly higher, she has validated her hypothesis. If they score the same or lower than the non-immigrants, the data have defeated her hypothesis. The important point to note is that any data she collects from groups (a), (b) and (c) are irrelevant. They cannot answer the question the researcher has posed.

In short, we should not try to answer this particular question unless we can go to Portugal to collect the data we need. If we cannot go to Portugal, we should answer another question or study another topic. There is no way to complete *this* project with data collected only in Canada. This is the kind of problem a researcher can, and should, anticipate when designing research, because the trip to Portugal is a required built-in expense.

Experiments and Quasi-experiments

When designing our research, we need to decide on what method to use to obtain the information we need. Typically, social scientists will make use of methods such as an experiment, quasi-experiment, correlational analysis, or single case analysis. We shall consider each of these methods in turn, and show that each can bring particular insights to our research.

An **experiment** is a research method designed to investigate the effect of one variable on another. The experiment takes place under well-controlled, carefully regulated conditions, in an artificial setting, usually a laboratory. In brief, the experimenter introduces the independent variable, then observes and measures its effect on the dependent variable.

The experimental method allows the researcher to control any extrinsic factors that might influence the phenomenon under study. One of the ways of controlling variables is by assigning each subject to one of two groups — an experimental group and a control group — in an unbiased way: either by random assignment or careful matching. The *experimental group* is exposed to the effects of the independent variable introduced by the researcher. The *control group* may be closely matched to the experimental group, and contains the same mix of ages, genders, educational levels and so on. The experimenter does *not* expose control subjects to the independent variable whose effects are being studied.

Often, sociologists argue that the experimental method is artificial: it is hard to imagine a real-life situation similar to the experimental ones research subjects find themselves in. For this reason, they prefer a research design that is more natural: for example, a quasi-experiment. A *quasi-experiment* modifies the experimental design, to study a problem that does not lend itself readily or naturally to an experiment.

Like an experiment, the quasi-experiment uses experimental and control groups, and compares people's behaviours before and after the experimental group receives their special treatment. However, the quasi-experiment does not randomly select or match experimental and control-group subjects. Nor can it control other changes in the environment.

Consider the following example. A group called the Canadian Alliance for Chastity, described in Applied Sociology, below, is promoting sexual abstinence among Canadian teenagers. Members of the group visit high schools and try, by emphasizing the risky nature of contraception, to persuade listeners to avoid sex. They claim that condoms fail eighteen times in a hundred trials, which (supposedly) results in eighteen unwanted pregnancies per hundred sex acts. We can view each sex act as a quasi-experiment which, 18 per cent of the time, allegedly produces an unwanted result. What the speaker doesn't mention is that other research shows condoms work almost perfectly when people *want* to prevent pregnancy. They mainly "fail" when users are poorly motivated to prevent pregnancies because they want to have a child "sooner or later": that is, when they are using condoms to space their childbirths rather than prevent them.

So, implicit in this report is a quasi-experimental design. One group, which isn't trying very hard to prevent pregnancy, is observed to suffer a high *failure* rate with condoms. The other group — unreported by the Chastity Alliance but observed by us anyway — is trying hard to prevent pregnancy and achieves a high *success* rate with condoms. What this quasi-experiment really shows, then, is that people who are having sex should be clear on whether they want to prevent pregnancy.

Substitutes for Experiments

Neither the experiment nor the quasi-experiment is common in sociological research. Far more common is *correlational analysis*, a type of research design that measures the association between two phenomena (cross-sectional analysis) or associated changes in two phenomena (longitudinal analysis).

In general, a *longitudinal study* involves gathering data from the same sample at intervals over time. It is a useful method for studying trends and the effects of particular changes. One form of longitudinal analysis, called a *panel study*, is the basis for Statistics Canada's monthly Labour Force Survey. Each month

Canadian Alliance for Chastity

APPLIED SOCIOLOGY

Of all sociologists, applied sociologists are probably the most cautious. They are always asking themselves questions like: What is the problem to be solved? What is the best way to solve it? And what are the likely side effects, or unwanted consequences, of trying to solve it that way? Just for a moment, play "applied sociologist" and ask yourself these questions while reading the excerpt below.

The message is simple: Wait until marriage. Marry for life.

Mr. Kun is one of 33 abstinent young adults (their ages range from 18 to 24) who are nearing the end of a national four-week chastity road trip, speaking to more than 100,000 students in nearly 500 schools.

It's difficult to know exactly how many Canadian students are adopting sexual abstinence, although the Canada Youth and AIDS study published in 1988, the last year comprehensive statistics on youth sex were compiled, found that 51 per cent of males and 54 per cent of females in Grade 11 had never had intercourse. The figures for college and university students were 23 and 26 per cent respectively.

In Canada, the idea of abstinence has captured a prominent place in sex education, as teachers try to persuade students that heartache, pregnancy and disease can be avoided by postponing sex. The first national guidelines on sexual health education, quietly published by Health Canada last November, twice mention abstinence counselling as one form of effective education.

Alex McKay, research co-ordinator with the Sex Information and Education Council of Canada, discerns a sexist subtext in the presentations and says many of the facts used are simply wrong. The opinions are one-sided, using scare tactics and distortion, he says. One aspect of the tour's message to which Mr. McKay objects is that it implicitly encourages early marriage and early childbearing, which he says can have a detrimental effect on a woman's career prospects.

Back at Our Lady Queen of Peace School, Mr. Kun is telling the students that society and even sex educators are pushing them to have sex, and that the chastity message is a voice in the wilderness.

He and his co-lecturer, Anna Piorecky, 19, also take a dim view of condoms. He tells the 200 students present that the failure rate of condoms is 18.4 per cent. Then he chooses five audience members to join him up front. He hands each a die. Each is to roll it 10 times, representing 10 years of sexual activity. Each time a four appears, he or she is to shout: "It's a boy!"

Six times a four appears and the shout is heard. Using condoms, six unplanned children would have been born to those five couples over 10 years, Mr. Kun says. "That's what they're calling safe sex."

Linda Smith, director of the sexual and reproductive health program of Calgary's public health system, and one of the 15 people who helped develop the national sex education guidelines, says she worries that this sort of lecture will persuade teens not to use condoms if they do become sexually active.

Source: Abridged from Alanna Mitchell, *The Globe and Mail*, Fri., June 2, 1995, pp. A1, A5

Statistics Canada surveys a new batch of respondents, as well as some of the respondents it surveyed the month before. In this way it can keep a running record of employment changes over time.

However, even panel studies are rare in sociology. There are problems with the initial selection of people, because most people do not want to commit themselves to repeated study. Moreover, the group, or panel, may undergo changes as a result of being on the panel, and therefore becomes less representative of the general population. Most important, it costs a great deal of money to re-interview people after a lapse of time, especially if many of the original sample have died, moved away or lost interest in the project, and must be tracked down. Of course, if they loathed the project, they will even resist being tracked down.

Average Weekly Usage of Automated Teller Machines

Respondents were asked:
In an average week, how often would you say you use an automatic teller machine to do your banking?

A. Percentage who use ATMs, by age:

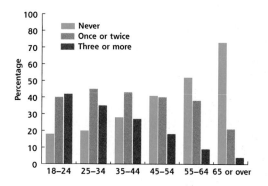

B. Percentage who use ATMs, by education:

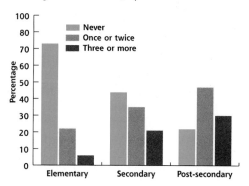

C. Percentage who use ATMs, by sex:

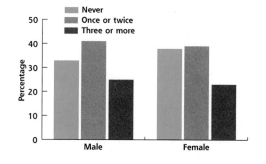

1,518 Canadian residents 18 years of age and over surveyed June 3–13, July 8–18, Aug. 5–16, 1994. Results are accurate to 2.65 percentage points, 95 times out of 100.

Source: Based on statistics appearing in *The Decima Quarterly Report/Summer 1994*

More common is the *retrospective survey*, where respondents are asked to report what has happened to them in the last month, year or other period, but all at one time: now. This method is used to collect valuable data about family life, as, for example, in the Family History Survey, and about work life, as in the Annual Work Pattern Survey.

Such research has produced interesting results that could not have been gained in another way. For example, at any given moment, the proportion of people who are unemployed is large. However, until recently, unemployment was a brief and common experience for most. For a minority — the chronically unemployed — frequent and long-term unemployment occurs whenever the economy worsens. It is they who are pushed into poverty when jobs become scarce. What's more, with a good research design, we can identify who these high-risk people are.

The most common research design in sociology is cross-sectional analysis. A *cross-sectional* study gathers evidence on subjects at just one point in time. The researcher tries to discover and explain the pattern of associations among variables. So, for example, the data in Social Profile 12-2 shows that the frequent use of automated (bank) teller machines (ATMs) is *highly* related to age and education: younger, more highly educated people use the machines more often than older, less educated people. However, the use of ATMs is virtually unrelated to gender: men and women use them almost equally often. Can you propose a theory to account for these findings?

The problem with this kind of research is that it is difficult to sort out causes from effects, because the data give no clue about the time sequence. The researcher cannot know which variable changed first — presumably, it is the cause — and which changed next — and is therefore the effect. For example, does higher education lead people to make more use of computerized machines? Or does familiarity with computerized machines enable people to get a higher education?

As we see in this example, a related problem of "spuriousness" may arise: in cross-sectional analysis, it is more difficult to determine whether both the supposed cause and effect are, in fact, the result of a third factor researchers are failing to measure. For example, it may be exposure to computerized technology — a third factor — which accounts for the apparent influence of age on ATM use.

Despite these problems, cross-sectional analysis remains attractive because of its low cost and easy execution. The researcher has to collect data only once, which means he or she can afford to collect a lot of data at one time, instead of "thinner" data on several occasions.

Single Case Analysis

The study of a single case — whether a single person, a group or a society — has a great deal of appeal for other sociologists. *Single case analysis* is a type of research design that involves a detailed, in-depth examination of a single example of a class of phenomena. By getting to know a lot about that single case, we learn not only about the "why" of something, but also about the "how." That is, we learn more about the process by which a cause creates an effect.

Single case analysis is reasonably common in sociology, although less common than in certain applied fields like clinical psychology, social work and management studies. The reason sociologists shy away from it is because you cannot be certain that the case you have studied truly represents all of the cases you might have studied. So you run a great risk when you try to generalize from these findings to other cases.

One solution is to make a smaller claim for the truth value of what you have discovered by this method. Instead of calling your work an explanatory or theory-testing project, you might be wiser to call it an exploratory or theory-building project.

We are in a slightly stronger position if we conduct a type of single case analysis called deviant case analysis. *Deviant case analysis* is a research design that studies a single case that fails to conform to an expected pattern. By failing to support a given hypothesis, the case forces us to revise and enrich the original hypothesis.

We start a deviant case analysis by conceding that there is truth to the theory we are testing. For example, most sociological research finds a very weak relationship between income and happiness. Since this runs against common sense, we may feel we need more insight into this finding. We could start with a study that focused on a particular subpopulation, such as the very rich or the very poor. To do this, Diener, Horowitz, and Emmons (1985) sampled people from *Forbes* business magazine's list of the wealthiest Americans, and compared them with people selected randomly from telephone directories. Those agreeing to participate completed a questionnaire about life concerns and life satisfaction.

In their survey, wealthy respondents prove to be happy a higher percentage of the time, score significantly higher on two different life-satisfaction scales and report significantly lower levels of "negative affect" — that is, unhappiness. Not all the wealthy are happy, of course; some are just as unhappy as unhappy ordinary persons sampled. Furthermore, few respondents, whether wealthy or ordinary, believe that money is a major source of happiness.

This research finds that wealthy and ordinary people also differ in what satisfies them. Wealthy respondents more often mention self-esteem and self-actualization as sources of their satisfaction, while ordinary people more often mention food, shelter and other basic human needs and safety concerns as sources of satisfaction. In short, a close study of the very rich seems to contradict the findings of research on the happiness of most ordinary people.

Here, the single case method of study, which encourages closely detailed work and a deeper understanding, would help sort out this confusion. Consider,

Graffiti gives sociologists an unobtrusive method of gauging people's opinions and moods.

for example, historian Michael Bliss's long biography of Canada's first million-aire, Sir Joseph Wesley Flavelle (Bliss, 1985). Flavelle rose from humble origins to become exceptionally rich and powerful. What we learn from his biography is the great importance of Methodist religion in his life. Flavelle was actively in-volved with his church and carried his religious beliefs into all his secular ac-tivities. His religion not only encouraged him to participate in social and political activity, it gave him recognition for his good works and success.

Armed with this insight, we can consider a new theory for testing. The the-ory might run as follows: For most people, income has little effect on happiness. For people with a high income, money has a positive effect on happiness if they (a) see their income as a heavenly reward or proof of their merit, and (b) use their income to engage in socially gratifying (and religiously meaningful) activi-ties. Stated otherwise, Scrooge was miserable not because he was rich but because he was socially isolated and irreligious (just as Dickens suggested!).

Note how much richer our understanding of the relationship between in-come and happiness becomes when we move from multiple case to single case analysis. Having said that, we have no right to generalize our results from data on Flavelle. With deviant case analysis, we have enriched our theory and found new variables. We must now study them more systematically with experimental, quasi-experimental or correlational methods. With single case analysis, we have only explored, not explained, happiness in a general sense.

MEASUREMENT

Not all research consists of explanation; much of it consists of gathering data with which to describe some activity, condition or event. Sometimes we gather data from documents, or observations, or processes. Sometimes variables can be presented in measurable form.

Measurement Scales

Measurement is a process of finding the extent, size or degree of some-thing. Quantitative sociological research depends on its ability to measure things:

the rate of suicide, the degree of integration of people into society, the level of satisfaction with life and so on. Unfortunately, measurement is often difficult, especially when the variables to be measured are abstract concepts such as satisfaction, alienation, segregation and inequality.

Measuring concepts well means, first, developing an operational definition of those concepts. As noted earlier, an *operational definition* links the meaning of a concept to procedures for measuring it. An operational definition of intelligence, for example, would be the score obtained on a set of specific questions answered in specific ways. The IQ score reflects the method used to measure intelligence. There may be something else we mean by intelligence that is independent of the means we use to measure it but, without a specific measure, the concept cannot be used for quantitative research.

In order to measure particular traits and characteristics, we need to identify variables which can be scaled. **Scales** are systems of units arranged in steps or degrees, allowing the researcher to assign numbers to observed events or responses. After reducing them to number scores, the researcher can manipulate response patterns to bring out whatever relationships exist among them. There are a number of ways in which this can be done.

One of the most common types of scales used by sociologists to arrange variables is a *nominal* or *categorical scale*. A nominal scale arranges a set of categories that we cannot order from high to low, large to small. For example, to the question "What language do you speak at home?" people may answer English, French, German, Polish, Italian, Greek and so on. A score on a nominal scale indicates the category into which a person falls. We would not say that speaking English gives one a higher or lower score than speaking Greek. The numbers we would assign to these scores would simply identify them and allow us to correlate language spoken with other social characteristics.

An *ordinal scale* contains categories that do range from high to low, so that movement along the scale indicates an increasing or decreasing size on some dimension. For example, eligible answers to the question "How often do you telephone your grandmother?" may include "very often," "occasionally" and "rarely." We know that "very often" is more than "occasionally" and that "occasionally" is more often than "rarely." This ordering, from high to low, is what characterizes an ordinal scale.

Like an ordinal scale, an *interval scale* contains categories that range from high to low. In the ordinal scale, we cannot be certain of the distance between categories. We do not know if the person phoning his grandmother "very often" does so eight times as often as the person who phones his grandmother "occasionally," or if the person phoning his grandmother "occasionally" does so only twice as often as the person who phones "rarely." However, in an interval scale, the distances or intervals between neighbouring categories are the same.

Finally, a *ratio scale* has both characteristics of an interval scale — hierarchical ordering and equal distances between categories — and one more as well: an absolute zero point. (For example, "How many glasses of water do you drink per day, on average?" Answer: 0, 1, 2, 3, 4, 5 . . . 1,000.)

On an interval scale, respondents cannot indicate a complete absence of something: of work satisfaction, for example. For some variables, no absolute zero exists. For example, no one has absolutely no intelligence, energy or physical attractiveness. Judgments on these issues are always bound to be relative. However, in a great many cases, absolute zero does exist. Last month, you may have earned absolutely no dollars, drunk no water and telephoned your grandmother zero times. Maybe no one among the people you know will name you as their "best friend." Where an absolute zero does exist, it is better to use a ratio scale than any other.

Unobtrusive Measures

Remember that research is a social enterprise. Even physicists, who study inanimate objects, realize that the act of measurement itself can disturb the thing being measured. As a result, researchers may never be able to get a truly accurate measure of something in its natural state. If this is true of atoms and molecules, imagine how serious the problem is when studying people. For this reason, it is often important that the measurement process itself be unobtrusive. An *unobtrusive measure* is one in which there is no interaction between the investigator and the people being studied. Because it does not require interaction, the responses of the people studied are not "reactive."

People are not only objects of sociological study, they are students of their own lives. People usually know when researchers are studying them. They judge the purpose and meaning of questions they are asked, and answer in ways that relate to the researcher's goals. In short, people play a role when they are aware of being studied. Occasionally, they give the researcher answers they think the researcher is looking for; or, they give the exact opposite, to shake the researcher up a bit. Often they think about things they have never considered before, and are transformed by the research process. In none of these cases is the respondent a passive object of study.

It is difficult for researchers to avoid or minimize such reactions from the people they study. It is far better to avoid the problem than to have to remedy it. That is where unobtrusive measures come in. Sociologists look for unobtrusive measures and often find them. They already exist in nature, if we are willing to look.

In their classic work on the topic, *Unobtrusive Measures*, Webb et al. (1966) discuss the strengths and weaknesses of several types of unobtrusive measure. One type is the "physical trace," the proof of erosion or accretion. A pathway worn through grass, over a carpet, or even on wood or stone shows where a great many people have been heading. By definition, the best-worn path is most popular; sociologists might want to find out why. Likewise, the largest line-up, the most graffiti on a wall, or most pennies in a wishing well — these accretions show where the most people (or the most active people) are spending their time. Again, sociologists might want to find out why.

A recent piece of unobtrusive research examined garbage to find out the relationship between what people *said* they ate and what they *actually* ate. As Social Profile 12.3 shows, if you ask people what they eat, they tend to report healthy eating practices — for example, a lot of cottage cheese and not a lot of chips and candy. But if you check their garbage, you find there's a gap between what people say and what they do. The moral of this story: Be prepared to check the quality of your data in as many ways as you can afford to. (Also, wear a gas mask to the research site.)

A second type of unobtrusive measure is the archival record, particularly any running record officially collected for public use such as records of births, deaths and marriages, tax records, Census forms, court records and records of parliamentary debate. A third type is offered by data that are usually not part of the public record, such as sales records, institutional records and personal documents (such as diaries, letters sent and received). Other forms of unobtrusive research include the observation of external physical signs (beards, tattoos, clothing, expressive movements), physical locations (for example, clustering versus segregation) and the sampling of overheard conversation.

SOCIAL PROFILE 12.3

The Lean Cuisine Syndrome

When asked to describe consumption habits, people tend to provide inaccurate reports about themselves, by underreporting consumption of food items that have a more 'negative' image and overreporting consumption of the more 'positive' ones.

% Underreported		% Overreported	
Sugar	94	Cottage Cheese	311
Chips/popcorn	81	Liver	200
Candy	80	Tuna	184
Bacon	80	Vegetable soup	94
Ice cream	63	Corn bread	72
Ham/lunch meats	57	Skim milk	57
Sausage	56	High-fibre cereal	55

Source: From *Rubbish! The Archaeology of Garbage* by William Rathje and Cullen Murphy. Copyright © 1992 by William Rathje and Cullen Murphy. Reprinted by permission of HarperCollins Publishers Inc.

Knowing If a Measure Is "Good"

The first thing we must be concerned about when we make a good measure is to make sure that our procedures are appropriate for the question we are asking. Suppose we want to measure change in the number of common law marriages over time. Well, first of all, we have to be certain *we* know what we mean by "common law" marriage, then that our *respondents* know what we mean. Otherwise, an apparent change in the numbers may just show (1) a change in what we meant, or (2) what other people meant by the term — not a useful finding. To ensure we find out what we need to know, we need clear definitions and good measures based on these definitions.

Here's an example. The Gallup pollsters asked people the following question: "Out of every tax dollar that goes to the federal government in Ottawa, how many cents of each dollar would you say are wasted?" The average respondent said about 47 cents in every dollar were being wasted.

The result has a certain obvious meaning: people are angry and frustrated with the government. But when you start to analyze the responses, you see the problems. As one might expect, supporters of the Conservative Party — the party that was then in power — estimated the least amount of waste (about 37 cents per dollar, on average). Supporters of the Reform Party estimated the largest amount of waste (about 52 cents per dollar). But supporters of the Liberal, NDP and Bloc Québécois parties fell in between at different amounts (46, 41 and 38 cents, respectively). Why were their averages different from those of the Reform Party and different from one another?

In short, we are stuck with a measure that is far too simple for the phenomenon we are trying to understand. We cannot make and test good theories so long as our measurements are too simple for the concepts they are representing. Measuring well is difficult yet crucially important.

SAMPLING Surveys and Sampling

Accurate data are the essence of good social science. To get them, we need appropriate measures; we also need good and trustworthy samples. As we have seen, there are many ways to measure things in sociological research, yet no matter how you choose to measure something, you cannot expect to measure it for everyone. The population of Canada, let alone the population of the world, is too large. This is why researchers study samples of people, not entire populations.

A **population** is the set of all people who share a specific characteristic of interest to the researcher: for example, it may be all Canadians or only Canadians who are over age forty-five, speak Chinese at home, play bridge for recreation or drive sports cars. We define a population in relation to the specific research question we want to answer. Every research project may imply a different population.

A **sample** is a relatively small number of people drawn from the population of interest. Almost all research studies samples, not total populations. Pure research by academic sociologists, market research, political polls, labour market surveys by government — all use samples which may represent 1 per cent of the population under study, or even less.

Even with a sample that comprises only a small percentage of the total population, great accuracy is possible. Estimates of the total population characteristics based on a small sample are no more than a few percentage points off in nineteen times out of twenty, if the sample is drawn correctly. Thus, samples are accurate enough for most purposes, as well as convenient and cheap.

The only time that sampling is *not* used in social research is when complete enumeration is necessary and cost is no consideration. In practice, in Canada this occurs in only one case: a national Census, carried out on the total population once every ten years. However, for reasons of cost, the Census asks each household member only a few questions. A 20 per cent sample of the population that is questioned in more detail at the same time yields more complete and sociologically interesting information.

Yet even when Statistics Canada tries to survey the whole population of Canada, as in the Census, many people are missed: possibly 5 or 10 per cent of the population. The Census most often misses fugitives, transients, illiterates and people living in other people's households. In short, a Census misses the poorest, youngest and least educated part of the Canadian population.

Types of Samples

Of the many ways to draw a sample of the population, some are better than others. The question to be answered will determine the suitable sample type. The cost and time available will determine the feasibility of using one sampling method instead of another.

The simplest type of sample is a *convenience* (or *availability*) *sample*. People who are accessible or willing to participate in the survey make up the sample. Interviewers station themselves in a public place — a busy street corner, an airport waiting room, a museum lobby, student lounge or large shopping centre, for example — and ask everyone who passes to answer a few questions. A convenience sample may fairly well represent the population that passes through that public place. For this reason, a convenience sample is good for generating new ideas, trying out measurements and getting preliminary research findings: for exploring the problem. But this kind of sample is never good enough to test a theory.

Another easy but imperfect method is to use a snowball sample. A snowball sample is made up of people referred to the researcher by others already in the sample. Think of a snowball rolling downhill, getting bigger as it goes.

The obvious advantage of a snowball sample is its ease and low cost. A less obvious advantage is its usefulness in finding rare or hidden subjects. Imagine trying to put together a sample of cocaine users, chess players, Gypsies or parents of children with Nintendo 64. It would be much easier to sample them through networks of similar people than by advertising in the newspaper, stopping people on a street corner or telephoning names drawn at random from a phone book. Where researchers are studying illegal or deviant behaviour, an introduction to the potential subject by an existing subject may make all the difference between cooperation and a refusal.

However, as with the convenience sample, we cannot be sure a snowball sample really represents all members of the population. Sociologists will use a snowball sample cautiously and for purposes of exploration, not explanation.

A third type of sample is the quota sample. A *quota sample* begins by defining categories that are in the same proportion as one finds in the population, then draws a certain number of respondents within each category. Suppose we want to study attitudes towards a more traditional school curriculum. We know that the population of the school district is 51 per cent male, 49 per cent female; 25 per cent Catholic and 75 per cent Protestant; 90 per cent native-born and 10 per cent immigrant; and so on. To get our sample of one hundred adult respondents, we will continue selecting available people until we have one hundred with the same "statistical profile" as the population.

In some ways, this sampling method is much better than the pure convenience sample. For example, it is more likely than the convenience sample to yield a variety of characteristics and opinions. However, we have no guarantee that people sampled in this way accurately represent the opinions of the whole population.

To avoid unwanted biases, good surveys use randomly selected samples. Researchers draw *random samples* from the population so that every member has an equal chance of being selected for the survey. To draw a *simple random sample* at your college, we would start with a complete list of all the students. Blindfolded, we would draw names out of a hat until we had the number of names we needed. Or we would assign an identification number to every name

Interviewing is a common and effective way of getting social information. Here a woman is collecting data from a convenience or availability sample.

and use a table of random numbers, or a computerized random-number generator, to select the sample.

A *systematic sample* is just as good. If we need a sample of one hundred people and there are 5,000 students at your college, we would select our first respondent on the list randomly, then select every fiftieth name after that. Like the simple random sample, the systematic sample avoids introducing a bias into the selection process. Everyone has the same chance for an interview. However, in both cases, pure chance may fail to give us enough cases of a kind we need: enough graduating students, handicapped students or students in a particular field of study, for example. To prevent this from happening, we would use a stratified sampling procedure.

Stratified sampling divides the population into categories (or strata) according to a characteristic of interest — in this case, let's say field of study. In general,

APPLIED SOCIOLOGY

Counting In the Homeless

The least one expects of a mature science is that it can count and describe accurately, and on the face of it, this seems like little to ask. But in practice, counting accurately is often hard to do. In Canada and elsewhere, programs for the homeless require a reliable estimate of the people who need help. But counting homeless people is difficult precisely because they are homeless, with no phone number to call, front door to knock on or place to call their own.

Just how many people are actually homeless in Metro Toronto is a question that is going to take a lot of work to answer. "Despite our best efforts there is no definite count," said Chris Brooks of Statistics Canada's Toronto office. StatsCan tried to count people at 90 hostels and soup kitchens for the 1991 census. But the number was not published because it was considered too inaccurate to report.

In this year's census, an experiment was conducted in Vancouver by counting people sleeping in Stanley Park, but other cities don't have one central area favoured by the homeless. "People who don't stay in shelters, who brave –30-degree weather to stay out all night, are not inclined to stand up and be counted," Mr. Brooks said. "We won't do the dumpster enumeration, chasing people down alleys, like the U.S. does."

The Toronto Coalition Against Homelessness estimates about 25,000 people are homeless in Metro — double its estimate for 1984. The figure includes people staying in public and charitable hostels; people who sleep in stairwells, bank foyers and parks and under bridges; people who ride the transit system all night; and people who illegally stay in abandoned buildings. It does not include what coalition spokesman Michael Shapcott calls the "nearly homeless" — those who have doubled up with other families, for instance.

One of the problems with looking at homelessness through hostel admissions — 34,000 in 1982, 60,000 in 1991, and 68,000 last year in Metro-run hostels — is that they are full of duplications. The same people may stay in hostels regularly. John Jagt, director of hostel services for the Metro Toronto government, says the city knows that 28,000 different people used hostels last year. But some were without a home for only a matter of weeks, he said.

An average night in peak season saw 4,000 people staying in shelters, 1,600 of them single men and 1,400 of them in family groupings. Right now there are 3,000 people in hostels each night, he said.

Two homeless men outside downtown Toronto's Union Station a couple of weeks ago illustrate another major limitation in the hostel counting system.

Mr. Jagt said the stereotype of a homeless persons as someone sitting on a sidewalk laden with plastic bags does not accurately represent the reality.

"The typical homeless woman does not look like a bag lady; she's wearing ordinary clothes. You might see a bag lady on the street and think you've seen one homeless person, when in fact you've seen a dozen homeless people but you only noticed the bag lady."

Source: Abridged from Jane Gadd, *The Globe and Mail*, Wed., July 31, 1996, p. A8

the stratifying variable should be a major independent variable in the study. Then the researcher samples randomly within each category, using either the simple random or systematic sampling method. Doing this ensures the researcher will get no fewer (or more) respondents in a given category than are to be found in the population; and these will have been chosen without bias. In effect, a stratified sample is an unbiased version of the quota sample we discussed earlier.

Finally, there is the *cluster sample*, which divides the population into geographic locales, then samples randomly within each locale. The cluster sample is like a stratified sample in which the stratifying characteristic is location. Like the stratified sample, it is relatively unbiased. However, once a researcher chooses locales for sampling, people outside those locales have no chance of being studied. Like the convenience sample, the cluster sample reduces the costs associated with distance and travel. It is particularly useful, then, if distances are large, as in a national survey. Smaller distances do not require cluster sampling or justify it.

Read the excerpt in Applied Sociology, below, on the problems census-takers face in counting the number of homeless people. What strategy do you think would work best if you wanted to survey a sample of the homeless?

DATA COLLECTION STRATEGIES

Have you considered how difficult it is to collect reliable data? Without such data, you have no hope of testing your theories. Beyond that, you have no hope of developing good social policies and programs, since these rest on good theories. Just think of the practical consequences of policies that are based on wrong information about the extent of poverty, crime or discrimination, for example.

Sociologists collect many different kinds of data and collect them in a variety of different ways. This section will briefly touch on five particular data collection strategies: secondary data analysis, participant observation, content analysis, interviewing, and questionnaires.

Secondary Data Analysis

Sociologists often collect data first-hand to answer a question they are posing. Often, however, they also use data other researchers have collected to answer other questions. *Secondary data analysis* examines and interprets data that have been gathered by another researcher or by the federal government. For a small cost, researchers can buy computer-readable tapes of data from the Census or the monthly Labour Force Survey, for example. Statistics Canada currently makes available hundreds of high-quality data sets for both academic research and market research. Indeed, scholars outside government probably analyze government-collected data more thoroughly than does anyone else.

Secondary analysis of data collected by other academics is also common. Archives such as the one at York University (Toronto) enable scholars to share with one another the data they have collected. Given the enormous costs of collecting survey data, occasionally in the millions of dollars, such data-sharing is sensible and desirable.

Secondary data analysis can turn up some interesting results. For example, a simple re-analysis of the results of the Olympic Games, which takes into account the different sizes of the countries participating, concludes that the big winners were actually Tonga, the Bahamas, Jamaica, Cuba and Australia. (By this measure, Canada was a big loser even though it performed over 50 percent better than the U.S.! See for yourself in Social Profile 12-4, below.)

The disadvantage of secondary data analysis is that these data were not collected with the second researcher's goals in mind. For example, government-collected data rarely contain many of the variables that interest sociologists.

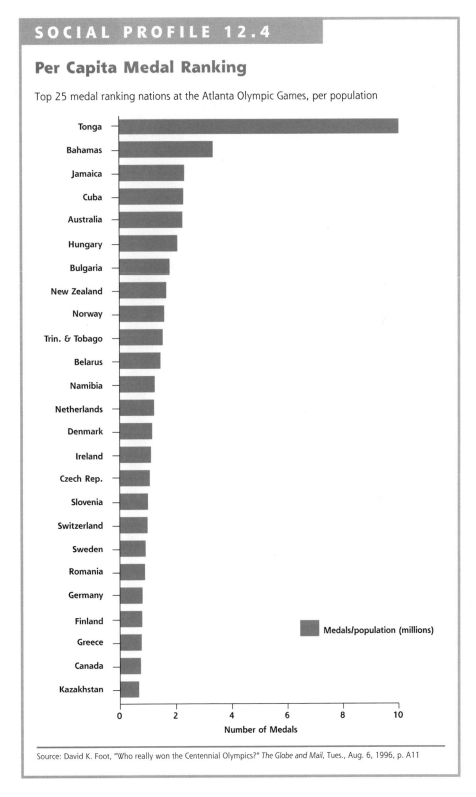

SOCIAL PROFILE 12.4

Per Capita Medal Ranking

Top 25 medal ranking nations at the Atlanta Olympic Games, per population

Source: David K. Foot, "Who really won the Centennial Olympics?" *The Globe and Mail*, Tues., Aug. 6, 1996, p. A11

Government data usually measure economic and demographic variables but shy away from data on people's feelings and attitudes. Government researchers avoid asking sensitive or intimate questions that might embarrass the government if a Member of Parliament attacked a Statistics Canada survey in Parliament.

Participant Observation

Observation has a longer history than any other form of social research. Since all of us can observe, it is also the easiest and least expensive form of research. But observation by itself can and usually does lead to distortions. We "read into" a situation more than might be there, or we fail to note subtle cues, gestures or meanings we do not know enough to catch.

Because observation has so many limitations, sociologists make use of a particular variation known as **participant observation** to gain first-hand information on forms of social interaction and social processes. Participant observation is a method of gathering data that requires the sociologist to become a participant in the social group being studied. The researcher takes part in the activities of the group, thereby gaining an insight into the subjective understandings of the group members.

The people being studied are usually unaware of being studied, and so they will behave in a typical, non-reactive manner. The participant observer might hang out with hustlers in bars, go to synagogue with orthodox Jews, smoke marijuana with jazz musicians, befriend slum kids or work in a mental hospital.

This research method assumes that researchers cannot understand a topic fully without intimately experiencing it first-hand. The method relies heavily on the skills, feelings, insights and intuition of the researcher. Since the researcher's subjective understanding of the situation is critical, one cannot easily generalize the findings to other groups or to the population at large. Still, participant observation provides a useful alternative or supplement to survey research — which rarely includes observation of actual behaviour — and to experimental research — which observes behaviour in an artificial setting.

In participant observation, the sociologist acts as both object (i.e., participant) and subject (i.e., observer) of the research process. This double role causes conflict and confusion for the new researcher. It also runs a double risk of distorting the research. On the one hand, by participating in the group, a researcher risks taking on the world-view of that group and losing an objective sense of what the group is doing. On the other hand, by observing the group while participating in it, the researcher risks changing the processes under study.

Like all activities that require an intimate knowledge of people's lives — law, medicine, social work, journalism, and the ministry, for example — participant observation raises many ethical questions. How should the researcher treat illegal behaviour, whether confessed or observed? How should the researcher respond to vicious and immoral behaviour? How should the researcher deal with conflicts and coalitions within the group, and whose side should the researcher take? There are no simple answers to these questions. That is why participant observation is much harder to learn and teach than any other type of research method.

Nevertheless, while participant observation is difficult, it has produced a significant legacy of excellent research. This particular research style was popularized among sociologists at the University of Chicago in the 1920s and came to be the method of choice for microsociologists such as symbolic interactionists. One microsociologist, Erving Goffman, produced such provocative and insightful research reports from his observations that his books remain among the best-selling sociology books to date (see, for example, Goffman 1959, 1961).

Content Analysis

Content analysis involves analyzing the content of communications such as private letters, books, speeches and conversations, scripts of television shows, comic books, magazine articles and popular songs. The researcher picks out the main themes and classifies them according to a predetermined set of categories.

Particular categories for classifying the data are chosen to illuminate the issues under study. For example, a researcher (Wilson, 1977) may study how women are stereotyped in magazine articles. Are they portrayed as less intelligent and more vain than men, or as sexual toys "created" for the pleasure of men? Answering these questions will mean classifying and analyzing the content of many articles in a consistent, systematic way.

Content analysis forces researchers to make judgments, both when drawing up lists of categories and when classifying the data according to those categories. Occasionally, people classifying or *coding* the content will judge the material differently. For example, in analyzing the content of children's television programs, different data coders may want to use different criteria for deciding what constitutes a "display of violence or aggression." The ways around this problem are, as always, preventive and remedial. To prevent the problem, the researcher must train the data coders thoroughly in how to use the coding scheme that has been devised. To remedy the problem, the researcher will check the consistency of the coded material: whether it shifts over time, and whether some coders are providing results that vary a great deal from the other coders' results. Badly flawed codework will have to be redone.

Interviews and Questionnaires

The interview is another important method of gathering data in sociology. In an *interview*, an interviewer asks subjects questions in a face-to-face encounter or over the telephone. An interview may collect qualitative or quantitative data, and it may ask structured or unstructured questions.

A *structured interview* asks each respondent a standard set of questions in the same form and the same order. This type of interview often forces the respondent to choose from among predetermined choices. Questions may also be open-ended, allowing the respondent to answer in his or her preferred way. An *unstructured interview* is more flexible than that. There are more open-ended questions the interviewee can answer freely. The interviewer often follows up on answers to gain more insight into the interviewee's views and feelings.

Structured interviews permit the researcher to easily tabulate and analyze responses on a computer. Unstructured interviews provide data that are harder to compare across respondents. As well, unstructured interviews are particularly liable to errors resulting from poor interviewing skills. As with content analysis, these problems are more easily prevented than remedied afterwards. To prevent them, researchers must carefully select and train their interviewers and evaluate the material they are collecting as the research goes on.

Researchers often use *questionnaires* in surveys, too. They are sets of questions given to respondents and designed to provide answers to the central research question. Usually, questionnaires are sent by mail and filled out by the respondent without the assistance of an interviewer.

A questionnaire can be short — a few questions — or long — running to dozens or even hundreds of questions. The longer a questionnaire is, the less willing a respondent is to complete it or even begin filling it out. This fact encourages the researcher to make a questionnaire as short and appealing as possible, and to offer the respondent incentives for completing the questionnaire.

Why sociology? To understand why different people do the same things in the same situations.

The researcher must avoid asking questions that are ambiguous or offensive, or that fail to permit a sufficiently wide variety of responses. Ambiguous questions on a political-attitude questionnaire might include "Would you vote for the Reform Party if it supported free trade but opposed an increase in immigration?" Unambiguous questions will use familiar words and ask the respondent to make only one judgment at a time; for example, "How old are you?" "How satisfied are you with your job?"

Questions offering too narrow a range of answers are hard to avoid, since it is difficult to anticipate how widely people's views will vary. One way around this is by using open-ended questions; for example, "What are some of the things you like about being a parent?" "What problems do you think people will face in the 21st century?" However, the answers to these questions must then be coded for analysis — a costly and error-prone procedure. Open-ended questions also slow down the rate at which respondents can answer, and therefore reduce their willingness to cooperate. The best way to prevent such problems is by pre-testing the questionnaire on people who are not part of your sample, and re-writing poor questions.

Some people are less willing to fill out a questionnaire than others. Even in a well-planned questionnaire survey, the response rate may fall well below 50 per cent, meaning that half of the people that have been approached are refusing to participate. This forces us to ask whether the non-response is random or systematic. Response bias can seriously mar a study's validity.

The great advantage of collecting data by questionnaire is the low cost. By using questionnaires, a careful researcher can collect a lot of good-quality information for much less money than an interview study would cost. It is for this reason that sociologists have thought, learned and written a great deal about questionnaire construction.

SOCIOLOGY FOR WHAT?   **Empowering the Public**   Now that we are near the end of the book, it is worthwhile to return to a theme that we stated at the very beginning.

It is the importance but enormous difficulty of doing sociological research that is unbiased and value-free.

Bias in sociology is rarely the result of intentional falsehood or even sloppy work. More often than not, the problem derives from the peculiarity of sociologists. Most people in the world *are not* white, middle-class, middle-aged men with Ph.D.'s and secure, well-paying jobs. On the other hand, most sociologists still *are*. The typical academic sociologist who writes books and articles is an "insider" in the sense that he has a lot of insight into, and skill in, the sociological analysis of white, middle-class, Canadian society. In particular, he is interested in and good at studying how large public organizations (like colleges) work since, typically, he works in one. However, he is not quite so good at studying how households, small businesses, communities, intimate relations or informal groups work.

Now contrast this "insider" with someone we could call an "outsider." There are many kinds of outsiders and they are not all the same; in fact, what they mainly have in common is that they are *not* insiders.

In Canada, "outsiders" include people who are non-white, non-male, non-middle-class, non-middle-aged, non-Canadian. Probably none of these outsiders has the same experience with, and perspective on, large public organizations as the typical male sociologist, but each is likely to have a variety of other valuable insights into such organizations. What's more, each is likely to have a better knowledge and understanding of *private spaces*, including households and small businesses, and of *social inequality*.

Each of these outsiders is a vulnerable member of Canadian society: in one way or another, a victim or potential victim of the way society is organized. In fact, "life on the outside" is characterized by uncertainty, dependency, prejudice, unfairness: it's not an ivory-tower kind of existence. What this means is that people who are on the outside are bound to be critical of people who are on the inside, and sceptical of the ways they view and explain everyday life. They are likely to have very different views and explanations of everyday life.

Whether outsiders' views and explanations of "life on the inside" are more or less valid than accounts provided by white, middle-aged, male professors may be debatable. What is much less debatable is their expertise about "life on the outside": for example, their understanding of sexual harassment, racial discrimination, living on welfare, going to prison, being unemployed and so on. In short, outsiders are much more likely than insiders to have a good, intuitive sense of what the "outside experience" is all about.

Now consider where these ideas take us. The discrepancy between the characteristics and everyday lives of typical people and typical sociologists leads to three particular problems in the majority of sociological studies:

- an overemphasis on the sociology of "life on the inside," the conventional wisdom of sociology, or what we could call "insider views;"

- a lack of scepticism about "life on the inside." Such research would benefit from what we might call "second opinions," critiques of insider views and/or outsiders writing about "the inside." For example, second opinions might include women analyzing men's institutions (i.e., attitudes, behaviour, organizations), blacks analyzing white people's institutions, poor people analyzing middle-class institutions and so on;

- a lack of understanding of "life on the outside." This problem would benefit from what we might call "social outsights," views provided by outsiders writing about the outside. For example, social outsights would include women analyzing housework, black people analyzing racial identity or black community organization, poor people analyzing unemployment or "making ends meet."

From a research standpoint, making these changes would result in better, less biased and more revealing research. From a teaching standpoint, these changes would (1) undermine the idea that any single sociologist, especially an "insider," could possibly give the entire, true story of everyday life in Canada; (2) make clear that sociology is a discipline which struggles to explain everyday life *despite* competing versions of reality; and (3) show students that they, as outsiders, can make a contribution to sociological debate.

If we are to do good research in sociology, it will have to be non-sexist, non-racist and non-classist, and the reason is simple: one-sided, biased research is bad research. Beyond that, participation in the sociological enterprise by a wider variety of people empowers the public. More of us become active producers, not merely passive consumers, of knowledge about the lives we lead. Just think of the different kinds of sociological discoveries we might make if we approached the task from different viewpoints that, according to market researcher Michael Adams, distinguish the "Generation X" readers of this book (see Applied Sociology on the next page).

The Feminist Critique of Demography

Take as an example of using alternative viewpoints the feminist critique of demography. Feminists argue that demography has been dominated by a male viewpoint, and S.C. Watkins suggests that traditional demographic research leads us to

> *conclude that women are primarily producers of children and of child services; that they produce with little assistance from men; that they are socially isolated from relatives and friends; and that their commitment to the production of children and child services is expected to be rather fragile.* (Watkins, 1993: 553)

Beyond that, Watkins writes, "[We] would learn even less about men" from demographic writings than we learn about women. Finally, she concludes that "to a surprising degree, our research draws on what we take for granted about women, men and the relations between them in order to pose our research questions, to collect our data and to interpret our results."

Some reasons for these problems are easy to identify. Demography developed with a "hard science" mentality. This is symbolized in a heavy reliance on quantitative data, the use of higher mathematics to develop models and a style of writing that strives to imitate the (male-dominated) physical and natural sciences. The implicit notion was that demography would be a science of birth, death and migration that was precise and almost timeless — like astronomy. Achieving this meant oversimplifying our notions about how, for example, people "decide" to have children. This, in turn, meant oversimplifying notions about the way in which power is distributed and decisions are made within a marriage when it comes to questions of sex and conception. And this, in turn, meant oversimplifying notions about what men and women want out of life and marriage, and how they go about getting it.

Its founders must have hoped demographic research would be cleansed of messy sociological concerns. They appear to have thought that investigations could be performed as though in isolated, sterile laboratories where men were

The Tribes of Generation X

Market research is an important branch of applied sociology. One of Canada's most successful market researchers, Michael Adams of Environics, has used data drawn from hundreds of surveys to characterize the various "types" of Canadian, in terms of their dominant social values. He distinguishes the following "tribes" among Gen-Xers:

Aimless Dependents

Who: 8 per cent (1.9 million) of pop.; 27 per cent of pop. 15 to 29
Motivators: financial independence, stability and security
Values: fear, desire for independence
Words to live by: "Couldn't care less"; "It's all meaningless"
Icons: hockey player Eric Lindros; actress/singer Courtney Love

Thrill-Seeking Materialists

Who: 7 per cent (1.7 million) of pop.; 25 per cent of pop. 15 to 29; many in Toronto
Motivators: traditional communities, social status and experience-seeking
Values: desire for money and material possessions, desire for recognition
Words to live by: "Live dangerously"; "Money is power"; "Second place is the first loser"
Icons: actress Pamela Lee Anderson; designer Calvin Klein

Autonomous Postmaterialists

Who: 6 per cent (1.4 million) of pop.; 20 per cent of pop. 15 to 29 years; often affluent
Motivators: personal autonomy and self-fulfilment
Values: freedom; respect for human rights
Words to live by: "Do your own thing"; "There's more to life than money"
Icons: cartoon character Bart Simpson; musician Ashley MacIsaac

Social Hedonists

Who: 4 per cent (900,000) of pop; 15 per cent of pop. 15 to 29; many in Ontario and Quebec
Motivators: experience-seeking and new communities
Values: esthetics, hedonism; sexual permissiveness; immediate gratification
Words to live by: "Don't worry, be happy"; "There is nothing deeper than the skin"
Icons: race-car drive Jacques Villeneuve; singer Janet Jackson

New Aquarians

Who: 4 per cent (900,000) of pop.; 13 per cent of pop. 15 to 29; many are teen-agers
Motivators: experience-seeking and new communities
Values: ecologism, hedonism
Words to live by: "There is no being, only becoming"; "Everything is interconnected"
Icons: author William Gibson; singer Tori Amos

Source: Adapted from *Sex in the Snow* by Michael Adams. Copyright © Michael Adams, 1997. Reprinted with permission of Penguin Books Canada Ltd.

"males" and women were "females" (and, for that matter, "females" existed only between the ages of fifteen to forty-nine, when they were capable of "reproduction"). The emotionally and conceptually messy facts of everyday life — love, sex, conflict, family violence — were ignored or given more clinical names.

A failure to address these issues — in effect, to wish them away — has led to problems in understanding reality. For example, demographers are still wondering why central theories, like demographic transition theory, failed to predict trends in population change adequately. From a feminist standpoint, the answer is plain enough: there are errors in the assumptions on which these theories are built. For example, demographic transition theory argued that industrial conditions and opportunities change people's valuation of children. But whose valuations change? The husband's? The wife's? Both? And in the event of differences, whose ideas prevail?

Beyond values, there are the non-familial influences on people's behaviour. Demographic research tends to ignore many characteristics that might explain people's behaviour. When it *does* examine a wider variety of characteristics, it often fails to compare women and men, to see whether they are similar or different. As we saw in Chapter 8, on gender relations, women's and men's lives are different in many ways. Yet the differences are rarely reflected in demographic research.

If traditional demographic approaches *were* hugely successful in explaining and predicting population growth, we might be willing to ignore these shortcomings but, in fact, these approaches have failed conspicuously. That means we have to go back and re-think first principles such as: Who has the power over child-bearing decisions? How are people influenced to change their values and behaviours? *Are* men different from women, and if so, in what (demographically relevant) respects? A feminist approach helps to re-focus the field and push it to ask new kinds of questions in line with how society is changing.

Planning the Future

Given the extraordinary rate at which the social world is changing, understanding what is going on around us and where it is leading becomes harder every day. Yet understanding the social world is essential to making informed decisions and acting responsibly. Because sociology gives us the information we need to make decisions, we believe it is becoming more important all the time.

Here's what Wendell Bell (1996: 140-157) has to say about the role of the sociologist in the future: The job of sociology and the other social sciences is to help us plan the future of the human race and bring life on earth as close as possible to what we desire. A grandiose and absurd goal? Perhaps, but this has been the goal of sociology at least since the days of Marx, Weber and Durkheim. We may fail in this goal, but we cannot sensibly avoid pursuing it, and sociology has been constructed to aid in this pursuit. Sociological research is the keystone in the edifice of social theory, policy and action.

CLOSING REMARKS

Why do sociological research? Because reality is more complicated, more interesting and more surprising than we might imagine.

Let's turn from cosmic concerns to something close to home. In September 1993, incoming students at the University of Toronto were asked a number of questions. About 60 per cent (nearly 4,000 students) responded. One question asked whether they rated themselves in "the highest 10 per cent" on academic ability; another, whether they rated themselves in "the highest 10 per cent" on mathematical ability; another, on writing ability; another still, on intellectual self-confidence; and finally, on the "drive to achieve." Here are some of the results:

- roughly one-quarter of the incoming University of Toronto men rated themselves in the top 10 per cent on academic ability, mathematical ability, intellectual self-confidence and drive to achieve;

- incoming men were twice as likely as incoming women to rate themselves in the top 10 per cent on academic ability, mathematical ability and intellectual confidence. Men and women rated themselves more similarly on writing ability and the drive to achieve;

- incoming men at (upper-middle-class) Trinity College were nearly twice as likely as incoming men in Engineering to rate themselves in the top 10 per cent in academic ability, writing ability, intellectual self-confidence and drive to achieve. Only in mathematical ability were the Engineering students likely to rate themselves as highly as the Trinity students.

Now that you have studied sociology, you may be able to explain some of these findings; maybe even to predict what will happen when these students find out that only 10 per cent can actually fit into "the highest 10 per cent" category.

In this chapter we have only scratched the surface as far as sociological research methods are concerned. Even so, we have presented what seems to be a bewildering number of methods for doing research and a large inventory of issues to keep in mind in order to assure that it is good research. Why this largesse? Why do sociologists not agree on a common set of methods they can apply to all research problems?

The reason is that sociologists study such a wide variety of social phenomena that no single set of methods and no simple set of guidelines are appropriate for all of them. As you have already seen in earlier chapters, sociology's field is extraordinarily wide and the issues with which it deals are both diverse and complex. Sociologists have made good use of all these methods to uncover a wide variety of facts about social life.

Although it is unlikely that all of you reading this book will become practising sociologists, as we noted at the beginning of this book, you are all sociologists of a kind.

We hope we have stretched your sociological imagination. Remember, that's your ability to see connections between large and small, changing and unchanging, portions of social life. It requires an awareness of the relation between individuals and the wider society. It helps us to look at our own personal experiences in a different, more objective way. It forces us to ask how our lives are shaped by the larger social context in which we live. Finally, the sociological imagination helps us to see society as the result of millions of people working out their own personal lives and making a connection between the MACRO and the MICRO levels of society.

We've told you the basics — a bare outline of the field and its riches. We hope we have whetted your curiosity. And now that we have led you to the water, we hope you will be moved, with the sociological resources at hand, to drink it.

Review Questions

1. What is the basic question asked by social research?

2. What is meant by "cause" and "effect"?

3. What is an explanation?

4. What is a hypothesis?

5. What is prediction?

6. What are "dependent" and "independent variables"?

7. What are "quantitative" and "qualitative data"?

8. What is a research design?

9. What are the different types of research design?

10. What are the different types of measurement scales?

11. How do we know when a measure is "good"?

12. How do concepts match up with measurements?

13. What are the different types of samples used in research?

14. What are the different research strategies used by sociologists?

15. What are some common forms of bias sociologists should try to avoid when engaging in research?

Discussion Questions

1. You will learn more by studying a small problem in depth than by studying a large problem superficially. Show this in respect to a particular case: for example, how the presence of a child with leukemia affects relations between family members versus the social effects of illness in Canadian society.

2. Discuss the arguments for and against experimenting on human beings. What useful information can we gain about social relationships only by experimenting? To what practical uses could we put this information?

3. Discuss how you might measure students' satisfaction with a college course they are taking. Should this measure be used to award promotions and cash bonuses for good teaching?

4. How would you select a sample of AIDS victims for study? That is, what type of sampling method would produce the required number of cases? Then, what would be your preferred method of collecting data? Why?

5. What difficulty would an (English-speaking) extraterrestrial have analyzing the content of this year's best-selling books and most-watched television programs? What would the extraterrestrial find out about North Americans by doing this?

6. Suppose a researcher has found that many juvenile delinquents have a low opinion of themselves, especially their intelligence and appearance. Give two interpretations of this finding and devise research that would prove only one was right.

Suggested Readings

Babbie, E. (1988) *Observing Ourselves*. Belmont, California: Wadsworth. This author has written a number of enjoyable textbooks on sociology and social research. This one focuses on the methods of qualitative research and does so very well.

Converse, J.M. and H. Schuman (1974) *Conversations at Random: Survey Research as Interviewers See It*. New York: John Wiley. In this witty and entertaining book, the vignettes, anecdotes and reflections of interviewers point out the dangers and challenges of data collection by interviewing.

Gray, George and Neil Guppy (1994) *Successful Surveys: Research Methods and Practice*. Toronto: Harcourt Brace and Company. This very useful book discusses all the important topics connected with carrying out surveys: sampling, data collection strategies and questionnaire design, among others.

Hammond, P. (1964) *Sociologists at Work: Essays on the Craft of Social Research*. New York: Basic Books. This highly readable ac-

count of some important sociological research projects includes information that rarely comes to the attention of readers.

Majchrzak, A. (1984) *Methods of Policy Research*. Beverly Hills: Sage Publications. This easy-to-read book discusses the problems of doing social research for a client in an organizational setting. The author finds that identifying points of conflict and "stakeholders" is critical for the research to succeed.

Whyte, W. F. (1955) *Street Corner Society: The Social Structure of an Italian Slum*. Chicago: University of Chicago Press. Whyte studied youth in an Italian slum of Boston during the 1930s. This is a classic study using participant observation, and shows the strengths and weaknesses of the method.

Yin, R.K. (1984) *Case Study Research: Design and Methods*. Beverly Hills: Sage Publications. This author develops the notion of "pattern-matching" to test competing theories on only one case — a single person or organization. The writing is energetic, the research advice practical and thorough.

Internet Resources

The following Web sites are good places to find more information about topics discussed in this chapter:

CyberPages Poll allows you to participate in a variety of surveys on many different issues, Canadian and international. http://www.cyberpages.com/poll

Statistics Canada Homepage includes media releases, frequently asked-for statistics, research papers and issues of *The Daily*, a daily publication Homepage containing new data and publication releases. http://www.statcan.ca

The CIA's World Factbook contains basic and not so basic statistics about every country in the world. http://www.odci.gov/cia/publications/nsolo/wfb-all.htm

The World Bank's "Social Indicators of Development" contains social indicators for over 170 economies. http://www.ciesin.org/IC/wbank/sid-home.html

Doing Research in Sociology provides links to a variety of sources discussing how to do research in sociology, e.g., effective library research and using electronic databases. http://129.97.58.10/discipline/sociology/research.html

APPENDIX

How to Write an Essay in Sociology

What we have to tell you now will be immediately useful in this course. What's more, it will be useful in writing essays for other courses, this academic year and in the future. And it will also be useful in writing good examination answers for this and other courses. In fact, it will be useful in whatever writing you do in life — business reports, letters to the editor, and so on. The problems of writing well and clearly are common across different writing assignments, however long or short they may be, however much or little time you may have.

Writing — actually facing a blank piece of paper, then filling it with intelligent words and ideas — is *hard* work. In a way, it's like magic. You are making something new, perhaps something quite unique and terrific, out of a few simple materials — a pen and paper, say, and some serious effort. That is exciting stuff — real magic. Still, doing magic is hard work. That's why you need to know some ways to make it easier.

The first thing you have to know is that you can't write something good if you don't have anything to say. So thinking has to come before writing; the better the thinking, the better the written product will be. Don't do your best thinking while, or even worse, *after* you have written your essay. Do it beforehand. Give yourself enough time to think. A paper written in one evening, without any good thinking in advance, looks like what it is: poor work.

The key to good thinking about a writing assignment is that you have to know very clearly (1) what the question is you are trying to answer, and (2) what you think the answer is. That may sound obvious and silly to you, but we guarantee we have read hundreds of essays, and books, where it is difficult to know what question is being answered and what answer is being offered. That kind of writing is a recipe for disaster. Do not set pen to paper, or fingertips to computer keyboard, before you are absolutely certain you know what the question is, and what the answer is.

Another thing we have learned from many years of reading and writing is that *any* question can be answered in *any* amount of time: in three minutes, three hours, three days, three months, or three years. There is no such thing as a question that *must* take a week, or six months, or ten years. Any question can be answered in the time you have available.

Obviously, an intelligent answer that took three hours to complete will be better — more insightful, more thought-provoking, more complete — than an intelligent answer that took only three minutes. If you have only three minutes to answer, do the best you can in the time available and you will be respected for the result. But if you have three hours to answer, by all means use that three hours to its fullest. Your instructor will be expecting more from a three-hour answer than from a three-minute answer.

Here's something that's much less obvious: when you are writing something — whatever it is, exam answer, essay, report or book — always follow the "Rule of Equal Thirds." Always spend about one-third of your time thinking, reading and preparing to answer; the middle third of your time actually answering in first draft; and a final third of your time cleaning up and revising.

So, if you are writing a three-month essay, spend one month thinking about the problem, collecting information at the library and collecting whatever other data you may need. Spend your second month writing a first draft of the essay. And spend your final month reorganizing, revising, re-reading and checking your essay for errors and typos. And, incidentally, every essay should be submitted in typed form.

Let's spend a little time thinking about each of these thirds.

THE FIRST THIRD

In the first third of your available time, you should put to work all the things you know about sociological methods of research. This is the time for background reading, designing your research, measuring your variables, collecting your data and analyzing the data in a preliminary way.

A lot of post-secondary students do not know how to use a library. Before you get started on your essay, you need to know how to find out what you do not know. You also have to develop strategies for limiting what you need to know. If, for example, you decide you want to write something on modern family life, you will find hundreds of books and thousands of articles on that topic at the library. Obviously you cannot read all of that material; you need a strategy to narrow down the question you are going to answer, and a way to decide which things you have to read and which things you can ignore.

The rise of the Internet as a source of information — a kind of "cyber-library" — offers us all new opportunities and also new problems. Nothing can beat the Internet for making recent information easily available. Books are slow and expensive to publish; as a result, they often take years to prepare and, often, years to appear in print. Journal articles are shorter, quicker to write and cheaper to produce, so they bring research findings into print faster, but they too are frequently out-of-date by the time they are published. However, cost and delay are minimal on the Internet, where all kinds of research findings flow instantly and continuously.

On the other hand, no quality control is exercised on the Net: no peer review of findings, no editing and (for any given document) few second thoughts by the author. So any given document can be deeply flawed, yet there it is — ready to misinform you. Moreover, there is no overall structure to cyberspace which will guide you away from bad-quality research findings towards good-quality research findings. (The best that "search engines" do is direct you to places where you are likely to find *some* kind of relevant material, whatever its quality.)

So don't hesitate to use the Internet for information, but don't assume that any two research reports you find on the net are of equal validity, or indeed that either is trustworthy. Beyond that, everything we have said about print libraries also applies to the cyber-library: you still need a strategy for narrowing down your research question and deciding what to read.

You may have a chance to do additional reading, data collection or data analysis at the next stage, but at least two-thirds of all that kind of work should be done in the first third of your available time. You may complete your research in the first third of the writing process.

THE SECOND THIRD

Once you have narrowed down your question and read and thought about your topic, you are ready to start writing your three-month essay.

No, let's put that point more strongly: If you look at your calendar and it tells you that today is the first day of month number two, then you *must* lay down your books and start writing. Force yourself to obey the "equal thirds" rule. Eventually, when you have a lot of experience writing, you will know how and when to relax that rule. But at the beginning, follow the rule mechanically. If it is the start of month number two, start writing.

Some people insist on making a detailed plan of their essay before they start to write anything at all. That works for some people; and when they are ready to write, everything just flows into the appropriate boxes. However, by far a more common problem is getting the stuff to start flowing at all. Lots of people — all the way from beginning writers up to professionals — suffer anxiety about starting to fill the blank page in front of them. That is the biggest problem you are going to face.

So we are going to urge you *not* to worry about making a highly detailed outline before you start to write. After all, you have thought and read about your problem for a month; it is time to start writing. In the second third of your time available, sit down and start filling pages. But when you do so, follow certain rules that will make the actual writing process much easier and more systematic.

What distinguishes a good three-hour answer from a good three-minute answer, or a good three-month answer from a good three-week answer is *not* whether the answer is "right." It is how thoroughly you explore your reasons for giving the answer you do. That is the most important thing you are going to take care of during this second third of your work on an essay, report, book or whatever. In fact, learning to make good arguments is what post-secondary education is all about.

There's an excellent book called *Writing Under Pressure*, by Sanford Kaye, a fellow who has been teaching writing to students, professors and executives for many years; and we agree with everything he has to say.

One thing Kaye discusses in his book is the importance of "because clauses" in writing. "Because clauses," he says, should make up at least two-thirds of anything you write. So, any good written answer will have:

(1) *a beginning* — What is the question to be answered? What does it mean? What do I have to show? What is my tentative answer to the question?

(2) *a middle* — many because clauses arguing on one side of the question; many because clauses arguing on the other side.

(3) *an end* — What is the final answer to the question? What are the implications of the answer, if any, for theory, for social policy, for everyday life?

As a rough estimate, in a ten-page, 2,500-word essay, no more than two pages (or 500 words) should be spent on the beginning and no more than two pages should be spent on the ending. All the rest — six pages or more — should be spent on the middle part, the "because clauses."

What are these "because clauses" we keep talking about? They are the reasons why you are about to answer the question in one way rather than another. "I think the reason for this happening is because . . . and because . . . and because. . . ." Those are the because clauses in support of your position. Let's call them "supporting because clauses."

Also, you are going to supply lots of "opposing because clauses" that say "Other people argue the opposite view because . . . and because . . . and because. . . ." You will review opposing positions, and discuss them fairly and thoroughly in your essay, because your instructor expects it of you. If you do *not* do so, your work will appear one-sided, shallow and laughable, and you will get a rotten mark in the course. (That's our "because clause" explaining why you should take this advice.)

But after reviewing all those "opposing because clauses," you get your revenge: a chance to rebut the opposing views to show why you do not find them persuasive — why they do not lead you to support their position, rather than the one you declared at the outset of the essay.

People differ in the way they do things. Usually we prefer to give the opposing argument first, then shoot it down, then give the argument that supports our side. That strategy is like ripping down an old building and clearing the land before you start putting up your own new house. So, our hypothetical ten-page essay might look like this:

Beginning (one to two pages)

(1) What is the question, and what is our rough answer to that question? — one to two pages

Middle (six to eight pages)

(2) Arguments against our answer — one to two pages

(3) Arguments against those arguments — one to two pages

(4) Arguments in favour of our answer — two to four pages

End (one to two pages)

(5) What is our final answer? This includes refinements, modifications, implications.

You should proportion your time to this use of space. Remember, the middle or "because" part should receive at least 60 per cent of your writing time (as well as space). And this rule applies whether we are talking about 60 per cent of one minute, one week or one year; or ten pages, a hundred pages or a thousand pages.

The Nature of "Becauses"   What is the nature of this important "because part" of the essay, exam question or book? Obviously it has something to do with the presentation of evidence. It can be logical evidence, but mainly it is empirical evidence — data specifically collected to support your argument or destroy your opponent's argument.

You can gather a lot of interesting information if you have a month to collect it and two months to write it up.

What happens when you have more *time* to write an answer is that you can collect better-*quality* data to support your argument: you can review more books and journals, maybe even collect some new data of your own through on-line sources, interviews or questionnaires or first-hand observation.

Remember that an essay or written answer that takes a hundred pages should differ from one that takes ten pages only in terms of *quantity*, not quality. You can simply display more because-information in a hundred pages than you can in ten pages. A typical undergraduate-course essay should be high on quality (after all, you have three months to write it), but low on quantity (you may have only ten pages to write it on). Whatever you do, don't give your instructor a lot of quantity but not much quality.

As you go along giving your because clauses, you may find that there is reading you should have done, data you should have collected or data you have collected and now have to analyze. Go ahead: make these final adjustments to your database. But remember, this stage of work — the middle third of your time — is primarily a writing stage. If you find you are spending a lot of time doing additional reading or data collection, you have organized your time poorly. Most of that work should have been done in the first third of your time.

THE THIRD THIRD

Some people may wonder why we have allotted as much as a third of our writing time to the cleaning-up stage. It is because this is an important stage, and many students overlook it or give it short shrift.

We know they have done this because many essays come to us that are messy, full of grammatical errors and spelling errors, and that lack a careful bibliography. And, once we start reading for content, we often find glaring holes in the logic and large gaps in the evidence presented. This makes us think that the student wrote the entire essay in a single evening — something instructors find very irritating — when, in some cases, the student may simply have failed to do a clean-up on the essay and may have devoted all his or her time reading, then writing a first draft.

Never hand in a first draft of an essay. Teachers were not put on earth to correct, or even read, your typos and spelling mistakes. Making us read such incomplete work is disrespectful; worse still, it makes us readers angry and disinclined to believe what you are arguing. It makes us graders believe you are a sloppy thinker — a C student at best. So, after you have written your draft of the essay, there are several things you should be sure to do:

First, submit your essay to the laugh test. This is important and can be done in a number of ways. Imagine reading your essay out loud to your parents, your friends or, even, to a public audience. If the thought of this makes you cringe in horror, or feel terrible embarrassment, that may be because you have written a silly essay — one that does not truly express thoughts you are willing to take responsibility for. If you are afraid to take responsibility for these thoughts, you should not be turning them in for a grade.

Think of your essay as a conversation with the grader and rewrite your essay so that no part of it is embarrassing, no matter who might read it. After rewriting, the thoughts you express should not be embarrassing. To help achieve this, the language you use in your essay should be your own language, not puffed up and fancy talk full of ten-dollar words.

Second, read the revised essay out loud to your family or friends, or give it to a friend you respect, and ask that person to read it and criticize it. Of course, nobody likes criticism. Everyone feels bad when they are criticized and happy when they are praised. However, when you are submitting something for criticism by a stranger — as you are doing with the essay you are writing — you may prefer to get criticism from a friend first. The criticism you get from a friend will not only be more friendly, it may save you from losing marks. So tell your friendly reader that you *want* criticism: it will help you out.

Some people — friends included — just love criticizing other people. Some even enjoy humiliating their friends. Too bad if this is the only kind of friend you have! But whatever your friend's motives and personality flaws, you should be able to deal with criticism. If your friend says, "Here are eight things that are wrong with your essay," you should deal with every one of these eight things before you turn in the essay for grading.

You will probably find that you can easily agree with *some* of your friend's points. If your friend is right, you need to re-think, or research further, some particular issues. Go do it! And, some of the points your friend makes may simply require clarification — you did not express your views clearly enough. Fine; re-write the confusing passages so that your friend (and other people) can understand them.

Finally, some of the points your friend makes may seem just plain wrong to you: your friend is misinformed, or suffering from a defect in logic. Nonetheless, go and re-write the passages in question — or add new information — so that even an average or stupid reader (like your friend) will go along with your argument.

You see, when you are writing something, you cannot control who is going to read the piece, or what ideas they bring to the reading. Even though you may be writing your essay for a professor with a background in the area, you should clearly develop your terms and ideas. Writers are *always* at the mercy of their readers, and you must prepare for the worst.

In our time, we authors have received some glowing reviews of our work and some absolutely damning, humiliating reviews, and everything in between. But we have to deal with all criticisms. What's more, as writers, you (and we) must always anticipate what readers may say, and deal with their possible criticisms before they have a chance to make them.

So submit your work to the laugh test; undergo friendly criticism; re-write and re-think as much as you have time for in that final one-third of your time. Then take care of cosmetic details.

A lot of you probably use word-processing software, and if you do, you should run your essay through a spell-checker to eliminate spelling errors in your written work. If you have serious trouble speaking or writing English, you must seek out help; there are courses to help you with this. If you are an English speaker but do not understand how to write two logical sentences in a row, there are writing clinics to help you, and you should take advantage of them.

Finally, and remember this, your instructor wants to see no typos or scratch-outs or things taped together. The essay should look as if you spent a month cleaning it up, because (according to the rule of equal thirds) you did!

THE ESSAY YOU ARE GOING TO WRITE

Suppose the essay you are going to write is worth 20 per cent of your final mark in the course. If so, you should spend about 20 per cent of your time in this course writing it. If you are spending about eight or nine hours a week on *each* of your courses, you should spend about 220 hours on a full-year course, and, therefore, about 44 hours on an essay for that course. Let's make this 45 hours, to keep the calculations simple. (Cut these numbers in half if you are taking a half-year [or 1-semester] course.)

When you write your essay, keep a log of the hours you are spending on it and force yourself to follow the time budget we have laid out. Following what we have said above, it should look like this:

First stage: 15 hours. Thinking, reading, making notes, preparing to answer.

Second stage: 15 hours. Writing the first draft of your essay. This comprises the following:

The beginning. Stating the question and approximate answer your essay will give: 2.5 hours.

The middle. Writing the "because clauses" portion. A total of 10 hours, comprising

    2.5 hours to state the case against your answer,

    2.5 hours to rebut the case against your answer, and

    5.0 hours to support your own case.

The end. Refining and modifying your opening position. Stating the implications of your conclusion: 2.5 hours.

Third stage: 15 hours. Doing the laugh test. Cleaning up and revising your essay. Adding new evidence, where needed. Fixing spelling and typing errors, making accurate footnotes and references.

WRITING AN EXAM ANSWER

When you are answering an exam question, things are slightly different, but not much. You still have an opportunity to prepare, to write and to clean up; and you should still follow the equal thirds rule when you do this.

Suppose you are writing an essay-type test. You read through the test paper completely to get your brain cells fired up. You find you have to answer two half-hour questions and you decide which question you are going to answer first. This is what you should do next:

Prepare: Spend ten minutes just thinking about the question and making little notes to yourself on the backs of pages, or on scratch paper. Make sure you understand the question and make sure you have decided on an answer by the end of the first ten-minute period.

Write: Spend ten minutes writing an answer: about one or two minutes to open the discussion; six to eight minutes for because clauses; another one or two minutes for closing statements.

Clean-up: Spend ten minutes reading through your answer, checking for errors, things you have left out, spelling mistakes and so on. Make the appropriate corrections.

You will find it is easier doing a clean-up if, when you answer the exam question, you leave two or three lines between each line you write. This allows you to add stuff in a neat way, if you have to. If you have prepared well, argued your "becauses" well and cleaned up well, you should impress your reader and get a good grade.

An Example

So far we have been somewhat abstract, and now it is time to give an example. Here's what goes through the mind of one student — Jennifer — as she answers an examination question.

She has to write an answer to the following question: "Does Canada have a race problem?" Time available is thirty minutes. Maximum space available is ten pages. There's no time to do background reading or collect data. She has to go with what she has in her head right now.

Prepare: Jennifer takes ten minutes to get ready and spends a few minutes asking herself "What do I think about this question? Does Canada have a race problem?" Whew, big question, she thinks. Yes, Canada *does* have a race problem.

Write:

Beginning: Time to write a two-page introduction. Yes, I think Canada has a race problem. Before I explain why I think so, I will explain what I think this question is about: namely, how people of African or Asian origins, or native peoples, get along in Canadian society.

I think Canada's visible minorities definitely have a problem. But is there a problem for the white majority? And is there a problem for Canadian society as a whole? I'm not sure. I'll come back to that issue — the issue of what kind of problem it is — at the end of the essay.

In the body of my essay, I am going to show that, by many different standards — jobs, health, living conditions, self-image, life chances — non-whites have a real problem in Canada.

Middle. I have about six or seven minutes to write this part. First, I will spend two minutes putting forward opposing arguments: the reasons why someone else might think Canada does *not* have a race problem.

(1) There are no lynchings or race riots.

(2) Most Canadians seem pretty tolerant towards racial minorities.

(3) Canada has a long history of racial tolerance; no history of slavery like the United States, for example.

(4) Canada has no laws that make racism officially okay, as South Africa did for a long time.

(5) If Canadians were racists, they wouldn't let so many non-whites come into the country.

(6) If there was a race problem in Canada, you would hear a lot about it on the news.

That's all I can come up with off the top of my head in two minutes. Now I have to destroy these points in two more minutes. Here goes:

(1) The fact that there are no lynchings or race riots may simply mean that the conflict has taken on more polite forms.

(2) The personal tolerance of Canadians may be irrelevant. After all, it is possible to be nice and tolerant but still ignore or exploit poor racial minorities.

(3) Canadians don't want anyone to be slaves. But that doesn't mean we want to have much to do with visible minorities, especially if they are poor.

(4) Canada does not have apartheid laws like the ones South Africa had, but many native people think Canada's Indian Act is discriminatory. And don't forget "systemic discrimination": many laws discriminate without necessarily intending to.

(5) Open immigration only proves that Canadians need cheap, highly educated labour from the Third World.

(6) The mass media are part business, part fantasy. You cannot rely on them to tell you if there is *really* a race problem.

Now I have two minutes to put forward my preferred position: namely, there *is* a race problem in Canada.

(1) Economic inequality. There is lots of evidence of high unemployment, poverty and demoralization among the non-white communities. Often, it shows up as bad health, poor nutrition, poor school attendance, high suicide rates.

(2) Job discrimination. The evidence provided by Henry and Ginzberg shows that Toronto whites do discriminate against blacks in hiring. The evidence by Peter Li shows that this results in lower-than-average incomes for blacks and Asians.

(3) Many non-whites — especially blacks and native peoples — *believe* there is a race problem; and they see signs of it in the behaviour of the police towards blacks and native people, in job discrimination and in the disputes over land claims.

End. Now I have a minute or two to finish off. "I have shown that, while there is some merit to the opposing arguments, on balance I am persuaded by evidence of economic inequality, job discrimination and white reactions to non-white concerns, that there is a race problem in Canada. Only time will tell whether the problem will get much worse before we take serious action to improve it. We would do well to see what has worked in other countries facing similar problems at earlier times in history."

Clean-up: Now I have ten minutes to read my answer through, correct errors, add any new ideas I may have and take out stuff that is truly dumb.

I am also doing my own laugh test: what would my mother or my best friend say about this exam answer, I ask myself. Well, she might say that she didn't agree with my last point — just because people *think* there is a race problem doesn't make it so. For example, most Quebecers think there is a problem with French-English relations in Canada, but most non-Quebecers do not think so, except that the Quebecers keep making such a fuss about things and want to destroy the country. Or take any two groups that are fighting — Israeli Jews and Palestinians, Irish Protestants and Catholics, Shiite and Sunni Moslems, and so on. They are always fighting and blaming each other for problems.

But, Mom, that is exactly the point I am making. I don't have to decide whether I agree more with the whites or the non-whites. The point is, the two groups are not equal and they probably don't agree on the reasons why. That's a race problem and some day it may grow into a race war.

I wish I had a chance to think about this some more, because it seems like a good issue to explore. It makes me remember what the sociologist W. I. Thomas said, "Things that are defined as real have real consequences." If non-whites think all whites are racists, and behave as though this is true, whites will be forced into behaving like racists. And if whites think all non-whites are trying to threaten them, or shame them, into sharing the wealth, and behave as though this is true, non-whites will harden their position and become more confrontational. Funny, isn't it, that we become what people think we are.

Now I have just a minute or two to write a few lines on this theme. If it doesn't fit on the page, I'll write it on the facing page and, with clear arrows, indicate where this new piece fits in. As I re-read, fix spelling and grammar and so on, I get some more ideas — good ones, I think. I put in a few words here and there.

My thoughts are getting really interesting, but I have to stop now. I am out of time. I have to go on to the next question. I don't want to use up any more of my precious time on the first answer. I can only hope that I did a good enough job on it in the time available.

CLOSING REMARKS

What have you learned from Jennifer's experience? Have you learned that writing an answer can be exciting and also frustrating because of all those great ideas you start to get just when it is time to stop?

Don't be frightened when all your ideas start tumbling out — all those different because clauses, arguments and counter-arguments. Most sociology instructors *love* seeing alternative interpretations, competing theories and important facts in search of a theoretical home. So let it all hang out, but be sure to tie everything together in a sensible way by the time you are finished.

Remember, you have to discipline yourself, and that is true whether you have thirty minutes or three years to answer a question. You have to get the work out and then, go on to the next assignment. That is the secret of success in writing. Try to follow the rules we have given you and you will find that exams and essays go very smoothly indeed.

Glossary

absolute poverty a condition that occurs when people have too little of the basic necessities (food, shelter and medicine, for example) for physical survival (*see also* relative poverty)

agents of socialization institutions and other structured relationships within which socialization takes place

alienation estrangement of workers from the product of their work, from the work process, from themselves and other workers

anomie according to Durkheim, a lack of regulation, or a lack of norms; anomie increases the likelihood of suicide and other "pathological" behaviours

anomie theory as developed by Robert Merton, this theory argues that inequality causes deviance by creating a gap between culturally defined *goals* and socially approved *means* for attaining those goals

anticipatory socialization socialization that prepares a person for roles they may eventually have to perform

assimilation the process by which members of a minority group abandon their own cultural traits and adopt those of the dominant culture

authority the ability of an individual or group to issue commands and have them obeyed because their control is perceived as legitimate

baby boom a sudden and considerable rise in the birth rate occurring in the 1950s and early 1960s; it was a response to economic prosperity, and the end of restraints on marriage and childbearing caused by the Depression and the Second World War

band a grouping the government has created to administer status Indians, who are typically native people under the jurisdiction of the Indian Act

biological determinism the view that differences among individuals or cultures exist because nature has selected for them; any genetic explanation of behaviour (*see also* social determinism)

bourgeoisie in Marxist terminology, the group of people who own the means of production (capitalists); sometimes also used to refer to the middle class in a capitalist society; the bourgeoisie employ the proletariat (*see also* proletariat)

bureaucracy a hierarchically organized formal organization found throughout industrial societies

bureaucratic control a way of controlling workers that relies on a large number of written rules and the promise of career rewards for conformity and effective performance

carrying capacity the number of people a geographic area can support, given the current level of available resources and technology

caste system a hierarchy of groups separated from each other by rules of ritual purity and prevented from intermarrying, changing castes through mobility, or carrying out inappropriate jobs

charismatic leader a leader who has an exceptional capacity to inspire devotion and enthusiasm among followers

Charter Groups Canadians of British and French ancestry, so named because settlers from England and France first came to Canada with royal permission to trade and settle (royal charters)

class inequality based on the distribution of material resources

class system a hierarchy of groups with different market conditions, work situations and life chances; in Marxist theory, classes stand in different relations to the means of production

cognitive development the development of abilities to think, believe, remember, perceive and reason

cohabitation a sexual union in which two people live together without marrying

cohort a group of people who share similar life experiences as the result of a major common experience (such as birth, marriage, graduation or migration in the same year or decade)

comprador an elite made up of the people who run corporations located in Canada but owned or controlled by foreign concerns

conflict theory a theoretical paradigm that emphasizes conflict and change as the regular and permanent features of society, because society is made up of various groups who wield varying amounts of power

corporate capitalism an economic system in which the key players are corporate groups and their directors; under corporate capitalism, monopolies and oligopolies also become common (*see also* laissez-faire capitalism)

counterculture a subculture that rejects conventionally accepted norms and values in favour of alternative ones crime   any act formally prohibited by criminal law

cultural capital   a set of beliefs and skills that help people get ahead in an unequal society

cultural literacy   a solid knowledge of our traditional culture; the ability to learn and communicate in our society

culture   the objects, artifacts, institutions, organizations, ideas and beliefs that make up the symbolic and learned aspects of human society

demographic transition   a fall in birth and death rates that accompanies industrialization, with the death rates falling first

demography   the scientific study of the size, composition (structure), distribution and patterns of change in a human population

dependency ratio   the ratio of economically dependent people (ages 17 and under and 65 and over) to people of working age (ages 18 through 64)

deviance   behaviour that leads to a negative reaction or response from a community or group

deviant subculture   a subculture whose members conform to norms, values and beliefs that the larger society considers deviant

differentiation   the process whereby various sets of activities are divided up and performed by a number of separate institutions (*see also* integration)

discrimination   the denial of access to opportunities that would be available to equally qualified members of the dominant group

division of labour   the breaking up of a job into a number of smaller jobs which are done by separate individuals (*see also* gendered division of labour)

divorce   the legal and formal dissolution of a legal marriage

domination   the exercise of control over an individual or group who must submit to that person's power; can be seen as inequality based on the distribution of authoritative resources

double standard   the application of different rules, or standards of behaviour, to men and women

dyad   a two-person group

economic order   the institutionalized system which produces, distributes and consumes material resources

elite   a small group that has power or influence over others and that is regarded as being superior in some way

endogamy   the tendency for people to marry partners within their own kin group, clan, race, ethnic group or class (*see also* exogamy)

endogenous   causes of death that are internal to the organism, not a result of externally induced trauma or infection

equalitarian (or egalitarian) family   a family in which the husband and wife jointly make all the important decisions; their opinions are equally important and mutually respected

equality of condition   equality in the distribution of goods such as food, housing, health, wealth, respect, authority, power and so on

equality of opportunity   equality of access to that which society values; a situation in which all people may compete equally for all positions in society

ethnicity   an ethnic group's distinctive cultural features, such as language, religion, sense of collective existence and shared historical heritage

ethnocentrism   a tendency to view life from the point of view of one's own culture; ethnocentrism enters into both common thought and social research

exogamy   the tendency for people to marry partners from outside their own kin group, clan, race, ethnic group or class (reverse of enogamy)

experiment   a research method designed to investigate the effect of one variable on another under well-controlled and regulated conditions; a control and experimental group are compared before and after the experimental treatment

explanation   something that gives the meaning of, gives reasons for, accounts for or interprets something else

extended family   one in which two or more generations of relatives live together

family   traditionally, a group of people who are related to one another through marriage, descent or legal adoption; increasingly, any group of people who, over a long period, depend on one another for emotional and material support

femininity   that package of traits people expect to find in a "typical" woman (*see also* masculinity)

feminism   an ideology that supports equality of the sexes and opposes patriarchy and sexism (*see also* patriarchy; sexism)

feminization of poverty   the growing tendency of poor people to be women, due to lone parenthood or impoverished old age

fertility rate   the average number of children a woman of childbearing age bears during her lifetime

folkways   norms whose violation are punished informally, if at all

formal social control an authorized procedure that defines how specific people (such as police officers) will enforce the rules and laws of a society (*see also* informal social control)

functionalism see structural functionalism

gender human traits that are linked by culture to each sex; the social, cultural and psychological aspects of masculinity and femininity

gendered division of labour the cultural separation of work (whether inside the home or in public) into "men's work" and "women's work"

gender identity the ways males and females learn to think of themselves; the learned part of the self that results from a person's recognition that he or she is a man or woman, boy or girl

gender roles (sex roles) attitudes and activities that a culture links to each sex, or are typically expected of members of a particular sex

gender socialization (or sex role socialization) the process of learning "appropriate" sex-specific behaviour

generation gap a difference in world views between parents and their children, or between the older and younger generations

generalized other a person's general idea of how the society, or surrounding group, expects him or her to behave

goal displacement in bureaucracies, the substitution of concerns about the survival of the organization for concerns about the goals for which the organization was created

groups on a micro level, a collection of people who interact regularly face-to-face; on a macro level, a category of people who share some important trait in common

growth rate the (annual) rate at which the number of people in a population increases; negative growth rate is the (annual) rate at which population size declines

heterogamy a pattern of mating between people who differ in important respects, especially in their social characteristics (*see also* homogamy)

high culture the set of tastes, values and norms that are characteristic of high-status groups in society; they include the fine arts, classical music, ballet and other "highbrow" concerns

homogamy a pattern of mating between people who are like each other, especially in their social characteristics (*see also* heterogamy)

human capital the level of people's well-being, as influenced by their health, education and welfare, which affects their value as members of the work force

hypothesis a proposition or tentative statement about the relationship between two or more variables that we can test through research

ideal culture the set of values people claim to believe in, as expressed in holy books, laws, institutions, novels and mass media presentations (*see also* real culture)

ideology an emotionally charged belief that either explains and justifies existing arrangements, or in the case of a counter ideology, calls for and justifies alternative ways of doing things

I and me the "I" is the spontaneous, creative and unsocialized aspect of the self; the "me" is the socialized aspect of the self, acting out social roles

impression management the use of wealth, power, authority and cultural capital to appear virtuous and normal; according to labelling theory, influences the way deviant behaviour will be handled

indigenous elites control firms that are Canadian-owned

Industrial Revolution a system of production that began around 1775 in England; it used machinery and inanimate forms of energy (such as electric power) to mass produce goods, often in large factories

industrial society a society characterized by large-scale mechanized production and an extensive division of labour

informal social control the maintenance of order through gossip, praise or blame (*see also* formal social control)

institutional completeness a measure of the degree to which an ethnic group provides its members with all the services they require through their own institutions separate from those of the larger society

integration the complement to differentiation, whereby various elements of a society are combined to form a unified whole (*see also* differentiation)

internalization the process by which a person learns and accepts as binding the norms and values of a group or society

labelling theory a theory that assumes everyone behaves in a deviant manner occasionally, and labelling people "deviant" locks them into repeated norm violation

laissez-faire capitalism an economic system, dominant in 19th-century England and America, that claimed government avoided interfering in the economy (*see also* corporate capitalism)

legitimate authority general and unquestioned belief that the exercise of control by government — the police and courts included — is justified; also a belief that those in positions of authority have a right to be there

life cycle a recognized, predictable sequence of stages through which individuals pass in the course of their lives

looking-glass self a sense of oneself formed through interaction with others, by assessing how they view us

macrosociology the study of large groups, processes that characterize whole societies and the system of arrangements that exists in a given society

marriage an acknowledged sexual and economic union between two or more people

masculinity the package of traits that people in our society expect to find in a "typical man" (*see also* femininity)

mass production the production of goods in large quantities, by means of division of labour, mechanization and large productive units (factories or offices)

material culture the artifacts and physical objects created or used by members of a culture, to be distinguished from what goes on in the minds of the people (non-material culture)

matriarchal family a structure in which the mother is the formal head of the household

matrilocal a residence pattern whereby married couples reside with or very near the brides' parents

microsociology the study of small groups, and of the processes and patterns of face-to-face interactions that take place within these groups in everyday life

migration (internal) the movement of people from one part of a country to another

monogamy marriage between one woman and one man (*see also* polygamy; serial monogamy)

monopoly one group's exclusive control over the production and sales of a commodity or service; both monopolies and cartels are limits to free competition

mores norms that carry moral significance, and are therefore cause for severe punishment when violated (*see also* folkways)

multiculturalism a philosophy of ethnic and race relations that promote the development of distinct cultural communities; sees each person as the member of an ethnic or racial group and undertakes to protect the group, not the individual

natural increase the excess of births over deaths in a population

neolocal residence a family household that is set up separate from the households of the spouses' parents

net migration rate the number of immigrants to a certain area, minus the number of emigrants from that area, per year per thousand inhabitants

norm an expectation about correct or proper behaviour in a particular situation, which serves as a guideline for an individual's actions

nuclear family a family household consisting of two spouses (with or without children) or a parent and his or her children

organic solidarity community cohesion that is based on the interdependence between people who are socially different

organized crime a centralized and formal structure within which individuals devote themselves to the pursuit of goals by illegal means; centrally organized, professional crime

paradigm a general way of seeing the world that embodies broad assumptions about the nature of society and people's behaviour. It suggests which questions sociologists should ask and how they should interpret the answers

participant observation a research technique in which the sociologist becomes a member of a group in order to observe and study it first-hand

patriarchal family a family structure in which the father is the formal head of the household

patriarchy a form of organization in which men dominate women

patrilocal describes a residence pattern whereby married couples reside with, or very near the grooms' parents

peer group a group of companions with whom one interacts, particularly from late childhood through adolescence into early adulthood, and who relate to one another as equals

pluralism a philosophy of ethnic and race relations that urges tolerance for group differences and protects the rights of minority individuals through provincial human rights codes and other legislation

polyandry the marriage of one woman to more than one man

polygamy the union of a spouse to two or more spouses at the same time (*see also* monogamy)

polygyny the marriage of more than one woman to one man

popular (or mass) culture the culture of average people; includes those preferences and tastes that are widespread in a society

population in research, the set of all individuals who share some specific characteristic of interest to the researcher (*see also* sample)

positive checks occurrences (such as war, famine, pestilence and disease) which have the effect of reducing the population or limiting its growth (*see also* preventive checks)

poverty see absolute poverty; relative poverty

power the capacity to exercise one's will despite resistance; in Marxist theory, power is the capacity of one class to realize its interests in opposition to other classes

prediction the process of forecasting by inference from scientific, especially statistical, analysis of past events

prejudice a negative or hostile attitude towards members of a particular group simply because they belong to that group, based on untested assumptions about their characteristics

prestige honour and respect, a type of stratification that is separate from income, authority or class position

preventive checks in Malthusian theory, processes (like late marriage, abstinence or abortion) which reduce population growth by limiting the number of live births (see also positive checks)

price-fixing a secret (and usually illegal) agreement between producers to charge the same price for a product or service they all offer, in order to keep the prices high

primary labour market that set of jobs which offer high wages, good opportunities for advancement and job security (see also secondary labour market)

primary socialization the early socialization of children, much of which takes place in a family setting

professionalization the conversion of jobs to professions, through group mobilization and the raising of educational requirements. As a result, the group gains income, respectability and the right to regulate itself

proletariat in Marx's theory, the working class who must sell their labour for wages; they own none of the means of production but their own labour power (see also bourgeoisie)

propaganda information, ideas or doctrines disseminated for the purpose of influencing the opinions and actions of others

push factors those factors that encourage people to leave an area, which include famine, a lack of job opportunities, discrimination and fear of oppression

pull factors those factors that encourage people to move to a particular area, which include better job opportunities, more tolerance for ethnic or religious minorities and greater freedom

qualitative data data that do not require, or do not lend themselves to, precise measurement

quantitative data data that are based on precise measurement and to which rigorous statistical methods can be applied

race a group whose members are defined as sharing the same physical characteristics; term is used as a biological concept, not a cultural one

racism the belief that one's own race is superior to all others

rationalization the process by which all human action, especially decision-making, becomes subject to calculation, measurement and control

real culture the ways people actually dress, talk, act, relate and think, which may differ markedly from the values and norms they claim to believe in (see also ideal culture)

recidivism a repeated lapse into crime and delinquency

reconstituted family a family to which one or both spouses bring children from a former union

relative poverty a condition defined by the general living standards of the society or group; a low standard of living compared to most (see also absolute poverty)

research design an orderly plan for collecting, analyzing and interpreting data

reserve where a band of status Indians live ("reservation" is the American term), under the terms of a treaty with the federal or provincial government

resocialization a learning process that reshapes the individual's personality by teaching radically different values, norms and role expectations, often within a total institution

resource mobilization the ability of a group to gather, organize and use necessary resources (such as money, leadership, support and connections) to promote its views

routinization a process by which a bureaucratic structure emerges in a (formerly) charismatic movement, to better administer the day-to-day goals of the movement

sample a relatively small number of people drawn from the population of interest

scale a system of units arranged in steps or degrees; measurement scales include nominal, ordinal, interval and ratio

scientific method a systematic series of steps in research that ensures maximum objectivity, and involves collecting evidence, making theories and testing predictions against careful observations

secondary deviation deviance by a person who perceives him- or herself as deviant, because of reactions to primary deviation, the initial deviant behaviour

secondary (or marginal) labour market contains all the jobs that are characterized by low wages, few opportunities for advancement and little job security (see also primary labour market)

secondary socialization the ongoing and lifelong process of socialization, including accumulated learning in adolescence and adulthood (see also primary socialization)

segregation   the act or process of setting apart two or more groups of people within the same territory

serial (sequential) monogamy   the union of a person to two or more spouses in a lifetime, one after another

sex   the division of humanity into biological categories of male and female; the biological and anatomical differences that distinguish males from females

sexism   the ideology or belief that people of one sex are naturally superior to people of the other, including beliefs that attribute certain characteristics to one or the other sex, thereby justifying inequality

sexual harassment   any unwanted behaviour, especially at work or school, which calls attention to a person's sexuality, thereby creating discomfort, or demands sexual favours in return for some work-related benefit (such as a promotion)

sign   a gesture, artifact or word that meaningfully represents something else

simple control   a kind of control that relies on the close supervision of workers, it is often found in small workplaces with a simple division of labour

single-parent family   a family containing one parent (typically a mother) and his or her children (typically young and dependent)

social determinism   a theoretical approach that denies human free will and assumes that society causes people to act the way they do (*see also* biological determinism)

social distance   reserve in interactions between people who belong to groups ranked as superior and inferior in status

social mobility   the movement of individuals among different levels of the occupational hierarchy; movement may be vertical or horizontal, across generations or within a generation

social movements   forms of collective action that are aimed at promoting or resisting change in a given society

social statics   processes that keep societies stable or which develop and spread the culture of a society

social structure   any enduring, predictable pattern of relations; the participants may be people, roles, groups or institutions

socialization   the learning process through which an individual becomes a capable member of society (*see also* primary socialization; resocialization; secondary socialization)

socio-economic status (SES)   a method of ranking people which combines measures of wealth, authority (or power) and prestige

sociological imagination   an awareness of how individual experiences, values, beliefs, attitudes and aspirations influence and are influenced by society

specialization   expertise in doing one particular job which has previously been part of a larger job category

status (social)   people's standing in the community, as measured by the amount of respect, deference or prestige they are granted; status differences create inequality based on the unequal distribution of symbolic resources

stereotype   a fixed mental image embracing all that is believed to be typical of members of a given group

stratification system   a system of inequality that integrates class, status and domination with other forms of differentiation, such as gender, race, ethnicity

structural functionalism (or functionalism)   a theoretical paradigm that emphasizes the way each part of a society functions to fulfill the needs of society as a whole

subculture   a group in society that shares some of the cultural traits of the larger society but also has its own distinctive values, beliefs, norms, style of dress and behaviour

submission   subjection to control by another group or individual whose power is based on a higher class position or higher status position

symbol   a sign that generates some emotion (*see also* sign)

symbolic interactionism   a theoretical paradigm that studies the process by which individuals interpret and respond to the actions of others, and that conceives of society as the product of this continuous face-to-face interaction

systemic discrimination   the unintended denial of opportunities to members of particular groups because of certain physical or cultural characteristics

taboo   the powerful belief that a particular act, food, place (and so on) is totally repulsive; violation is supposed to result in immediate punishment by the group or even by God

technical control   a kind of worker control that relies on the productive technology to maintain the pace of work; it is often found where there is an assembly line

total fertility rate   an estimate of the average number of live children a woman will bear as she passes through the age-specific fertility rates of a society

underdevelopment   the effect on the periphery of unequal exchanges with the core; an underdeveloped society is one that has lost the capacity to take care of its own needs

underemployment   employment in a job which requires far less expertise, skill or ability than the job-holder typically has

values   shared conceptions of what is considered good, right and desirable, which influence people's behaviour and serve as standards for evaluating the actions of others

variable   any trait, quality or characteristic which can vary in size over time or across individuals or groups

vertical mosaic   a society in which ethnic-group membership overlaps with class or socio-economic status, such that we can predict a person's position in society from that individual's ethnic origins

white-collar crimes   crimes committed by high-status people, often in the course of their work; they include fraud, forgery, tax evasion, price-fixing, work safety violations and embezzlement

World System theory   a theory that analyzes the change of societies by reference to their relation with other societies

zero population growth   a phenomenon that occurs when the factors leading to population growth are exactly balanced by the factors leading to population decline; it is also known as replacement, as the population size remains constant

References

Abler, Thomas S. (1992) "Scalping, torture, cannibalism and rape: Ethnohistorical analysis of conflicting cultural values in war," *Anthropologica*, XXXIV, 3-120

Armstrong, P. and H. Armstrong (1993) *The Double Ghetto*, third edition. Toronto: McClelland and Stewart

Baer, D., E. Grabb and W. Johnston (1993) "National character, regional culture and the values of Canadians," *Canadian Review of Sociology and Anthropology*, 30 (1), February, 13-36

Baldus, B. and V. Tribe (1978) "Perceptions of social inequality among public school children," *Canadian Review of Sociology and Anthropology*, 15 (1), 50-60

Beaujot, R. (1988) "Canada's demographic profile," pp. 39-70 in J. Curtis and L. Tepperman (eds.), *Understanding Canadian Society*. Toronto: McGraw-Hill Ryerson

Becker, G.S. (1981) *A Treatise on the Family*. Cambridge, Mass.: Harvard University Press

Becker, H.S. (1963) *Outsiders: Studies in the Sociology of Deviance*. New York: Free Press

Bell, D. (1960) "Crime as an American way of life," Reprinted in *The End of Ideology*. New York: Free Press

_____ (1973) *The Coming of Post-industrial Society*. New York: Basic Books

Bell, W. (1996) *Foundations of Futures Studies: Human Science for a New Era. Volume 1: History, Purposes, and Knowledge*. New Brunswick, N.J.: Transaction Publishers

Berger, J. (1972) *Ways of Seeing*. New York: Viking

Bernard, J. (1973) *The Future of Marriage*. New York: Bantam Books

Bibby, Reginald W. (1995) *The Bibby Report: Social Trends Canadian Style*. Toronto: Stoddart Publishing

Blain, J. (1993) "I can't come in today, the baby has chickenpox: Gender and class processes in how parents in the labour force deal with the problem of sick children," *Canadian Journal of Sociology*, 18, 4, 405-429

Bliss, M. (1985) *Canada's First Millionaire*. Toronto: McClelland and Stewart

Blumer, H. (1937) "Social psychology," in E.P. Schmidt, ed. *Man and Society: A Substantive Introduction to the Social Sciences*, New York: Prentice-Hall

Bogardus, E.S. (1959) *Social Distance*. Yellow Springs, Ohio: Antioch College Press

Bourdieu, P. (1977) *Reproduction in Education, Society and Culture*. Beverly Hills: Sage

Braverman, H. (1974) *Labor and Monopoly Capital*. New York: Monthly Review Press

Brenner, M.H. (1984) *Estimating the Effects of Economic Change on National Health and Social Wellbeing*. Washington: United States Congress, Joint Economic Committee (June)

Bretl, D.J. and J. Cantor (1988) "The portrayal of men and women in U.S. television commercials: A recent content analysis and trends over 15 years," *Sex Roles*, 18, 9-10, May, 595-609

Breton, R. (1964) "Institutional completeness of ethnic communities and personal relations of immigrants," *American Journal of Sociology*, vol. 70, 193-205

_____ W. Isajiw, W. Kalbach and J. Reitz (1990) *Ethnic Identity and Equality: Varieties of Experience in a Canadian City*. Toronto: University of Toronto Press

Brym, R.J. and B.J. Fox (1989) *From Culture to Power: The Sociology of English Canada*. Studies in Canadian Sociology. Toronto: Oxford University Press

Campbell, A. (1980) *The Sense of Well-being in America*: Recent Patterns and Trends. New York: McGraw-Hill Ryerson

Carroll, William K. and Robert S. Ratner, "Master frames and counter-hegemony: Political sensibilities in contemporary social movements," *Canadian Review of Sociology and Anthropology*, 1996, 33, 4, Nov., 407-435

Centerwall, Brandon S. (1992) "Television and violent crime," *The Public Interest*, 56-71

Clark, T.N. and S.M. Lipset (1991) "Are social classes dying?" *International Sociology*, 6 (4), Dec., 397-410

_____ and M. Rempel (1993) "The declining political significance of social class," *International Sociology*, 8 (3), Sept., 293-316

Clement, W. (1975) *The Canadian Corporate Elite: Economic Power in Canada*. Toronto: McClelland and Stewart

_____ (1977) *Continental Corporate Power: An Analysis of Economic Power*. Toronto: McClelland and Stewart

Collins, R. (1982). *Sociological Insight: An Introduction to Non-obvious Sociology*. New York: Oxford University Press

Comstock, G. and V.C. Strasburger (1990) "Deceptive appearances: Television violence and aggressive behavior," *Journal of Adolescent Health Care*, 11, 31-44

Cooley, C.H. (1902) *Human Nature and Social Order*. New York: Charles Scribners

Corak, M. and A. Heisz (1996) "The intergenerational income mobility of Canadian men," Working Paper No. 89, Business and Labour Market Analysis, Ottawa: Statistics Canada

Crispell, D. (1992) "Myths of the 1950s," *American Demographics*, Aug., 38-43

Davis, K. and W.E. Moore (1945) "Some principles of stratification," *American Sociological Review*, 10 (April), 242-249

Diener, E., J. Horowitz, and R.A. Emmons (1985) "Happiness of the very wealthy," *Social Indicators Research*, 16, 263-274

Durkheim, E. (1938) *The Rules of Sociological Method*. Chicago: University of Chicago Press

_____ (1951) *Suicide*. New York: Free Press

_____ (1964) *The Division of Labor in Society*. New York: Free Press

Easterlin, R.A. (1980) *Birth and Fortune: The Impact of Numbers on Personal Welfare*. New York: Basic Books

Edwards, R. (1979) *Contested Terrain: The Transformation of the Workplace in the Twentieth Century*. New York: Basic Books

Engels, F. (1978 [1884]) "The origins of the family, private property and the state," pp. 734-759 in R.C. Tucker, ed. *The Marx-Engels Reader*, second edition. New York: W.W. Norton

Felson, Richard B. and Natalie Russo (1988) "Parental punishment and sibling aggression," *Social Psychology Quarterly*, 51, 1, March, 11-18

Ferguson, K.E. (1984) *The Feminist Case Against Bureaucracy*. Philadelphia: Temple University Press

Frideres, J. (1993) *Native Peoples in Canada: Contemporary Conflicts*, fourth edition. Scarborough: Prentice Hall Canada

Galtung, J. (1971) "A structural theory of imperialism," *Journal of Peace Research*, 8(2), 135-149

_____ and R. Vincent (1992) *Global Glasnost: Toward a New International Information/Communications Order?* Cresskill, N.J.: Hampton

Garfinkel, H. (1967) *Studies in Ethnomethodology*. Englewood Cliffs, N.J.: Prentice Hall

Gartner, R. (1989) "Patterns of victimization," 138-147 in L. Tepperman and J. Curtis (eds.), *Everyday Life: A Reader*. Toronto: McGraw-Hill Ryerson

Gerber, L. (1984) "Community characteristics and out-migration from Canadian Indian reserves: path analyses," *Canadian Review of Sociology and Anthropology*, 21(2) May, 145-165

Gerbner, G., L. Gross, M. Morgan and N. Signorelli (1980) "The mainstreaming of America: Violence Profile No. 11," *Journal of Communication*, 30, 3, summer, 10-29

Goffman, E. (1959) *Presentation of Self in Everyday Life*. Garden City, N.Y.: Doubleday

_____ (1961) *Asylums: Essays on the Social Situation of Mental Patients and Other Inmates*. Garden City, N.Y.: Anchor

_____ (1964) *Stigma: Notes on the Management of Spoiled Identity*. Englewood Cliffs, N.J.: Prentice Hall

Gusfield, J. (1963) *Symbolic Crusade*. Urbana: University of Illinois Press

Hagan, J. (1984) *Disreputable Pleasures: Crime and Deviance in Canada*, second edition. Toronto: McGraw-Hill Ryerson

_____ (1994) *Crime and Disrepute*. Sociology for a New Century series. Thousand Oaks, Calif.: Pine Forge Press

Harris, M. (1991) *Cannibals and Kings: The Origins of Cultures*. New York: Vintage Books

Heath, A. (1981) *Social Mobility*. Glasgow: Fontana Books

Held, D. (1989) *Political Theory and the Modern State*. Stanford: Stanford University Press

Henry, F. and E. Ginzberg (1990) "Racial discrimination in employment", pp. 302-309 in J. Curtis and L. Tepperman (eds.) *Images of Canada: The Sociological Tradition*. Scarborough: Prentice Hall Canada

Hirsch, E.D., Jr. (1988) *Cultural Literacy*. New York: Vintage Books

Johnson, H. (1987) "Homicide in Canada," *Canadian Social Trends*, winter, 2-6

_____ (1988) "Wife abuse," *Canadian Social Trends*, spring, 17-20

_____ and P. Chisholm (1989) "Family Homicide," *Canadian Social Trends*, autumn, 17, 18

Karp, D. (1986) "'You can take the boy out of Dorchester, but you can't take Dorchester out of the boy: Toward a social psychology of mobility," *Symbolic Interaction*, 9, 1, 19-36

Kasper, A. (1994) "A feminist, qualitative methodology: A study of women with breast cancer," *Qualitative Sociology*, 17, 3, 263-281

Kerr, J. and J. MacPhail (1991) *Canadian Nursing: Issues and Perspectives*. Ottawa: Canadian Nurses Association

Lash, S. and J. Urry (1987) *The End of Organized Capitalism*. Madison, Wisconsin: University of Wisconsin Press

Larzelere, Robert E. (1986) "Moderate spanking: Model or deterrent of children's aggression in the family?" *Journal of Family Violence*, 1, 1, March, 27-36

Li, P. (1982) "Chinese immigrants on the Canadian prairie, 1910-47," *Canadian Review of Sociology and Anthropology*, 19 (4), 527-540

Lipset, S.M. (1990) *Continental Divide: The Values and Institutions of the United States and Canada*. New York: Routledge

Locke, E.A. (1976) "The nature and causes of job satisfaction," pp. 1297-1349 in M.D. Dunnette (ed.), *Handbook of Industrial and Organizational Psychology*. Chicago: Rand McNally

Luxton, M. (1983) "Two hands for the clock: Changing patterns in the gendered division of labour in the home," *Studies in Political Economy*, 12, fall, 27-44

Macpherson, C.B. (1962) *The Political Theory of Possessive Individualism: Hobbes to Locke*. Oxford: Clarendon Press

Malthus, T.R. (1959 [1798]) *Population: The First Essay*. Ann Arbor: University of Michigan Press

Mandell, N. (1987) "The family" pp. 145-196 in M.M. Rosenberg et al (eds.), *An Introduction to Sociology*. Toronto: Methuen

Marx, K. (1936) *Capital*. New York: Modern Library

_____ (1969) *The German Ideology*. New York: International Publishers

_____ and F. Engels (1955) *The Communist Manifesto*, S.H. Beer (ed.) New York: Appleton Century Crofts

Mead, G.H. (1934) *Mind, Self and Society*. Chicago: University of Chicago Press

Merton, R.K. (1957a) "Manifest and latent functions," Chapter 1 in *Social Theory and Social Structure*, revised edition. New York: Free Press

_____ (1957b) "Social structure and anomie," Chapter 4 in *Social Theory and Social Structure*, revised edition. New York: Free Press

Michalos, A.C. (1988) "Optimism in thirty countries over a decade," *Social Indicators Research*, 20 (2), April, 177-180

Mills, C.W. (1959) *The Sociological Imagination*. New York: Oxford University Press

Moore, M. (1989) "Female lone parenting over the life course," *Canadian Journal of Sociology*, 14 (3), 335-352

Murdock, G.P. (1945) "The common denominator of cultures," pp. 123-142 in R. Linton (ed.), *The Science of Man in the World Crisis*. New York: Columbia University Press

Newson, John, Elizabeth Newson and Mary Adams (1993) "The social origins of delinquency," *Criminal Behaviour and Mental Health*, 3, 1, 19-29

Ornstein, M. (1988) "Social class and economic inequality," Chapter 7 in J. Curtis and L. Tepperman (eds.), *Understanding Canadian Society*. Toronto: McGraw-Hill Ryerson

Parker, M. and J. Slaughter (1990) "Management by stress: The team concept in the US auto industry," *Science as Culture*, 8, 27-58

Parsons, T. (1951) "Social structure and dynamic process: the case of modern medical practice," Chapter 10 in *The Social System*. New York: Free Press

_____ (1975) "Some theoretical considerations on the nature and trends of changes of ethnicity," pp. 53-85 in N. Glazer and D. Moynihan (eds.), *Ethnicity: Theory and Experience*. Cambridge, Mass.: Harvard University Press

_____ and R.F. Bales (1955) *Family Socialization and Interaction Process*. New York: Free Press

Pearl, D. (1984) "Violence and aggression," *Society*, Sept./Oct., 17-22

Perimenis, L. (1991) "The ritual of anorexia nervosa in cultural context," *Journal of American Culture*, 14, 4, winter, 49-59

Phillips, D.P. (1980) "Airplane accidents, murder, and the mass media: Towards a theory of imitation and suggestion," *Social Forces*, 58, 4, June, 1001-1024

Piaget, J. (1932) *The Moral Judgement of the Child*. New York: Free Press

Polanyi, K. (1944) *The Great Transformation*. New York: Farrar and Rinehart

Porter, J. (1965) *The Vertical Mosaic*. Toronto: University of Toronto Press

Quarantelli, E.L. (1996) "Basic themes derived from survey findings on human behavior in the Mexico City earthquake," *International Sociology*, 11, 4, Dec., 481-499

Reid, P. and G. Finchilescu (1995) "The disempowering effects of media violence against women on college women," *Psychology of Women Quarterly*, 19, 397-411

Reiter, E. (1986) "Life in a fast-food factory," pp. 309-326 in C. Heron and R. Storey (eds.), *On the Job: Confronting the Labour Process in Canada*. Kingston and Montreal: McGill-Queen's University Press

Reitz, J. (1980) *The Survival of Ethnic Groups*. Toronto: McGraw-Hill Ryerson

_____ (1988) "Less racial discrimination in Canada or simply less racial conflict? Implications of comparisons with Britain," *Canadian Public Policy*, XIV (4), 424-441

_____ and R. Breton (1994) *The Illusion of Difference: Realities of Ethnicity in Canada and the United States*. Toronto: C.D. Howe Institute

Rosenthal, R. (1986) "Media violence, antisocial behavior, and the social consequences of small effects," *Journal of Social Issues*, 42, 3, 141-154

Rubington, E. and M. Weinberg (1968) *Deviance: The Interactionist Perspective*. New York: Macmillan

Rudman, W.J. and A.F. Hagiwara (1992) "Sexual exploitation in advertising health and wellness products," *Women and Health*, 18, 4, 77-89

_____ and P. Verdi (1993) "Exploitation: Comparing sexual and violent imagery of females and males in advertising," *Women and Health*, 20, 4, 1-14

Runciman, W.G. (1966) *Relative Deprivation and Social Justice*. London: Routledge and Kegan Paul

Sacco, V.F. and H. Johnson (1990) *Patterns of Criminal Victimization in Canada*. General Social Survey Analysis Series, Catalogue 11-612E, No. 2. Ottawa: Statistics Canada

Sapir, E. (1929) "The status of linguistics as a science," *Language*, 5(4), 207-214

Satzewich, V. (1992) *Deconstructing a nation: Immigration, multiculturalism and racism in 90s Canada*, Halifax, N.S.: Fernwood Publishing

_____ (1993) *First Nations: Race, Class, and Gender Relations*. Scarborough: Nelson Canada

Sennett, R. and J. Cobb (1973) *The Hidden Injuries of Class*. New York: Vintage

Sharma, S.S. (1986) "Untouchability, a myth or a reality: A study of interaction between scheduled castes and Brahmins in a Western U.P. village," *Sociological Bulletin*, 35 (1), March, 68-79

Shibutani, T. and K.M. Kwan (1965) *Ethnic Stratification: A Comparative Approach*, New York: Macmillan

Sieber, S. (1981) *Fatal Remedies: The Ironies of Social Intervention*. New York: Plenum

Stasiulis, D. (1988) "Capitalism, democracy and the Canadian state," pp. 223-26 in D. Forcese and S. Richer (eds.), *Social Issues: Sociological Views of Canada*. Scarborough: Prentice Hall Canada

_____ (1990) "Theorizing Connections: Gender, Race, Ethnicity, and Class," pp. 269-305 in P. Li (ed.), *Race and Ethnic Relations in Canada*. Toronto: Oxford University Press

Stone, G. (1970) "The circumstances and situation of social status" pp. 250-59 in G. Stone and H. Faberman (eds.), *Social Psychology Through Symbolic Interaction*. Waltham, Mass.: Xerox College Publishing

Swaan, A. de (1989) "Jealousy as a class phenomenon: The petite bourgeoisie and social security," *International Sociology*, 4 (3), 259-271

Sydie, R. (1987) "Sociology and Gender," in M. Rosenberg, W. Shaffir, A. Turowetz and M. Weinfeld (eds.), *An Introduction to Sociology*. Toronto: Methuen

Thio, A. (1983) *Deviant Behaviour*. Boston: Houghton Mifflin

Thomas, W.I. (1967) *The Unadjusted Girl*. New York: Harper and Row

_____ and D.S. Thomas (1928) *The Child in America*. New York: Alfred A. Knopf

United Nations (1991) *The World's Women, 1970-1990: Trends and Statistics*. New York: United Nations Publications

Vincent, R.C. (1989) "Clio's consciousness raised? Portrayal of women in rock videos, re-examined," *Journalism Quarterly*, 66, 1, spring, 155-160

von Glinow, M. (1988) *The New Professionals: Managing Today's High-Tech Employees*. Cambridge, Mass.: Ballinger Publishing Company

Watkins, S.C. (1993) "If all we knew about women was what we read in Demography, what would we know?" *Demography*, 30, 4, Nov., 551-577

Webb, E.J. et al. (1966) *Unobtrusive Measures: Nonreactive Research in the Social Sciences*. Chicago: Rand McNally

Weber, M. (1946), from *Max Weber: Essays in Sociology*, trans. and edited by H.H. Gerth and C.W. Mills. New York: Oxford University Press

_____ (1958a) "Class, status, party," Chapter 7 in H. Gerth and C.W. Mills (eds.), from *Max Weber: Essays in Sociology*, New York: Oxford University Press

_____ (1958b) "Science as a vocation," Chapter 5 in H. Gerth and C.W. Mills (eds.), from *Max Weber: Essays in Sociology*, New York: Oxford University Press

_____ (1958c) "Bureaucracy," Section 8 in H. Gerth and C.W. Mills (eds.), from *Max Weber: Essays in Sociology*. New York: Oxford University Press

_____ (1961) *General Economic History*. New York: Collier Books

_____ (1964) "The types of authority and imperative coordination," Section 3 in T. Parsons (ed.), *The Theory of Social and Economic Organization*. New York: Free Press

_____ (1974) *The Protestant Ethic and the Spirit of Capitalism*. London: George Allen and Unwin

Weiss, M.J. (1988) *The Clustering of America*. New York: Harper and Row. A Tilden Press Book

Wilson, S.J. (1977) "The changing image of women in Canadian mass circulating magazines" *Atlantis* 2 (2), 33-44

Wright, E.O. (1985) *Classes*. London: Verso

Wrong, D. (1961) "The oversocialized conception of man in modern sociology," *American Sociological Review*, 26 (April), 183-193

Photo Credits

Index